German Military Travel Papers of the Second World War

German Military Travel Papers of the Second World War

Matt DiPalma

Schiffer Publishing Ltd

4880 Lower Valley Road • Atglen, PA 19310

Dedicated to the memory of

Martin Strasser Caidin

who didn't teach me how to write,
so much as he taught me that I could.

Library of Congress Control Number: 2016935660

Book design by Matt DiPalma
Cover design by Justin Watkinson
Type set in Humnst777 BT/LubalGraph Bd BT
ISBN: 978-0-7643-5086-3
Printed in China

Published by Schiffer Publishing, Ltd.
4880 Lower Valley Road
Atglen, PA 19310
Phone: (610) 593-1777; Fax: (610) 593-2002
E-mail: Info@schifferbooks.com
Web: www.schifferbooks.com

For our complete selection of fine books on this and related subjects, please visit our website at www.schifferbooks.com. You may also write for a free catalog.

Schiffer Publishing's titles are available at special discounts for bulk purchases for sales promotions or premiums. Special editions, including personalized covers, corporate imprints, and excerpts, can be created in large quantities for special needs. For more information, contact the publisher.

We are always looking for people to write books on new and related subjects. If you have an idea for a book, please contact us at proposals@schifferbooks.com.

A Note on Type

This book has been set in 12-point Monotype Bembo, originally cut at the end of the fifteenth century by Francesco Griffo and Italian renaissance printer Aldus Manutius, and revived in the late 1920s. It was used extensively throughout the Third Reich.

Captions are set in *DIN 1451 Mittelschrift*, a typeface created originally for standardization of railway car markings for the Prussian railway in 1905 for its legibility at a distance. It was adopted by the *Reichsbahn* in the 1920s and *Autobahn* in the 1930s, and remains in use in many countries today.

These typefaces were chosen for their cultural and historic significance as representations of common letter forms used during the Third Reich era.

Contents

German soldiers departing for home from Russia for Easter leave. Note the signs on the building behind them denoting the directions for those leaving for or returning from leave beside the larger sign with the timetable for departing trains.

Foreword

Your papers are not in order!

For seven decades now a belief has existed about the German military during the Second World War that remembers it as an extremely well organized, almost ritualistically bureaucratic machine that achieved levels of efficiency no other country could. In fact, the hyper-efficient and simultaneously repressive police state created by National Socialist Germany is often thought of as reflecting innate cultural characteristics unique to the German people. We think of them as born organizers with a unique gift for implementing the all-encompassing administrative culture that reached its apotheosis during the years stretching from 1934 to 1945.

While this kind of primordialist narrative—the idea that Germans were born with order and discipline as instincts—is certainly a tempting theory, the ordered bureaucracy of the National Socialist German state actually derived from an enormous amount of effort. Like other nation states, Nazi Germany sought to exert state control over a large and diverse population, and it sought to do so in an age when the only means available was analog.

This meant paperwork—lots and lots of paperwork. Nazi Germany could not have done what it did without the extensive paper trail of official documents that allowed it to bring its people and its military under positive state control. Nowhere is this methodical organizational culture more apparent than in the world of the Third Reich's wartime military travel documents. With a comprehensive range of forms and passes authorizing leave, travel between units, or travel between assigned posts, the *Wehrmacht* (all branches) created a regulated system capable of monitoring its soldiers, sailors, airmen, and *Waffen-SS panzergrenadiers* while they were en route between point A and point B.

In the pages that follow, Matt DiPalma explains this complex, esoteric, and nevertheless important subject in a way that it has never been explained before. With *German Military Travel Papers of the Second World War*, he has provided the English-language reader with an indispensable guide to understanding documents like the *Kriegsurlaubsschein* (Wartime Leave Permit), the *Sonderausweis* (Specialized Identity Paper), and the *Wehrmachtfahrschein* (*Wehrmacht* Travel Pass). He also places these documents within the context of items like the *Soldbuch* (Pay Book) and the *Erkennungsmarke* (the *Wehrmacht*'s two-piece style of dog tag) to indicate how they all related to one another and created a system for controlling the cumbersome apparatus of the Third Reich's war machine.

This book also helps to unlock the mystery behind the constellation of acronyms and abbreviations that the German military created during the conflict in a form of National Socialist shorthand. Here, the truncation *1./228.Pz.Jäg.Btl.* is deciphered as referring to 1st *Kompanie*, 228th *Panzerjäger Bataillon* (or Company A, 228th Tank Destroyer Battalion). For anyone attempting to make sense of Nazi documents, this is an aspect of the book that makes it particularly useful.

But this book is not just valuable as a tool for comprehending what the Third Reich's military travel papers did and did not do: it is also a handy desk reference for the curator or collector who might need to determine the authenticity of a particular National Socialist document. By detailing the colors of ink and the card stock used, and the even the size of genuine travel documents produced by the *Wehrmacht* during the war, Mr. DiPalma has provided the means for determining if a particular example is legitimate, or a clever forgery. In these ways, *German Military Travel Papers of the Second World War* contributes meaningfully to a subject that is typically the target of broad generalizations and even broader misunderstanding.

Martin K.A. Morgan
Luxembourg City
December 14, 2014

cher
3
Kosmos
Ich komme auf Urlaub

Acknowledgments

Understandably, the list to whom praise is owed on a work such as this is quite extensive.

First, I would like to express my most sincere appreciation to my editor Bob Biondi, my publisher Pete Schiffer, and the entire family at Schiffer Publishing, not just for giving me this opportunity, but for being the guiding, friendly people that they are. I could not have hoped for a better bunch to work with in the publication of my first book!

I'd like to thank William Zukauskas, a highly knowledgeable collector who first introduced me to World War II collecting and reenacting, without which my interest in collecting paperwork probably wouldn't have coalesced.

Many thanks to Emilie Caldwell Stewart and Jeff Young, both authors of several well-respected books on paperwork of the Third Reich, and who have always been willing to share time and answers with me when I had the courage to ask.

I'd also like to thank a number of fellow living historians and reenactors who have encouraged me in this hobby: Ryan Blocker, Museum Collections Assistant in the Curatorial Department at the Alabama Department of Archives and History, whose love of history is one that rivals even my own; Brian Kepner, whose encouragement and guidance have always been appreciated; and Don Bowman and Tom Jesse, both of whom I can call nothing less than truly inspirational. To the tremendously long list of friends and fellow living historians, all of whom have been constant sources of friendship and encouragement in this and other endeavors, I wish I could list you all! I treasure our time together and extend my warmest and most appreciative regards.

I cannot give enough thanks to the late Martin Caidin, author of over 140 historical books and fiction novels, and his widow DeeDee. Marty's life was an inspiration in its own right, but their friendship and tutelage on how to be shining examples of human beings shall never be forgotten. Thanks also to Joe and Gay Haldeman, the entire Halde-clan actually, who have been a wealth of knowledge to me on the writing industry and true friends who have welcomed me into their lives not just as a pupil but as extended family.

My undying thanks to Linda Evans, Bill Hatfield, Lori Haldeman, Jeff Granger, Joanne Clark, and the late Gloria Evans, fellow writers and loyal and talented editors, proofreaders, and just plain good friends. I cannot thank you nor praise you enough for all you have done for my development as a writer.

Speaking of good friends, no work would be completed without the encouragement of such. There is a countless list of those who have offered encouragement, and who have always been there to call and brag to without even once thinking of telling me to stop calling, but special, heart-felt thanks must go to Glen Purdy and Scott "Mole" Marvin. The two of them have supported me through thick, thin, and then some, not just with encouragement when things went well, but more for their unending support and love when things weren't going at all right. I am truly blessed to have such wonderful people in my life.

Lastly, I really want to thank my family: my mom Anne, my father Bob, my two brothers, Tony and Nic, and my beloved wife, Penny, who have not only tolerated my obsessions, but have even gone so far as to encourage them. An undertaking such as this takes time, often a great deal of it; I cannot begin to repay you all the time you've lost while I trudged along in my pursuits. I shall always love and cherish you for being the wonderful and loving blessings to me that you are!

An Ausgabestelle, or issue location, for the Führer's Gift to those leaving for home from the front. This station was located at Pogegen in the district of Tilsit, formerly East Prussia, now in Lithuania.

Introduction

For as long as I can remember, I have always been fascinated with the Second World War. Seeking to find a relatively inexpensive way to invest in original articles from that conflict, I began collecting paperwork of both the Allies and the Axis, though I admit my collection tends to overly represent the Third Reich.

I bought reference books on the *Soldbuch*, the *Wehrpass*, and other documents to become as knowledgeable on the subject as I could, but I couldn't find as much as I would have liked on the day-to-day papers carried by the average *Soldat*. To my knowledge, this is the only work that concentrates solely on leave and travel documents.

Throughout my career as a graphic designer and illustrator, I have studied the print and design conventions of numerous countries and time periods, especially how layout, illustration, artistic style, and font choices reflect and are typical of specific eras. I combined a love of design with my love of history to create an online business selling reproductions of items in my collection, but it is my sets of German leave and travel papers that I sell most. I have also produced period paperwork with The History Bunker for the Imperial War Museum, television, and the movies.

For purposes of this work, the term *Wehrmacht* refers to the German armed forces of the Third Reich, and not just the army. The army was referred to as *das Heer*, the air force as *die Luftwaffe*, and the navy as *die Kriegsmarine*. Military vehicle license plates reflect this, as they always reference the branch to which that vehicle belonged: WH for *Wehrmacht-Heer*, WL for *Wehrmacht-Luftwaffe*, and WM for *Wehrmacht-Kriegsmarine*.

I have attempted to keep translations as true to their original intent; they are not necessarily word-for-word literal translations, except in instances where such might allow additional understanding of the phrase. Each phrase or word will be translated, either parenthetically or in the body of the text; if you don't see a direct translation right away, I have also provided a glossary. Also, I have opted to spell German words that use the "ß" as "ss," per the recently adopted convention, not because I am new to German (I've been speaking it on and off since 1973), but because many English-speaking people tend to confuse it with the letter "B." I hope this doesn't upset the purists among my readers.

Figures are noted in the captions, the first number of which indicates the chapter; for example, figure 2-15 refers to the fifteenth figure in chapter 2. All documents in this book are at full size unless otherwise noted. When reduced, their actual size has been added to the captions.

This book is not meant to be an end-all attempt to identify every travel document ever used by the Third Reich, but rather an overview of the more common military forms, as well as an informative guide to the many original items available to collectors and enthusiasts today. It concentrates on military and paramilitary travel forms and associated papers of interest; adding civilian paperwork associated with travel would expand this volume to astronomical proportions. If you have anything to add to this work or wish to note any errors you might find, I would be more than happy to receive them for future editions.

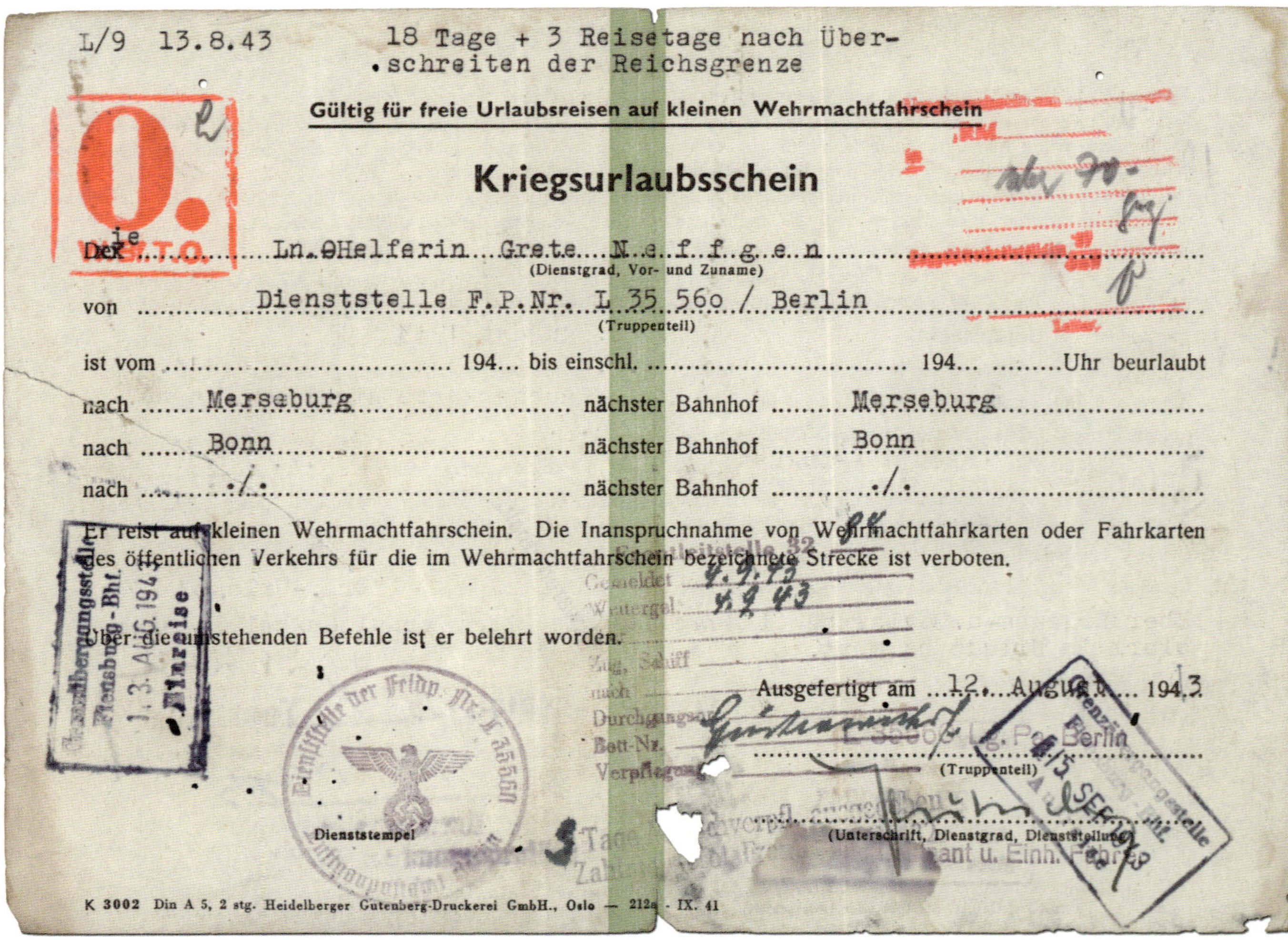
L/9 13.8.43 18 Tage + 3 Reisetage nach Überschreiten der Reichsgrenze

O. W.T.O.

Gültig für freie Urlaubsreisen auf kleinen Wehrmachtfahrschein

Kriegsurlaubsschein

Die Ln.-Helferin Grete Neffgen
(Dienstgrad, Vor- und Zuname)

von Dienststelle F.P.Nr. L 35 560 / Berlin
(Truppenteil)

ist vom .... 194... bis einschl. .... 194... ......Uhr beurlaubt

nach Merseburg nächster Bahnhof Merseburg

nach Bonn nächster Bahnhof Bonn

nach ./. nächster Bahnhof ./.

Er reist auf kleinen Wehrmachtfahrschein. Die Inanspruchnahme von Wehrmachtfahrkarten oder Fahrkarten des öffentlichen Verkehrs für die im Wehrmachtfahrschein bezeichnete Strecke ist verboten.

Über die umstehenden Befehle ist er belehrt worden.

Gemeldet 4.9.43
Weitergel. 4.9.43

Ausgefertigt am 12. August 1943

(Truppenteil)

Dienststempel

(Unterschrift, Dienstgrad, Dienststellung)

Grenzübergangsstelle Flensburg-Bhf. 13. AUG 1943 Einreise

K 3002 Din A 5, 2 stg. Heidelberger Gutenberg-Druckerei GmbH., Oslo — 212a · IX. 41

The Wehrmacht recognized that everyone needed leave. This Kriegsurlaubsschein for Luftwaffe-Nachrichten Helferin Grete Naffgen, one of the many women working as a radio technician for the Luftwaffe against Allied bombers, permitted her an eighteen-day leave and three additional travel days within the Reich.

1

The Details of Paperwork

The German Mindset

My uncle, David Pennington, served in the U.S. Army during the Second World War with the 36th Infantry Division. He landed at Salerno in 1943 and fought at San Pietro, the Rapido River, Anzio, with the Lost Battalion at the Rhône Valley, and was awarded the Silver Star for gallantry at the Siegfried Line. When I was about twelve, I once asked him who had the best army in Europe during the war. Without hesitation, he said, "Germany."

Figure 1-1. Photograph of the author's uncle, David Pennington, who was awarded the Silver Star for gallantry while crossing the Siegfried Line into Germany. He respected the Soldat a great deal.

To my surprise, he told me that the Germans had better weapons, better discipline, and were more efficient than anyone else at that time. He had a great deal of respect for the German soldier, and felt that they were "the most professional army in Europe."

To this day, Germans seem to follow an unwritten national directive for that level of professionalism. When meeting German friends of ours in Salzburg, Austria, we asked them to join us at our hotel at 10:00 am. To our amusement, they met us at the exact time, nearly to the second.

They were a little taken aback when we said, "You're here already."

"Of course," he replied. "It is ten o'clock, and I am German."

Nowhere is this meticulous attention to detail more obvious than in the mountains of paperwork the Third Reich generated to run not just the military, but the nation itself. For example, the *Heeres Dienstvorschrift 159, Reiseverordnung für die Wehrmacht* (H.Dv.159 for short, Military Service Manual 159, Travel Regulations for the Military) has over fifty-eight pages describing the regulations, conditions, and pay for a single man to go on leave or travel at military expense.

Yet, since captured paperwork would be a godsend to enemy intelligence analysts, it was discouraged to carry all your paperwork with you. In *Der Dienstunterricht in der Luftwaffe* (The Service Instruction in the *Luftwaffe*) for instance, page 297 references L.Dv.29, the *Luftwaffe Dienstvorschrift* that regulates transfer and travel between duty stations. It states that soldiers are required to turn all official paperwork over to the command of one's new duty station upon arrival, especially any travel papers:

> "*2. Bei Versetzungen und Versetzungskommandos sind dem neuen Truppenteil folgende Papiere zu übersenden:...*
> *...g.) Urlaubsnachweis und Nachweis über gewährte freie Urlaubsreisen,...*"
> 2. In transfers and transfer commands, the following papers are to be turned over to the new duty station:...
> ...g.) Proof of leave and proof of free leave travel granted,...

There are those that might consider this the antithesis of organization. Such a store of directives, especially those that appear to contradict one another, would present a barrier to efficiency, yet such procedures served a number of purposes.

For one, it was expected. In any military organization, regulations provide routine, structure, codes of conduct, and so on, to build unit cohesion and combat efficiency. Germany, being the regimented culture that it is, would naturally accept nothing less. For instance, there are over 652 *Heeres Dienstvorschriften*, some of which had over fifty volumes. H.Dv.481 alone had 180 separate *Merkblätter*, informational leaflets, on the handling peculiarities of every caliber of ammunition in *Wehrmacht* inventory, from pistol ammo to ammunition for the larger field artillery.

Second, since a soldier on leave or traveling between duty stations was required to have several different forms with him during his trip, it made desertion extremely difficult. Specific forms were required for certain modes and purposes of travel, and many required verification throughout the trip. Acquiring these forms by any means other than legitimate was quite challenging, and often ensured that a soldier was not away from his unit unless he was supposed to be. That's not to say that desertion wasn't possible or didn't occur, but the accountability of German soldiers as a result was rather high, even as the nation crumbled during the closing months of the war.

Finally, the overall system made infiltration by foreign agents extremely difficult. The elaborate set of forms required were difficult to forge unless one was intimately familiar with the layout, convention and location of various identifying stamps, and the unique markings of each. The best known example of successful Allied circumvention of this system was the escape from *Stalag Luft III* in October of 1943, better known as the Great Escape, popularized by the 1963 movie of the same name. Still, of the seventy-six airmen who escaped, all but three were recaptured, executed, or killed.

The system was hardly new. Handwritten furlough notes and passes were used throughout Europe as early as the middle ages, expanded by the printing press during the sixteenth century, and used by many nations throughout the 1800s. By World War I, the majority of printing conventions that would be used by the *Wehrmacht* had been perfected by the *Reichsheer*, so much so that one must sometimes examine dates and stamps to determine whether a document dates to the First World War or the Second. It was the additional required paperwork that was expanded so thoroughly during the Third Reich.

Travel papers of the armed forces of any nation can be broken down into four main classifications: leave papers that allowed one to be away from one's unit (often for rest or recuperation), forms

Marschbefehl.

Das Ers.M.G.Batl.XII setzt am 6. Dezbr. 1916

gem. St.G.K.O.XII Nr. ...

zum ... in Marsch

Fahrtziel: ... Fahrtnummer: ...

Bemerkungen: ...

Leutnant u. Adjutant.

Figure 1-2. At first glance, this mimeographed Marschbefehl from the First World War, dated December 6, 1916, is practically identical to its counterpart from the Second. One should always examine a document closely before purchasing it! (6 9/16" x 8 1/4")

that allocated travel at either one's own or military expense, orders for individuals or small groups of individuals to relocate, and paperwork delineating special situations in which a soldier might be required to be away from his unit.

The *Wehrmacht* required forms from many of these categories for travel to be legitimate, much like other armies, however; each condition required a different collection of forms. The form needed to travel at one's own expense varied from that for traveling at military expense, which in turn varied, depending on how far a soldier was going. If a soldier was transferring to a different unit but stopping at home along the way on leave, an entirely different set of forms were required, and so on.

Size

These and a good many other documents were printed throughout the Reich by a number of individual contractors and government agencies. Information can often be located in the lower left hand corner of each, and it identifies the characteristics of the form, not the form itself. The details most frequently noted are the size by DIN 476 classification (*Deutsches Institut für Normung, Nr. 476 [Papierformate],* German Institute for Standardization, Number 476 [Paper Formats]) such as A5, B6, etc.; the company or agency responsible for printing the form; the city in which it was located; the year it was printed or approved; and on occasion, the contract number under which the form was produced. Use of such information was itself not standardized; some companies incorporated all of this information while others included very little.

Most German paperwork of the Third Reich is trimmed to sizes in the DIN 476 "A" series. The parent sheet, DIN A0, the sheet of paper produced by a mill to be trimmed later into smaller sizes, is one square meter in area at an aspect ratio of 1:$\sqrt{2}$, or 0.707; 841mm x 1149mm (approximately 33⅛" x 44¼"). By folding or cutting the parent sheet in half, the result is the A1 size, 594mm x 841mm. By folding or cutting the A1 sheet in half, we get the A2 size, and so on, all the way to A10 at 26mm x 37mm. The same fashion of division and nomenclature is used for the B0 parent sheet (1000mm x 1414mm), the C0 parent sheet (917mm x 1297mm), and the D0 parent sheet (771mm x 1091mm). "C" series sizes usually refer to envelopes and correspond to the appropriate "A" series size as an insert; for example, a flat A7 sheet will fit into a C7 envelope.

The primary advantage of this system can be most appreciated in printing, photography, and graphic design, fields in which Germany excelled since the turn of the century and set many standards. Regardless of what percentage an image is enlarged or reduced, it will fit onto a corresponding size without having to crop the image or trim excess paper. Using the common American paper sizes, an image scaled to a tabloid sheet of 11" x 17" can be reduced to 8½" x 11" letter size, but one would have to trim almost ½" from either side to maintain the same aspect ratio.

The DIN 476 system of paper sizes was created in 1922, but not standardized throughout Europe until 1975 with the creation of ISO 216 (International Standards Organization, number 216), which was, for all intents and purposes, just a redefinition of DIN 476; the sizes and nomenclature are identical, except that the "D" series was discarded. If one purchases letter paper in Germany or Austria today, it is still sold and referred to specifically as DIN A4 paper.

The majority of German travel forms were trimmed to A5 size (148mm x 210mm, roughly 5⅞" x 8¼") and

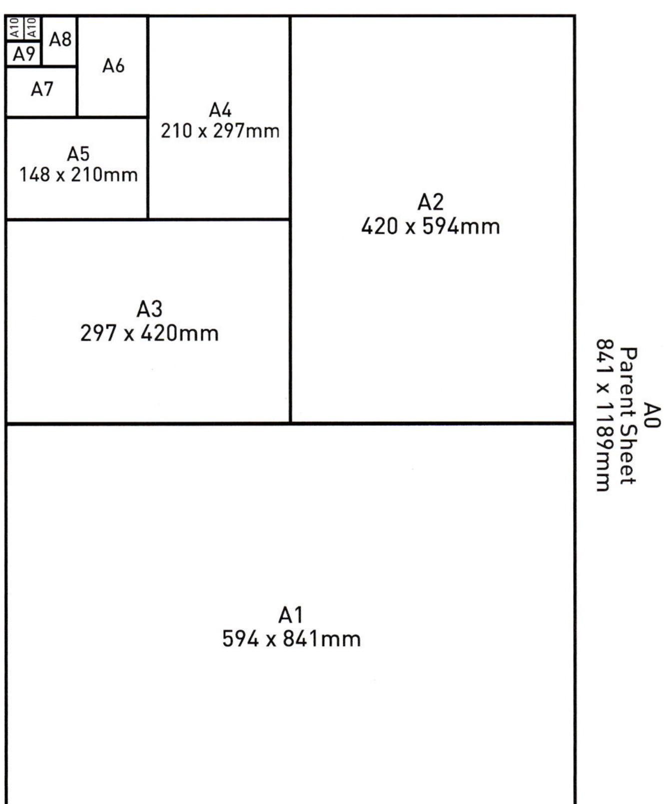

Figure 1-3. How the DIN 476 "A-series" of paper sizes are determined: the 33⅛" x 46$^{13}/_{16}$" parent sheet, size A0, cut in half results in two A1 sized sheets. An A1 sized sheet cut in half results in two A2 sheets, and so on. Each size is exactly half of the previous size, so each sheet retains the same aspect ratio.

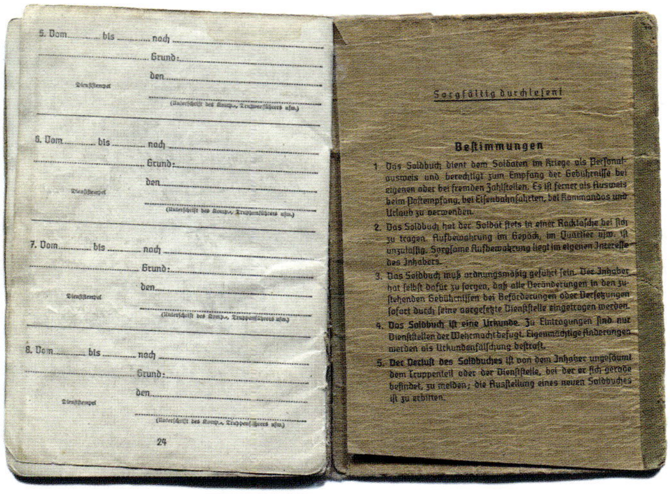

Figure 1-4. DIN sizing made it easy to keep travel papers, which were frequently cut to A5 or A6 size, in the accordion pocket in the back cover of the Soldbuch, the German soldier's primary form of identification.

could be folded in half to A6 size, then placed within the small accordion pocket at the back of one's *Soldbuch*, the primary mode of identification for the German soldier. Towards the end of the war, as resources and facilities became scarce, certain forms were combined into one larger form. These combined forms were often printed on A4 size (210mm x 297mm, or about 8¼" x 11⅝"), which is a bit narrower and taller than a standard US letter-size paper. An A4 sheet of paper folded twice is also A6 sized, and fits within the pocket of the *Soldbuch*.

Other travel documents, particularly temporary leave cards or permission cards, were printed and trimmed to A7 size: 74mm x 105mm, roughly 2⅞" x 4⅛." These were usually reserved for *Stadt-Urlaubskarten* (City Leave Cards), *Nacht-Urlaubskarten* (Night Leave Cards), and temporary *Ausweiskarten* (Identity Cards) as this reduced size added to their ease of handling.

Paper

The paper that German travel documents were printed on varies, depending on the form. Small A7 cards, such as the *Stadt-Urlaubskarte,* were often printed on a fine-toothed heavy stock that is quite similar to modern 80 to 100 lb cover or card stock, such as what can be found in modern art or craft stores. Tooth refers to its texture; a fine-toothed paper is soft and smooth to the touch, whereas a coarse-toothed paper feels rougher. The weight or poundage listed is the approximate weight of 500 sheets (one ream) of paper cut to its basic size. In the case of modern card stock, the basic size is 20" x 26," even though it is often sold in packages of 8½" x 11" or 12" x 12."

When not printed on card stock (each *Standortstelle* or duty station often contracted for cards to be printed on their own and use was far from standardized), smaller A7 cards would have been printed on the same paper as larger A5 and A4 travel papers. These forms were printed almost exclusively on a fine-toothed, lightweight 25 lb newsprint about the same weight as what one would expect for a daily newspaper, but with a smoother finish. It was not coated, or "slick," as it's often called, like an advertising insert, though some were printed on a semi-coated stock to achieve a finer tooth.

Color varies from dull white to ivory to oyster-colored paper to a light brown, kraft, terra cotta, and ginkgo green cover stock. A stark, pure white is rare, often

Figure 1-5. An example of the watermark found in a 20 Reichsmark note from 1939. Watermarks can only be seen when held to the light. The view on the right shows what the bill looks like in normal light. (3" x 6⅛")

due to wartime scarcity of bleaching agents necessary for its production.

The more specialized forms such as the *Sonderausweis "I"* (Special Identity Paper "I") or *Grenzübertrittsausweis* (Border Crossing Identity Form) used a more finished, brighter, semi-coated newsprint, the tooth of which is similar to a modern 60 lb resume paper. The result is reduced ink absorption during the printing process, so colors tend to be brighter and offer more contrast than when printed on other papers. Oddly enough, for a form that needed verifiable accuracy, very few travel forms are watermarked, while all special issued ration cards are. A watermark is a pattern in paper that forms during production, often by design, which shows up as light and dark regions when that document is held up to a light, as in the 20 *Reichsmark* note on the previous page.

Watermarks have long been used to prevent forgeries, particularly in money. Bills held aloft usually reveal the faces of royalty and political figures; official documents when held to a light source often disclose a coat of arms or other official sigil. To this day, watermarks remain one of the primary stumbling blocks for forgers and counterfeiters.

Ersatzteilen

If the exact forms were not available, clerks had the authority to type their own versions, or even use mimeograph (a cheap, short-run office printing process used prior to the introduction of photocopiers), depending on the availability of the required machinery. The layout followed that of the original forms, as can be expected, since the clerks would simply replicate the already established format. These temporary documents were sometimes trimmed to inconsistent sizes, depending on what was available.

The clerk would type the form on the kind of paper that one would expect in any clerk's office, from rough, 20 lb bond to a translucent 25% rag stock commonly referred to as "onion skin" paper. Some examples exist as originally typed documents, though many are carbons. For those not familiar with the process, a stack of four or five sheets of blank paper would have carbon paper interleaved between them and inserted into a typewriter. When a clerk types the original document, the impact of each letter creates a carbon impression on them.

These *Ersatzteilen* (substitute pages) were kept on hand and filled out the same as their printed equivalent, signed by the appropriate authority, and validated with unit-specific stamps known as a *Dienststempel*.

Dienststempeln

A *Dienststempel*, at least the common round stamp with the recognizable eagle and swastika, was standardized in size at 35mm in diameter. Few examples of military *Dienststempel* exist outside that dimension (though many different civilian stamps do), and can usually assist in spotting a faked document.

Some were inscribed with a unit's military designation, or *Truppenteil*, often abbreviated per *Wehrmacht* conventions to fit within the border and still be legible; for example, the 1st *Kompanie* of the 228th *Panzerjäger Bataillon* would be abbreviated *1.Kom./228. PanzerJäg.-Btl.*, or shortened even further to *1./228. Pz.Jäg.Btl.* The *Truppenteil* would arc across the top of the eagle and a small diamond, stylized leaf, or asterisk would be centered at the bottom. If a unit's title required both the top and bottom of the circle to adequately describe its designation, that legend would be broken at a convenient point and an asterisk or "+" placed to the left and right of the circle, centered between the ends of the two lines of type.

Another common circular-eagle-and-swastika *Dienststempel* format was the unit's *Feldpost* stamp. *Feldpost* was the *Wehrmacht's* method of identifying the unit from which free mail for soldiers circulated, but it was also used to identify the unit itself, as each unit down to the battalion level, and at times even down to the company level, had their own *Feldpostnummer* (Field Mail Number).

Figure 1-6. Reconstructed variations of Dienststempel, in this case for the 1st Company of the 228th Panzerjäger (anti-tank) Battalion. Any of these layouts would have been used. Standardization of formats for stamps was minimal at best, especially when using the Feldpostnummer, a counterespionage tactic used quite successfully to obfuscate a unit's designation.

This five- to six-digit alphanumeric designation was unique to that unit (unless that unit had been destroyed or reclassified, in which case the number might be reassigned), so it was a quick, simple, and secure manner with which to identify. A *Feldpostnummer* preceded by an "L" designated a *Luftwaffe* unit, while *Kriegsmarine* units were preceded by an "M." Using our previous example, the 1st *Kompanie* of the 228th *Panzerjäger Bataillon* could simply be identified as *Feldpostnummer 26775*. If any documents bearing that stamp were to fall into enemy hands, identification by enemy intelligence would be immensely difficult if they did not know that number had been assigned to that particular unit.

Issuing units could also be identified by their *Dienstellenummer*, sometimes written as *Dienstelle der Feldpostnummer* (Service Office of the Field Mail Number), which is the "official" longhand designation for the *Feldpostnummer*. Stamps bearing this nomenclature may be written in one arc across the top, e.g. *Dienstelle Feldpostnummer 26775* with an asterisk centered at the bottom, or broken into two lines, top and bottom, such that *Dienstelle* lies alone at the top or the 26775 lies alone at the bottom.

Many travel forms also required identification of a soldier's *Truppenteil* in the body of the document, so the unit's *Soldbuch* stamp might be used for that purpose. Again, this could be the full *Truppenteil* of the unit, or simply its *Feldpostnummer*. It was stamped about as often as it was typed or written in the required space, as well as at the bottom below the preparation date, awaiting the commanding officer's signature.

These *Stempel* were far from standardized, often appearing as if each unit had been left to its own devices

Figure 1-6. Typefaces typical of Truppenteilstempel in Fraktur, broken script, and sans serif fonts, all of which were in use in Germany at that time. The names to the left of the reconstructed examples are the names of modern computer equivalents.

Fette Fraktur	1. Kom./228. Panzerjäger-Btl.
Alte Schwabacher	1. Kom./228. Panzerjäger-Btl.
Brokenscript	1. Kom./228. Panzerjäger-Btl.
Potsdam	1. Kom./228. Panzerjäger-Btl.
Tannenberg	1. Kom./228. Panzerjäger-Btl.
DIN 1451 Mittelschrift	1. Kom./228. Panzerjäger-Btl.
Berthold Akzidenz Grotesk	1. Kom./228. Panzerjäger-Btl.
Alte Haas Grotesk	1. Kom./228. Panzerjäger-Btl.

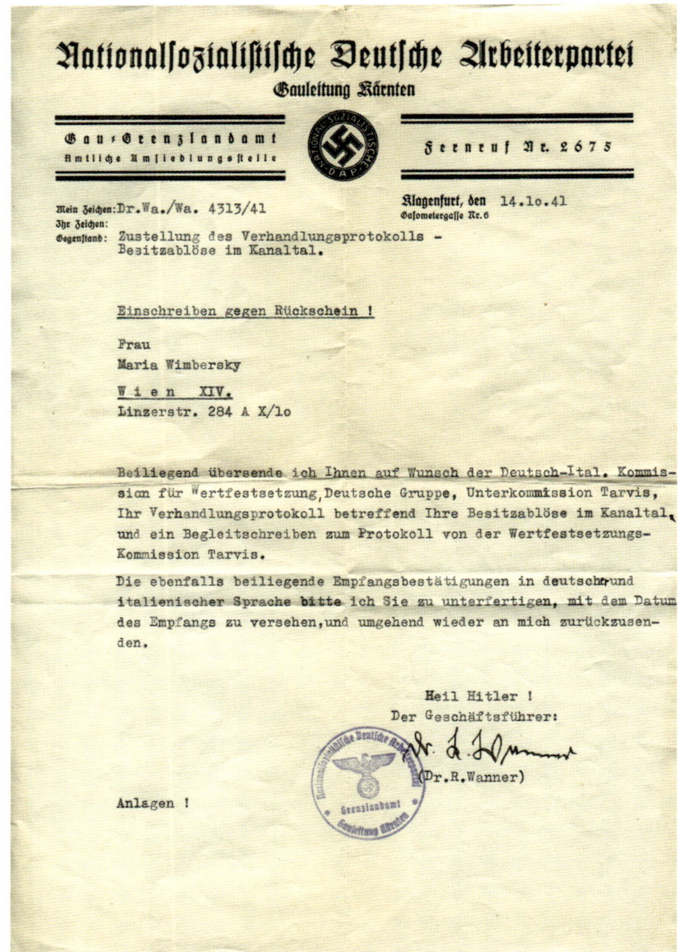
Nationalsozialistische Deutsche Arbeiterpartei
Gauleitung Kärnten

Gau-Grenzlandamt
Amtliche Umsiedlungsstelle

Fernruf Nr. 2675

Mein Zeichen: Dr.Wa./Wa. 4313/41
Ihr Zeichen:
Gegenstand: Zustellung des Verhandlungsprotokolls - Besitzablöse im Kanaltal.

Klagenfurt, den 14.10.41
Gasometergasse Nr. 6

Einschreiben gegen Rückschein !

Frau
Maria Wimbersky
Wien XIV.
Linzerstr. 284 A X/10

Beiliegend übersende ich Ihnen auf Wunsch der Deutsch-Ital. Kommission für Wertfestsetzung, Deutsche Gruppe, Unterkommission Tarvis, Ihr Verhandlungsprotokoll betreffend Ihre Besitzablöse im Kanaltal, und ein Begleitschreiben zum Protokoll von der Wertfestsetzungs-Kommission Tarvis.

Die ebenfalls beiliegende Empfangsbestätigungen in deutsch und italienischer Sprache bitte ich Sie zu unterfertigen, mit dem Datum des Empfangs zu versehen, und umgehend wieder an mich zurückzusenden.

Heil Hitler !
Der Geschäftsführer:
(Dr.R.Wanner)

Anlagen !

Figure 1-8. An example of NSDAP (Nazi Party) letterhead from Vienna, Austria. Note the use of the traditional, yet "degenerate," Fraktur heading instead of the officially sanctioned broken script. (A4)

to acquire. Size was often limited to whatever would fit into the small spaces for *Bescheinigungen* on page 3 of the *Soldbuch* (certifications; in this case, certifications of duty stations), and are usually only 20–25mm wide (about ¾"), though some are comparatively large, being at least 60mm or even 80mm across (2½" to 3¼").

Furthermore, it appears that the fonts used for the typesetting of these *Dienststempel* were not standardized in the least.

Few are set in *Fraktur*, the heavy, characteristically German typeface used since the sixteenth century, and fonts such as *Fette Fraktur*, *Schwabacher*, and *Unger* had fallen out of favor with the Nazis in the mid-1930s. Hitler denounced the use of *Fraktur* as "degenerate" and "Jewish" as early as 1934. The problem was that *Fraktur* was traditional; almost all books printed in Germany were set in *Fraktur*, and for the most part people preferred it. It wasn't until *Chef der Parteikanzlei* Martin Bormann (Chief of the Party Chancellory) banned the use of *Fraktur* on printed documents by issuing his decree of January 1941 on Nazi Party stationery, the letterhead of which was set in, of all things, *Fraktur*.

So the majority of *Truppenteilstempel* were set in heavy, black-letter or "broken script" fonts similar to modern fonts such as *Schaftstiefel*, *Potsdam*, and *Tannenberg*. These angular typefaces looked much more like that designed by Albrecht Dürer in the sixteenth century in his books *Unterweysung der Messung* (1532–38, Instruction on Measures), composed of thick lines and angled squares to compose letters, and was a precursor to *Fraktur*.

Others still were set in sans serif fonts, increasingly popular among designers during the 1920s and 1930s, such as *Dinschrift*, *Akzidenz*, *Haas*, and *Schelter* (the latter of which would later be the primary model for Helvetica, introduced in 1957). These are often condensed or compressed horizontally between three-quarters to almost half their normal width, to allow the typesetter to render as much of the *Truppenteil* as possible on a single line.

The last *Dienststempel* one normally finds on many travel forms can be found just below the date and *Truppenteil* at the bottom: the commanding officer's stamp. This *Stempel* has both the commander's rank and position to identify him as the authority granting permission or otherwise authorizing travel, such as *Hauptmann und Kompanie-Führer* (Captain and Company Leader). Normally located directly below the commanding officer's signature, it is frequently stamped in the same color as the date and *Truppenteil*. A larger unit might have a single *Stempel* made with the *Truppenteil* and the commanding officer's information together, but this is far more rare than the use of two separate stamps.

Ink Colors

The color of the ink pads for stamps varied. Deep purple or rich violet were by far the most frequently used, though other colors and black were used on occasion. The *Kriegsmarine* used a very dark navy blue from time to time, as did many of the world's navies, as well as the *Luftwaffe* and some hospitals.

Several shades of green were used exclusively by *Gebirgsjäger* units (Mountain Infantry), though these units did from time to time use black, purple, or violet as well, probably depending on the state of the clerk's green ink supply.

Few examples exist of red ink being used; these seem to have only been brought out when the usual inkpads ran dry or to call attention to specific conditions, such as the example in figure 2-72 from *Organization Todt*, a civil and military engineering group named after its founder Dr. Fritz Todt. Civilian organizations such as the *Reichsarbeitsdienst* (RAD, the Reich Work Force, similar to the American Civil Conservation Corps), the *Deutsche Arbeits Front* (German Work Front), and *Reichsbahn* (German State Rail System), like the military, used purple and violet ink with far more regularity.

Bright royal blue ink, lighter shades of purple, and magenta were for all practical purposes never used, and are usually a good indicator of a forgery.

It should be pointed out that it was not unusual to find different colors for different stamps on the same document. Blank forms might be stamped with a *Dienststempel* in bulk when received, and additional stamps would be added when the form was actually issued. In fact, the back of many forms would be stamped to note additional pay, rations, or other essential items given to a soldier for the duration of his travel whenever that information wasn't already printed, by using *Sonderstempel*.

Sonderstempeln

Sonderstempeln, or special stamps, can most often be found on the *Kriegsurlaubsschein* (Wartime Leave Permit) and the *Sonderausweis* (Specialized Identity Paper). These stamps were used to indicate additional conditions or information regarding the Soldat's travel.

If a soldier was traveling directly from the front, he would need to be deloused before he could board a train, so he would pass through an *Entlausungsstelle*, or delousing station. A special stamp on his travel permit was one way to indicate that he had successfully completed this procedure.

Soldaten traveling from the front or certain duty stations between October 1942 and September 1944 would be given either the *Führer-Paket* (Führer's Package) or *Führergeschenk* (Führer's Present). Once received, usually at a rail stop on the way home or upon crossing the border, a stamp was added to both the travel papers and the Soldbuch to prevent a soldier from receiving

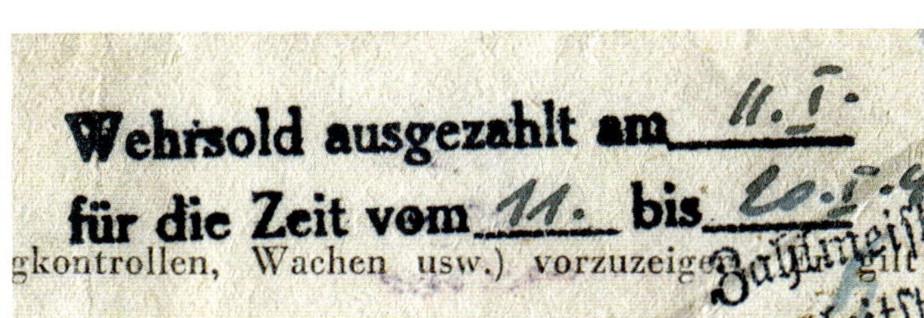

Figure 1-9. An example of a Sonderstempel, denoting the payment of additional Military Pay, or Wehrsold, issued on January 11th for the period of January 11-20, 1944.

more than one. Detailed information on the contents of such packages can be found in *Rations of the German Wehrmacht in World War II* by Jim Pool and Tom Bock (Schiffer), and is well worth the read.

Other noted additions were for *Wehrsold* (Military Wages in addition to a base pay, similar to modern hazardous duty pay), *Marschverpflegung* (Marching Provisions), *Raucherkarten* (Smoker Cards; tobacco rations), *Rasierseife* (Shaving Soap), and so on. These are almost exclusively stamped in shades of purple and violet. Few stamps were added in a dark navy blue, and fewer still in black. *Entlausungsstelle* used red stamps to indicate the fact that a *Soldat* had indeed been deloused, as this color stands out among other stamps likely to already be on the form.

Stamps might also be added by *Reichsbahn Durchgangsstelle* (Railway Transfer or Throughway Stations) to indicate that a traveler had passed through certain train stations. These tend to be in black ink and, on occasion, purple or violet.

Completion

How papers were filled out differed also, primarily as to whether they were typed or filled out by hand. This in turn varied, not because, the diverse handwriting of different clerks, but because there were different styles of handwriting in use in Germany at the time.

The most frequently used style of handwriting on existing paperwork was *Normalschrift* or *Romanischeschrift* (Normal or Roman script), the standard handwriting form used today by the majority of the western world. One rarely finds papers filled out in the late-nineteenth- and early twentieth-century *Kupferstichschrift* (Copper plate script) or *Kurrent* (i.e., current style), as might have been used by a clerk who had been a World War I veteran. Mash-ups between *Romanische* and *Kurrent*, where someone might interchange letters from one style of handwriting the other, are frequently found. Rarest, however, are

Figure 1-10. Although the majority of travel papers were filled out by hand, a number of forms were also completed by Schreibmaschine (literally "writing machine") or typewriter. By law, all typewriters sold in Germany after 1935 were required to have a key with the SS runes; this includes typewriters manufactured outside the Reich. This example of a German-made Schuster & Walther Triumph typewriter from Nürnberg has the SS runes on the number 3 key—the majority of typewriters had them on the 5 key.

Figure 1-11. A postcard from the Western Front during the First World War, written on August 16, 1918 in the Kurrent handwriting style compared to a printed version of the Sütterlinschrift handwriting from the January 1936 Deutsche Jugendburg, the German equivalent to the American Weekly Reader. The letterforms are the same, but Sütterlin is much rounder to make it easier for children to learn to write, much like the wide loops of the Palmer method taught in the United States when compared to the older Spencerian handwriting of the 19th century.

forms completed in *Sütterlinschrift*, of which I have only seen a few. *Sütterlin* replaced *Kurrent* between 1915 and 1923 in German schools, and is noticeably rounder and more open, in much the same way that letters of the Palmer method taught in the U.S. since 1923 are more rounded than nineteenth-century Spencerian script. The teaching of *Sütterlin* was banned by the Führer himself in 1941; people of the conquered territories simply couldn't read it, and since the Reich was supposed to last another 992 years, it would behoove German schools to replace it to something more universally legible.

Ultraviolet Flouresence

Many collectors rely on ultraviolet light to check the authenticity of paperwork from the 1930s and 1940s. By shining UV light onto a document, one can often determine whether it is a clever fake or an original piece of paperwork.

Mills use brighteners and dyes to color and finish paper. Prior to the Third Reich era, these dyes do not glow or fluoresce under ultraviolet light; after the Third Reich era, they do. The problem for collectors is that the transition from a non-fluorescing process to fluorescing ones occurred in many nations during the 1930s and 1940s.

Although this method is, for the most part, a very good indicator, it is not 100% reliable, and should not be used as a "make or break" determination of a document's authenticity. Some forgers use prewar paper stocks to print modern reproductions, so these will not fluoresce at all and appear under UV light as original. Because of the transition to more modern brighteners throughout this time period, some documents that I know are original because of their source (veterans, museums, and reputable dealers) fluoresce rather nicely.

Use UV light as one of many indicators, but not your sole test for authenticity. As with any document, examine all factors: paper finish and weight, ink color, stamp quality, handwriting, the unit represented, and so on. Together they will let you know whether an article is original. If any number of these don't look right, there could very well be a good reason.

Figure 2-1. The Soldbuch was the primary identity form for the German soldier, sailor, or airman. Pages were cut to A5 size, then folded, bound, and trimmed to roughly A6 size.

2

The Details of Documents Required to Travel

Das Soldbuch

Since the primary identity document of the German soldier was the *Soldbuch* (Pay Book), it comes as no surprise that this vital document should be considered absolutely necessary for one to travel. A number of the travel passes and permits often refer an inspector to the *Soldbuch* for purposes of identification, rather than an additional *Ausweis* (Identity Affidavit).

A number of books have already been written about the *Soldbuch*, many of which are excellent references, especially Emily Caldwell Stuart's *Wehrpasses and Soldbuchs*, Young & Meinz's *German Third Reich Era Documents, Volume Two: Military Documents*, and Scapini and Gorzanelli's *The Wehrpass and Soldbuch of the Wehrmacht*. For brevity's sake, I won't attempt to go into great detail, but the *Soldbuch* identified the soldier by name, rank, *Erkennungsmarke* (the *Wehrmacht's* two-piece style of dog tag), and the *Wehrnummer*, a uniquely German method of identifying the soldier by his home town and by the page and number on that town's *Wehrstammrolle*, or Military Draft Register, that the soldier's name appears.

The *Soldbuch* noted other particulars of a soldier's service (his duty stations, training history, clothing and equipment issued, etc.), but of specific interest to this work are the last two to four pages, the pages upon which leave was recorded. The exact page numbers vary because the *Soldbuch* themselves varied from service to service, but all reserve the last pages to record leave.

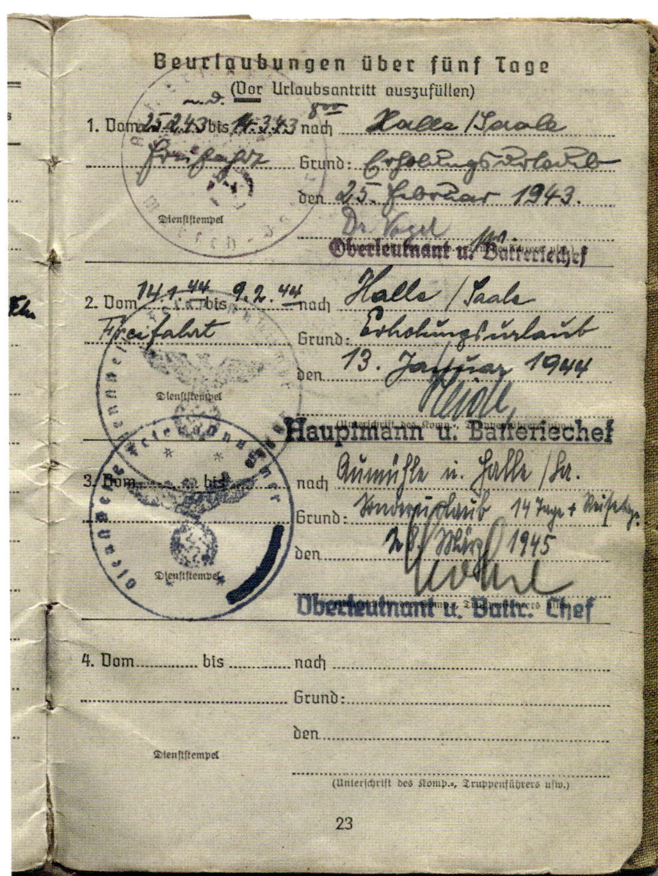
Beurlaubungen über fünf Tage
(Vor Urlaubsantritt auszufüllen)
1. Vom 25.2.43 bis 14.3.43 nach Halle/Saale
Grund: Erholungsurlaub
den 25. Februar 1943.
Dienststempel
Oberleutnant u. Batteriechef
2. Vom 14.1.44 bis 9.2.44 nach Halle/Saale
Freifahrt
Grund: Erholungsurlaub
den 13. Januar 1944
Dienststempel
Hauptmann u. Batteriechef
3. Vom ... bis ... nach
Grund:
den ... 1945
Dienststempel
Oberleutnant u. Battr. Chef
4. Vom ... bis ... nach
Grund:
den
Dienststempel
(Unterschrift des Komp.-, Truppenführers usw.)
23

Figure 2-2. The Urlaubsseiten (Leave Pages) from the Soldbuch of Obergefreiter Carl Kahle, Artillerie Regiment 194. Of the three Urlauben recorded in his Soldbuch, two were recorded as Erholungsurlaub (Recreational Leave) and one Sonderurlaub (Special Leave).

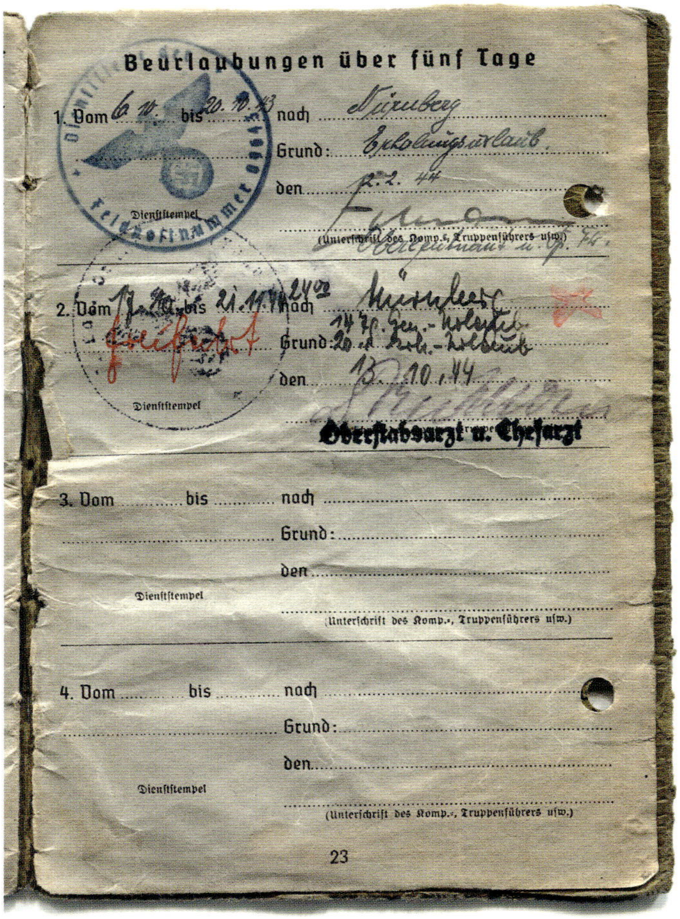

Figure 2-3. Two Urlauben recorded in Grenadier Kurt Bürckner's Soldbuch. This was Bürkner's second Soldbuch (noted at the top of page 1), hence the disjointed dates of the first leave recorded; he was granted Erholungsurlaub from October 6–20, 1943, though the leave was recorded in this Soldbuch when it was issued on February 12, 1944. The second, two separate Erholungsurlaub that ran concurrently from October 17 until November 21, 1944, was issued by the Reserve-Lazarett (Reserve Hospital) Regensburg, where he recovered from grenade or artillery fragments for almost a year, from March 10, 1944 until his discharge on February 10, 1945.

Figure 2-4. Some fortunate Soldaten, such as Obergefreiter Erik Jurreil of Artillerie Regiment 255, were granted leave frequently enough that a blank page was removed from a blank Soldbuch and glued into his, just to record them all. Obergefreiter Jurreil "earned" these 13 separate Urlauben between December 14, 1940, until January 23, 1945, due to multiple bouts of pneumonia recorded in his Soldbuch.

Four separate sections on each page are provided for a clerk to record all leave granted in excess of five days (*Beurlauben über fünf Tage*), prior to the solder's departure. The duration and destination was noted, as well as the grounds for travel, usually in a single word; for example, *Erholungsurlaub* (Recreational Leave) or *Heiratsurlaub* (Marriage Leave). The date would be entered, along with the *Dienststempel*, *Truppenteil*, and commanding officer's signature, and the *Soldbuch* given back to the soldier, eager for departure.

Die Reiseverordnung

The *Wehrmacht* depended on a series of regulations to govern travel, pay while traveling, how long one was permitted to remain during travel, etc., and the primary source for this was the *Reiseverordnung für die Wehrmacht*. There were three different designations for this one set of rules, the *Heeres Dienstvorschrift 159* (H.Dv.159 - Army Service Manual 159), the Marine *Dienstvorschrift Nr. 283* (M.Dv.Nr.283 - Navy Service Manual Number 283), and the *Luftwaffe Dienstvorschrift 39* (L.Dv.39 - Air Force Service Manual 39). There were not three different books, but rather a single volume with three different designations given by each branch.

The *Reiseverordnung* listed all regulations governing travel in the military. It regulated *Dienstreisen* (Service Travel), *Urlaubsreisen* (Leave Travel), and transfers between duty stations using the *Marschbefehl* (Marching Orders). Other regulations covered those traveling sick or wounded, reimbursable expenses, who was permitted to travel in first, second, or third class railcars, overnight pay, disbursements given to married or single soldiers, travel expenses, and so on.

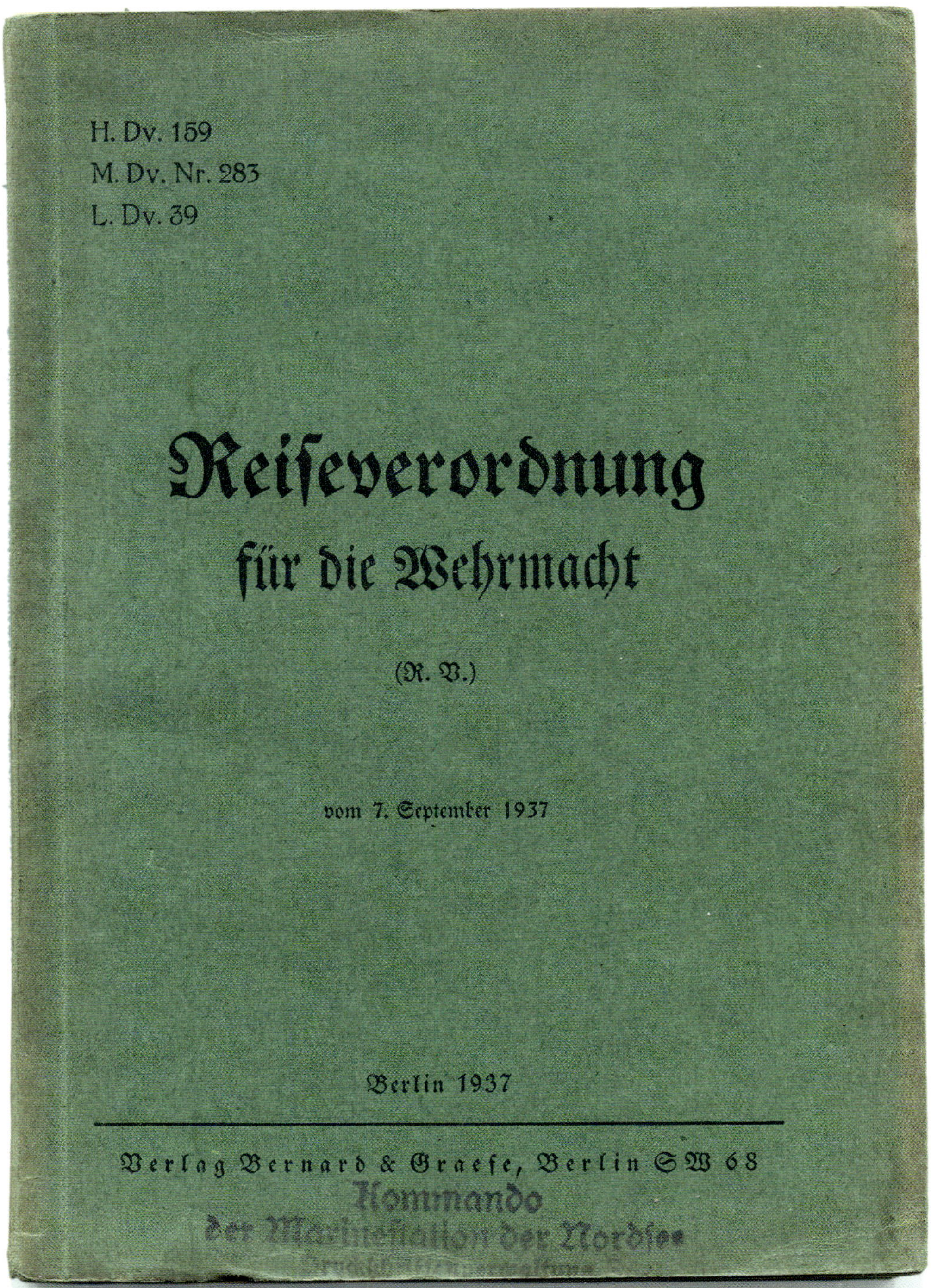

Figure 2-5. Cover of the Reiseverordnung für die Wehrmacht; note the three different military branches' designations in the upper left corner. This particular issue comes from the Oberkommando der Marinestation der Nordsee (Commander of the Navy Station of the North Sea), which is stamped at the bottom. ($5\frac{7}{8}$" x $8\frac{1}{4}$")

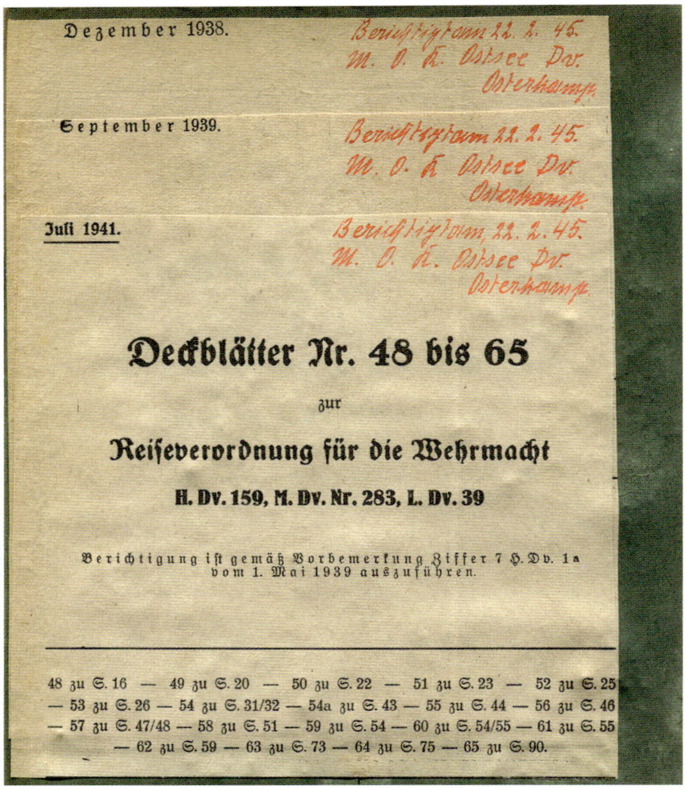

Dezember 1938.

September 1939.

Juli 1941.

Deckblätter Nr. 48 bis 65

zur

Reiseverordnung für die Wehrmacht

H. Dv. 159, M. Dv. Nr. 283, L. Dv. 39

Berichtigung ist gemäß Vorbemerkung Ziffer 7 H.Dv. 1a vom 1. Mai 1939 auszuführen.

48 zu S. 16 — 49 zu S. 20 — 50 zu S. 22 — 51 zu S. 23 — 52 zu S. 25 — 53 zu S. 26 — 54 zu S. 31/32 — 54a zu S. 43 — 55 zu S. 44 — 56 zu S. 46 — 57 zu S. 47/48 — 58 zu S. 51 — 59 zu S. 54 — 60 zu S. 54/55 — 61 zu S. 55 — 62 zu S. 59 — 63 zu S. 73 — 64 zu S. 75 — 65 zu S. 90.

Figure 2-6. Saved and mounted title pages of the three Deckblätter (Cover Sheets), which updated the Reiseverordnung in 1938, 1939, and 1941.

Regulations enumerated in the *Reiseverordnung* are further augmented, updated, and clarified through five *Beilagen* (Enclosures), five *Anhangen* (Supplements) and three *Deckblätter* (literally Cover Sheets, but more appropriately translated to Addenda and Corrections), which the original owner of my particular copy was kind enough to cut, organize, and glue over the appropriate sections updated. Did I mention how meticulous Germans can be?

The majority of the book is printed in *Fraktur*, though certain sections and paragraphs are printed in a light serif typeface as seen below, which is a very interesting combination when next to *Fraktur*.

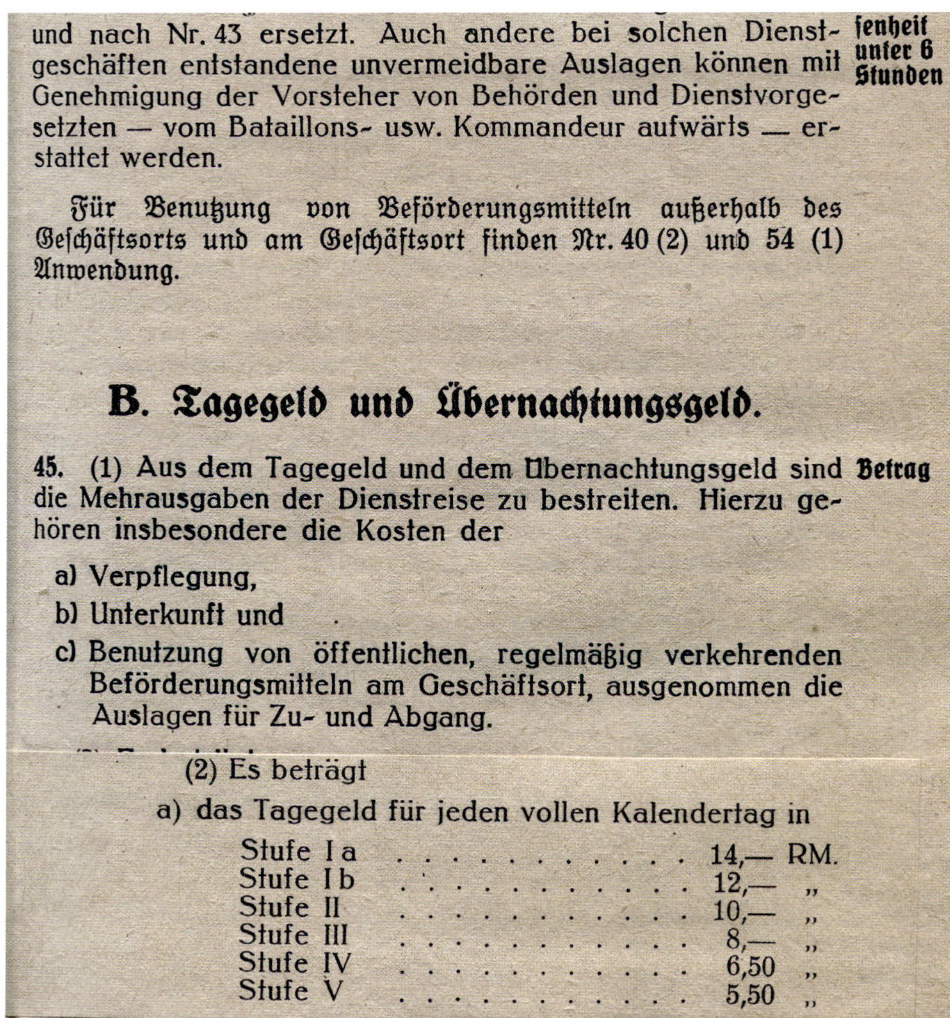

und nach Nr. 43 ersetzt. Auch andere bei solchen Dienstgeschäften entstandene unvermeidbare Auslagen können mit Genehmigung der Vorsteher von Behörden und Dienstvorgesetzten — vom Bataillons- usw. Kommandeur aufwärts — erstattet werden. **fenheit unter 6 Stunden**

Für Benutzung von Beförderungsmitteln außerhalb des Geschäftsorts und am Geschäftsort finden Nr. 40 (2) und 54 (1) Anwendung.

B. Tagegeld und Übernachtungsgeld.

45. (1) Aus dem Tagegeld und dem Übernachtungsgeld sind die Mehrausgaben der Dienstreise zu bestreiten. Hierzu gehören insbesondere die Kosten der **Betrag**

a) Verpflegung,

b) Unterkunft und

c) Benutzung von öffentlichen, regelmäßig verkehrenden Beförderungsmitteln am Geschäftsort, ausgenommen die Auslagen für Zu- und Abgang.

(2) Es beträgt

a) das Tagegeld für jeden vollen Kalendertag in

Stufe I a	14,— RM.
Stufe I b	12,— „
Stufe II	10,— „
Stufe III	8,— „
Stufe IV	6,50 „
Stufe V	5,50 „

Figure 2-7. A randomly selected page which shows the juxtaposition of typefaces used, along with the pasted table at the bottom, a correction from a Deckblatt issued after publication of the Reiseverordnung.

Figure 2-8. An illustration of the two things near and dear to every Soldat's heart, as caught by a cartoonist for the Nazi Party newspaper Völkischer Beobachter's (People's Observer) Feldpost series of soldiers' entertainment books, specifically Heft 4: Landser lachen – Fronthumor dieses Krieges (Notebook 4: Soldiers Laugh – Humor From the Front of This War).

Leave Passes

There are only two things that soldiers of every nation crave, the second of which is leave. To go on leave, however, required permission from one's unit, which one had to request. As such, the first form a homesick *Soldat* might encounter would commonly be the *Urlaubsgesuch* (Leave Request; literally, the "Leave Search").

This would have been filled out and handed in to the *Verwaltungsstelle* (Administrative Office) of one's unit. The *Urlaubsgesuch* required the soldier's rank and name and the dates he wished to be absent. Units often had their own forms printed and few are identical to one another, so depending on the form, there might also be a section requiring specific grounds for requesting leave. If no printed forms were available, pre-typed or pre-written forms were often available for the *Soldat* to fill out.

The leave request would either be approved or denied, the details of which would often be printed

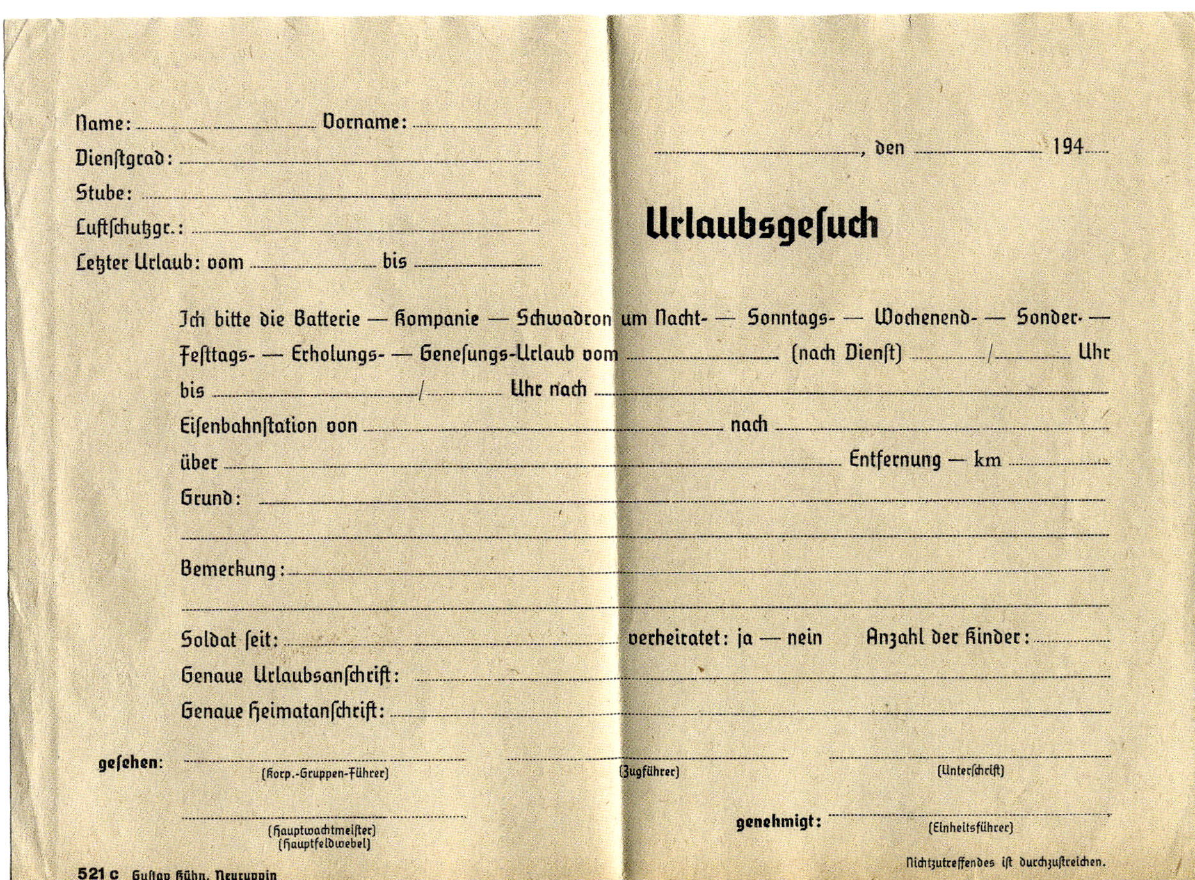

Name: .... Vorname: ....

Dienstgrad: ....

Stube: ....

Luftschutzgr.: ....

Letzter Urlaub: vom .... bis ....

........, den .... 194....

Urlaubsgesuch

Ich bitte die Batterie — Kompanie — Schwadron um Nacht- — Sonntags- — Wochenend- — Sonder- — Festtags- — Erholungs- — Genesungs-Urlaub vom .... (nach Dienst) ..../.... Uhr bis ..../.... Uhr nach ....

Eisenbahnstation von .... nach ....

über .... Entfernung — km ....

Grund: ....

Bemerkung: ....

Soldat seit: .... verheiratet: ja — nein Anzahl der Kinder: ....

Genaue Urlaubsanschrift: ....

Genaue Heimatanschrift: ....

gesehen: .... (Korp.-Gruppen-Führer) .... (Zugführer) .... (Unterschrift)

.... (Hauptwachtmeister) (Hauptfeldwebel)

genehmigt: .... (Einheitsführer)

521 c Gustav Kühn, Neuruppin

Nichtzutreffendes ist durchzustreichen.

Figure 2-9. A Soldat's journey toward leave began with a request, which was completed in writing or by using a form such as this, an Urlaubsgesuch. This multi-service form was printed by Gustav Kühn in Neurippen; his mark is in the lower left corner beside his stock number. (A5)

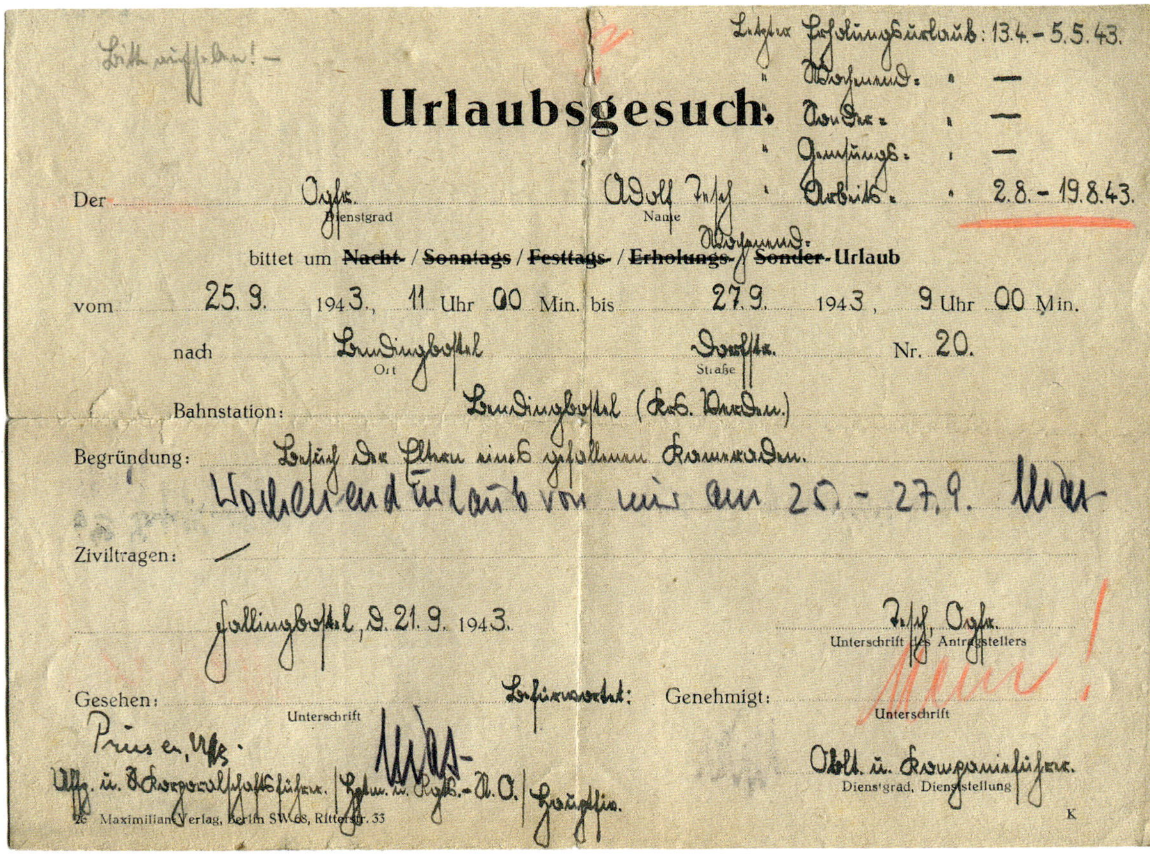

Urlaubsgesuch.

Letzter Erholungsurlaub: 13.4.–5.5.43.

Der Ogfr. (Dienstgrad) Adolf Fesch (Name)

bittet um ~~Nacht-~~ / ~~Sonntags~~ / ~~Festtags-~~ / ~~Erholungs-~~ / ~~Sonder-~~ Urlaub

vom 25.9. 1943., 11 Uhr 00 Min. bis 27.9. 1943, 9 Uhr 00 Min.

nach (Ort) (Straße) Nr. 20.

Bahnstation:

Begründung:

Wochenendurlaub von mir am 20.–27.9.

Ziviltragen: —

, d. 21.9. 1943.

Unterschrift des Antragstellers

Gesehen: Unterschrift

Genehmigt: Nein! Unterschrift

Oblt. u. Kompanieführer

Dienstgrad, Dienststellung

Maximilian Verlag, Berlin SW 68, Ritterstr. 33

K

Figure 2-10. Another Urlaubsgesuch, completed by Gefreiter Adolf Fesch in order to visit the parents of a fallen Kamerad. Note that the request was emphatically denied by his Oberleutnant (Nein!) where the signature would have gone; this would have been Fesch's third leave in four months. (A5)

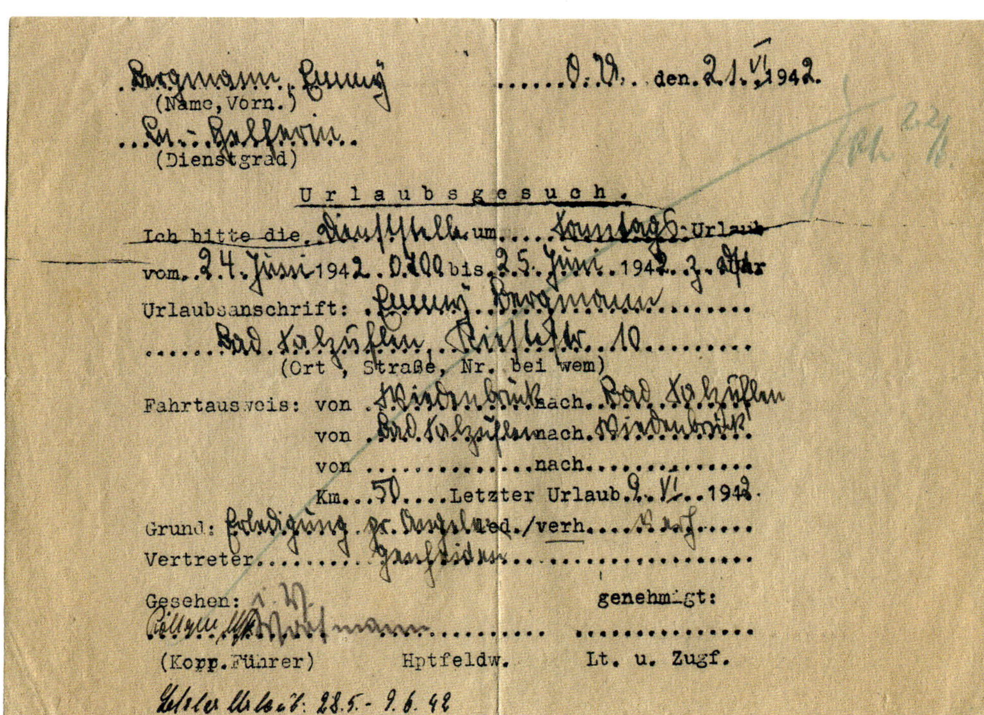

(Name, Vorn.) .... den 21.VI.1942.

(Dienstgrad)

Urlaubsgesuch.

Ich bitte die ...... um ...... Urlaub

vom 24. Juni 1942 0.700 bis 25. Juni 1942

Urlaubsanschrift: ....

Bad Salzuflen ....

(Ort, Straße, Nr. bei wem)

Fahrtausweis: von ...... nach Bad Salzuflen

von Bad Salzuflen nach ......

von .... nach ....

Km...50....Letzter Urlaub 9.VI..1942.

Grund: ...... /verh. ......

Vertreter. ....

Gesehen: genehmigt:

(Kopp.Führer) Hptfeldw. Lt. u. Zugf.

Letzter Urlaub: 28.5.–9.6.42

Figure 2-11. When no preprinted form was available, resourceful clerks would type their own. This series of Urlaubgesuchen was prepared by Luftwaffe Helferin (Helper, usually in radio communications) Bergmann, often to visit her parents some 50 km away in Bad Salzuflen. On this Urlaubsgesuch, Helfer-in Bergmann requested Sonntag-surlaub ("Sunday" leave) from 7:00 am on June 24 until 3:00 am, June 25, 1942. Her previous leave is noted in ink at the bottom of the form, from May 28 until June 9, 1942.

Figure 2-12. This request by Luftwaffe Helferin Bergmann for Heimaturlaub (home leave) from 7:00 am on July 27 until 3:00 am on July 28, 1942, was denied; note the lack of the Leutnant und Zugführer's – Lieutenant and Squad Leader) signature. At the top of the form, Bergmann's Heimleiterin (a Female Home Leader) noted, presumably to the Lieutenant, "What are you doing? We had given her Nachturlaub (Night's Leave) to get married."

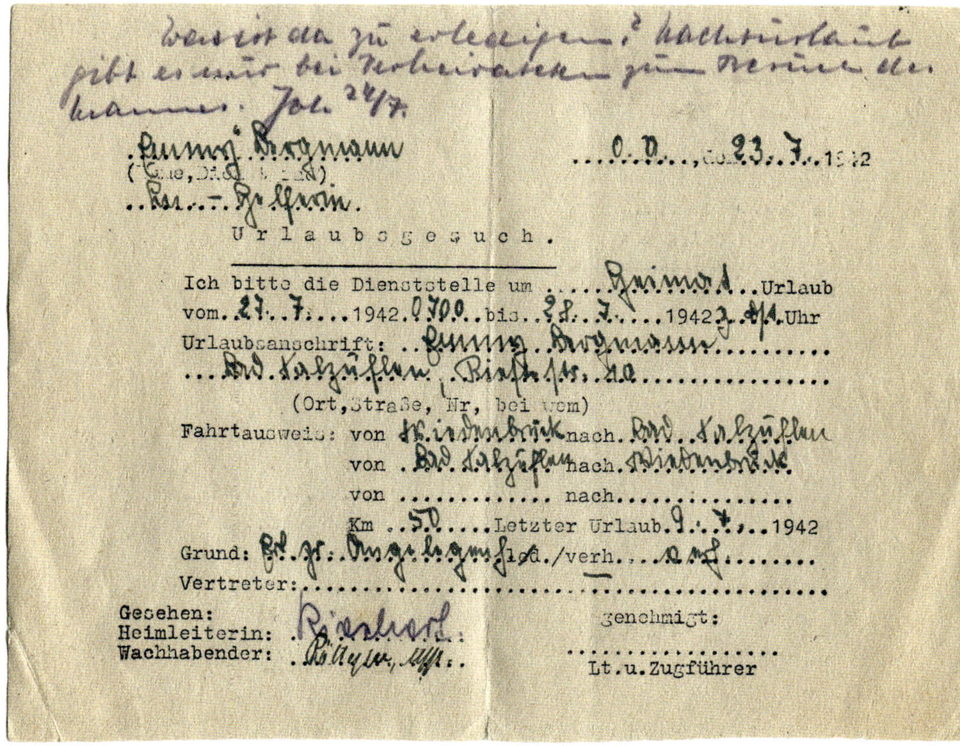
O.U., den 23.7.1942

(Name, Dienstgrad)

Urlaubsgesuch.

Ich bitte die Dienststelle um ....Urlaub

vom.27.7....1942.0700..bis..28.7.....1942....Uhr

Urlaubsanschrift: ....

(Ort, Straße, Nr, bei wem)

Fahrtausweis: von .... nach ....

von .... nach ....

von .... nach ....

Km ..50....Letzter Urlaub.9.7...1942

Grund: ....led./verh.........

Vertreter: ....

Gesehen:

Heimleiterin: ....

Wachhabender: ....

genehmigt:

....

Lt.u.Zugführer

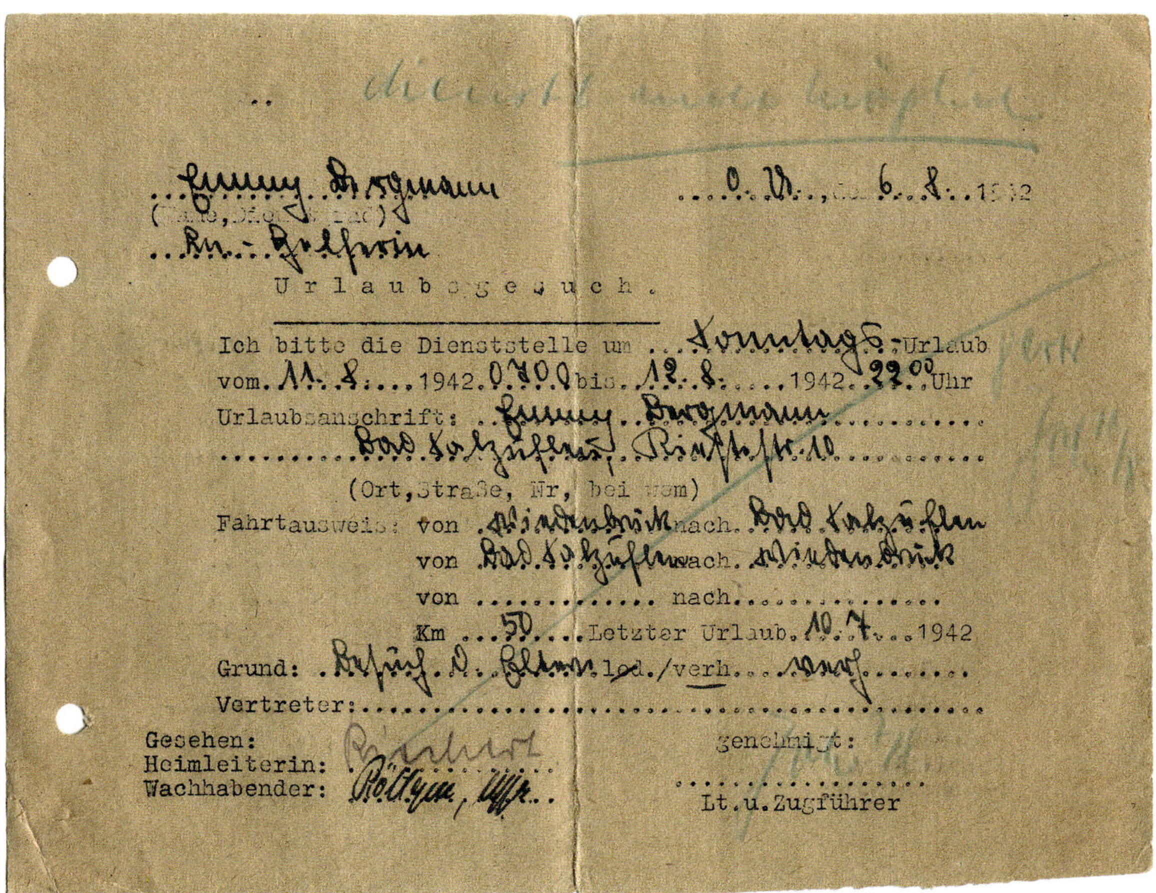
O.U., den 6.8.1942

(Name, Dienstgrad)

Urlaubsgesuch.

Ich bitte die Dienststelle um ...Sonntags-Urlaub

vom.11.8....1942.0700.bis..12.8.....1942.22⁰⁰Uhr

Urlaubsanschrift: ....

(Ort, Straße, Nr, bei wem)

Fahrtausweis: von .... nach ....

von .... nach ....

von .... nach ....

Km ...50....Letzter Urlaub.10.7...1942

Grund: ....led./verh.........

Vertreter: ....

Gesehen:

Heimleiterin: ....

Wachhabender: ....

genehmigt:

....

Lt.u.Zugführer

Figure 2-13. This last request by Helferin Bergmann, again for "Sunday leave," was for leave lasting from 7:00 am on August 11 until 10:00 pm on August 12, 1942. Her previous leave was noted as July 10, 1942, as her request for leave on July 27-28 had been denied. This request however was approved. (All three forms are approximately 6$^3/_8$" x 8$^1/_8$")

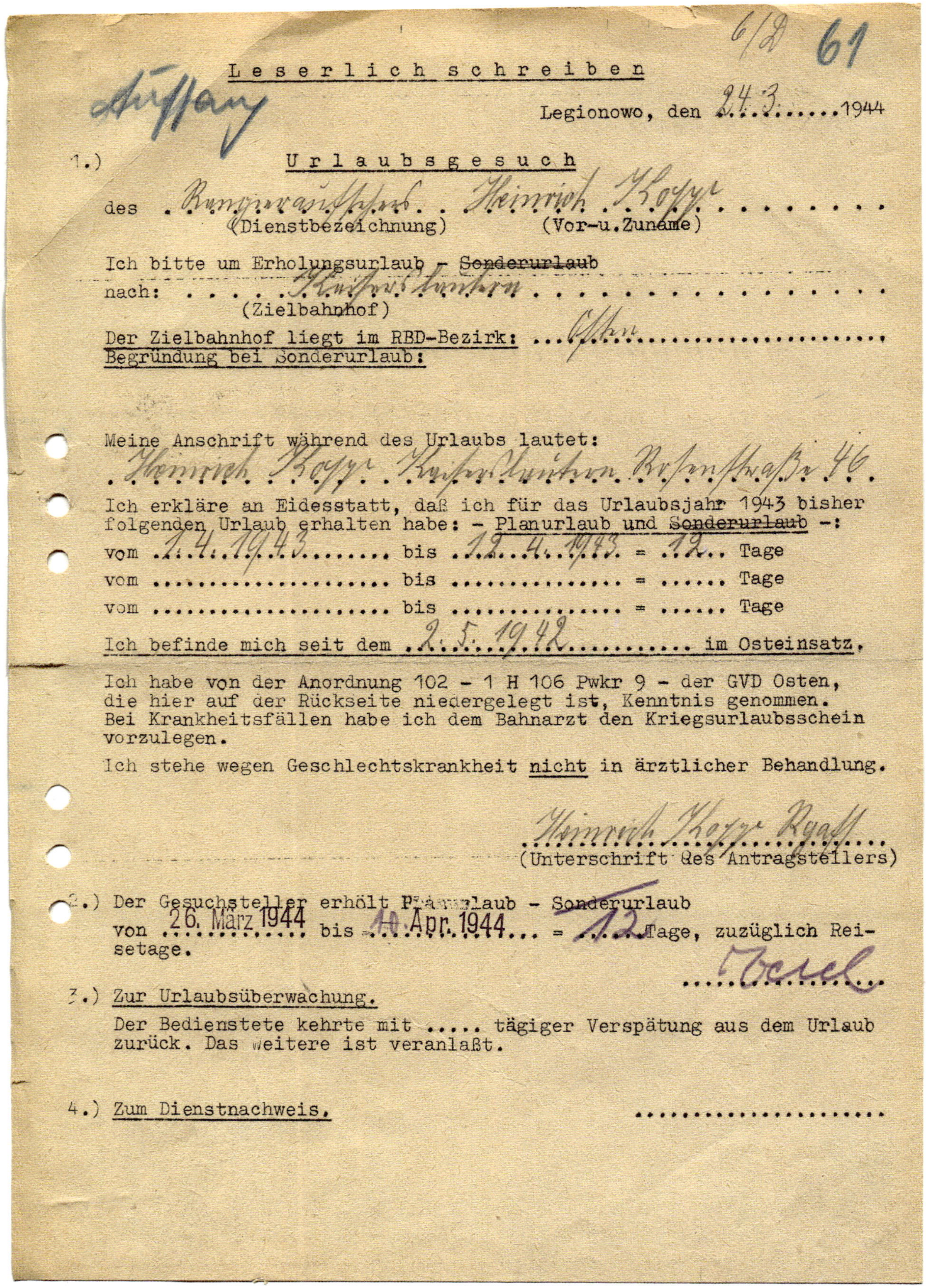

6/D 61

Leserlich schreiben

Legionowo, den 24.3.1944

1.) Urlaubsgesuch

des Rangieraufseher Heinrich Kopp
(Dienstbezeichnung) (Vor-u.Zuname)

Ich bitte um Erholungsurlaub - ~~Sonderurlaub~~
nach: Kaiserslautern
(Zielbahnhof)

Der Zielbahnhof liegt im RBD-Bezirk: Osten
Begründung bei Sonderurlaub:

Meine Anschrift während des Urlaubs lautet:
Heinrich Kopp Kaiserslautern Rosenstraße 46.

Ich erkläre an Eidesstatt, daß ich für das Urlaubsjahr 1943 bisher folgenden Urlaub erhalten habe: - Planurlaub und ~~Sonderurlaub~~ -:
vom 1.4.1943 bis 12.4.1943 = 12 Tage
vom .... bis .... = ... Tage
vom .... bis .... = ... Tage

Ich befinde mich seit dem 2.5.1942 im Osteinsatz.

Ich habe von der Anordnung 102 - 1 H 106 Pwkr 9 - der GVD Osten, die hier auf der Rückseite niedergelegt ist, Kenntnis genommen. Bei Krankheitsfällen habe ich dem Bahnarzt den Kriegsurlaubsschein vorzulegen.

Ich stehe wegen Geschlechtskrankheit nicht in ärztlicher Behandlung.

Heinrich Kopp Rgaff.
(Unterschrift des Antragstellers)

2.) Der Gesuchsteller erhält ~~Planurlaub~~ - Sonderurlaub von 26. März 1944 bis 10 Apr. 1944 = 12 Tage, zuzüglich Reisetage.

3.) Zur Urlaubsüberwachung.
Der Bedienstete kehrte mit ..... tägiger Verspätung aus dem Urlaub zurück. Das weitere ist veranlaßt.

4.) Zum Dienstnachweis.

Figures 2-14 & 2-15. Not all forms were half a page in size; these Ersatz Urlaubsgesuchen (Replacement Leave Requests) created by clerks for those serving in the Reichsbahn, used a full page. The legends at the top of the forms, Sehr deutlich schreiben or Leserlich schreiben, respectively encourage those filling out the forms to write clearly and legibly. (A4)

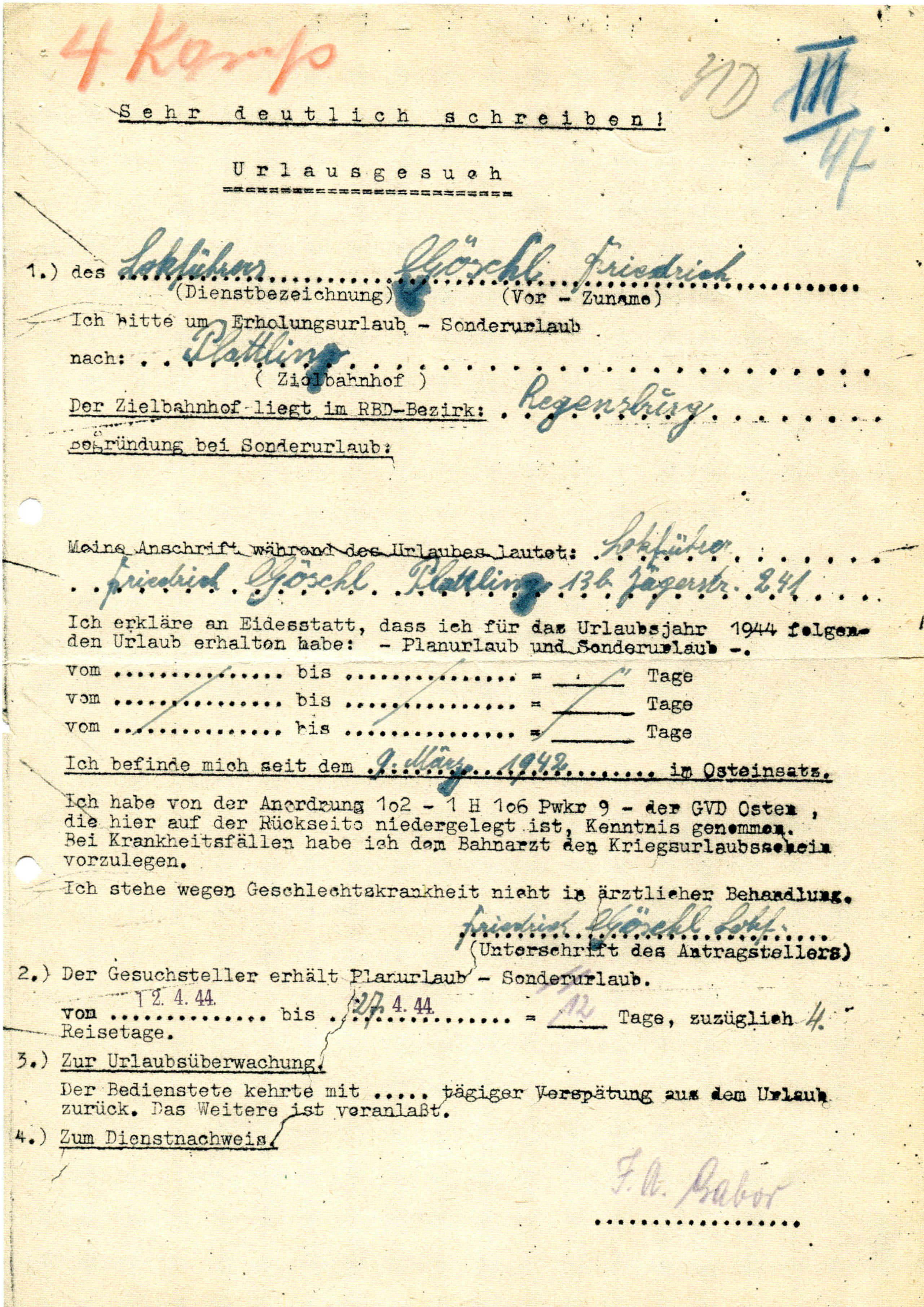

4 Kamp

Sehr deutlich schreiben!

Urlausgesuch

1.) des Lokführer Glöschl Friedrich
(Dienstbezeichnung) (Vor - Zuname)

Ich bitte um Erholungsurlaub - Sonderurlaub

nach: Plattling
(Zielbahnhof)

Der Zielbahnhof liegt im RBD-Bezirk: Regensburg

Begründung bei Sonderurlaub:

Meine Anschrift während des Urlaubes lautet: Lokführer Friedrich Glöschl Plattling 13b Jägerstr. 241

Ich erkläre an Eidesstatt, dass ich für das Urlaubsjahr 1944 folgenden Urlaub erhalten habe: - Planurlaub und Sonderurlaub -.

vom .... bis .... = ____ Tage
vom .... bis .... = ____ Tage
vom .... bis .... = ____ Tage

Ich befinde mich seit dem 9. März 1942 im Osteinsatz.

Ich habe von der Anordnung 1o2 - 1 H 1o6 Pwkr 9 - der GVD Osten, die hier auf der Rückseite niedergelegt ist, Kenntnis genommen. Bei Krankheitsfällen habe ich dem Bahnarzt den Kriegsurlaubsschein vorzulegen.

Ich stehe wegen Geschlechtskrankheit nicht in ärztlicher Behandlung.

Friedrich Glöschl Lokf.
(Unterschrift des Antragstellers)

2.) Der Gesuchsteller erhält Planurlaub - Sonderurlaub.
vom 12. 4. 44 bis 27. 4. 44 = 12 Tage, zuzüglich 4 Reisetage.

3.) Zur Urlaubsüberwachung.
Der Bedienstete kehrte mit ..... tägiger Verspätung aus dem Urlaub zurück. Das Weitere ist veranlaßt.

4.) Zum Dienstnachweis.

F.A. Babor

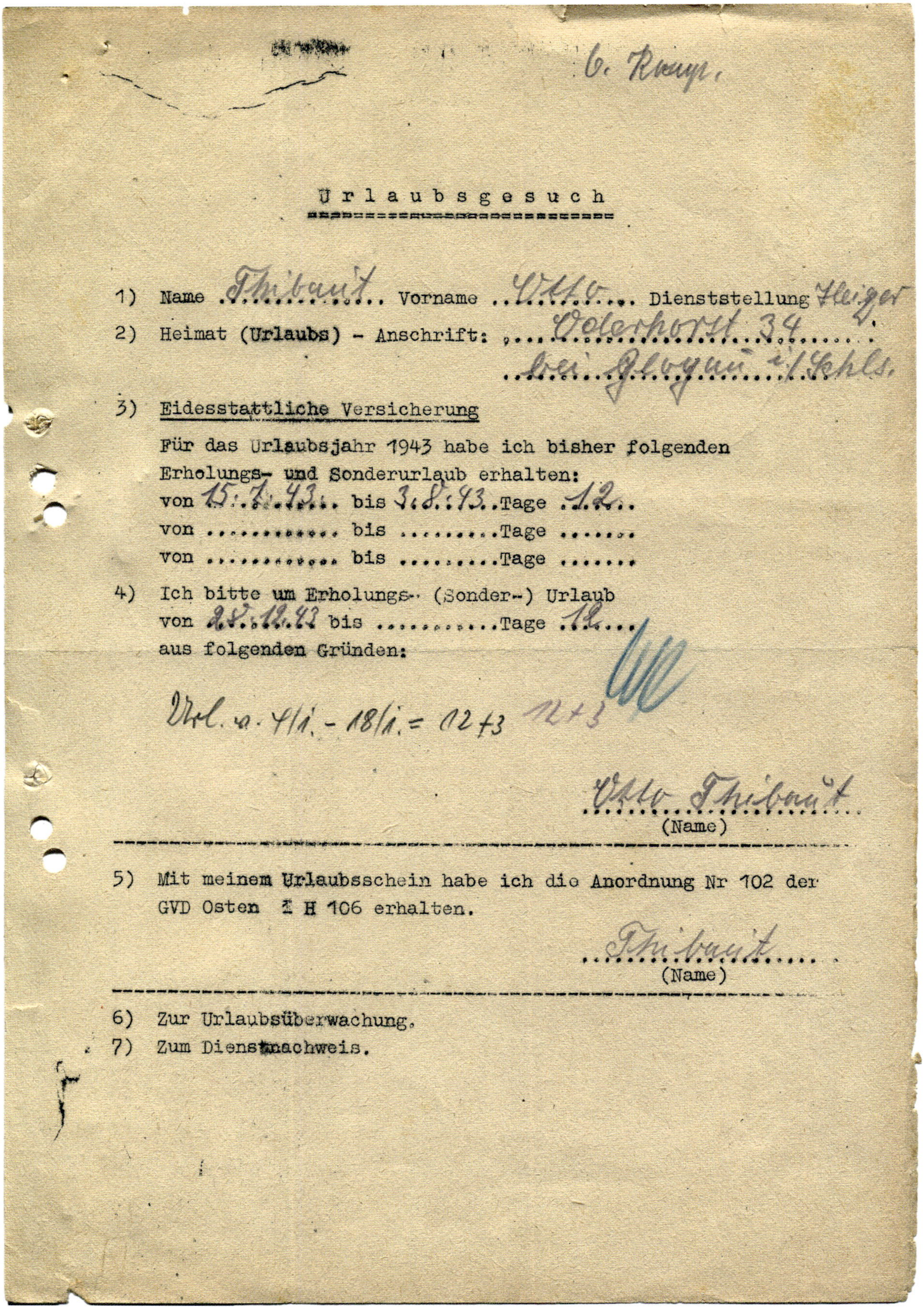

6. Komp.

U r l a u b s g e s u c h

1) Name Thibaut Vorname Otto Dienststellung Flieger
2) Heimat (Urlaubs) - Anschrift: Osterhorst 34
bei Glogau i. Schls.

3) Eidesstattliche Versicherung

Für das Urlaubsjahr 1943 habe ich bisher folgenden Erholungs- und Sonderurlaub erhalten:
von 15.7.43 bis 3.8.43 Tage 12
von .... bis ....Tage ....
von .... bis ....Tage ....

4) Ich bitte um Erholungs- (Sonder-) Urlaub
von 28.12.43 bis ....Tage 12
aus folgenden Gründen:

Vol. v. 4/1. - 18/1. = 12+3 12+3

Otto Thibaut
(Name)

5) Mit meinem Urlaubsschein habe ich die Anordnung Nr 102 der GVD Osten Z H 106 erhalten.

Thibaut
(Name)

6) Zur Urlaubsüberwachung.
7) Zum Dienstnachweis.

Figure 2-16. On this Ersatz Urlaubsgesuch, Flieger (Airman) Otto Thibaut, stationed at Osterhorst 34 (Eastern Airfield 34) near Glogau (now Glogów in southwest Poland), requested leave from July 15 until August 8, 1943. He request was granted and he was given three additional Reisetage (travel days) for a total of 15 days. (A4)

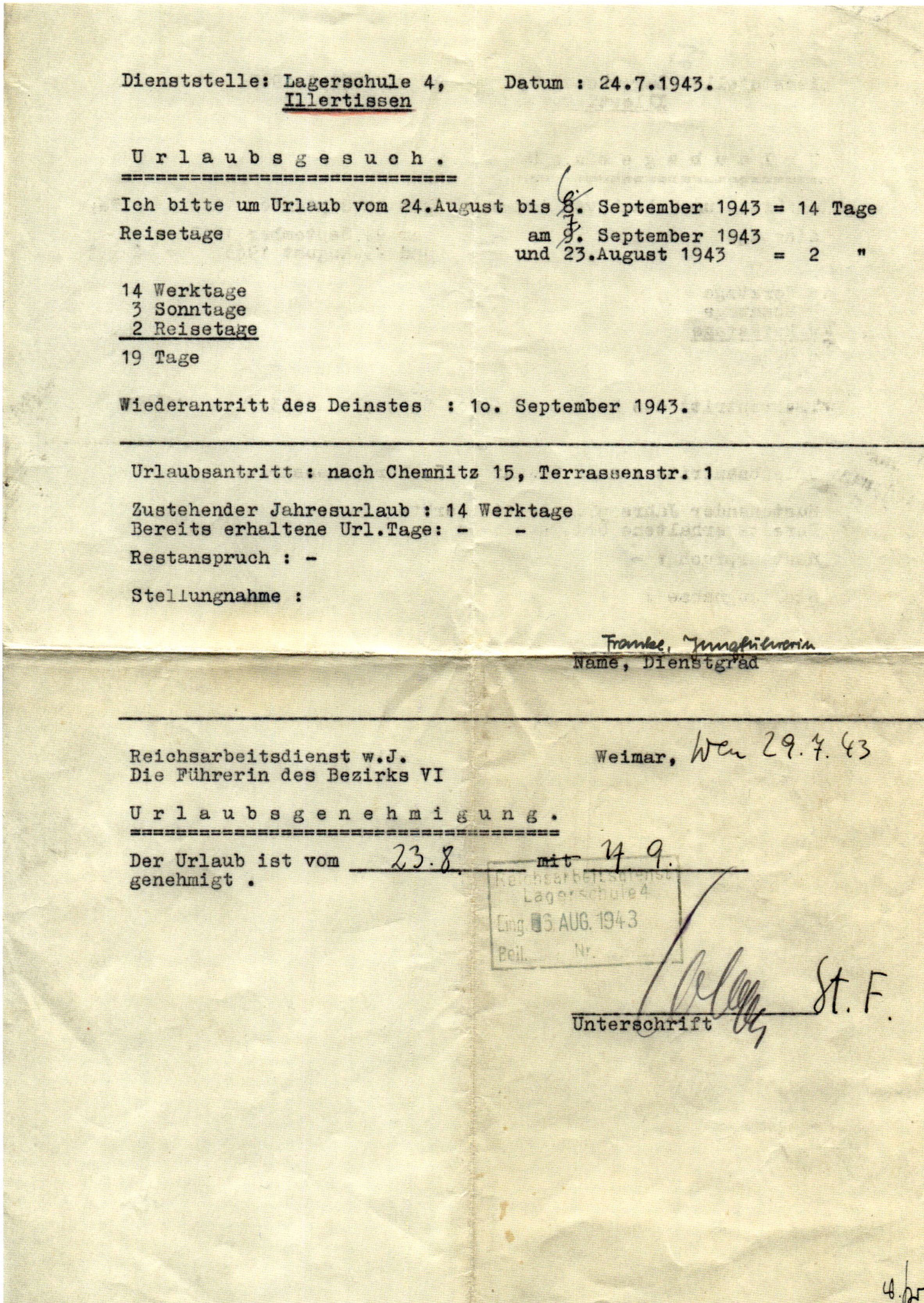

Dienststelle: Lagerschule 4, Illertissen

Datum : 24.7.1943.

Urlaubsgesuch.

Ich bitte um Urlaub vom 24.August bis 8. [6] September 1943 = 14 Tage

Reisetage am 9. [7] September 1943 und 23.August 1943 = 2 "

14 Werktage
3 Sonntage
2 Reisetage

19 Tage

Wiederantritt des Deinstes : 1o. September 1943.

Urlaubsantritt : nach Chemnitz 15, Terrassenstr. 1

Zustehender Jahresurlaub : 14 Werktage
Bereits erhaltene Url.Tage: - -

Restanspruch : -

Stellungnahme :

Franke, Jungführerin
Name, Dienstgrad

Reichsarbeitsdienst w.J.
Die Führerin des Bezirks VI

Weimar, den 29.7.43

Urlaubsgenehmigung.

Der Urlaub ist vom 23.8 mit 7.9. genehmigt .

Reichsarbeitsdienst Lagerschule 4 Eing. 6. AUG. 1943 Beil. Nr.

[signature] St.F.
Unterschrift

Figure 2-17. This letter, typed and signed by Reichsarbeitsdienst Jungführerin (Reich Work Sevice Female Junior Leader) Franke, requested a leave of fourteen work days, three Sundays, and two travel days for a total of nineteen days from August 24 until September 9, 1943, to return to duty on September 10, 1943. Note that Franke's commanding officer corrected her math at the top of her letter, changing the dates from September 9 to September 7. The request was approved on July 29, 1943. (A4)

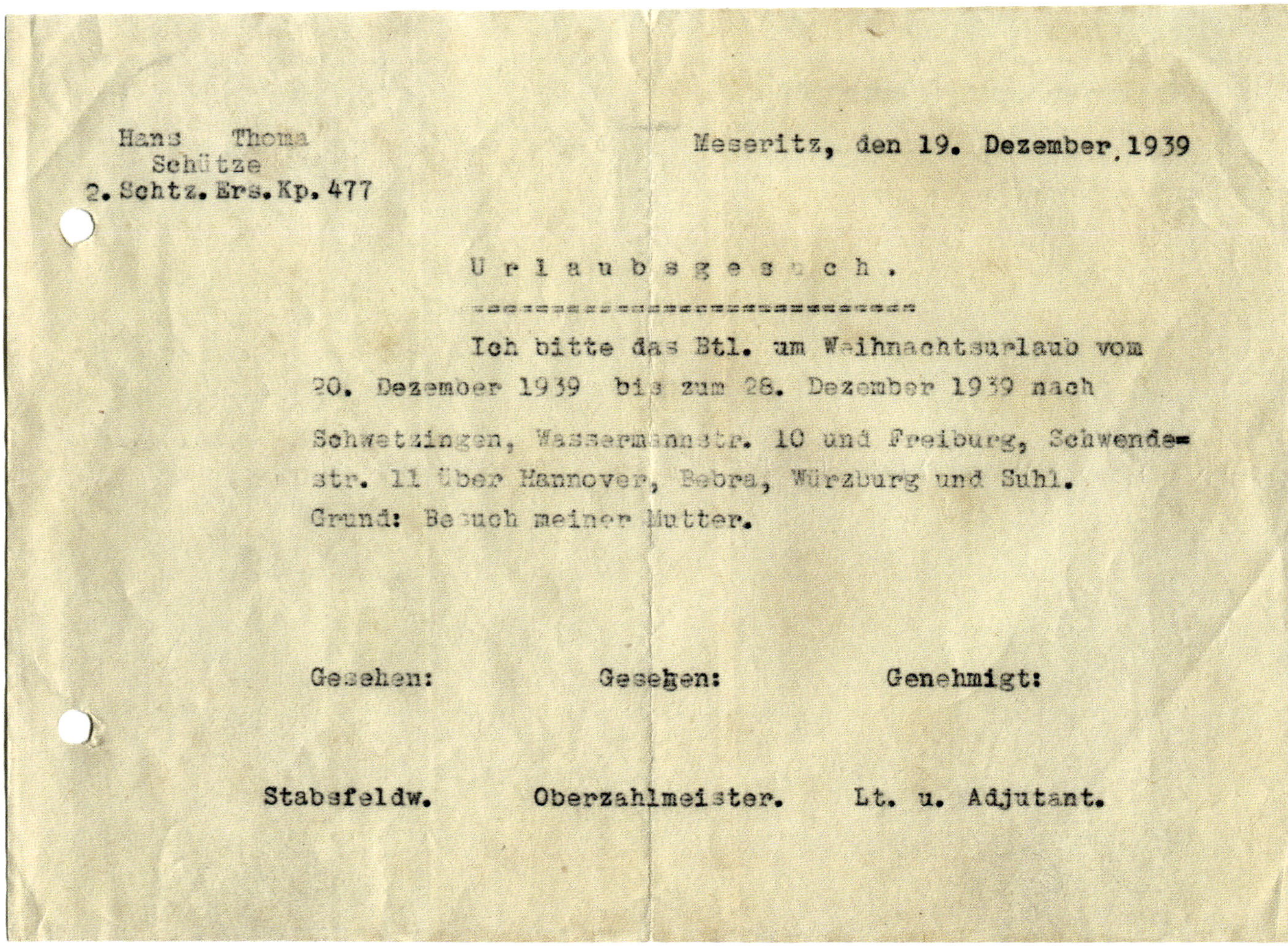

Hans Thoma
Schütze
2. Schtz.Ers.Kp.477

Meseritz, den 19. Dezember 1939

Urlaubsgesuch.

Ich bitte das Btl. um Weihnachtsurlaub vom 20. Dezember 1939 bis zum 28. Dezember 1939 nach Schwetzingen, Wassermannstr. 10 und Freiburg, Schwendestr. 11 über Hannover, Bebra, Würzburg und Suhl.
Grund: Besuch meiner Mutter.

Gesehen: Gesehen: Genehmigt:

Stabsfeldw. Oberzahlmeister. Lt. u. Adjutant.

Figure 2-18. This is a carbon copy of a leave request by Schütze (Private) Hans Thoma for Weihnachtsurlaub, or Christmas Leave, from December 20 until December 28, 1939, to visit his mother (noted at the line which reads "Grund: Besuch meiner Mutter.") This early in the war, it was probably granted; however, there is no way to know for sure. (A5)

at the bottom of the same *Urlaubsgesuch*. If leave was granted, the approved dates would be indicated and usually included a number of days added to the leave for estimated travel time (*Reisetage*).

The *Urlaubsgesuch* would not have been required for special leave such as transfer to a new duty station or convalescence following an injury this would have been automatically granted but special leave such as bereavement leave, Christmas leave, or even sick leave would have required that the soldier submit a request by way of this form.

Use of the prepared form was not necessarily the only way one could request leave, however. On pages 89–91 of the *Dienstunterricht in der Luftwaffe*, under the section for composing messages, two examples of leave requests are given as an illustration of clarity in writing:

Ich bitte um Erholungsurlaub vom 10.4. bis 20.4. nach Friedrichshafen, Bahnhofstrasse 2.
Ich bitte um Austellung folgender Urlaubsscheine: Jütterbog–Ulm, Ulm–Friedrichshafen, Friedrichshafen–München, München–Jütterbog.
Zustehend: 14 Tage
Bereits bewilligt: ___ Tage Wohlfahrt.

May I please go on recreational leave from 10 April until 20 April to Friedrichshafen, at Bahnhof Street, number 2.
May I please have the Leave Pass for the following itinerary: Jütterbog to Ulm, Ulm to Friedrichshafen, and Friedrichshafen to Munich, Munch to Jütterbog (for the return trip).
Leave to last 14 days
Already permitted: ___ days travel time.

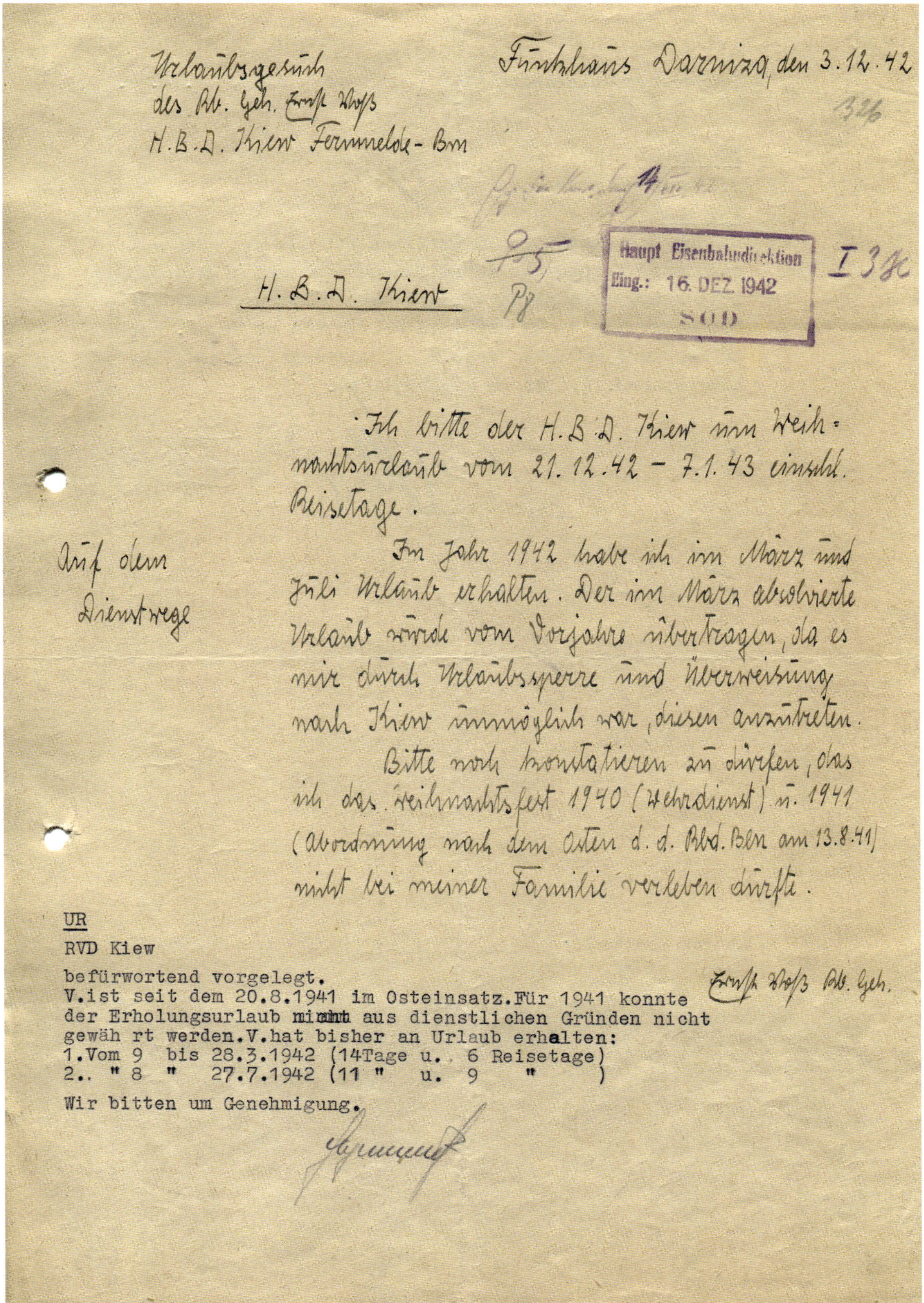

Urlaubsgesuch
des Rb. Geh. Ernst Woß
H.B.D. Kiew Fernmelde-Bm

Funkhaus Darniza, den 3.12.42

Haupt Eisenbahndirektion
Eing.: 16. DEZ. 1942
SOD

H.B.D. Kiew

Ich bitte der H.B.D. Kiew um Weihnachtsurlaub vom 21.12.42 – 7.1.43 einschl. Reisetage.

Auf dem Dienstwege

Im Jahr 1942 habe ich im März und Juli Urlaub erhalten. Der im März absolvierte Urlaub wurde vom Vorjahre übertragen, da es mir durch Urlaubssperre und Überweisung nach Kiew unmöglich war, diesen anzutreten.

Bitte noch konstatieren zu dürfen, das ich das Weihnachtsfest 1940 (Wehrdienst) u. 1941 (Abordnung nach dem Osten d. d. Bbd. Bln am 13.8.41) nicht bei meiner Familie verleben durfte.

Ernst Woß Rb. Geh.

UR
RVD Kiew
befürwortend vorgelegt.
V.ist seit dem 20.8.1941 im Osteinsatz.Für 1941 konnte
der Erholungsurlaub nicht aus dienstlichen Gründen nicht
gewäh rt werden.V.hat bisher an Urlaub erhalten:
1.Vom 9 bis 28.3.1942 (14Tage u. 6 Reisetage)
2.. " 8 " 27.7.1942 (11 " u. 9 ")
Wir bitten um Genehmigung.

Figure 2-19. An interesting letter, written by hand at the Funkhaus (Radio station) in Darniza, a suburb of Kiev, and mistakenly directed to the Reichsbahn official at Haupteisenbahndirektion Kiew (HBD) (Main Railway Directorate Kiev) requesting Christmas leave from December 21, 1942, until January 7, 1943. The typewritten notation at the bottom by the RVD Kiew (Reichsbahnverkehrsdirektion – Railway Traffic Directorate) notes that the requestor has been serving honorably since August 20, 1941, with only two short periods of leave (March 9-28 and July 8-27, 1942), and that they are pleased to grant his request. (A4)

Meldung
Ich bin an Grippe erkrankt und nicht reisefähig. Voraussichliche Dauer: 10 Tage.
Behandelnder Artz: Dr. Lehmann, Kreisartz. Zuegnis liegt bei. Ich liege in der Wohnung bei meiner Eltern.

Message
I have become sick with the flu and am not capable of traveling. Expected duration: 10 days.
Attending physician: Dr. Lehman, district doctor. The Doctor's proof is included with this message. I am at the home of my parents.

Once leave was approved, the clerk would locate the soldiers *Urlaubs- und Freifahrnachweis* (Leave and Free Travel Report). This A4 document is something that a soldier would rarely, if ever, see; it was kept on file with everyone else's *Nachweis*.

It listed the name and rank of the individual, as well as particulars about him: birthdate, rank, wife's name, number of children, etc. The clerk would record the details about the approved travel, and keep a running total of all leave granted. At the end of the year, the total amount of leave time would be added and indicated at the top.

Each soldier in the unit had an *Urlaubs- und Freifahrnachweis* available for the commanding officer to review, allowing him to identify anyone who might be abusing leave privileges.

Once leave was granted and recorded, a *Soldat* could collect his papers from the *Verwaltungsstelle*, where the leave would be noted by the clerk on the last two pages in a soldier's *Soldbuch*, a preventive measure against desertion or absenteeism as noted before. If one had travel papers but the leave had not been recorded in his *Soldbuch*, or vice versa, one might find himself answering a vast number of questions.

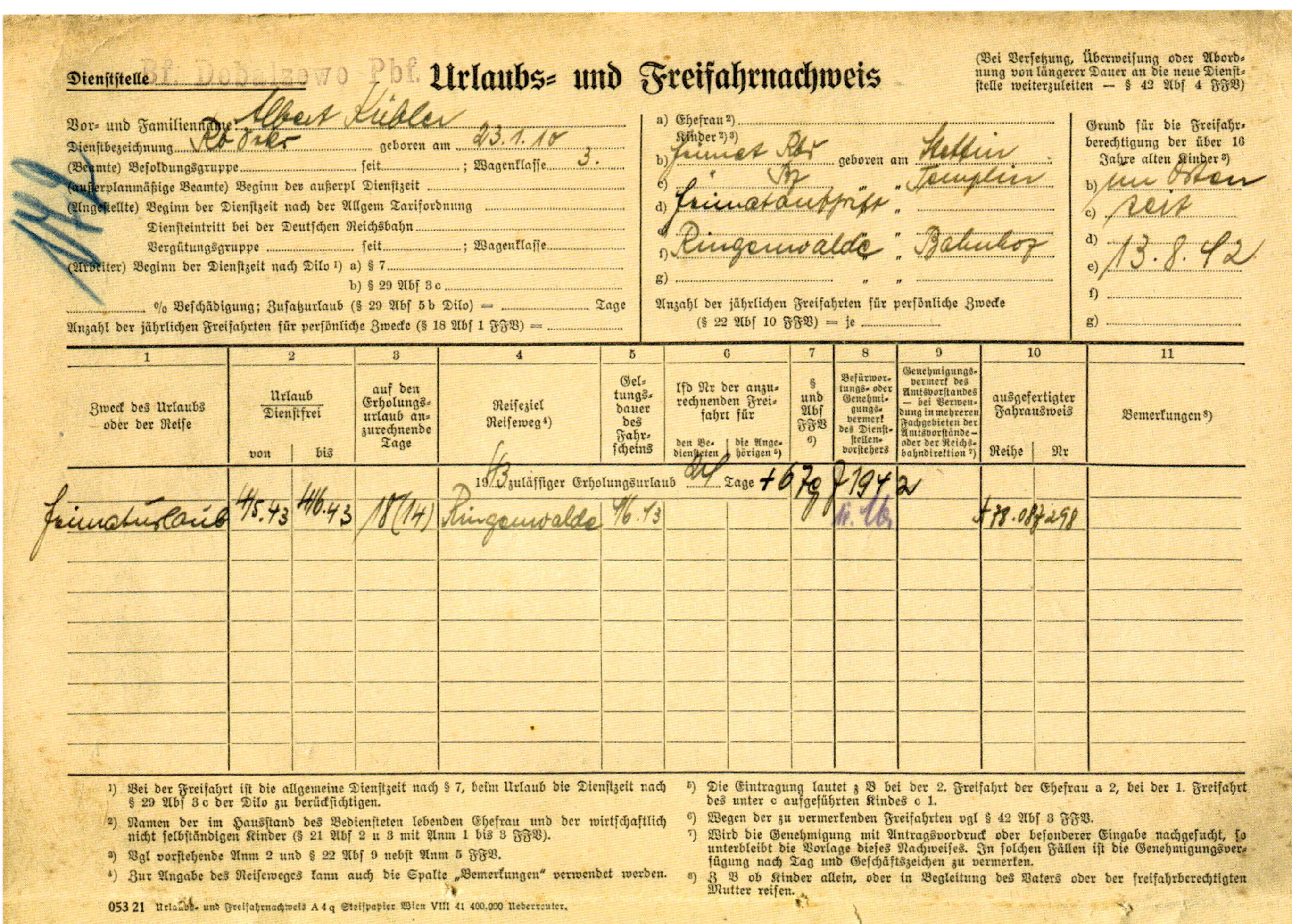

Dienststelle Bf. Dobalzewo Pbf.

Urlaubs- und Freifahrnachweis

(Bei Versetzung, Überweisung oder Abordnung von längerer Dauer an die neue Dienststelle weiterzuleiten — § 42 Abf 4 FFV)

Vor- und Familienname: Albert Kübler
Dienstbezeichnung .... geboren am 23.1.10
(Beamte) Besoldungsgruppe .... seit ....; Wagenklasse 3.
(außerplanmäßige Beamte) Beginn der außerpl Dienstzeit ....
(Angestellte) Beginn der Dienstzeit nach der Allgem Tarifordnung ....
Diensteintritt bei der Deutschen Reichsbahn ....
Vergütungsgruppe .... seit ....; Wagenklasse ....
(Arbeiter) Beginn der Dienstzeit nach Dilo [1]) a) § 7 ....
b) § 29 Abf 3c ....
.... % Beschädigung; Zusatzurlaub (§ 29 Abf 5b Dilo) = ... Tage
Anzahl der jährlichen Freifahrten für persönliche Zwecke (§ 18 Abf 1 FFV) = ...

a) Ehefrau [2]) ....
Kinder [2]) [3])
b) .... geboren am ....
c) .... " " ....
d) .... " " ....
e) .... " " ....
f) Ringenwalde " " ....
g) .... " " ....
Anzahl der jährlichen Freifahrten für persönliche Zwecke (§ 22 Abf 10 FFV) = je ....

Grund für die Freifahrberechtigung der über 16 Jahre alten Kinder [3])
b) ....
c) ....
d) ....
e) 13.8.42
f) ....
g) ....

1 Zweck des Urlaubs oder der Reise	2 Urlaub / Dienstfrei von	bis	3 auf den Erholungsurlaub anzurechnende Tage	4 Reiseziel Reiseweg [4])	5 Geltungsdauer des Fahrscheins	6 lfd Nr der anzurechnenden Freifahrt für den Bediensteten	die Angehörigen [5])	7 § und Abf FFV [6])	8 Befürwortungs- oder Genehmigungsvermerk des Dienststellenvorstehers	9 Genehmigungsvermerk des Amtsvorstandes — bei Verwendung in mehreren Fachgebieten der Amtsvorstände — oder der Reichsbahndirektion [7])	10 ausgefertigter Fahrausweis Reihe	Nr	11 Bemerkungen [8])
1943 zulässiger Erholungsurlaub ... Tage +6 Tg f 1942													
Heimaturlaub	4/5.43	4/6.43	18 (14)	Ringenwalde	4/6.43						[illegible]	[illegible]	

[1]) Bei der Freifahrt ist die allgemeine Dienstzeit nach § 7, beim Urlaub die Dienstzeit nach § 29 Abf 3c der Dilo zu berücksichtigen.
[2]) Namen der im Hausstand des Bediensteten lebenden Ehefrau und der wirtschaftlich nicht selbständigen Kinder (§ 21 Abf 2 u 3 mit Anm 1 bis 3 FFV).
[3]) Vgl vorstehende Anm 2 und § 22 Abf 9 nebst Anm 5 FFV.
[4]) Zur Angabe des Reiseweges kann auch die Spalte „Bemerkungen" verwendet werden.
[5]) Die Eintragung lautet z B bei der 2. Freifahrt der Ehefrau a 2, bei der 1. Freifahrt des unter c aufgeführten Kindes c 1.
[6]) Wegen der zu vermerkenden Freifahrten vgl § 42 Abf 3 FFV.
[7]) Wird die Genehmigung mit Antragsvordruck oder besonderer Eingabe nachgesucht, so unterbleibt die Vorlage dieses Nachweises. In solchen Fällen ist die Genehmigungsverfügung nach Tag und Geschäftszeichen zu vermerken.
[8]) Z B ob Kinder allein, oder in Begleitung des Vaters oder der freifahrberechtigten Mutter reisen.

053 21 Urlaubs- und Freifahrnachweis A 4 q Steifpapier Wien VIII 41 400.000 Ueberreuter.

Figure 2-20. This is a Reichsbahn Urlaubs- und Freifahrnachweis (Railroad Leave and Proof of Free Travel) for Locomotive Engineer Albert Kübler. (A4)

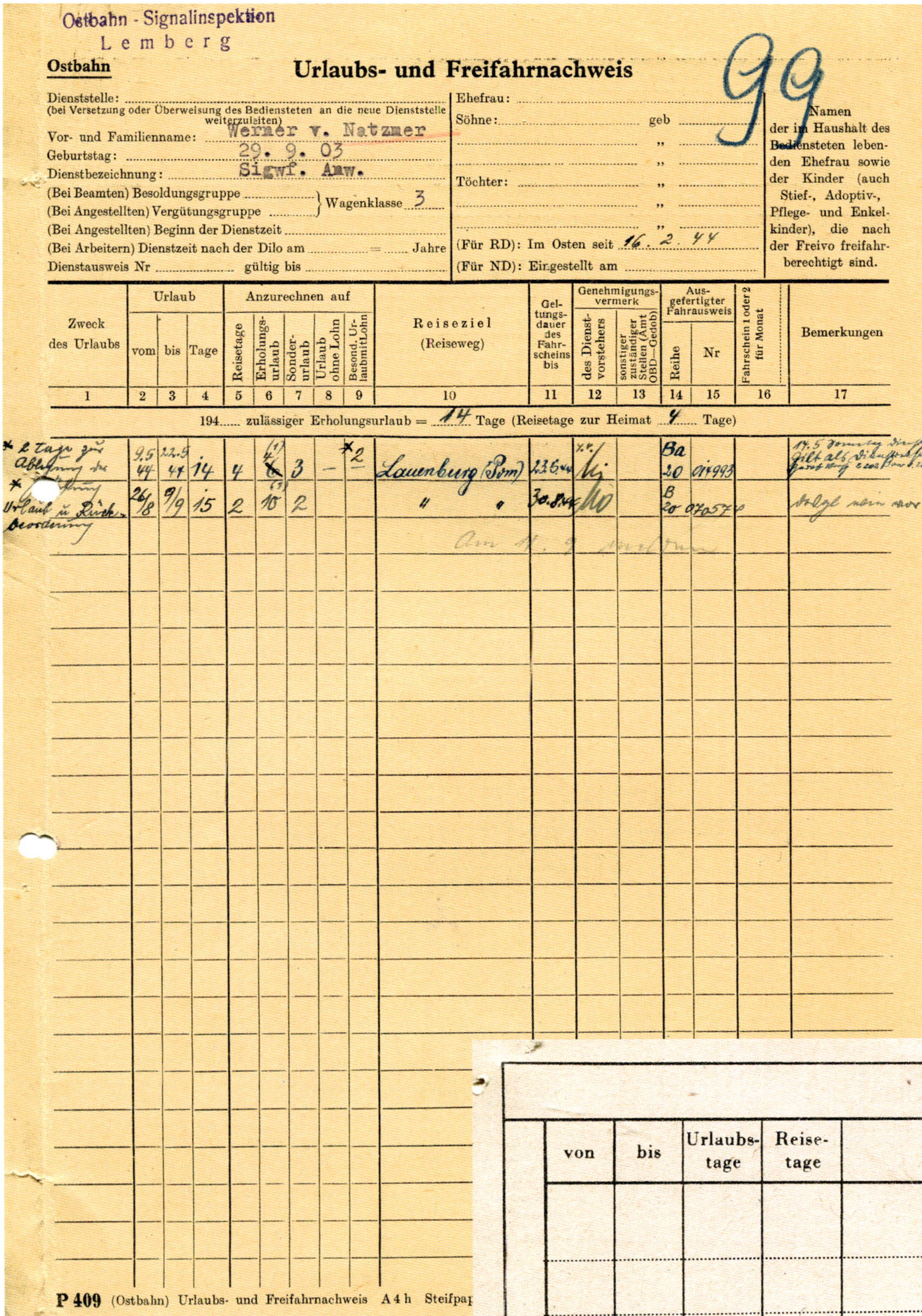

Ostbahn - Signalinspektion
Lemberg

Ostbahn **Urlaubs- und Freifahrnachweis** 99

Dienststelle:
(bei Versetzung oder Überweisung des Bediensteten an die neue Dienststelle weiterzuleiten)
Vor- und Familienname: Werner v. Natzmer
Geburtstag: 29. 9. 03
Dienstbezeichnung: Sigwf. Anw.
(Bei Beamten) Besoldungsgruppe
(Bei Angestellten) Vergütungsgruppe } Wagenklasse 3
(Bei Angestellten) Beginn der Dienstzeit
(Bei Arbeitern) Dienstzeit nach der Dilo am ... = ... Jahre
Dienstausweis Nr ... gültig bis

Ehefrau:
Söhne: ... geb
Töchter:
(Für RD): Im Osten seit 16. 2. 44
(Für ND): Eingestellt am

Namen der im Haushalt des Bediensteten lebenden Ehefrau sowie der Kinder (auch Stief-, Adoptiv-, Pflege- und Enkelkinder), die nach der Freivo freifahrberechtigt sind.

Zweck des Urlaubs	Urlaub vom	Urlaub bis	Urlaub Tage	Anzurechnen auf: Reisetage	Erholungsurlaub	Sonderurlaub	Urlaub ohne Lohn	Besond. Urlaub mit Lohn	Reiseziel (Reiseweg)	Geltungsdauer des Fahrscheins bis	Genehmigungsvermerk: des Dienstvorstehers	sonstiger zuständiger Stellen (Amt OBD—Gedob)	Ausgefertigter Fahrausweis: Reihe	Nr	Fahrschein 1 oder 2 für Monat	Bemerkungen
1	2	3	4	5	6	7	8	9	10	11	12	13	14	15	16	17

194...... zulässiger Erholungsurlaub = 14 Tage (Reisetage zur Heimat 4 Tage)

Zweck des Urlaubs	vom	bis	Tage	5	6	7	8	9	Reiseziel	11	12	13	Reihe	Nr	16	Bemerkungen
* 2 Tage zur Ablehnung ... * ...	9.5 44	22.5 44	14	4	8	3	–	*2	Lauenburg (Pom)	23.6.44	[illegible]		Ba 20	01993		14.5 ... gilt als Dienstreise ...
Urlaub z. Rückbeorderung	26/8	9/9	15	2	10	2			" "	30.8.44	[illegible]		B 20	070570		...

Am 4. 9 ...

P 409 (Ostbahn) Urlaubs- und Freifahrnachweis A 4 h Steifpap

Figure 2-21.
Another Urlaubs- und Freifahrnachweis, this time for signalman Werner Natzmer, who worked for the Reichsbahn on the Eastern Front. Although these forms were from the Reichsbahn, the Wehrmacht versions were very similar. (A4)

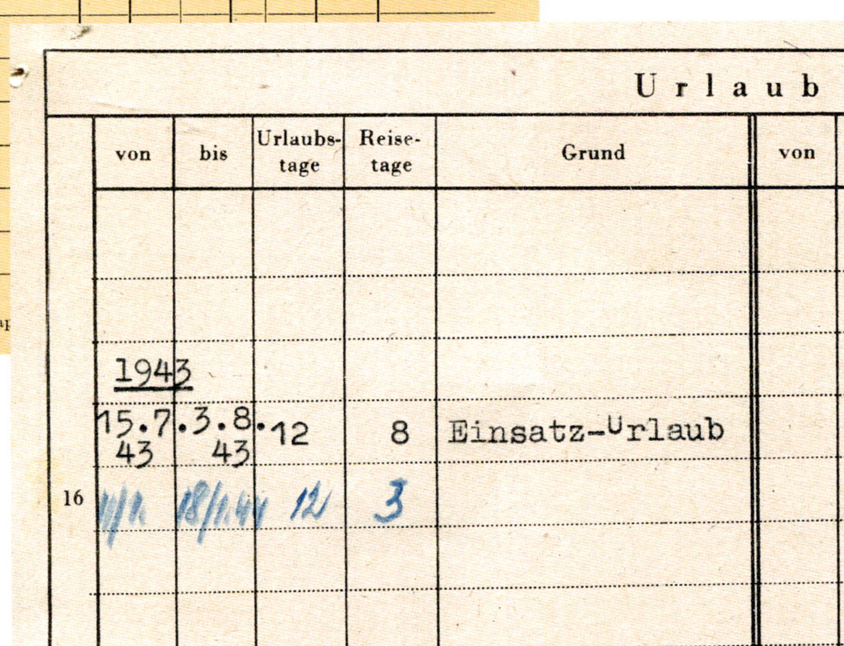

	Urlaub					
	von	bis	Urlaubs-tage	Reise-tage	Grund	von
	1943					
	15.7.43	3.8.43	12	8	Einsatz-Urlaub	
16	1/1.44	18/1.44	12	3		

Figure 2-22. An enlargement from an Urlaubs- und Freifahrnachweis noting the dates leave had been granted, the number of leave days, the number of travel days, and the grounds for which leave had been granted. (A4)

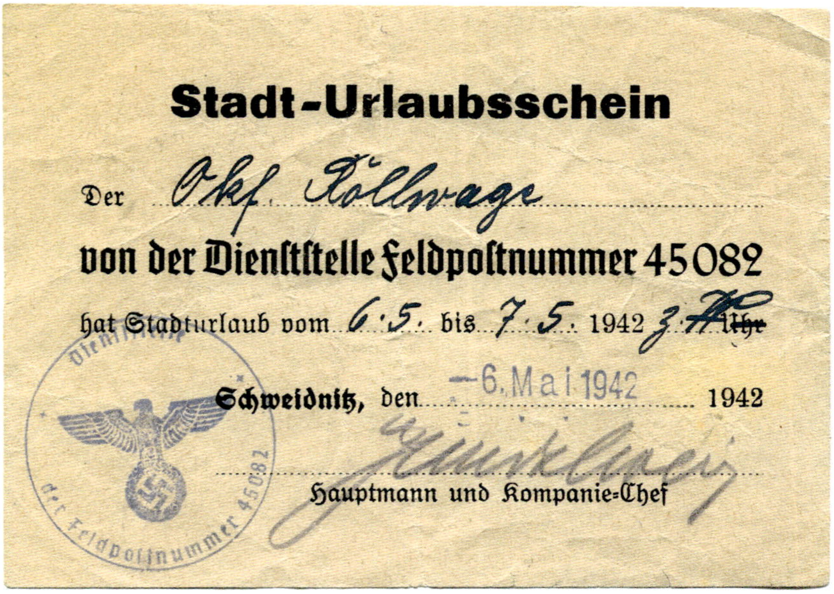

Stadt-Urlaubsschein

Der Okf. Köllwage

von der Dienststelle Feldpostnummer 45082

hat Stadturlaub vom 6.5. bis 7.5. 1942 3 Uhr

Schweidnitz, den —6. Mai 1942 1942

Hauptmann und Kompanie-Chef

Figure 2-23. This overnight Stadt-Urlaubsschein (City Leave Pass) for the city of Schweidnitz (what is now Swidnica in Poland) was granted to Oberkompanieführer (Senior Company Leader) Kollwage from May 6 until 3:00 am on May 7, 1942. This form had been printed specifically for Dienststelle Feldpostnummer 45082, or the 4. Kompanie, 5. Kolonne des Kraftwagen Transport Abteilung (4th Company, 5th Column of Motor Transport Section).

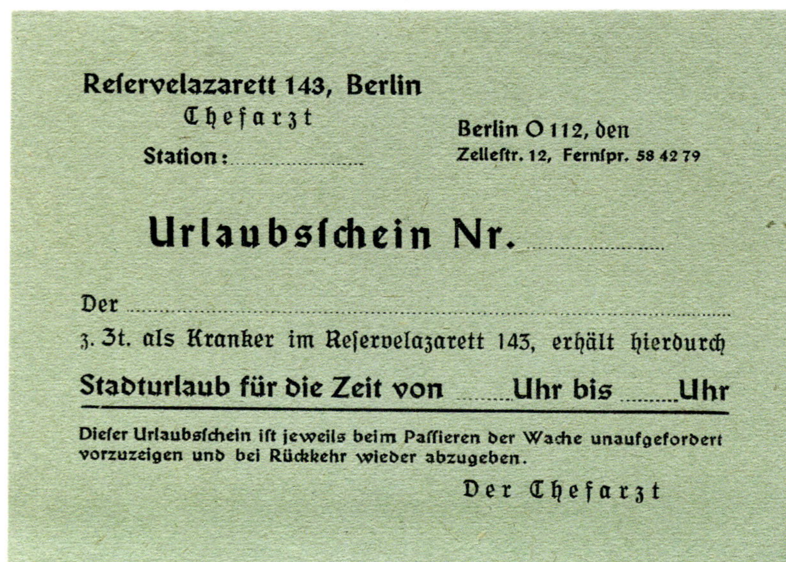

Reservelazarett 143, Berlin
Chefarzt
Station: ....

Berlin O 112, den
Zellestr. 12, Fernspr. 58 42 79

Urlaubsschein Nr. ....

Der ....
z. Zt. als Kranker im Reservelazarett 143, erhält hierdurch
Stadturlaub für die Zeit von .... Uhr bis .... Uhr

Dieser Urlaubsschein ist jeweils beim Passieren der Wache unaufgefordert vorzuzeigen und bei Rückkehr wieder abzugeben.

Der Chefarzt

Figure 2-24. This unissued Stadt-Urlaubsschein had been printed for Reservelazarett 143 (Military Reserve Hospital 143) in Berlin and was issued to patients of that hospital by order of the Chefarzt (Chief Doctor).

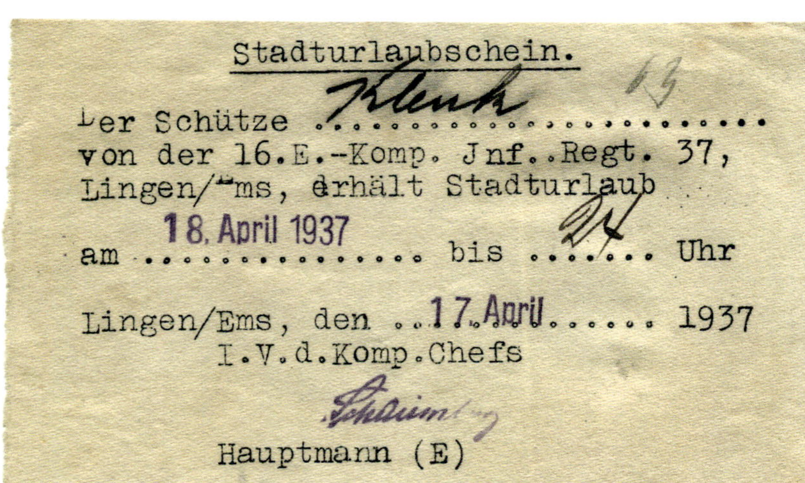

Stadturlaubschein.

Der Schütze Klenk
von der 16.E.-Komp. Jnf.-Regt. 37,
Lingen/Ems, erhält Stadturlaub
am 18. April 1937 bis 24 Uhr

Lingen/Ems, den 17. April 1937
I.V.d.Komp.Chefs

Hauptmann (E)

Figure 2-25. This pre-war Ersatz Stadturlaubsschein was issued to Schütze (Private) Klenk, training with the 16. Ersatz-Kompanie (Training Company; literally "Replacement" Company) of Infanterie Regiment 37.

Figure 2-26. This Bescheinigung or Certificate issued by the Reservelazarett Augsburg to Obergefreiter Georg Stadelmain granted him leave in the city from 1:00 pm on November 18 until 8:00 am November 20, 1944. (A6)

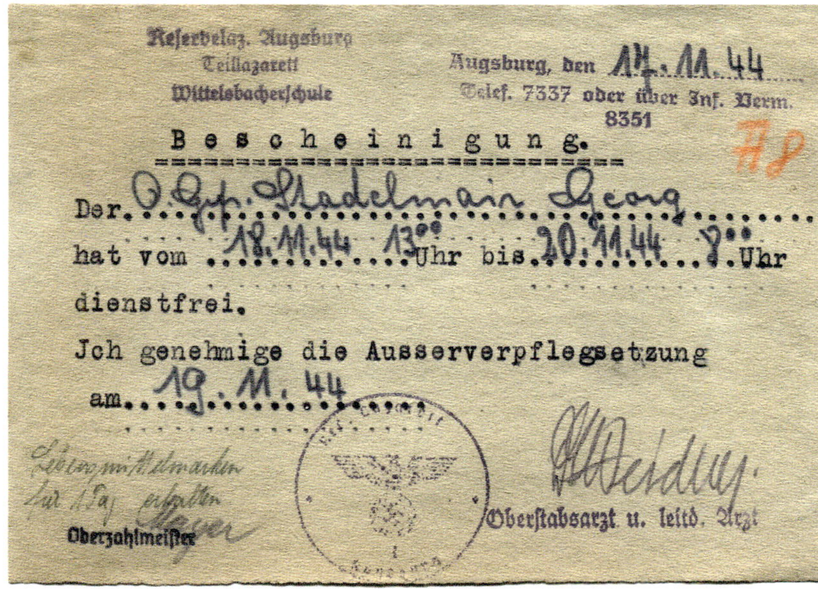
Reservelaz. Augsburg
Teillazarett
Wittelsbacherschule
Augsburg, den 17.11.44
Telef. 7337 oder über Inf. Verm. 8351
Bescheinigung.
Der O.Gfr. Stadelmain Georg
hat vom 18.11.44 13[00] Uhr bis 20.11.44 8[00] Uhr
dienstfrei.
Jch genehmige die Ausserverpflegsetzung
am 19.11.44
Oberzahlmeister
Oberstabsarzt u. leitd. Arzt

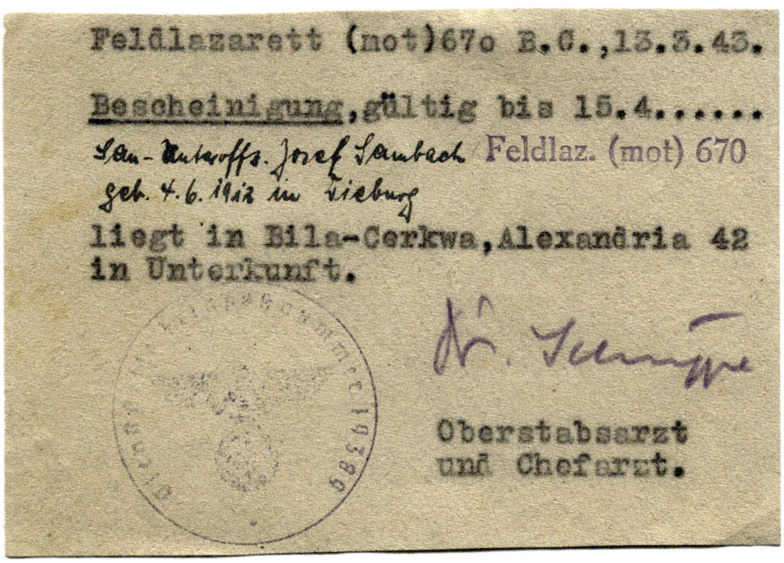
Feldlazarett (mot)670 B.G.,13.3.43.
Bescheinigung, gültig bis 15.4......
San-Unteroffz. Josef Sambach Feldlaz. (mot) 670
liegt in Bila-Cerkwa, Alexandria 42
in Unterkunft.
Oberstabsarzt
und Chefarzt.

Figure 2-27. This leave pass was for Sanitäts-Unteroffizier (Medical Corporal) Josef Sambach of Feldlazarett 670 (Motoriziert) (the 670th Motorized Field Hospital) for leave in the city of Bila-Cerka on April 15, 1943, the headquarters of which was on Alexandria Street, number 42. The information typed onto this small card completely negates any counterintelligence offered by using the unit's stamp for Feldpostnummer 19389.

Nr. 32 D
Nachturlaubskarte
Inhaber dieses Ausweises
hat Urlaub innerhalb des
Standortes bis 1 Uhr.
3. Kompanie
Inf.-Ers.-Btl. 173
Weißenfels
Hauptmann und Kompanie-Führer

Figure 2-28. A bound and reusable Nachturlaubskarte (Night Leave Card), permitting the bearer leave for one hour within the base, printed for the 3. Kompanie, Infanterie Ersatz Bataillon 173 (Infantry Training Battalion 173), in the city of Weissenfels, Germany.

Figure 2-29. Another pre-printed, bound Nacht-Urlaubskarte, this time prepared for Cavalry Reit- und Fahrschule XI (Riding School 11) in Gardelegen, granted the bearer (in this case Obergefreiter Brademann) leave until midnight. This particular pass was sold at one time at a European flea market (Flohmarkt), evidenced by the Entnazifizierten or "De-Nazified" unit stamp. It's against the law today to sell items bearing the swastika throughout much of Europe.

Figure 2-30. This small Ersatz leave card typed on thick, rough mat board, granted the bearer night-time leave until 7:00 a.m. by order of the Standortarzt (base doctor) of this Heeres-Sanitätsstaffel (Army Medical Squadron).

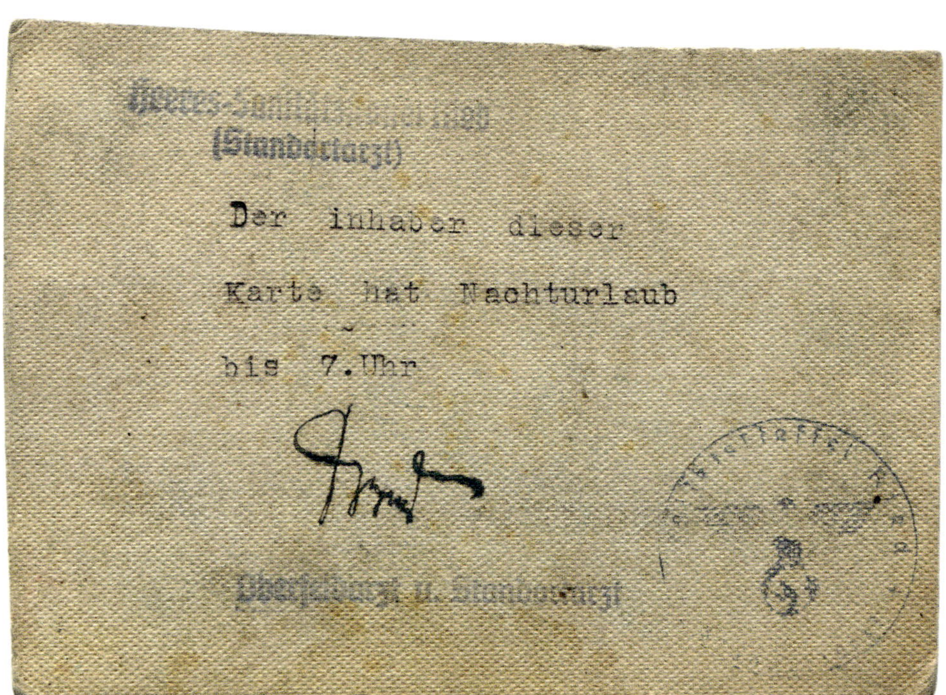

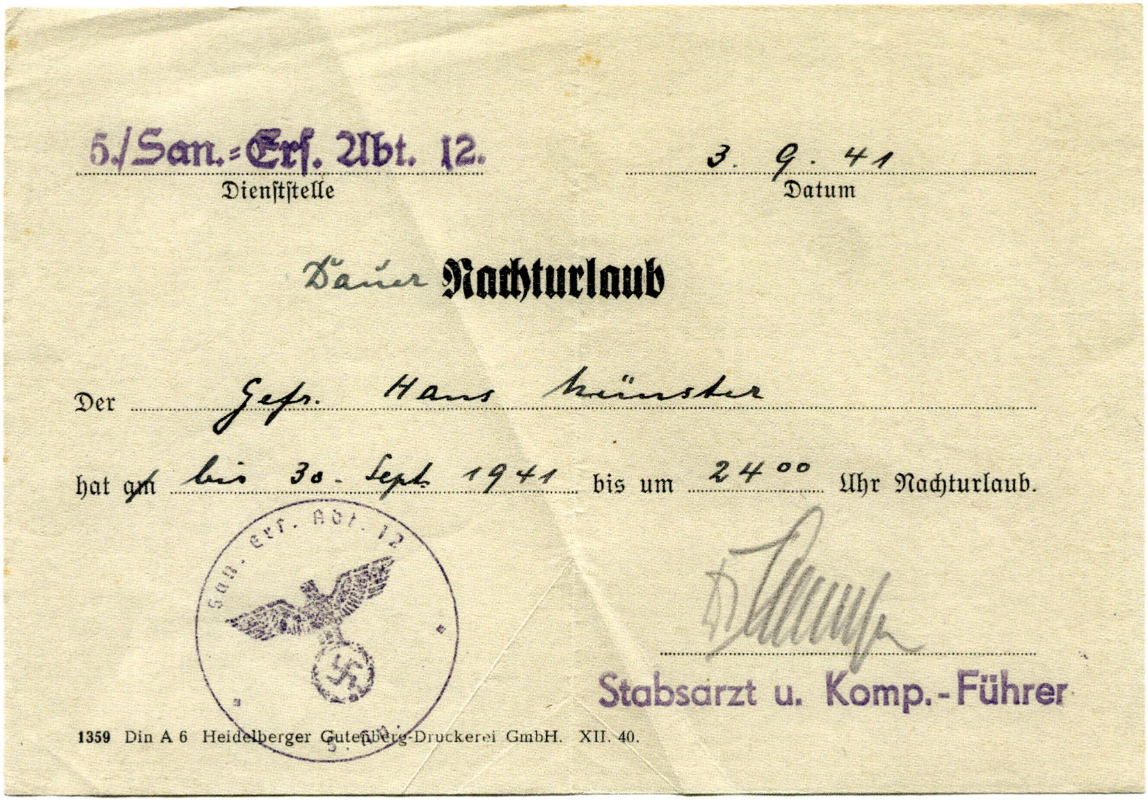

5./San.=Erf. Abt. 12. 3. 9. 41
Dienststelle Datum

Dauer Nachturlaub

Der Gefr. Hans Künster

hat ~~am~~ bis 30. Sept. 1941 bis um 24⁰⁰ Uhr Nachturlaub.

Stabsarzt u. Komp.-Führer

1359 Din A 6 Heidelberger Gutenberg-Druckerei GmbH. XII. 40.

Figure 2-31. Night-time leave cards could sometimes be turned into leave cards lasting much longer, as is the case for Gefreiter Hans Künster of the 5. Kompanie of the Medical Training Section 12 (Sanitäts-Ersatz Abteilung 12), who was granted a Dauer Nachturlaub ("Lasting" night Leave) from September 3 until midnight of September 30, 1941.

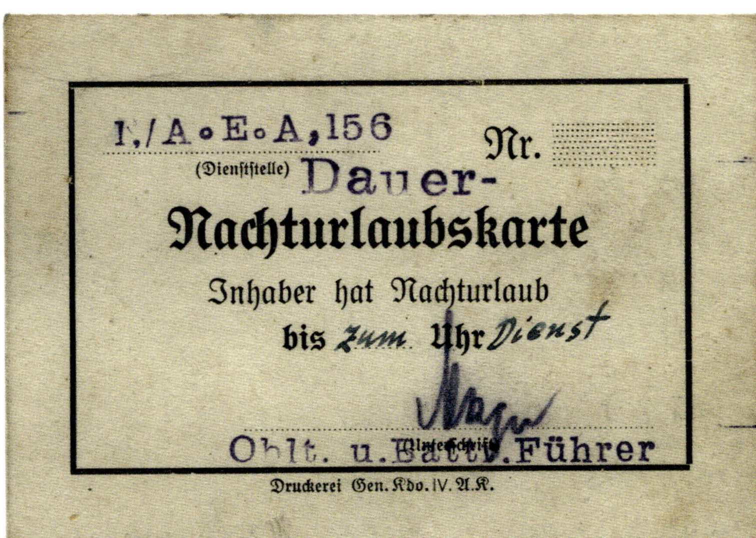

I./A.E.A,156 Nr.
(Dienststelle) Dauer-
Nachturlaubskarte
Inhaber hat Nachturlaub
bis zum Uhr Dienst
(Unterschrift)
Oblt. u. Battr.Führer
Druckerei Gen.Kdo.IV.A.K.

Figure 2-32. Another Dauer-Nachturlaubskarte, though this one is more official; issued by Artillerie-Ersatz-Abteilung 156 (Artillery Training Section 156 – note the stamp on the back), the bearer of this card was permitted to remain in town "until the hour of duty" (bis zum Uhr Dienst).

5./San.=Ers. Abt. 12

(Dienststelle, Truppenteil) 24.10.41 (Datum)

Nachturlaubschein

Der San. Uffz. Künster, Hans

hat am 25.X.41 bis um 2 00 Uhr Nachturlaub.

Grund:

Unterschrift des Komp.- usw. Führers, Dienststellenleiters.

(Dienstsiegel)

(Name und Dienstgrad)

Bestell-Nr. 655. Wkr.-Dr. XII Wiesbaden

Figure 2-33. Another nighttime leave granted to Herr Künster, this time on October 25, 1941 until 2:00 a.m. You can tell that a clerk filled out a number of leave cards, but left the name blank behind the rank of Sanitäts-Unteroffizier, which was filled in later, possibly before graduation from field medic training.

Fliegerhorst Werl

Obgefr. Schubert

Kontrollkarte Nr. 56

S. 1356 Heidelberger Gutenberg-Druckerei GmbH. 3. 41

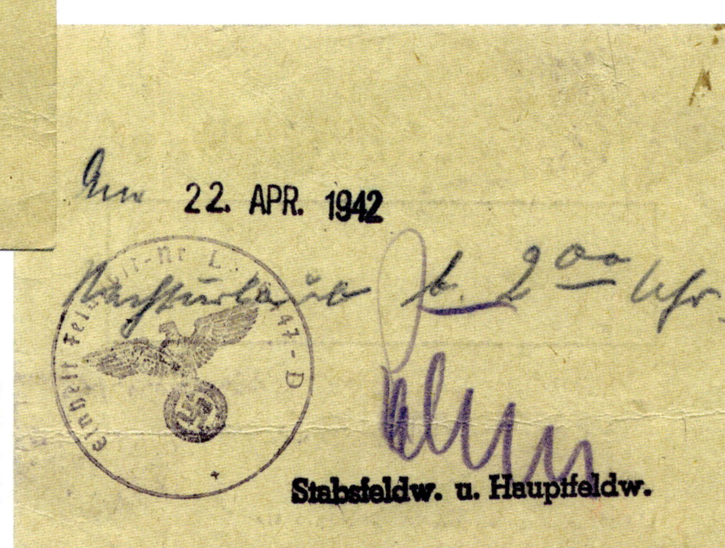

Am 22. APR. 1942

Nachturlaub b. 2 00 Uhr

Stabsfeldw. u. Hauptfeldw.

Figure 2-34. This Kontrollkarte (Control or Accountability Card) for Obergefreiter Schubert of Fliegerhorst Werl (Werl Air Force base) was temporarily used as a Nachturlaubskarte on on April 22, 1942. Note on the back that Nachturlaub b. 200 (Night leave until 2:00 am) has been written in by the Hauptfeldwebel (Top Sergeant) or "Spiess."

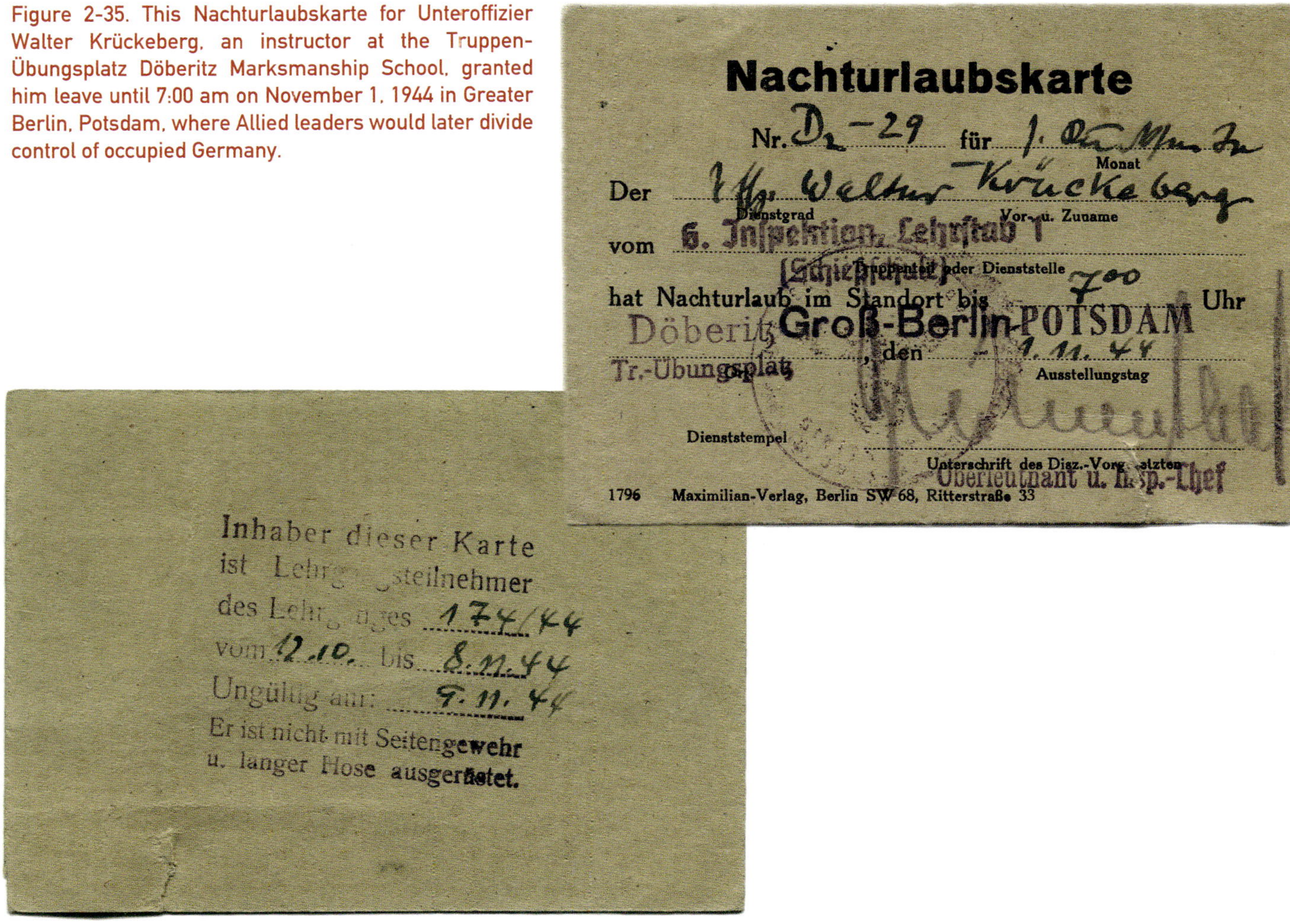
Nachturlaubskarte
Nr. D2-29 für 1. Okt. Monat
Monat
Der Uffz. Walter Krückeberg
Dienstgrad Vor- u. Zuname
vom 6. Inspektion, Lehrstab I (Schießschule)
Truppenteil oder Dienststelle
hat Nachturlaub im Standort bis 7⁰⁰ Uhr
Groß-Berlin POTSDAM
Döberitz Tr.-Übungsplatz, den 1.11.44
Ausstellungstag
Dienststempel
Unterschrift des Disz.-Vorgesetzten
Oberleutnant u. Insp.-Chef
1796 Maximilian-Verlag, Berlin SW 68, Ritterstraße 33

Inhaber dieser Karte
ist Lehr[illegible]steilnehmer
des Lehr[illegible]es 174/44
vom 12.10. bis 8.11.44
Ungültig am: 9.11.44
Er ist nicht mit Seitengewehr
u. langer Hose ausgerüstet.

Figure 2-35. This Nachturlaubskarte for Unteroffizier Walter Krückeberg, an instructor at the Truppen-Übungsplatz Döberitz Marksmanship School, granted him leave until 7:00 am on November 1, 1944 in Greater Berlin, Potsdam, where Allied leaders would later divide control of occupied Germany.

Short periods of leave might be granted, especially at training facilities and bases. A soldier may be given permission to go into town for a day or two and would be required to return at an appointed date and time. As such, those individuals would be granted a *Stadt-Urlaubsschein* (City Leave Permit) and it would be valid until the date and hour noted for return.

Like other permits, the *Stadt-Urlaubsschein* bore the soldier's name, was dated, validated with a *Dienststempel*, and signed by the commanding officer. The *Soldat* was required to keep the permit with him; if he was stopped by the *Feldgendarmerie* (Military Police) or local authorities, he would need it to prove that he had permission to be away from his base, even if only for a short time.

A *Stadt-Urlaubsschein* might also be given to soldiers recuperating from combat wounds. A *Reserve-Lazarett*, or military hospital, might grant a patient a chance to get out for a few hours as part of their convalescence. This was noted on the *Stadt-Urlaubsschein: von ___ Uhr bis ___ Uhr* (from ___ o'clock until ___ o'clock). Because the pass was written for a wounded soldier, it noted only a span of hours, not days; it would not help a recovering soldier to be gone from the hospital for longer than that.

Evening-only privileges might also be granted to an individual, and so a *Nacht-Urlaubsschein* (Night Leave Permit) might be issued. It granted the same permissions as a *Stadt-Urlaubsschein*, and was usually a preprinted form or card, but was often of a much shorter duration, and usually expired that night. Any number of different kinds of *Kontrollkarten* (Control Cards) might be used as a *Nacht-Urlaubsschein*, with the notation for *Nachturlaub* written on the face of the card.

These passes were produced by local printers, and at times were imprinted with the *Truppenteil* for individual units that had contracted them. Sizes vary but most seem to have been an A7-sized pass that has been trimmed, as if to allow it to fit into a wallet or pocket. It is uncertain whether the pass was issued this size or trimmed by the soldier after receiving it.

Before the war, the standard pass issued to soldiers for an extended period (usually two weeks to one month) was the *Urlaubsschein*. There were two different versions

Figure 2-36. This postcard, sent via Feldpost (free Field Mail) to Robert Hautelmann, who was recovering from wounds in Reserve Lazarett 113 in Berlin-Dahlem, proclaimed every Soldat's favorite phrase: Hurrah! Der Urlaubsschein ist da! (Hurray! The leave pass has arrived!)

of this form, one imprinted with a green stripe, and one without. The green stripe indicated that travel had been paid for by the *Wehrmacht*, while the form without had been paid by the *Soldat* himself. A travel pass was required to accompany the *Urlaubsschein*, regardless of whether the soldier had paid for his own transport or not.

As with the *Stadt-* or *Nacht-Urlaubsschein*, the *Urlaubsschein* might be imprinted with the *Truppenteil*, or left blank to be filled out or stamped. It listed the rank and name of the soldier on leave, the dates between which he was permitted to be away from his duty station, where he was traveling from and where he was traveling to, as well as any train stations where he might be transferring. The pass was dated and signed at the bottom.

Forms without a green stripe had space reserved on the lower right for the *Sationsstempel*, where personnel of the *Reichsbahn* would stamp the train station, time, and date of departure.

The reverse of the form listed the conditions of travel, that if a soldier used the pass for unauthorized purposes he would lose the pass, that he was to travel in third-class accommodations, and so on.

Following the opening of the war, the *Urlaubsschein* was replaced by the *Kriegsurlaubsschein* (Wartime Leave Permit). The information noted was identical to the prewar variation, though it was often expanded and was rarely preprinted with the *Truppenteil*. Forms without the green stripe remained reserved for travel at one's own cost: "*Gültig nur für Urlaubreisen auf eigene Kosten.*" In addition to the previously mentioned information, the *Kriegsurlaubsschein* also indicated whether the pass would be used for a return trip, and for the specific train number and times reserved. The term *Sationsstempel* was replaced by the *Bahnhofstagestempel* (Train Station Date Stamp), but this was merely a change in terminology; the two were identical.

In comparison, the fronts of a *Kriegsurlaubsschein* with the green stripe were simplified, removing the *Sationsstempel* and *Bahnhofstagestempel* entirely. "*Gültig für freie Urlaubsreisen auf Kleinen Wehrmachtfahrschein*" was printed at the top of the form, and meant that the form was valid for free leave travel with the small *Wehrmacht* travel pass. In order for a soldier to travel free of charge with the *Kriegsurlaubsschein*, he must also have a valid small *Wehrmacht* travel pass with him. More on that form later.

The backs of the two *Kriegsurlaubsschein* were nearly identical. Conditions for travel, particularly who was paying for the trip and in which class the soldier was authorized to travel, are explained in detail. In addition to the same conditions that were printed on the prewar version, the *Kriegsurlaubsschein* included spaces to indicate the issuance of travel fees, rations given out as food or

Figure 2-37. (Opposite) An example of a pre-printed, pre-war Urlaubsschein for the 2nd Battery of Flakregiment 7 (Anti-Aircraft Regiment 7), stationed in Wolfenbüttel, granting leave for Gefreiter Turkap leave from September 25-27, 1937 until 7:00 am. The handwritten notation at the top (Mit Verpflegung) indicates that he is to be fed at Wehrmacht expense while travelling. (A5)

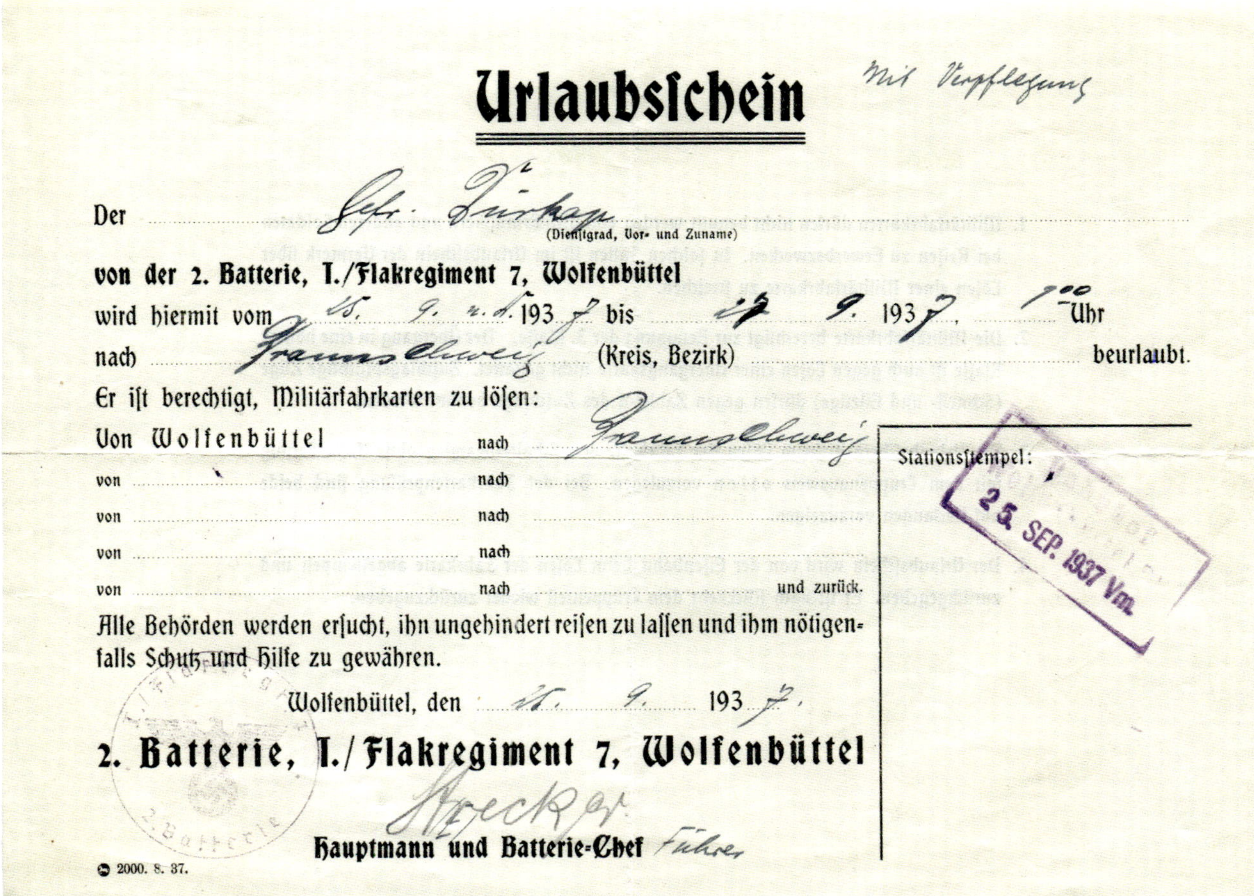

Urlaubsschein Mit Verpflegung

Der Gefr. Dürkop (Dienstgrad, Vor- und Zuname)

von der 2. Batterie, I./Flakregiment 7, Wolfenbüttel

wird hiermit vom 15. 9. 1937 bis 27. 9. 1937, 1°° Uhr

nach Braunschweig (Kreis, Bezirk) beurlaubt.

Er ist berechtigt, Militärfahrkarten zu lösen:

Von Wolfenbüttel nach Braunschweig

von ... nach ...

von ... nach ...

von ... nach ...

von ... nach ... und zurück.

Stationsstempel: 25. SEP. 1937 Vm.

Alle Behörden werden ersucht, ihn ungehindert reisen zu lassen und ihm nötigenfalls Schutz und Hilfe zu gewähren.

Wolfenbüttel, den 15. 9. 1937.

2. Batterie, I./Flakregiment 7, Wolfenbüttel

Hauptmann und Batterie-Chef Führer

2000. 8. 37.

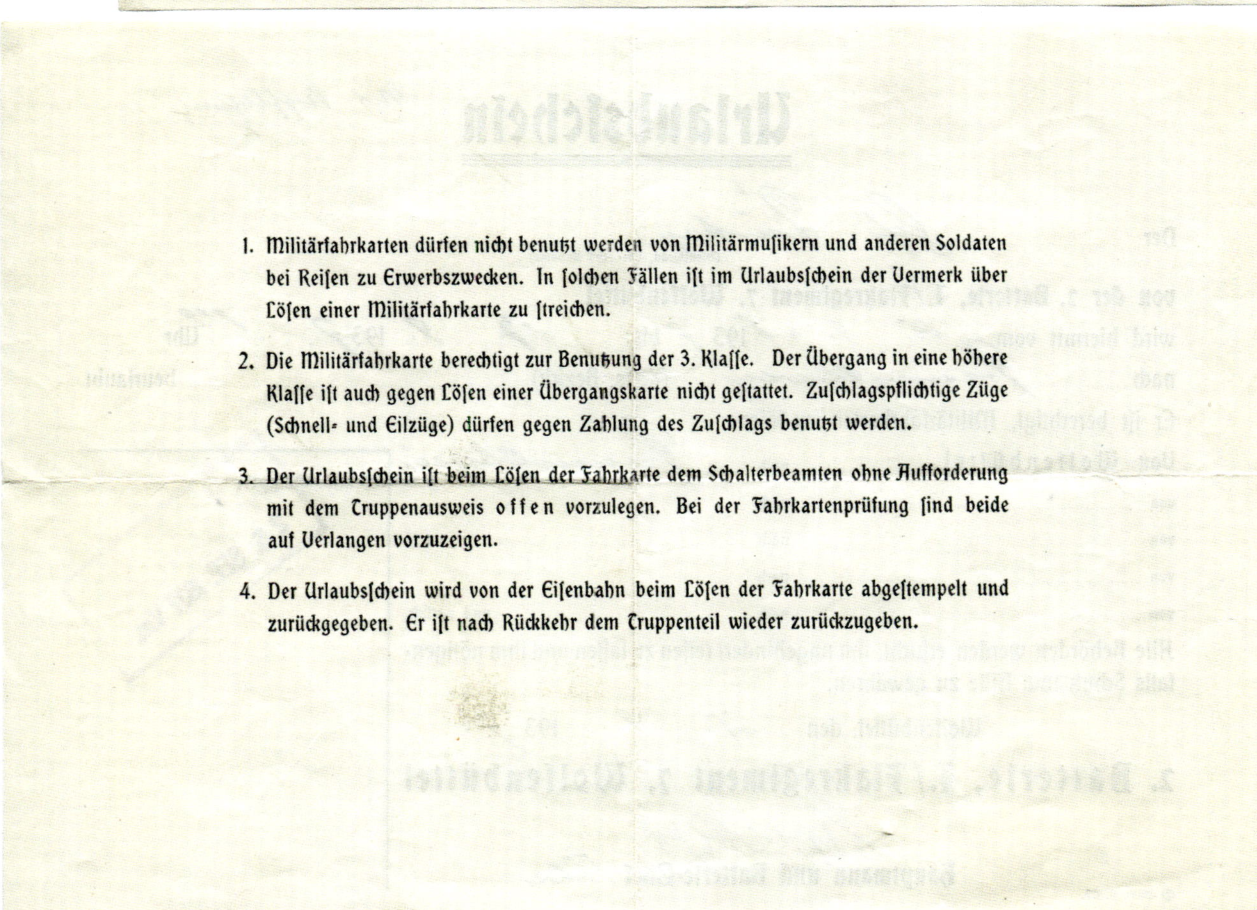

1. Militärfahrkarten dürfen nicht benutzt werden von Militärmusikern und anderen Soldaten bei Reisen zu Erwerbszwecken. In solchen Fällen ist im Urlaubsschein der Vermerk über Lösen einer Militärfahrkarte zu streichen.
2. Die Militärfahrkarte berechtigt zur Benutzung der 3. Klasse. Der Übergang in eine höhere Klasse ist auch gegen Lösen einer Übergangskarte nicht gestattet. Zuschlagspflichtige Züge (Schnell- und Eilzüge) dürfen gegen Zahlung des Zuschlags benutzt werden.
3. Der Urlaubsschein ist beim Lösen der Fahrkarte dem Schalterbeamten ohne Aufforderung mit dem Truppenausweis offen vorzulegen. Bei der Fahrkartenprüfung sind beide auf Verlangen vorzuzeigen.
4. Der Urlaubsschein wird von der Eisenbahn beim Lösen der Fahrkarte abgestempelt und zurückgegeben. Er ist nach Rückkehr dem Truppenteil wieder zurückzugeben.

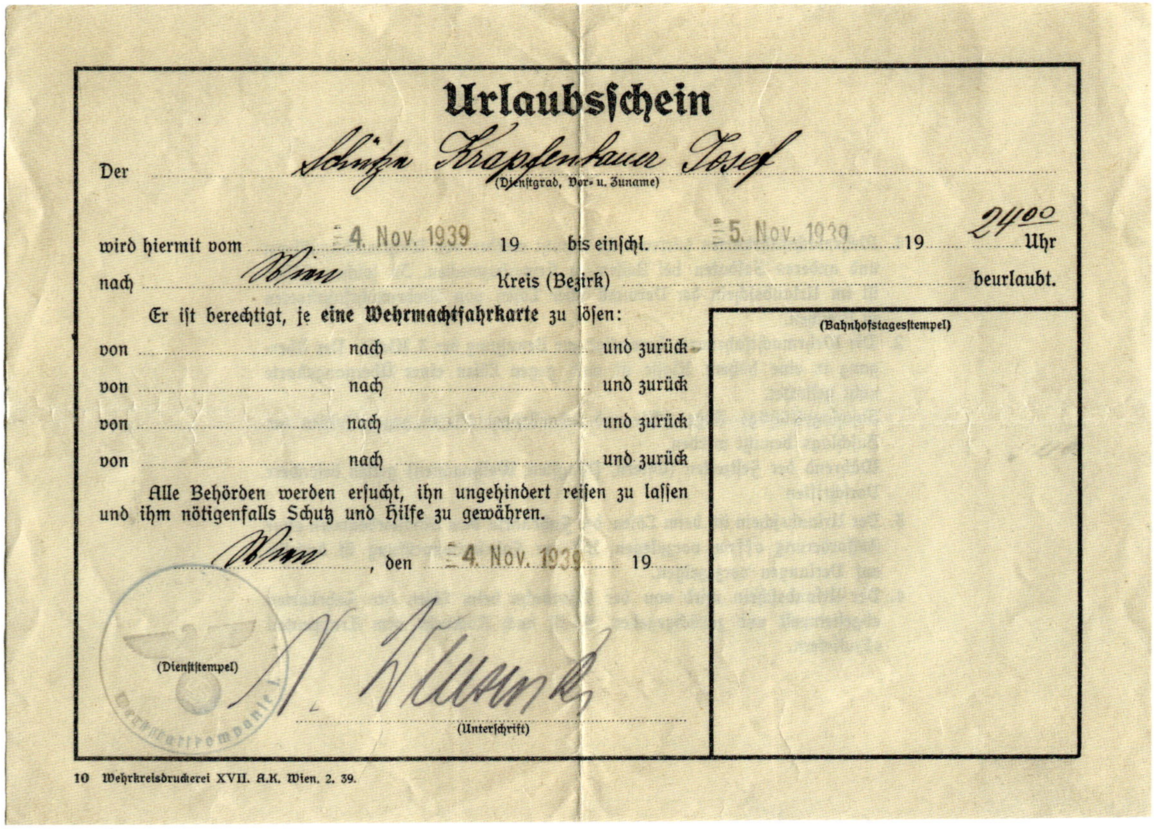

Urlaubsschein

Der Schütze Krapfenhauer Josef
(Dienstgrad, Vor- u. Zuname)

wird hiermit vom 4. Nov. 1939 19 bis einschl. 5. Nov. 1939 19 24⁰⁰ Uhr

nach Wien Kreis (Bezirk) beurlaubt.

Er ist berechtigt, je eine Wehrmachtfahrkarte zu lösen:

von ... nach ... und zurück

von ... nach ... und zurück

von ... nach ... und zurück

von ... nach ... und zurück

Alle Behörden werden ersucht, ihn ungehindert reisen zu lassen und ihm nötigenfalls Schutz und Hilfe zu gewähren.

Wien, den 4. Nov. 1939 19

(Dienststempel)

(Unterschrift)

(Bahnhofstagesstempel)

10 Wehrkreisdruckerei XVII. A.K. Wien. 2. 39.

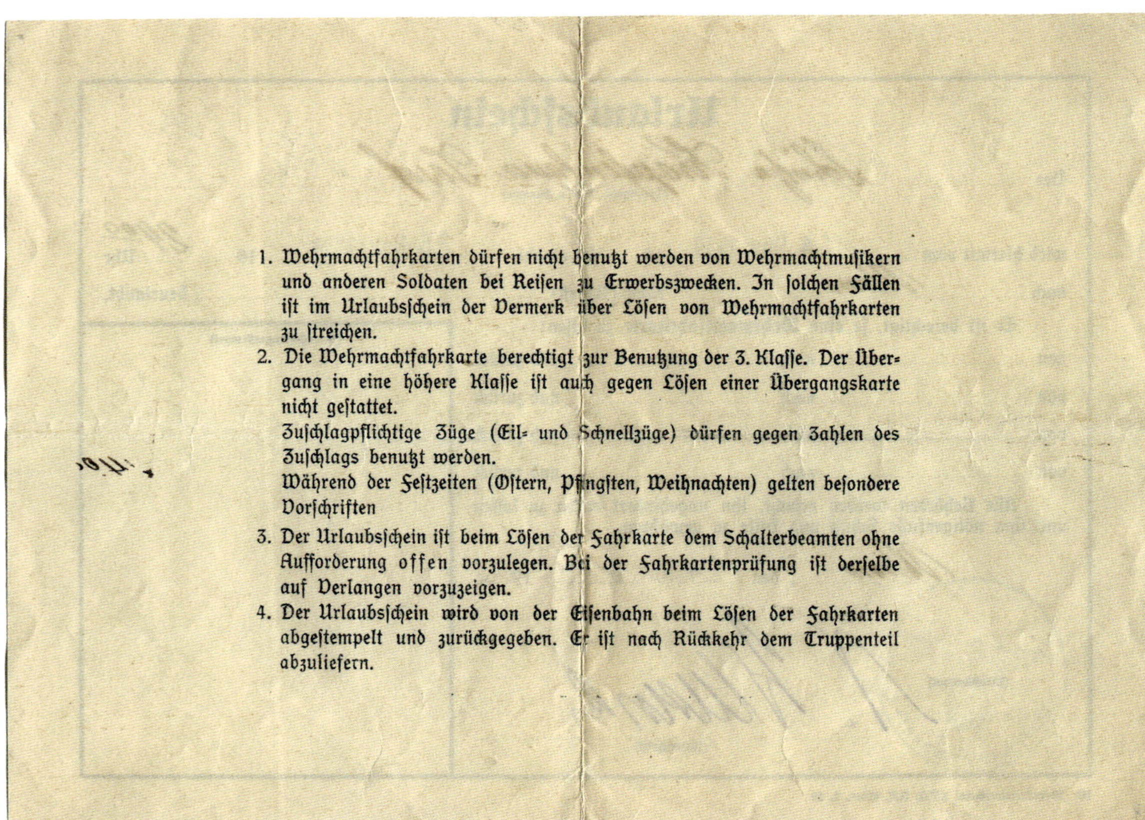

1. Wehrmachtfahrkarten dürfen nicht benutzt werden von Wehrmachtmusikern und anderen Soldaten bei Reisen zu Erwerbszwecken. In solchen Fällen ist im Urlaubsschein der Vermerk über Lösen von Wehrmachtfahrkarten zu streichen.
2. Die Wehrmachtfahrkarte berechtigt zur Benutzung der 3. Klasse. Der Übergang in eine höhere Klasse ist auch gegen Lösen einer Übergangskarte nicht gestattet.
   Zuschlagpflichtige Züge (Eil- und Schnellzüge) dürfen gegen Zahlen des Zuschlags benutzt werden.
   Während der Festzeiten (Ostern, Pfingsten, Weihnachten) gelten besondere Vorschriften
3. Der Urlaubsschein ist beim Lösen der Fahrkarte dem Schalterbeamten ohne Aufforderung offen vorzulegen. Bei der Fahrkartenprüfung ist derselbe auf Verlangen vorzuzeigen.
4. Der Urlaubsschein wird von der Eisenbahn beim Lösen der Fahrkarten abgestempelt und zurückgegeben. Er ist nach Rückkehr dem Truppenteil abzuliefern.

Figure 2-38. Another example of a pre-war Urlaubsschein, though this one was issued to Schützer (Private) Josef Krapfenhauer after the war had started, before the correct Kriegsurlaubsschein (Wartime Leave Pass) had been issued to his unit. (A5)

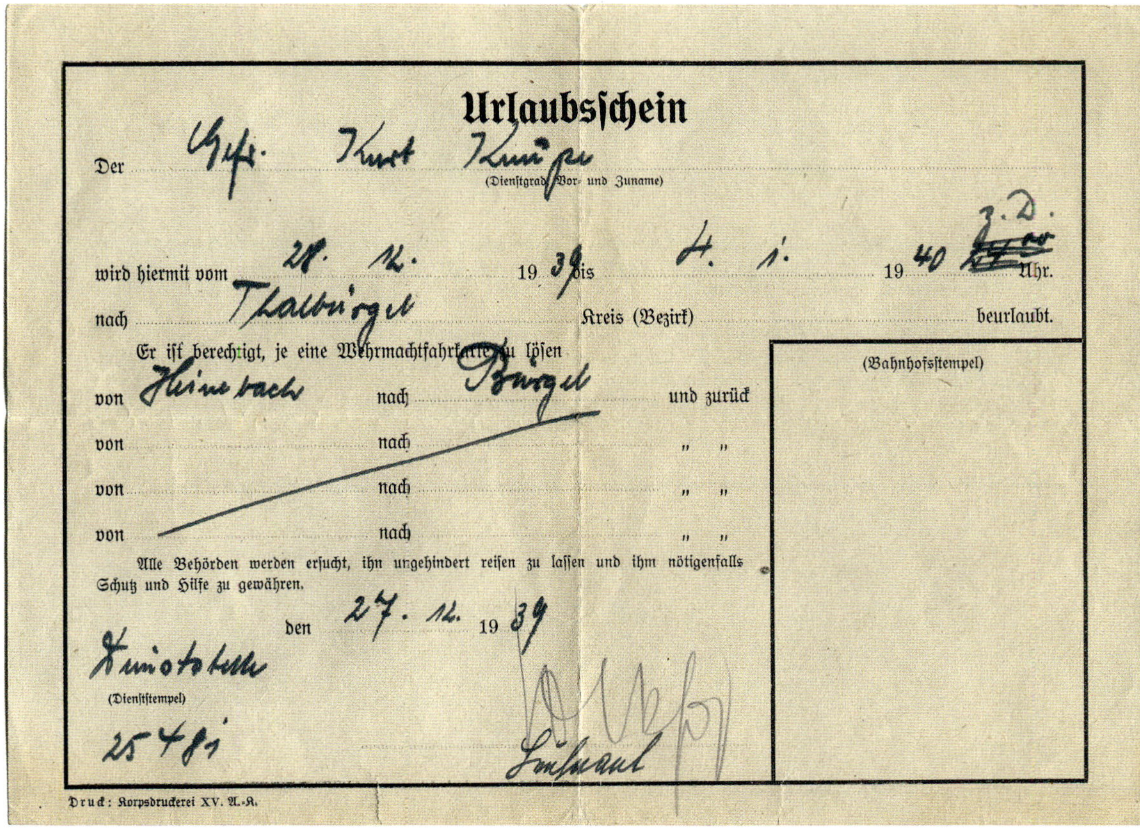

Urlaubsschein

Der .... (Dienstgrad, Vor- und Zuname)

wird hiermit vom 28. 12. 1939 bis 4. 1. 1940 .... Uhr.

nach .... Kreis (Bezirk) .... beurlaubt.

(Bahnhofsstempel)

Er ist berechtigt, je eine Wehrmachtfahrkarte zu lösen

von .... nach .... und zurück

von .... nach .... " "

von .... nach .... " "

von .... nach .... " "

Alle Behörden werden ersucht, ihn ungehindert reisen zu lassen und ihm nötigenfalls Schutz und Hilfe zu gewähren.

den 27. 12. 1939

(Dienststempel)

Druck: Korpsdruckerei XV. A.-K.

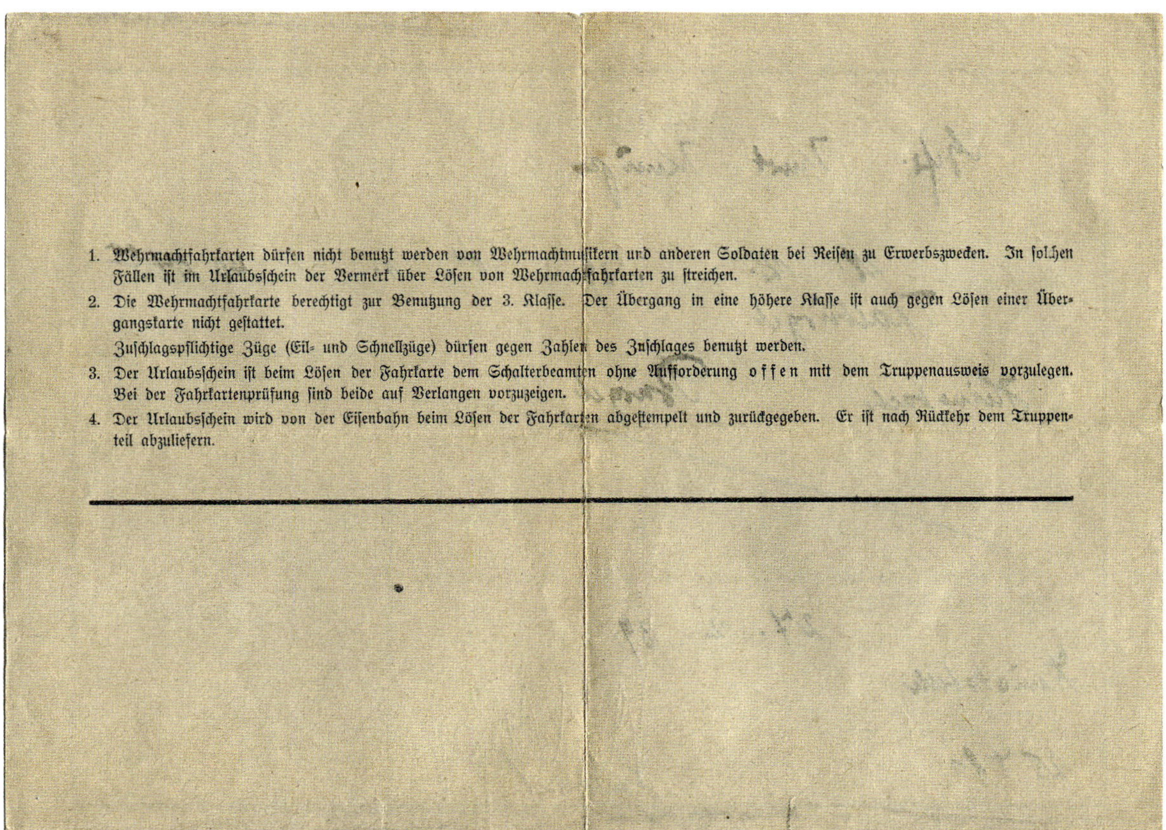

1. Wehrmachtfahrkarten dürfen nicht benutzt werden von Wehrmachtmusikern und anderen Soldaten bei Reisen zu Erwerbszwecken. In solchen Fällen ist im Urlaubsschein der Vermerk über Lösen von Wehrmachtfahrkarten zu streichen.
2. Die Wehrmachtfahrkarte berechtigt zur Benutzung der 3. Klasse. Der Übergang in eine höhere Klasse ist auch gegen Lösen einer Übergangskarte nicht gestattet.
   Zuschlagspflichtige Züge (Eil- und Schnellzüge) dürfen gegen Zahlen des Zuschlages benutzt werden.
3. Der Urlaubsschein ist beim Lösen der Fahrkarte dem Schalterbeamten ohne Aufforderung o f f e n mit dem Truppenausweis vorzulegen. Bei der Fahrkartenprüfung sind beide auf Verlangen vorzuzeigen.
4. Der Urlaubsschein wird von der Eisenbahn beim Lösen der Fahrkarten abgestempelt und zurückgegeben. Er ist nach Rückkehr dem Truppenteil abzuliefern.

Figure 2-39. One has to wonder whether this leave pass was ever honored. Issued to Gefreiter Kurt Knupe for leave from December 28,1939 until January 4. 1940. this pre-wartime pass issued during the Sitzkrieg was never officially stamped but marked only as Dienstelle 25481 (1. Schwadron Kavallerie-Schutzen-Regiment 7 or the 1st Squadron of Cavalry Regiment 7). It bears no signs of use, and Bahnhofstempeln (train station stamps) such as date stamps.

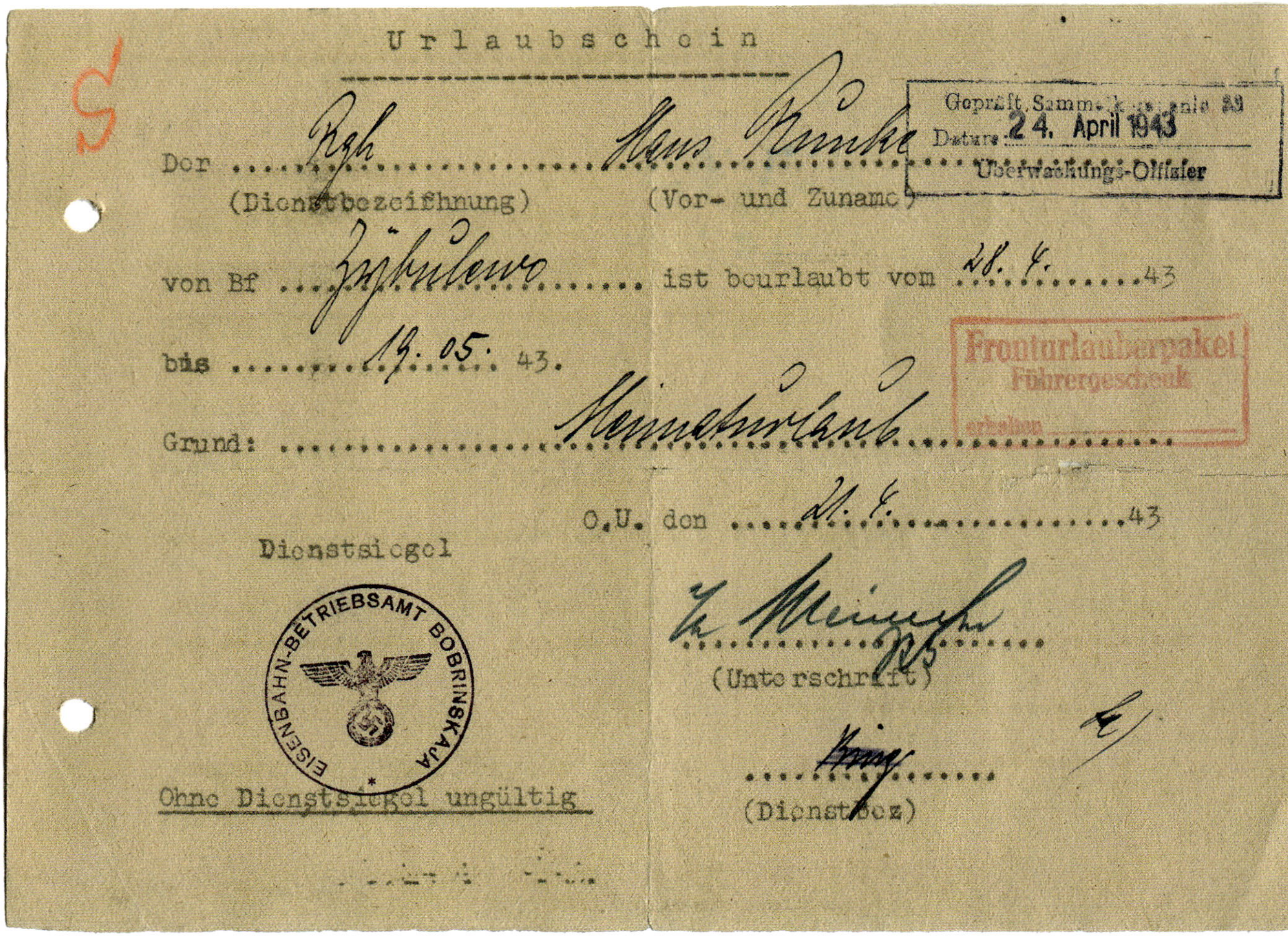

Figure 2-40. An excellent example of an Ersatz Urlaubsschein issued by the Reichsbahn at the Railway Business Office at Bobrinskia in occupied Russia to Hans Runke for Heimaturlaub (Home Leave) from April 28 until May 19, 1943. Note that even though he was in the Reichsbahn, Herr Runke was issued the Fronturlauberpaket (Front Soldier's Leave Package) normally reserved for front line soldiers. (A5)

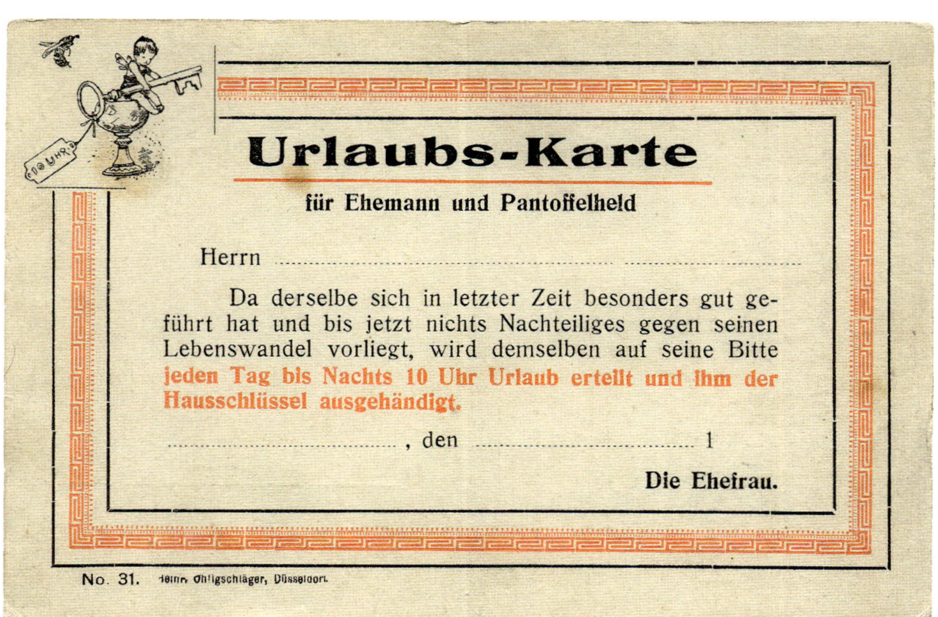

Figure 2-41. Although leave papers were taken very seriously, a great degree of humor still surrounded them. This humorous postcard and fake leave card granted leave to the Ehemann und Pantoffelheld (Husband and the Henpecked One; literally "Slippers Hero") and stated that he was entitled to leave every night until 10:00 pm, at which time he was to hand over the keys to the house; the card has been issued by Die Ehefrau (the wife). ($3^5/_8$" x $5^1/_2$")

money for its purchase, as well as ration cards or stamps, soap, and even shaving soap.

Also added are two blocks at the bottom. To the left was the certification for the receipt of a soldier's pay upon arriving at the leave location (*Bescheinigung über Meldung am Urlaubsort*) and to the right was space for the certification that one had been given the appropriate ration cards (*Bescheinigung der Kartenausgabestelle*).

Stamps in these locations, especially as shortages increased during the war, guaranteed that the soldier had indeed been given pay and food. Second, it prevented the soldier from collecting more pay or food than he was allotted. Third, since a soldier's destination was clearly marked on the front of the form, it ensured that he could only collect pay and food at the train station he was supposed to arrive at, thus preventing or complicating any thoughts of desertion.

As mentioned in the introduction, *Sonderstempel* were added to the *Kriegsurlaubsschein* to indicate additional information pertinent to the soldier's travel. Such *Sonderstempel* might be used to indicate whether a soldier had passed through a delousing station or a *Feldlazarett* (Field Hospital) to confirm that he was free of contagion and healthy enough to travel. (Typhus was a serious threat on the front and Germany had a vested interest in soldiers not sharing it with friends and families within the Reich.)

Other stamps might include where and when he had been paid and for which period of time, as well as the issuance of rations not noted on the printed form, especially tobacco. A soldier being granted a *Fronturlauberpaket* (Vacationing Soldier from the Front's Package) or *Führergeschenk* (Führer's Present) would have a stamp on the *Kriegsurlaubsschein* indicating such a gift as well.

The *Kriegsurlaubsschein* was used by all branches of the military. Civilian paramilitary organizations, especially those serving alongside the *Wehrmacht* in the completion of their duties, seemed to have used the same forms. Some organizations, particularly the *Reichsarbeitsdienst* (*RAD*, Reich Work Service) and *Reichsbahn*, had their own forms printed; the format is nearly identical but the name of the organizations are printed on the form itself. This also served to prevent it from being used by wayward *Soldaten*.

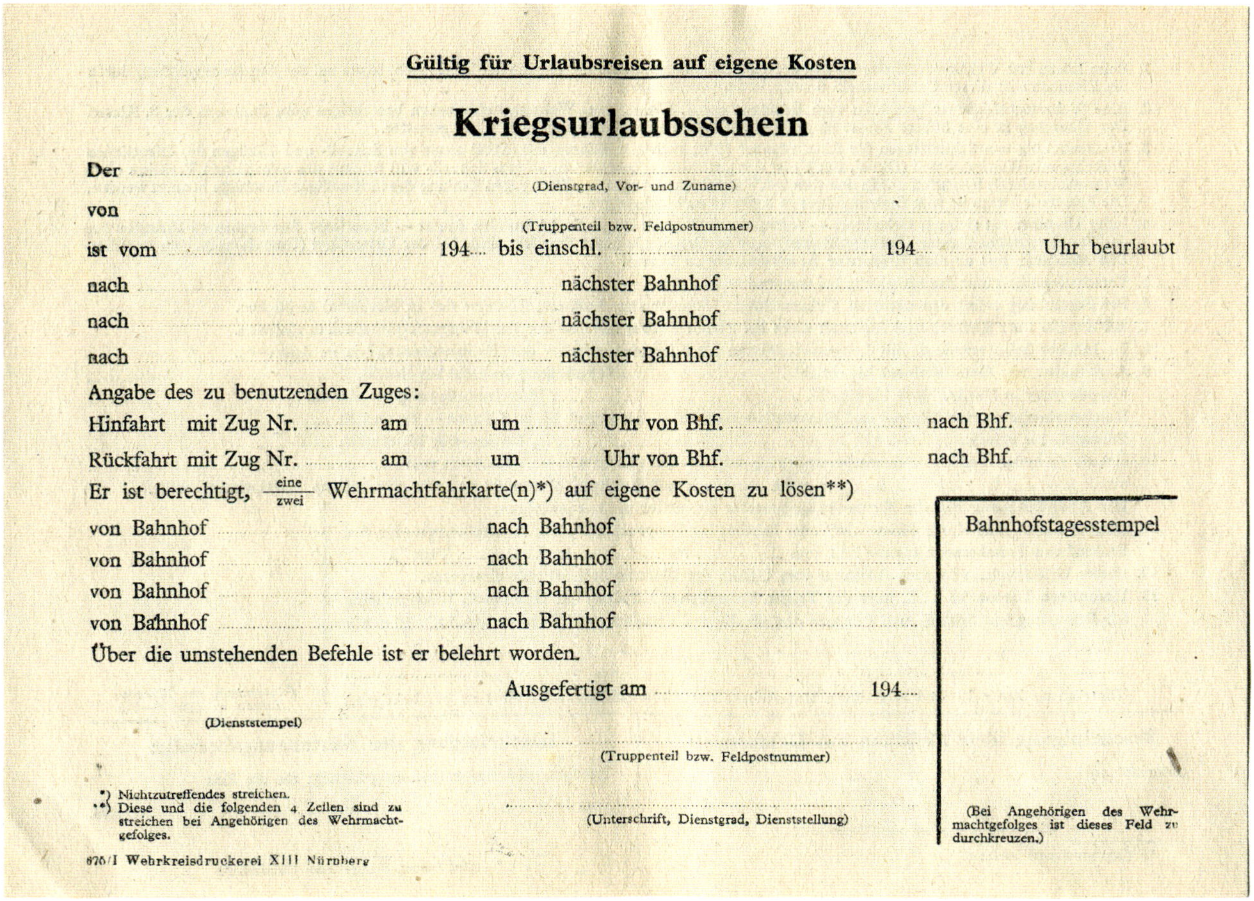

Gültig für Urlaubsreisen auf eigene Kosten

Kriegsurlaubsschein

Der ....
(Dienstgrad, Vor- und Zuname)
von ....
(Truppenteil bzw. Feldpostnummer)
ist vom .... 194... bis einschl. .... 194... .... Uhr beurlaubt
nach .... nächster Bahnhof ....
nach .... nächster Bahnhof ....
nach .... nächster Bahnhof ....
Angabe des zu benutzenden Zuges:
Hinfahrt mit Zug Nr. ..... am ..... um ..... Uhr von Bhf. .... nach Bhf. ....
Rückfahrt mit Zug Nr. ..... am ..... um ..... Uhr von Bhf. .... nach Bhf. ....
Er ist berechtigt, eine/zwei Wehrmachtfahrkarte(n)*) auf eigene Kosten zu lösen**)
von Bahnhof .... nach Bahnhof ....
von Bahnhof .... nach Bahnhof ....
von Bahnhof .... nach Bahnhof ....
von Bahnhof .... nach Bahnhof ....
Über die umstehenden Befehle ist er belehrt worden.
Ausgefertigt am .... 194...
(Dienststempel)
....
(Truppenteil bzw. Feldpostnummer)
....
(Unterschrift, Dienstgrad, Dienststellung)

Bahnhofstagesstempel

(Bei Angehörigen des Wehrmachtgefolges ist dieses Feld zu durchkreuzen.)

*) Nichtzutreffendes streichen.
**) Diese und die folgenden 4 Zeilen sind zu streichen bei Angehörigen des Wehrmachtgefolges.

676/I Wehrkreisdruckerei XIII Nürnberg

Figure 2-42. A blank Kriegsurlaubsschein für Urlaubsreisen auf eigene Kosten (Wartime Leave Pass for travel at one's own cost). This form has been printed using a serif typeface rather than the more common Fraktur. It was printed at Wehrkreisdruckerei XIII (Military District Printer) in Nürnberg. The reverse (following page) lists specific conditions of travel and has space for notations for the issuance of rations, payment, soap, and shaving soap. (A5)

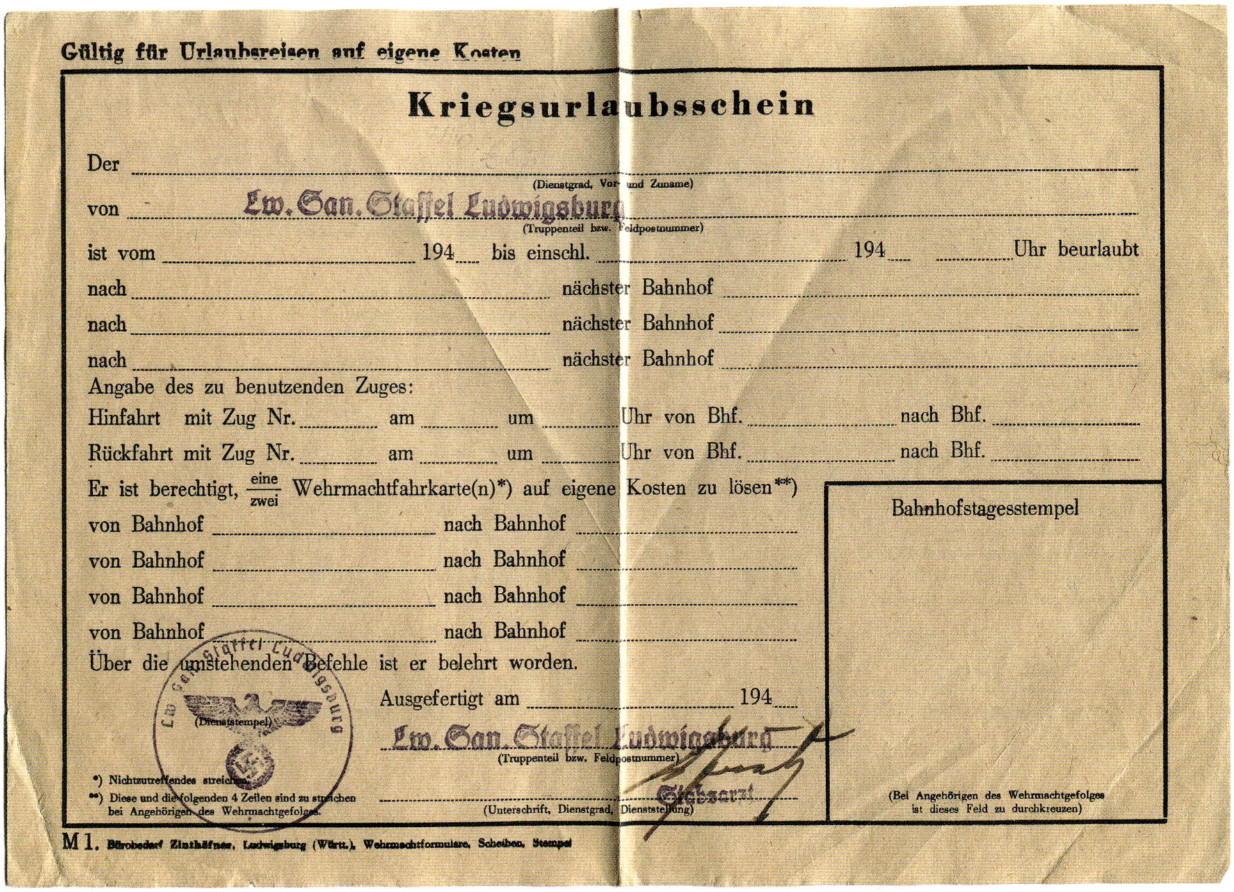

Gültig für Urlaubsreisen auf eigene Kosten

Kriegsurlaubsschein

Der ...
(Dienstgrad, Vor- und Zuname)

von Lw. San. Staffel Ludwigsburg
(Truppenteil bzw. Feldpostnummer)

ist vom ... 194... bis einschl. ... 194... ... Uhr beurlaubt

nach ... nächster Bahnhof ...

nach ... nächster Bahnhof ...

nach ... nächster Bahnhof ...

Angabe des zu benutzenden Zuges:

Hinfahrt mit Zug Nr. ... am ... um ... Uhr von Bhf. ... nach Bhf. ...

Rückfahrt mit Zug Nr. ... am ... um ... Uhr von Bhf. ... nach Bhf. ...

Er ist berechtigt, eine/zwei Wehrmachtfahrkarte(n)*) auf eigene Kosten zu lösen**)

von Bahnhof ... nach Bahnhof ...

von Bahnhof ... nach Bahnhof ...

von Bahnhof ... nach Bahnhof ...

von Bahnhof ... nach Bahnhof ...

Über die umstehenden Befehle ist er belehrt worden.

Bahnhofstagesstempel

(Bei Angehörigen des Wehrmachtgefolges ist dieses Feld zu durchkreuzen)

(Dienststempel) Lw. San. Staffel Ludwigsburg

Ausgefertigt am ... 194...

Lw. San. Staffel Ludwigsburg
(Truppenteil bzw. Feldpostnummer)

Stabsarzt
(Unterschrift, Dienstgrad, Dienststellung)

*) Nichtzutreffendes streichen.
**) Diese und die folgenden 4 Zeilen sind zu streichen bei Angehörigen des Wehrmachtgefolges.

M 1. Bürobedarf Zinthäfner, Ludwigsburg (Württ.), Wehrmachtformulare, Scheiben, Stempel

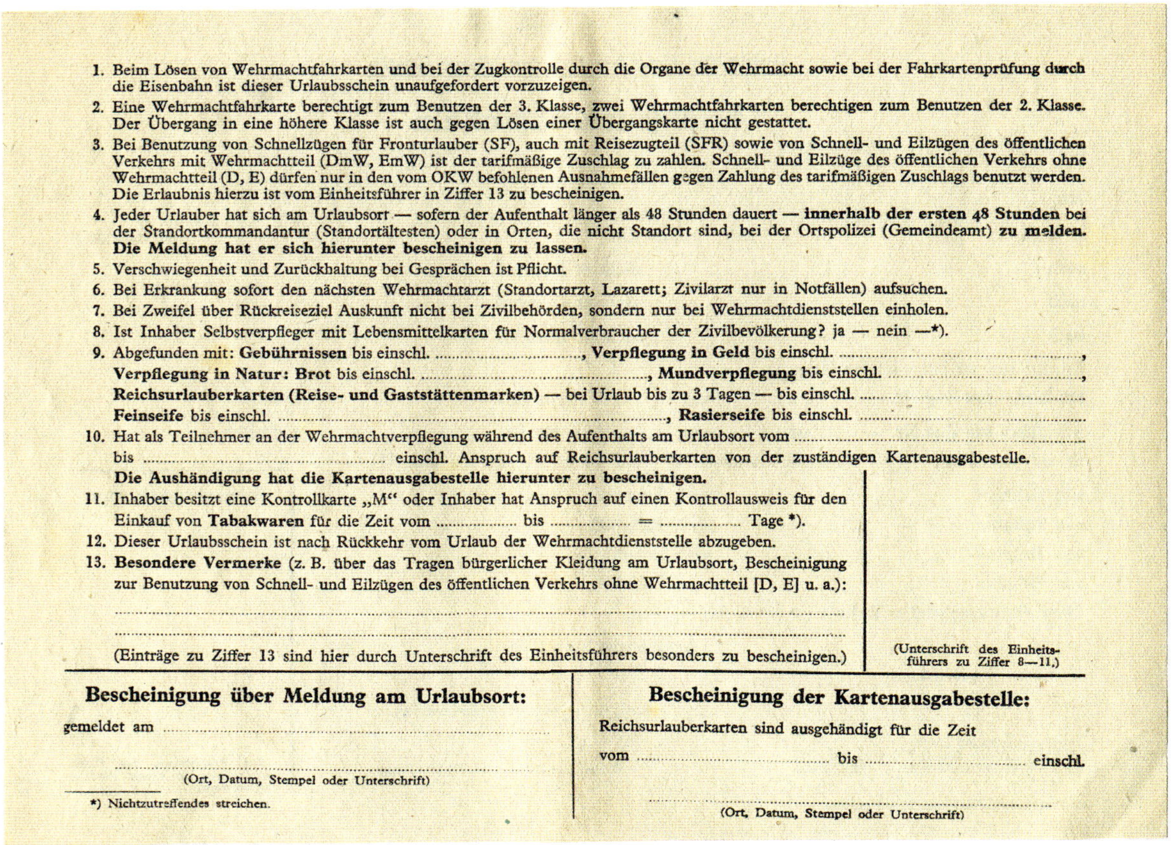

1. Beim Lösen von Wehrmachtfahrkarten und bei der Zugkontrolle durch die Organe der Wehrmacht sowie bei der Fahrkartenprüfung durch die Eisenbahn ist dieser Urlaubsschein unaufgefordert vorzuzeigen.
2. Eine Wehrmachtfahrkarte berechtigt zum Benutzen der 3. Klasse, zwei Wehrmachtfahrkarten berechtigen zum Benutzen der 2. Klasse. Der Übergang in eine höhere Klasse ist auch gegen Lösen einer Übergangskarte nicht gestattet.
3. Bei Benutzung von Schnellzügen für Fronturlauber (SF), auch mit Reisezugteil (SFR) sowie von Schnell- und Eilzügen des öffentlichen Verkehrs mit Wehrmachtteil (DmW, EmW) ist der tarifmäßige Zuschlag zu zahlen. Schnell- und Eilzüge des öffentlichen Verkehrs ohne Wehrmachtteil (D, E) dürfen nur in den vom OKW befohlenen Ausnahmefällen gegen Zahlung des tarifmäßigen Zuschlags benutzt werden. Die Erlaubnis hierzu ist vom Einheitsführer in Ziffer 13 zu bescheinigen.
4. Jeder Urlauber hat sich am Urlaubsort — sofern der Aufenthalt länger als 48 Stunden dauert — **innerhalb der ersten 48 Stunden** bei der Standortkommandantur (Standortältesten) oder in Orten, die nicht Standort sind, bei der Ortspolizei (Gemeindeamt) **zu melden. Die Meldung hat er sich hierunter bescheinigen zu lassen.**
5. Verschwiegenheit und Zurückhaltung bei Gesprächen ist Pflicht.
6. Bei Erkrankung sofort den nächsten Wehrmachtarzt (Standortarzt, Lazarett; Zivilarzt nur in Notfällen) aufsuchen.
7. Bei Zweifel über Rückreiseziel Auskunft nicht bei Zivilbehörden, sondern nur bei Wehrmachtdienststellen einholen.
8. Ist Inhaber Selbstverpfleger mit Lebensmittelkarten für Normalverbraucher der Zivilbevölkerung? ja — nein —*).
9. Abgefunden mit: **Gebührnissen** bis einschl. ..., **Verpflegung in Geld** bis einschl. ...,
   Verpflegung in Natur: Brot bis einschl. ..., **Mundverpflegung** bis einschl. ...,
   Reichsurlauberkarten (Reise- und Gaststättenmarken) — bei Urlaub bis zu 3 Tagen — bis einschl. ...
   Feinseife bis einschl. ..., **Rasierseife** bis einschl. ...
10. Hat als Teilnehmer an der Wehrmachtverpflegung während des Aufenthalts am Urlaubsort vom ... bis ... einschl. Anspruch auf Reichsurlauberkarten von der zuständigen Kartenausgabestelle. **Die Aushändigung hat die Kartenausgabestelle hierunter zu bescheinigen.**
11. Inhaber besitzt eine Kontrollkarte „M" oder Inhaber hat Anspruch auf einen Kontrollausweis für den Einkauf von **Tabakwaren** für die Zeit vom ... bis ... = ... Tage *).
12. Dieser Urlaubsschein ist nach Rückkehr vom Urlaub der Wehrmachtdienststelle abzugeben.
13. **Besondere Vermerke** (z. B. über das Tragen bürgerlicher Kleidung am Urlaubsort, Bescheinigung zur Benutzung von Schnell- und Eilzügen des öffentlichen Verkehrs ohne Wehrmachtteil [D, E] u. a.):

(Einträge zu Ziffer 13 sind hier durch Unterschrift des Einheitsführers besonders zu bescheinigen.)

(Unterschrift des Einheitsführers zu Ziffer 8—11.)

Bescheinigung über Meldung am Urlaubsort:

gemeldet am ...

(Ort, Datum, Stempel oder Unterschrift)

*) Nichtzutreffendes streichen.

Bescheinigung der Kartenausgabestelle:

Reichsurlauberkarten sind ausgehändigt für die Zeit vom ... bis ... einschl.

(Ort, Datum, Stempel oder Unterschrift)

Figure 2-43. Another blank Kriegsurlaubsschein, partially filled out for use by Luftwaffe Sanitäts Staffel (Medical Squadron) Ludwigsburg. Note how different the layout is from the previous example, yet the information is identical. (A5)

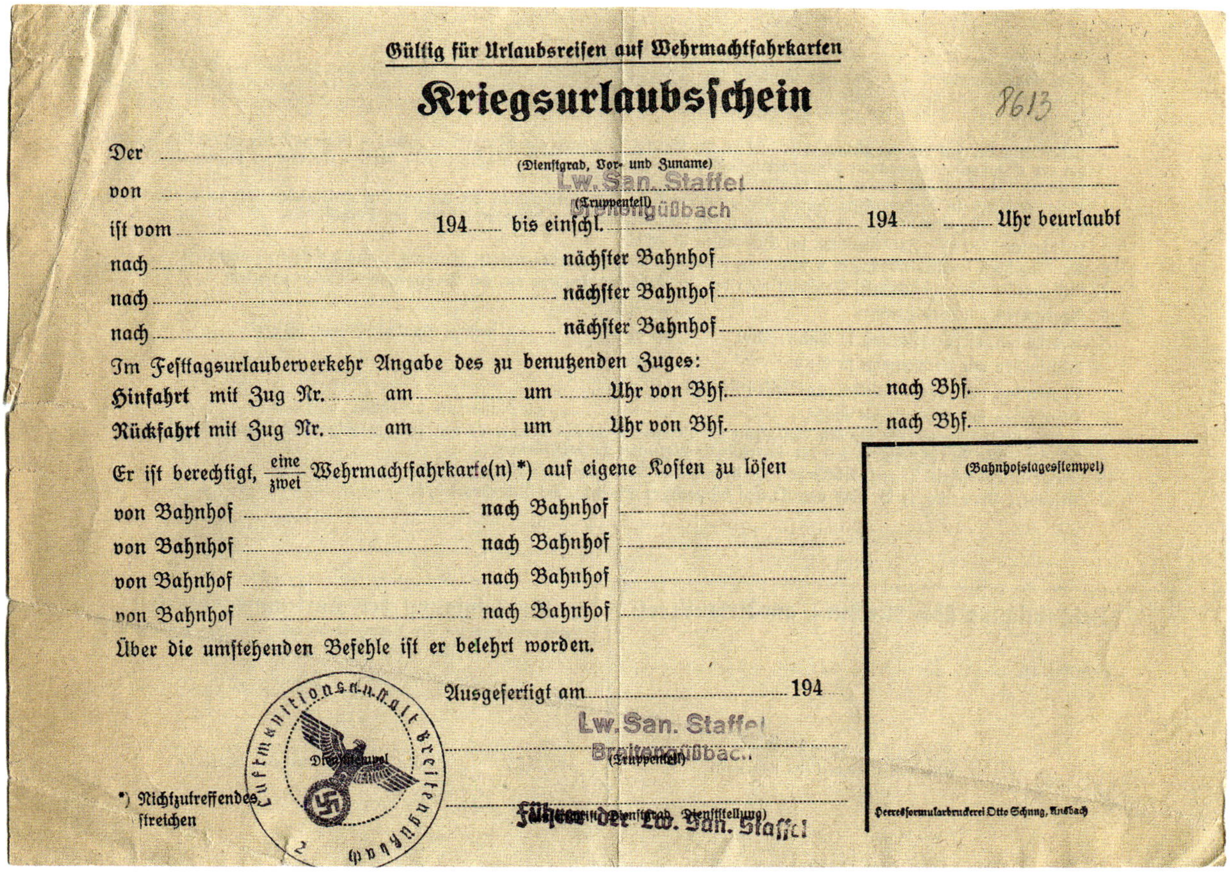

Gültig für Urlaubsreisen auf Wehrmachtfahrkarten

Kriegsurlaubsschein

8613

Der ....
(Dienstgrad, Vor- und Zuname)

von .... Lw.San. Staffel Breitengüßbach
(Truppenteil)

ist vom .... 194...... bis einschl. .... 194...... .... Uhr beurlaubt

nach .... nächster Bahnhof ....

nach .... nächster Bahnhof ....

nach .... nächster Bahnhof ....

Im Festtagsurlauberverkehr Angabe des zu benutzenden Zuges:

Hinfahrt mit Zug Nr. .... am .... um .... Uhr von Bhf. .... nach Bhf. ....

Rückfahrt mit Zug Nr. .... am .... um .... Uhr von Bhf. .... nach Bhf. ....

Er ist berechtigt, eine/zwei Wehrmachtfahrkarte(n)*) auf eigene Kosten zu lösen

von Bahnhof .... nach Bahnhof ....

von Bahnhof .... nach Bahnhof ....

von Bahnhof .... nach Bahnhof ....

von Bahnhof .... nach Bahnhof ....

Über die umstehenden Befehle ist er belehrt worden.

(Bahnhofstagesstempel)

Ausgefertigt am 194

Dienststempel

Lw.San. Staffel Breitengüßbach
(Truppenteil)

*) Nichtzutreffendes streichen

Führer der Lw. San. Staffel
(Dienstgrad, Dienststellung)

Heeresformulardruckerei Otto Schnug, Ansbach

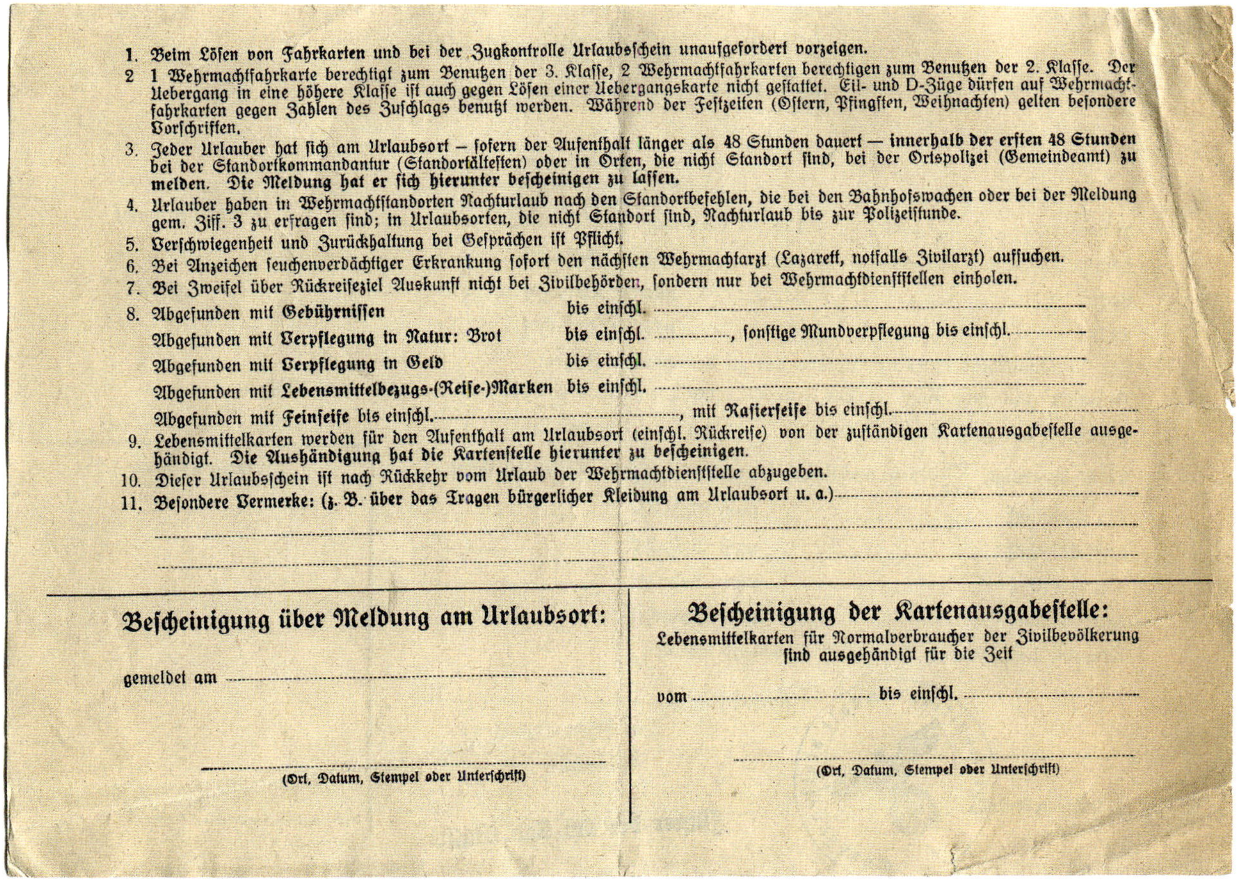

1. Beim Lösen von Fahrkarten und bei der Zugkontrolle Urlaubsschein unaufgefordert vorzeigen.
2. 1 Wehrmachtfahrkarte berechtigt zum Benutzen der 3. Klasse, 2 Wehrmachtfahrkarten berechtigen zum Benutzen der 2. Klasse. Der Uebergang in eine höhere Klasse ist auch gegen Lösen einer Uebergangskarte nicht gestattet. Eil- und D-Züge dürfen auf Wehrmachtfahrkarten gegen Zahlen des Zuschlags benutzt werden. Während der Festzeiten (Ostern, Pfingsten, Weihnachten) gelten besondere Vorschriften.
3. Jeder Urlauber hat sich am Urlaubsort – sofern der Aufenthalt länger als 48 Stunden dauert — **innerhalb der ersten 48 Stunden** bei der Standortkommandantur (Standortältesten) oder in Orten, die nicht Standort sind, bei der Ortspolizei (Gemeindeamt) **zu melden. Die Meldung hat er sich hierunter bescheinigen zu lassen.**
4. Urlauber haben in Wehrmachtstandorten Nachturlaub nach den Standortbefehlen, die bei den Bahnhofswachen oder bei der Meldung gem. Ziff. 3 zu erfragen sind; in Urlaubsorten, die nicht Standort sind, Nachturlaub bis zur Polizeistunde.
5. Verschwiegenheit und Zurückhaltung bei Gesprächen ist Pflicht.
6. Bei Anzeichen seuchenverdächtiger Erkrankung sofort den nächsten Wehrmachtarzt (Lazarett, notfalls Zivilarzt) aufsuchen.
7. Bei Zweifel über Rückreiseziel Auskunft nicht bei Zivilbehörden, sondern nur bei Wehrmachtdienststellen einholen.
8. Abgefunden mit **Gebührnissen** bis einschl. ....
   Abgefunden mit **Verpflegung in Natur:** Brot bis einschl. ...., sonstige Mundverpflegung bis einschl. ....
   Abgefunden mit **Verpflegung in Geld** bis einschl. ....
   Abgefunden mit **Lebensmittelbezugs-(Reise-)Marken** bis einschl. ....
   Abgefunden mit **Feinseife** bis einschl. ...., mit **Rasierseife** bis einschl. ....
9. Lebensmittelkarten werden für den Aufenthalt am Urlaubsort (einschl. Rückreise) von der zuständigen Kartenausgabestelle ausgehändigt. **Die Aushändigung hat die Kartenstelle hierunter zu bescheinigen.**
10. Dieser Urlaubsschein ist nach Rückkehr vom Urlaub der Wehrmachtdienststelle abzugeben.
11. **Besondere Vermerke: (z. B. über das Tragen bürgerlicher Kleidung am Urlaubsort u. a.)** ....

Bescheinigung über Meldung am Urlaubsort:

gemeldet am ....

....
(Ort, Datum, Stempel oder Unterschrift)

Bescheinigung der Kartenausgabestelle:

Lebensmittelkarten für Normalverbraucher der Zivilbevölkerung sind ausgehändigt für die Zeit

vom .... bis einschl. ....

....
(Ort, Datum, Stempel oder Unterschrift)

Figure 2-44. Another Kriegsurlaubsschein, this time printed using the Fraktur typeface and filled out for use by Luftwaffe Sanitäts Staffel in Breitengussbach. Except for the typeface, its layout is practically identical to that of figure 2-43.

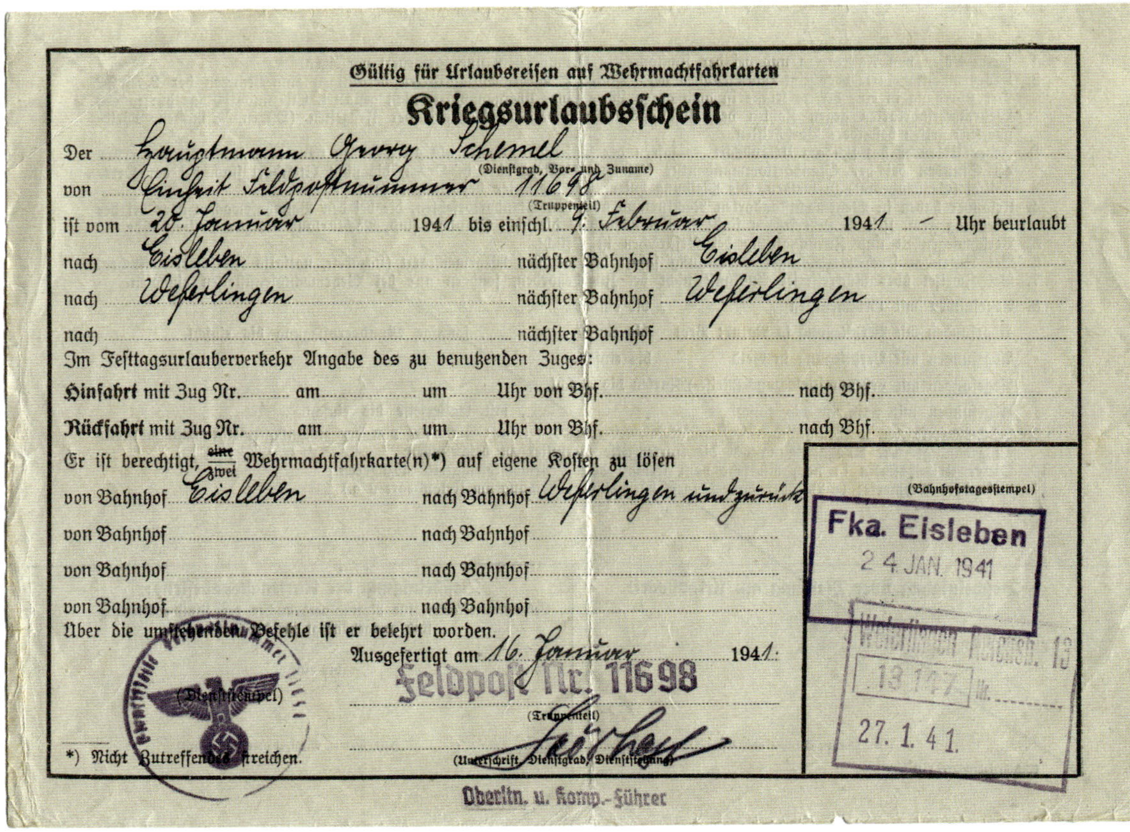

Gültig für Urlaubsreisen auf Wehrmachtfahrkarten

Kriegsurlaubsschein

Der Hauptmann Georg Schemel (Dienstgrad, Vor- und Zuname)

von Einheit Feldpostnummer 11698 (Truppenteil)

ist vom 20. Januar 1941 bis einschl. 9. Februar 1941 – Uhr beurlaubt

nach Eisleben nächster Bahnhof Eisleben

nach Weferlingen nächster Bahnhof Weferlingen

nach ..... nächster Bahnhof .....

Im Festtagsurlauberverkehr Angabe des zu benutzenden Zuges:

Hinfahrt mit Zug Nr. ..... am ..... um ..... Uhr von Bhf. ..... nach Bhf. .....

Rückfahrt mit Zug Nr. ..... am ..... um ..... Uhr von Bhf. ..... nach Bhf. .....

Er ist berechtigt, eine/zwei Wehrmachtfahrkarte(n)*) auf eigene Kosten zu lösen

von Bahnhof Eisleben nach Bahnhof Weferlingen und zurück

von Bahnhof ..... nach Bahnhof .....

von Bahnhof ..... nach Bahnhof .....

von Bahnhof ..... nach Bahnhof .....

Über die umstehenden Befehle ist er belehrt worden.

Ausgefertigt am 16. Januar 1941

Feldpost Nr. 11698 (Truppenteil)

(Dienststempel)

(Unterschrift, Dienstgrad, Dienststellung)

Oberltn. u. Komp.-Führer

*) Nicht Zutreffendes streichen.

(Bahnhofstagesstempel)

Fka. Eisleben 24 JAN. 1941

13 1 47

27. 1. 41.

Figure 2-45. A Fraktur Kriegsurlaubsschein issued to Hauptmann (Captain) Georg Schemel for leave from January 20 until February 9, 1941 by the 1st Company of Wach-Bataillon or Watch Battalion 608 (Feldpost Nr. 11698) for travel from Eisleben to Wesserling and back. (A5)

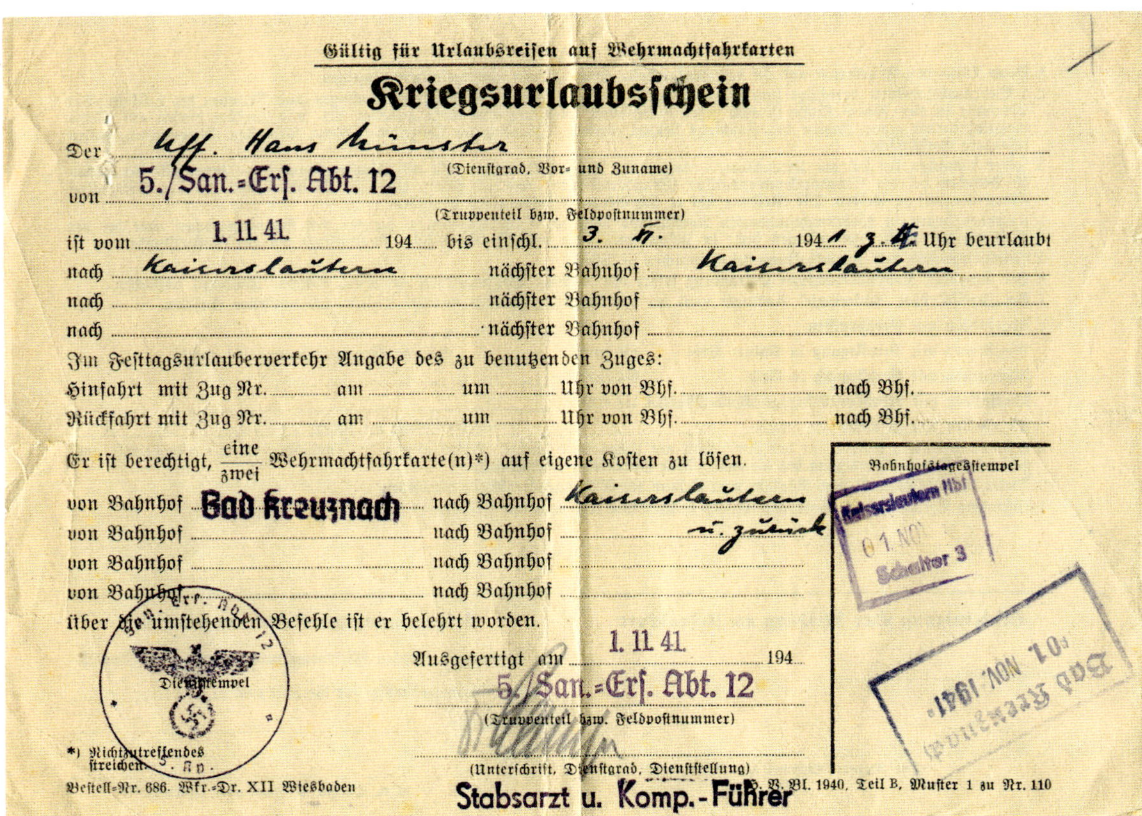

Gültig für Urlaubsreisen auf Wehrmachtfahrkarten

Kriegsurlaubsschein

Der Uffz. Hans Künster (Dienstgrad, Vor- und Zuname)

von 5./San.-Ers. Abt. 12 (Truppenteil bzw. Feldpostnummer)

ist vom 1. 11. 41. 194 bis einschl. 3. 11. 1941 3 h Uhr beurlaubt

nach Kaiserslautern nächster Bahnhof Kaiserslautern

nach ..... nächster Bahnhof .....

nach ..... nächster Bahnhof .....

Im Festtagsurlauberverkehr Angabe des zu benutzenden Zuges:

Hinfahrt mit Zug Nr. ..... am ..... um ..... Uhr von Bhf. ..... nach Bhf. .....

Rückfahrt mit Zug Nr. ..... am ..... um ..... Uhr von Bhf. ..... nach Bhf. .....

Er ist berechtigt, eine/zwei Wehrmachtfahrkarte(n)*) auf eigene Kosten zu lösen.

von Bahnhof **Bad Kreuznach** nach Bahnhof Kaiserslautern

von Bahnhof ..... nach Bahnhof ..... u. zurück

von Bahnhof ..... nach Bahnhof .....

von Bahnhof ..... nach Bahnhof .....

über die umstehenden Befehle ist er belehrt worden.

Ausgefertigt am 1. 11. 41 194

5./San.-Ers. Abt. 12 (Truppenteil bzw. Feldpostnummer)

Dienststempel

(Unterschrift, Dienstgrad, Dienststellung)

Stabsarzt u. Komp.-Führer

*) Nichtzutreffendes streichen.

Bestell-Nr. 686. Wkr.-Dr. XII Wiesbaden

H. V. Bl. 1940, Teil B, Muster 1 zu Nr. 110

Bahnhofstagesstempel

Kaiserslautern Hbf 01 NOV Schalter 3

Bad Kreuznach 01 NOV 1941

Figure 2-46. Unteroffizier Hans Künster (see figures 2-31 and 2-33) used this Kriegsurlaubsschein to travel from Bad Kreuznach to Kaiserslautern and back.

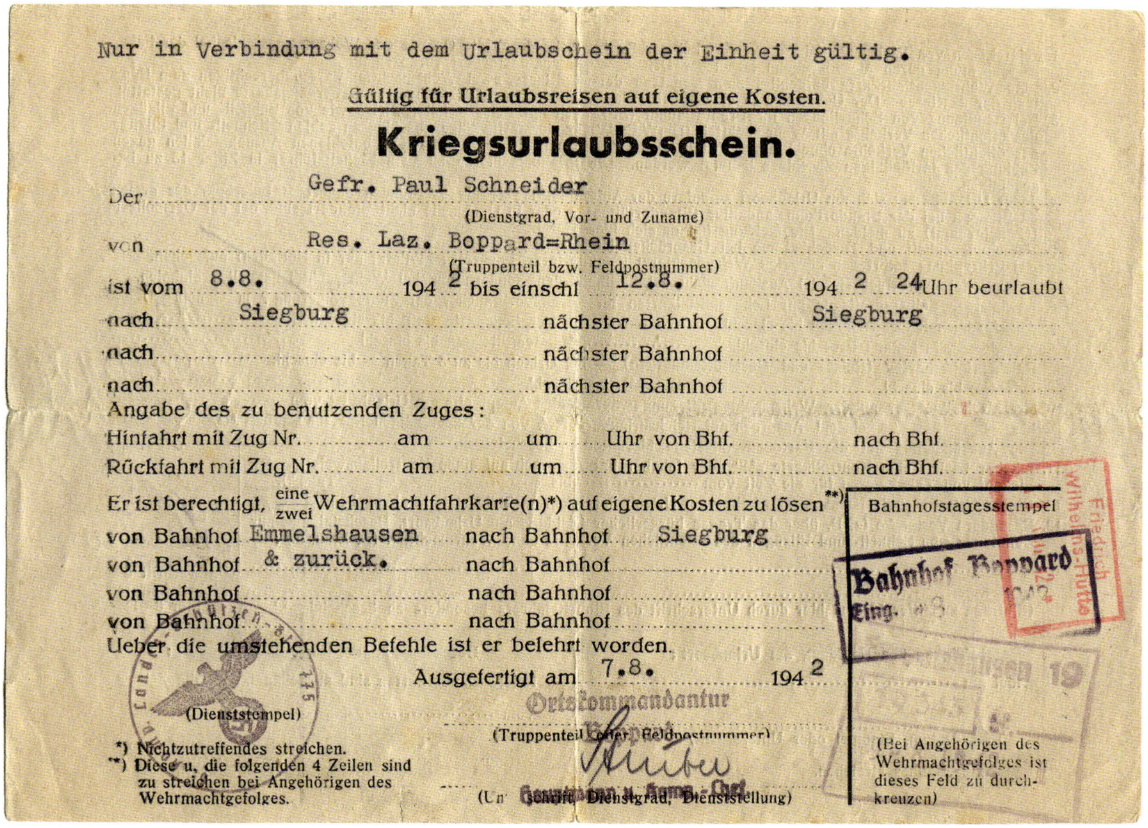

Nur in Verbindung mit dem Urlaubschein der Einheit gültig.

Gültig für Urlaubsreisen auf eigene Kosten.

Kriegsurlaubsschein.

Der Gefr. Paul Schneider
(Dienstgrad, Vor- und Zuname)

von Res. Laz. Boppard=Rhein
(Truppenteil bzw. Feldpostnummer)

ist vom 8.8. 1942 bis einschl 12.8. 1942 24 Uhr beurlaubt

nach Siegburg nächster Bahnhof Siegburg

nach .... nächster Bahnhof ....

nach .... nächster Bahnhof ....

Angabe des zu benutzenden Zuges:

Hinfahrt mit Zug Nr. ...... am ...... um ...... Uhr von Bhf. ...... nach Bhf. ......

Rückfahrt mit Zug Nr. ...... am ...... um ...... Uhr von Bhf. ...... nach Bhf. ......

Er ist berechtigt, eine/zwei Wehrmachtfahrkarte(n)*) auf eigene Kosten zu lösen**)

von Bahnhof Emmelshausen nach Bahnhof Siegburg

von Bahnhof & zurück. nach Bahnhof

von Bahnhof .... nach Bahnhof ....

von Bahnhof .... nach Bahnhof ....

Ueber die umstehenden Befehle ist er belehrt worden.

Ausgefertigt am 7.8. 1942

(Dienststempel)

Ortskommandantur

(Truppenteil oder Feldpostnummer)

(Unterschrift, Dienstgrad, Dienststellung)

*) Nichtzutreffendes streichen.
**) Diese u. die folgenden 4 Zeilen sind zu streichen bei Angehörigen des Wehrmachtgefolges.

Bahnhofstagesstempel

Bahnhof Boppard

Eing.

(Bei Angehörigen des Wehrmachtgefolges ist dieses Feld zu durchkreuzen)

Figure 2-47. Gefreiter Paul Schneider travelled from Emmelshausen to Siegburg and back using this Kriegsurlaubsschein in August of 1942. The typewritten notation at the top states that this pass is only valid in association with unit business. Note the use of a more decorative typeface in the printing, one that harkens more to the previous war than that of the 1940s, but the back of the form is printed much like other examples, using a standard serif print.

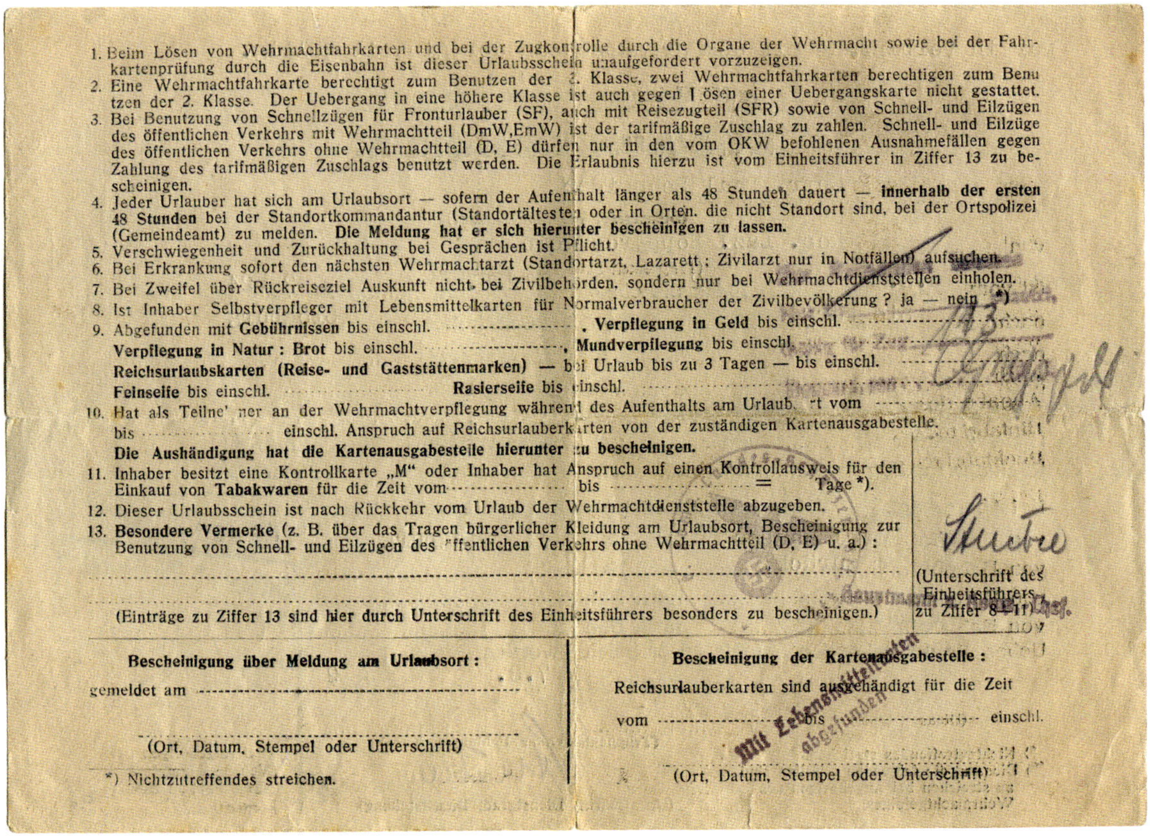

1. Beim Lösen von Wehrmachtfahrkarten und bei der Zugkontrolle durch die Organe der Wehrmacht sowie bei der Fahrkartenprüfung durch die Eisenbahn ist dieser Urlaubsschein unaufgefordert vorzuzeigen.
2. Eine Wehrmachtfahrkarte berechtigt zum Benutzen der 3. Klasse, zwei Wehrmachtfahrkarten berechtigen zum Benutzen der 2. Klasse. Der Uebergang in eine höhere Klasse ist auch gegen Lösen einer Uebergangskarte nicht gestattet.
3. Bei Benutzung von Schnellzügen für Fronturlauber (SF), auch mit Reisezugteil (SFR) sowie von Schnell- und Eilzügen des öffentlichen Verkehrs mit Wehrmachtteil (DmW,EmW) ist der tarifmäßige Zuschlag zu zahlen. Schnell- und Eilzüge des öffentlichen Verkehrs ohne Wehrmachtteil (D, E) dürfen nur in den vom OKW befohlenen Ausnahmefällen gegen Zahlung des tarifmäßigen Zuschlags benutzt werden. Die Erlaubnis hierzu ist vom Einheitsführer in Ziffer 13 zu bescheinigen.
4. Jeder Urlauber hat sich am Urlaubsort — sofern der Aufenthalt länger als 48 Stunden dauert — **innerhalb der ersten 48 Stunden** bei der Standortkommandantur (Standortältesten oder in Orten, die nicht Standort sind, bei der Ortspolizei (Gemeindeamt) zu melden. **Die Meldung hat er sich hierunter bescheinigen zu lassen.**
5. Verschwiegenheit und Zurückhaltung bei Gesprächen ist Pflicht.
6. Bei Erkrankung sofort den nächsten Wehrmachtarzt (Standortarzt, Lazarett; Zivilarzt nur in Notfällen) aufsuchen.
7. Bei Zweifel über Rückreiseziel Auskunft nicht bei Zivilbehörden, sondern nur bei Wehrmachtdienststellen einholen.
8. Ist Inhaber Selbstverpfleger mit Lebensmittelkarten für Normalverbraucher der Zivilbevölkerung? ja — nein *)
9. Abgefunden mit **Gebührnissen** bis einschl. ...., **Verpflegung in Geld** bis einschl. ....
Verpflegung in Natur: Brot bis einschl. ...., **Mundverpflegung** bis einschl. ....
Reichsurlaubskarten (Reise- und Gaststättenmarken) — bei Urlaub bis zu 3 Tagen — bis einschl. ....
Feinseife bis einschl. .... **Rasierseife** bis einschl. ....
10. Hat als Teilnehmer an der Wehrmachtverpflegung während des Aufenthalts am Urlaubsort vom .... bis .... einschl. Anspruch auf Reichsurlauberkarten von der zuständigen Kartenausgabestelle.
Die Aushändigung hat die Kartenausgabestelle hierunter zu bescheinigen.
11. Inhaber besitzt eine Kontrollkarte „M" oder Inhaber hat Anspruch auf einen Kontrollausweis für den Einkauf von **Tabakwaren** für die Zeit vom .... bis .... = Tage *).
12. Dieser Urlaubsschein ist nach Rückkehr vom Urlaub der Wehrmachtdienststelle abzugeben.
13. **Besondere Vermerke** (z. B. über das Tragen bürgerlicher Kleidung am Urlaubsort, Bescheinigung zur Benutzung von Schnell- und Eilzügen des öffentlichen Verkehrs ohne Wehrmachtteil (D, E) u. a.):

(Einträge zu Ziffer 13 sind hier durch Unterschrift des Einheitsführers besonders zu bescheinigen.)

(Unterschrift des Einheitsführers zu Ziffer 8–11)

Bescheinigung über Meldung am Urlaubsort:

gemeldet am ....

(Ort, Datum, Stempel oder Unterschrift)

*) Nichtzutreffendes streichen.

Bescheinigung der Kartenausgabestelle:

Reichsurlauberkarten sind ausgehändigt für die Zeit

vom .... bis .... einschl.

(Ort, Datum, Stempel oder Unterschrift)

Mit Lebensmittelkarten abgefunden

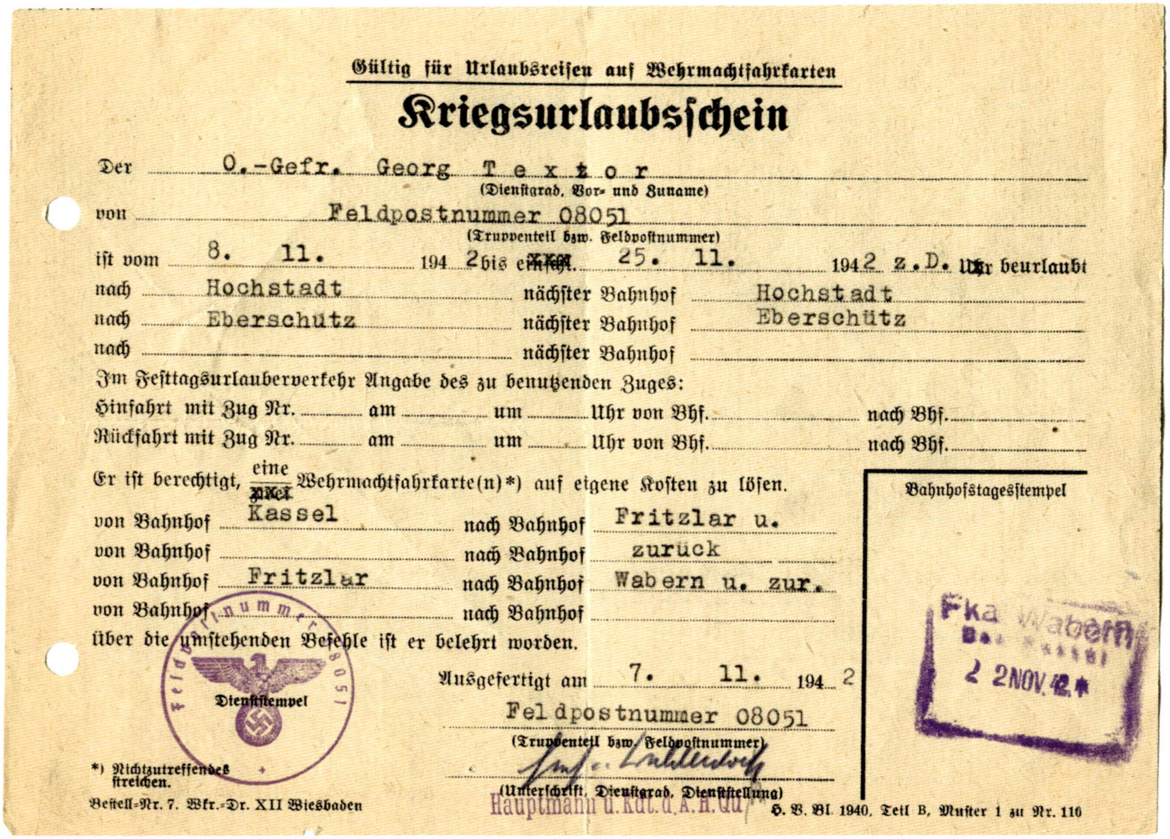

Gültig für Urlaubsreisen auf Wehrmachtfahrkarten

Kriegsurlaubsschein

Der O.-Gefr. Georg T e x t o r
(Dienstgrad, Vor- und Zuname)

von Feldpostnummer 08051
(Truppenteil bzw. Feldpostnummer)

ist vom 8. 11. 1942 bis einschl. 25. 11. 1942 z.D. Uhr beurlaubt

nach Hochstadt nächster Bahnhof Hochstadt

nach Eberschütz nächster Bahnhof Eberschütz

nach .... nächster Bahnhof ....

Im Festtagsurlauberverkehr Angabe des zu benutzenden Zuges:

Hinfahrt mit Zug Nr. .... am .... um .... Uhr von Bhf. .... nach Bhf. ....

Rückfahrt mit Zug Nr. .... am .... um .... Uhr von Bhf. .... nach Bhf. ....

Er ist berechtigt, eine ~~zwei~~ Wehrmachtfahrkarte(n)*) auf eigene Kosten zu lösen.

von Bahnhof Kassel nach Bahnhof Fritzlar u.

von Bahnhof .... nach Bahnhof zurück

von Bahnhof Fritzlar nach Bahnhof Wabern u. zur.

von Bahnhof .... nach Bahnhof ....

über die umstehenden Befehle ist er belehrt worden.

Bahnhofstagesstempel

Fka Wabern ... 2 2NOV.42.

Dienststempel

Ausgefertigt am 7. 11. 1942

Feldpostnummer 08051

(Truppenteil bzw. Feldpostnummer)

(Unterschrift, Dienstgrad, Dienststellung)

Hauptmann u. Kdt. d. A.K.St.

*) Nichtzutreffendes streichen.

Bestell-Nr. 7. Wkr.-Dr. XII Wiesbaden

H. V. Bl. 1940, Teil B, Muster 1 zu Nr. 116

2-48. Obergefreiter Georg Textor of Armee-Kartenstelle 518 (Army Map Depot, Feldpostnummer 08051, July 15, 1942 to January 24, 1943) travelled quite a bit using this Kriegsurlaubsschein, going from Hochstadt to Eberschutz, but travelling at his own expense from Kassel to Fritzlar and back, and then from Fritzlar to Wabern and back in November of 1942. The handwritten note on the back states that the pass did not entitle Obergefreiter Textor to food ration cards. (A5)

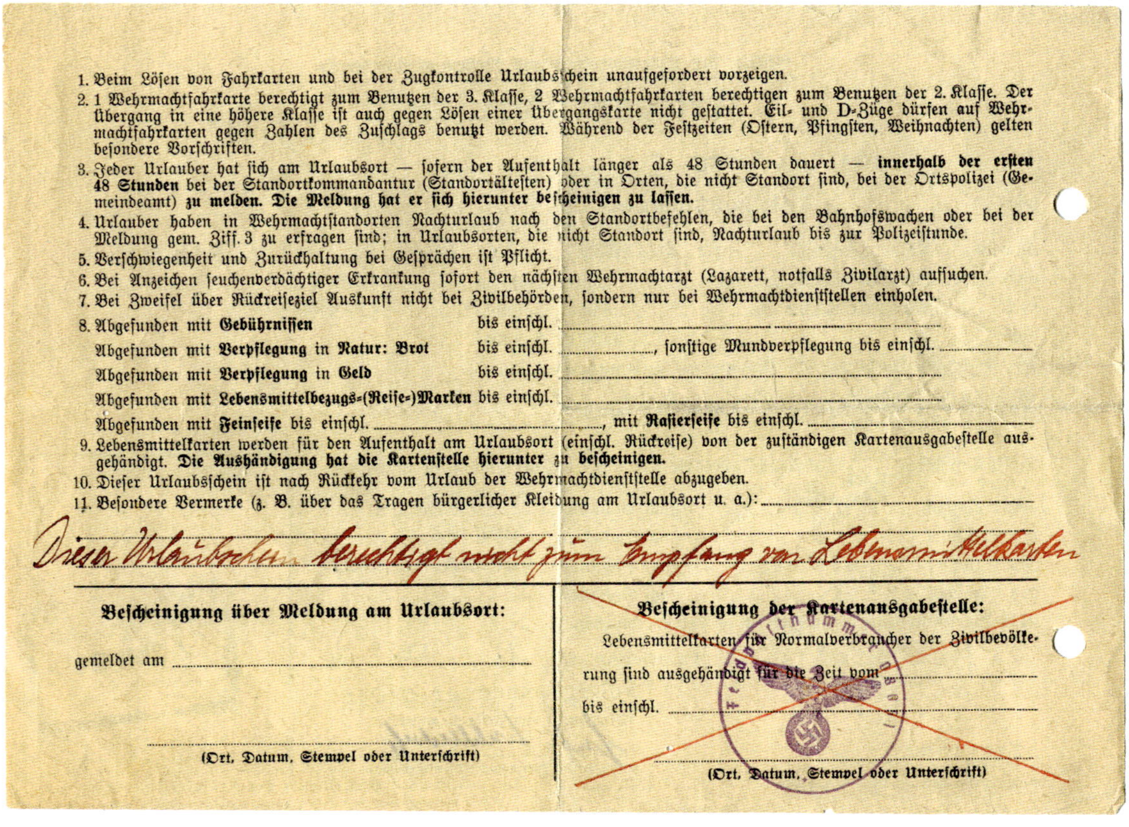

1. Beim Lösen von Fahrkarten und bei der Zugkontrolle Urlaubsschein unaufgefordert vorzeigen.
2. 1 Wehrmachtfahrkarte berechtigt zum Benutzen der 3. Klasse, 2 Wehrmachtfahrkarten berechtigen zum Benutzen der 2. Klasse. Der Übergang in eine höhere Klasse ist auch gegen Lösen einer Übergangskarte nicht gestattet. Eil- und D-Züge dürfen auf Wehrmachtfahrkarten gegen Zahlen des Zuschlags benutzt werden. Während der Festzeiten (Ostern, Pfingsten, Weihnachten) gelten besondere Vorschriften.
3. Jeder Urlauber hat sich am Urlaubsort — sofern der Aufenthalt länger als 48 Stunden dauert — **innerhalb der ersten 48 Stunden** bei der Standortkommandantur (Standortältesten) oder in Orten, die nicht Standort sind, bei der Ortspolizei (Gemeindeamt) **zu melden. Die Meldung hat er sich hierunter bescheinigen zu lassen.**
4. Urlauber haben in Wehrmachtstandorten Nachturlaub nach den Standortbefehlen, die bei den Bahnhofswachen oder bei der Meldung gem. Ziff. 3 zu erfragen sind; in Urlaubsorten, die nicht Standort sind, Nachturlaub bis zur Polizeistunde.
5. Verschwiegenheit und Zurückhaltung bei Gesprächen ist Pflicht.
6. Bei Anzeichen seuchenverdächtiger Erkrankung sofort den nächsten Wehrmachtarzt (Lazarett, notfalls Zivilarzt) aufsuchen.
7. Bei Zweifel über Rückreiseziel Auskunft nicht bei Zivilbehörden, sondern nur bei Wehrmachtdienststellen einholen.
8. Abgefunden mit **Gebührnissen** bis einschl. ....
   Abgefunden mit **Verpflegung in Natur: Brot** bis einschl. ...., sonstige Mundverpflegung bis einschl. ....
   Abgefunden mit **Verpflegung in Geld** bis einschl. ....
   Abgefunden mit **Lebensmittelbezugs-(Reise-)Marken** bis einschl. ....
   Abgefunden mit **Feinseife** bis einschl. ...., mit **Rasierseife** bis einschl. ....
9. Lebensmittelkarten werden für den Aufenthalt am Urlaubsort (einschl. Rückreise) von der zuständigen Kartenausgabestelle ausgehändigt. **Die Aushändigung hat die Kartenstelle hierunter zu bescheinigen.**
10. Dieser Urlaubsschein ist nach Rückkehr vom Urlaub der Wehrmachtdienststelle abzugeben.
11. Besondere Vermerke (z. B. über das Tragen bürgerlicher Kleidung am Urlaubsort u. a.): ....

Dieser Urlaubschein berechtigt nicht zum Empfang von Lebensmittelkarten

Bescheinigung über Meldung am Urlaubsort:

gemeldet am ....

(Ort, Datum, Stempel oder Unterschrift)

Bescheinigung der Kartenausgabestelle:

Lebensmittelkarten für Normalverbraucher der Zivilbevölkerung sind ausgehändigt für die Zeit vom ....

bis einschl. ....

(Ort, Datum, Stempel oder Unterschrift)

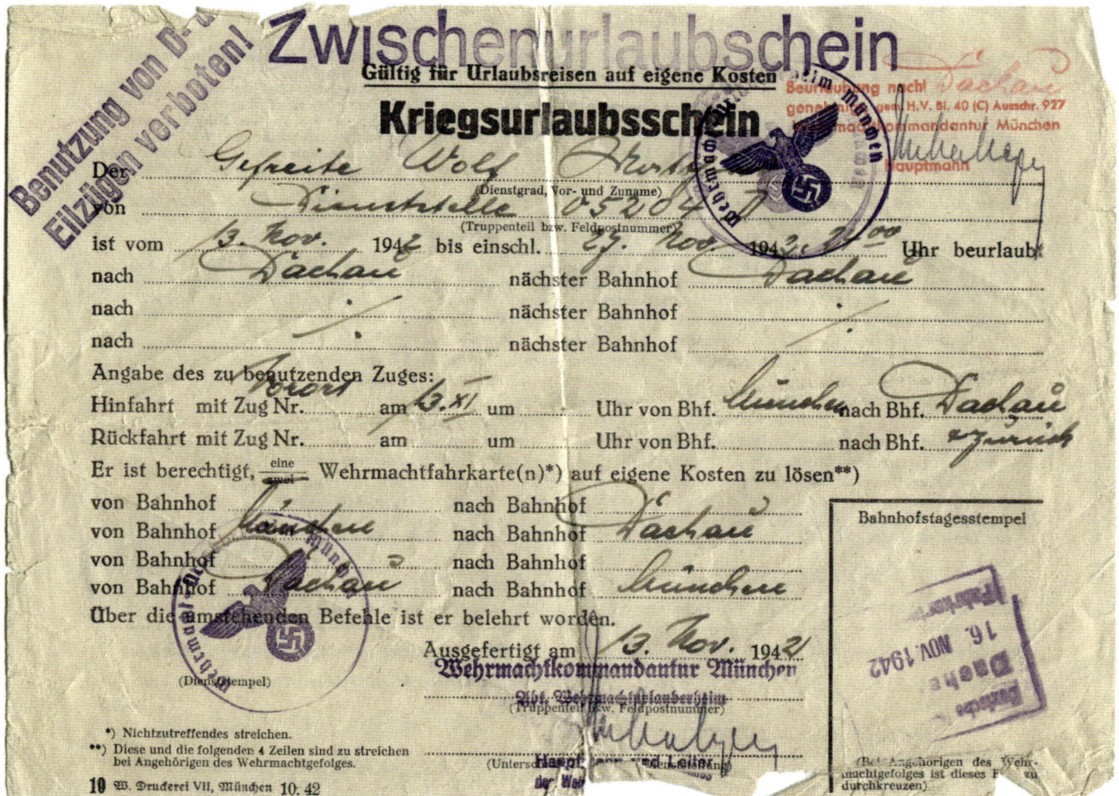
Benutzung von D- u. Eilzügen verboten!

Zwischenurlaubschein

Gültig für Urlaubsreisen auf eigene Kosten

Kriegsurlaubsschein

Beurlaubung nach: Dachau genehmigt gem. H.V. Bl. 40 (C) Ausschr. 927 Wehrmachtkommandantur München Hauptmann

Der Gefreite Wolf ...
(Dienstgrad, Vor- und Zuname)

von Dienststelle 05204
(Truppenteil bzw. Feldpostnummer)

ist vom 13. Nov. 1942 bis einschl. 27. Nov. 1942 ... Uhr beurlaubt

nach Dachau nächster Bahnhof Dachau

nach ./. nächster Bahnhof ./.

nach nächster Bahnhof

Angabe des zu benutzenden Zuges:

Hinfahrt mit Zug Nr. Vorort am 13.XI um ... Uhr von Bhf. München nach Bhf. Dachau

Rückfahrt mit Zug Nr. ... am ... um ... Uhr von Bhf. ... nach Bhf. zurück

Er ist berechtigt, eine / zwei Wehrmachtfahrkarte(n)*) auf eigene Kosten zu lösen**)

von Bahnhof ... nach Bahnhof ...

von Bahnhof München nach Bahnhof Dachau

von Bahnhof ... nach Bahnhof ...

von Bahnhof Dachau nach Bahnhof München

Über die umstehenden Befehle ist er belehrt worden.

Ausgefertigt am 13. Nov. 1942

Wehrmachtkommandantur München

(Dienststempel)

(Truppenteil bzw. Feldpostnummer)

(Unterschrift ...) Hauptmann und Leiter der Wehrmacht...

Bahnhofstagesstempel

16. NOV. 1942 Dachau

(Bei Angehörigen des Wehrmachtgefolges ist dieses Feld zu durchkreuzen)

*) Nichtzutreffendes streichen.

**) Diese und die folgenden 4 Zeilen sind zu streichen bei Angehörigen des Wehrmachtgefolges.

10 W. Druckerei VII, München 10. 42

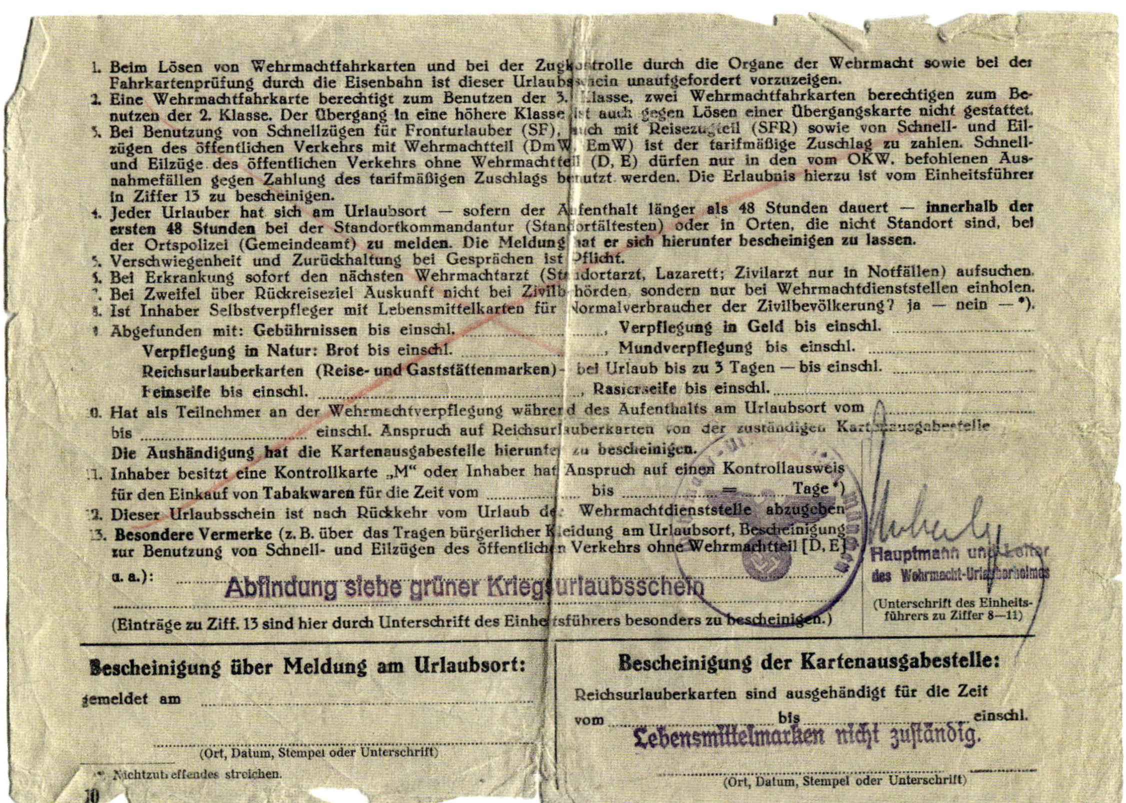
1. Beim Lösen von Wehrmachtfahrkarten und bei der Zugkontrolle durch die Organe der Wehrmacht sowie bei der Fahrkartenprüfung durch die Eisenbahn ist dieser Urlaubsschein unaufgefordert vorzuzeigen.

2. Eine Wehrmachtfahrkarte berechtigt zum Benutzen der 3. Klasse, zwei Wehrmachtfahrkarten berechtigen zum Benutzen der 2. Klasse. Der Übergang in eine höhere Klasse ist auch gegen Lösen einer Übergangskarte nicht gestattet.

3. Bei Benutzung von Schnellzügen für Fronturlauber (SF), auch mit Reisezugteil (SFR) sowie von Schnell- und Eilzügen des öffentlichen Verkehrs mit Wehrmachtteil (DmW, EmW) ist der tarifmäßige Zuschlag zu zahlen. Schnell- und Eilzüge des öffentlichen Verkehrs ohne Wehrmachtteil (D, E) dürfen nur in den vom OKW. befohlenen Ausnahmefällen gegen Zahlung des tarifmäßigen Zuschlags benutzt werden. Die Erlaubnis hierzu ist vom Einheitsführer in Ziffer 13 zu bescheinigen.

4. Jeder Urlauber hat sich am Urlaubsort — sofern der Aufenthalt länger als 48 Stunden dauert — **innerhalb der ersten 48 Stunden** bei der Standortkommandantur (Standortältesten) oder in Orten, die nicht Standort sind, bei der Ortspolizei (Gemeindeamt) **zu melden. Die Meldung hat er sich hierunter bescheinigen zu lassen.**

5. Verschwiegenheit und Zurückhaltung bei Gesprächen ist Pflicht.

6. Bei Erkrankung sofort den nächsten Wehrmachtarzt (Standortarzt, Lazarett; Zivilarzt nur in Notfällen) aufsuchen.

7. Bei Zweifel über Rückreiseziel Auskunft nicht bei Zivilbehörden, sondern nur bei Wehrmachtdienststellen einholen.

8. Ist Inhaber Selbstverpfleger mit Lebensmittelkarten für Normalverbraucher der Zivilbevölkerung? ja — nein —*).

9. Abgefunden mit: **Gebührnissen** bis einschl. ..., **Verpflegung in Geld** bis einschl. ...
Verpflegung in Natur: Brot bis einschl. ..., **Mundverpflegung** bis einschl. ...
Reichsurlauberkarten (Reise- und Gaststättenmarken) - bei Urlaub bis zu 3 Tagen — bis einschl. ...
Feinseife bis einschl. ..., **Rasierseife** bis einschl. ...

10. Hat als Teilnehmer an der Wehrmachtverpflegung während des Aufenthalts am Urlaubsort vom ... bis ... einschl. Anspruch auf Reichsurlauberkarten von der zuständigen Kartenausgabestelle
Die Aushändigung hat die Kartenausgabestelle hierunter zu bescheinigen.

11. Inhaber besitzt eine Kontrollkarte „M" oder Inhaber hat Anspruch auf einen Kontrollausweis für den Einkauf von **Tabakwaren** für die Zeit vom ... bis ... = ... Tage*)

12. Dieser Urlaubsschein ist nach Rückkehr vom Urlaub der Wehrmachtdienststelle abzugeben

13. **Besondere Vermerke** (z. B. über das Tragen bürgerlicher Kleidung am Urlaubsort, Bescheinigung zur Benutzung von Schnell- und Eilzügen des öffentlichen Verkehrs ohne Wehrmachtteil [D, E] u. a.): Abfindung siehe grüner Kriegsurlaubsschein

(Einträge zu Ziff. 13 sind hier durch Unterschrift des Einheitsführers besonders zu bescheinigen.)

Hauptmann und Leiter des Wehrmacht-Urlauberheims
(Unterschrift des Einheitsführers zu Ziffer 8—11)

Bescheinigung über Meldung am Urlaubsort:

gemeldet am ...

(Ort, Datum, Stempel oder Unterschrift)

Bescheinigung der Kartenausgabestelle:

Reichsurlauberkarten sind ausgehändigt für die Zeit vom ... bis ... einschl.

Lebensmittelmarken nicht zuständig.

(Ort, Datum, Stempel oder Unterschrift)

*) Nichtzutreffendes streichen.

10

Figure 2-49. This Kriegsurlaubsschein authorized this Gefreite (sic) of Dienststelle 05204 (Pionier Bataillon 561) to travel between Munich and Dachau (not the infamous camp, but the town in the vicinity of it). The reverse of the form states that all rations and supplies have been issued according to the "green" leave pass, the Kriegsurlaubsschein with a green stripe authorizing travel paid for by the Wehrmacht. Many times a second "between" leave pass (Zwischenurlaubsschein) was issued when a Soldat was granted personal leave at his own expense while on official business. The Sonderstempel "Benutzung von D- und Eilzügen verboten!" forbade the Soldat from using trains reserved for troops. (A5)

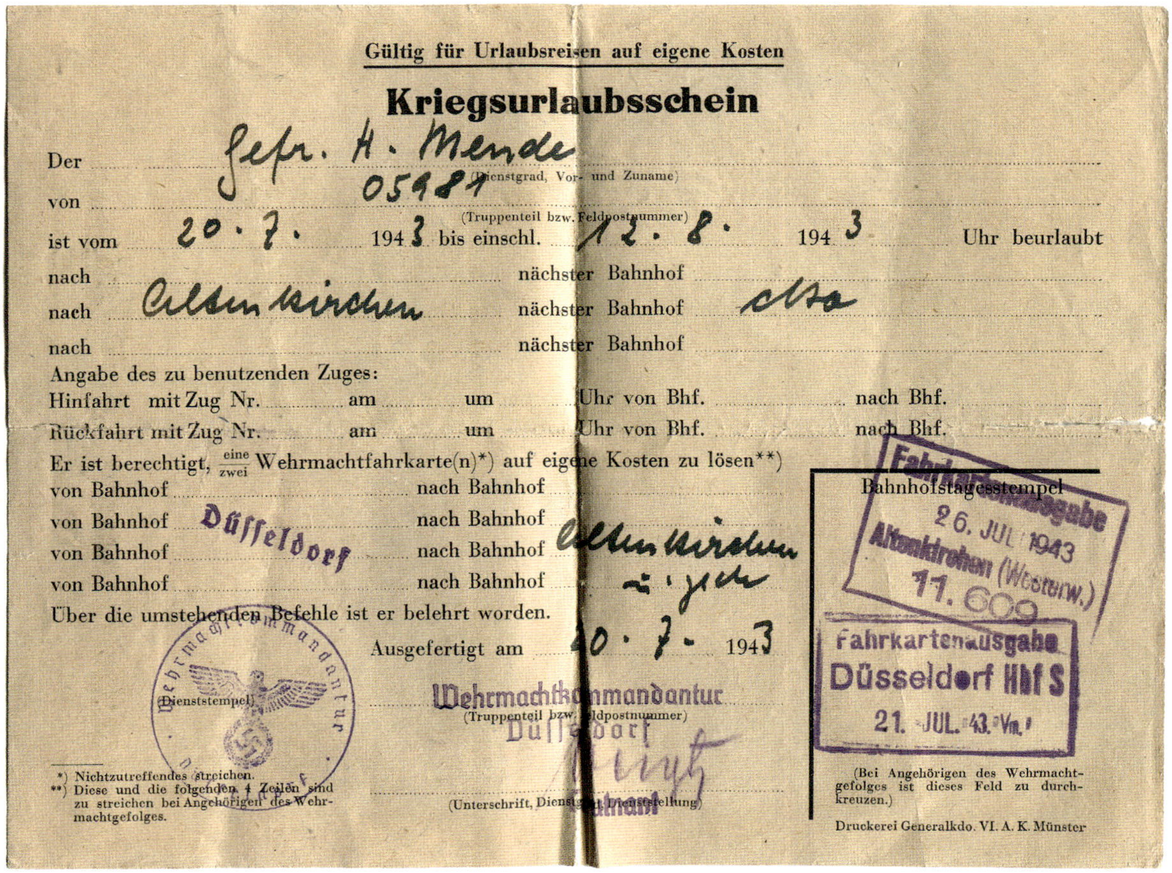

Gültig für Urlaubsreisen auf eigene Kosten

Kriegsurlaubsschein

Der Gefr. H. Mende (Dienstgrad, Vor- und Zuname)

von 05981 (Truppenteil bzw. Feldpostnummer)

ist vom 20.7. 1943 bis einschl. 12.8. 1943 Uhr beurlaubt

nach ... nächster Bahnhof ...

nach Altenkirchen nächster Bahnhof ebda

nach ... nächster Bahnhof ...

Angabe des zu benutzenden Zuges:

Hinfahrt mit Zug Nr. ... am ... um ... Uhr von Bhf. ... nach Bhf. ...

Rückfahrt mit Zug Nr. ... am ... um ... Uhr von Bhf. ... nach Bhf. ...

Er ist berechtigt, eine/zwei Wehrmachtfahrkarte(n)*) auf eigene Kosten zu lösen**)

von Bahnhof ... nach Bahnhof ...

von Bahnhof ... nach Bahnhof ...

von Bahnhof Düsseldorf nach Bahnhof Altenkirchen

von Bahnhof ... nach Bahnhof u. zurück

Über die umstehenden Befehle ist er belehrt worden.

Ausgefertigt am 20.7. 1943

(Dienststempel) Wehrmachtkommandantur

Wehrmachtkommandantur Düsseldorf (Truppenteil bzw. Feldpostnummer)

(Unterschrift, Dienstgrad und Dienststellung) Leutnant

*) Nichtzutreffendes streichen.
**) Diese und die folgenden 4 Zeilen sind zu streichen bei Angehörigen des Wehrmachtgefolges.

Bahnhofstagesstempel

Fahrkartenausgabe 26. JUL 1943 Altenkirchen (Westerw.) 11.609

Fahrkartenausgabe Düsseldorf Hbf S 21. JUL. 43. Vm.

(Bei Angehörigen des Wehrmachtgefolges ist dieses Feld zu durchkreuzen.)

Druckerei Generalkdo. VI. A. K. Münster

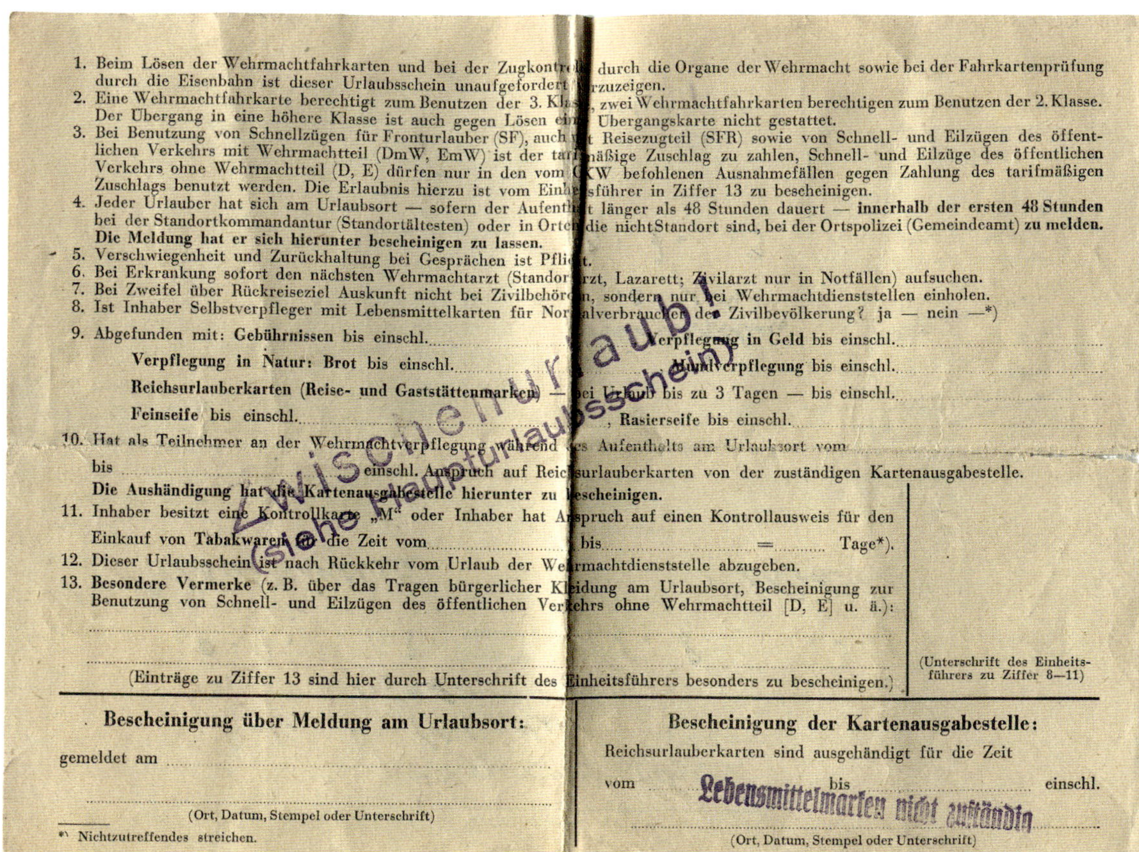

1. Beim Lösen der Wehrmachtfahrkarten und bei der Zugkontrolle durch die Organe der Wehrmacht sowie bei der Fahrkartenprüfung durch die Eisenbahn ist dieser Urlaubsschein unaufgefordert vorzuzeigen.
2. Eine Wehrmachtfahrkarte berechtigt zum Benutzen der 3. Klasse, zwei Wehrmachtfahrkarten berechtigen zum Benutzen der 2. Klasse. Der Übergang in eine höhere Klasse ist auch gegen Lösen einer Übergangskarte nicht gestattet.
3. Bei Benutzung von Schnellzügen für Fronturlauber (SF), auch mit Reisezugteil (SFR) sowie von Schnell- und Eilzügen des öffentlichen Verkehrs mit Wehrmachtteil (DmW, EmW) ist der tarifmäßige Zuschlag zu zahlen, Schnell- und Eilzüge des öffentlichen Verkehrs ohne Wehrmachtteil (D, E) dürfen nur in den vom OKW befohlenen Ausnahmefällen gegen Zahlung des tarifmäßigen Zuschlags benutzt werden. Die Erlaubnis hierzu ist vom Einheitsführer in Ziffer 13 zu bescheinigen.
4. Jeder Urlauber hat sich am Urlaubsort — sofern der Aufenthalt länger als 48 Stunden dauert — **innerhalb der ersten 48 Stunden** bei der Standortkommandantur (Standortältesten) oder in Orten, die nicht Standort sind, bei der Ortspolizei (Gemeindeamt) **zu melden. Die Meldung hat er sich hierunter bescheinigen zu lassen.**
5. Verschwiegenheit und Zurückhaltung bei Gesprächen ist Pflicht.
6. Bei Erkrankung sofort den nächsten Wehrmachtarzt (Standortarzt, Lazarett; Zivilarzt nur in Notfällen) aufsuchen.
7. Bei Zweifel über Rückreiseziel Auskunft nicht bei Zivilbehörden, sondern nur bei Wehrmachtdienststellen einholen.
8. Ist Inhaber Selbstverpfleger mit Lebensmittelkarten für Normalverbraucher der Zivilbevölkerung? ja — nein —*)
9. Abgefunden mit: **Gebührnissen** bis einschl. ... **Verpflegung in Geld** bis einschl. ...
   Verpflegung in Natur: Brot bis einschl. ... **Mundverpflegung** bis einschl. ...
   Reichsurlauberkarten (Reise- und Gaststättenmarken) — bei Urlaub bis zu 3 Tagen — bis einschl. ...
   Feinseife bis einschl. ..., **Rasierseife** bis einschl. ...
10. Hat als Teilnehmer an der Wehrmachtverpflegung während des Aufenthalts am Urlaubsort vom ... bis ... einschl. Anspruch auf Reichsurlauberkarten von der zuständigen Kartenausgabestelle. **Die Aushändigung hat die Kartenausgabestelle hierunter zu bescheinigen.**
11. Inhaber besitzt eine Kontrollkarte „M" oder Inhaber hat Anspruch auf einen Kontrollausweis für den Einkauf von Tabakwaren für die Zeit vom ... bis ... = ... Tage*).
12. Dieser Urlaubsschein ist nach Rückkehr vom Urlaub der Wehrmachtdienststelle abzugeben.
13. **Besondere Vermerke** (z. B. über das Tragen bürgerlicher Kleidung am Urlaubsort, Bescheinigung zur Benutzung von Schnell- und Eilzügen des öffentlichen Verkehrs ohne Wehrmachtteil [D, E] u. ä.):

(Einträge zu Ziffer 13 sind hier durch Unterschrift des Einheitsführers besonders zu bescheinigen.)

(Unterschrift des Einheitsführers zu Ziffer 8—11)

Zwischenurlaubsschein (siehe Haupturlaubsschein)

Bescheinigung über Meldung am Urlaubsort:

gemeldet am ...

(Ort, Datum, Stempel oder Unterschrift)

*) Nichtzutreffendes streichen.

Bescheinigung der Kartenausgabestelle:

Reichsurlauberkarten sind ausgehändigt für die Zeit vom ... bis ... einschl.

Lebensmittelmarken nicht zuständig

(Ort, Datum, Stempel oder Unterschrift)

Figure 2-50. Another Zwischenurlaubsschein (note the stamp on the back directing one to see the Haupturlaubsschein, main leave pass, to certify ration cards and other items) issued to Gefreiter Mende of Infanterie-Divisions-Nachrichten-Abteilung 304, or Infantry Division Communication Section 304. (A5)

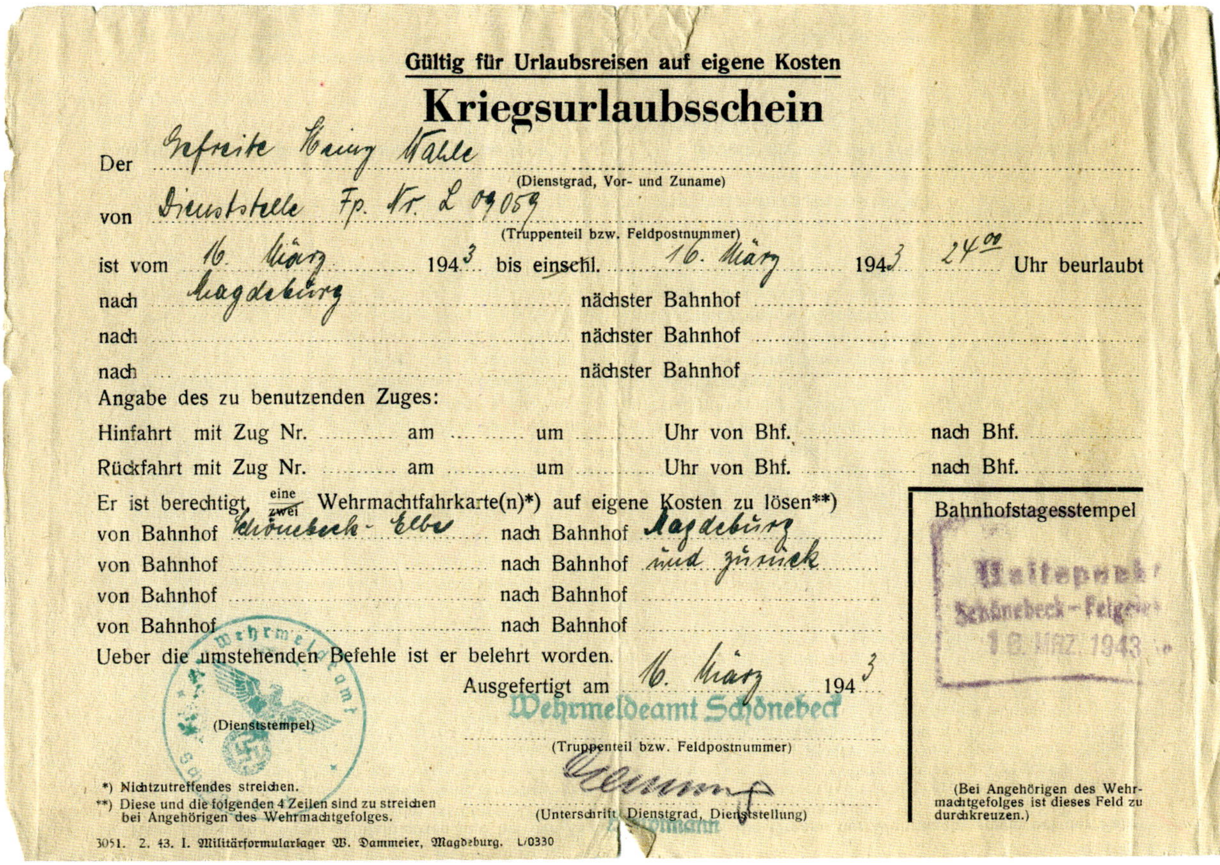

Gültig für Urlaubsreisen auf eigene Kosten

Kriegsurlaubsschein

Der Gefreite Heinz Wahle
(Dienstgrad, Vor- und Zuname)

von Dienststelle Fp. Nr. L 09059
(Truppenteil bzw. Feldpostnummer)

ist vom 16. März 1943 bis einschl. 16. März 1943 24⁰⁰ Uhr beurlaubt

nach Magdeburg nächster Bahnhof ....

nach .... nächster Bahnhof ....

nach .... nächster Bahnhof ....

Angabe des zu benutzenden Zuges:

Hinfahrt mit Zug Nr. ...... am ...... um ...... Uhr von Bhf. ...... nach Bhf. ......

Rückfahrt mit Zug Nr. ...... am ...... um ...... Uhr von Bhf. ...... nach Bhf. ......

Er ist berechtigt, eine/zwei Wehrmachtfahrkarte(n)*) auf eigene Kosten zu lösen**)

von Bahnhof Schönebeck-Elbe nach Bahnhof Magdeburg

von Bahnhof .... nach Bahnhof und zurück

von Bahnhof .... nach Bahnhof ....

von Bahnhof .... nach Bahnhof ....

Ueber die umstehenden Befehle ist er belehrt worden.

Ausgefertigt am 16. März 1943

Wehrmeldeamt Schönebeck
(Truppenteil bzw. Feldpostnummer)

(Dienststempel)

(Unterschrift, Dienstgrad, Dienststellung)

Bahnhofstagesstempel

Haltepunkt Schönebeck-Felgeleben 16. MRZ. 1943

(Bei Angehörigen des Wehrmachtgefolges ist dieses Feld zu durchkreuzen.)

*) Nichtzutreffendes streichen.
**) Diese und die folgenden 4 Zeilen sind zu streichen bei Angehörigen des Wehrmachtgefolges.

3051. 2. 43. I. Militärformularlager W. Dammeier, Magdeburg. L/0330

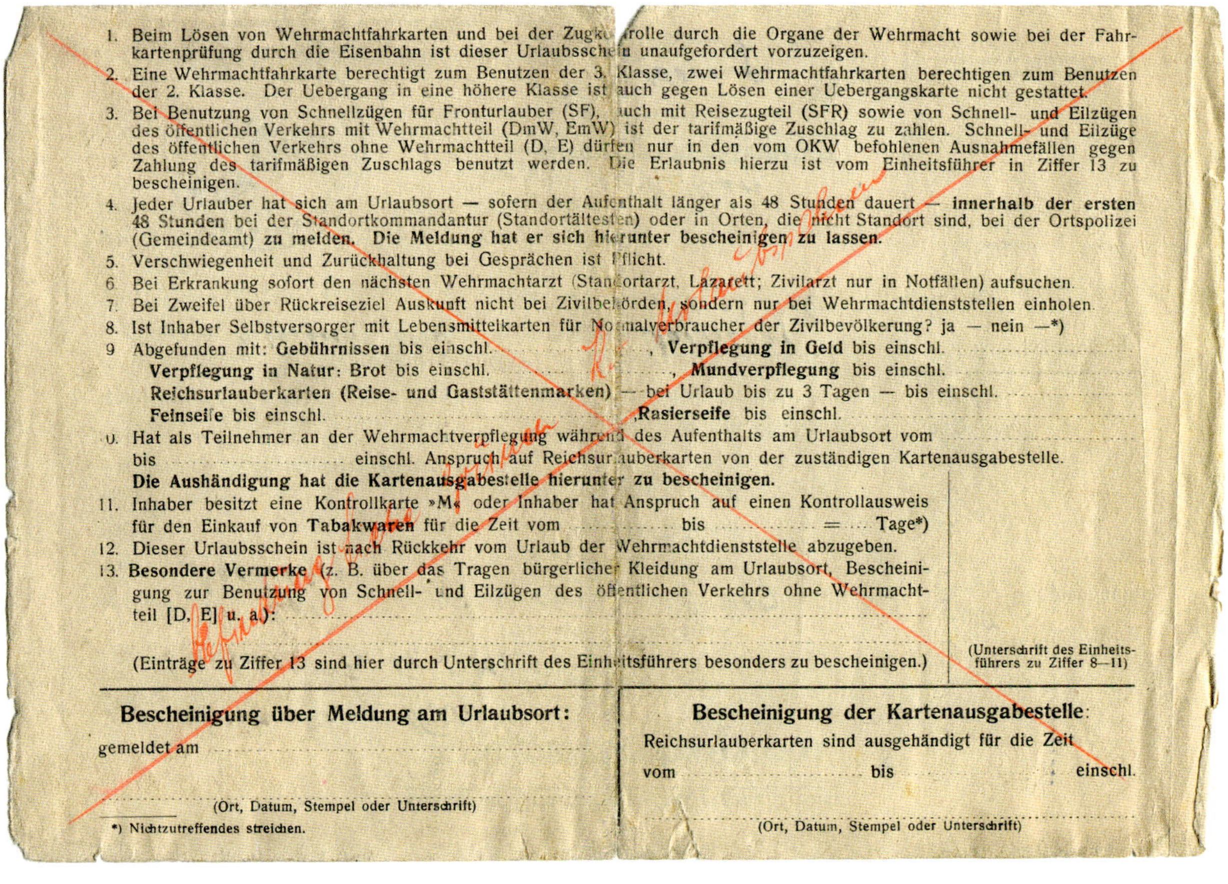

1. Beim Lösen von Wehrmachtfahrkarten und bei der Zugkontrolle durch die Organe der Wehrmacht sowie bei der Fahrkartenprüfung durch die Eisenbahn ist dieser Urlaubsschein unaufgefordert vorzuzeigen.
2. Eine Wehrmachtfahrkarte berechtigt zum Benutzen der 3. Klasse, zwei Wehrmachtfahrkarten berechtigen zum Benutzen der 2. Klasse. Der Uebergang in eine höhere Klasse ist auch gegen Lösen einer Uebergangskarte nicht gestattet.
3. Bei Benutzung von Schnellzügen für Fronturlauber (SF), auch mit Reisezugteil (SFR) sowie von Schnell- und Eilzügen des öffentlichen Verkehrs mit Wehrmachtteil (DmW, EmW) ist der tarifmäßige Zuschlag zu zahlen. Schnell- und Eilzüge des öffentlichen Verkehrs ohne Wehrmachtteil (D, E) dürfen nur in den vom OKW befohlenen Ausnahmefällen gegen Zahlung des tarifmäßigen Zuschlags benutzt werden. Die Erlaubnis hierzu ist vom Einheitsführer in Ziffer 13 zu bescheinigen.
4. Jeder Urlauber hat sich am Urlaubsort — sofern der Aufenthalt länger als 48 Stunden dauert — **innerhalb der ersten 48 Stunden** bei der Standortkommandantur (Standortältesten) oder in Orten, die nicht Standort sind, bei der Ortspolizei (Gemeindeamt) **zu melden. Die Meldung hat er sich hierunter bescheinigen zu lassen.**
5. Verschwiegenheit und Zurückhaltung bei Gesprächen ist Pflicht.
6. Bei Erkrankung sofort den nächsten Wehrmachtarzt (Standortarzt, Lazarett; Zivilarzt nur in Notfällen) aufsuchen.
7. Bei Zweifel über Rückreiseziel Auskunft nicht bei Zivilbehörden, sondern nur bei Wehrmachtdienststellen einholen.
8. Ist Inhaber Selbstversorger mit Lebensmittelkarten für Normalverbraucher der Zivilbevölkerung? ja — nein —*)
9. Abgefunden mit: **Gebührnissen** bis einschl. ...., **Verpflegung in Geld** bis einschl. ....
   Verpflegung in Natur: Brot bis einschl. ...., **Mundverpflegung** bis einschl. ....
   Reichsurlauberkarten (Reise- und Gaststättenmarken) — bei Urlaub bis zu 3 Tagen — bis einschl. ....
   Feinseife bis einschl. .... **Rasierseife** bis einschl. ....
10. Hat als Teilnehmer an der Wehrmachtverpflegung während des Aufenthalts am Urlaubsort vom .... bis .... einschl. Anspruch auf Reichsurlauberkarten von der zuständigen Kartenausgabestelle.
    Die Aushändigung hat die Kartenausgabestelle hierunter zu bescheinigen.
11. Inhaber besitzt eine Kontrollkarte »M« oder Inhaber hat Anspruch auf einen Kontrollausweis für den Einkauf von **Tabakwaren** für die Zeit vom .... bis .... = ... Tage*)
12. Dieser Urlaubsschein ist nach Rückkehr vom Urlaub der Wehrmachtdienststelle abzugeben.
13. **Besondere Vermerke** (z. B. über das Tragen bürgerlicher Kleidung am Urlaubsort, Bescheinigung zur Benutzung von Schnell- und Eilzügen des öffentlichen Verkehrs ohne Wehrmachtteil [D, E] u. a.): ....

(Einträge zu Ziffer 13 sind hier durch Unterschrift des Einheitsführers besonders zu bescheinigen.)

(Unterschrift des Einheitsführers zu Ziffer 8—11)

Bescheinigung über Meldung am Urlaubsort:

gemeldet am ....

(Ort, Datum, Stempel oder Unterschrift)

*) Nichtzutreffendes streichen.

Bescheinigung der Kartenausgabestelle:

Reichsurlauberkarten sind ausgehändigt für die Zeit

vom .... bis .... einschl.

(Ort, Datum, Stempel oder Unterschrift)

2-051. Like the pass in figure 2-50, this pass notes that all rations, pay, etc. issued to Gefreite (sic) Heinz Wahle have been noted on his "Green" Kriegsurlaubsschein, although it hasn't been noted as a Zwischenurlaubsschein. (A5)

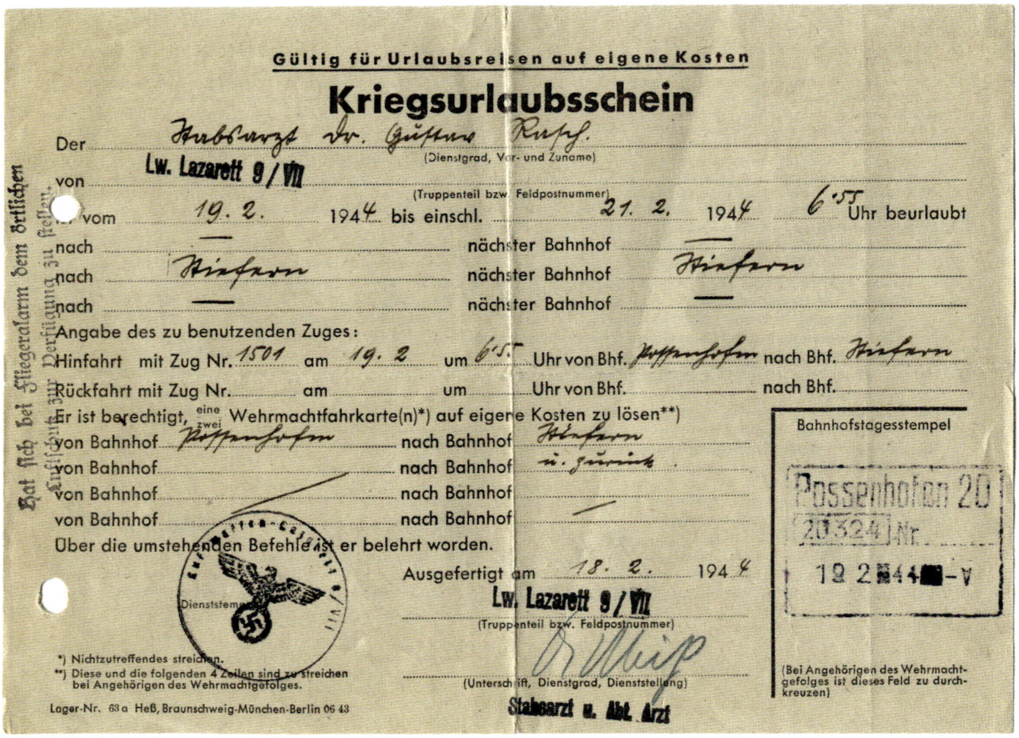

Gültig für Urlaubsreisen auf eigene Kosten

Kriegsurlaubsschein

Der Stabsarzt Dr. Gustav Rusch (Dienstgrad, Vor- und Zuname)

von Lw. Lazarett 9/VII (Truppenteil bzw. Feldpostnummer)

vom 19. 2. 1944 bis einschl. 21. 2. 1944 6.55 Uhr beurlaubt

nach — nächster Bahnhof —

nach Stiefern nächster Bahnhof Stiefern

nach — nächster Bahnhof —

Angabe des zu benutzenden Zuges:

Hinfahrt mit Zug Nr. 1501 am 19. 2 um 6.55 Uhr von Bhf. Possenhofen nach Bhf. Stiefern

Rückfahrt mit Zug Nr. am um Uhr von Bhf. nach Bhf.

Er ist berechtigt, eine/zwei Wehrmachtfahrkarte(n)*) auf eigene Kosten zu lösen**)

von Bahnhof Possenhofen nach Bahnhof Stiefern

von Bahnhof nach Bahnhof u. zurück

von Bahnhof nach Bahnhof

von Bahnhof nach Bahnhof

Über die umstehenden Befehle ist er belehrt worden.

Ausgefertigt am 18. 2. 1944

Lw. Lazarett 9/VII (Truppenteil bzw. Feldpostnummer)

(Unterschrift, Dienstgrad, Dienststellung) Stabsarzt u. Abt. Arzt

Dienststempel

Bahnhofstagesstempel: Possenhofen 20 / 20324 Nr. / 19 2 44 -V

(Bei Angehörigen des Wehrmachtgefolges ist dieses Feld zu durchkreuzen)

*) Nichtzutreffendes streichen.
**) Diese und die folgenden 4 Zeilen sind zu streichen bei Angehörigen des Wehrmachtgefolges.

Lager-Nr. 63a Heß, Braunschweig-München-Berlin 06 43

Hat sich bei Fliegeralarm dem örtlichen Luftschutz zur Verfügung zu stellen.

Figure 2-52. Kriegsurlaubsschein issued to Staff Doctor Gustav Rusch of Luftwaffe Lazarett 9/VII to Stiefern February 19-21, 1944 bears the stamp along the left side that states that in the event of air raid, one is expected to assist the Luftschutz, or Air Raid Service. By the end of the war, such notations were routinely printed on the forms, rather than relying on the use of Sonderstempeln. (A5)

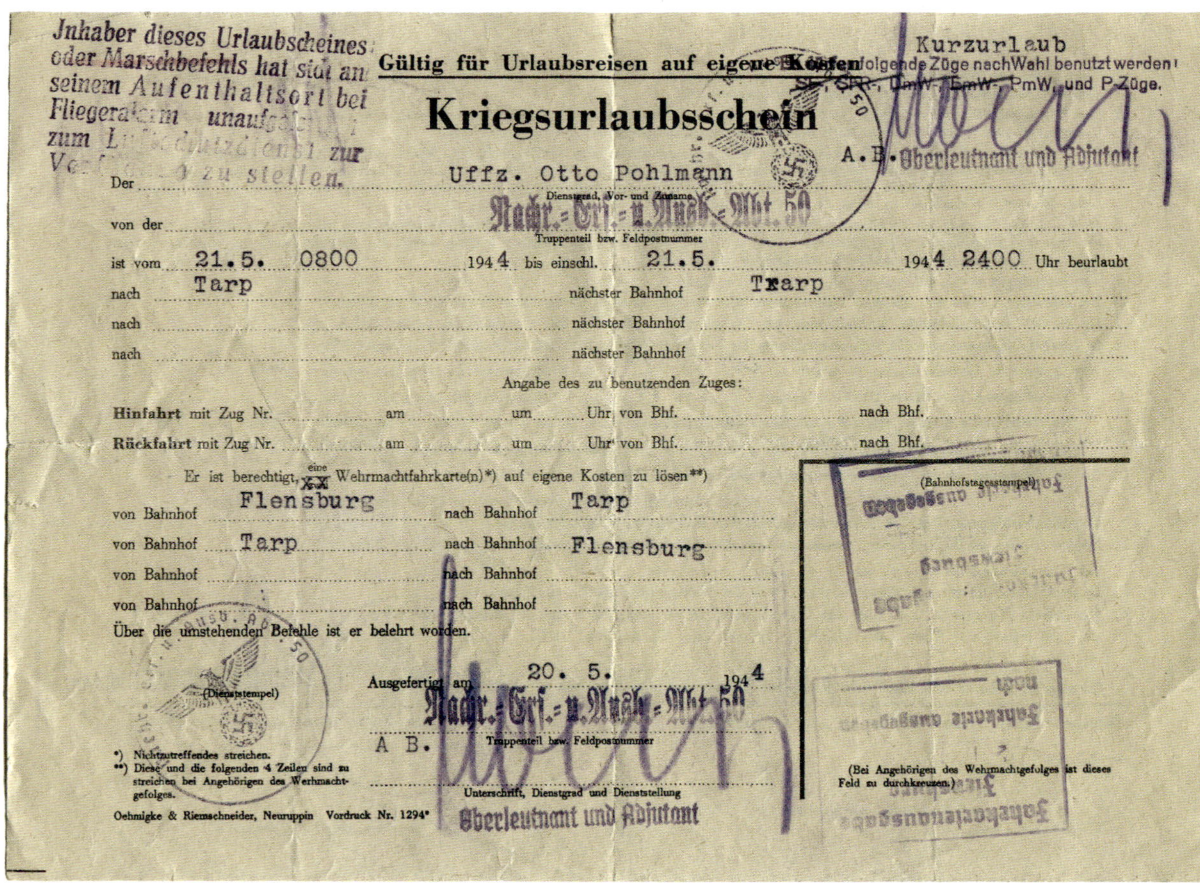

Jnhaber dieses Urlaubscheines oder Marschbefehls hat sich an seinem Aufenthaltsort bei Fliegeralarm unaufgefordert zum Luftschutzdienst zur Verfügung zu stellen.

Kurzurlaub

Gültig für Urlaubsreisen auf eigene Kosten

folgende Züge nach Wahl benutzt werden: SF, SFR, DmW, EmW, PmW, und P-Züge.

Kriegsurlaubsschein

Der Uffz. Otto Pohlmann (Dienstgrad, Vor- und Zuname)

von der Nachr.-Ers.-u.Ausb.-Abt. 50 (Truppenteil bzw. Feldpostnummer)

ist vom 21.5. 0800 1944 bis einschl. 21.5. 1944 2400 Uhr beurlaubt

nach Tarp nächster Bahnhof Tarp

nach nächster Bahnhof

nach nächster Bahnhof

Angabe des zu benutzenden Zuges:

Hinfahrt mit Zug Nr. am um Uhr von Bhf. nach Bhf.

Rückfahrt mit Zug Nr. am um Uhr von Bhf. nach Bhf.

Er ist berechtigt, eine/zwei Wehrmachtfahrkarte(n)*) auf eigene Kosten zu lösen**)

von Bahnhof Flensburg nach Bahnhof Tarp

von Bahnhof Tarp nach Bahnhof Flensburg

von Bahnhof nach Bahnhof

von Bahnhof nach Bahnhof

Über die umstehenden Befehle ist er belehrt worden.

Ausgefertigt am 20. 5. 1944

Nachr.-Ers.-u.Ausb.-Abt. 50 (Truppenteil bzw. Feldpostnummer)

A. B.

(Dienststempel)

Unterschrift, Dienstgrad und Dienststellung: Oberleutnant und Adjutant

A. B. Oberleutnant und Adjutant

(Bahnhofstagesstempel)

(Bei Angehörigen des Wehrmachtgefolges ist dieses Feld zu durchkreuzen.)

*) Nichtzutreffendes streichen.
**) Diese und die folgenden 4 Zeilen sind zu streichen bei Angehörigen des Wehrmachtgefolges.

Oehmigke & Riemschneider, Neuruppin Vordruck Nr. 1294*

Figure 2-53. Unteroffizier Otto Pohlmann of Nachrichten Ersatz und Ausbildungs Abteilung 50 (Communications Replacement and Training Section 50) was granted this pass for Kurzurlaub, or short leave, which was only valid on May 21, 1944 from 8:00 am until midnight. As on Dr. Rusch's pass, Otto Pohlmann's pass was stamped with instructions to assist the Air Raid Service in the event of an air raid. (A5)

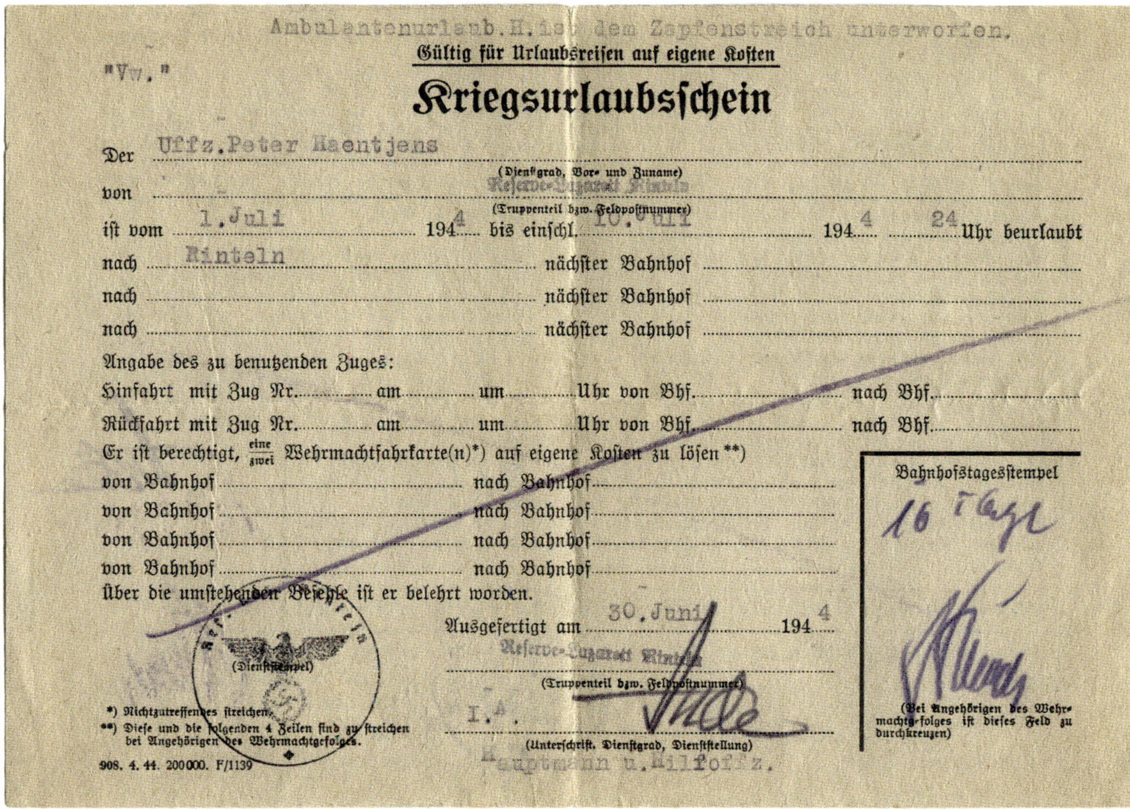

Ambulantenurlaub.H.ist dem Zapfenstreich unterworfen.

Gültig für Urlaubsreisen auf eigene Kosten

"Vw."

Kriegsurlaubsschein

Der Uffz.Peter Haentjens
(Dienstgrad, Vor- und Zuname)
von Reserve-Lazarett Rinteln
(Truppenteil bzw. Feldpostnummer)
ist vom 1.Juli 1944 bis einschl. 10.Juli 1944 24 Uhr beurlaubt
nach Rinteln nächster Bahnhof
nach .... nächster Bahnhof ....
nach .... nächster Bahnhof ....

Angabe des zu benutzenden Zuges:
Hinfahrt mit Zug Nr. .... am .... um .... Uhr von Bhf. .... nach Bhf. ....
Rückfahrt mit Zug Nr. .... am .... um .... Uhr von Bhf. .... nach Bhf. ....
Er ist berechtigt, eine/zwei Wehrmachtfahrkarte(n)*) auf eigene Kosten zu lösen**)
von Bahnhof .... nach Bahnhof ....
von Bahnhof .... nach Bahnhof ....
von Bahnhof .... nach Bahnhof ....
von Bahnhof .... nach Bahnhof ....
Über die umstehenden Befehle ist er belehrt worden.

Bahnhofstagesstempel
16 Tage
(Bei Angehörigen des Wehrmachtgefolges ist dieses Feld zu durchkreuzen)

Ausgefertigt am 30.Juni 1944
Reserve-Lazarett Rinteln
(Truppenteil bzw. Feldpostnummer)
I.A.
(Unterschrift, Dienstgrad, Dienststellung)
Hauptmann u.Hilfoffz.

(Dienststempel)

*) Nichtzutreffendes streichen.
**) Diese und die folgenden 4 Zeilen sind zu streichen bei Angehörigen des Wehrmachtgefolges.

908. 4. 44. 200000. F/1139

Figure 2-54. Unteroffizier Peter Häntjens' pass from Reserve-Lazarett Rinteln granted him Ambulantenurlaub or "ambulatory" or "walking wounded" leave, July 1-10, 1944, during which time the injured Soldat was not exempt from evening formations, dem Zapfenstreich. The red stamp on the back indicates that a Verpflegungskarte, a military ration card for July 1944, has been issued to him. (A5)

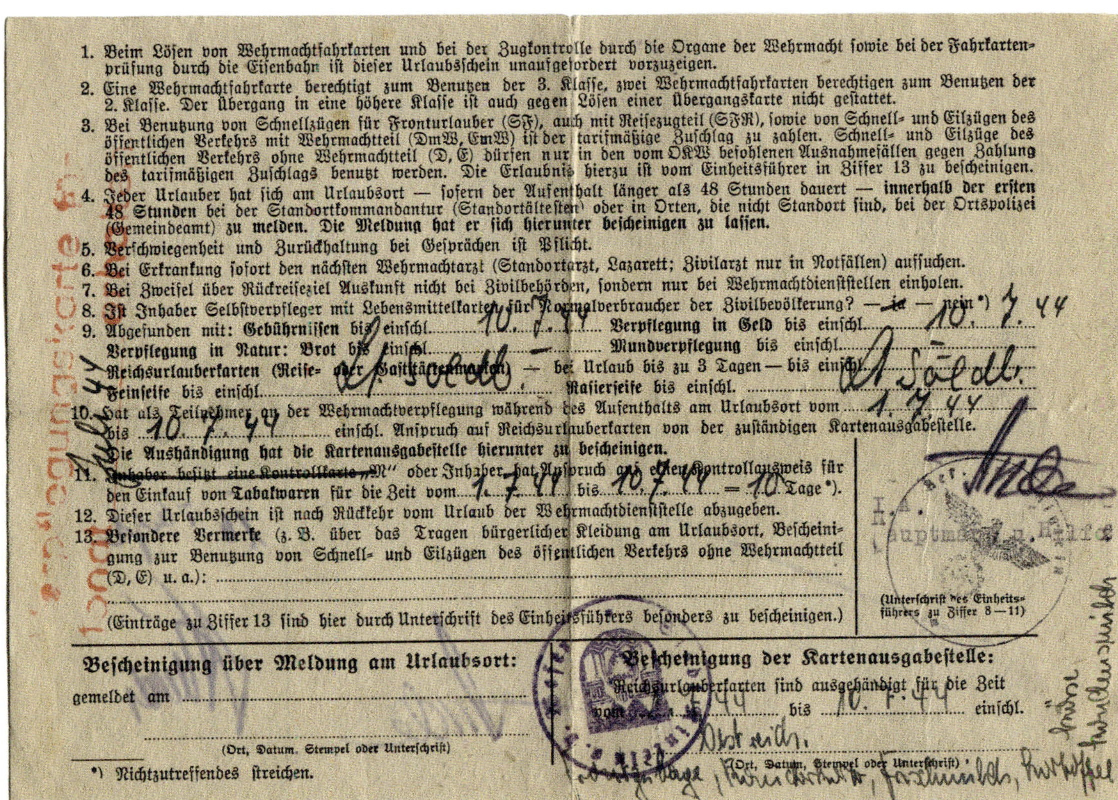

1. Beim Lösen von Wehrmachtfahrkarten und bei der Zugkontrolle durch die Organe der Wehrmacht sowie bei der Fahrkartenprüfung durch die Eisenbahn ist dieser Urlaubsschein unaufgefordert vorzuzeigen.
2. Eine Wehrmachtfahrkarte berechtigt zum Benutzen der 3. Klasse, zwei Wehrmachtfahrkarten berechtigen zum Benutzen der 2. Klasse. Der Übergang in eine höhere Klasse ist auch gegen Lösen einer Übergangskarte nicht gestattet.
3. Bei Benutzung von Schnellzügen für Fronturlauber (SF), auch mit Reisezugteil (SFR), sowie von Schnell- und Eilzügen des öffentlichen Verkehrs mit Wehrmachtteil (DmW, EmW) ist der tarifmäßige Zuschlag zu zahlen. Schnell- und Eilzüge des öffentlichen Verkehrs ohne Wehrmachtteil (D, E) dürfen nur in den vom OKW befohlenen Ausnahmefällen gegen Zahlung des tarifmäßigen Zuschlags benutzt werden. Die Erlaubnis hierzu ist vom Einheitsführer in Ziffer 13 zu bescheinigen.
4. Jeder Urlauber hat sich am Urlaubsort — sofern der Aufenthalt länger als 48 Stunden dauert — **innerhalb der ersten 48 Stunden** bei der Standortkommandantur (Standortältesten) oder in Orten, die nicht Standort sind, bei der Ortspolizei (Gemeindeamt) **zu melden. Die Meldung hat er sich hierunter bescheinigen zu lassen.**
5. Verschwiegenheit und Zurückhaltung bei Gesprächen ist Pflicht.
6. Bei Erkrankung sofort den nächsten Wehrmachtarzt (Standortarzt, Lazarett; Zivilarzt nur in Notfällen) aufsuchen.
7. Bei Zweifel über Rückreiseziel Auskunft nicht bei Zivilbehörden, sondern nur bei Wehrmachtdienststellen einholen.
8. Ist Inhaber Selbstverpfleger mit Lebensmittelkarten für Normalverbraucher der Zivilbevölkerung? — ~~ja~~ — nein*) 7.44
9. Abgefunden mit: **Gebührnissen** bis einschl. 10.7.44 **Verpflegung in Geld** bis einschl. 10.7.
Verpflegung in Natur: Brot bis einschl. — **Mundverpflegung** bis einschl. —
Reichsurlauberkarten (Reise- oder Gaststättenmarken) — bei Urlaub bis zu 3 Tagen — bis einschl. Lt. Soldb.
Feinseife bis einschl. Lt. Soldb. **Rasierseife** bis einschl.
10. Hat als Teilnehmer an der Wehrmachtverpflegung während des Aufenthalts am Urlaubsort vom 1.7.44 bis 10.7.44 einschl. Anspruch auf Reichsurlauberkarten von der zuständigen Kartenausgabestelle. **Die Aushändigung hat die Kartenausgabestelle hierunter zu bescheinigen.**
11. ~~Inhaber besitzt eine Kontrollkarte „M"~~ oder Inhaber hat Anspruch auf einen Kontrollausweis für den Einkauf von **Tabakwaren** für die Zeit vom 1.7.44 bis 10.7.44 = 10 Tage*).
12. Dieser Urlaubsschein ist nach Rückkehr vom Urlaub der Wehrmachtdienststelle abzugeben.
13. **Besondere Vermerke** (z. B. über das Tragen bürgerlicher Kleidung am Urlaubsort, Bescheinigung zur Benutzung von Schnell- und Eilzügen des öffentlichen Verkehrs ohne Wehrmachtteil (D, E) u. a.):

(Einträge zu Ziffer 13 sind hier durch Unterschrift des Einheitsführers besonders zu bescheinigen.)

I.A.
Hauptmann u.Hilfo...
(Unterschrift des Einheitsführers zu Ziffer 8—11)

Bescheinigung über Meldung am Urlaubsort:
gemeldet am ....
(Ort, Datum, Stempel oder Unterschrift)

*) Nichtzutreffendes streichen.

Bescheinigung der Kartenausgabestelle:
Reichsurlauberkarten sind ausgehändigt für die Zeit vom 1.7.44 bis 10.7.44 einschl.
(Ort, Datum, Stempel oder Unterschrift)

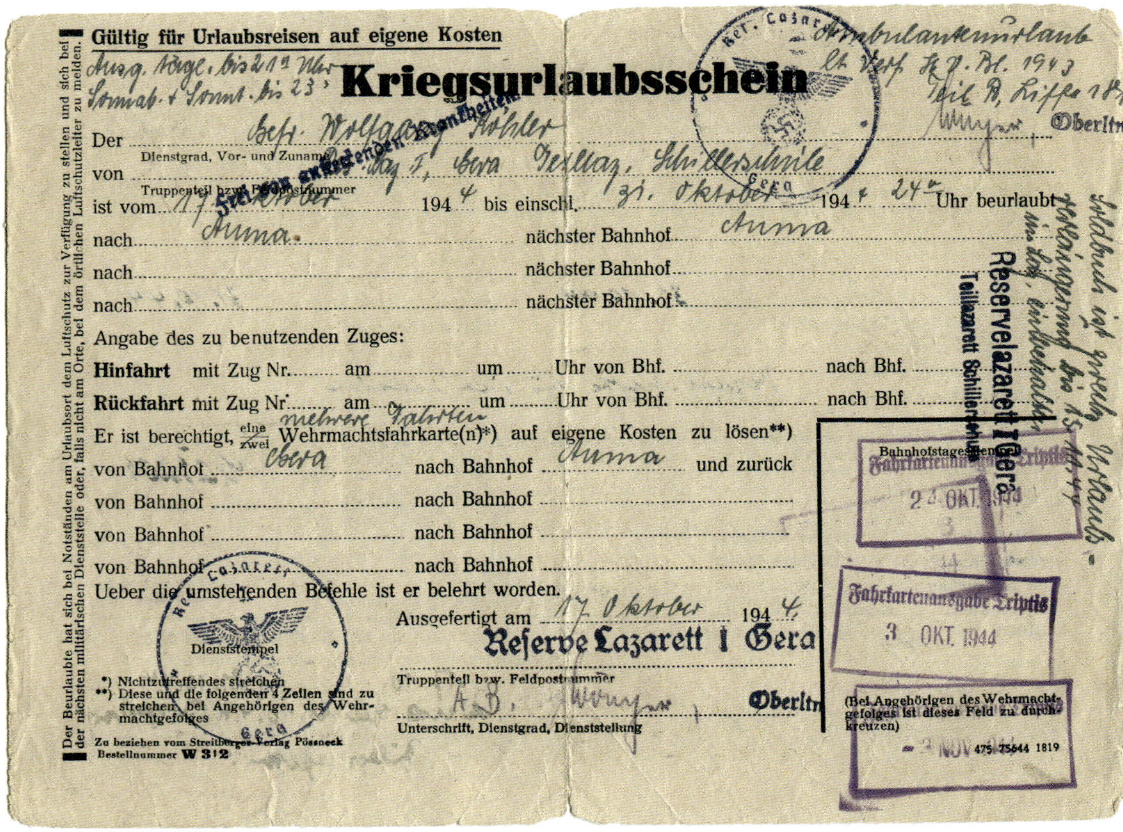

Gültig für Urlaubsreisen auf eigene Kosten

Kriegsurlaubsschein

Der .... Oberltn
Dienstgrad, Vor- und Zuname
von ....
Truppenteil bzw. Feldpostnummer
ist vom .... 194 .. bis einschl. .... 194 .. .... Uhr beurlaubt
nach .... nächster Bahnhof ....
nach .... nächster Bahnhof ....
nach .... nächster Bahnhof ....

Angabe des zu benutzenden Zuges:

Hinfahrt mit Zug Nr. ...... am ...... um ...... Uhr von Bhf. ...... nach Bhf. ......
Rückfahrt mit Zug Nr. ...... am ...... um ...... Uhr von Bhf. ...... nach Bhf. ......

Er ist berechtigt, eine/zwei Wehrmachtsfahrkarte(n)*) auf eigene Kosten zu lösen**)
von Bahnhof .... nach Bahnhof .... und zurück
von Bahnhof .... nach Bahnhof ....
von Bahnhof .... nach Bahnhof ....
von Bahnhof .... nach Bahnhof ....

Ueber die umstehenden Befehle ist er belehrt worden.

Ausgefertigt am .... 194 ..

Reserve Lazarett I Gera

Truppenteil bzw. Feldpostnummer

Oberltn

Unterschrift, Dienstgrad, Dienststellung

Dienststempel

*) Nichtzutreffendes streichen
**) Diese und die folgenden 4 Zeilen sind zu streichen bei Angehörigen des Wehrmachtgefolges

(Bei Angehörigen des Wehrmachtgefolges ist dieses Feld zu durchkreuzen)

Zu beziehen vom Streitberger-Verlag Pössneck
Bestellnummer W 312

475/25644 1819

Frei von ansteckenden Krankheiten

Reservelazarett I Gera
Teillazarett Schillerschule

Fahrkartenausgabe Triptis
3 OKT. 1944

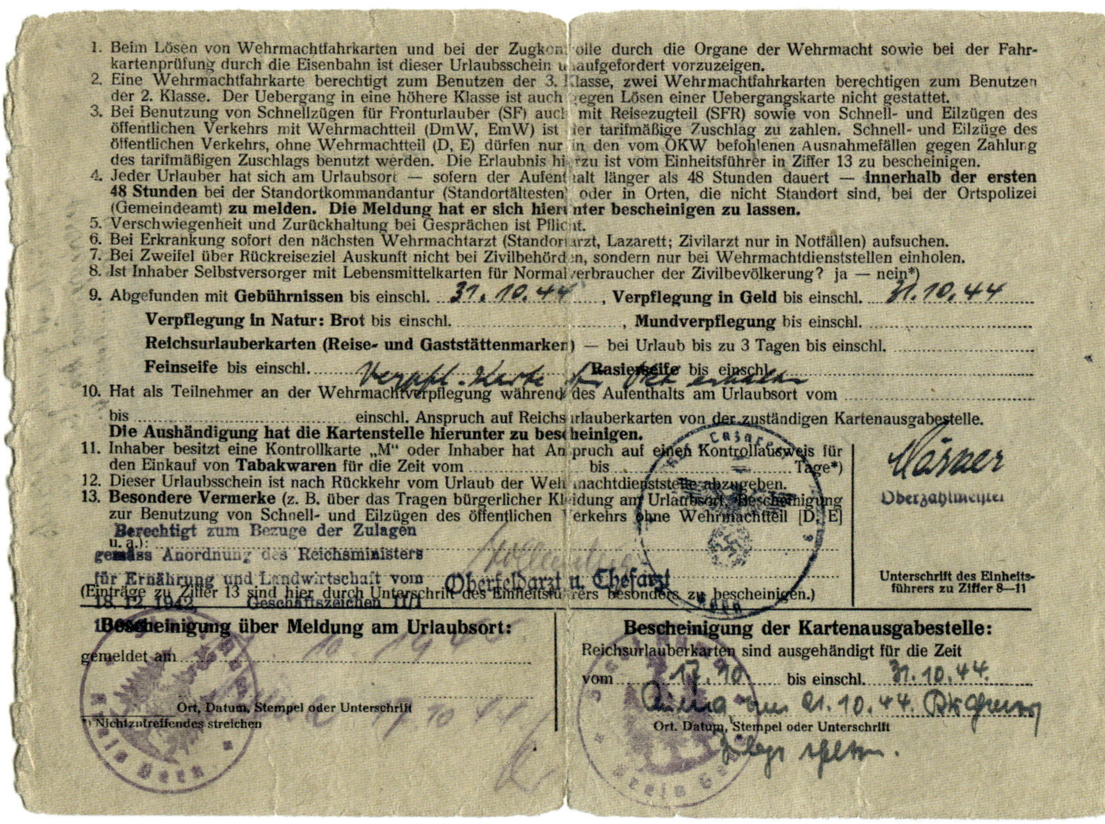

1. Beim Lösen von Wehrmachtfahrkarten und bei der Zugkontrolle durch die Organe der Wehrmacht sowie bei der Fahrkartenprüfung durch die Eisenbahn ist dieser Urlaubsschein unaufgefordert vorzuzeigen.
2. Eine Wehrmachtfahrkarte berechtigt zum Benutzen der 3. Klasse, zwei Wehrmachtfahrkarten berechtigen zum Benutzen der 2. Klasse. Der Uebergang in eine höhere Klasse ist auch gegen Lösen einer Uebergangskarte nicht gestattet.
3. Bei Benutzung von Schnellzügen für Fronturlauber (SF) auch mit Reisezugteil (SFR) sowie von Schnell- und Eilzügen des öffentlichen Verkehrs mit Wehrmachtteil (DmW, EmW) ist der tarifmäßige Zuschlag zu zahlen. Schnell- und Eilzüge des öffentlichen Verkehrs, ohne Wehrmachtteil (D, E) dürfen nur in den vom OKW befohlenen Ausnahmefällen gegen Zahlung des tarifmäßigen Zuschlags benutzt werden. Die Erlaubnis hierzu ist vom Einheitsführer in Ziffer 13 zu bescheinigen.
4. Jeder Urlauber hat sich am Urlaubsort — sofern der Aufenthalt länger als 48 Stunden dauert — **innerhalb der ersten 48 Stunden** bei der Standortkommandantur (Standortältesten) oder in Orten, die nicht Standort sind, bei der Ortspolizei (Gemeindeamt) **zu melden. Die Meldung hat er sich hierunter bescheinigen zu lassen.**
5. Verschwiegenheit und Zurückhaltung bei Gesprächen ist Pflicht.
6. Bei Erkrankung sofort den nächsten Wehrmachtarzt (Standortarzt, Lazarett; Zivilarzt nur in Notfällen) aufsuchen.
7. Bei Zweifel über Rückreiseziel Auskunft nicht bei Zivilbehörden, sondern nur bei Wehrmachtdienststellen einholen.
8. Ist Inhaber Selbstversorger mit Lebensmittelkarten für Normalverbraucher der Zivilbevölkerung? ja — nein*)
9. Abgefunden mit **Gebührnissen** bis einschl. 31.10.44, **Verpflegung in Geld** bis einschl. 31.10.44
   Verpflegung in Natur: Brot bis einschl. ...., **Mundverpflegung** bis einschl. ....
   Reichsurlauberkarten (Reise- und Gaststättenmarken) — bei Urlaub bis zu 3 Tagen bis einschl. ....
   Feinseife bis einschl. .... **Rasierseife** bis einschl. ....
10. Hat als Teilnehmer an der Wehrmachtverpflegung während des Aufenthalts am Urlaubsort vom .... bis .... einschl. Anspruch auf Reichsurlauberkarten von der zuständigen Kartenausgabestelle. **Die Aushändigung hat die Kartenstelle hierunter zu bescheinigen.**
11. Inhaber besitzt eine Kontrollkarte „M" oder Inhaber hat Anspruch auf einen Kontrollausweis für den Einkauf von **Tabakwaren** für die Zeit vom .... bis .... Tage*)
12. Dieser Urlaubsschein ist nach Rückkehr vom Urlaub der Wehrmachtdienststelle abzugeben.
13. **Besondere Vermerke** (z. B. über das Tragen bürgerlicher Kleidung am Urlaubsort, Bescheinigung zur Benutzung von Schnell- und Eilzügen des öffentlichen Verkehrs ohne Wehrmachtteil [D, E]

Berechtigt zum Bezuge der Zulagen u. a.):
gemäss Anordnung des Reichsministers für Ernährung und Landwirtschaft vom 18.12.1942, Geschäftszeichen II/1

Oberfeldarzt u. Chefarzt

(Einträge zu Ziffer 13 sind hier durch Unterschrift des Einheitsführers besonders zu bescheinigen.)

Oberzahlmeister

Unterschrift des Einheitsführers zu Ziffer 8—11

Bescheinigung über Meldung am Urlaubsort:

gemeldet am ....

Ort, Datum, Stempel oder Unterschrift

*) Nichtzutreffendes streichen

Bescheinigung der Kartenausgabestelle:

Reichsurlauberkarten sind ausgehändigt für die Zeit vom .... bis einschl. 31.10.44

Ort, Datum, Stempel oder Unterschrift

Figure 2-55. By the time this Kriegsurlaubsschein had been issued, printed instructions to assist in air raids had begun to appear along the left side of the pass, though not exclusively. This pass, issued by Reserve Lazarett Gera to Gefreiter Wolfgang Röhler for ambulatory leave, also states that in the bearer's Soldbuch his leave has been extended by the hospital until November 15, 1944 (Urlaubsverlängerung bis 15.11.44 ins Lazarett einbehalten) but is "Frei von ansteckenden Krankenheiten" (free from infectious diseases). (A5)

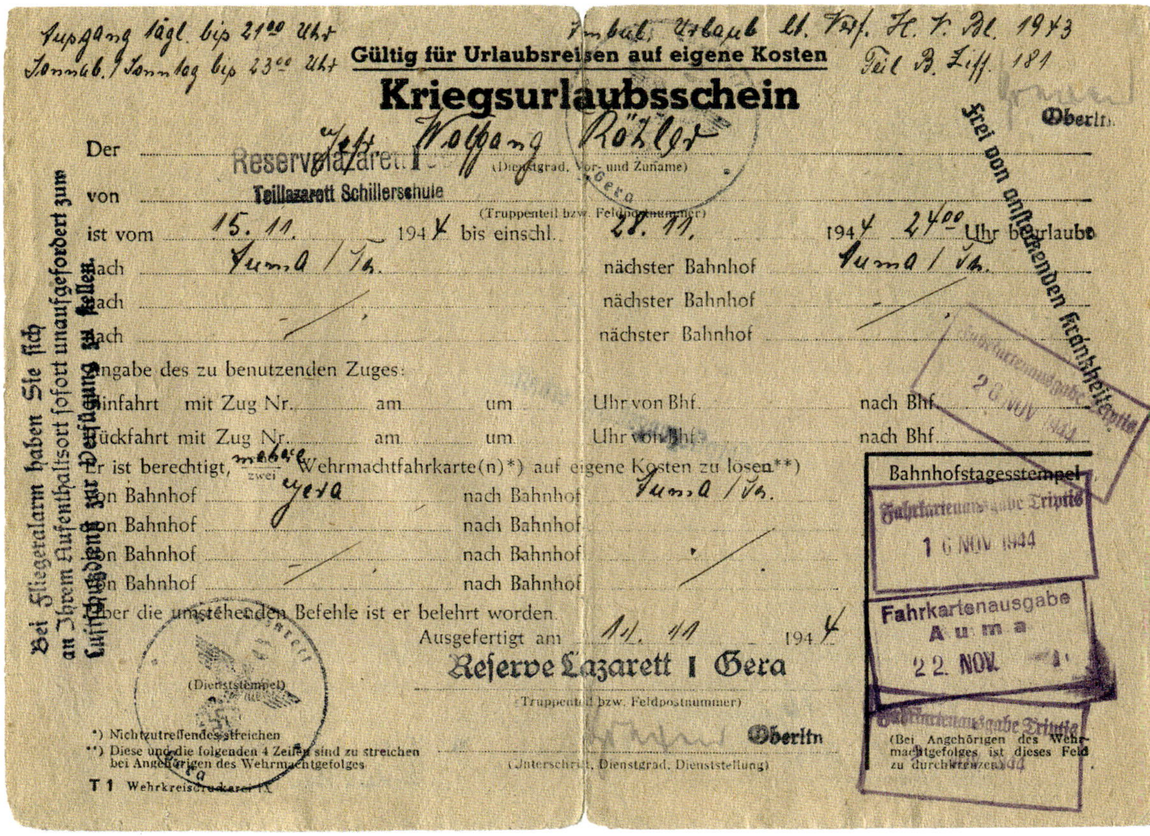
Ausgang tägl. bis 21⁰⁰ Uhr
Sonnab./Sonntag bis 23⁰⁰ Uhr
Gültig für Urlaubsreisen auf eigene Kosten
Ambul. Urlaub U. Vorf. H. V. Bl. 1943 Teil B. Ziff. 181

Kriegsurlaubsschein

Der Gefr. Wolfgang Röhler (Dienstgrad, Vor- und Zuname)
von Reservelazarett I — Teillazarett Schillerschule (Truppenteil bzw. Feldpostnummer)
ist vom 15. 11. 1944 bis einschl. 28. 11. 1944 24⁰⁰ Uhr beurlaubt
nach Auma / Th. nächster Bahnhof Auma / Th.
nach — nächster Bahnhof —
nach nächster Bahnhof
Angabe des zu benutzenden Zuges:
Hinfahrt mit Zug Nr. am um Uhr von Bhf. nach Bhf.
Rückfahrt mit Zug Nr. am um Uhr von Bhf. nach Bhf.
Er ist berechtigt, mehrere zwei Wehrmachtfahrkarte(n)*) auf eigene Kosten zu lösen**)
von Bahnhof Gera nach Bahnhof Auma / Th.
von Bahnhof nach Bahnhof
von Bahnhof — nach Bahnhof —
von Bahnhof nach Bahnhof
Über die umstehenden Befehle ist er belehrt worden.
Ausgefertigt am 14. 11. 1944
Reserve Lazarett I Gera
(Truppenteil bzw. Feldpostnummer)
(Dienststempel)
Oberin
(Unterschrift, Dienstgrad, Dienststellung)
*) Nichtzutreffendes streichen
**) Diese und die folgenden 4 Zeilen sind zu streichen bei Angehörigen des Wehrmachtgefolges
T 1 Wehrkreisdruckerei IX

Bei Fliegeralarm haben Sie sich an Ihrem Aufenthaltsort sofort unaufgefordert zum Luftschutzdienst zur Verfügung zu stellen.

Frei von ansteckenden Krankheiten

Bahnhofstagesstempel
Fahrkartenausgabe Triptis 16 NOV 1944
Fahrkartenausgabe Auma 22. NOV.
Fahrkartenausgabe Triptis 26 NOV 1944
(Bei Angehörigen des Wehrmachtgefolges ist dieses Feld zu durchkreuzen)

Figure 2-56. Gefreiter Röhler's second pass, issued once again by Reserve Lazarett Gera upon expiration of the previous pass (figure 2-055). (A5)

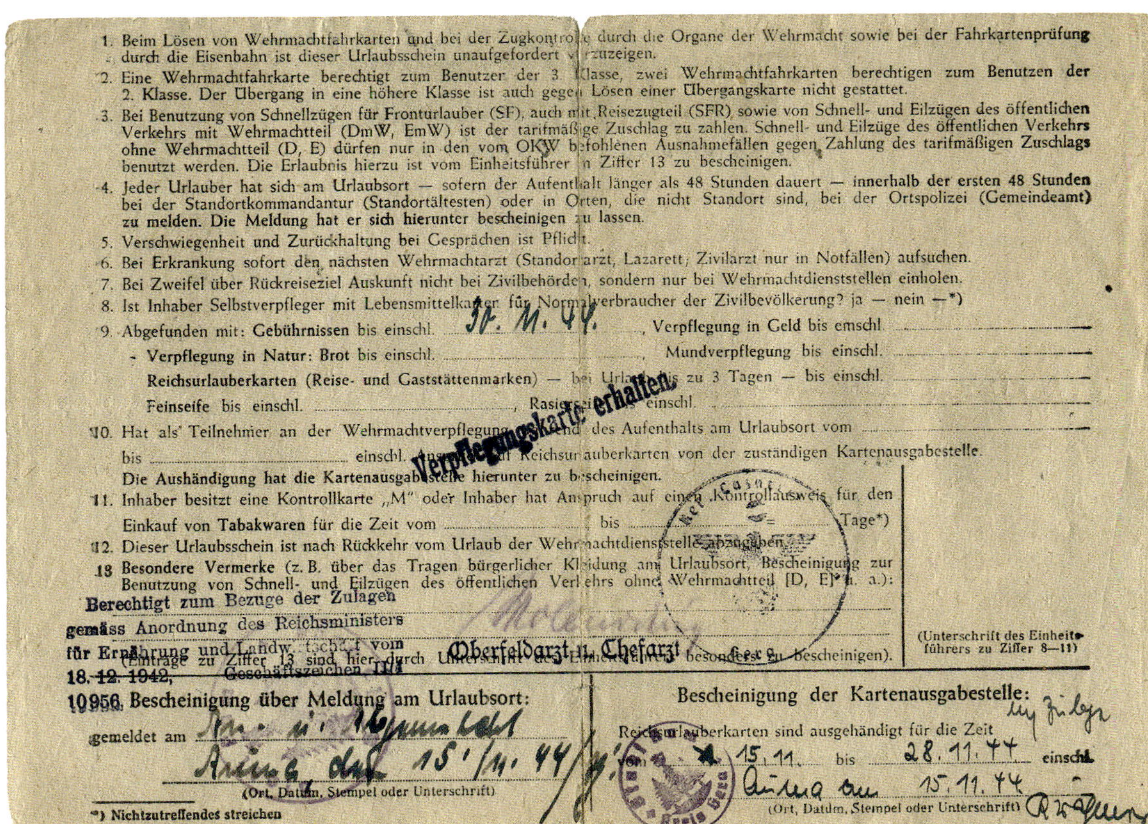
1. Beim Lösen von Wehrmachtfahrkarten und bei der Zugkontrolle durch die Organe der Wehrmacht sowie bei der Fahrkartenprüfung durch die Eisenbahn ist dieser Urlaubsschein unaufgefordert vorzuzeigen.
2. Eine Wehrmachtfahrkarte berechtigt zum Benutzen der 3. Klasse, zwei Wehrmachtfahrkarten berechtigen zum Benutzen der 2. Klasse. Der Übergang in eine höhere Klasse ist auch gegen Lösen einer Übergangskarte nicht gestattet.
3. Bei Benutzung von Schnellzügen für Fronturlauber (SF), auch mit Reisezugteil (SFR), sowie von Schnell- und Eilzügen des öffentlichen Verkehrs mit Wehrmachtteil (DmW, EmW) ist der tarifmäßige Zuschlag zu zahlen. Schnell- und Eilzüge des öffentlichen Verkehrs ohne Wehrmachtteil (D, E) dürfen nur in den vom OKW befohlenen Ausnahmefällen gegen Zahlung des tarifmäßigen Zuschlags benutzt werden. Die Erlaubnis hierzu ist vom Einheitsführer in Ziffer 13 zu bescheinigen.
4. Jeder Urlauber hat sich am Urlaubsort — sofern der Aufenthalt länger als 48 Stunden dauert — innerhalb der ersten 48 Stunden bei der Standortkommandantur (Standortältesten) oder in Orten, die nicht Standort sind, bei der Ortspolizei (Gemeindeamt) zu melden. Die Meldung hat er sich hierunter bescheinigen zu lassen.
5. Verschwiegenheit und Zurückhaltung bei Gesprächen ist Pflicht.
6. Bei Erkrankung sofort den nächsten Wehrmachtarzt (Standortarzt, Lazarett; Zivilarzt nur in Notfällen) aufsuchen.
7. Bei Zweifel über Rückreiseziel Auskunft nicht bei Zivilbehörden, sondern nur bei Wehrmachtdienststellen einholen.
8. Ist Inhaber Selbstverpfleger mit Lebensmittelkarten für Normalverbraucher der Zivilbevölkerung? ja — nein —*)
9. Abgefunden mit: Gebührnissen bis einschl. 30. 11. 44, Verpflegung in Geld bis einschl.
- Verpflegung in Natur: Brot bis einschl. Mundverpflegung bis einschl.
Reichsurlauberkarten (Reise- und Gaststättenmarken) — bei Urlaub bis zu 3 Tagen — bis einschl.
Feinseife bis einschl. Rasierseife bis einschl.
10. Hat als Teilnehmer an der Wehrmachtverpflegung während des Aufenthalts am Urlaubsort vom bis einschl. Anspruch auf Reichsurlauberkarten von der zuständigen Kartenausgabestelle. Die Aushändigung hat die Kartenausgabestelle hierunter zu bescheinigen.
11. Inhaber besitzt eine Kontrollkarte „M" oder Inhaber hat Anspruch auf einen Kontrollausweis für den Einkauf von Tabakwaren für die Zeit vom bis (Tage*)
12. Dieser Urlaubsschein ist nach Rückkehr vom Urlaub der Wehrmachtdienststelle abzugeben.
13. Besondere Vermerke (z. B. über das Tragen bürgerlicher Kleidung am Urlaubsort, Bescheinigung zur Benutzung von Schnell- und Eilzügen des öffentlichen Verkehrs ohne Wehrmachtteil [D, E]*) u. a.):
Berechtigt zum Bezuge der Zulagen gemäss Anordnung des Reichsministers für Ernährung und Landwirtschaft vom 18. 12. 1942, Geschäftszeichen II B 10956.
Oberfeldarzt u. Chefarzt
(Eintrage zu Ziffer 13 sind hier durch Unterschrift des Einheitsführers besonders zu bescheinigen).
(Unterschrift des Einheitsführers zu Ziffer 8—11)

Verpflegungskarte erhalten.

Bescheinigung über Meldung am Urlaubsort:
gemeldet am Nur i. Ausweis/Aufenthalt
Auma, den 15. 11. 44
(Ort, Datum, Stempel oder Unterschrift)

Bescheinigung der Kartenausgabestelle:
Reichsurlauberkarten sind ausgehändigt für die Zeit vom 15. 11. bis 28. 11. 44 einschl.
Auma am 15. 11. 44
(Ort, Datum, Stempel oder Unterschrift)

*) Nichtzutreffendes streichen

Figure 2-57. An original photograph of a Cavalry Gefreiter (note his riding boots and spurs) as he awaits a train at the Paris Bahnhofsüberwachung (Railway Monitoring Station).

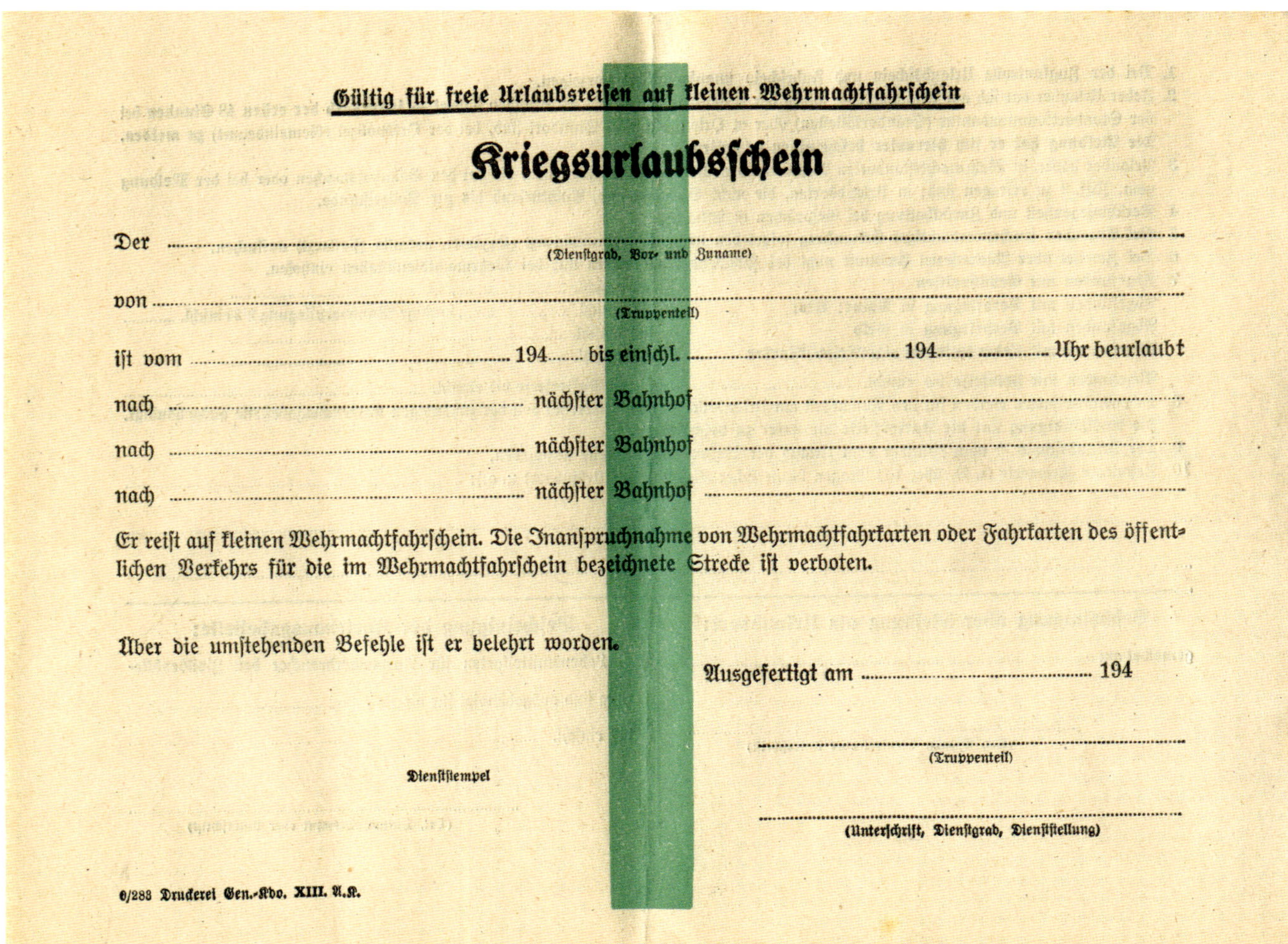

Gültig für freie Urlaubsreisen auf kleinen Wehrmachtfahrschein

Kriegsurlaubsschein

Der ....
(Dienstgrad, Vor- und Zuname)

von ....
(Truppenteil)

ist vom .... 194....... bis einschl. .... 194....... .... Uhr beurlaubt

nach .... nächster Bahnhof ....

nach .... nächster Bahnhof ....

nach .... nächster Bahnhof ....

Er reist auf kleinen Wehrmachtfahrschein. Die Inanspruchnahme von Wehrmachtfahrkarten oder Fahrkarten des öffentlichen Verkehrs für die im Wehrmachtfahrschein bezeichnete Strecke ist verboten.

Über die umstehenden Befehle ist er belehrt worden.

Ausgefertigt am 194

Dienststempel

....
(Truppenteil)

....
(Unterschrift, Dienstgrad, Dienststellung)

6/288 Druckerei Gen.-Kdo. XIII. A.K.

Figure 2-58. Kriegsurlaubsscheinen with a green stripe down the middle were reserved for travel that had been paid for by the Wehrmacht. These forms were not valid as tickets however, and had to be presented along with a ticket, either the kleinen Wehrmachtfahrkarte or some other ticket issued by the Wehrmacht. (A5)

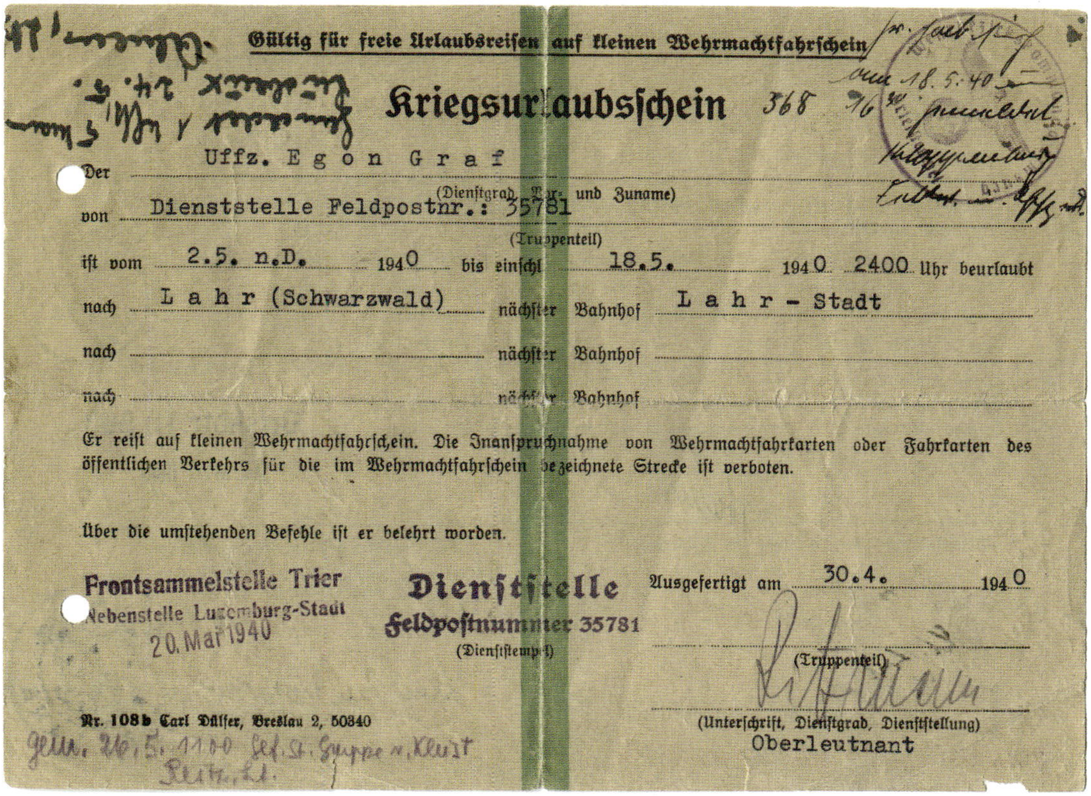

Gültig für freie Urlaubsreisen auf kleinen Wehrmachtfahrschein

Kriegsurlaubsschein 368

Der Uffz. Egon Graf (Dienstgrad, Vor- und Zuname)

von Dienststelle Feldpostnr.: 35781 (Truppenteil)

ist vom 2.5. n.D. 1940 bis einschl. 18.5. 1940 2400 Uhr beurlaubt

nach Lahr (Schwarzwald) nächster Bahnhof Lahr - Stadt

nach ... nächster Bahnhof ...

nach ... nächster Bahnhof ...

Er reist auf kleinen Wehrmachtfahrschein. Die Inanspruchnahme von Wehrmachtfahrkarten oder Fahrkarten des öffentlichen Verkehrs für die im Wehrmachtfahrschein bezeichnete Strecke ist verboten.

Über die umstehenden Befehle ist er belehrt worden.

Frontsammelstelle Trier Nebenstelle Luxemburg-Stadt 20. Mar 1940

Dienststelle Feldpostnummer 35781 (Dienststempel)

Ausgefertigt am 30.4. 1940

(Truppenteil)

(Unterschrift, Dienstgrad, Dienststellung) Oberleutnant

Nr. 108b Carl Dülfer, Breslau 2, 50840

Figure 2-59. This Kriegsurlaubsschein was issued to Unteroffizier Egon Graf by 4. Kompanie, Korps-Nachrichten-Abteilung 441 (4th Company, Corps Communications Section 441, Dienststelle Feldpostnummer 35781), valid from May 2 until May 18, 1940 to Lahr, Germany, near the contested Alsace-Lorraine region of France. Stamps on the back indicate that Uffz. Graf's pass had been extended by Ortskommandantur (I) 636 (Office of the Local Commandant, Number 636 Feldpostnummer 33592). No explanation is given on this form, though a notation (if original) at the bottom left corner on the front notes that Graf was wounded at 11:00 am on May 26 serving in Gruppe von Kleist. (A5)

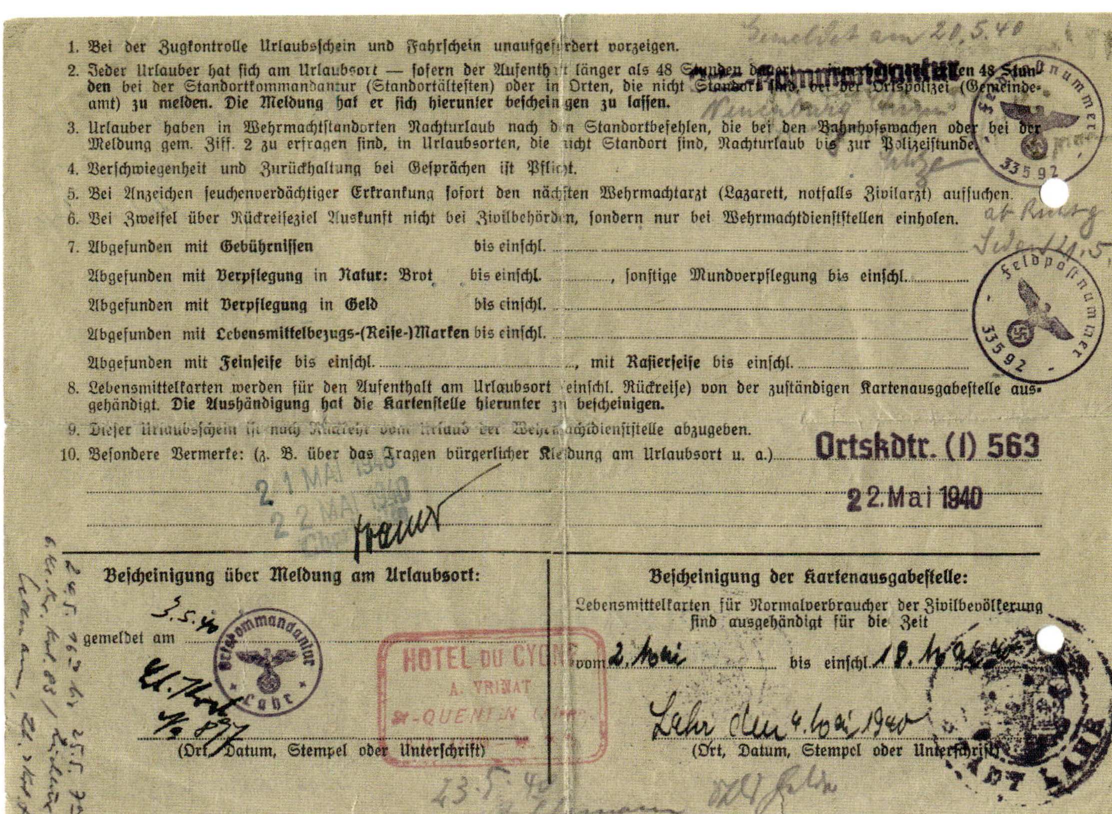

1. Bei der Zugkontrolle Urlaubsschein und Fahrschein unaufgefordert vorzeigen.
2. Jeder Urlauber hat sich am Urlaubsort — sofern der Aufenthalt länger als 48 Stunden dauert — innerhalb der ersten 48 Stunden bei der Standortkommandantur (Standortältesten) oder in Orten, die nicht Standorte sind, bei der Ortspolizei (Gemeindeamt) zu melden. Die Meldung hat er sich hierunter bescheinigen zu lassen.
3. Urlauber haben in Wehrmachtstandorten Nachturlaub nach den Standortbefehlen, die bei den Bahnhofswachen oder bei der Meldung gem. Ziff. 2 zu erfragen sind, in Urlaubsorten, die nicht Standort sind, Nachturlaub bis zur Polizeistunde.
4. Verschwiegenheit und Zurückhaltung bei Gesprächen ist Pflicht.
5. Bei Anzeichen seuchenverdächtiger Erkrankung sofort den nächsten Wehrmachtarzt (Lazarett, notfalls Zivilarzt) aufsuchen.
6. Bei Zweifel über Rückreiseziel Auskunft nicht bei Zivilbehörden, sondern nur bei Wehrmachtdienststellen einholen.
7. Abgefunden mit Gebührnissen bis einschl. ...
   Abgefunden mit Verpflegung in Natur: Brot bis einschl. ..., sonstige Mundverpflegung bis einschl. ...
   Abgefunden mit Verpflegung in Geld bis einschl. ...
   Abgefunden mit Lebensmittelbezugs-(Reise-)Marken bis einschl. ...
   Abgefunden mit Feinseife bis einschl. ..., mit Rasierseife bis einschl. ...
8. Lebensmittelkarten werden für den Aufenthalt am Urlaubsort (einschl. Rückreise) von der zuständigen Kartenausgabestelle ausgehändigt. Die Aushändigung hat die Kartenstelle hierunter zu bescheinigen.
9. Dieser Urlaubsschein ist nach Rückkehr vom Urlaub bei der Wehrmachtdienststelle abzugeben.
10. Besondere Vermerke: (z. B. über das Tragen bürgerlicher Kleidung am Urlaubsort u. a.) Ortskdtr. (I) 563

22. Mai 1940

Bescheinigung über Meldung am Urlaubsort:

gemeldet am ...

(Ort, Datum, Stempel oder Unterschrift)

HOTEL DU CYGNE ... ST-QUENTIN

Bescheinigung der Kartenausgabestelle:

Lebensmittelkarten für Normalverbraucher der Zivilbevölkerung sind ausgehändigt für die Zeit vom 2. Mai bis einschl. ...

(Ort, Datum, Stempel oder Unterschrift)

Figure 2-60. Kriegsurlaubsschein for Junior Doctor Johann Teufl. Note that the green stripe is a different shade than previous examples. This could be due to age, but it's more likely that Wehrkreisdruckerei XVII in Wien (Military District Printer in Vienna, Austria) simply stocked different green ink; regulations required a green stripe but did not stipulate specific shades. (A5)

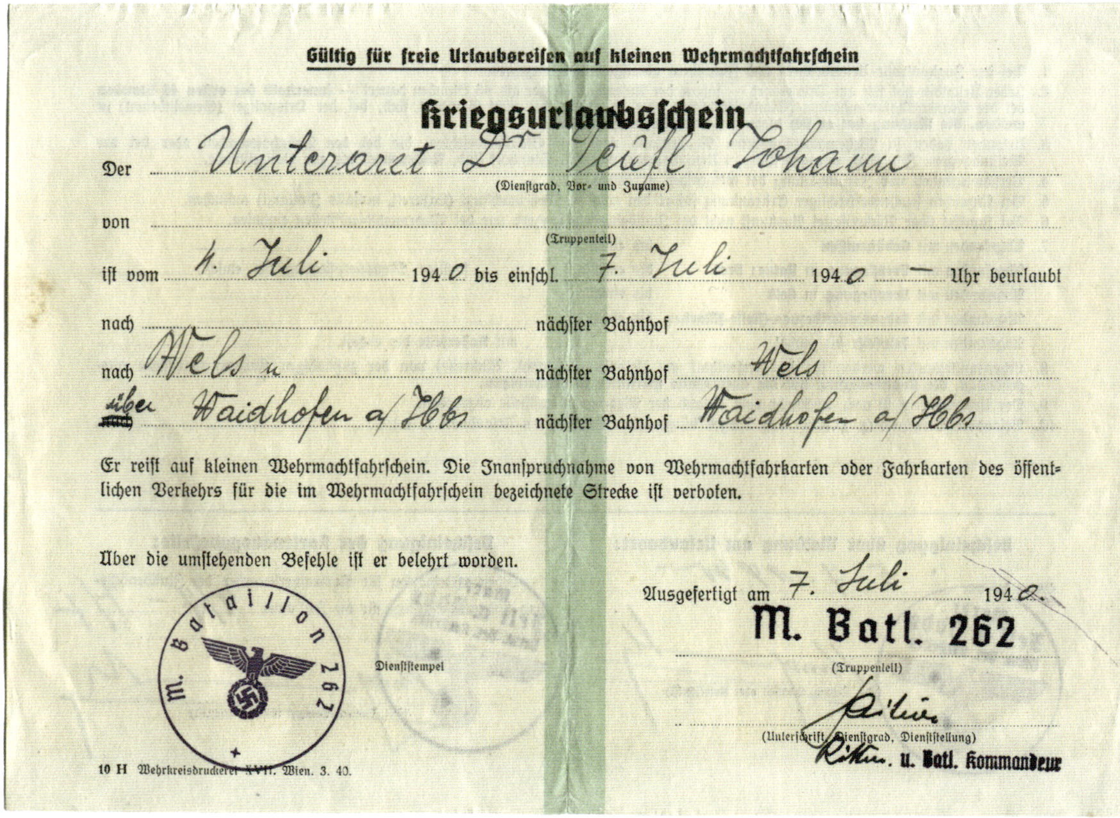

Gültig für freie Urlaubsreisen auf kleinen Wehrmachtfahrschein

Kriegsurlaubsschein

Der Unterarzt Dr Teufl Johann
(Dienstgrad, Vor- und Zuname)

von
(Truppenteil)

ist vom 4. Juli 1940 bis einschl. 7. Juli 1940 — Uhr beurlaubt

nach ... nächster Bahnhof ...

nach Wels u nächster Bahnhof Wels

über Waidhofen a/Ybbs nächster Bahnhof Waidhofen a/Ybbs

Er reist auf kleinen Wehrmachtfahrschein. Die Inanspruchnahme von Wehrmachtfahrkarten oder Fahrkarten des öffentlichen Verkehrs für die im Wehrmachtfahrschein bezeichnete Strecke ist verboten.

Über die umstehenden Befehle ist er belehrt worden.

Ausgefertigt am 7. Juli 1940.

M. Batl. 262
(Truppenteil)

M. Bataillon 262

Dienststempel

(Unterschrift, Dienstgrad, Dienststellung)
Rittm. u. Batl. Kommandeur

10 H Wehrkreisdruckerei XVII. Wien. 3. 40.

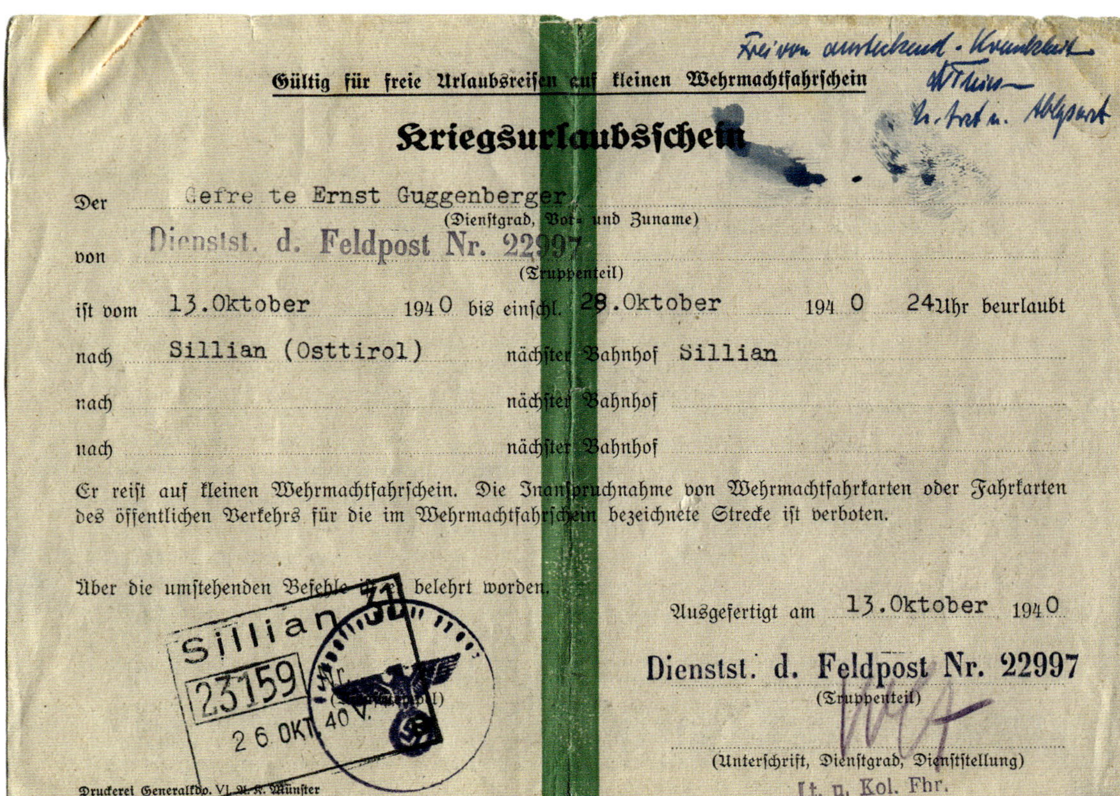

Gültig für freie Urlaubsreisen auf kleinen Wehrmachtfahrschein

Kriegsurlaubsschein

Der Gefre te Ernst Guggenberger
(Dienstgrad, Vor- und Zuname)

von Dienstst. d. Feldpost Nr. 22997
(Truppenteil)

ist vom 13.Oktober 1940 bis einschl. 28.Oktober 1940 24 Uhr beurlaubt

nach Sillian (Osttirol) nächster Bahnhof Sillian

nach nächster Bahnhof

nach nächster Bahnhof

Er reist auf kleinen Wehrmachtfahrschein. Die Inanspruchnahme von Wehrmachtfahrkarten oder Fahrkarten des öffentlichen Verkehrs für die im Wehrmachtfahrschein bezeichnete Strecke ist verboten.

Über die umstehenden Befehle ist er belehrt worden.

Sillian 23159 26 OKT. 40 V.

Ausgefertigt am 13.Oktober 1940

Dienstst. d. Feldpost Nr. 22997
(Truppenteil)

(Unterschrift, Dienstgrad, Dienststellung)
Lt. u. Kol. Fhr.

Druckerei Generalkdo. VI A. K. Münster

Figure 2-61. As noted above, this Kriegsurlaubsschein issued in October of 1940 by Artillerie-Ersatz-Abteilung 24 of Infanterie Division 174 (Feldpost Nummer 22997) uses yet another shade of green ink. (A5)

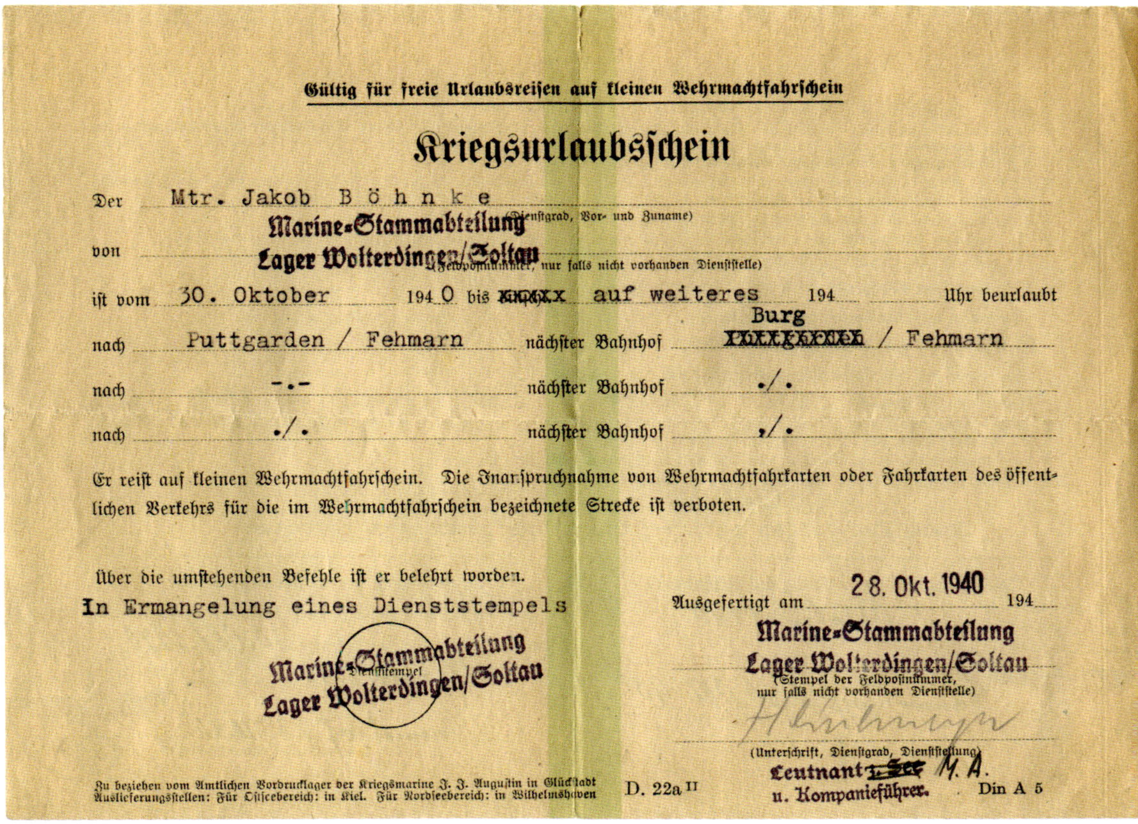

Gültig für freie Urlaubsreisen auf kleinen Wehrmachtfahrschein

Kriegsurlaubsschein

Der Mtr. Jakob Böhnke
(Dienstgrad, Vor- und Zuname)

von Marine-Stammabteilung Lager Wolterdingen/Soltau
(Feldpostnummer, nur falls nicht vorhanden Dienststelle)

ist vom 30. Oktober 1940 bis ~~xxxxx~~ auf weiteres 194 Uhr beurlaubt

nach Puttgarden / Fehmarn nächster Bahnhof ~~xxxxxxxxx~~ Burg / Fehmarn

nach -.- nächster Bahnhof ./.

nach ./. nächster Bahnhof ./.

Er reist auf kleinen Wehrmachtfahrschein. Die Inanspruchnahme von Wehrmachtfahrkarten oder Fahrkarten des öffentlichen Verkehrs für die im Wehrmachtfahrschein bezeichnete Strecke ist verboten.

Über die umstehenden Befehle ist er belehrt worden.

In Ermangelung eines Dienststempels
Marine-Stammabteilung Lager Wolterdingen/Soltau
(Dienststempel)

Ausgefertigt am 28. Okt. 1940 194

Marine-Stammabteilung Lager Wolterdingen/Soltau
(Stempel der Feldpostnummer, nur falls nicht vorhanden Dienststelle)

(Unterschrift, Dienstgrad, Dienststellung)
Leutnant ~~z. See~~ M.A. u. Kompanieführer.

Zu beziehen vom Amtlichen Vordrucklager der Kriegsmarine J. J. Augustin in Glückstadt
Auslieferungsstellen: Für Ostseebereich: in Kiel. Für Nordseebereich: in Wilhelmshaven

D. 22a II Din A 5

Figure 2-62. Using probably the lightest shade of green yet, this pass was issued to Matrose (Seaman) Jakob Böhnke by Marine-Stammabteilung (Naval Holding Section) at Camp Wolterdingen in Soltau, south of Hamburg. Notice that the Truppenteil stamp has been used in the absence (In Ermagelung) of the Dienststempel, but duly noted by the clerk. The back notes that Böhke is on Arbeitsurlaub (work leave) and that once he has arrived at his work district, he is forbidden to wear his Naval uniform while working. (A5)

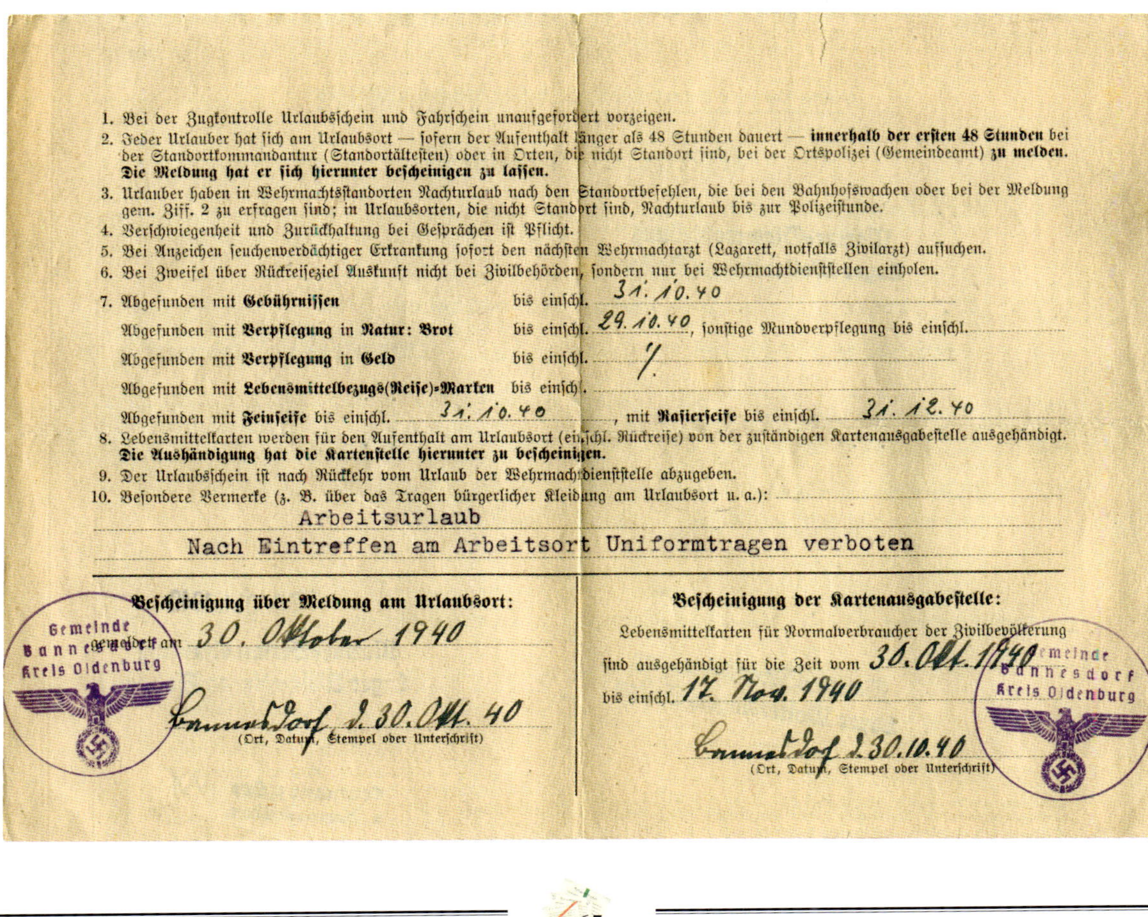

1. Bei der Zugkontrolle Urlaubsschein und Fahrschein unaufgefordert vorzeigen.
2. Jeder Urlauber hat sich am Urlaubsort — sofern der Aufenthalt länger als 48 Stunden dauert — **innerhalb der ersten 48 Stunden** bei der Standortkommandantur (Standortältesten) oder in Orten, die nicht Standort sind, bei der Ortspolizei (Gemeindeamt) **zu melden. Die Meldung hat er sich hierunter bescheinigen zu lassen.**
3. Urlauber haben in Wehrmachtsstandorten Nachturlaub nach den Standortbefehlen, die bei den Bahnhofswachen oder bei der Meldung gem. Ziff. 2 zu erfragen sind; in Urlaubsorten, die nicht Standort sind, Nachturlaub bis zur Polizeistunde.
4. Verschwiegenheit und Zurückhaltung bei Gesprächen ist Pflicht.
5. Bei Anzeichen seuchenverdächtiger Erkrankung sofort den nächsten Wehrmachtarzt (Lazarett, notfalls Zivilarzt) aufsuchen.
6. Bei Zweifel über Rückreiseziel Auskunft nicht bei Zivilbehörden, sondern nur bei Wehrmachtdienststellen einholen.
7. Abgefunden mit **Gebührnissen** bis einschl. 31.10.40
   Abgefunden mit **Verpflegung in Natur: Brot** bis einschl. 29.10.40, sonstige Mundverpflegung bis einschl.
   Abgefunden mit **Verpflegung in Geld** bis einschl. /
   Abgefunden mit **Lebensmittelbezugs(Reise)-Marken** bis einschl.
   Abgefunden mit **Feinseife** bis einschl. 31.10.40, mit **Rasierseife** bis einschl. 31.12.40
8. Lebensmittelkarten werden für den Aufenthalt am Urlaubsort (einschl. Rückreise) von der zuständigen Kartenausgabestelle ausgehändigt. **Die Aushändigung hat die Kartenstelle hierunter zu bescheinigen.**
9. Der Urlaubsschein ist nach Rückkehr vom Urlaub der Wehrmachtdienststelle abzugeben.
10. Besondere Vermerke (z. B. über das Tragen bürgerlicher Kleidung am Urlaubsort u. a.):
    Arbeitsurlaub
    Nach Eintreffen am Arbeitsort Uniformtragen verboten

Bescheinigung über Meldung am Urlaubsort:
Gemeldet am 30. Oktober 1940
Bannesdorf d. 30. Okt. 40
(Ort, Datum, Stempel oder Unterschrift)
Gemeinde Bannesdorf Kreis Oldenburg

Bescheinigung der Kartenausgabestelle:
Lebensmittelkarten für Normalverbraucher der Zivilbevölkerung sind ausgehändigt für die Zeit vom 30. Okt. 1940 bis einschl. 17. Nov. 1940
Bannesdorf d. 30.10.40
(Ort, Datum, Stempel oder Unterschrift)
Gemeinde Bannesdorf Kreis Oldenburg

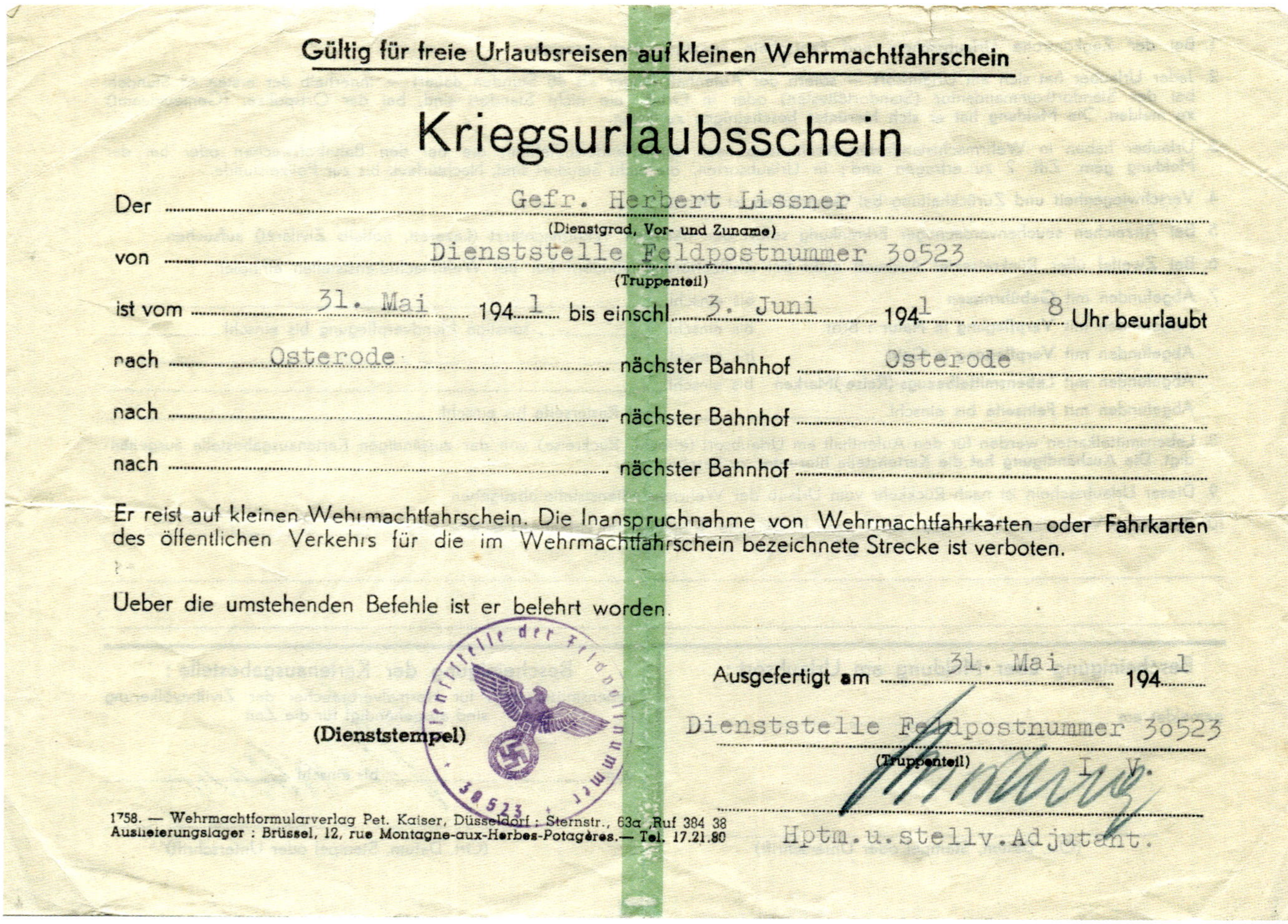

Gültig für freie Urlaubsreisen auf kleinen Wehrmachtfahrschein

Kriegsurlaubsschein

Der .... Gefr. Herbert Lissner ....
(Dienstgrad, Vor- und Zuname)

von .... Dienststelle Feldpostnummer 30523 ....
(Truppenteil)

ist vom .... 31. Mai .... 1941 bis einschl. .... 3. Juni .... 1941 .... 8 Uhr beurlaubt

nach .... Osterode .... nächster Bahnhof .... Osterode ....

nach .... nächster Bahnhof ....

nach .... nächster Bahnhof ....

Er reist auf kleinen Wehrmachtfahrschein. Die Inanspruchnahme von Wehrmachtfahrkarten oder Fahrkarten des öffentlichen Verkehrs für die im Wehrmachtfahrschein bezeichnete Strecke ist verboten.

Ueber die umstehenden Befehle ist er belehrt worden.

(Dienststempel)

Ausgefertigt am .... 31. Mai 1941

Dienststelle Feldpostnummer 30523
(Truppenteil)

I. V.

Hptm.u.stellv.Adjutant.

1758. — Wehrmachtformularverlag Pet. Kaiser, Düsseldorf; Sternstr., 63a, Ruf 384 38
Auslieferungslager : Brüssel, 12, rue Montagne-aux-Herbes-Potagères.— Tel. 17.21.80

Figure 2-63. Just as the shade of green ink was not specified in regulations, neither were typefaces. This pass has been set in DIN Schriften Neuzeit Grotesk, an easy to read sans serif typestyle. Gefreiter Herbert Lissner, serving Kommandant rückwärtigen Armeegebiet 582 (Commander, Rear Army Area 582, Feldpostnummer 30523), was granted leave from May 31 until June 3, 1941 prior to the invasion of Russia. (A5)

Dienststelle Feldpost Nr. 22320

Frei von ansteckenden Krankheiten nicht seuchenverdächtig

Reserve-Kriegs-Lazarett NEAPEL

Gültig für freie Urlaubsreise auf kleinen Wehrmachtfahrschein

Kriegsurlaubsschein

Der Ogfr. Franz Becker (Dienstgrad, Vor- und Zuname)

von Dienststelle 08045 (Truppenteil)

ist vom 4. Oktober 1941 bis einschl. 24. Oktober 1941 ..... Uhr beurlaubt

nach Mainz-Gonsenheim nächster Bahnhof Mainz

nach Darmstadt nächster Bahnhof Darmstadt

nach ..... nächster Bahnhof .....

Er reist auf kleinen Wehrmachtfahrschein. Die Inanspruchnahme von Wehrmachtfahrkarten oder Fahrkarten des öffentlichen Verkehrs für die im Wehrmachtfahrschein bezeichnete Strecke ist verboten.

Weitergeleitet am ... um ... Uhr Frontleitstelle Neapel

Über die umstehenden Befehle ist er belehrt worden.

Afrika-Urlauber Urlaubsdatum eingetr. bzw. geändert. Entlaust am: 3.10. Frontleitstelle Neapel Hauptmann; Oberleutnant

Dienststelle Feldpostnummer 08045 Dienstsiegel

Ausgefertigt am 23. Sept. 1941

Dienststelle 08045 (Truppenteil)

(Unterschrift, Dienstgrad, Dienststellung)

Oblt. u. stellv. Kdt. d. Stabsq.

1. Bei der Zugkontrolle Urlaubsschein und Fahrschein unaufgefordert vorzeigen.
2. Jeder Urlauber hat sich am Urlaubsort — sofern der Aufenthalt länger als 48 Stunden dauert — innerhalb der ersten 48 Stunden bei der Standortkommandantur (Standortältesten) oder in Orten, die nicht Standort sind, bei der Ortspolizei (Gemeindeamt) zu melden. Die Meldung hat er sich hierunter bescheinigen zu lassen.
3. Urlauber haben in Wehrmachtsstandorten Nachturlaub nach den Standortbefehlen, die bei den Bahnhofswachen oder bei der Meldung gem. Ziff. 2 zu erfragen sind; in Urlaubsorten, die nicht Standort sind, Nachturlaub bis zur Polizeistunde.
4. Verschwiegenheit und Zurückhaltung bei Gesprächen ist Pflicht.
5. Bei Anzeichen seuchenverdächtiger Erkrankung sofort den nächsten Wehrmachtarzt (Lazarett, notfalls Zivilarzt) aufsuchen.
6. Bei Zweifel über Rückreiseziel Auskunft nicht bei Zivilbehörden, sondern nur bei Wehrmachtdienststellen einholen.
7. Abgefunden mit Gebührnissen bis einschl. 30. Oktober 1941
   Abgefunden mit Verpflegung in Natur: Brot bis einschl. 3 Tage, sonstige Mundverpflegung bis einschl. .....
   Abgefunden mit Verpflegung in Geld bis einschl. 21. Oktober 1941
   Abgefunden mit Lebensmittelbezugs(Reise-)Marken bis einschl. keine
   Abgefunden mit Feinseife bis einschl. August ....., mit Rasierseife bis einschl. .....
8. Lebensmittelkarten werden für den Aufenthalt am Urlaubsort (einschl. Rückreise) von der zuständigen Kartenausgabestelle ausgehändigt. Die Aushändigung hat die Kartenstelle hierunter zu bescheinigen.
9. Der Urlaubsschein ist nach Rückkehr vom Urlaub der Wehrmachtdienststelle abzugeben.
10. Besondere Vermerke (z.B. über das Tragen bürgerlicher Kleidung am Urlaubsort u. a.):
    Das Tragen bürgerlicher Kleidung ist gestattet.

Oberzahlmeister

Oblt. u. stellv. Kdt. d. Stabsq.

Bescheinigung über Meldung am Urlaubsort:

Gemeldet am Mainz-Gonsenheim, 6. Okt. 1941

Rev. Zweigstelle

22. Okt. 1941

(Ort, Datum, Stempel oder Unterschrift)

Bescheinigung der Kartenausgabestelle:

Lebensmittelkarten für Normalverbraucher der Zivilbevölkerung sind ausgehändigt für die Zeit vom 4.10.41. bis einschl. 21.10.41.

-6.10.41

(Ort, Datum, Stempel oder Unterschrift)

Figure 2-64. Though difficult to read, Sonderstempeln often allow one to trace the movements of a Soldat in his travels. Obergefreiter Franz Becker of the 15th Panzer Division (Dienststelle 08045) was granted leave from North Africa and was flown via Fliegerhorst 6/IV (Air Base 6/IV) to Naples, Italy via Messina. He was seen at the Reserve-Kriegs-Lazarett in Naples and deloused on October 3, 1941 and declared free of infectious diseases. From there, he took the train to Gonsenheim near Mainz (where he was issued rations and other essentials) and continued to Darmstadt. Upon his return to Naples, he was given additional rations on October 30 at the Auskunftsstelle (Information Office) in Naples (Feldpostnummer 45500) and paid upon his return by the Oberzahlmeister (Senior Pay Master) of the 15th Panzer Division. (A5)

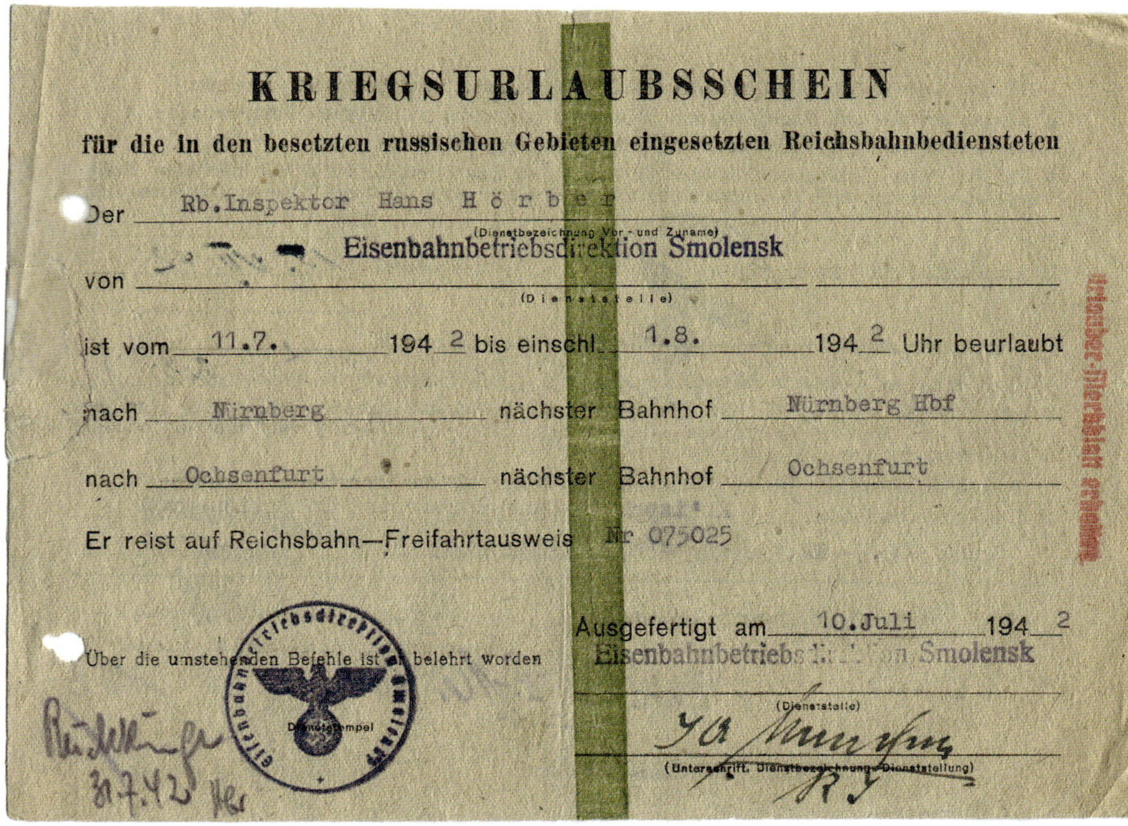

KRIEGSURLAUBSSCHEIN

für die in den besetzten russischen Gebieten eingesetzten Reichsbahnbediensteten

Der Rb.Inspektor Hans Hörber
(Dienstbezeichnung Vor- und Zuname)

von Eisenbahnbetriebsdirektion Smolensk
(Dienststelle)

ist vom 11.7. 194 2 bis einschl. 1.8. 194 2 Uhr beurlaubt

nach Nürnberg nächster Bahnhof Nürnberg Hbf

nach Ochsenfurt nächster Bahnhof Ochsenfurt

Er reist auf Reichsbahn—Freifahrtausweis Nr 075025

Ausgefertigt am 10.Juli 194 2

Eisenbahnbetriebs... Smolensk
(Dienststelle)

(Unterschrift, Dienstbezeichnung, Dienststellung)

Über die umstehenden Befehle ist er belehrt worden

Dienststempel

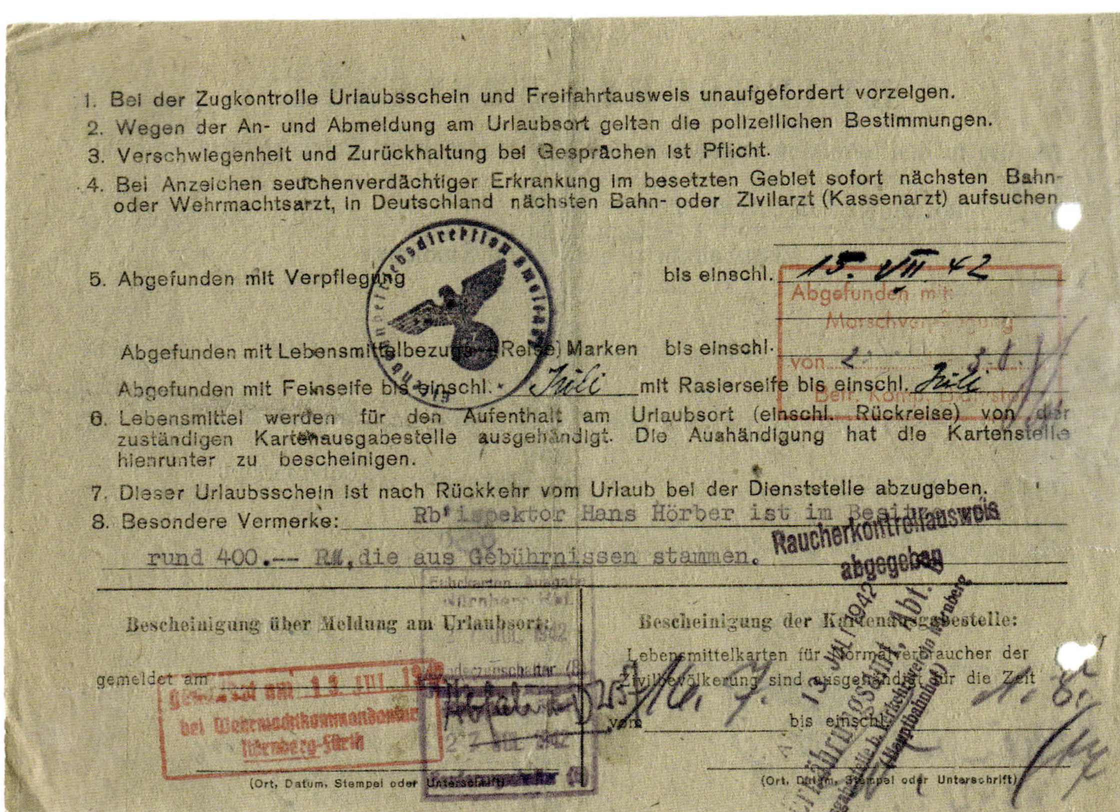

1. Bei der Zugkontrolle Urlaubsschein und Freifahrtausweis unaufgefordert vorzeigen.
2. Wegen der An- und Abmeldung am Urlaubsort gelten die polizeilichen Bestimmungen.
3. Verschwiegenheit und Zurückhaltung bei Gesprächen ist Pflicht.
4. Bei Anzeichen seuchenverdächtiger Erkrankung im besetzten Gebiet sofort nächsten Bahn- oder Wehrmachtsarzt, in Deutschland nächsten Bahn- oder Zivilarzt (Kassenarzt) aufsuchen.
5. Abgefunden mit Verpflegung bis einschl. 15. VII 42

   Abgefunden mit Lebensmittelbezug (Reise) Marken bis einschl.

   Abgefunden mit Feinseife bis einschl. Juli mit Rasierseife bis einschl. Juli
6. Lebensmittel werden für den Aufenthalt am Urlaubsort (einschl. Rückreise) von der zuständigen Kartenausgabestelle ausgehändigt. Die Aushändigung hat die Kartenstelle hierunter zu bescheinigen.
7. Dieser Urlaubsschein ist nach Rückkehr vom Urlaub bei der Dienststelle abzugeben.
8. Besondere Vermerke: Rb'inspektor Hans Hörber ist im Besitz von rund 400.-- RM, die aus Gebührnissen stammen.

Rauchercontrollausweis abgegeben

Bescheinigung über Meldung am Urlaubsort: gemeldet am 13. JUL 1942 bei Wehrmachtkommandantur Nürnberg-Fürth
(Ort, Datum, Stempel oder Unterschrift)

Bescheinigung der Kartenausgabestelle: Lebensmittelkarten für Normalverbraucher der Zivilbevölkerung sind ausgehändigt für die Zeit vom 16. 7. bis einschl. 1. 8.
(Ort, Datum, Stempel oder Unterschrift)

Figure 2-65. Very similar to those issued by the Wehrmacht, Kriegsurlaubschein issued by the Reichsbahn, the German State Railway system, were often printed for the occupied areas they were valid, in this case occupied Russia ("besetzten russischen Gebiet"). This pass from Smolensk for railway inspector Hans Hörber notes on the reverse that he is in possession of roughly 400 Reichsmarks that have been collected as fees! (A5)

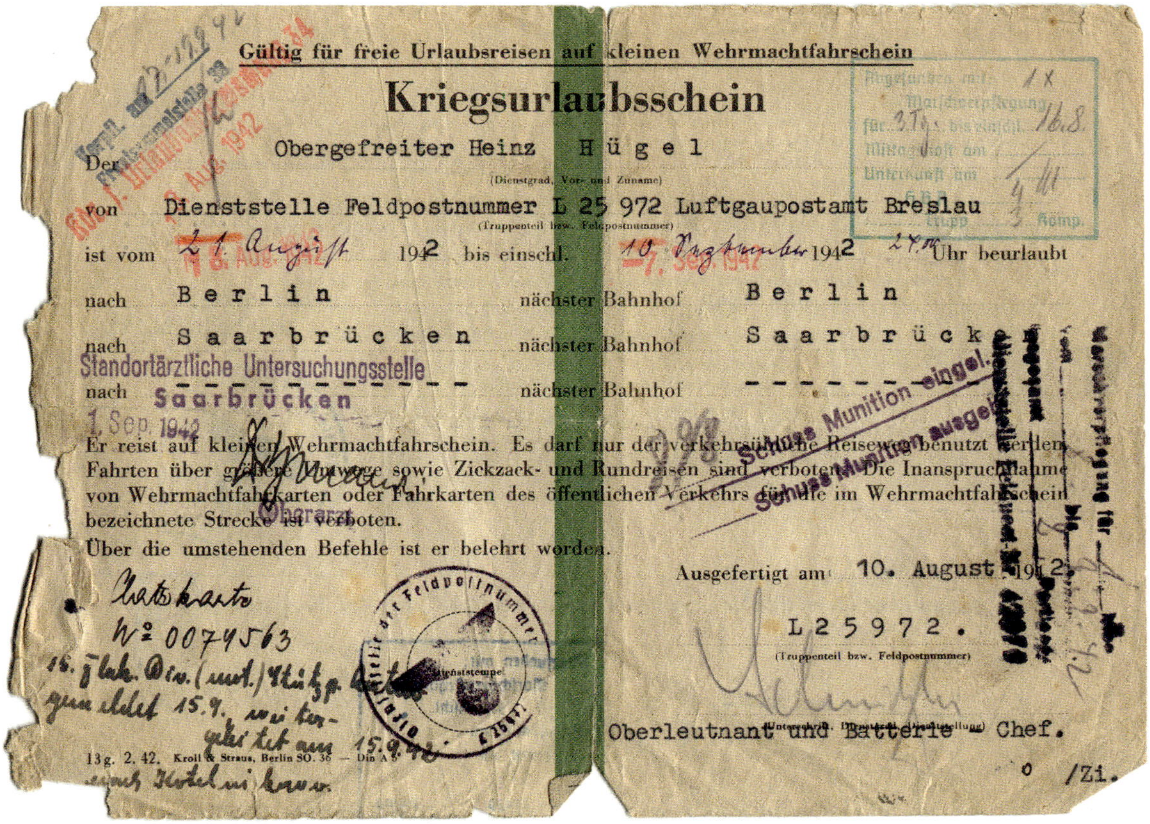

Gültig für freie Urlaubsreisen auf kleinen Wehrmachtfahrschein

Kriegsurlaubsschein

Der Obergefreiter Heinz Hügel
(Dienstgrad, Vor- und Zuname)

von Dienststelle Feldpostnummer L 25 972 Luftgaupostamt Breslau
(Truppenteil bzw. Feldpostnummer)

ist vom 21. August 1942 bis einschl. 10. September 1942 24.00 Uhr beurlaubt

nach Berlin nächster Bahnhof Berlin

nach Saarbrücken nächster Bahnhof Saarbrücken

nach ------- nächster Bahnhof -------

Er reist auf kleinen Wehrmachtfahrschein. Es darf nur der verkehrsübliche Reiseweg benutzt werden. Fahrten über größere Umwege sowie Zickzack- und Rundreisen sind verboten. Die Inanspruchnahme von Wehrmachtfahrkarten oder Fahrkarten des öffentlichen Verkehrs für die im Wehrmachtfahrschein bezeichnete Strecke ist verboten.

Über die umstehenden Befehle ist er belehrt worden.

Ausgefertigt am: 10. August 1942

L25972.
(Truppenteil bzw. Feldpostnummer)

Oberleutnant und Batterie - Chef.
(Unterschrift, Dienstgrad, Dienststellung)

o /Zi.

13g. 2. 42. Kroll & Straus, Berlin SO. 36 — Din A 5

Figure 2-66. Again, stamps and notations on travel documents opened a window onto the history of the individual Soldat. In this case, Obergefreiter Heinz Hügel of Flak Regiment 12 and his pay, which exceeded 1,000 Reichsmarks due to accumulated back pay of Wehrsold (service pay), Frontzulage (front pay), and Verpflegungsgeld (ration money), noted at the top of the reverse of this pass and paid on September 15, 1942 (notation on the lower left corner of the front). The majority of the Sonderstempeln here are from various Frontleistellen (front control center) for Marschverpflegung, the issuance of march rations. (A5)

1. Dieser Urlaubsschein ist nur den Kontrollorganen der Wehrmacht vorzuzeigen.
2. Jeder Urlauber hat sich am Urlaubsort — sofern der Aufenthalt länger als 48 Stunden dauert — innerhalb der ersten 48 Stunden bei der Standortkommandantur (Standortältesten) oder in Orten, die nicht Standort sind, bei der Ortspolizei (Gemeindeamt) anzumelden. Die Meldung hat er sich hierunter bescheinigen zu lassen.
3. Verschwiegenheit und Zurückhaltung bei Gesprächen ist Pflicht.
4. Bei Erkrankung sofort den nächsten Wehrmachtarzt (Standortarzt, Lazarett; Zivilarzt nur in Notfällen) aufsuchen.
5. Bei Zweifel über Rückreiseziel Auskunft nicht bei Zivilbehörden, sondern nur bei Wehrmachtdienststellen einholen.
6. Ist Inhaber Selbstverpfleger mit Lebensmittelkarten für Normalverbraucher der Zivilbevölkerung? ja — nein —*)
7. Abgefunden mit Gebührnissen bis einschl. 31.8.1942., Verpflegung in Geld bis einschl. 31.8.1942.
Verpflegung in Natur: Brot bis einschl. 12.8.1942, Mundverpflegung bis einschl. 12.8.1942.
Reichsurlauberkarten (Reise- und Gaststättenmarken) — bei Urlaub bis zu 3 Tagen — bis einschl. August 1942.
Feinseife bis einschl. August 1942, Rasierseife bis einschl. August 1942.
8. Hat als Teilnehmer an der Wehrmachtverpflegung während des Aufenthalts am Urlaubsort vom siehe umseitig bis siehe umseitig einschl. Anspruch auf Reichsurlauberkarten von der zuständigen Kartenausgabestelle. Die Aushändigung hat die Kartenausgabestelle hierunter zu bescheinigen.
9. Inhaber besitzt eine Kontrollkarte „M" oder Inhaber hat Anspruch auf einen Kontrollausweis für den Einkauf von Tabakwaren für die Zeit vom ------ bis ------ (Tage*).
10. Dieser Urlaubsschein ist nach Rückkehr vom Urlaub der Wehrmachtdienststelle abzugeben.
11. Besondere Vermerke: (z. B. über das Tragen bürgerlicher Kleidung am Urlaubsort u. a.):

Oblt. u. Battr.-
(Unterschrift des Einheitsführers zu Ziffer 11)

(Einträge zu Ziffer 11 sind hier durch Unterschrift des Einheitsführers besonders zu bescheinigen.)

Bescheinigung über Meldung am Urlaubsort:	Bescheinigung der Kartenausgabestelle:
gemeldet am 21. Aug. 1942	Reichsurlauberkarten sind ausgehändigt für die Zeit vom 20.8.42 bis [illegible] einschl.
(Ort, Datum, Stempel oder Unterschrift)	(Ort, Datum, Stempel oder Unterschrift)

*) Nichtzutreffendes streichen.

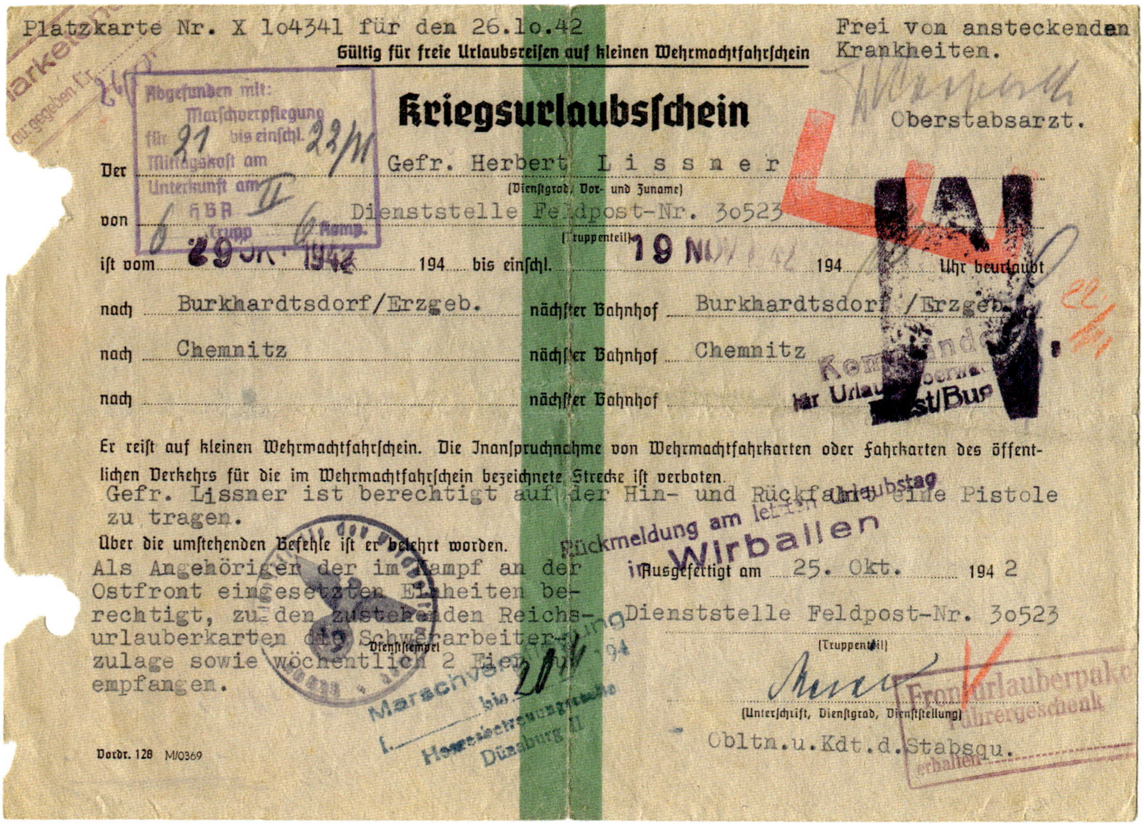

Platzkarte Nr. X 104341 für den 26.10.42
Gültig für freie Urlaubsreisen auf kleinen Wehrmachtfahrschein

Frei von ansteckenden Krankheiten.
Oberstabsarzt.

Kriegsurlaubsschein

Der Gefr. Herbert Lissner
(Dienstgrad, Vor- und Zuname)
von Dienststelle Feldpost-Nr. 30523
(Truppenteil)
ist vom 29 OKT. 1942 194.... bis einschl. 19 NOV. 1942 194.... Uhr beurlaubt
nach Burkhardtsdorf/Erzgeb. nächster Bahnhof Burkhardtsdorf/Erzgeb.
nach Chemnitz nächster Bahnhof Chemnitz
nach .... nächster Bahnhof ....

Er reist auf kleinen Wehrmachtfahrschein. Die Inanspruchnahme von Wehrmachtfahrkarten oder Fahrkarten des öffentlichen Verkehrs für die im Wehrmachtfahrschein bezeichnete Strecke ist verboten.
Gefr. Lissner ist berechtigt auf der Hin- und Rückfahrt eine Pistole zu tragen.
Über die umstehenden Befehle ist er belehrt worden.
Als Angehörigen der im Kampf an der Ostfront eingesetzten Einheiten berechtigt, zu den zustehenden Reichsurlauberkarten die Schwerarbeiterzulage sowie wöchentlich 2 Eier zu empfangen.

Ausgefertigt am 25. Okt. 1942
Dienststelle Feldpost-Nr. 30523
(Truppenteil)
(Dienststempel)
(Unterschrift, Dienstgrad, Dienststellung)
Oblt.n.u.Kdt.d.Stabsqu.

Vordr. 128 M/0369

Abgefunden mit: Marschverpflegung für 21 bis einschl. 22/11 Mittagskost am Unterkunft am
Rückmeldung am letzten Urlaubstag Wirballen
Marschverpflegung ... bis ... 194
Fronturlauberpaket Führergeschenk erhalten

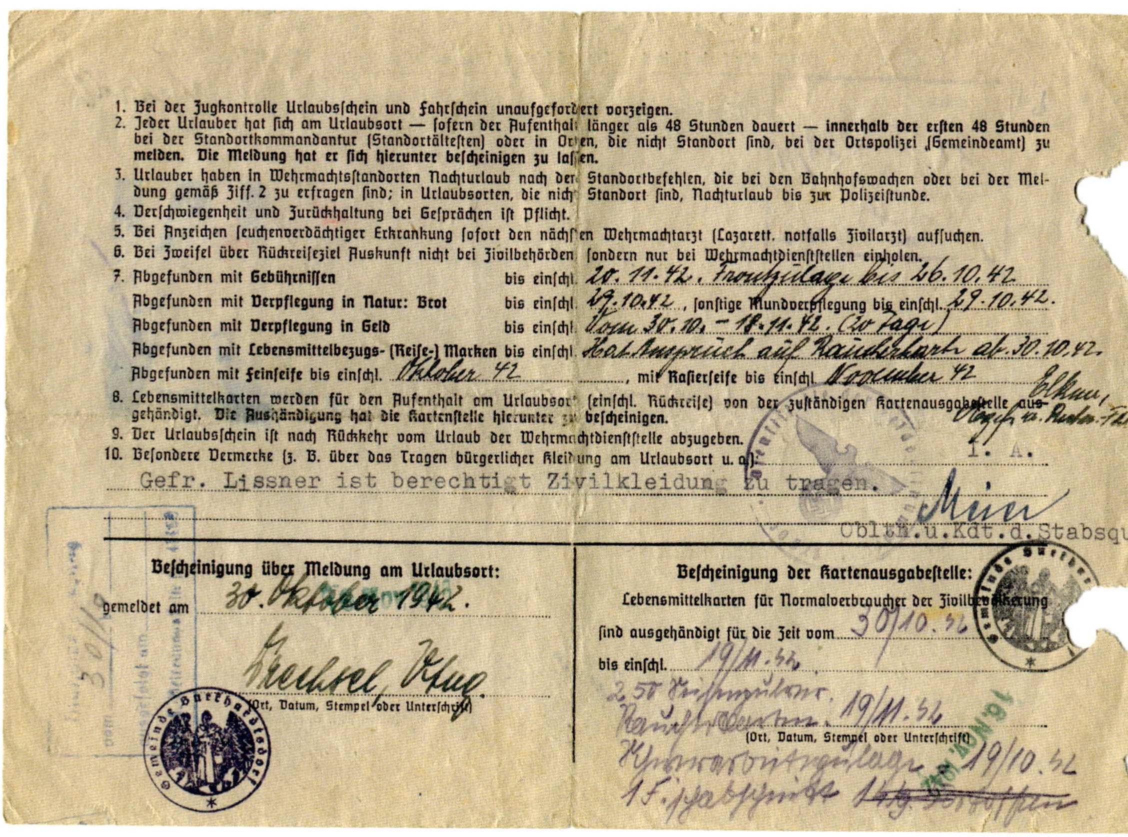

1. Bei der Zugkontrolle Urlaubsschein und Fahrschein unaufgefordert vorzeigen.
2. Jeder Urlauber hat sich am Urlaubsort — sofern der Aufenthalt länger als 48 Stunden dauert — **innerhalb der ersten 48 Stunden** bei der Standortkommandantur (Standortältesten) oder in Orten, die nicht Standort sind, bei der Ortspolizei (Gemeindeamt) zu **melden. Die Meldung hat er sich hierunter bescheinigen zu lassen.**
3. Urlauber haben in Wehrmachtsstandorten Nachturlaub nach den Standortbefehlen, die bei den Bahnhofswachen oder bei der Meldung gemäß Ziff. 2 zu erfragen sind; in Urlaubsorten, die nicht Standort sind, Nachturlaub bis zur Polizeistunde.
4. Verschwiegenheit und Zurückhaltung bei Gesprächen ist Pflicht.
5. Bei Anzeichen seuchenverdächtiger Erkrankung sofort den nächsten Wehrmachtarzt (Lazarett, notfalls Zivilarzt) aufsuchen.
6. Bei Zweifel über Rückreiseziel Auskunft nicht bei Zivilbehörden, sondern nur bei Wehrmachtdienststellen einholen.
7. Abgefunden mit **Gebührnissen** bis einschl. 20.11.42. Frontzulage bis 26.10.42
   Abgefunden mit **Verpflegung in Natur: Brot** bis einschl. 29.10.42, sonstige Mundverpflegung bis einschl. 29.10.42.
   Abgefunden mit **Verpflegung in Geld** bis einschl. Vom 30.10. – 18.11.42. (20 Tage)
   Abgefunden mit **Lebensmittelbezugs- (Reise-) Marken** bis einschl. Hat Anspruch auf Raucherkarte ab 30.10.42.
   Abgefunden mit **Feinseife** bis einschl. Oktober 42, mit **Rasierseife** bis einschl. November 42
8. Lebensmittelkarten werden für den Aufenthalt am Urlaubsort (einschl. Rückreise) von der zuständigen Kartenausgabestelle ausgehändigt. **Die Aushändigung hat die Kartenstelle hierunter zu bescheinigen.**
9. Der Urlaubsschein ist nach Rückkehr vom Urlaub der Wehrmachtdienststelle abzugeben.
10. Besondere Vermerke (z. B. über das Tragen bürgerlicher Kleidung am Urlaubsort u. a.):
Gefr. Lissner ist berechtigt Zivilkleidung zu tragen.
I. A.
Oblt.n.u.Kdt.d.Stabsqu

Bescheinigung über Meldung am Urlaubsort:
gemeldet am 30. Oktober 1942.
(Ort, Datum, Stempel oder Unterschrift)

Bescheinigung der Kartenausgabestelle:
Lebensmittelkarten für Normalverbraucher der Zivilbevölkerung sind ausgehändigt für die Zeit vom 30/10.42
bis einschl. 19/11.42
(Ort, Datum, Stempel oder Unterschrift)

Figure 2-67. Gefreiter Herbert Lissner, who in 1941 had been granted leave prior to the invasion of Russia (see figure 2-64), must have led a very interesting life; on this pass, it is stated that he is authorized to wear civilian clothing and to carry his pistol with him while travelling. The large "E" and "M" stamped on the front of the form indicate that he has been deloused and given rations (Entlaussten and Marschverpflegung). Note too that he has been given the Führergeschenk, "Führer's gift," for his service at the front. (A5)

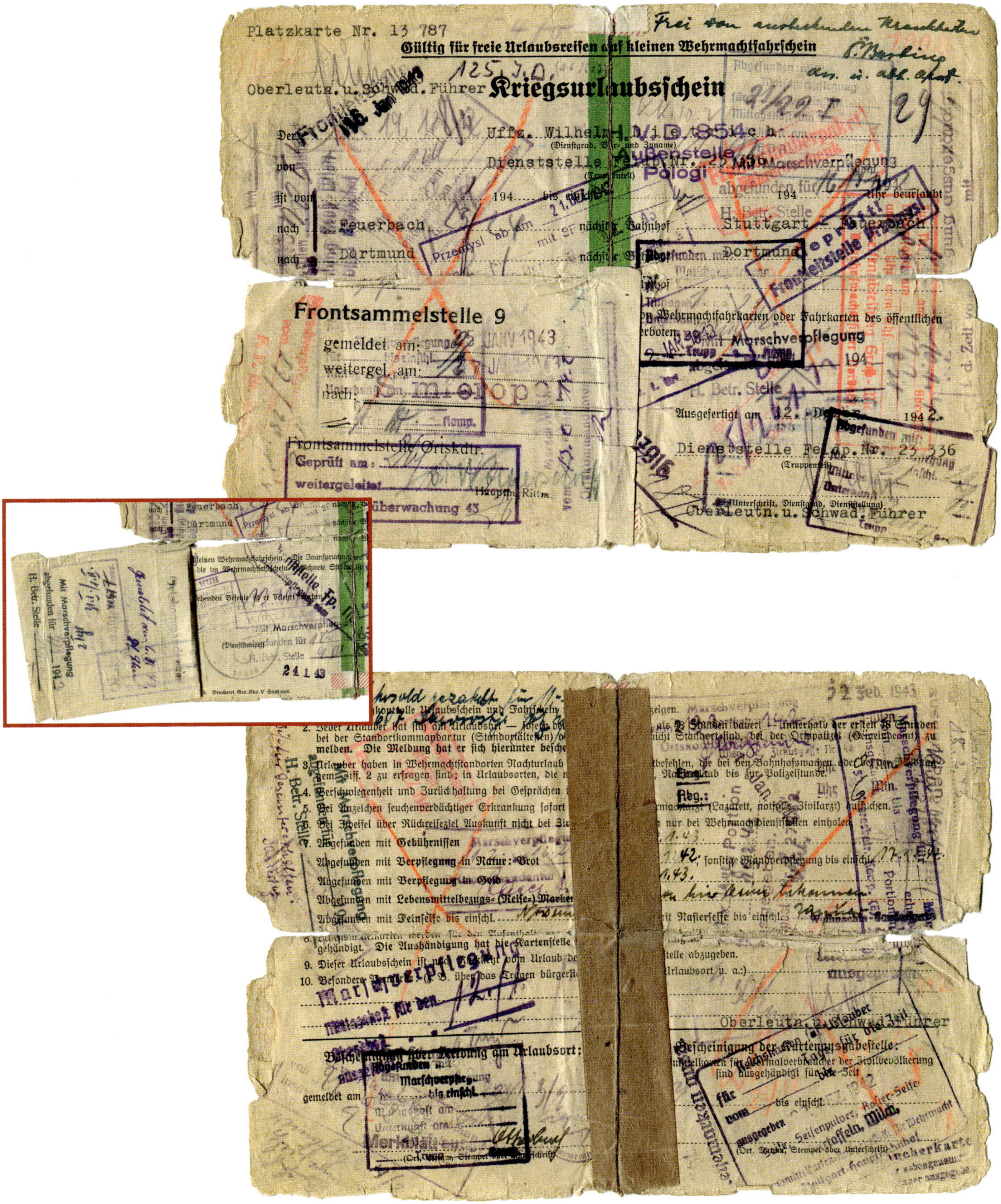

Figure 2-68. Where does one even start with an example such as this? Unteroffizier Wilhelm Dietrich of the 3rd Squadron of Aufklärungs-Abteilung 125 (Reconnaissance Section 125) of the 125. Infanterie-Division travelled through Feuerbach to Dortmund in December of 1942 and January of 1943, during which time he passed through a number of different Frontleitstellen (front control centers) and Frontsammelstellen (front collection centers) throughout Russia and Poland, where he was issued pay, marching rations, ration cards, tobacco rations, etc. (A5)

Figure 2-69. This particular pass for Leutenant Walter Juzmann of the 4th Company of Artillery Regiment 60 was glued into his diary, where he notes that rather than being returned to his unit: "The Frontleitstele sent me to the Crimea! Without great delay it's march straight on to Ssnamenka (Znamenka, Ukraine)." (A5)

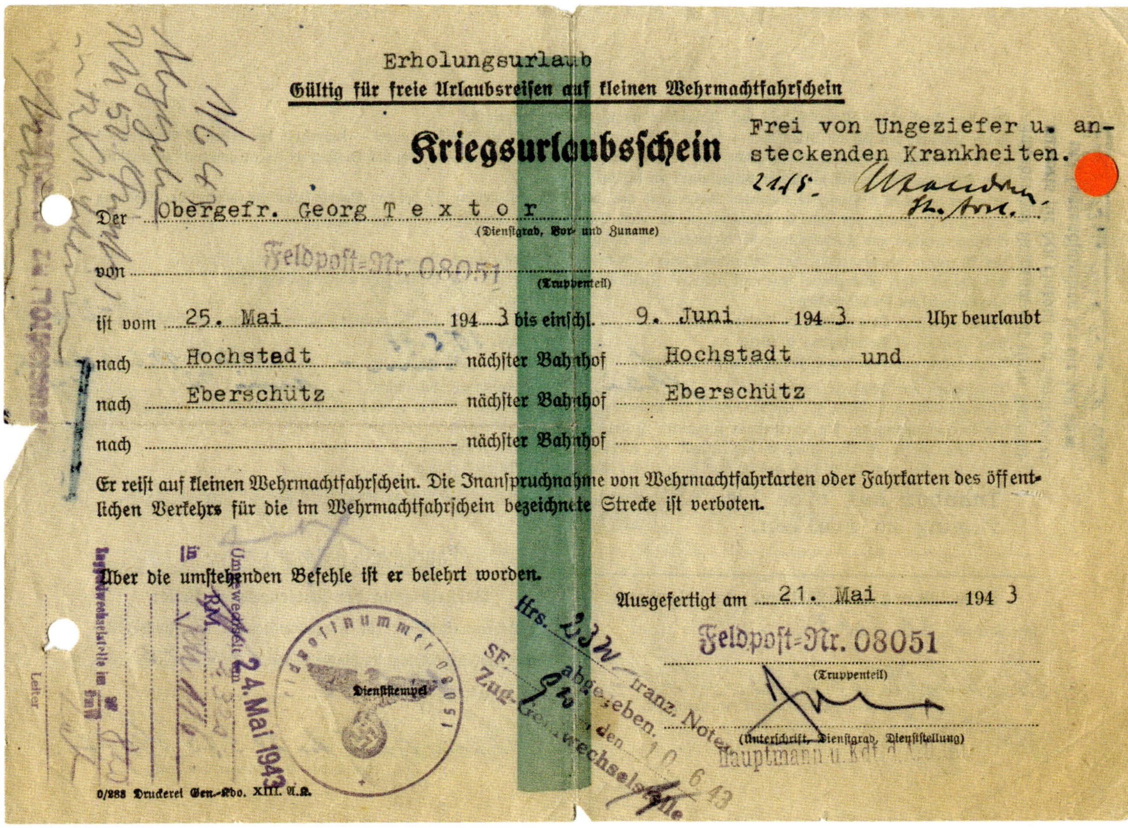

Erholungsurlaub

Gültig für freie Urlaubsreisen auf kleinen Wehrmachtfahrschein

Kriegsurlaubsschein

Frei von Ungeziefer u. ansteckenden Krankheiten.

Der Obergefr. Georg T e x t o r (Dienstgrad, Vor- und Zuname)

von Feldpost-Nr. 08051 (Truppenteil)

ist vom 25. Mai 1943 bis einschl. 9. Juni 1943 Uhr beurlaubt

nach Hochstadt nächster Bahnhof Hochstadt und

nach Eberschütz nächster Bahnhof Eberschütz

nach nächster Bahnhof

Er reist auf kleinen Wehrmachtfahrschein. Die Inanspruchnahme von Wehrmachtfahrkarten oder Fahrkarten des öffentlichen Verkehrs für die im Wehrmachtfahrschein bezeichnete Strecke ist verboten.

Über die umstehenden Befehle ist er belehrt worden.

Ausgefertigt am 21. Mai 1943

Feldpost-Nr. 08051 (Truppenteil)

(Unterschrift, Dienstgrad, Dienststellung) Hauptmann u. Kdt.

Dienststempel

24. Mai 1943

0/288 Druckerei Gen.-Kdo. XIII. A.K.

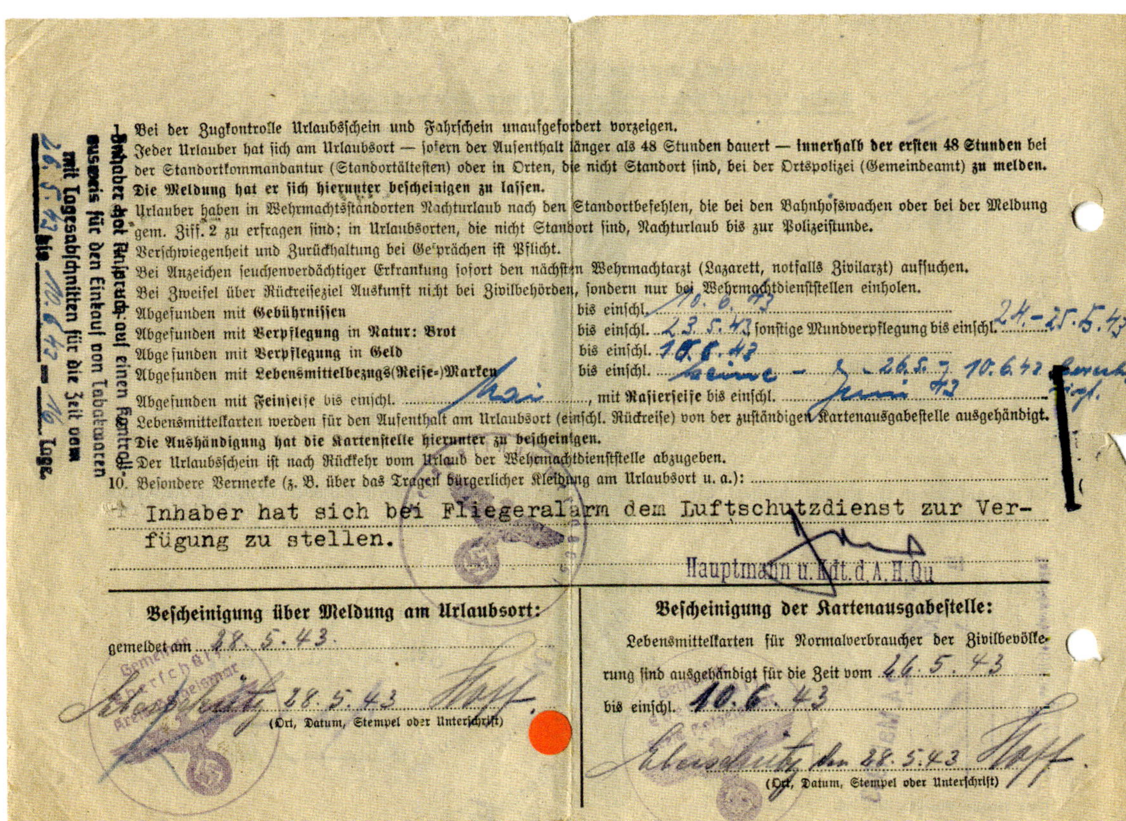

1. Bei der Zugkontrolle Urlaubsschein und Fahrschein unaufgefordert vorzeigen.
2. Jeder Urlauber hat sich am Urlaubsort — sofern der Aufenthalt länger als 48 Stunden dauert — **innerhalb der ersten 48 Stunden** bei der Standortkommandantur (Standortältesten) oder in Orten, die nicht Standort sind, bei der Ortspolizei (Gemeindeamt) **zu melden. Die Meldung hat er sich hierunter bescheinigen zu lassen.**
3. Urlauber haben in Wehrmachtsstandorten Nachturlaub nach den Standortbefehlen, die bei den Bahnhofswachen oder bei der Meldung gem. Ziff. 2 zu erfragen sind; in Urlaubsorten, die nicht Standort sind, Nachturlaub bis zur Polizeistunde.
4. Verschwiegenheit und Zurückhaltung bei Gesprächen ist Pflicht.
5. Bei Anzeichen seuchenverdächtiger Erkrankung sofort den nächsten Wehrmachtarzt (Lazarett, notfalls Zivilarzt) aufsuchen.
6. Bei Zweifel über Rückreiseziel Auskunft nicht bei Zivilbehörden, sondern nur bei Wehrmachtdienststellen einholen.
7. Abgefunden mit **Gebührnissen** bis einschl. 10. 6. 43
   Abgefunden mit **Verpflegung** in **Natur: Brot** bis einschl. 23. 5. 43 sonstige Mundverpflegung bis einschl. 24.–25. 5. 43
   Abgefunden mit **Verpflegung** in **Geld** bis einschl. 10. 6. 43
   Abgefunden mit **Lebensmittelbezugs(Reise-)Marken** bis einschl. keine – 26. 5. – 10. 6. 43
   Abgefunden mit **Feinseife** bis einschl. Mai, mit **Rasierseife** bis einschl. Juni 43
8. Lebensmittelkarten werden für den Aufenthalt am Urlaubsort (einschl. Rückreise) von der zuständigen Kartenausgabestelle ausgehändigt. **Die Aushändigung hat die Kartenstelle hierunter zu bescheinigen.**
9. Der Urlaubsschein ist nach Rückkehr vom Urlaub der Wehrmachtdienststelle abzugeben.
10. Besondere Vermerke (z. B. über das Tragen bürgerlicher Kleidung am Urlaubsort u. a.):

Inhaber hat sich bei Fliegeralarm dem Luftschutzdienst zur Verfügung zu stellen.

Hauptmann u. Kdt. d. A. H. Qu.

Inhaber hat Anspruch auf einen Kontrollausweis für den Einkauf von Tabakwaren mit Tagesabschnitten für die Zeit vom 26. 5. 43 bis 10. 6. 43 = 16 Tage.

Bescheinigung über Meldung am Urlaubsort:	**Bescheinigung der Kartenausgabestelle:**
gemeldet am 28. 5. 43	Lebensmittelkarten für Normalverbraucher der Zivilbevölkerung sind ausgehändigt für die Zeit vom 26. 5. 43 bis einschl. 10. 6. 43
Eberschütz 28. 5. 43 (Ort, Datum, Stempel oder Unterschrift)	Eberschütz, den 28. 5. 43 (Ort, Datum, Stempel oder Unterschrift)

Figure 2-70. Obergfreiter Georg Textor of the Army Map Depot (see figure 2-50), this time travelling at Wehrmacht expense during May and June of 1943, was paid an accumulated 2,320 Reichsmarks on May 24, 1943. (A5)

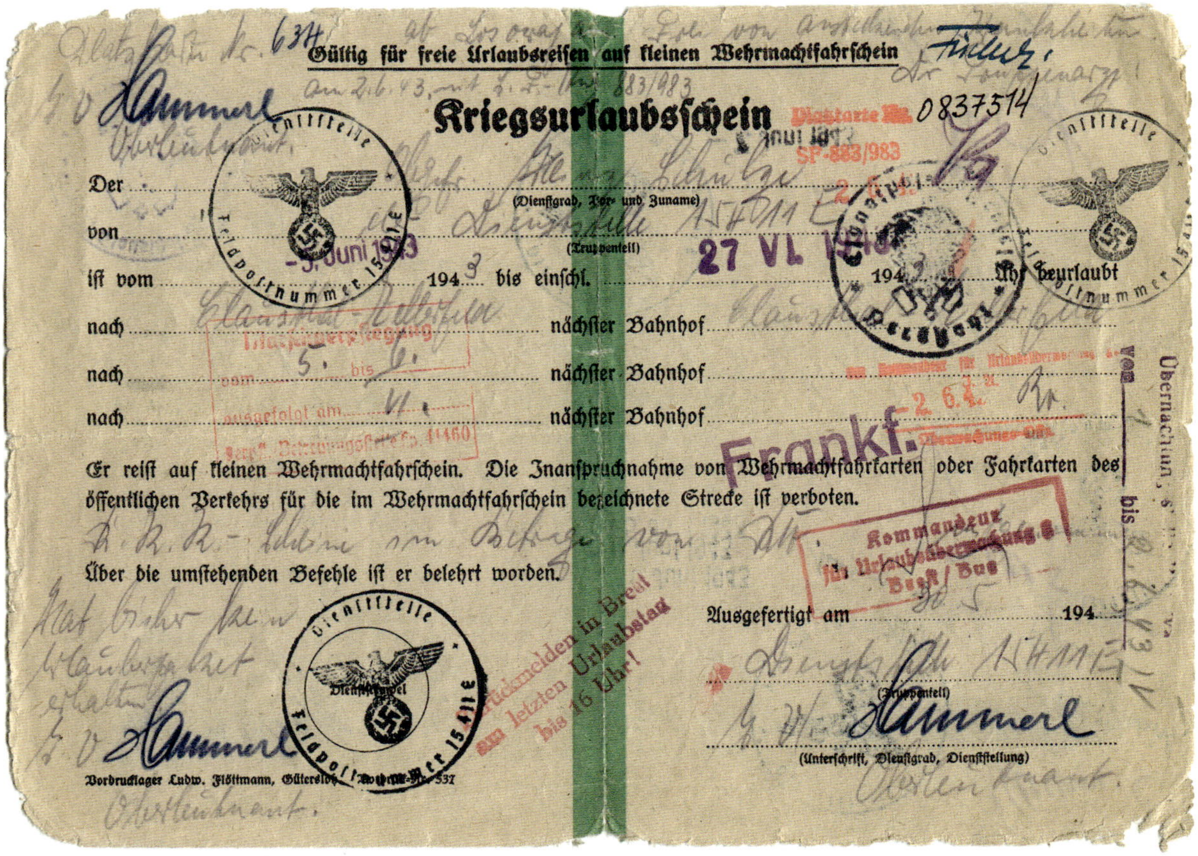

Gültig für freie Urlaubsreisen auf kleinen Wehrmachtfahrschein

Kriegsurlaubsschein

Der .... (Dienstgrad, Vor- und Zuname)

von .... (Truppenteil)

ist vom .... 194 bis einschl. .... 194 .... beurlaubt

nach .... nächster Bahnhof ....

nach .... nächster Bahnhof ....

nach .... nächster Bahnhof ....

Er reist auf kleinen Wehrmachtfahrschein. Die Inanspruchnahme von Wehrmachtfahrkarten oder Fahrkarten des öffentlichen Verkehrs für die im Wehrmachtfahrschein bezeichnete Strecke ist verboten.

Über die umstehenden Befehle ist er belehrt worden.

Ausgefertigt am 194

(Truppenteil)

(Unterschrift, Dienstgrad, Dienststellung)

Vordrucklager Ludw. Flöttmann, Gütersloh ... 537

Figure 2-71. Of particular interest on Obergefreiter Heinz Schulze's leave pass, in addition to the many Stempeln for rations and the other issue items, is the Sonderstempel on the front stating that he has been paid for his return trip on the last day of his leave from 4:00 pm. Note also that the form flips up to be legible, not left to right. (A5)

1. Beim Lösen von Fahrkarten und bei der Zugkontrolle Urlaubsschein und Fahrschein unaufgefordert vorzeigen.
2. Jeder Urlauber hat sich am Urlaubsort — sofern der Aufenthalt länger als 48 Stunden dauert — innerhalb der ersten 48 Stunden bei der Standortkommandantur (Standortältesten) oder in Orten, die nicht Standort sind, bei der Ortspolizei (Gemeindebeamt) zu melden. Die Meldung hat er sich hierunter bescheinigen zu lassen.
3. Urlauber haben in Wehrmachtstandorten Nachturlaub nach den Standortbefehlen, die bei den Bahnhofswachen oder bei der Meldung gemäß Ziff. 2 zu erfragen sind; in Urlaubsorten, die nicht Standort sind, Nachturlaub bis zur Polizeistunde.
4. Verschwiegenheit und Zurückhaltung bei Gesprächen ist Pflicht.
5. Bei Anzeichen seuchenverdächtiger Erkrankung sofort den nächsten Wehrmachtarzt (Lazarett, notfalls Zivilarzt) aufsuchen.
6. Bei Zweifel über Rückreiseziel Auskunft nicht bei Zivilbehörden, sondern nur bei Wehrmachtdienststellen einholen.
7. Abgefunden mit Gebührnissen bis einschl. 30. Juni 1943
   Abgefunden mit Verpflegung in Natur: Brot bis einschl. 4. Juni 1943 übrige Mundverpflegung bis einschl.
   Abgefunden mit Verpflegung in Geld bis einschl. 25. Juni 1943
   Abgefunden mit Lebensmittelbezugs-(Reise-)Marken bis einschl.
   Abgefunden mit Feinseife bis einschl. Mai 43, mit Rasierseife bis einschl. Juni 43
8. Lebensmittelkarten werden für den Aufenthalt am Urlaubsort (einschl. Rückreise) von der zuständigen Kartenausgabestelle ausgehändigt. Die Aushändigung hat die Kartenstelle hierunter zu bescheinigen.
9. Dieser Urlaubsschein ist nach Rückkehr vom Urlaub der Wehrmachtdienststelle abzugeben.
10. Besondere Vermerke: (z. B. über das Tragen bürgerlicher Kleidung am Urlaubsort u. a.)

Bescheinigung über Meldung am Urlaubsort: gemeldet am 7. Juni 1943

Zellerfeld 7. Juni 1943

(Ort, Datum, Stempel oder Unterschrift)

Bescheinigung der Kartenausgabestelle: Lebensmittelkarten für Normalverbraucher der Zivilbevölkerung sind ausgehändigt für die Zeit vom 7.6.43 bis einschl. ...6.43

— 7. Juni 1943

Ort, Datum, Stempel oder Unterschrift

Tabak-Kontrollausweis Nr. ... erhalten

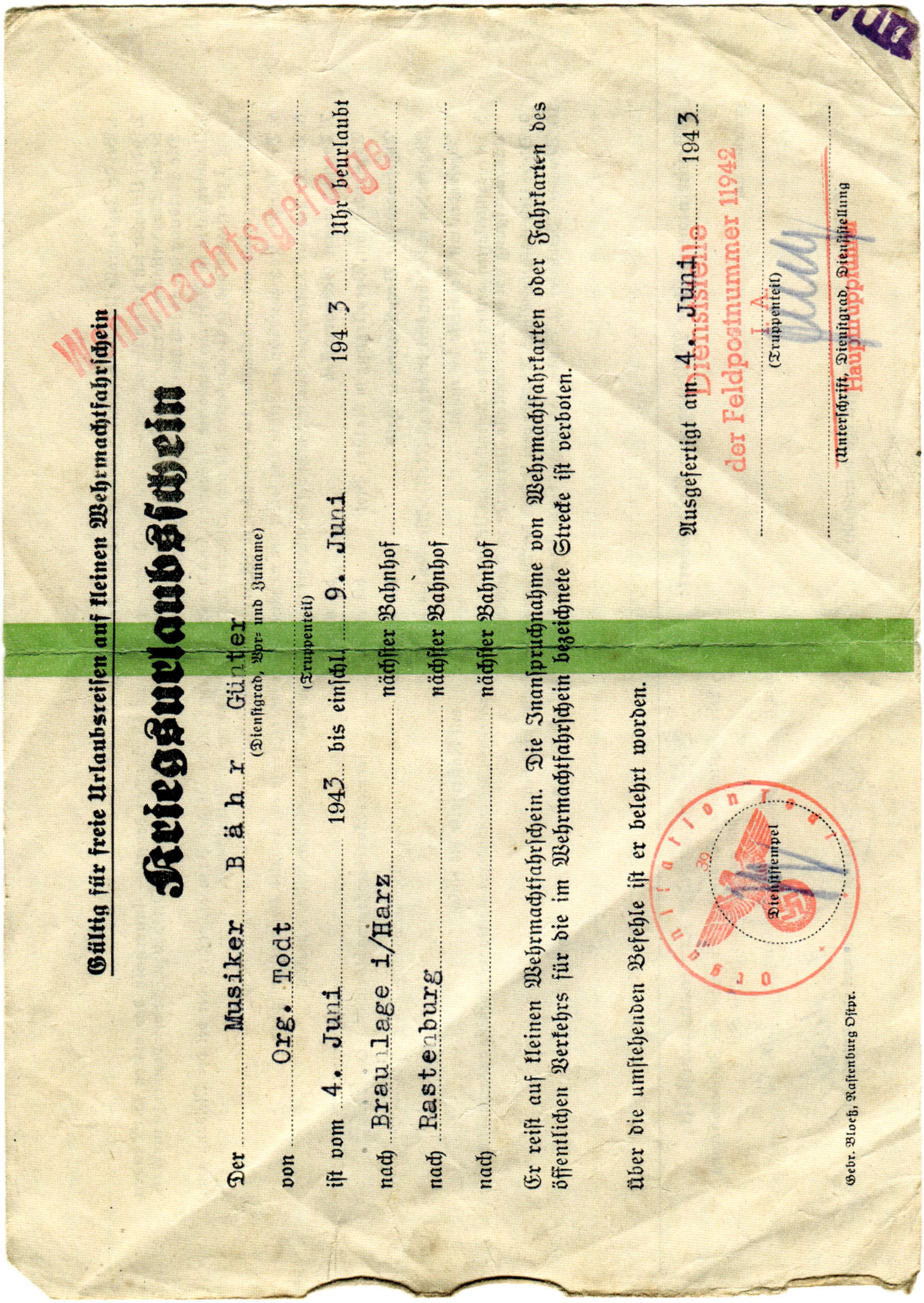
Gültig für freie Urlaubsreisen auf kleinen Wehrmachtfahrschein

Wehrmachtsgefolge

Kriegsurlaubsschein

Der Musiker Bähr Günter
(Dienstgrad, Vor- und Zuname)

von Org. Todt
(Truppenteil)

ist vom 4. Juni 1943 bis einschl. 9. Juni 1943 Uhr beurlaubt

nach Braunlage i/Harz nächster Bahnhof

nach Rastenburg nächster Bahnhof

nach nächster Bahnhof

Er reist auf kleinen Wehrmachtfahrschein. Die Inanspruchnahme von Wehrmachtfahrkarten oder Fahrkarten des öffentlichen Verkehrs für die im Wehrmachtfahrschein bezeichnete Strecke ist verboten.

Über die umstehenden Befehle ist er belehrt worden.

Ausgefertigt am 4. Juni 1943

Dienststelle der Feldpostnummer 11942

I. A.

(Truppenteil)

Haupttruppführer

Unterschrift, Dienstgrad, Dienststellung

Organisation Todt

39

Dienststempel

Gebr. Bloeß, Rastenburg Ostpr.

Figure 2-72. This is an especially interesting pass, primarily because the bearer, Musician Günter Bähr, who was not part of the Wehrmacht, but rather Organization Todt, a civil and military engineering group. His pass, however, is stamped that he was a member of a Wehrmacht entourage (Wehrmachtgefolge), presumably as part of a band touring the front. (Full size - A5)

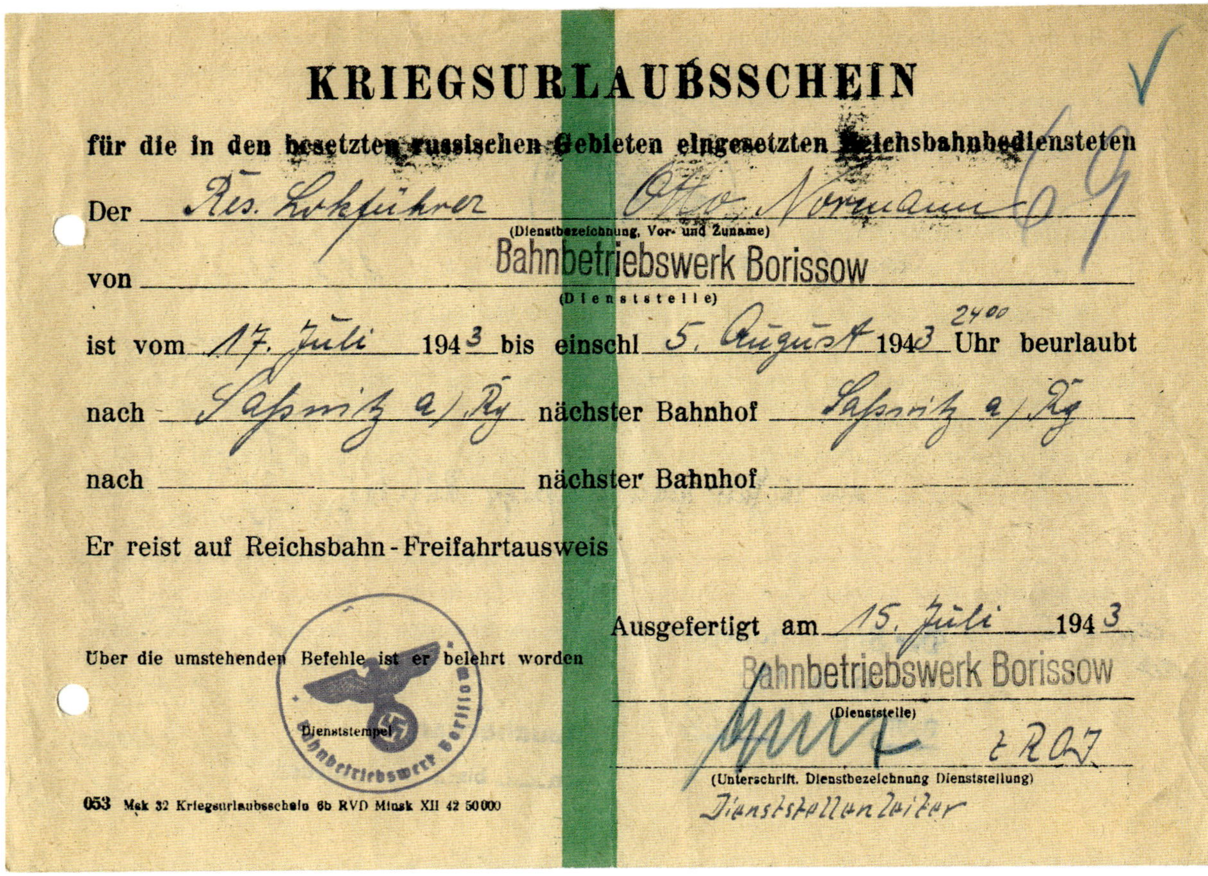

KRIEGSURLAUBSSCHEIN

für die in den besetzten russischen Gebieten eingesetzten Reichsbahnbediensteten

Der Res. Lokführer Otto Normann 69
(Dienstbezeichnung, Vor- und Zuname)

von Bahnbetriebswerk Borissow
(Dienststelle)

ist vom 17. Juli 1943 bis einschl 5. August 1943 2400 Uhr beurlaubt

nach Saßnitz a/Rg nächster Bahnhof Saßnitz a/Rg

nach ______ nächster Bahnhof ______

Er reist auf Reichsbahn-Freifahrtausweis

Über die umstehenden Befehle ist er belehrt worden

Dienststempel

Ausgefertigt am 15. Juli 1943

Bahnbetriebswerk Borissow
(Dienststelle)

(Unterschrift, Dienstbezeichnung Dienststellung)
Dienststellenleiter

053 Mck 32 Kriegsurlaubsschein 6b RVD Minsk XII 42 50000

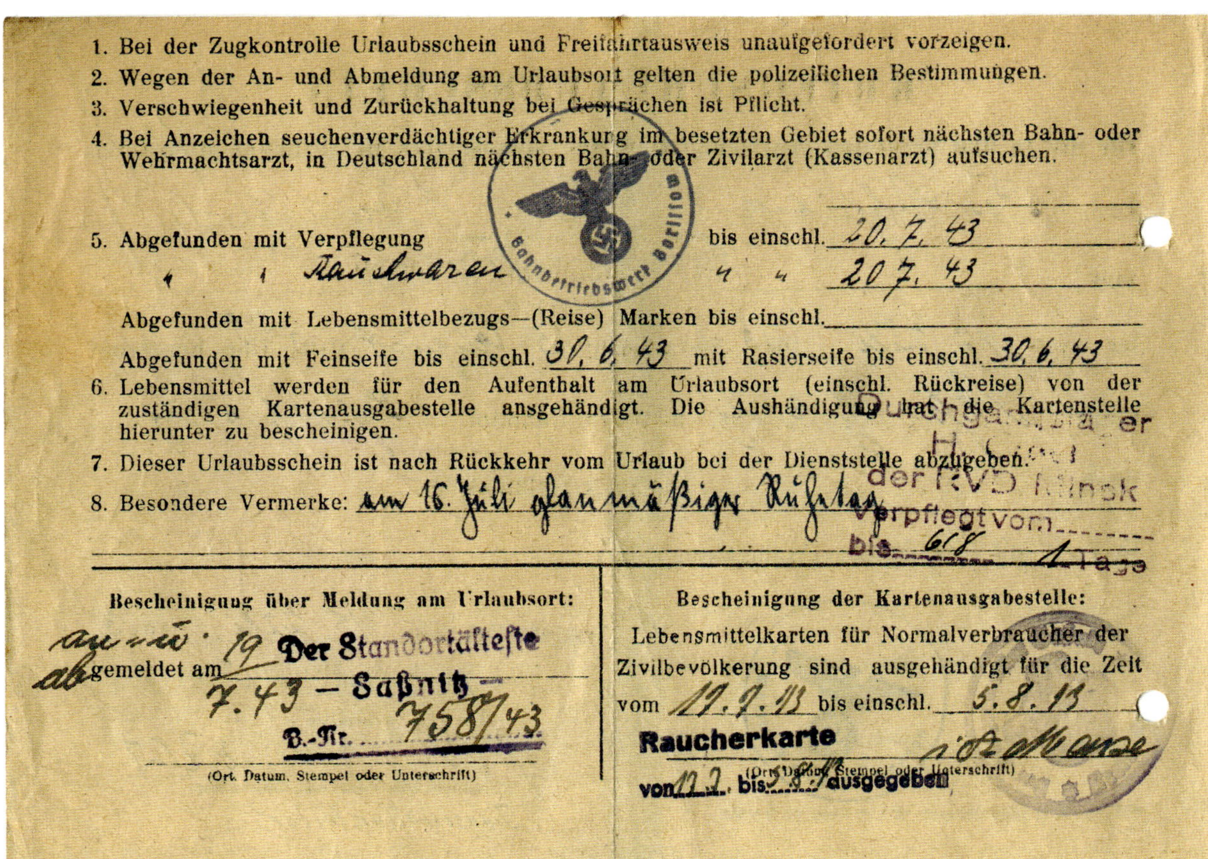

1. Bei der Zugkontrolle Urlaubsschein und Freifahrtausweis unaufgefordert vorzeigen.
2. Wegen der An- und Abmeldung am Urlaubsort gelten die polizeilichen Bestimmungen.
3. Verschwiegenheit und Zurückhaltung bei Gesprächen ist Pflicht.
4. Bei Anzeichen seuchenverdächtiger Erkrankung im besetzten Gebiet sofort nächsten Bahn- oder Wehrmachtsarzt, in Deutschland nächsten Bahn- oder Zivilarzt (Kassenarzt) aufsuchen.
5. Abgefunden mit Verpflegung bis einschl. 20.7.43
   " " Rauchwaren " " 20.7.43
   Abgefunden mit Lebensmittelbezugs—(Reise) Marken bis einschl. ______
   Abgefunden mit Feinseife bis einschl. 30.6.43 mit Rasierseife bis einschl. 30.6.43
6. Lebensmittel werden für den Aufenthalt am Urlaubsort (einschl. Rückreise) von der zuständigen Kartenausgabestelle ausgehändigt. Die Aushändigung hat die Kartenstelle hierunter zu bescheinigen.
7. Dieser Urlaubsschein ist nach Rückkehr vom Urlaub bei der Dienststelle abzugeben.
8. Besondere Vermerke: am 16. Juli planmäßiger Ruhetag

Durchgangslager der RVD Minsk
Verpflegt vom ______ bis 6/8 1 Tage

Bescheinigung über Meldung am Urlaubsort:	Bescheinigung der Kartenausgabestelle:
an- ab- gemeldet am 19.7.43 Der Standortälteste Saßnitz B.-Nr. 758/43	Lebensmittelkarten für Normalverbraucher der Zivilbevölkerung sind ausgehändigt für die Zeit vom 19.7.43 bis einschl. 5.8.43
(Ort, Datum, Stempel oder Unterschrift)	(Ort, Datum, Stempel oder Unterschrift) Raucherkarte von 19.7. bis 5.8. ausgegeben

Figure 2-73. A Reichsbahn-issued leave pass for Reserve Locomotive Engineer Otto Normann. Note that the lower left hand corner shows that the printer is (was) located in RVD Minsk (Reichsverkehrsdirektion or Reich Traffic Director). (A5)

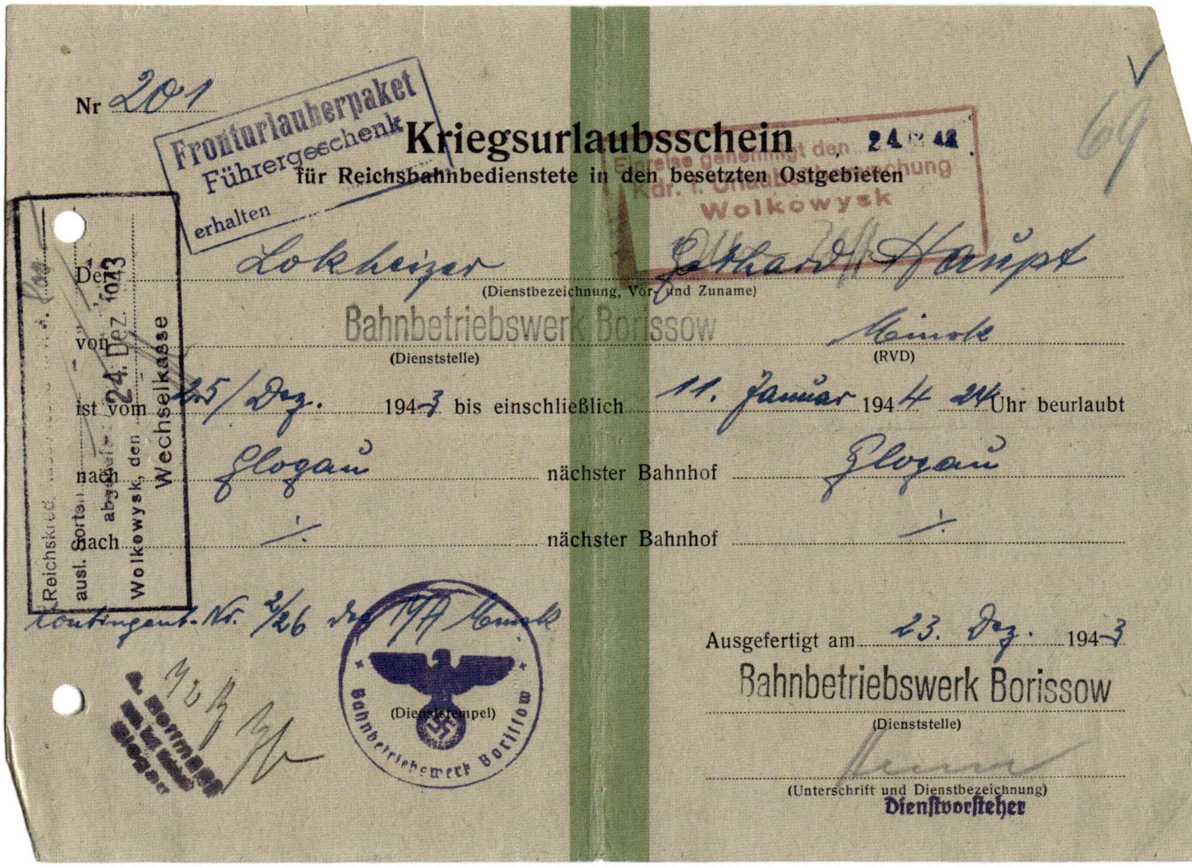

Nr 201

Fronturlauberpaket Führergeschenk erhalten

Kriegsurlaubsschein

24.12.43

für Reichsbahnbedienstete in den besetzten Ostgebieten

Einreise genehmigt den [illegible] Kdr. f. [illegible] Wolkowysk

Der Lokheizer Gothard Haupt
(Dienstbezeichnung, Vor- und Zuname)

von Bahnbetriebswerk Borissow — Minsk
(Dienststelle) (RVD)

ist vom 25/Dez. 1943 bis einschließlich 11. Januar 1944 24 Uhr beurlaubt

nach Glogau nächster Bahnhof Glogau

nach -/- nächster Bahnhof -/-

Reichskred. [illegible] ausl. Sorten abgef. [illegible] Wolkowysk, den 24. Dez 1943 Wechselkasse

Kontingent-Nr. 2/26 der RVD Minsk

(Dienststempel) Bahnbetriebswerk Borissow

Ausgefertigt am 23. Dez. 1943

Bahnbetriebswerk Borissow
(Dienststelle)

(Unterschrift und Dienstbezeichnung)
Dienstvorsteher

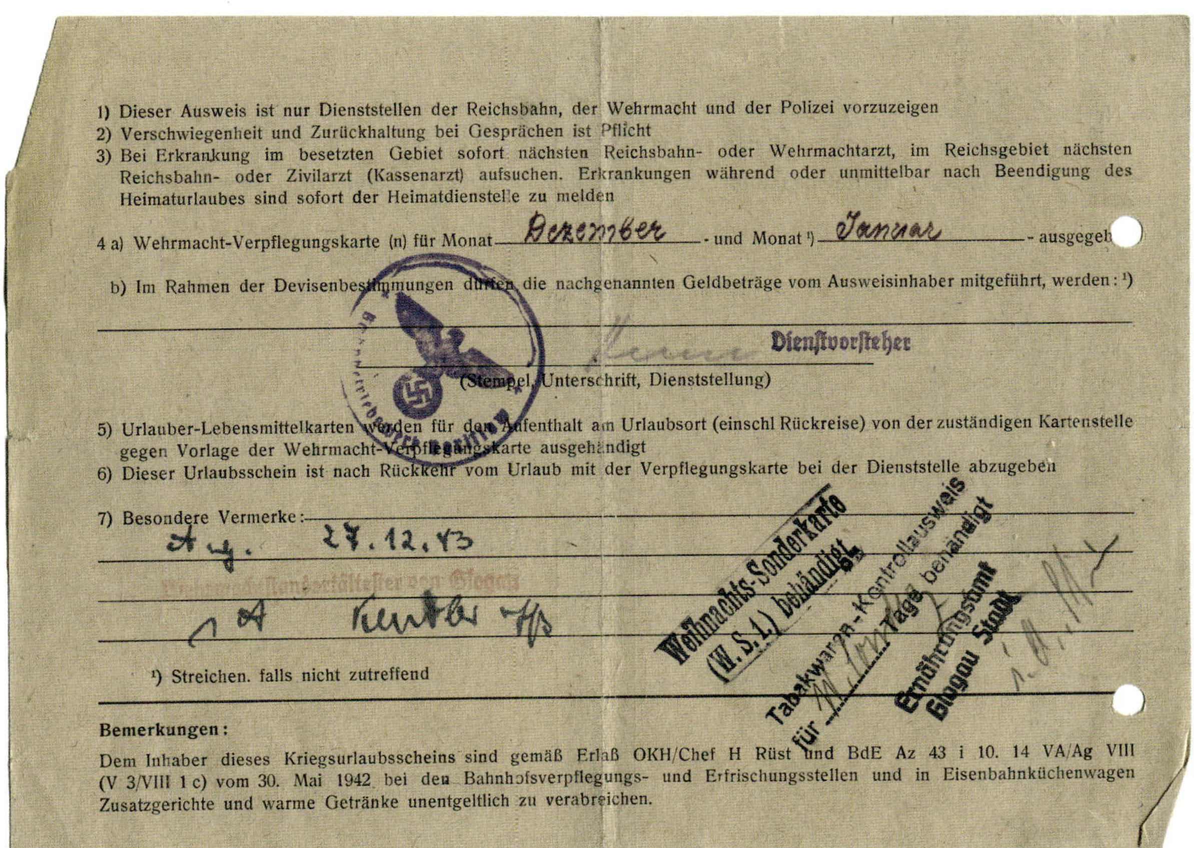

1) Dieser Ausweis ist nur Dienststellen der Reichsbahn, der Wehrmacht und der Polizei vorzuzeigen
2) Verschwiegenheit und Zurückhaltung bei Gesprächen ist Pflicht
3) Bei Erkrankung im besetzten Gebiet sofort nächsten Reichsbahn- oder Wehrmachtarzt, im Reichsgebiet nächsten Reichsbahn- oder Zivilarzt (Kassenarzt) aufsuchen. Erkrankungen während oder unmittelbar nach Beendigung des Heimaturlaubes sind sofort der Heimatdienststelle zu melden

4 a) Wehrmacht-Verpflegungskarte (n) für Monat Dezember und Monat [1]) Januar - ausgegeb

b) Im Rahmen der Devisenbestimmungen dürfen die nachgenannten Geldbeträge vom Ausweisinhaber mitgeführt, werden: [1])

Dienstvorsteher
(Stempel, Unterschrift, Dienststellung)

5) Urlauber-Lebensmittelkarten werden für den Aufenthalt am Urlaubsort (einschl Rückreise) von der zuständigen Kartenstelle gegen Vorlage der Wehrmacht-Verpflegungskarte ausgehändigt
6) Dieser Urlaubsschein ist nach Rückkehr vom Urlaub mit der Verpflegungskarte bei der Dienststelle abzugeben

7) Besondere Vermerke: Ang. 27.12.43

Wehrmeldestelle [illegible] Glogau

Weihnachts-Sonderkarte (W.S.K.) behändigt

Tabakwaren-Kontrollausweis für [illegible] Tage behändigt

Ernährungsamt Glogau Stadt

[1]) Streichen, falls nicht zutreffend

Bemerkungen:

Dem Inhaber dieses Kriegsurlaubsscheins sind gemäß Erlaß OKH/Chef H Rüst und BdE Az 43 i 10. 14 VA/Ag VIII (V 3/VIII 1 c) vom 30. Mai 1942 bei den Bahnhofsverpflegungs- und Erfrischungsstellen und in Eisenbahnküchenwagen Zusatzgerichte und warme Getränke unentgeltlich zu verabreichen.

Figure 2-74. A Reichsbahn issued leave pass, this one for Lokomotivheizer (Stoker) Gothard Haupt. The dates are not specified, but Herr Haupt was given the Führergeschenk as well as the Weihnachts-Sonderkarte (Christmas "Special" Ration Card). (A5)

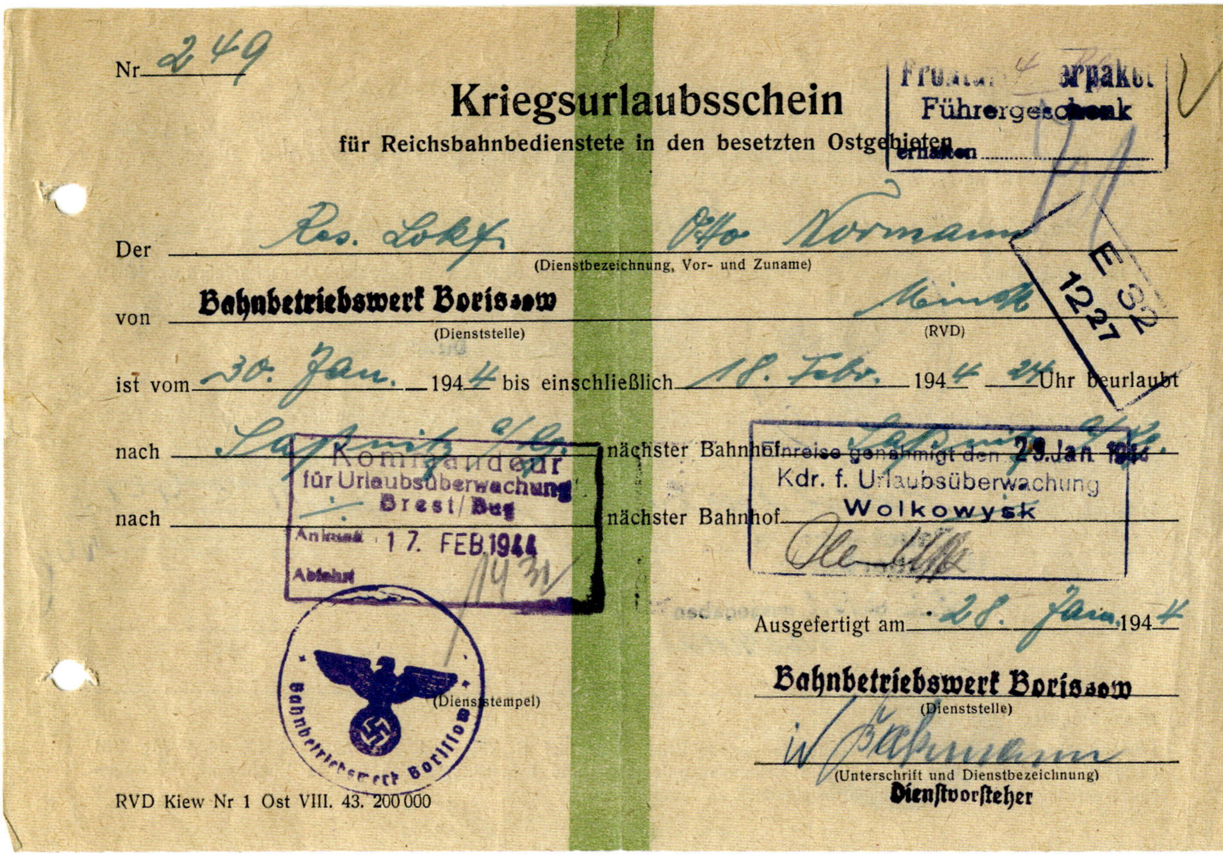

Nr. 249

Kriegsurlaubsschein

für Reichsbahnbedienstete in den besetzten Ostgebieten

Frontarbeiterpaket / Führergeschenk erhalten

Der Res. Lokf. Otto Normann
(Dienstbezeichnung, Vor- und Zuname)

von Bahnbetriebswerk Borissow (Dienststelle) Minsk (RVD)

ist vom 30. Jan. 1944 bis einschließlich 18. Febr. 1944 24 Uhr beurlaubt

nach .... nächster Bahnhof ....

nach .... nächster Bahnhof ....

Kommandeur für Urlaubsüberwachung Brest/Bug — Ankunft 17. FEB 1944 — Abfahrt

Einreise genehmigt den 29. Jan. 1944 — Kdr. f. Urlaubsüberwachung Wolkowysk

E S2 1227

(Dienststempel) Bahnbetriebswerk Borissow

Ausgefertigt am 28. Jan. 1944

Bahnbetriebswerk Borissow
(Dienststelle)

(Unterschrift und Dienstbezeichnung)
Dienstvorsteher

RVD Kiew Nr 1 Ost VIII. 43. 200000

Figure 2-75. Another pass belonging to Reserve Locomotive Engineer Normann, this time for leave lasting almost three full weeks, January 30, until February 18, 1944. The stamp for Bahnbetriebswerk (Railway Operation Factory) in Borissow is in Fraktur, compared to the other in figure 2-74, which is in DIN 1451. (A5)

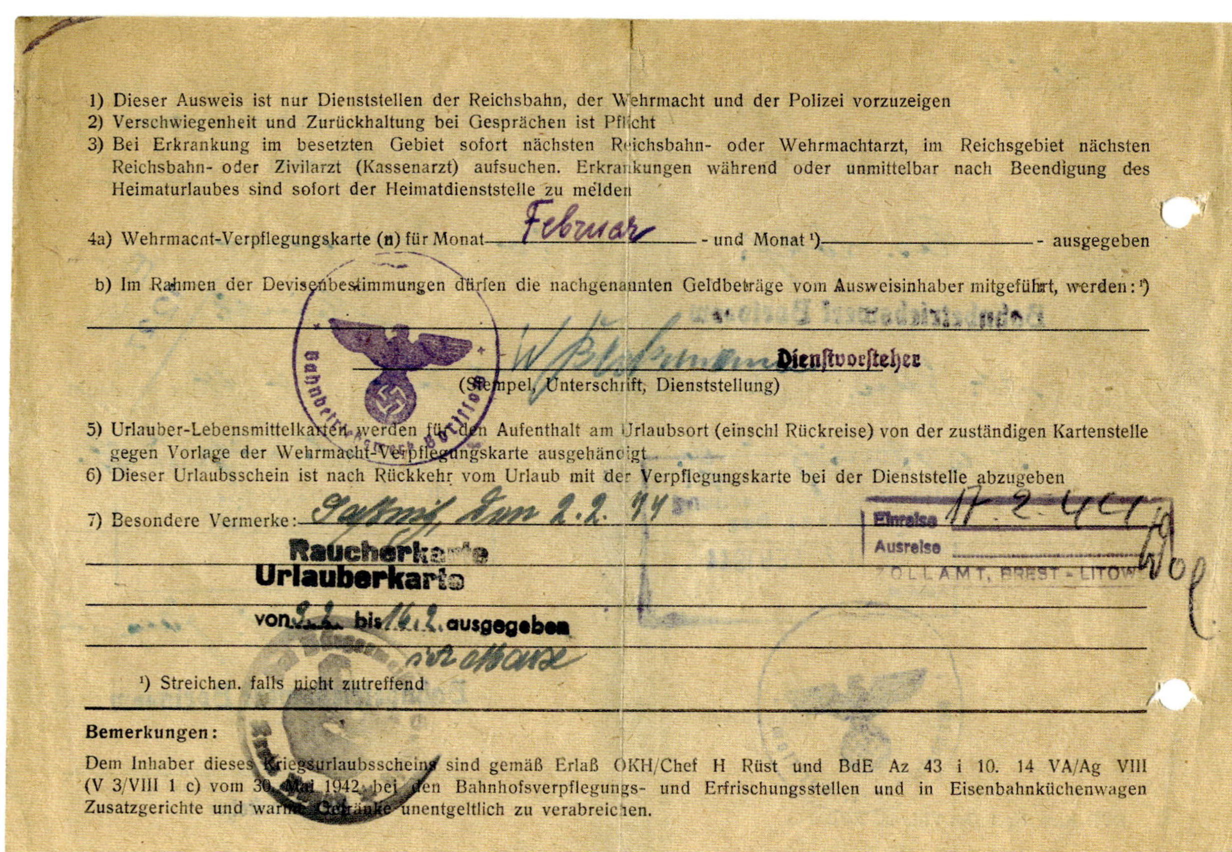

1) Dieser Ausweis ist nur Dienststellen der Reichsbahn, der Wehrmacht und der Polizei vorzuzeigen
2) Verschwiegenheit und Zurückhaltung bei Gesprächen ist Pflicht
3) Bei Erkrankung im besetzten Gebiet sofort nächsten Reichsbahn- oder Wehrmachtarzt, im Reichsgebiet nächsten Reichsbahn- oder Zivilarzt (Kassenarzt) aufsuchen. Erkrankungen während oder unmittelbar nach Beendigung des Heimaturlaubes sind sofort der Heimatdienststelle zu melden

4a) Wehrmacht-Verpflegungskarte (n) für Monat Februar - und Monat [1] - ausgegeben

b) Im Rahmen der Devisenbestimmungen dürfen die nachgenannten Geldbeträge vom Ausweisinhaber mitgeführt werden: [1]

Dienstvorsteher
(Stempel, Unterschrift, Dienststellung)

5) Urlauber-Lebensmittelkarten werden für den Aufenthalt am Urlaubsort (einschl Rückreise) von der zuständigen Kartenstelle gegen Vorlage der Wehrmacht-Verpflegungskarte ausgehändigt
6) Dieser Urlaubsschein ist nach Rückkehr vom Urlaub mit der Verpflegungskarte bei der Dienststelle abzugeben

7) Besondere Vermerke: Saßnitz ... 2. 2. 44

Raucherkarte
Urlauberkarte
von 2.2. bis 16.2. ausgegeben

Einreise 17. 2. 44 — Ausreise — ZOLLAMT BREST-LITOWSK

[1]) Streichen, falls nicht zutreffend

Bemerkungen:

Dem Inhaber dieses Kriegsurlaubsscheins sind gemäß Erlaß OKH/Chef H Rüst und BdE Az 43 i 10. 14 VA/Ag VIII (V 3/VIII 1 c) vom 30. Mai 1942 bei den Bahnhofsverpflegungs- und Erfrischungsstellen und in Eisenbahnküchenwagen Zusatzgerichte und warme Getränke unentgeltlich zu verabreichen.

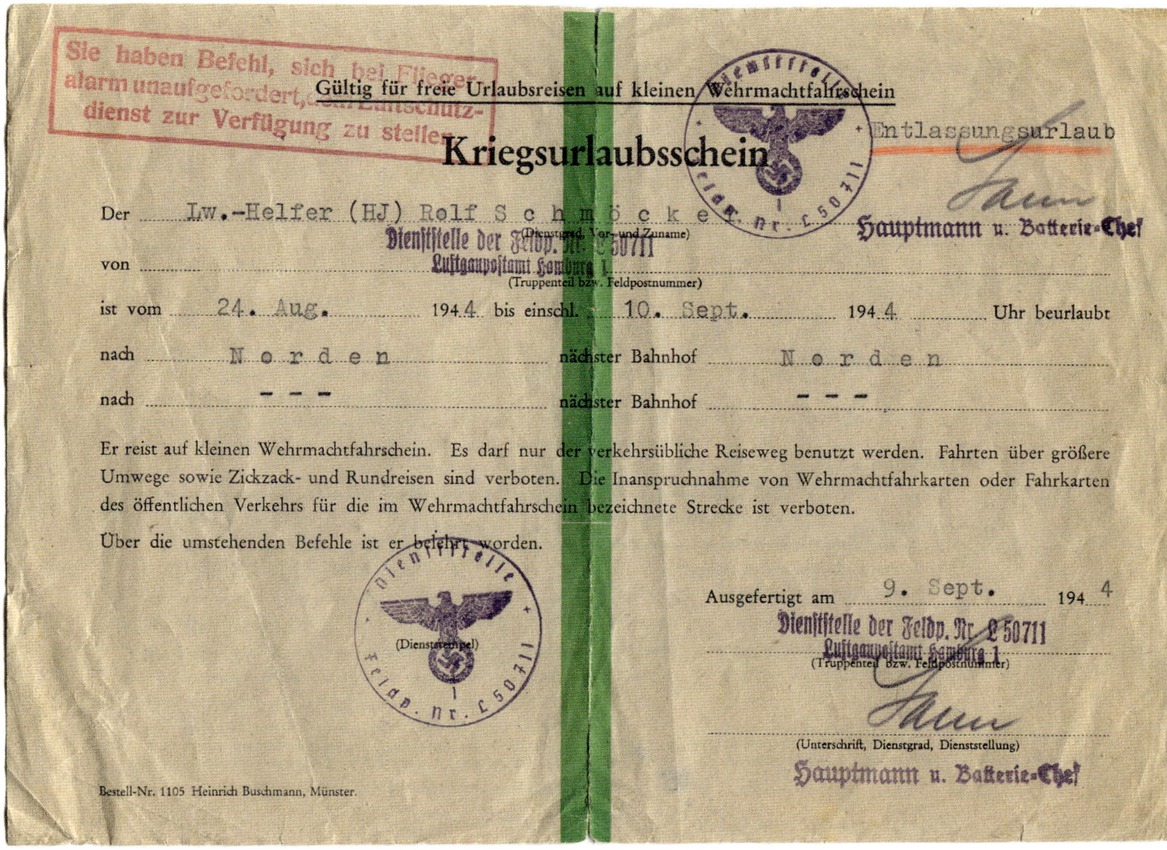

Sie haben Befehl, sich bei Fliegeralarm unaufgefordert, dem Luftschutzdienst zur Verfügung zu stellen.

Gültig für freie Urlaubsreisen auf kleinen Wehrmachtfahrschein

Entlassungsurlaub

Kriegsurlaubsschein

Der Lw.-Helfer (HJ) Rolf Schmöcke (Dienstgrad, Vor- und Zuname)

von Dienststelle der Feldp. Nr. L 50711 Luftgaupostamt Hamburg 1 (Truppenteil bzw. Feldpostnummer)

ist vom 24. Aug. 1944 bis einschl. 10. Sept. 1944 Uhr beurlaubt

nach Norden nächster Bahnhof Norden

nach --- nächster Bahnhof ---

Er reist auf kleinen Wehrmachtfahrschein. Es darf nur der verkehrsübliche Reiseweg benutzt werden. Fahrten über größere Umwege sowie Zickzack- und Rundreisen sind verboten. Die Inanspruchnahme von Wehrmachtfahrkarten oder Fahrkarten des öffentlichen Verkehrs für die im Wehrmachtfahrschein bezeichnete Strecke ist verboten.

Über die umstehenden Befehle ist er belehrt worden.

(Dienststempel)

Ausgefertigt am 9. Sept. 1944

Dienststelle der Feldp. Nr. L 50711 Luftgaupostamt Hamburg 1 (Truppenteil bzw. Feldpostnummer)

(Unterschrift, Dienstgrad, Dienststellung)

Hauptmann u. Batterie-Chef

Bestell-Nr. 1105 Heinrich Buschmann, Münster.

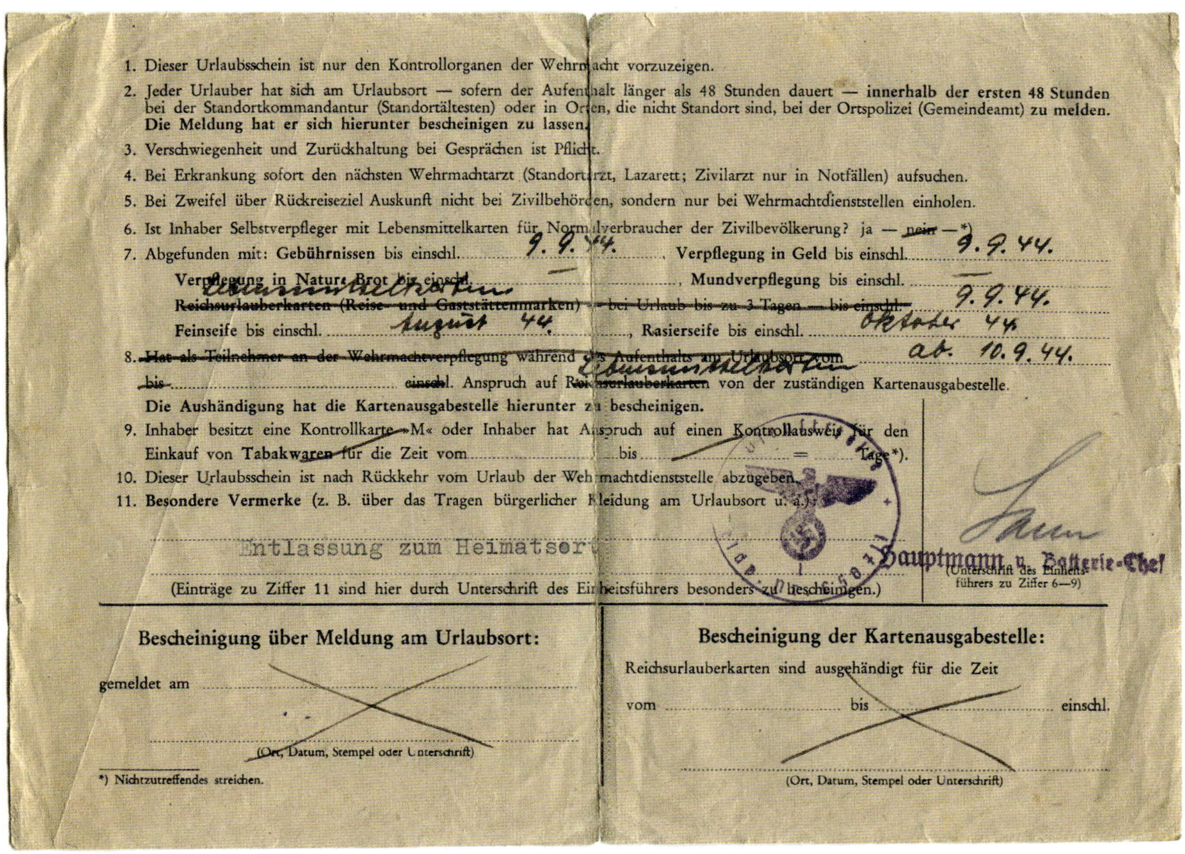

1. Dieser Urlaubsschein ist nur den Kontrollorganen der Wehrmacht vorzuzeigen.
2. Jeder Urlauber hat sich am Urlaubsort — sofern der Aufenthalt länger als 48 Stunden dauert — **innerhalb der ersten 48 Stunden** bei der Standortkommandantur (Standortältesten) oder in Orten, die nicht Standort sind, bei der Ortspolizei (Gemeindeamt) zu melden. **Die Meldung hat er sich hierunter bescheinigen zu lassen.**
3. Verschwiegenheit und Zurückhaltung bei Gesprächen ist Pflicht.
4. Bei Erkrankung sofort den nächsten Wehrmachtarzt (Standortarzt, Lazarett; Zivilarzt nur in Notfällen) aufsuchen.
5. Bei Zweifel über Rückreiseziel Auskunft nicht bei Zivilbehörden, sondern nur bei Wehrmachtdienststellen einholen.
6. Ist Inhaber Selbstverpfleger mit Lebensmittelkarten für Normalverbraucher der Zivilbevölkerung? ja — ~~nein~~ —*)
7. Abgefunden mit: Gebührnissen bis einschl. 9.9.44., Verpflegung in Geld bis einschl. 9.9.44.
   Verpflegung in Natur: Brot bis einschl. Lebensmittelkarten, Mundverpflegung bis einschl. —
   ~~Reichsurlauberkarten (Reise- und Gaststättenmarken) — bei Urlaub bis zu 3 Tagen — bis einschl.~~ 9.9.44.
   Feinseife bis einschl. August 44, Rasierseife bis einschl. Oktober 44
8. ~~Hat als Teilnehmer an der Wehrmachtverpflegung während des Aufenthalts am Urlaubsort vom~~ ab. 10.9.44.
   ~~bis~~ einschl. Anspruch auf ~~Reichsurlauberkarten~~ Lebensmittelkarten von der zuständigen Kartenausgabestelle.
   Die Aushändigung hat die Kartenausgabestelle hierunter zu bescheinigen.
9. Inhaber besitzt eine Kontrollkarte »M« oder Inhaber hat Anspruch auf einen Kontrollausweis für den Einkauf von Tabakwaren für die Zeit vom ... bis ... = ... Tage*).
10. Dieser Urlaubsschein ist nach Rückkehr vom Urlaub der Wehrmachtdienststelle abzugeben.
11. **Besondere Vermerke** (z. B. über das Tragen bürgerlicher Kleidung am Urlaubsort u. ä.):

Entlassung zum Heimatsort

(Einträge zu Ziffer 11 sind hier durch Unterschrift des Einheitsführers besonders zu bescheinigen.)

Hauptmann u. Batterie-Chef (Unterschrift des Einheitsführers zu Ziffer 6—9)

Bescheinigung über Meldung am Urlaubsort:

gemeldet am

(Ort, Datum, Stempel oder Unterschrift)

*) Nichtzutreffendes streichen.

Bescheinigung der Kartenausgabestelle:

Reichsurlauberkarten sind ausgehändigt für die Zeit

vom ... bis ... einschl.

(Ort, Datum, Stempel oder Unterschrift)

Figure 2-76. As the war dragged on, manpower reserves fell short, as one can see in this pass for Luftwaffe-Helfer Rolf Schmöcke of the Hitler Jugend (HJ), the Hitler Youth. Young Rolf was probably about 16 at the time; many boys at that age were already being called up into the Wehrmacht. This pass is marked Entlassungsurlaub, Discharge Leave; he was likely being discharged from his duties in the Hitler Youth to be drafted. (A5)

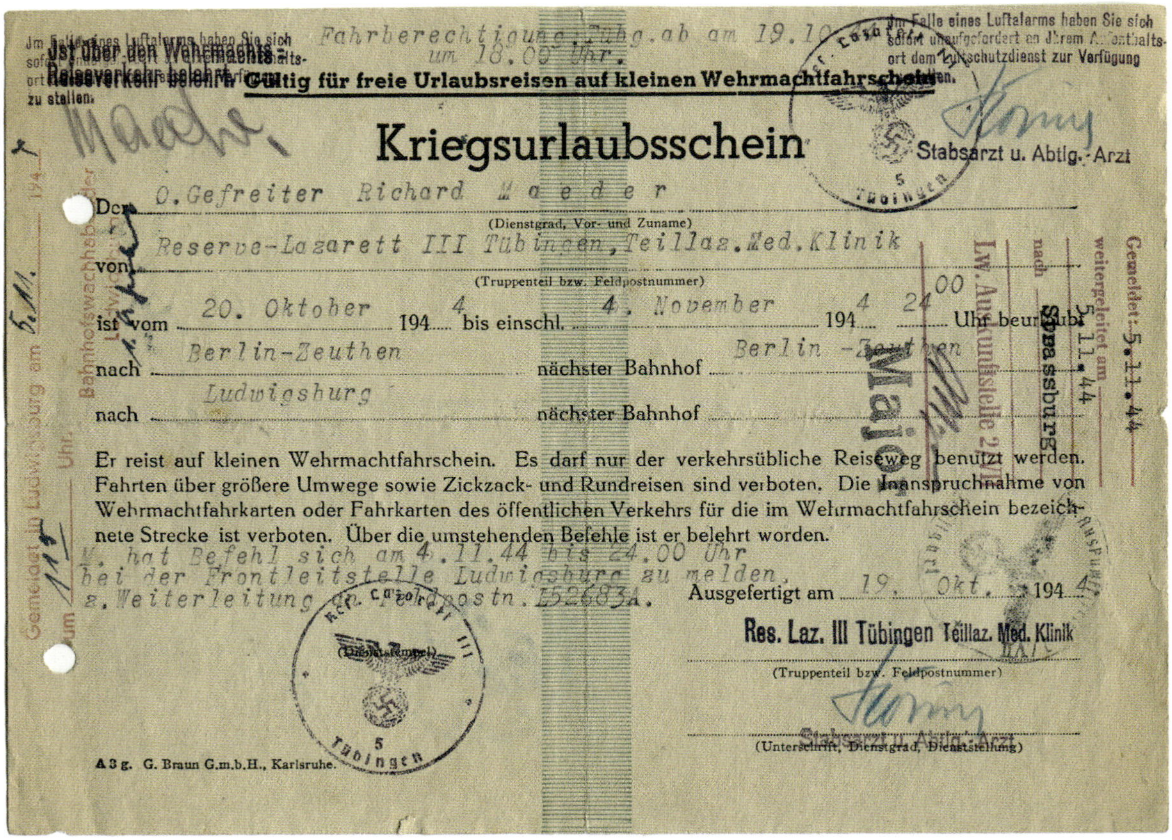

Im Falle eines Luftalarms haben Sie sich sofort unaufgefordert an Ihrem Aufenthaltsort dem Luftschutzdienst zur Verfügung zu stellen.

Ist über den Wehrmachts-Reiseverkehr belehrt

Fahrberechtigung: Tübg. ab am 19.10. um 18.00 Uhr.

Gültig für freie Urlaubsreisen auf kleinen Wehrmachtfahrschein

Kriegsurlaubsschein

Stabsarzt u. Abtlg.-Arzt

Der O.Gefreiter Richard Maeder
(Dienstgrad, Vor- und Zuname)

von Reserve-Lazarett III Tübingen, Teillaz. Med. Klinik
(Truppenteil bzw. Feldpostnummer)

ist vom 20. Oktober 1944 bis einschl. 4. November 1944 24.00 Uhr beurlaubt

nach Berlin-Zeuthen nächster Bahnhof Berlin-Zeuthen

nach Ludwigsburg nächster Bahnhof

Er reist auf kleinen Wehrmachtfahrschein. Es darf nur der verkehrsübliche Reiseweg benutzt werden. Fahrten über größere Umwege sowie Zickzack- und Rundreisen sind verboten. Die Inanspruchnahme von Wehrmachtfahrkarten oder Fahrkarten des öffentlichen Verkehrs für die im Wehrmachtfahrschein bezeichnete Strecke ist verboten. Über die umstehenden Befehle ist er belehrt worden.

M. hat Befehl sich am 4.11.44 bis 24.00 Uhr bei der Frontleitstelle Ludwigsburg zu melden, z. Weiterleitung an Feldpostn. L52683A.

Ausgefertigt am 19. Okt. 1944

Res. Laz. III Tübingen Teillaz. Med. Klinik
(Truppenteil bzw. Feldpostnummer)

Stabsarzt u. Abtlg.-Arzt
(Unterschrift, Dienstgrad, Dienststellung)

A 3 g. G. Braun G.m.b.H., Karlsruhe.

Gemeldet am 5.11. um 1 Uhr. Bahnhofswachhabender

Lw. Auffangstelle 2/VII Major

nach Strassburg weitergeleitet am 5.11.44

Gemeldet: 5.11.44

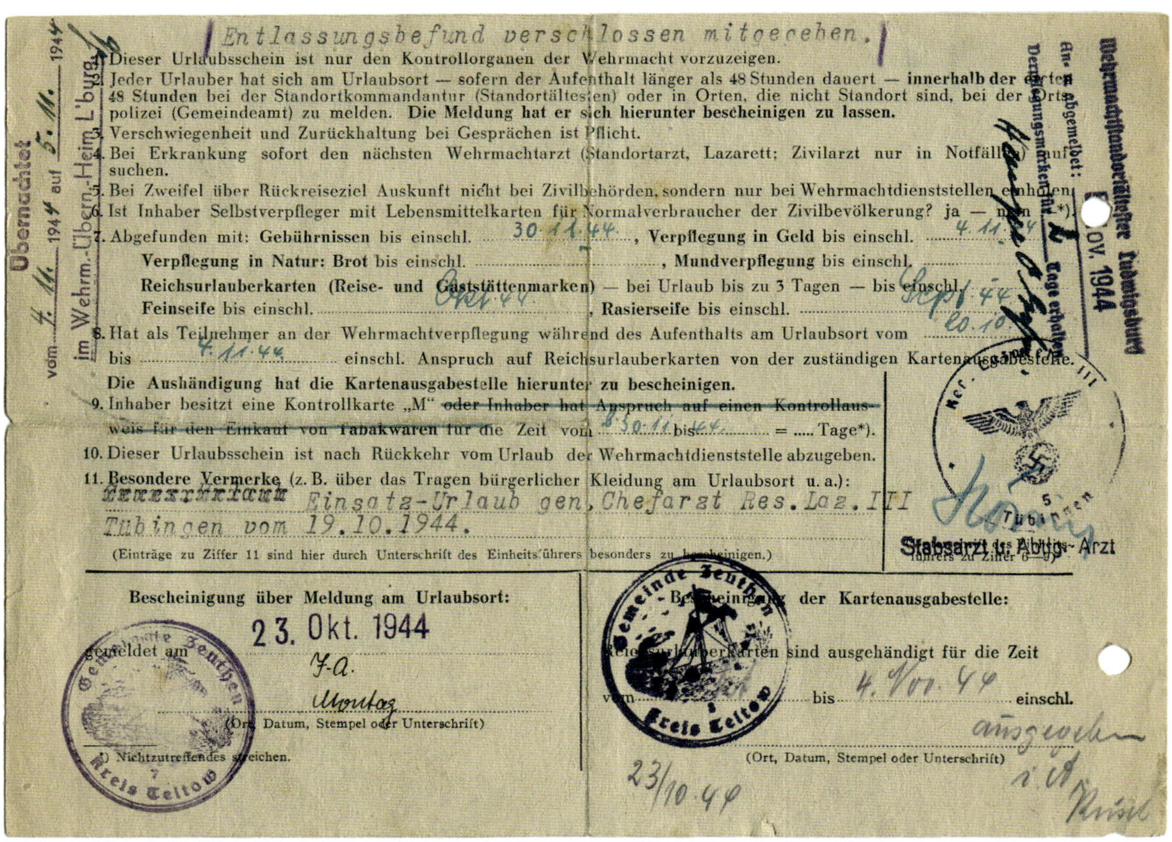

Entlassungsbefund verschlossen mitgegeben.

1. Dieser Urlaubsschein ist nur den Kontrollorganen der Wehrmacht vorzuzeigen.
2. Jeder Urlauber hat sich am Urlaubsort — sofern der Aufenthalt länger als 48 Stunden dauert — **innerhalb der ersten 48 Stunden** bei der Standortkommandantur (Standortältesten) oder in Orten, die nicht Standort sind, bei der Ortspolizei (Gemeindeamt) zu melden. **Die Meldung hat er sich hierunter bescheinigen zu lassen.**
3. Verschwiegenheit und Zurückhaltung bei Gesprächen ist Pflicht.
4. Bei Erkrankung sofort den nächsten Wehrmachtarzt (Standortarzt, Lazarett; Zivilarzt nur in Notfällen) aufsuchen.
5. Bei Zweifel über Rückreiseziel Auskunft nicht bei Zivilbehörden, sondern nur bei Wehrmachtdienststellen einholen.
6. Ist Inhaber Selbstverpfleger mit Lebensmittelkarten für Normalverbraucher der Zivilbevölkerung? ja — nein*)
7. Abgefunden mit: Gebührnissen bis einschl. 30.11.44, Verpflegung in Geld bis einschl. 4.11.
   Verpflegung in Natur: Brot bis einschl. ......, Mundverpflegung bis einschl. ......
   Reichsurlauberkarten (Reise- und Gaststättenmarken) — bei Urlaub bis zu 3 Tagen — bis einschl. ......
   Feinseife bis einschl. Okt. 44, Rasierseife bis einschl. Sept. 44
8. Hat als Teilnehmer an der Wehrmachtverpflegung während des Aufenthalts am Urlaubsort vom 20.10. bis 4.11.44 einschl. Anspruch auf Reichsurlauberkarten von der zuständigen Kartenausgabestelle.
   Die Aushändigung hat die Kartenausgabestelle hierunter zu bescheinigen.
9. Inhaber besitzt eine Kontrollkarte „M" ~~oder Inhaber hat Anspruch auf einen Kontrollausweis für den Einkauf von Tabakwaren für die~~ Zeit vom ...... bis ...... = ... Tage*).
10. Dieser Urlaubsschein ist nach Rückkehr vom Urlaub der Wehrmachtdienststelle abzugeben.
11. Besondere Vermerke (z. B. über das Tragen bürgerlicher Kleidung am Urlaubsort u. a.):
    Einsatz-Urlaub gen. Chefarzt Res. Laz. III Tübingen vom 19.10.1944.
    (Einträge zu Ziffer 11 sind hier durch Unterschrift des Einheitsführers besonders zu bescheinigen.)

Stabsarzt u. Abtlg.-Arzt

Bescheinigung über Meldung am Urlaubsort:

gemeldet am 23. Okt. 1944

I.A.

(Ort, Datum, Stempel oder Unterschrift)

*) Nichtzutreffendes streichen.

Bescheinigung der Kartenausgabestelle:

Reichsurlauberkarten sind ausgehändigt für die Zeit vom ...... bis 4. Nov. 44 einschl.

ausgegeben i. A.

(Ort, Datum, Stempel oder Unterschrift)

23/10.44

Übernachtet vom 4.11.1944 auf 5.11. im Wehrm.-Übern.-Heim L'burg.

Wehrmachtstandortältester Tübingen

Figure 2-77. Obergefreiter Richard Mäder (spelled in this document without the typical umlaut) was issued this pass when he was discharged from the Reserve-Lazarett in Tübingen through Ludwigsburg and on to his next duty station with Flieger Regiment 91 (L52683). Note that the green stripe is composed of a number of smaller green stripes; the printer apparently misunderstood the instructions given in the regulations, though this mistake was not severe enough to cause the order form to be rejected. (A5)

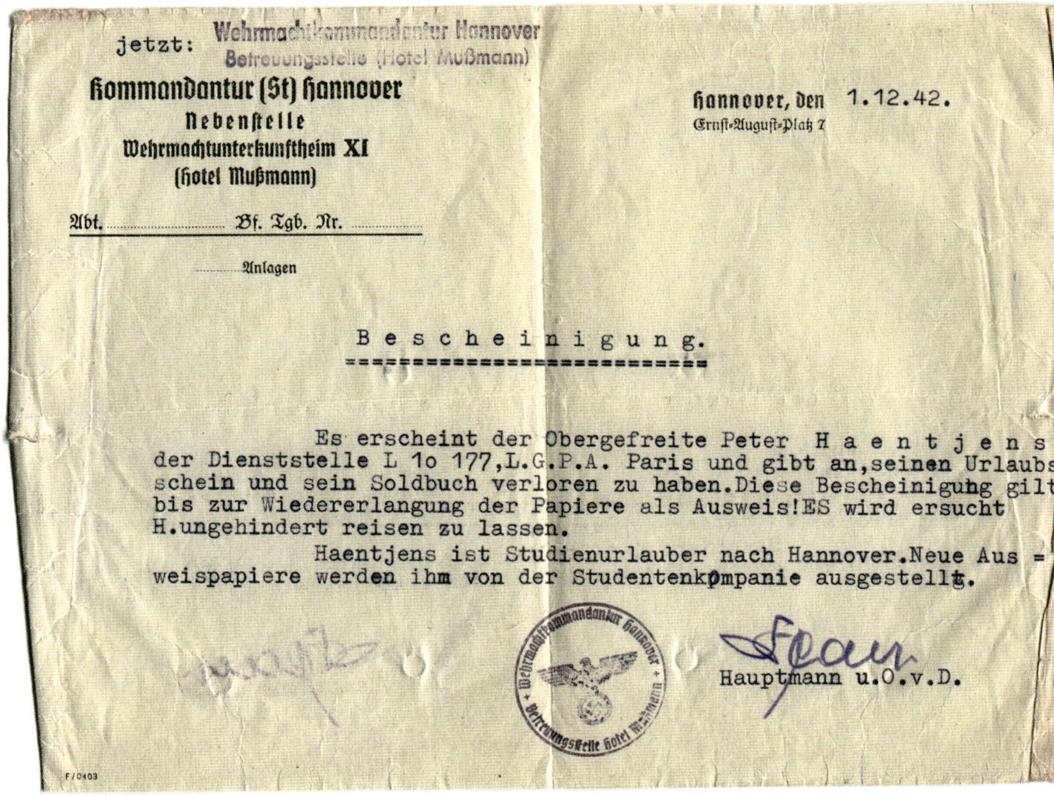

jetzt: Wehrmachtkommandantur Hannover
Betreuungsstelle (Hotel Mußmann)

Kommandantur (St) Hannover
Nebenstelle
Wehrmachtunterkunftheim XI
(Hotel Mußmann)

Hannover, den 1.12.42.
Ernst-August-Platz 7

Abt. .... Bf. Tgb. Nr. ....

.... Anlagen

Bescheinigung.

Es erscheint der Obergefreite Peter H a e n t j e n s der Dienststelle L 1o 177, L.G.P.A. Paris und gibt an, seinen Urlaubsschein und sein Soldbuch verloren zu haben. Diese Bescheinigung gilt bis zur Wiedererlangung der Papiere als Ausweis! ES wird ersucht H. ungehindert reisen zu lassen.

Haentjens ist Studienurlauber nach Hannover. Neue Ausweispapiere werden ihm von der Studentenkompanie ausgestellt.

Hauptmann u.O.v.D.

F/0403

Figure 2-78. As can be expected, paperwork would sometimes go missing. This Bescheingung (Certificate) attests to that fact, noting that Luftwaffe Obergefreite (sic) Peter Häntjens lost his travel papers and Soldbuch while on leave, and that this paper shall act as his identity papers until they can be properly replaced. (A5)

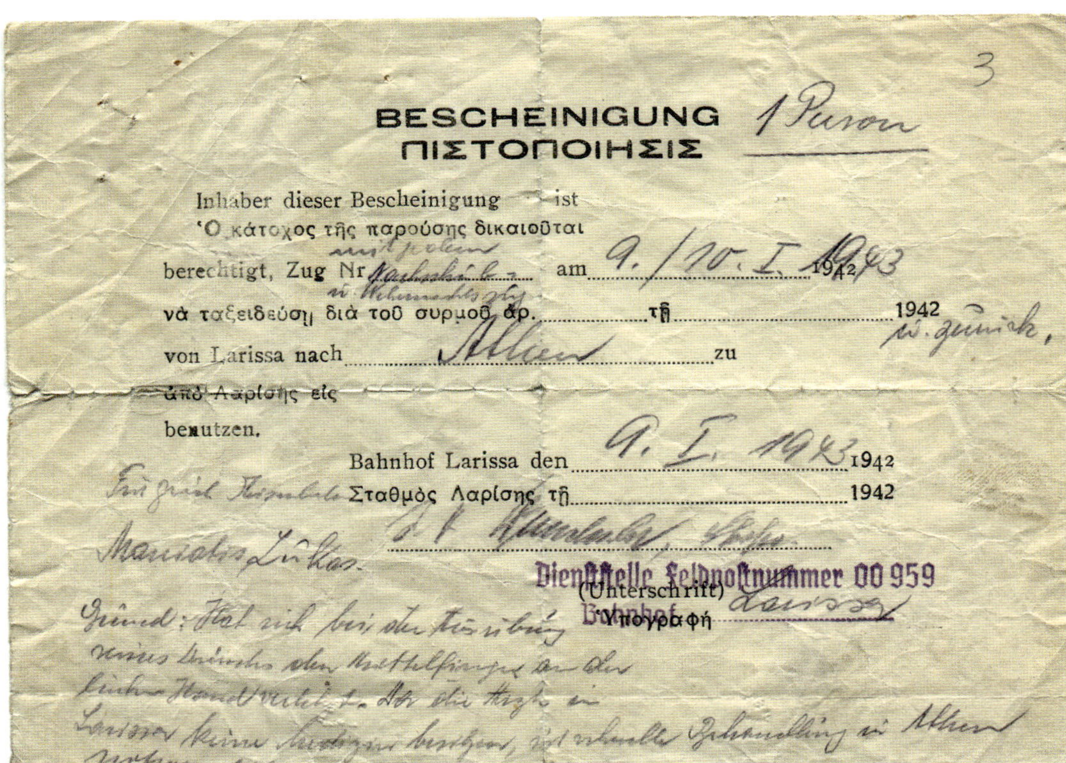

BESCHEINIGUNG
ΠΙΣΤΟΠΟΙΗΣΙΣ

Inhaber dieser Bescheinigung ist
Ὁ κάτοχος τῆς παρούσης δικαιοῦται
berechtigt, Zug Nr. .... am 1942
νὰ ταξειδεύσῃ διὰ τοῦ συρμοῦ ἀρ. .... τῇ 1942
von Larissa nach .... zu
ἀπὸ Λαρίσης εἰς
benutzen.

Bahnhof Larissa den 1942
Σταθμὸς Λαρίσης τῇ 1942

(Unterschrift)
Ὑπογραφή

Dienststelle Feldpostnummer 00 959

Figure 2-79. This bilingual German-Greek certificate indicates that the bearer (no name is indicated, though a name does appear in pencil on the side: Maniatis Linkas) is permitted to travel from Larissa to Athens on January 9-10, 1942, issued by the military field railway office Feldeisenbahn-Betriebsamt 10 (FPN 00959). (A5)

Travel Passes

A soldier traveling within the *Reich*, like anyone else, was required to prove that such travel was paid for, either by himself or by the *Wehrmacht*. Civilians could buy a train ticket, as could soldiers traveling at their own expense (though in such cases, soldiers could purchase a *Wehrmacht-Fahrkarte* ticket at reduced rates). Whenever the *Wehrmacht* required a soldier to travel, it was the military that paid the bill, and four different forms were used to indicate this.

The *Wehrmachtfahrschein* (Wehrmacht Travel Pass) was the first of these documents. The *Wehrmachtfahrschein* was a two page form folded to A6 size (hinged either at the top—A5 size—and folded to A6, or hinged at the side to create a form 105 mm x 296 mm and folded to A6), and was used to identify and permit a small number of troops to travel. Spaces were provided on the front to indicate the number of officers authorized to travel in second class cars and another space to indicate the number of soldiers traveling in third class. At the top right corner was the phrase "*Gilt als Fahrausweis*," meaning that the pass also served as a ticket.

Figure 2-80. These sailors from one of the many Kriegsmarine Kriegschule (Naval Training School, barely discernable on their hat tallies) await their train to return from leave. The two signs alert travellers to be wary of pickpockets (Taschendieb: "pocket thieves") and to ring the bell for baggage handlers.

Gilt als Fahrausweis!

Wehrmachtfahrschein, Teil 2

(Bei Beendigung der Reise abzugeben)

Personenzug*) / Eilzug*) / Schnellzug*)

für ./. Offiziere usw. in der 2. Klasse

für ein Unteroffiziere und Mannschaften in der 3. Klasse

zur einmaligen Fahrt

von Crimmitschau

nach Orleans

über

Das Fahrgeld ist zu stunden.

Ausgefertigt am 5. 7. 1940

(Dienststempel)

Dienststelle Feldpost-Nr. 21760

(Truppenteil usw.)

Auf der Rückseite, Namen der Reisenden und den Zweck der Reise kurz angeben.

(Unterschrift, Dienstgrad, Dienststellung)

Leutnant u. Adjutant

*) Nichtzutreffendes streichen

Form. Nr. 599 a. Gabler & Köhler, Leipzig N 22

Figure 2-81. A Wehrmachfahrschein (Military Ticket) was valid for a number of officers or soldiers, but in this case a single Soldat (Private Schaffrath) was issued this form to travel from Crimmitschau in Germany to Orleans, France.

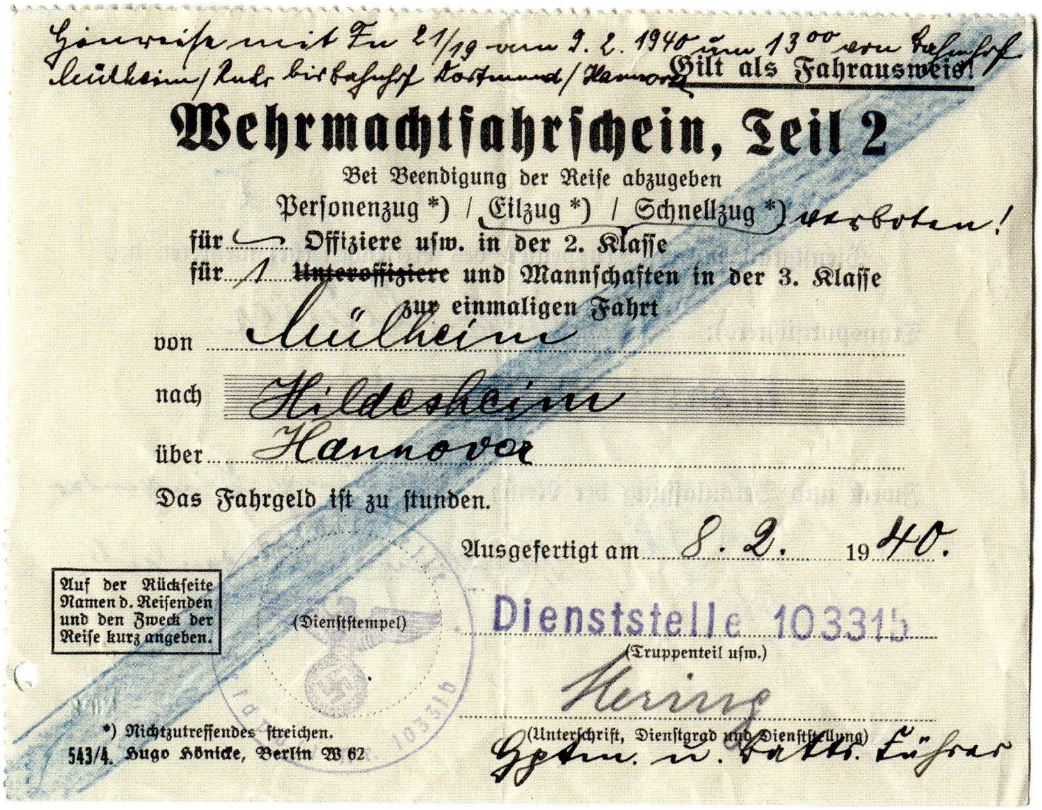

Gilt als Fahrausweis!

Wehrmachtfahrschein, Teil 2

Bei Beendigung der Reise abzugeben

Personenzug *) / Eilzug *) / Schnellzug *) verboten!

für — Offiziere usw. in der 2. Klasse

für 1 ~~Unteroffiziere~~ und Mannschaften in der 3. Klasse

zur einmaligen Fahrt

von Mülheim

nach Hildesheim

über Hannover

Das Fahrgeld ist zu stunden.

Ausgefertigt am 8. 2. 1940.

Auf der Rückseite Namen d. Reisenden und den Zweck der Reise kurz angeben.

(Dienststempel)

Dienststelle 10331b

(Truppenteil usw.)

(Unterschrift, Dienstgrad und Dienststellung)

*) Nichtzutreffendes streichen.

543/4. Hugo Hönicke, Berlin W 62

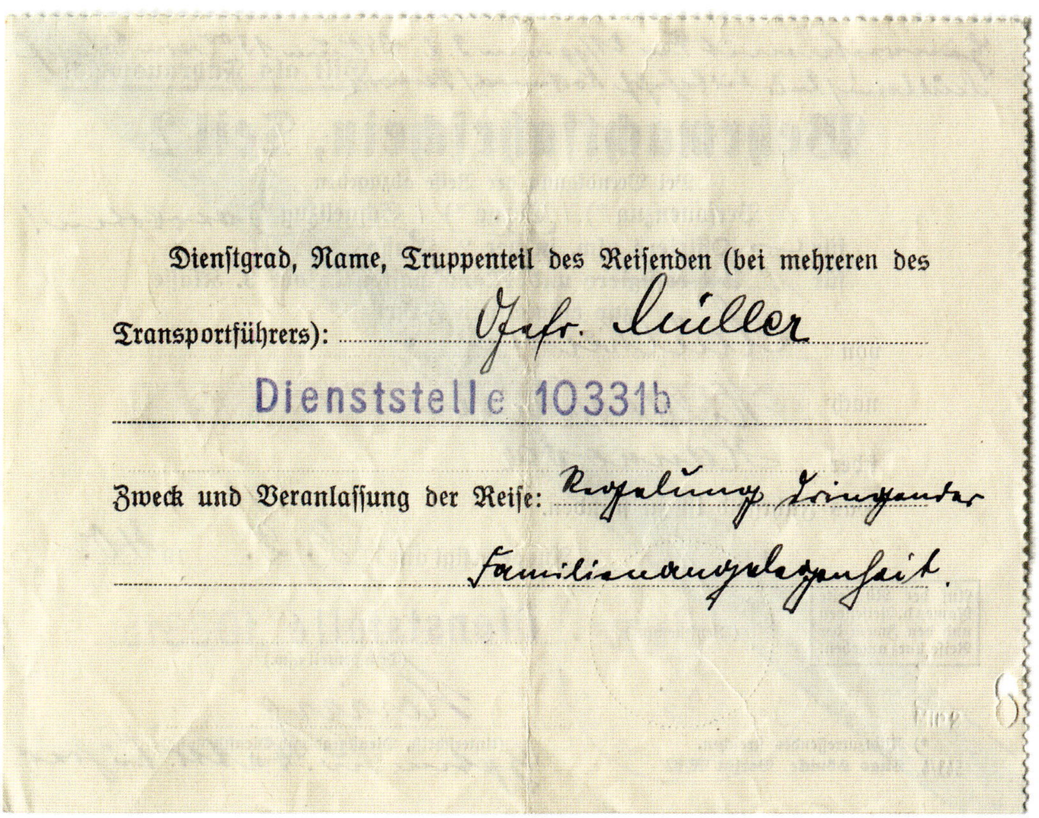

Dienstgrad, Name, Truppenteil des Reisenden (bei mehreren des Transportführers): Gefr. Müller

Dienststelle 10331b

Zweck und Veranlassung der Reise: Regelung dringender Familienangelegenheit.

Figure 2-82. Although not intended for this sort of use, this Wehrmachtfahrschein has been pressed into service as a Kleine Wehrmachtfahrschein (see figure 2-92 et. seq.). A resourceful clerk has added a blue line with a colored pencil to indicate that this ticket shall be used under those travel conditions; note that use of the ticket on Eilzug and Schnellzug (swifter trains with fewer stops) are "verboten!"

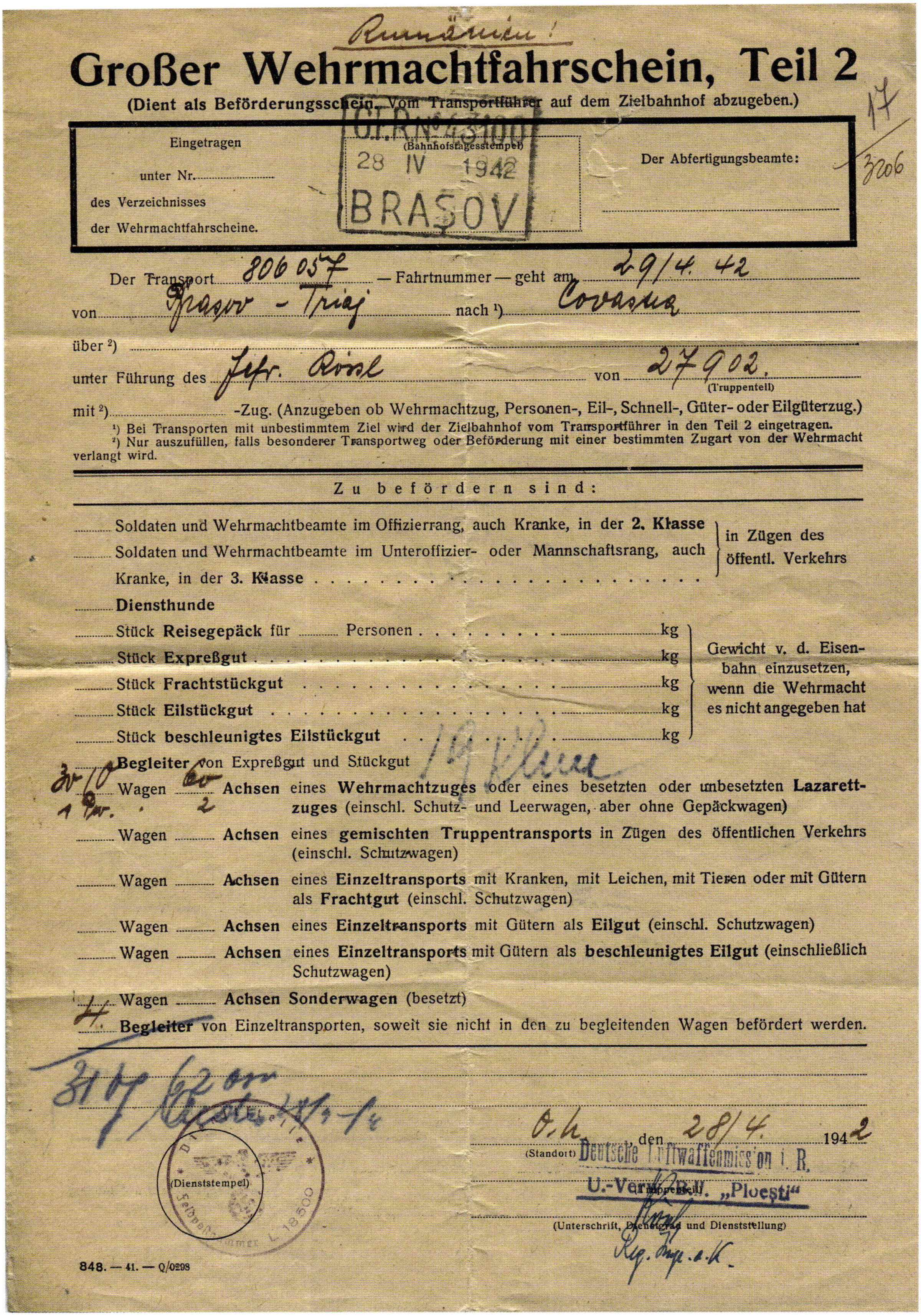

Rumänien!

Großer Wehrmachtfahrschein, Teil 2

(Dient als Beförderungsschein. Vom Transportführer auf dem Zielbahnhof abzugeben.)

17 / 3206

Eingetragen unter Nr. .... des Verzeichnisses der Wehrmachtfahrscheine.	(Bahnhofstagesstempel) CFR Nº 43100 28 IV 1942 BRAŞOV	Der Abfertigungsbeamte: ....

Der Transport 806 057 — Fahrtnummer — geht am 29/4. 42

von Brasov - Triaj nach ¹) Covasna

über ²) ....

unter Führung des Gefr. Rösl von 27902. (Truppenteil)

mit ²) .... -Zug. (Anzugeben ob Wehrmachtzug, Personen-, Eil-, Schnell-, Güter- oder Eilgüterzug.)

¹) Bei Transporten mit unbestimmtem Ziel wird der Zielbahnhof vom Transportführer in den Teil 2 eingetragen.
²) Nur auszufüllen, falls besonderer Transportweg oder Beförderung mit einer bestimmten Zugart von der Wehrmacht verlangt wird.

Zu befördern sind:

.... Soldaten und Wehrmachtbeamte im Offizierrang, auch Kranke, in der **2. Klasse** } in Zügen des öffentl. Verkehrs
.... Soldaten und Wehrmachtbeamte im Unteroffizier- oder Mannschaftsrang, auch Kranke, in der **3. Klasse** } in Zügen des öffentl. Verkehrs

.... **Diensthunde**

.... Stück **Reisegepäck** für .... Personen .... kg
.... Stück **Expreßgut** .... kg
.... Stück **Frachtstückgut** .... kg
.... Stück **Eilstückgut** .... kg
.... Stück **beschleunigtes Eilstückgut** .... kg
} Gewicht v. d. Eisenbahn einzusetzen, wenn die Wehrmacht es nicht angegeben hat

19 Pkw.

.... **Begleiter** von Expreßgut und Stückgut

30 / 1 Pkw. Wagen 60 / 2 **Achsen** eines **Wehrmachtzuges** oder eines besetzten oder unbesetzten **Lazarettzuges** (einschl. Schutz- und Leerwagen, aber ohne Gepäckwagen)

.... Wagen .... **Achsen** eines **gemischten Truppentransports** in Zügen des öffentlichen Verkehrs (einschl. Schutzwagen)

.... Wagen .... **Achsen** eines **Einzeltransports** mit Kranken, mit Leichen, mit Tieren oder mit Gütern als **Frachtgut** (einschl. Schutzwagen)

.... Wagen .... **Achsen** eines **Einzeltransports** mit Gütern als **Eilgut** (einschl. Schutzwagen)

.... Wagen .... **Achsen** eines **Einzeltransports** mit Gütern als **beschleunigtes Eilgut** (einschließlich Schutzwagen)

.... Wagen .... **Achsen Sonderwagen** (besetzt)

4 **Begleiter** von Einzeltransporten, soweit sie nicht in den zu begleitenden Wagen befördert werden.

31 / 62 ...

(Dienststempel)

O.U., den 28/4. 1942
(Standort) Deutsche Luftwaffenmission i. R.
U.-Verw. B.V. „Ploesti"
(Unterschrift, Dienstgrad und Dienststellung)
Reg. Insp. a.K.

848. — 41. — Q/0298

Figure 2-83. This Grosser Wehrmachtfahrschein (Large Military Train Ticket) was used whenever large numbers of troops or equipment was being transported. This example shows a shipment by 31 military railway cars in April 28, 1942, bound from Brasov to Covasna in Romania, authorized by the Deutsche Luftwaffemission in Rumänien, German Air Force Mission in Romania, based in Ploesti. (A4)

Bescheinigung des Abfertigungsbeamten

Im Beisein des Zugsführers und des Transportführers ist festgestellt worden:

a) daß die Stärke des Transports mit den Angaben im Wehrmachtschein übereinstimmt,

b) daß die vorgeschriebenen Wagenausrüstungsstücke, die Ladegeräte und Lademittel vollzählig und in gutem Zustand vorhanden sind.

(Nichtzutreffendes ist zu streichen)

...., den .... 194....

C.F.R. № 43100 28 IV 1942 BRAŞOV

Der Abfertigungsbeamte

....

Bescheinigung des Transportführers

über Aenderungen in der Stärke des Transports oder über Aenderungen im Transportweg:

....

(Unterschrift des Transportführers)

Die Richtigkeit vorstehender Bescheinigung wird anerkannt:

Der Abgangsbahnhof
Der Zugsführer

....

(Unterschrift)

Abfahrt am .... 194.... ......Uhr ....Min.
Ankunft am .... 194.... ......Uhr ....Min.
(Vom Transportführer auszufüllen)

The heading of the form noted *Teil 1* or *Teil 2*, the page number, one and two, and was used for travel to and from a destination. Both pages were filled out, front and back, with identical information, normally with the use of carbon paper, though examples do exist of *Teil 2* having been filled out by hand. Upon departure, the pages would be separated; page one would be kept by the *Reichsbahn*, and page two would be kept by the soldier to allow him to return. A soldier was supposed to turn page two in at the end of his return travel (*Bei Beendung der Reise abzugeben* - At the end of this trip, please return this form), but whether it was because of souvenir hoarding *Soldaten* or complacent conductors, many still exist.

The *Wehrmachtfahrschein* also noted for which trains travel was approved, in this case, *Personenzug* (Civilian Passenger Train), *Eilzug* (Fast Train with a few swift stops), or *Schnellzug* (Fast or Express Train with limited stops). Riding on any of these would have been space permitting; if the train was sold out, the soldier would have to wait for the next available one, unless some well-meaning civilian relinquished his place.

The back of the document was kept very simple; the only information required was rank, name, the soldier's unit, and the purpose for the trip.

A second form was the *Grosser Wehrmachtfahrschein* (Large *Wehrmacht* Travel Pass - *see previous pages*) and it was appropriately named, being A4 size, four times the size of the *Wehrmachtfahrschein*. This was also a two page document, subject to the same conditions as the *Wehrmachtfahrschein* (i.e., presenting page one for the outbound trip and page two for the return, provided one was required).

The *Grosser Wehrmachtfahrschein* served as a travel ticket for large numbers of men, usually a platoon or more, or a significant amount of heavy equipment. The types of trains on which travel was authorized was also indicated, and consisted of *Wehrmachtzug* (Military Transport Train), *Personenzug*, *Eilzug*, *Schnellzug*, *Güterzug* (Freight Train), and *Eilgüterzug* (Freight Train with few, swift stops).

It had spaces provided to indicate the number of officers in second class and sergeants and men in third class, but it also had a space to note the number of *Diensthunde* (Service Dogs).

The larger portion of the form was reserved for freight information, particularly the personal gear and equipment of the soldiers traveling. Spaces were provided to list the overall weight of travel packs (such as backpacks and rucksacks), express goods, and so on. Below that was a segment to be completed to identify rolling stock allocated by the number of cars and axels (*Achsen*), and on what style of train: *Lazarettzuges* (Hospital Train), *Truppentransports* (Troop Trains), *Einzeltransports* (Individualized Loads), and so forth.

The bottom of the form was available for the *Truppenteil* and officer's signature authorizing the transportation of the men and/or equipment, along with the *Dienststempel* of the unit.

The back is reserved for certifications and notations by the *Reichsbahn*. It was divided into two sections. The first was reserved for the preparing departure station to certify that the information on the front of the form was correct, and that the cars in question were serviceable and in good condition. The second, larger area allowed the *Transportführer* (literally, Transport Leader – loading officer) to note or otherwise certify any particular conditions or situations out of the ordinary.

Naturally, if the Third Reich created a *Grosser* (Large) *Wehrmachtfahrschein*, there had to be a *Kleiner* (Small) *Wehrmachtfahrschein*. This is the travel ticket most often acquired by collectors because so many were produced and used. It is identical in size to the *Wehrmachtfahrschein*, namely a sheet hinged at either the top or side and folded to A6 size. This form was generally reserved for a single *Soldat* or small group of soldiers to travel.

There are three variations of the *Kleiner Wehrmachtfahrschein*, one with no stripe and two with different colored stripes, one blue and one red. The stripe, or lack thereof, indicates whether travel is authorized at *Wehrmacht* expense (striped) or at one's own expense (no stripe).

The top of the *Kleiner Wehrmachtfahrschein* indicated upon which trains travel was authorized. In the case of the form with no stripe, all trains were permissible, depending on available space ("*Gültig für alle Züge, auch Eil- und D-Züge*" – Valid for all trains, including fast trains with limited stops and D-trains or *Durchgangszug* – Through Train).

The front of all three forms, both *Teil 1* and *Teil 2*, had spaces provided to indicate the number of people traveling in first, second, or third class, depending on which was authorized. Below that was a space to indicate the number of *Diensthunden* accompanying the soldier, as well as the number of pieces of luggage authorized to be transported (which was rarely filled out).

At the middle of the form was room to indicate departure and arrival stations, as well as an additional blank to indicate a transfer station if needed. The bottom was reserved for date stamp, *Dienststempel*, *Truppenteil*, and officer's signature and *Stempel*.

This information is standard, save for the legend at the top regarding authorized trains, which varied on the striped forms.

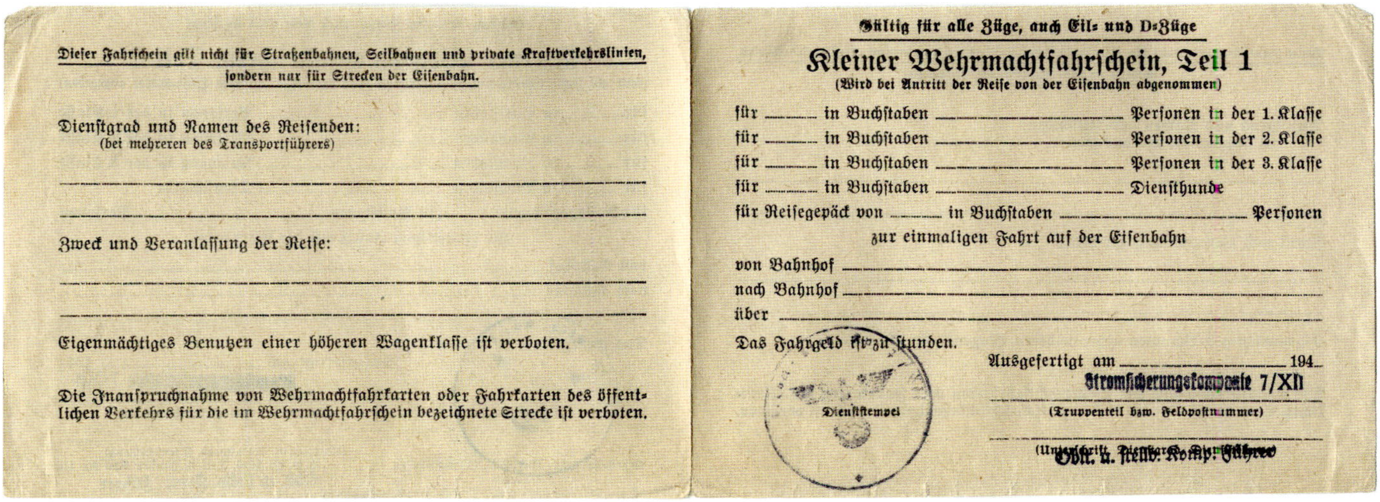

Dieser Fahrschein gilt nicht für Straßenbahnen, Seilbahnen und private Kraftverkehrslinien, sondern nur für Strecken der Eisenbahn.

Dienstgrad und Namen des Reisenden:
(bei mehreren des Transportführers)

Zweck und Veranlassung der Reise:

Eigenmächtiges Benutzen einer höheren Wagenklasse ist verboten.

Die Inanspruchnahme von Wehrmachtfahrkarten oder Fahrkarten des öffentlichen Verkehrs für die im Wehrmachtfahrschein bezeichnete Strecke ist verboten.

Gültig für alle Züge, auch Eil- und D-Züge

Kleiner Wehrmachtfahrschein, Teil 1
(Wird bei Antritt der Reise von der Eisenbahn abgenommen)

für ______ in Buchstaben ______ Personen in der 1. Klasse
für ______ in Buchstaben ______ Personen in der 2. Klasse
für ______ in Buchstaben ______ Personen in der 3. Klasse
für ______ in Buchstaben ______ Diensthunde
für Reisegepäck von ______ in Buchstaben ______ Personen
zur einmaligen Fahrt auf der Eisenbahn
von Bahnhof ______
nach Bahnhof ______
über ______
Das Fahrgeld ist zu stunden.

Dienststempel

Ausgefertigt am ______ 194_
Stromsicherungskompanie 7/XII
(Truppenteil bzw. Feldpostnummer)
(Unterschrift, Dienstgrad, Dienststellung)
Oblt. u. stellv. Komp.-Führer

Figure 2-83. The Kleiner Wehrmachtfahrschein (Small Military Ticket) with no stripe; this ticket is valid for all trains including Eilzüge and D-Züge (Swift Trains and "D" Trains). The front and back, which made up pages 1 and 2, were identical; often the pages were filled out separately, but a piece of carbon paper could be inserted between the two halves prior to being filled out by typewriter. ($4^{1}/_{8}$" x $11^{3}/_{4}$")

Figure 2-84. A prewar photo of a Mercedes Omnibus in the Sudeten city of Rumburg (now the Czech city of Rumburk), showing that it's more than just a truck but not quite as much as a bus.

The blue-striped *Kleiner Wehrmachtfahrschein* authorized free travel for distances in excess of 200 km, so travel on the faster *Schnellzüge* (Fast or Express Trains) was authorized. The form also allowed soldiers to upgrade at their own expense. The *Soldat* was not allowed to use the *Kleiner Wehrmachtfahrschein* to travel for free on the *Strassenbahn*, *Seilbahn*, or *Omnibus* (Street Trains or Trolleys, Cable Cars, or Semi-busses) once he had arrived at his destination.

The red-striped *Kleiner Wehrmachtfahrschein* authorized free travel for distances less than 200 km, so travel was restricted to the slower *Personenzüge* (Passenger Trains). Passage on *Schnellzüge* was permitted, but only in specially marked cars for *Wehrmacht* personnel, and even then, only when space was available. Like the blue-striped form, free travel was limited to the trains themselves, and not valid for local transit once one had arrived.

The backs of the forms required the same information to be filled out: the rank and name of the person traveling, as well as the purpose for the trip. Additionally, information and restrictions were included on the backs of the striped forms that delineated the exact trains and cars available for free travel.

Towards the end of the war, as resources and travel opportunities became scarcer and life more difficult, the *Wehrmacht* sought to lessen the stress of travel throughout the *Reich*, not to mention the draw on resources and manpower required to fill out multiple forms. The OKW (*Oberkommando der Wehrmacht* - Central Command of the *Wehrmacht*) created a form late in 1943 that combined the *Kriegsurlaubsschein*, the *Sonderausweis*

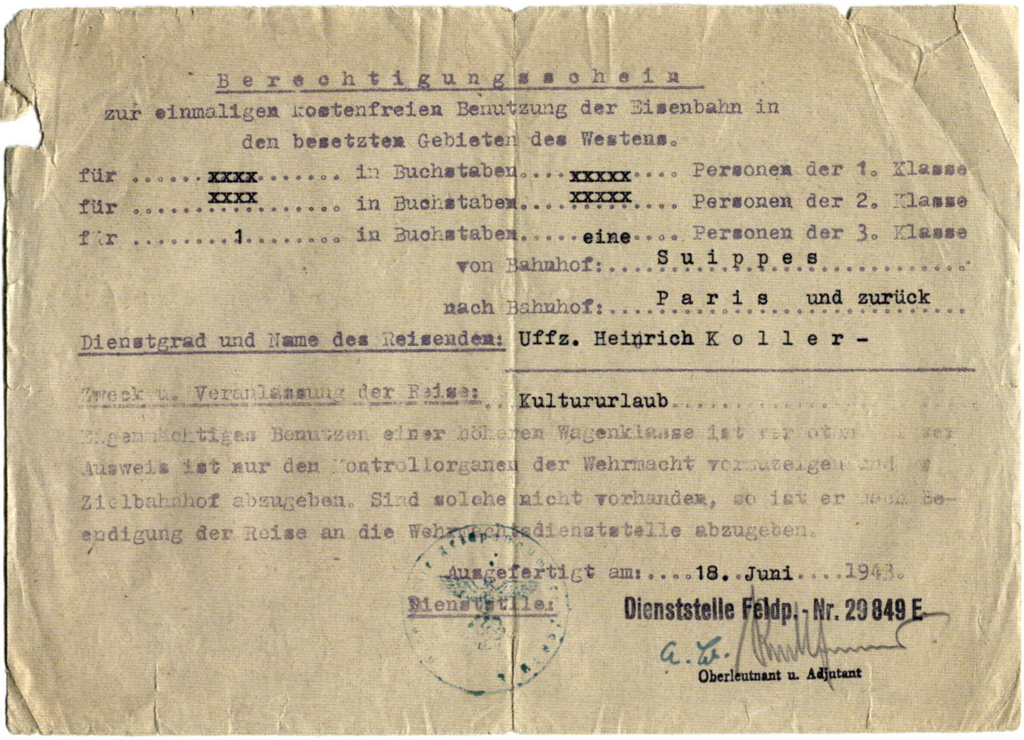

Berechtigungsschein
zur einmaligen kostenfreien Benutzung der Eisenbahn in
den besetzten Gebieten des Westens.
für ......xxxx....... in Buchstaben.....xxxxx.... Personen der 1. Klasse
für ......xxxx....... in Buchstaben.....xxxxx.... Personen der 2. Klasse
für ....1........ in Buchstaben.....eine.... Personen der 3. Klasse
von Bahnhof: ...Suippes...
nach Bahnhof: ...Paris und zurück...
Dienstgrad und Name des Reisenden: Uffz. Heinrich Koller -
Zweck u. Veranlassung der Reise: Kultururlaub
Eigenmächtiges Benutzen einer höheren Wagenklasse ist verboten. Der Ausweis ist nur den Kontrollorganen der Wehrmacht vorzuzeigen und am Zielbahnhof abzugeben. Sind solche nicht vorhanden, so ist er nach Beendigung der Reise an die Wehrmachtdienststelle abzugeben.
Ausgefertigt am: ....18. Juni....1943.
Dienststelle: Dienststelle Feldp.-Nr. 29 849 E
a. W. [signature]
Oberleutnant u. Adjutant

Figure 2-85. Unteroffizier Heinrich Koller used this mimeographed Berechtigungsschein (Certificate of Eligibility) in lieu of a Wehrmachtfahrschein to travel from Artillery School III (FPN 29849) in Suippes to Paris on Kultururlaub ("Cultural" Leave). (A5)

Figure 2-86. A blank military ticket with the blue stripe, which limited travel to specific trains. This particular form was printed in Heidelberg in July of 1942 (note the legend on the lower left corner).

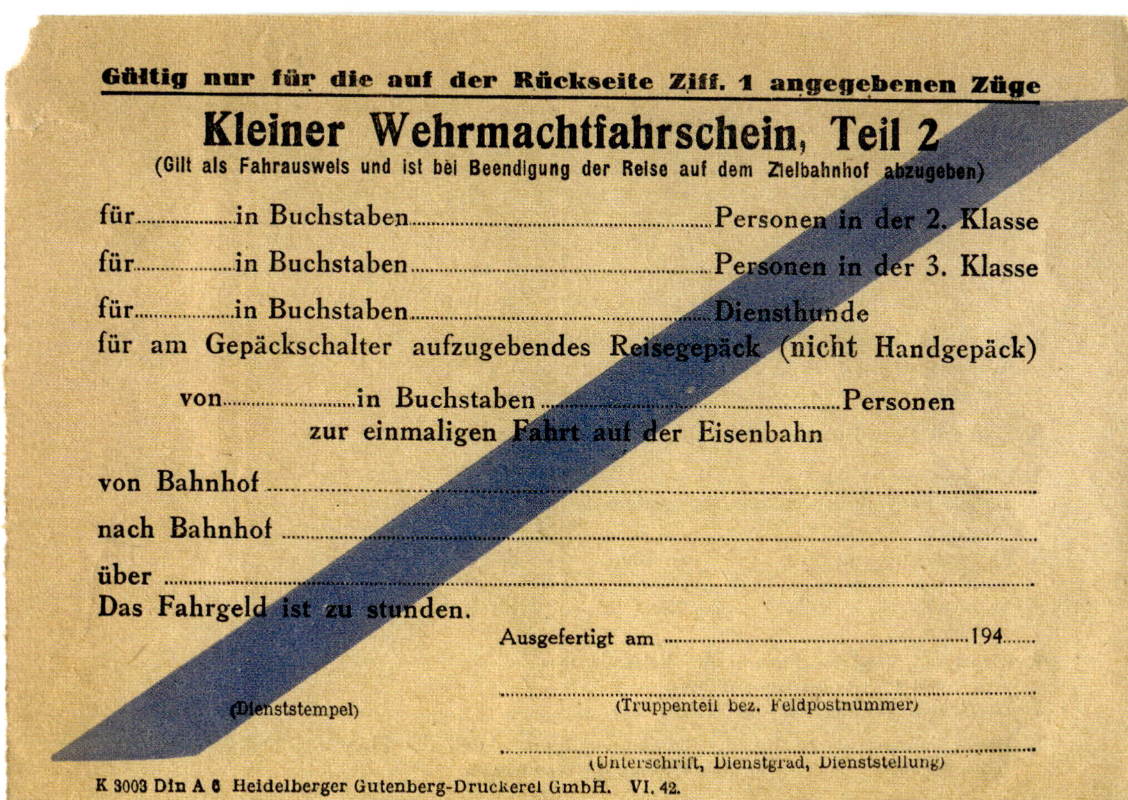

Gültig nur für die auf der Rückseite Ziff. 1 angegebenen Züge
Kleiner Wehrmachtfahrschein, Teil 2
(Gilt als Fahrausweis und ist bei Beendigung der Reise auf dem Zielbahnhof abzugeben)
für..................in Buchstaben..Personen in der 2. Klasse
für..................in Buchstaben..Personen in der 3. Klasse
für..................in Buchstaben..Diensthunde
für am Gepäckschalter aufzugebendes Reisegepäck (nicht Handgepäck)
von..........................in Buchstaben ....Personen
zur einmaligen Fahrt auf der Eisenbahn
von Bahnhof ....
nach Bahnhof ....
über ....
Das Fahrgeld ist zu stunden.
Ausgefertigt am ....194......
(Dienststempel) .... (Truppenteil bez. Feldpostnummer)
.... (Unterschrift, Dienstgrad, Dienststellung)
K 3003 Din A 6 Heidelberger Gutenberg-Druckerei GmbH. VI. 42.

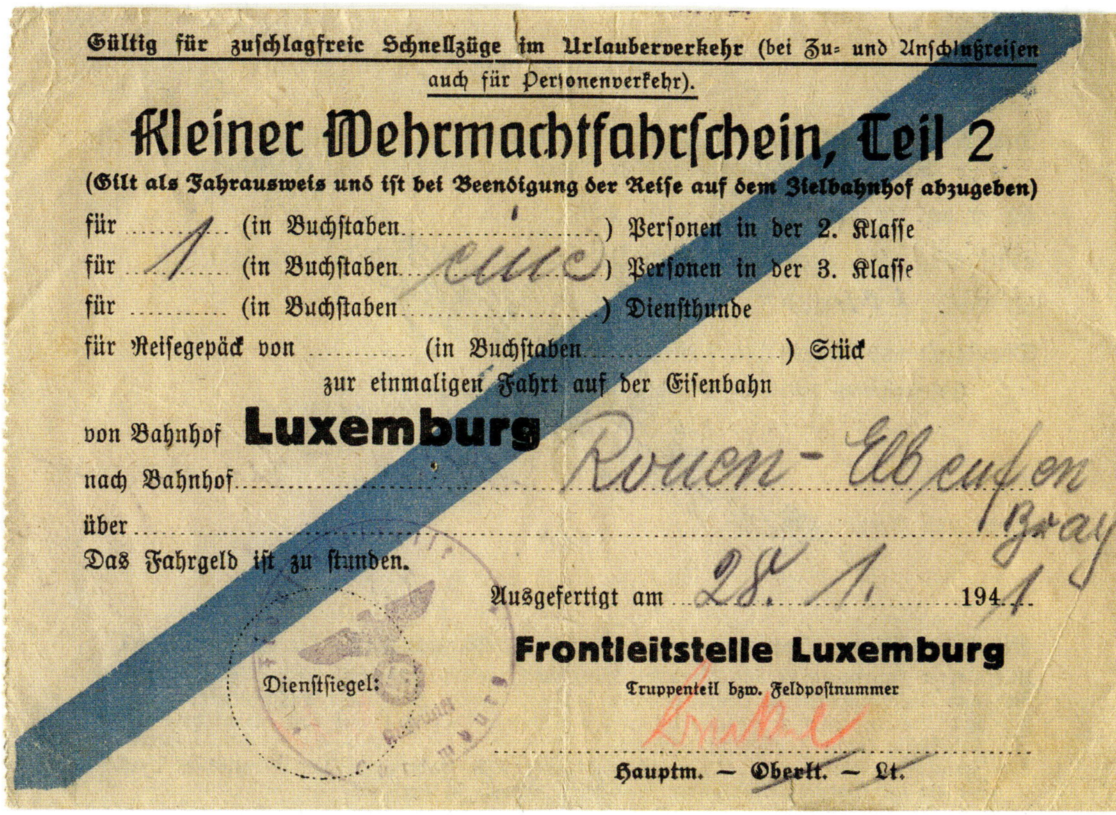

Gültig für zuschlagfreie Schnellzüge im Urlauberverkehr (bei Zu- und Anschlußreisen auch für Personenverkehr).

Kleiner Wehrmachtfahrschein, Teil 2

(Gilt als Fahrausweis und ist bei Beendigung der Reise auf dem Zielbahnhof abzugeben)

für .... (in Buchstaben ....) Personen in der 2. Klasse

für ...1... (in Buchstaben ...eine...) Personen in der 3. Klasse

für .... (in Buchstaben ....) Diensthunde

für Reisegepäck von .... (in Buchstaben ....) Stück

zur einmaligen Fahrt auf der Eisenbahn

von Bahnhof **Luxemburg**

nach Bahnhof ...... Rouen-Elbeuf en

über ...... Gray

Das Fahrgeld ist zu stunden.

Ausgefertigt am ...28. 1. ... 1941

Dienstsiegel:

Frontleitstelle Luxemburg

Truppenteil bzw. Feldpostnummer

Hauptm. — Oberlt. — Lt.

Figure 2-87. A ticket printed for use in Luxembourg, probably printed in Luxembourg, valid for a third class return trip from Rouen, France. The reverse states that the purpose of travel is for Unteroffizier Lissner to return to his troop.

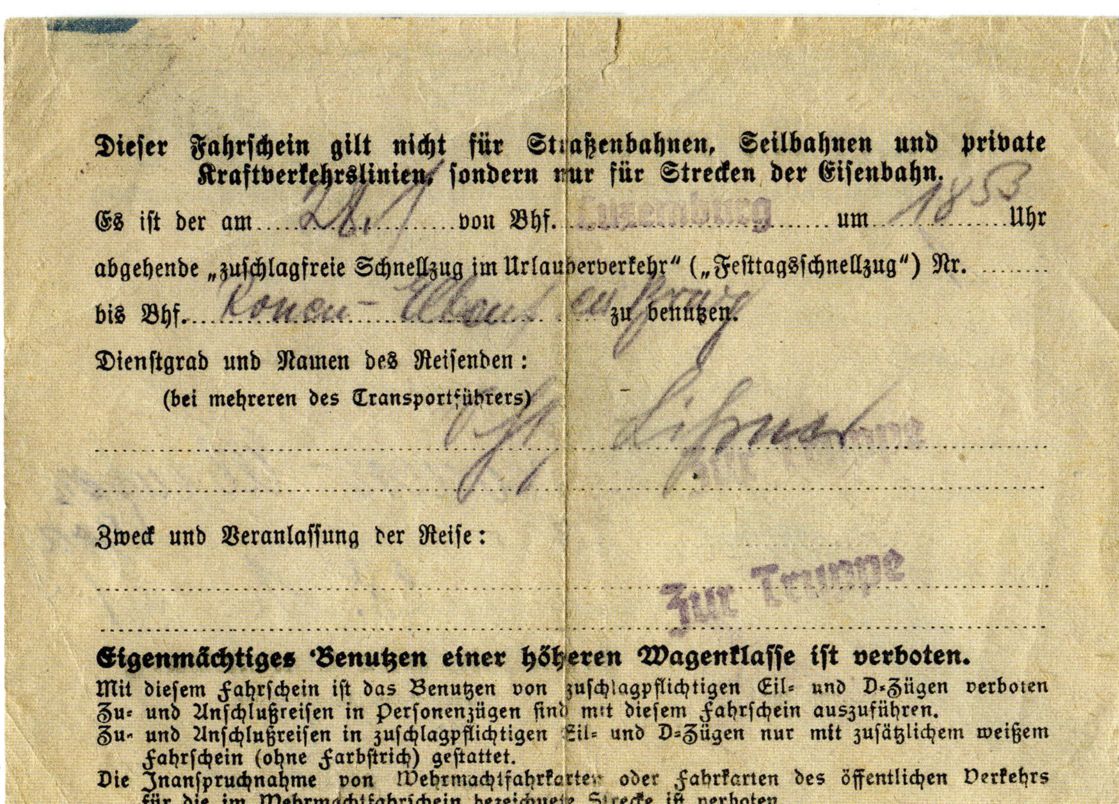

Dieser Fahrschein gilt nicht für Straßenbahnen, Seilbahnen und private Kraftverkehrslinien, sondern nur für Strecken der Eisenbahn.

Es ist der am ...28.1... von Bhf. ...Luxemburg... um ...18.53... Uhr

abgehende „zuschlagfreie Schnellzug im Urlauberverkehr" („Festtagsschnellzug") Nr. ....

bis Bhf. ...Rouen-Elbeuf en Gray... zu benutzen.

Dienstgrad und Namen des Reisenden:

(bei mehreren des Transportführers)

...Uffz. Lissner...

Zweck und Veranlassung der Reise:

...Zur Truppe...

Eigenmächtiges Benutzen einer höheren Wagenklasse ist verboten.

Mit diesem Fahrschein ist das Benutzen von zuschlagpflichtigen Eil- und D-Zügen verboten
Zu- und Anschlußreisen in Personenzügen sind mit diesem Fahrschein auszuführen.
Zu- und Anschlußreisen in zuschlagpflichtigen Eil- und D-Zügen nur mit zusätzlichem weißem Fahrschein (ohne Farbstrich) gestattet.
Die Inanspruchnahme von Wehrmachtfahrkarten oder Fahrkarten des öffentlichen Verkehrs für die im Wehrmachtfahrschein bezeichnete Strecke ist verboten.

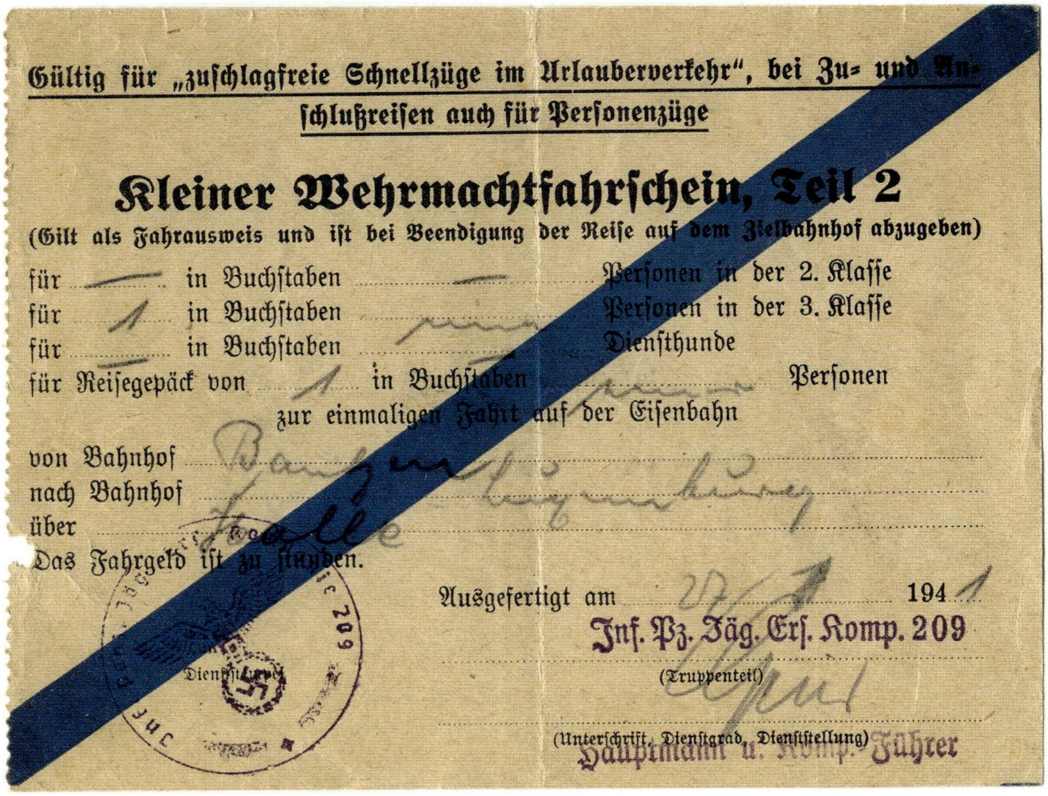

Gültig für „zuschlagfreie Schnellzüge im Urlauberverkehr", bei Zu- und Anschlußreisen auch für Personenzüge

Kleiner Wehrmachtfahrschein, Teil 2

(Gilt als Fahrausweis und ist bei Beendigung der Reise auf dem Zielbahnhof abzugeben)

für — in Buchstaben — Personen in der 2. Klasse
für 1 in Buchstaben Personen in der 3. Klasse
für in Buchstaben Diensthunde
für Reisegepäck von 1 in Buchstaben Personen
zur einmaligen Fahrt auf der Eisenbahn
von Bahnhof
nach Bahnhof
über Halle
Das Fahrgeld ist zu stunden.

Ausgefertigt am 194 1

Inf. Pz. Jäg. Ers. Komp. 209

(Truppenteil)

(Unterschrift, Dienstgrad, Dienststellung)

Hauptmann u. Komp.-Führer

Figure 2-88. This ticket was valid for travel from Bautzen through Luxembourg to Halle, in Germany, and was issued to Herbert Lissner by Infanterie-Panzerjäger (Infantry Anti-Tank) Training Company 209.

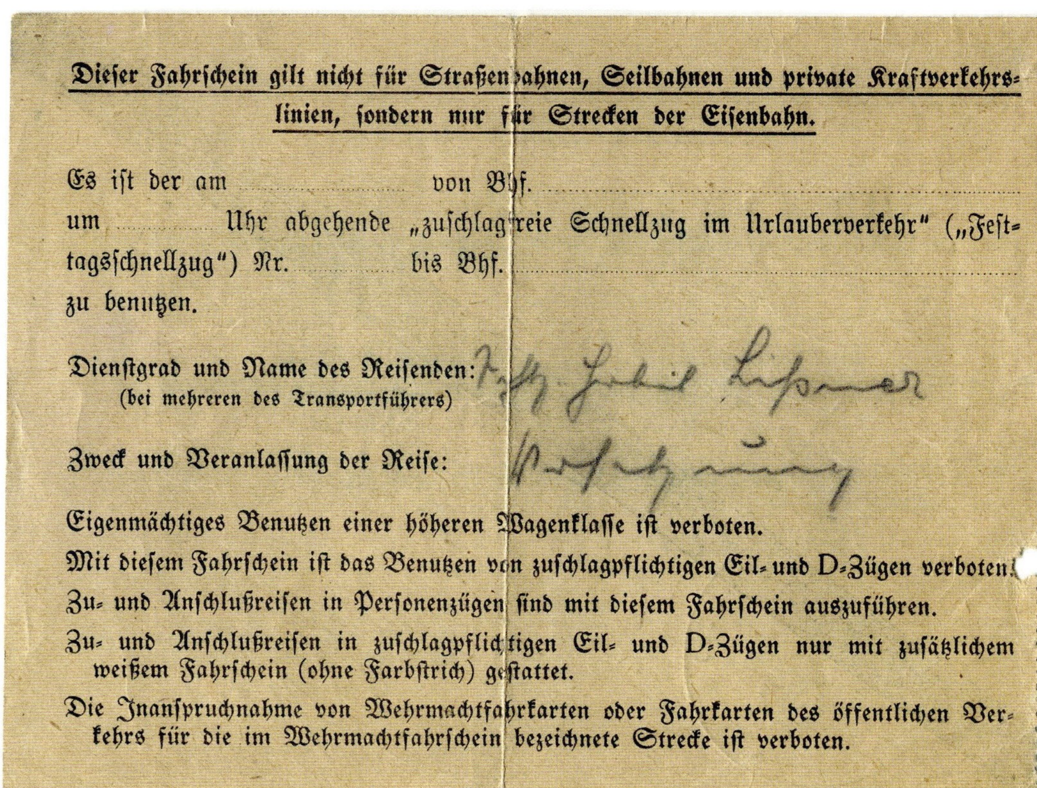

Dieser Fahrschein gilt nicht für Straßenbahnen, Seilbahnen und private Kraftverkehrslinien, sondern nur für Strecken der Eisenbahn.

Es ist der am von Bhf.
um Uhr abgehende „zuschlagfreie Schnellzug im Urlauberverkehr" („Festtagsschnellzug") Nr. bis Bhf.
zu benutzen.

Dienstgrad und Name des Reisenden:
(bei mehreren des Transportführers)

Zweck und Veranlassung der Reise:

Eigenmächtiges Benutzen einer höheren Wagenklasse ist verboten.

Mit diesem Fahrschein ist das Benutzen von zuschlagpflichtigen Eil- und D-Zügen verboten!

Zu- und Anschlußreisen in Personenzügen sind mit diesem Fahrschein auszuführen.

Zu- und Anschlußreisen in zuschlagpflichtigen Eil- und D-Zügen nur mit zusätzlichem weißem Fahrschein (ohne Farbstrich) gestattet.

Die Inanspruchnahme von Wehrmachtfahrkarten oder Fahrkarten des öffentlichen Verkehrs für die im Wehrmachtfahrschein bezeichnete Strecke ist verboten.

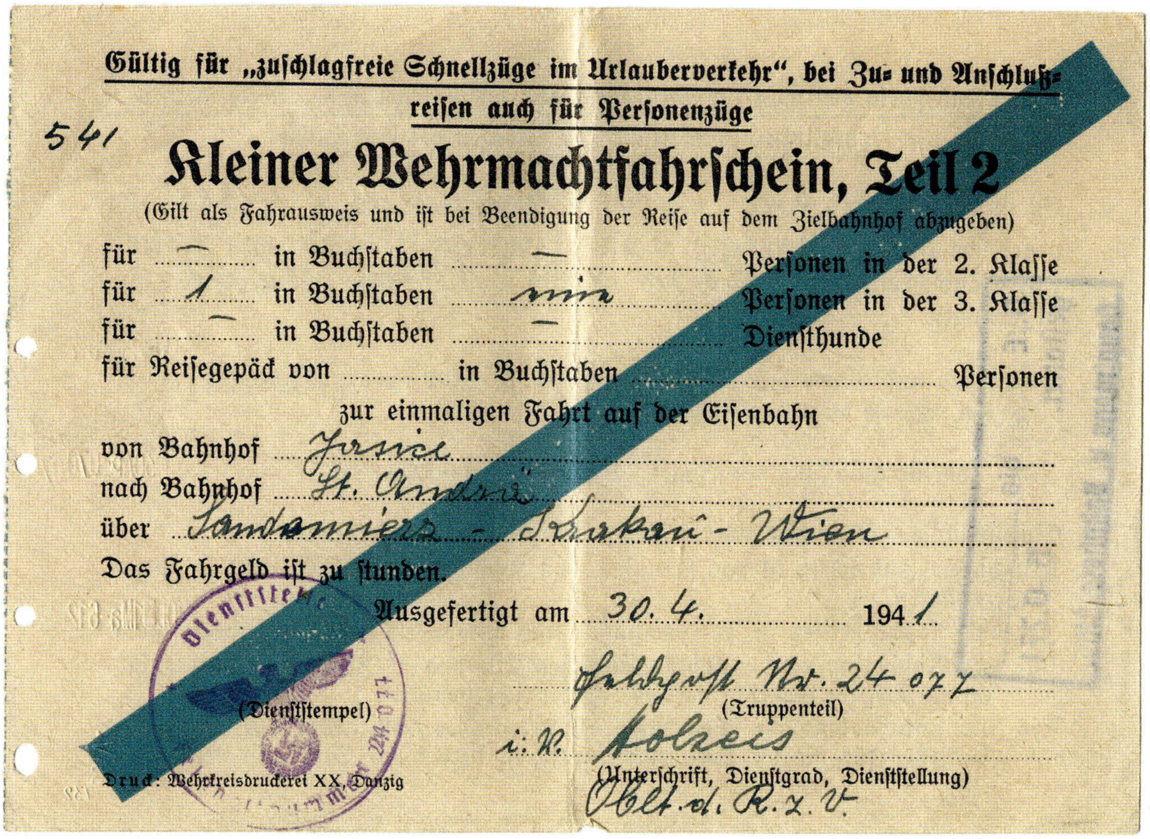

Gültig für „zuschlagfreie Schnellzüge im Urlauberverkehr", bei Zu- und Anschlußreisen auch für Personenzüge

541

Kleiner Wehrmachtfahrschein, Teil 2

(Gilt als Fahrausweis und ist bei Beendigung der Reise auf dem Zielbahnhof abzugeben)

für — in Buchstaben — Personen in der 2. Klasse
für 1 in Buchstaben eins Personen in der 3. Klasse
für — in Buchstaben — Diensthunde
für Reisegepäck von .... in Buchstaben .... Personen

zur einmaligen Fahrt auf der Eisenbahn

von Bahnhof Jasice
nach Bahnhof St. Andrä
über Sandomierz - Krakau - Wien

Das Fahrgeld ist zu stunden.

Ausgefertigt am 30. 4. 1941

(Dienststempel)

Feldpost Nr. 24 077
(Truppenteil)

i. V. Holzeis
(Unterschrift, Dienstgrad, Dienststellung)
Oblt. d. R. z. V.

Druck: Wehrkreisdruckerei XX, Danzig

Figure 2-89. Not all blue stripes were "entirely" blue, similarly to the issues of different shades of green ink shown in figure 2-61. This form printed by Wehrkreisdruckerei XX (Military District Printer XX), Danzig used what appears to be an almost green shade of ink, though this discoloration is almost certainly due to age.

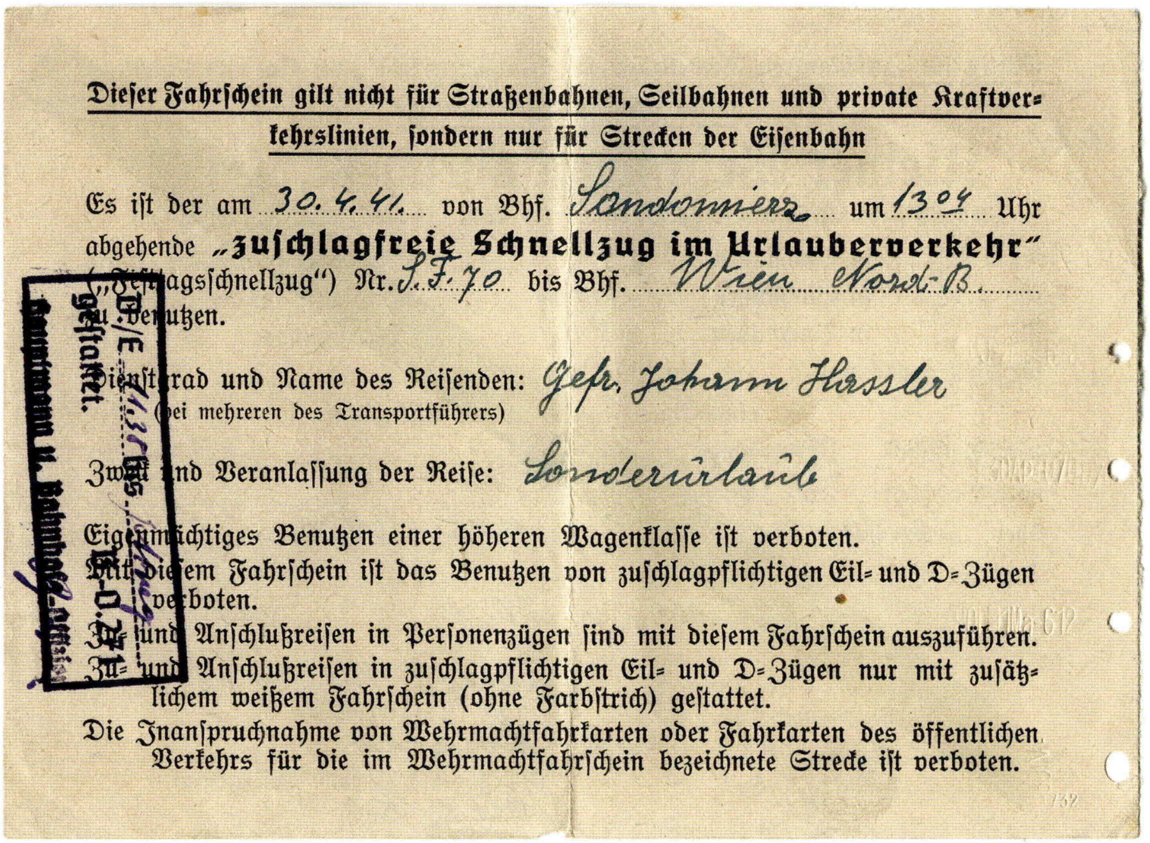

Dieser Fahrschein gilt nicht für Straßenbahnen, Seilbahnen und private Kraftverkehrslinien, sondern nur für Strecken der Eisenbahn

Es ist der am 30. 4. 41. von Bhf. Sandomierz um 13 04 Uhr abgehende „zuschlagfreie Schnellzug im Urlauberverkehr" („Feiertagsschnellzug") Nr. S. F. 70 bis Bhf. Wien Nord-B. zu benutzen.

Dienstgrad und Name des Reisenden: Gefr. Johann Hassler
(bei mehreren des Transportführers)

Zweck und Veranlassung der Reise: Sonderurlaub

Eigenmächtiges Benutzen einer höheren Wagenklasse ist verboten.
Mit diesem Fahrschein ist das Benutzen von zuschlagpflichtigen Eil- und D-Zügen verboten.
Zu- und Anschlußreisen in Personenzügen sind mit diesem Fahrschein auszuführen.
Zu- und Anschlußreisen in zuschlagpflichtigen Eil- und D-Zügen nur mit zusätzlichem weißem Fahrschein (ohne Farbstrich) gestattet.
Die Inanspruchnahme von Wehrmachtfahrkarten oder Fahrkarten des öffentlichen Verkehrs für die im Wehrmachtfahrschein bezeichnete Strecke ist verboten.

Gültig für „zuschlagfreie Schnellzüge im Urlauberverkehr", bei Zu- und Anschlußreisen auch für Personenzüge

Kleiner Wehrmachtfahrschein, Teil 1

(Wird bei Antritt der Reise von der Eisenbahn abgenommen)

für – in Buchstaben – Personen in der 2. Klasse
für 1 in Buchstaben Eine Personen in der 3. Klasse
für – in Buchstaben – Diensthunde
für Reisegepäck von – in Buchstaben – Personen
zur einmaligen Fahrt auf der Eisenbahn
von Bahnhof Saloniki
nach Bahnhof Roßwein
über Belgrad-Agram-Graz-Wien-Prag-Dresden-Döbeln
Das Fahrgeld ist zu stunden.
Ausgefertigt am 4. 11. 1941

Dienststempel

Truppenteil

Unterschrift, Dienstgrad, Dienststellung

Mil 504 c/kl.blau Vordruckverlag Karl W. Neumann, Freiberg i.Sa.

Figure 2-90. This ticket prepared for Gefreiter Alfred Böttcher under the conditions of "Leave for Special Occasion" was for quite a long trip, from Saloniki, Greece to Döbeln, Germany, a $17^{1/2}$ hour drive today, passing through a total of nine different train stations.

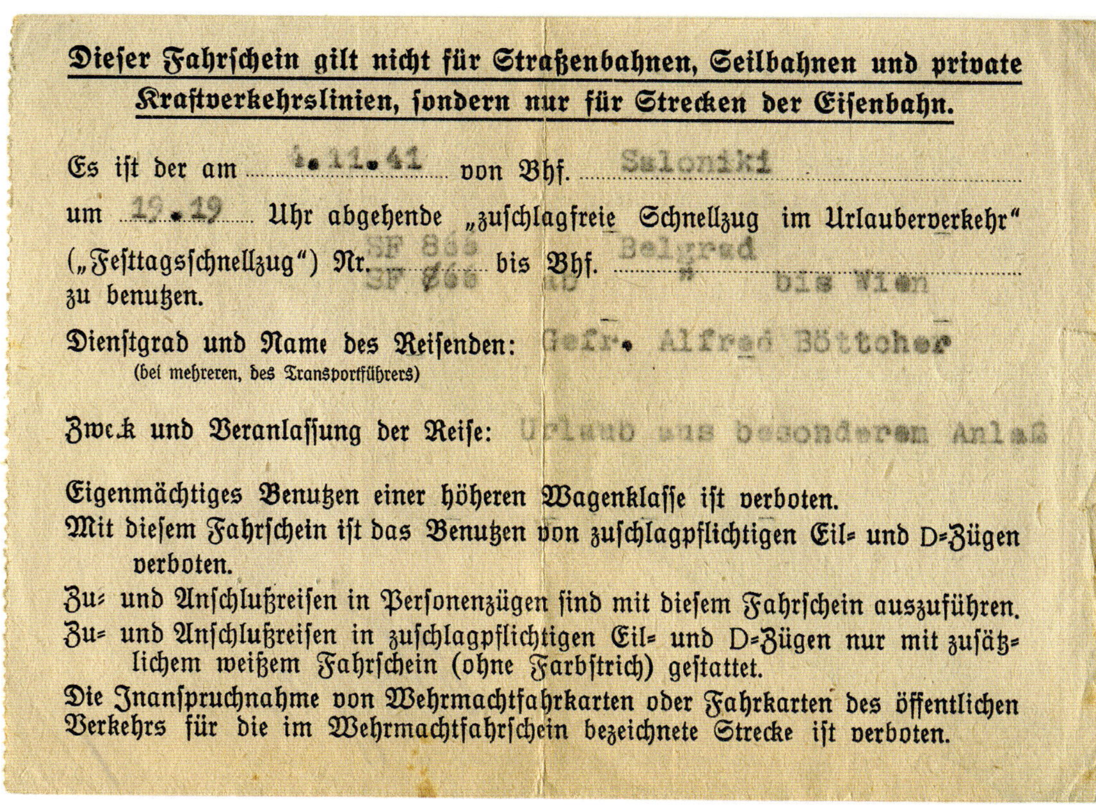

Dieser Fahrschein gilt nicht für Straßenbahnen, Seilbahnen und private Kraftverkehrslinien, sondern nur für Strecken der Eisenbahn.

Es ist der am 4.11.41 von Bhf. Saloniki
um 19.19 Uhr abgehende „zuschlagfreie Schnellzug im Urlauberverkehr" („Festtagsschnellzug") Nr. SF 865 bis Bhf. Belgrad
SF 866 ab " bis Wien
zu benutzen.

Dienstgrad und Name des Reisenden: Gefr. Alfred Böttcher
(bei mehreren, des Transportführers)

Zweck und Veranlassung der Reise: Urlaub aus besonderem Anlaß

Eigenmächtiges Benutzen einer höheren Wagenklasse ist verboten.
Mit diesem Fahrschein ist das Benutzen von zuschlagpflichtigen Eil- und D-Zügen verboten.
Zu- und Anschlußreisen in Personenzügen sind mit diesem Fahrschein auszuführen.
Zu- und Anschlußreisen in zuschlagpflichtigen Eil- und D-Zügen nur mit zusätzlichem weißem Fahrschein (ohne Farbstrich) gestattet.
Die Inanspruchnahme von Wehrmachtfahrkarten oder Fahrkarten des öffentlichen Verkehrs für die im Wehrmachtfahrschein bezeichnete Strecke ist verboten.

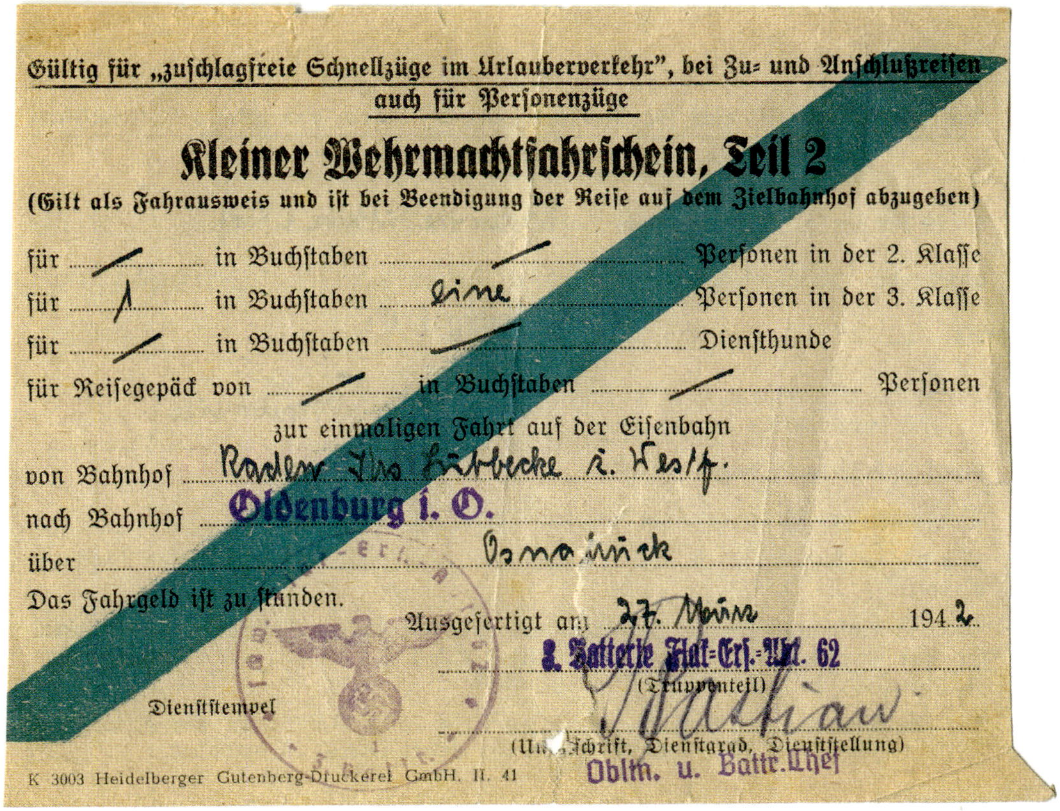
Gültig für „zuschlagfreie Schnellzüge im Urlauberverkehr", bei Zu- und Anschlußreisen auch für Personenzüge

Kleiner Wehrmachtfahrschein, Teil 2

(Gilt als Fahrausweis und ist bei Beendigung der Reise auf dem Zielbahnhof abzugeben)

für ....../...... in Buchstaben ....../...... Personen in der 2. Klasse
für ....1.... in Buchstaben ....eine.... Personen in der 3. Klasse
für ....../...... in Buchstaben ....../...... Diensthunde
für Reisegepäck von ....../...... in Buchstaben ....../...... Personen

zur einmaligen Fahrt auf der Eisenbahn

von Bahnhof Raden Ihr. Lübbecke i. Westf.
nach Bahnhof Oldenburg i. O.
über Osnabrück

Das Fahrgeld ist zu stunden.

Ausgefertigt am 27. März 1942

Dienststempel

1. Batterie Flak-Ers.-Abt. 62
(Truppenteil)

(Unterschrift, Dienstgrad, Dienststellung)
Oblt. u. Battr. Chef

K 3003 Heidelberger Gutenberg-Druckerei GmbH. II. 41

Figure 2-91. Wilhelm Tempelmeier travelled on March 27, 1942 using this ticket for the purpose of Landwirtschaftshilfe, an agricultural assistance program that permitted certain Wehrmacht personnel to take leave to help with crops and livestock in Germany.

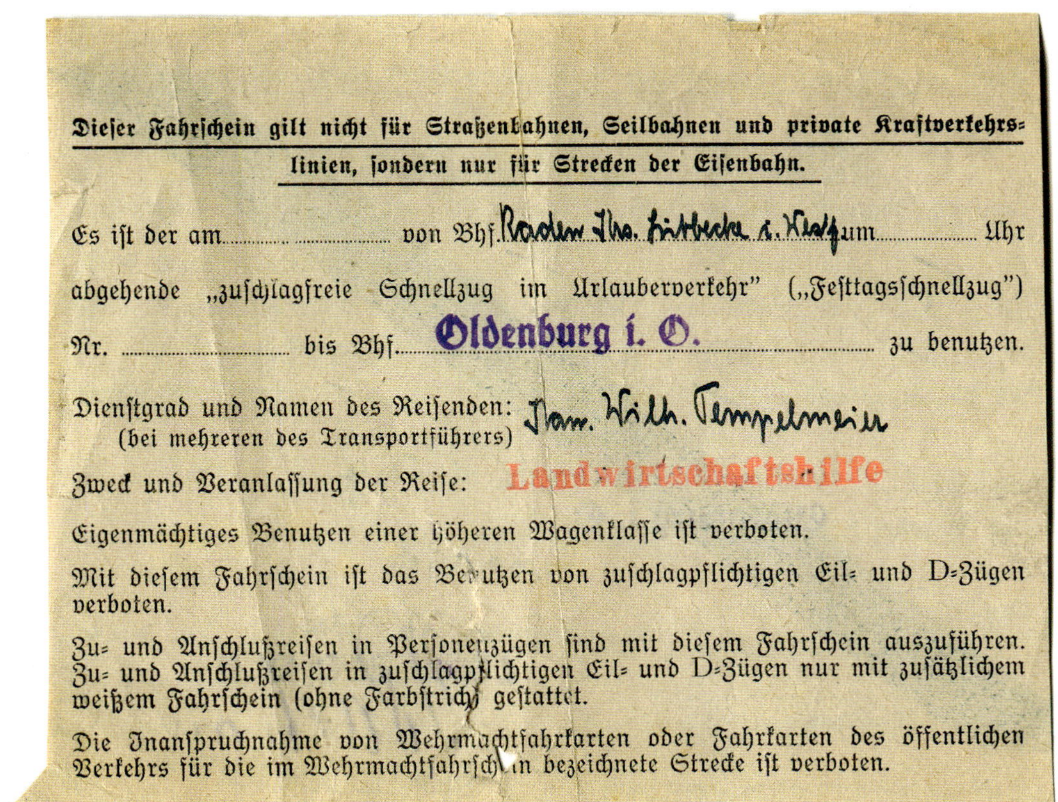
Dieser Fahrschein gilt nicht für Straßenbahnen, Seilbahnen und private Kraftverkehrslinien, sondern nur für Strecken der Eisenbahn.

Es ist der am .... von Bhf. Raden Ihr. Lübbecke i. Westf. um .... Uhr abgehende „zuschlagfreie Schnellzug im Urlauberverkehr" („Festtagsschnellzug") Nr. .... bis Bhf. Oldenburg i. O. zu benutzen.

Dienstgrad und Namen des Reisenden: (bei mehreren des Transportführers) Kan. Wilh. Tempelmeier

Zweck und Veranlassung der Reise: Landwirtschaftshilfe

Eigenmächtiges Benutzen einer höheren Wagenklasse ist verboten.

Mit diesem Fahrschein ist das Benutzen von zuschlagpflichtigen Eil- und D-Zügen verboten.

Zu- und Anschlußreisen in Personenzügen sind mit diesem Fahrschein auszuführen. Zu- und Anschlußreisen in zuschlagpflichtigen Eil- und D-Zügen nur mit zusätzlichem weißem Fahrschein (ohne Farbstrich) gestattet.

Die Inanspruchnahme von Wehrmachtfahrkarten oder Fahrkarten des öffentlichen Verkehrs für die im Wehrmachtfahrschein bezeichnete Strecke ist verboten.

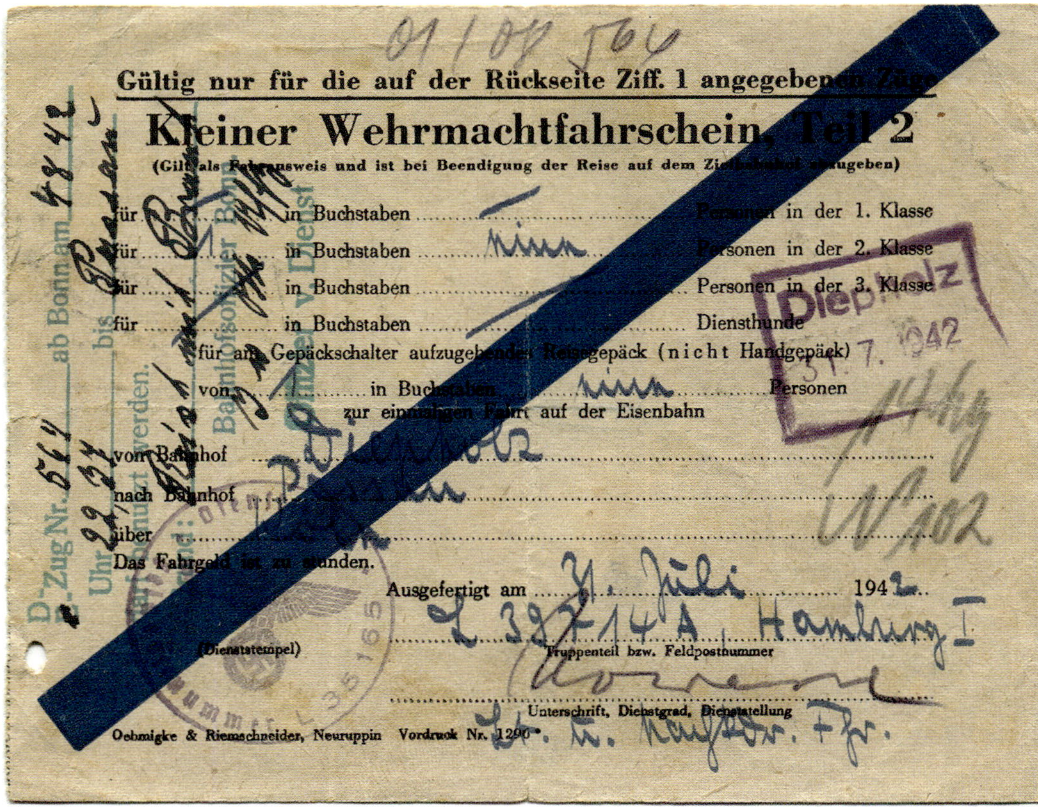
01/08 564

Gültig nur für die auf der Rückseite Ziff. 1 angegebenen Züge

Kleiner Wehrmachtfahrschein, Teil 2

(Gilt als Fahrausweis und ist bei Beendigung der Reise auf dem Zielbahnhof abzugeben)

für .... in Buchstaben .... Personen in der 1. Klasse

für ....1.... in Buchstaben ....eine.... Personen in der 2. Klasse

für .... in Buchstaben .... Personen in der 3. Klasse

für .... in Buchstaben .... Diensthunde

für am Gepäckschalter aufzugebendes Reisegepäck (nicht Handgepäck)

von .... in Buchstaben ....eine.... Personen

zur einmaligen Fahrt auf der Eisenbahn

vom Bahnhof ....Diepholz....

nach Bahnhof ....Passau....

über ....

Das Fahrgeld ist zu stunden.

Ausgefertigt am ....31. Juli.... 1942

(Dienststempel)

L 39714 A, Hamburg I

Truppenteil bzw. Feldpostnummer

Unterschrift, Dienstgrad, Dienststellung

Oehmigke & Riemschneider, Neuruppin Vordruck Nr. 1290

D-Zug Nr. 564 ab Bonn am 4.8.42 Uhr 22.34 bis Passau

Bahnhofsoffizier Bonn

Diepholz 31. 7. 1942

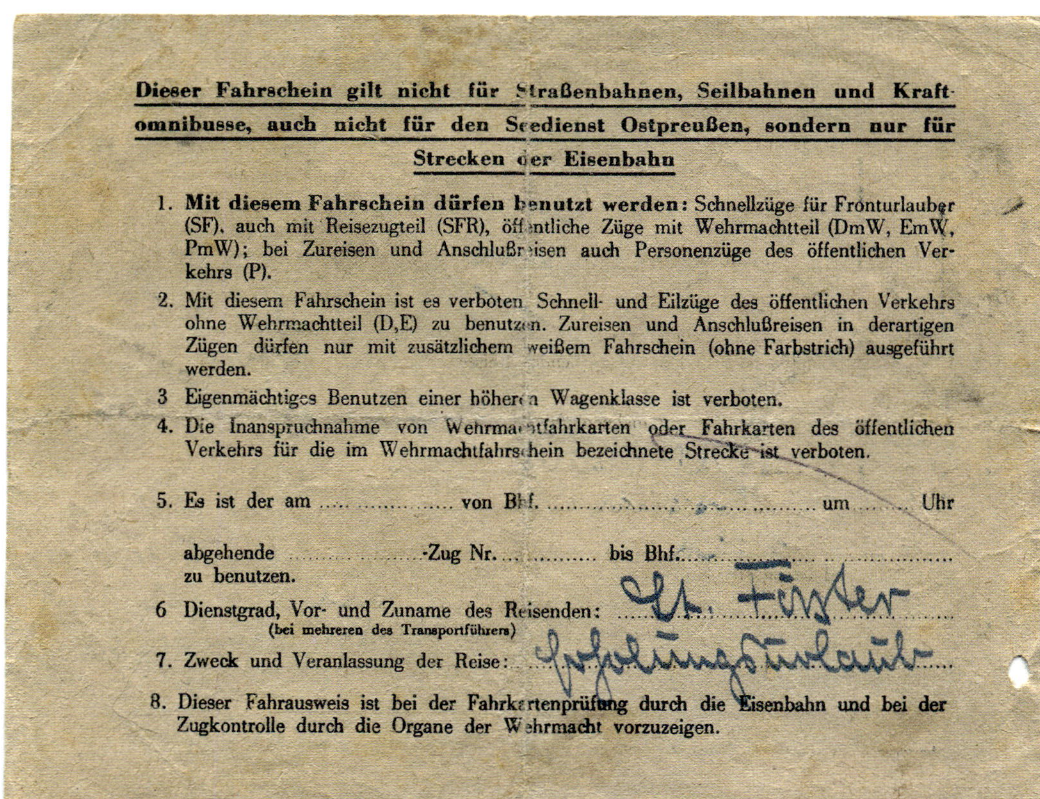
Dieser Fahrschein gilt nicht für Straßenbahnen, Seilbahnen und Kraftomnibusse, auch nicht für den Seedienst Ostpreußen, sondern nur für Strecken der Eisenbahn

1. **Mit diesem Fahrschein dürfen benutzt werden:** Schnellzüge für Fronturlauber (SF), auch mit Reisezugteil (SFR), öffentliche Züge mit Wehrmachtteil (DmW, EmW, PmW); bei Zureisen und Anschlußreisen auch Personenzüge des öffentlichen Verkehrs (P).
2. Mit diesem Fahrschein ist es verboten Schnell- und Eilzüge des öffentlichen Verkehrs ohne Wehrmachtteil (D,E) zu benutzen. Zureisen und Anschlußreisen in derartigen Zügen dürfen nur mit zusätzlichem weißem Fahrschein (ohne Farbstrich) ausgeführt werden.
3. Eigenmächtiges Benutzen einer höheren Wagenklasse ist verboten.
4. Die Inanspruchnahme von Wehrmachtfahrkarten oder Fahrkarten des öffentlichen Verkehrs für die im Wehrmachtfahrschein bezeichnete Strecke ist verboten.
5. Es ist der am .... von Bhf. .... um .... Uhr abgehende ....-Zug Nr. .... bis Bhf. .... zu benutzen.
6. Dienstgrad, Vor- und Zuname des Reisenden: Lt. Fuster (bei mehreren des Transportführers)
7. Zweck und Veranlassung der Reise: Erholungsurlaub
8. Dieser Fahrausweis ist bei der Fahrkartenprüfung durch die Eisenbahn und bei der Zugkontrolle durch die Organe der Wehrmacht vorzuzeigen.

Figure 2-92. This ticket allowed Luftwaffe Leutnant Fuster to travel from Dienhols through Passau to Köln for Erholungsurlaub (recreational leave). Note the green stamp along the left side that specified both train and seat number, to ensure the Leutnant would not lose his seat.

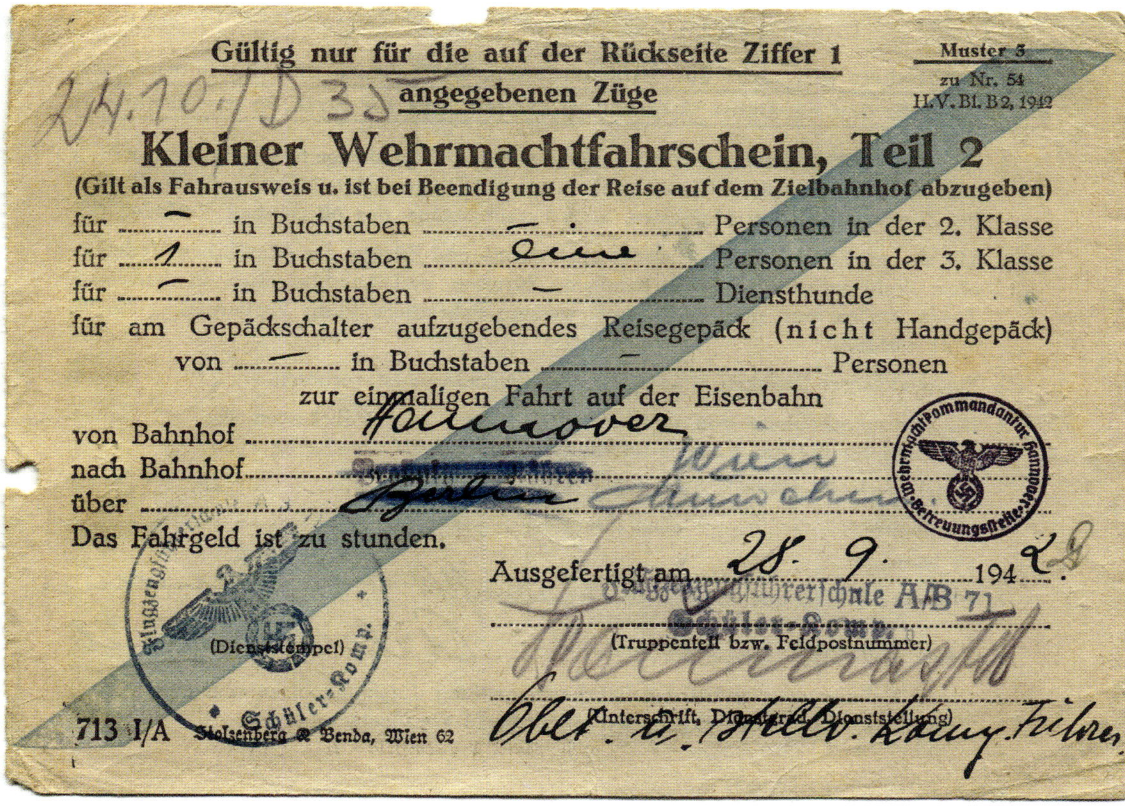

Gültig nur für die auf der Rückseite Ziffer 1 angegebenen Züge

Muster 3
zu Nr. 54
H.V.Bl.B2, 1942

Kleiner Wehrmachtfahrschein, Teil 2

(Gilt als Fahrausweis u. ist bei Beendigung der Reise auf dem Zielbahnhof abzugeben)

für — in Buchstaben — Personen in der 2. Klasse
für 1 in Buchstaben eine Personen in der 3. Klasse
für — in Buchstaben — Diensthunde
für am Gepäckschalter aufzugebendes Reisegepäck (nicht Handgepäck)
von — in Buchstaben — Personen
zur einmaligen Fahrt auf der Eisenbahn
von Bahnhof Hannover
nach Bahnhof Wien
über Berlin
Das Fahrgeld ist zu stunden.

Ausgefertigt am 28. 9. 1942

(Dienststempel)

(Truppenteil bzw. Feldpostnummer)

(Unterschrift, Dienstgrad, Dienststellung)

713 I/A Stolzenberg & Benda, Wien 62

Figure 2-93. A ticket for Gefreiter Wilhelm Kleeman to travel from Flugzeugführerschule (Pilots' School) in Hannover to Berlin for Arbeitsurlaub (Working Leave), though this was changed to Warsaw at some point.

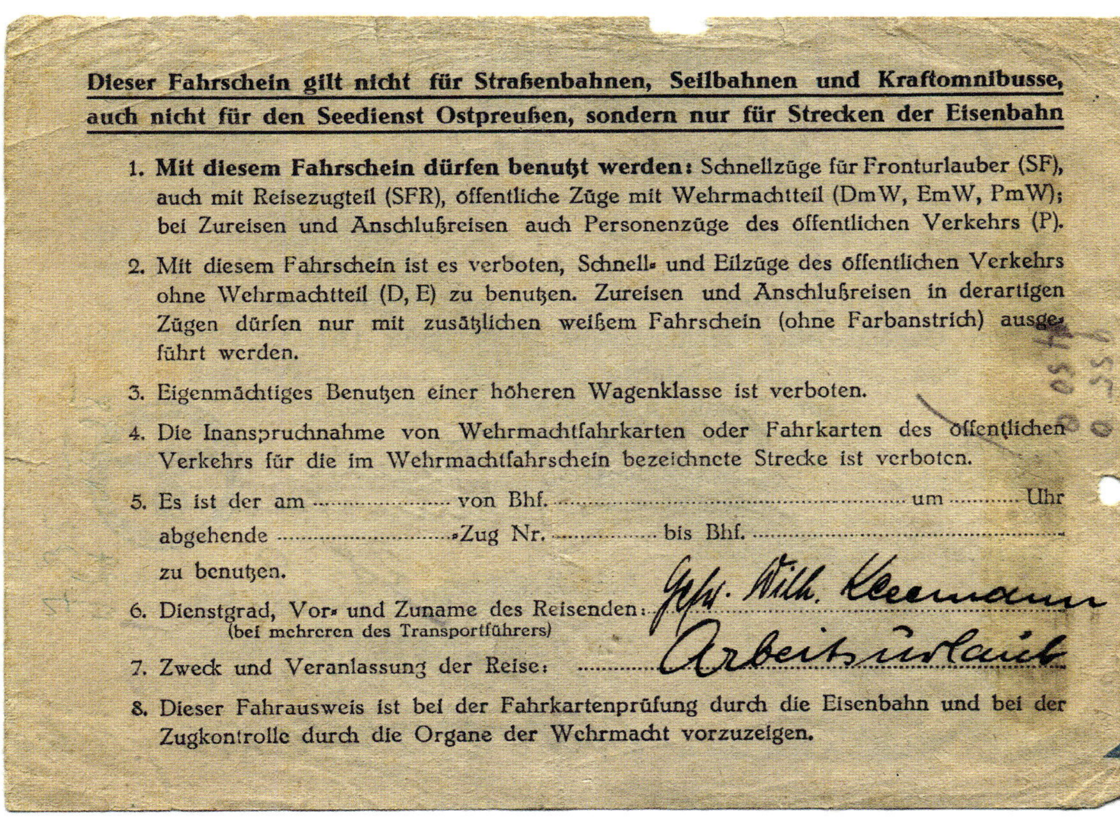

Dieser Fahrschein gilt nicht für Straßenbahnen, Seilbahnen und Kraftomnibusse, auch nicht für den Seedienst Ostpreußen, sondern nur für Strecken der Eisenbahn

1. **Mit diesem Fahrschein dürfen benutzt werden:** Schnellzüge für Fronturlauber (SF), auch mit Reisezugteil (SFR), öffentliche Züge mit Wehrmachtteil (DmW, EmW, PmW); bei Zureisen und Anschlußreisen auch Personenzüge des öffentlichen Verkehrs (P).
2. Mit diesem Fahrschein ist es verboten, Schnell- und Eilzüge des öffentlichen Verkehrs ohne Wehrmachtteil (D, E) zu benutzen. Zureisen und Anschlußreisen in derartigen Zügen dürfen nur mit zusätzlichem weißem Fahrschein (ohne Farbanstrich) ausgeführt werden.
3. Eigenmächtiges Benutzen einer höheren Wagenklasse ist verboten.
4. Die Inanspruchnahme von Wehrmachtfahrkarten oder Fahrkarten des öffentlichen Verkehrs für die im Wehrmachtfahrschein bezeichnete Strecke ist verboten.
5. Es ist der am .... von Bhf. .... um .... Uhr abgehende .... Zug Nr. .... bis Bhf. .... zu benutzen.
6. Dienstgrad, Vor- und Zuname des Reisenden: Gefr. Wilh. Kleemann (bei mehreren des Transportführers)
7. Zweck und Veranlassung der Reise: Arbeitsurlaub
8. Dieser Fahrausweis ist bei der Fahrkartenprüfung durch die Eisenbahn und bei der Zugkontrolle durch die Organe der Wehrmacht vorzuzeigen.

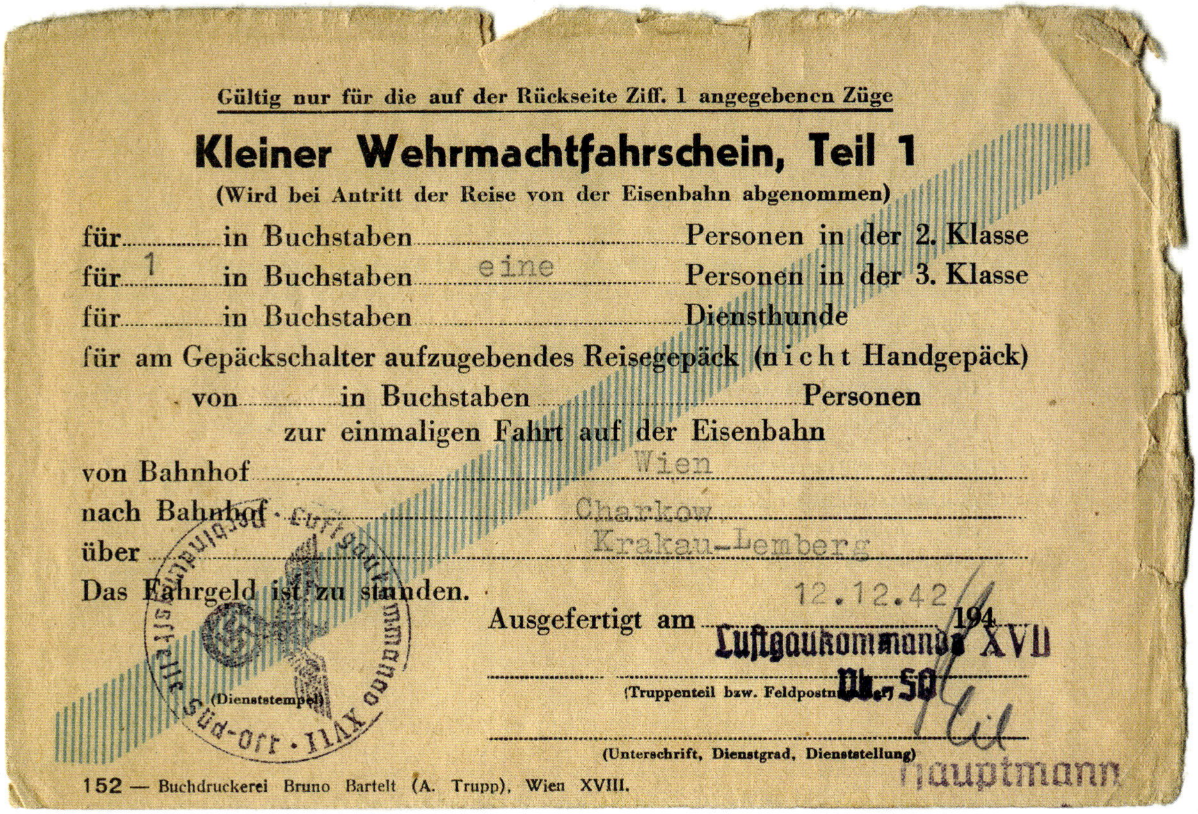

Gültig nur für die auf der Rückseite Ziff. 1 angegebenen Züge

Kleiner Wehrmachtfahrschein, Teil 1

(Wird bei Antritt der Reise von der Eisenbahn abgenommen)

für .... in Buchstaben .... Personen in der 2. Klasse

für 1 in Buchstaben eine Personen in der 3. Klasse

für .... in Buchstaben .... Diensthunde

für am Gepäckschalter aufzugebendes Reisegepäck (nicht Handgepäck)

von .... in Buchstaben .... Personen

zur einmaligen Fahrt auf der Eisenbahn

von Bahnhof Wien

nach Bahnhof Charkow

über Krakau-Lemberg

Das Fahrgeld ist zu stunden.

Ausgefertigt am 12.12.42 194

Luftgaukommando XVII

Ob. St.

(Truppenteil bzw. Feldpostnummer)

(Dienststempel)

(Unterschrift, Dienstgrad, Dienststellung)

Hauptmann

152 — Buchdruckerei Bruno Bartelt (A. Trupp), Wien XVIII.

A

B

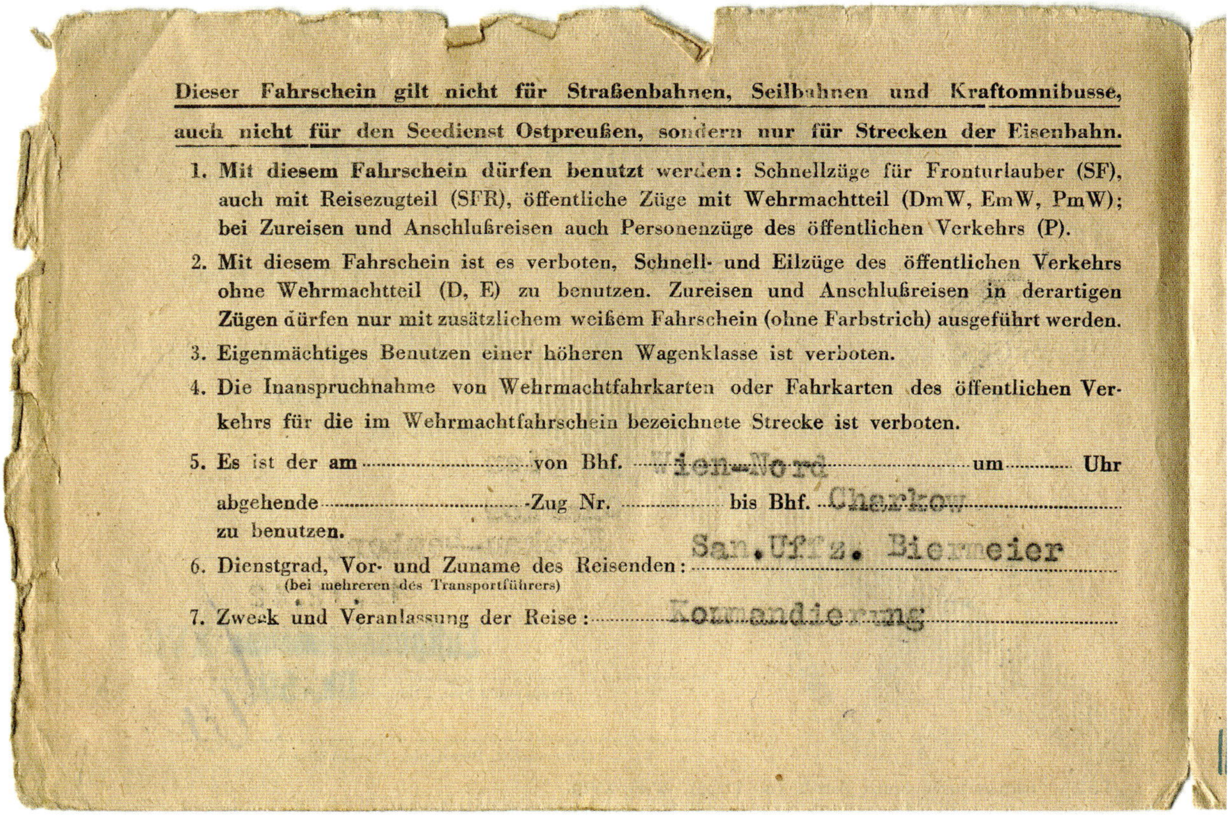

Dieser Fahrschein gilt nicht für Straßenbahnen, Seilbahnen und Kraftomnibusse, auch nicht für den Seedienst Ostpreußen, sondern nur für Strecken der Eisenbahn.

1. Mit diesem Fahrschein dürfen benutzt werden: Schnellzüge für Fronturlauber (SF), auch mit Reisezugteil (SFR), öffentliche Züge mit Wehrmachtteil (DmW, EmW, PmW); bei Zureisen und Anschlußreisen auch Personenzüge des öffentlichen Verkehrs (P).
2. Mit diesem Fahrschein ist es verboten, Schnell- und Eilzüge des öffentlichen Verkehrs ohne Wehrmachtteil (D, E) zu benutzen. Zureisen und Anschlußreisen in derartigen Zügen dürfen nur mit zusätzlichem weißem Fahrschein (ohne Farbstrich) ausgeführt werden.
3. Eigenmächtiges Benutzen einer höheren Wagenklasse ist verboten.
4. Die Inanspruchnahme von Wehrmachtfahrkarten oder Fahrkarten des öffentlichen Verkehrs für die im Wehrmachtfahrschein bezeichnete Strecke ist verboten.
5. Es ist der am .... von Bhf. Wien-Nord .... um .... Uhr abgehende .... Zug Nr. .... bis Bhf. Charkow zu benutzen.
6. Dienstgrad, Vor- und Zuname des Reisenden: San.Uffz. Biermeier (bei mehreren des Transportführers)
7. Zweck und Veranlassung der Reise: Kommandierung

Figure 2-94. This set of images show how the Wehrmachtfahrschein was frequently prepared. A piece of carbon paper was inserted between the two pages and typed, which transferred to Page 2 (image C). The form was flipped and the carbon paper reinserted and typed on the back of Page 2 (image D), which transferred to the back of Page 1 (image B). In this example of both pages, Sanitäts-Unteroffizier (Medical Corporal) Biermeier travelled from Vienna to Krakow, Poland in December 1942.

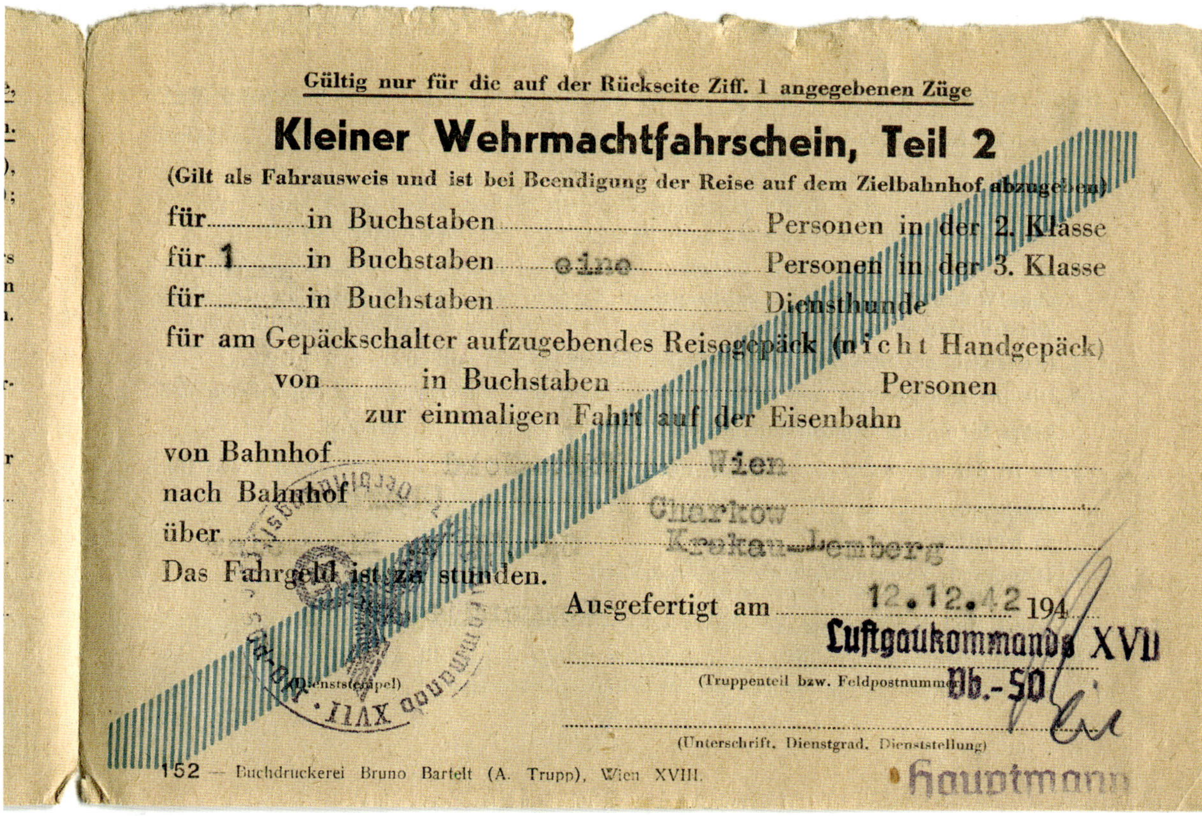

Gültig nur für die auf der Rückseite Ziff. 1 angegebenen Züge

Kleiner Wehrmachtfahrschein, Teil 2

(Gilt als Fahrausweis und ist bei Beendigung der Reise auf dem Zielbahnhof abzugeben)

für .... in Buchstaben .... Personen in der 2. Klasse

für 1 .... in Buchstaben eine .... Personen in der 3. Klasse

für .... in Buchstaben .... Diensthunde

für am Gepäckschalter aufzugebendes Reisegepäck (nicht Handgepäck)

von .... in Buchstaben .... Personen

zur einmaligen Fahrt auf der Eisenbahn

von Bahnhof .... Wien

nach Bahnhof .... Charkow

über .... Krakau-Lemberg

Das Fahrgeld ist zu stunden.

Ausgefertigt am 12.12.42 194

Luftgaukommando XVII

(Dienststempel)

(Truppenteil bzw. Feldpostnummer) Qb.-SO

(Unterschrift, Dienstgrad, Dienststellung)

Hauptmann

152 — Buchdruckerei Bruno Bartelt (A. Trupp), Wien XVIII.

C

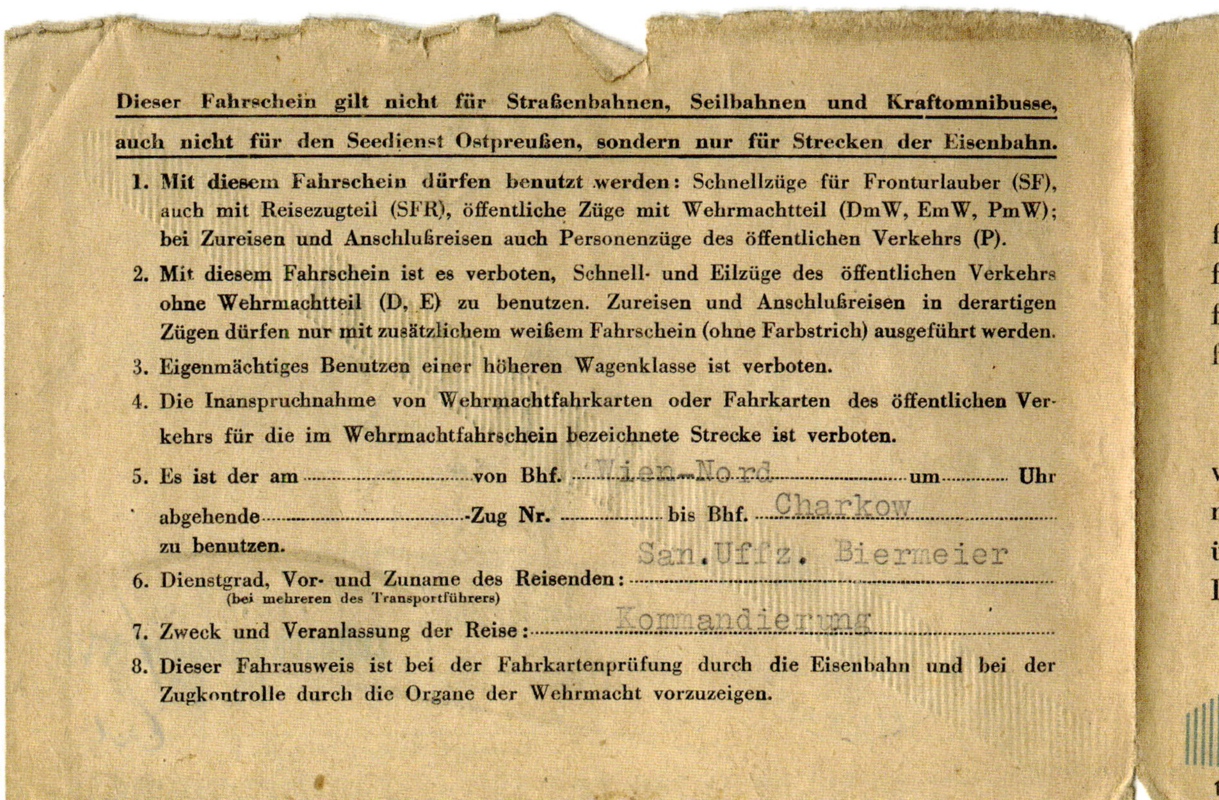

Dieser Fahrschein gilt nicht für Straßenbahnen, Seilbahnen und Kraftomnibusse, auch nicht für den Seedienst Ostpreußen, sondern nur für Strecken der Eisenbahn.

1. **Mit diesem Fahrschein dürfen benutzt werden:** Schnellzüge für Fronturlauber (SF), auch mit Reisezugteil (SFR), öffentliche Züge mit Wehrmachtteil (DmW, EmW, PmW); bei Zureisen und Anschlußreisen auch Personenzüge des öffentlichen Verkehrs (P).
2. **Mit diesem Fahrschein ist es verboten,** Schnell- und Eilzüge des öffentlichen Verkehrs ohne Wehrmachtteil (D, E) zu benutzen. Zureisen und Anschlußreisen in derartigen Zügen dürfen nur mit zusätzlichem weißem Fahrschein (ohne Farbstrich) ausgeführt werden.
3. Eigenmächtiges Benutzen einer höheren Wagenklasse ist verboten.
4. Die Inanspruchnahme von Wehrmachtfahrkarten oder Fahrkarten des öffentlichen Verkehrs für die im Wehrmachtfahrschein bezeichnete Strecke ist verboten.
5. Es ist der am .... von Bhf. Wien-Nord .... um .... Uhr abgehende .... Zug Nr. .... bis Bhf. Charkow .... zu benutzen.
6. Dienstgrad, Vor- und Zuname des Reisenden: San.Uffz. Biermeier
   (bei mehreren des Transportführers)
7. Zweck und Veranlassung der Reise: Kommandierung
8. Dieser Fahrausweis ist bei der Fahrkartenprüfung durch die Eisenbahn und bei der Zugkontrolle durch die Organe der Wehrmacht vorzuzeigen.

D

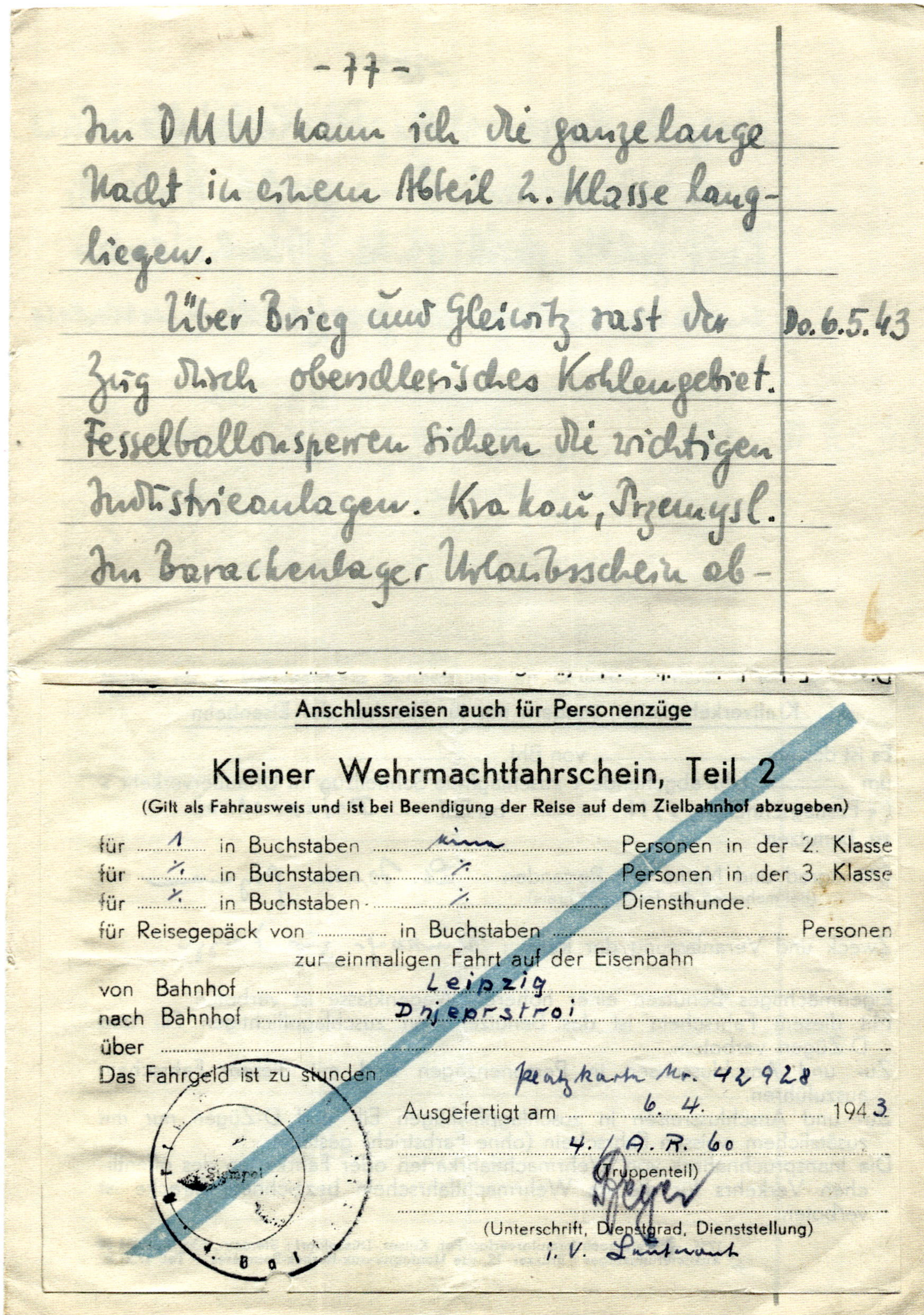

-77-

Im DMW kann ich die ganze lange Nacht in einem Abteil 2. Klasse lang-liegen.

Über Brieg und Gleiwitz rast der Zug durch oberschlesisches Kohlengebiet. Fesselballonsperren sichern die wichtigen Industrieanlagen. Krakau, Przemysl. Im Barackenlager Urlaubsschein ab- Do. 6.5.43

Anschlussreisen auch für Personenzüge

Kleiner Wehrmachtfahrschein, Teil 2

(Gilt als Fahrausweis und ist bei Beendigung der Reise auf dem Zielbahnhof abzugeben)

für 1 in Buchstaben eine Personen in der 2. Klasse
für ./. in Buchstaben ./. Personen in der 3. Klasse
für ./. in Buchstaben ./. Diensthunde
für Reisegepäck von .... in Buchstaben .... Personen
zur einmaligen Fahrt auf der Eisenbahn
von Bahnhof Leipzig
nach Bahnhof Dnjeprstroi
über ....
Das Fahrgeld ist zu stunden Platzkarte Nr. 42928

Ausgefertigt am 6. 4. 1943

4./A.R. 60
(Truppenteil)

(Unterschrift, Dienstgrad, Dienststellung)
i.V. Leutnant

Figure 2-95. This ticket was affixed to the first half of the diary entry of Leutnant Juzmann (see figure 2-72) which reads: "In DMW (?) I spent the entire night long in a 2nd class compartment of a passenger car. Through Brieg and Gleiwitz the train rested to take on a coal allotment, then on past flak balloon tethers in the industrial camps of Kracow and Przemysl. In Barachenlager (?) our leave passes were stamped."

Dieser Fahrschein gilt nicht für Strassenbahnen, Seilbahnen und Kraftomnibusse, auch nicht für den Seedienst Ostpreussen, sondern nur für Strecken der Eisenbahn

1. Mit diesem Fahrschein dürfen benutzt werden: Schnellzüge für Fronturlauber (SF), auch mit Reisezugteil (SFR), öffentliche Züge mit Wehrmachtteil (DmW, EmW, PmW); bei Zureisen und Anschlussreisen auch Personenzüge des öffentlichen Verkehrs (P).
2. Mit diesem Fahrschein ist es verboten, Schnell- und Eilzüge des öffentlichen Verkehrs ohne Wehrmachtteil (D, E) zu benutzen. Zureisen und Anschlussreisen in derartigen Zügen dürfen nur mit zusätzlichem weissem Fahrschein (ohne Farbanstrich) ausgeführt werden.
3. Eigenmächtiges Benutzen einer höheren Wagenklasse ist verboten.
4. Die Inanspruchnahme von Wehrmachtfahrkarten oder Fahrkarten des öffentlichen Verkehrs für die im Wehrmachtfahrschein bezeichnete Strecke ist verboten.
5. Es ist der am .... von Bhf. .... um ...... Uhr abgehende ....-Zug Nr. .... bis Bhf. .... zu benutzen.
6. Dienstgrad, Vor- und Zuname des Reisenden: Gefr. G. Kunze (bei mehreren des Transportführers)
7. Zweck und Veranlassung der Reise: Erholungsurlaub
8. Dieser Fahrausweis ist bei der Fahrkartenprüfung durch die Eisenbahn und bei der Zugkontrolle durch die Organe der Wehrmacht vorzuzeigen.

Gültig nur für die auf der Rückseite Ziff. 1 angegebenen Züge

Kleiner Wehrmachtfahrschein, Teil 1

(Wird bei Antritt der Reise von der Eisenbahn abgenommen)

für .-.-. in Buchstaben .-.-.-. Personen in der 2. Klasse
für ..1.. in Buchstaben .-.-. eine .-.-. Personen in der 3. Klasse
für .-.-. in Buchstaben .-.-.-. Diensthunde
für am Gepäckschalter aufzugebendes Reisegepäck (nicht Handgepäck) von .... in Buchstaben .... Personen
zur einmaligen Fahrt auf der Eisenbahn
von Bahnhof Berlin
nach Bahnhof Wien
über ....
Das Fahrgeld ist zu stunden.

Ausgefertigt am 6. September 1943

Dienststelle Feldpostnummer 41465
(Truppenteil bzw. Feldpostnummer)
(Dienststempel)
(Unterschrift, Dienstgrad, Dienststellung)
Oberzahlmeister u. Leiter

Figure 2-96. Here is another fine example of both pages of the Wehrmachtfahrschein and how carbon paper was used to ease the task of the clerk. In this case, Gefreiter Kunze travelled from Berlin to Vienna on Erholungsurlaub (Recreational Leave). (4 1/16" x 11 7/16")

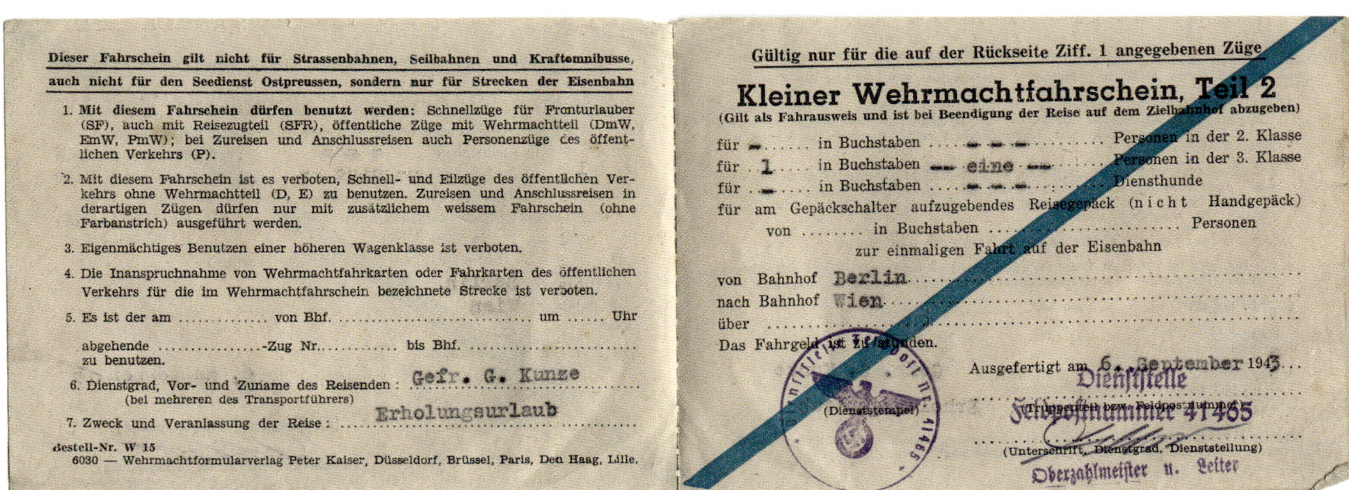

Dieser Fahrschein gilt nicht für Strassenbahnen, Seilbahnen und Kraftomnibusse, auch nicht für den Seedienst Ostpreussen, sondern nur für Strecken der Eisenbahn

1. Mit diesem Fahrschein dürfen benutzt werden: Schnellzüge für Fronturlauber (SF), auch mit Reisezugteil (SFR), öffentliche Züge mit Wehrmachtteil (DmW, EmW, PmW); bei Zureisen und Anschlussreisen auch Personenzüge des öffentlichen Verkehrs (P).
2. Mit diesem Fahrschein ist es verboten, Schnell- und Eilzüge des öffentlichen Verkehrs ohne Wehrmachtteil (D, E) zu benutzen. Zureisen und Anschlussreisen in derartigen Zügen dürfen nur mit zusätzlichem weissem Fahrschein (ohne Farbanstrich) ausgeführt werden.
3. Eigenmächtiges Benutzen einer höheren Wagenklasse ist verboten.
4. Die Inanspruchnahme von Wehrmachtfahrkarten oder Fahrkarten des öffentlichen Verkehrs für die im Wehrmachtfahrschein bezeichnete Strecke ist verboten.
5. Es ist der am .... von Bhf. .... um ...... Uhr abgehende ....-Zug Nr. .... bis Bhf. .... zu benutzen.
6. Dienstgrad, Vor- und Zuname des Reisenden: Gefr. G. Kunze (bei mehreren des Transportführers)
7. Zweck und Veranlassung der Reise: Erholungsurlaub

Bestell-Nr. W 15
6030 — Wehrmachtformularverlag Peter Kaiser, Düsseldorf, Brüssel, Paris, Den Haag, Lille.

Gültig nur für die auf der Rückseite Ziff. 1 angegebenen Züge

Kleiner Wehrmachtfahrschein, Teil 2

(Gilt als Fahrausweis und ist bei Beendigung der Reise auf dem Zielbahnhof abzugeben)

für .-.-. in Buchstaben .-.-.-. Personen in der 2. Klasse
für ..1.. in Buchstaben .-.-. eine .-.-. Personen in der 3. Klasse
für .-.-. in Buchstaben .-.-.-. Diensthunde
für am Gepäckschalter aufzugebendes Reisegepäck (nicht Handgepäck) von .... in Buchstaben .... Personen
zur einmaligen Fahrt auf der Eisenbahn
von Bahnhof Berlin
nach Bahnhof Wien
über ....
Das Fahrgeld ist zu stunden.

Ausgefertigt am 6. September 1943

Dienststelle Feldpostnummer 41465
(Truppenteil bzw. Feldpostnummer)
(Dienststempel)
(Unterschrift, Dienstgrad, Dienststellung)
Oberzahlmeister u. Leiter

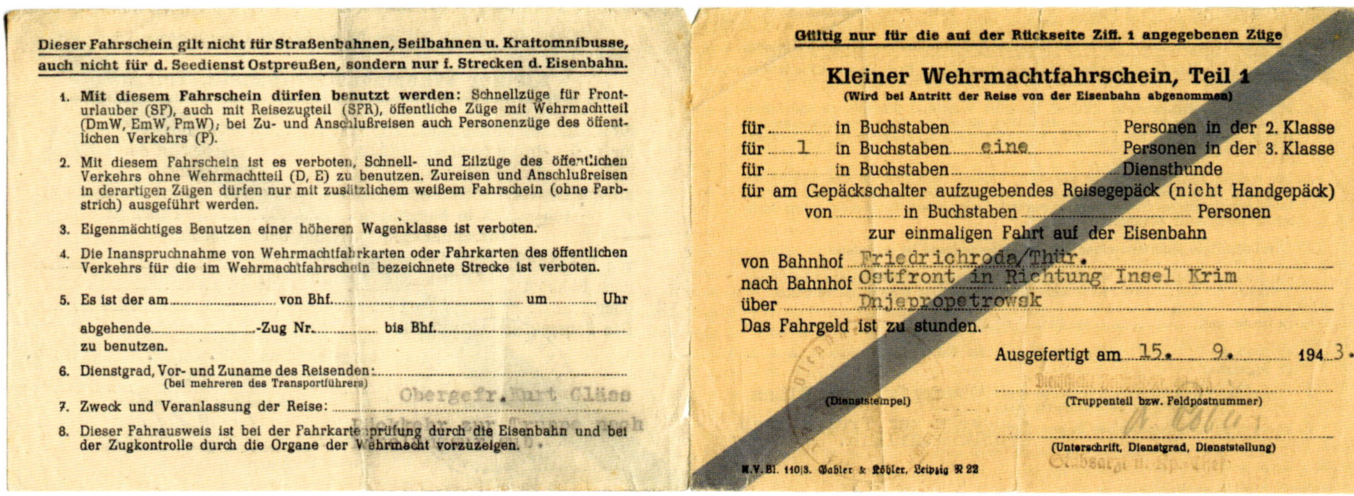

Dieser Fahrschein gilt nicht für Straßenbahnen, Seilbahnen u. Kraftomnibusse, auch nicht für d. Seedienst Ostpreußen, sondern nur f. Strecken d. Eisenbahn.

1. **Mit diesem Fahrschein dürfen benutzt werden:** Schnellzüge für Fronturlauber (SF), auch mit Reisezugteil (SFR), öffentliche Züge mit Wehrmachtteil (DmW, EmW, PmW); bei Zu- und Anschlußreisen auch Personenzüge des öffentlichen Verkehrs (P).
2. Mit diesem Fahrschein ist es verboten, Schnell- und Eilzüge des öffentlichen Verkehrs ohne Wehrmachtteil (D, E) zu benutzen. Zureisen und Anschlußreisen in derartigen Zügen dürfen nur mit zusätzlichem weißem Fahrschein (ohne Farbstrich) ausgeführt werden.
3. Eigenmächtiges Benutzen einer höheren Wagenklasse ist verboten.
4. Die Inanspruchnahme von Wehrmachtfahrkarten oder Fahrkarten des öffentlichen Verkehrs für die im Wehrmachtfahrschein bezeichnete Strecke ist verboten.
5. Es ist der am .... von Bhf. .... um .... Uhr abgehende ....-Zug Nr. .... bis Bhf. .... zu benutzen.
6. Dienstgrad, Vor- und Zuname des Reisenden: .... (bei mehreren des Transportführers) Obergefr. Kurt Gläss
7. Zweck und Veranlassung der Reise: .... Rückkehr zur Truppe nach
8. Dieser Fahrausweis ist bei der Fahrkartenprüfung durch die Eisenbahn und bei der Zugkontrolle durch die Organe der Wehrmacht vorzuzeigen.

Gültig nur für die auf der Rückseite Ziff. 1 angegebenen Züge

Kleiner Wehrmachtfahrschein, Teil 1

(Wird bei Antritt der Reise von der Eisenbahn abgenommen)

für .... in Buchstaben .... Personen in der 2. Klasse
für 1 in Buchstaben eine Personen in der 3. Klasse
für .... in Buchstaben .... Diensthunde
für am Gepäckschalter aufzugebendes Reisegepäck (nicht Handgepäck)
von .... in Buchstaben .... Personen
zur einmaligen Fahrt auf der Eisenbahn
von Bahnhof Friedrichroda/Thür.
nach Bahnhof Ostfront in Richtung Insel Krim
über Dnjepropetrowsk
Das Fahrgeld ist zu stunden.

Ausgefertigt am 15. 9. 1943.

(Dienststempel) (Truppenteil bzw. Feldpostnummer)

(Unterschrift, Dienstgrad, Dienststellung)

Stabsarzt u. Kp.-Chef

H.V.Bl. 110/3. Gabler & Kobler, Leipzig R 22

Figure 2-97. In this example, Obergefreiter Kurt Gläss returned to his troop following recreational leave (Sanitäts-Kompanie 14, Medical Company 14) and travelled from Thüringen to Dnepropetrovsk in the Crimea, a month before the Russian offensive. ($4^1/_8$" x $11^7/_{16}$")

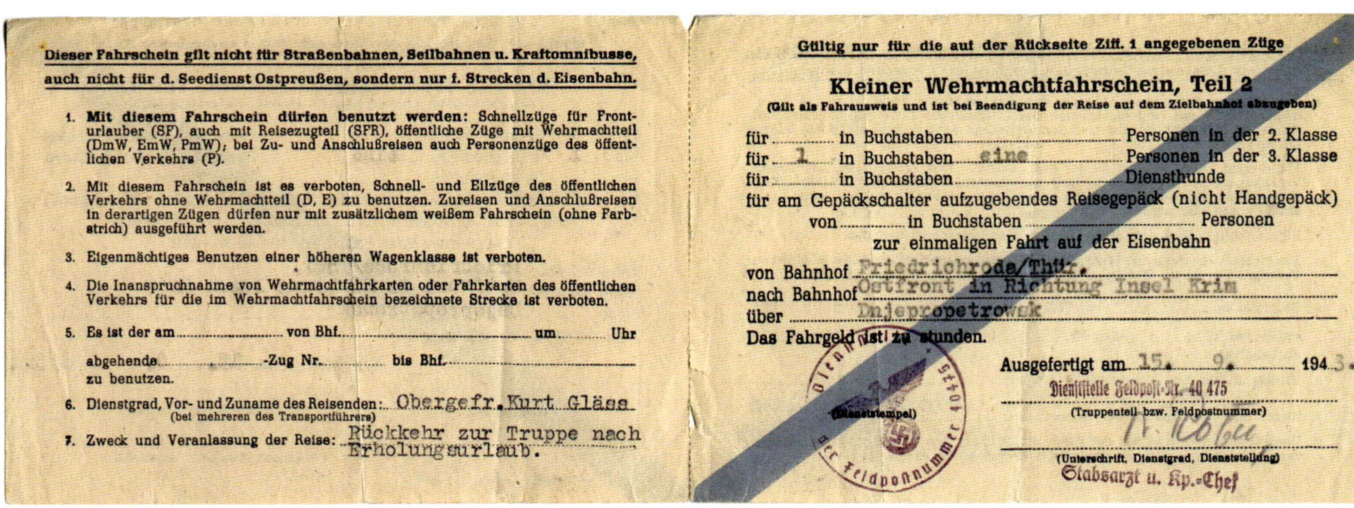

Dieser Fahrschein gilt nicht für Straßenbahnen, Seilbahnen u. Kraftomnibusse, auch nicht für d. Seedienst Ostpreußen, sondern nur f. Strecken d. Eisenbahn.

1. **Mit diesem Fahrschein dürfen benutzt werden:** Schnellzüge für Fronturlauber (SF), auch mit Reisezugteil (SFR), öffentliche Züge mit Wehrmachtteil (DmW, EmW, PmW); bei Zu- und Anschlußreisen auch Personenzüge des öffentlichen Verkehrs (P).
2. Mit diesem Fahrschein ist es verboten, Schnell- und Eilzüge des öffentlichen Verkehrs ohne Wehrmachtteil (D, E) zu benutzen. Zureisen und Anschlußreisen in derartigen Zügen dürfen nur mit zusätzlichem weißem Fahrschein (ohne Farbstrich) ausgeführt werden.
3. Eigenmächtiges Benutzen einer höheren Wagenklasse ist verboten.
4. Die Inanspruchnahme von Wehrmachtfahrkarten oder Fahrkarten des öffentlichen Verkehrs für die im Wehrmachtfahrschein bezeichnete Strecke ist verboten.
5. Es ist der am .... von Bhf. .... um .... Uhr abgehende ....-Zug Nr. .... bis Bhf. .... zu benutzen.
6. Dienstgrad, Vor- und Zuname des Reisenden: Obergefr. Kurt Gläss (bei mehreren des Transportführers)
7. Zweck und Veranlassung der Reise: Rückkehr zur Truppe nach Erholungsurlaub.

Gültig nur für die auf der Rückseite Ziff. 1 angegebenen Züge

Kleiner Wehrmachtfahrschein, Teil 2

(Gilt als Fahrausweis und ist bei Beendigung der Reise auf dem Zielbahnhof abzugeben)

für .... in Buchstaben .... Personen in der 2. Klasse
für 1 in Buchstaben eine Personen in der 3. Klasse
für .... in Buchstaben .... Diensthunde
für am Gepäckschalter aufzugebendes Reisegepäck (nicht Handgepäck)
von .... in Buchstaben .... Personen
zur einmaligen Fahrt auf der Eisenbahn
von Bahnhof Friedrichroda/Thür.
nach Bahnhof Ostfront in Richtung Insel Krim
über Dnjepropetrowsk
Das Fahrgeld ist zu stunden.

Ausgefertigt am 15. 9. 1943.

Dienststelle Feldpost-Nr. 40 475
(Truppenteil bzw. Feldpostnummer)

(Dienststempel) Feldpostnummer 40475

(Unterschrift, Dienstgrad, Dienststellung)
Stabsarzt u. Kp.-Chef

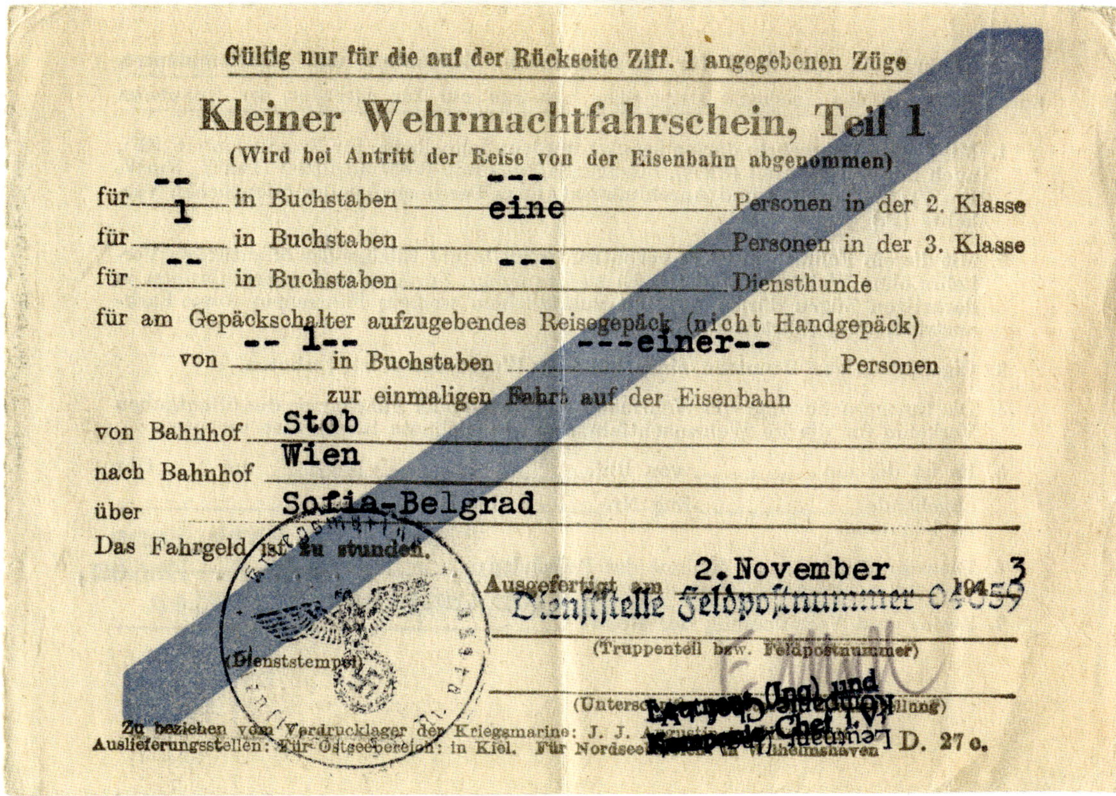

Gültig nur für die auf der Rückseite Ziff. 1 angegebenen Züge

Kleiner Wehrmachtfahrschein, Teil 1

(Wird bei Antritt der Reise von der Eisenbahn abgenommen)

für 1 in Buchstaben eine Personen in der 2. Klasse

für ___ in Buchstaben ___ Personen in der 3. Klasse

für -- in Buchstaben --- Diensthunde

für am Gepäckschalter aufzugebendes Reisegepäck (nicht Handgepäck)

von -- 1-- in Buchstaben ---einer-- Personen

zur einmaligen Fahrt auf der Eisenbahn

von Bahnhof Stob

nach Bahnhof Wien

über Sofia-Belgrad

Das Fahrgeld ist zu stunden.

(Dienststempel)

Ausgefertigt am 2.November 1943

Dienststelle Feldpostnummer 04859

(Truppenteil bzw. Feldpostnummer)

(Unterschrift ... Stellung)

Kapitänleutnant (Ing) und Kompanie Chef I.V.

Zu beziehen vom Vordrucklager der Kriegsmarine: J. J. Augustin ...

Auslieferungsstellen: Für Ostseebereich: in Kiel. Für Nordseebereich: in Wilhelmshaven D. 27 c.

Figure 2-98. Issued by 2. Marine-Kraftwagen-Einsatz-Abteilung (2nd Naval Transport Training Section), this ticket got Obergefreiter Hans Rath from Stob, Bulgaria to Vienna, Austria by way of Sofia-Belgrade in November 1943.

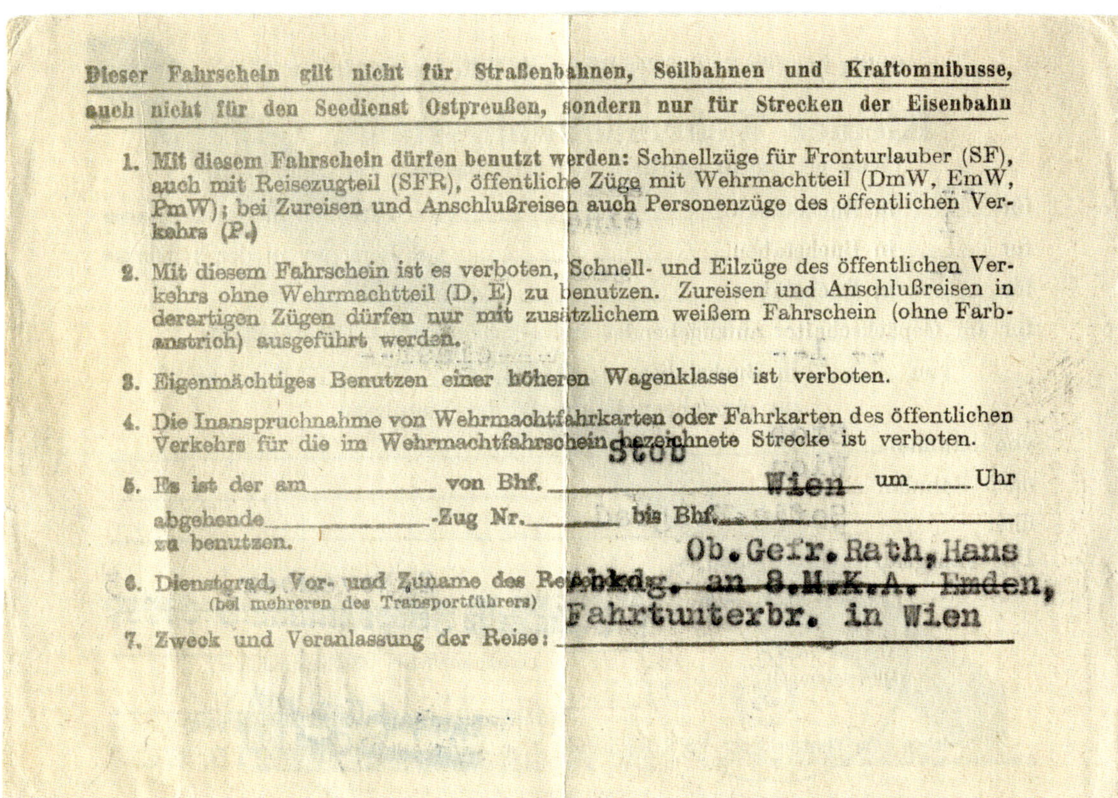

Dieser Fahrschein gilt nicht für Straßenbahnen, Seilbahnen und Kraftomnibusse, auch nicht für den Seedienst Ostpreußen, sondern nur für Strecken der Eisenbahn

1. Mit diesem Fahrschein dürfen benutzt werden: Schnellzüge für Fronturlauber (SF), auch mit Reisezugteil (SFR), öffentliche Züge mit Wehrmachtteil (DmW, EmW, PmW); bei Zureisen und Anschlußreisen auch Personenzüge des öffentlichen Verkehrs (P.)

2. Mit diesem Fahrschein ist es verboten, Schnell- und Eilzüge des öffentlichen Verkehrs ohne Wehrmachtteil (D, E) zu benutzen. Zureisen und Anschlußreisen in derartigen Zügen dürfen nur mit zusätzlichem weißem Fahrschein (ohne Farbanstrich) ausgeführt werden.

3. Eigenmächtiges Benutzen einer höheren Wagenklasse ist verboten.

4. Die Inanspruchnahme von Wehrmachtfahrkarten oder Fahrkarten des öffentlichen Verkehrs für die im Wehrmachtfahrschein bezeichnete Strecke ist verboten.

5. Es ist der am ___ von Bhf. Stob Wien um ___ Uhr abgehende ___-Zug Nr. ___ bis Bhf. ___ zu benutzen.

6. Dienstgrad, Vor- und Zuname des Reisenden (bei mehreren des Transportführers) Ob.Gefr.Rath,Hans

7. Zweck und Veranlassung der Reise: Abkdg. an 8.M.K.A. Emden, Fahrtunterbr. in Wien

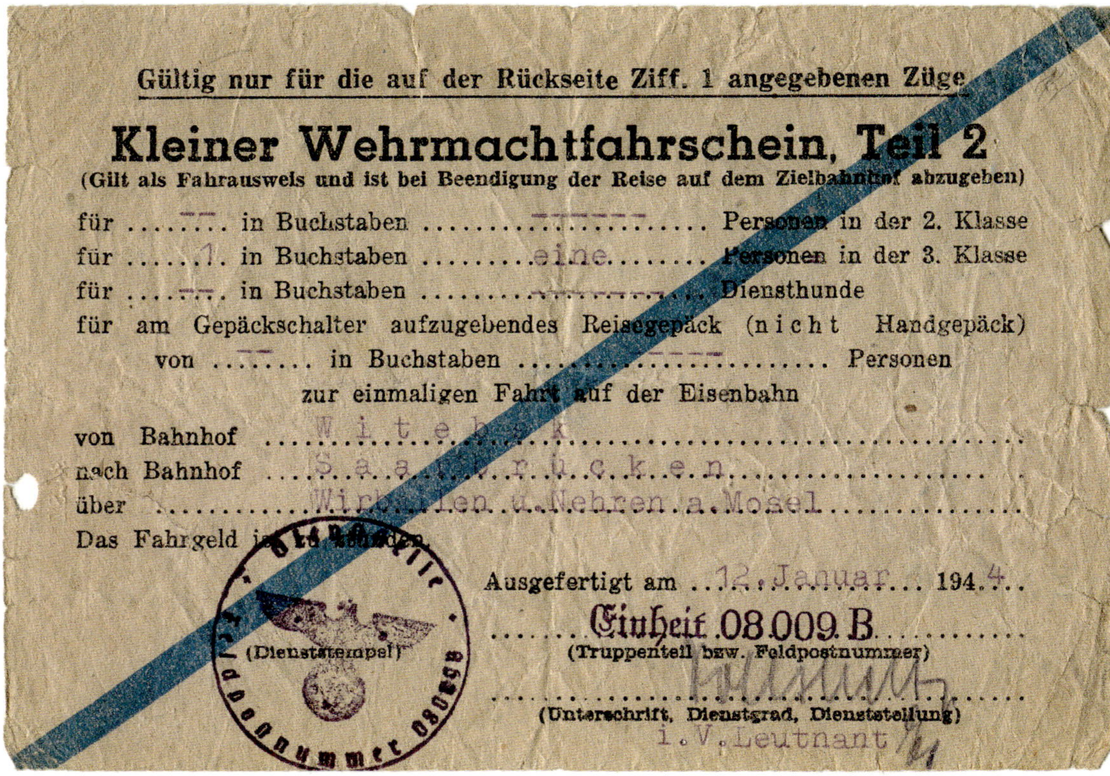

Gültig nur für die auf der Rückseite Ziff. 1 angegebenen Züge

Kleiner Wehrmachtfahrschein, Teil 2

(Gilt als Fahrausweis und ist bei Beendigung der Reise auf dem Zielbahnhof abzugeben)

für ....-.-.. in Buchstaben .... Personen in der 2. Klasse

für ......1. in Buchstaben ....eine......... Personen in der 3. Klasse

für ....-.-.. in Buchstaben .... Diensthunde

für am Gepäckschalter aufzugebendes Reisegepäck (nicht Handgepäck)

von .... in Buchstaben .... Personen

zur einmaligen Fahrt auf der Eisenbahn

von Bahnhof ......Witebsk......................................

nach Bahnhof ......Saarbrücken......................................

über ......Wirballen u. Wehren a. Mosel......................................

Das Fahrgeld ist zu stunden.

(Dienststempel)

Ausgefertigt am ...12. Januar... 194.4..

.......Einheit 08 009 B.......

(Truppenteil bzw. Feldpostnummer)

....

(Unterschrift, Dienstgrad, Dienststellung)

i.V. Leutnant

Figure 2-99. Feldwebel Hans Sichl, assigned to travel on SF-Zug 869 (SF Train 869), rode this train from Vitebsk, Russia to Virbalis, Lithuania, to Danzig, through Berlin, to finally come to a stop in Saarbrücken.

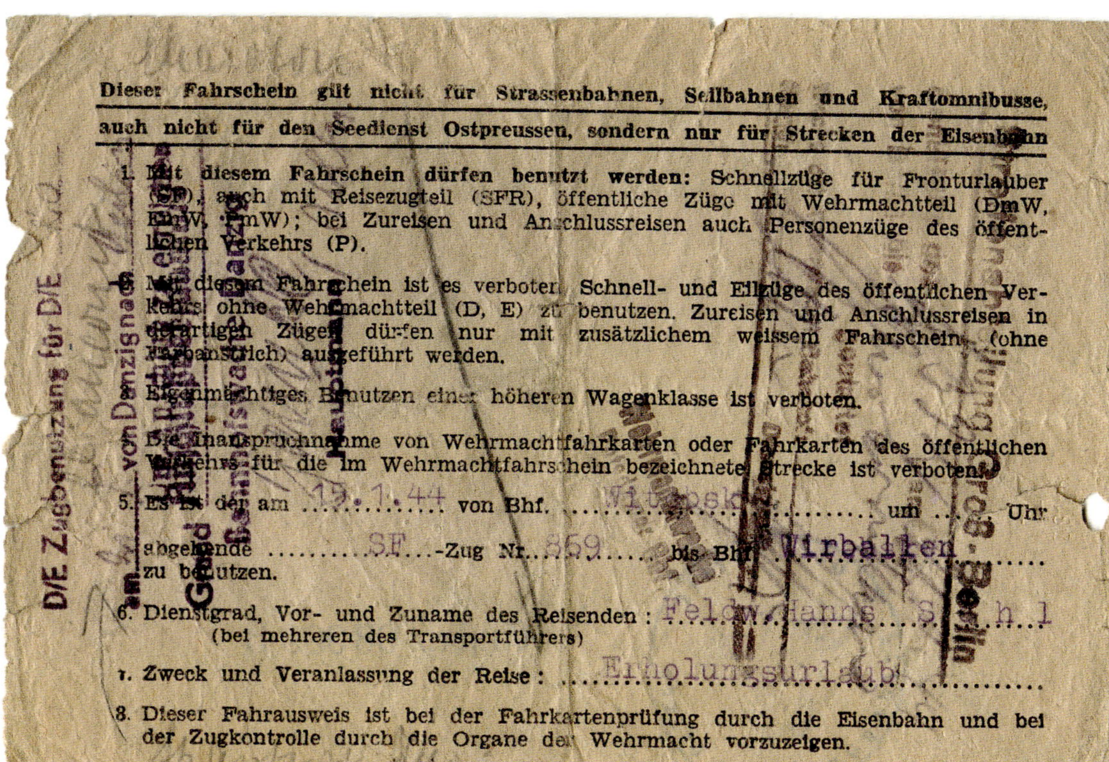

Dieser Fahrschein gilt nicht für Strassenbahnen, Seilbahnen und Kraftomnibusse, auch nicht für den Seedienst Ostpreussen, sondern nur für Strecken der Eisenbahn

1. Mit diesem Fahrschein dürfen benutzt werden: Schnellzüge für Fronturlauber (SF), auch mit Reisezugteil (SFR), öffentliche Züge mit Wehrmachtteil (DmW, EmW, PmW); bei Zureisen und Anschlussreisen auch Personenzüge des öffentlichen Verkehrs (P).

2. Mit diesem Fahrschein ist es verboten, Schnell- und Eilzüge des öffentlichen Verkehrs ohne Wehrmachtteil (D, E) zu benutzen. Zureisen und Anschlussreisen in derartigen Zügen dürfen nur mit zusätzlichem weissem Fahrschein (ohne Farbanstrich) ausgeführt werden.

3. Eigenmächtiges Benutzen einer höheren Wagenklasse ist verboten.

4. Die Inanspruchnahme von Wehrmachtfahrkarten oder Fahrkarten des öffentlichen Verkehrs für die im Wehrmachtfahrschein bezeichnete Strecke ist verboten.

5. Es ist der am ...13.1.44... von Bhf. ......Witebsk......... um ...... Uhr abgehende ....SF...-Zug Nr...869....... bis Bhf. ...Wirballen...... zu benutzen.

6. Dienstgrad, Vor- und Zuname des Reisenden: Feldw. Hanns S...h...l (bei mehreren des Transportführers)

7. Zweck und Veranlassung der Reise: ......Erholungsurlaub......

8. Dieser Fahrausweis ist bei der Fahrkartenprüfung durch die Eisenbahn und bei der Zugkontrolle durch die Organe der Wehrmacht vorzuzeigen.

D/E Zugbenutzung für D/E ... von Danzig nach ...

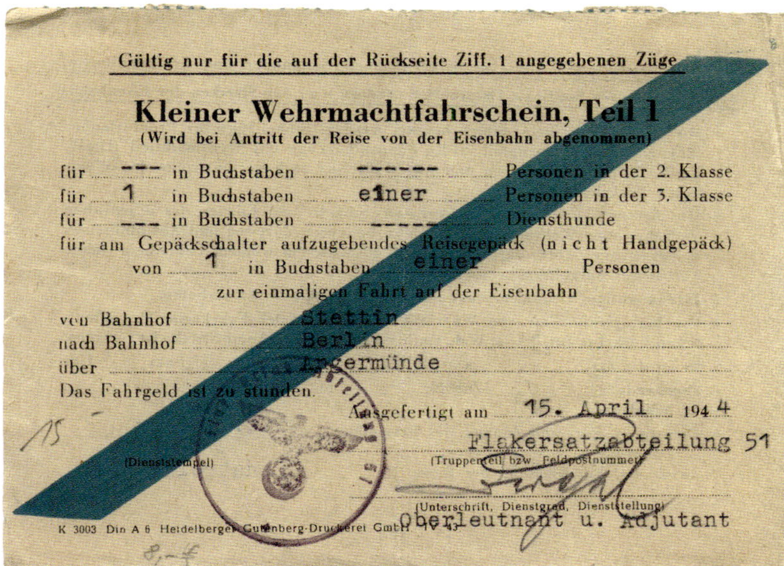
Gültig nur für die auf der Rückseite Ziff. 1 angegebenen Züge

Kleiner Wehrmachtfahrschein, Teil 1
(Wird bei Antritt der Reise von der Eisenbahn abgenommen)

für --- in Buchstaben ------- Personen in der 2. Klasse
für 1 in Buchstaben einer Personen in der 3. Klasse
für --- in Buchstaben ----- Diensthunde
für am Gepäckschalter aufzugebendes Reisegepäck (nicht Handgepäck)
von 1 in Buchstaben einer Personen
zur einmaligen Fahrt auf der Eisenbahn
von Bahnhof Stettin
nach Bahnhof Berlin
über Angermünde
Das Fahrgeld ist zu stunden.
Ausgefertigt am 15. April 1944
Flakersatzabteilung 51
(Dienststempel) (Truppenteil bzw. Feldpostnummer)
(Unterschrift, Dienstgrad, Dienststellung)
Oberleutnant u. Adjutant
K 3003 Din A 6 Heidelberger Gutenberg-Druckerei GmbH IV. 43

A

B

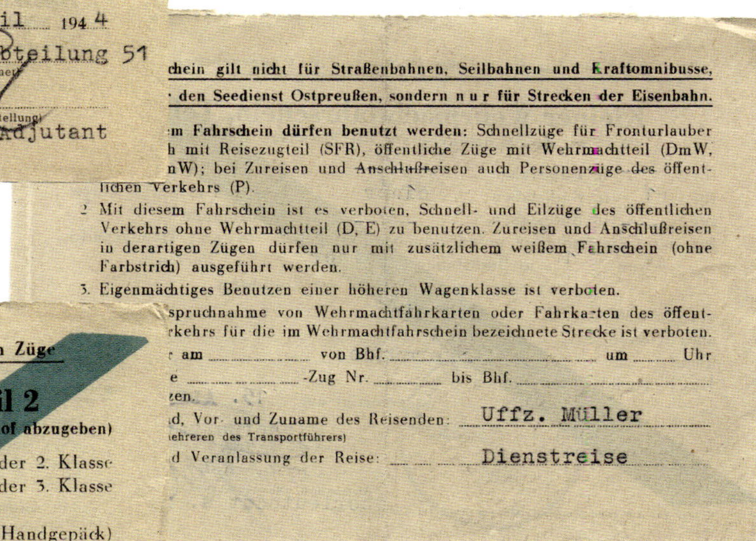
...chein gilt nicht für Straßenbahnen, Seilbahnen und Kraftomnibusse,
... den Seedienst Ostpreußen, sondern nur für Strecken der Eisenbahn.
...m Fahrschein dürfen benutzt werden: Schnellzüge für Fronturlauber ...h mit Reisezugteil (SFR), öffentliche Züge mit Wehrmachtteil (DmW, ...nW); bei Zureisen und Anschlußreisen auch Personenzüge des öffentlichen Verkehrs (P).
2. Mit diesem Fahrschein ist es verboten, Schnell- und Eilzüge des öffentlichen Verkehrs ohne Wehrmachtteil (D, E) zu benutzen. Zureisen und Anschlußreisen in derartigen Zügen dürfen nur mit zusätzlichem weißem Fahrschein (ohne Farbstrich) ausgeführt werden.
3. Eigenmächtiges Benutzen einer höheren Wagenklasse ist verboten.
...spruchnahme von Wehrmachtfahrkarten oder Fahrkarten des öffent... ...rkehrs für die im Wehrmachtfahrschein bezeichnete Strecke ist verboten.
... am ... von Bhf. ... um ... Uhr
...e ... -Zug Nr. ... bis Bhf. ...
...zen.
...d, Vor- und Zuname des Reisenden: Uffz. Müller
...ehreren des Transportführers)
...d Veranlassung der Reise: Dienstreise

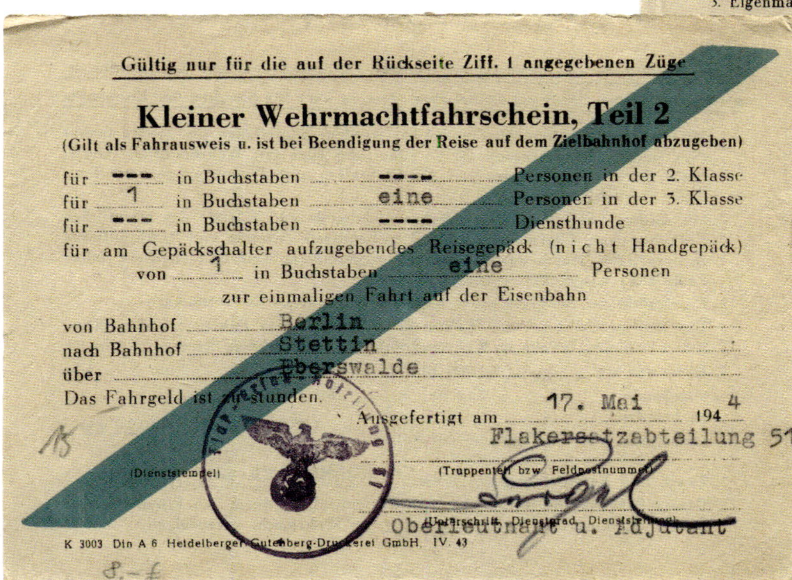
Gültig nur für die auf der Rückseite Ziff. 1 angegebenen Züge

Kleiner Wehrmachtfahrschein, Teil 2
(Gilt als Fahrausweis u. ist bei Beendigung der Reise auf dem Zielbahnhof abzugeben)

für --- in Buchstaben ---- Personen in der 2. Klasse
für 1 in Buchstaben eine Personen in der 3. Klasse
für --- in Buchstaben ---- Diensthunde
für am Gepäckschalter aufzugebendes Reisegepäck (nicht Handgepäck)
von 1 in Buchstaben eine Personen
zur einmaligen Fahrt auf der Eisenbahn
von Bahnhof Berlin
nach Bahnhof Stettin
über Eberswalde
Das Fahrgeld ist zu stunden.
Ausgefertigt am 17. Mai 1944
Flakersatzabteilung 51
(Dienststempel) (Truppenteil bzw. Feldpostnummer)
(Unterschrift, Dienstgrad, Dienststellung)
Oberleutnant u. Adjutant
K 3003 Din A 6 Heidelberger Gutenberg-Druckerei GmbH IV. 43

C

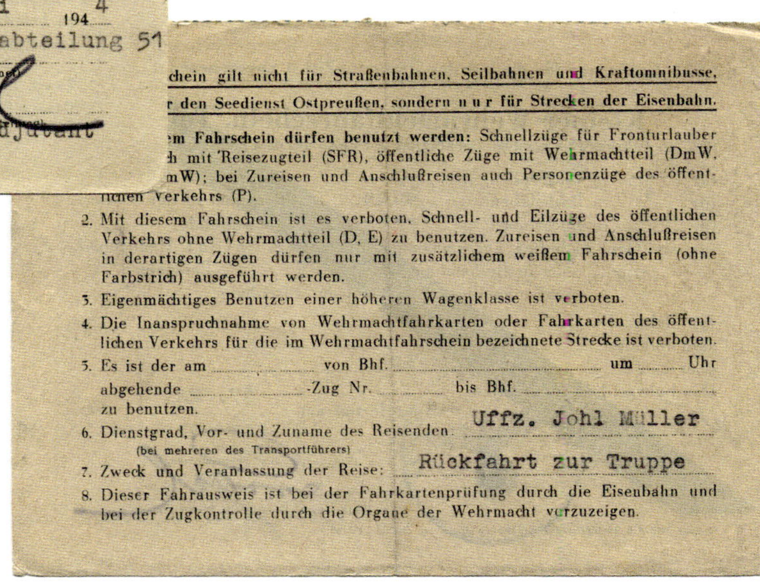
...chein gilt nicht für Straßenbahnen, Seilbahnen und Kraftomnibusse,
...r den Seedienst Ostpreußen, sondern nur für Strecken der Eisenbahn.
...m Fahrschein dürfen benutzt werden: Schnellzüge für Fronturlauber ...h mit Reisezugteil (SFR), öffentliche Züge mit Wehrmachtteil (DmW, ...mW); bei Zureisen und Anschlußreisen auch Personenzüge des öffentlichen Verkehrs (P).
2. Mit diesem Fahrschein ist es verboten, Schnell- und Eilzüge des öffentlichen Verkehrs ohne Wehrmachtteil (D, E) zu benutzen. Zureisen und Anschlußreisen in derartigen Zügen dürfen nur mit zusätzlichem weißem Fahrschein (ohne Farbstrich) ausgeführt werden.
3. Eigenmächtiges Benutzen einer höheren Wagenklasse ist verboten.
4. Die Inanspruchnahme von Wehrmachtfahrkarten oder Fahrkarten des öffentlichen Verkehrs für die im Wehrmachtfahrschein bezeichnete Strecke ist verboten.
5. Es ist der am ... von Bhf. ... um ... Uhr
abgehende ... -Zug Nr. ... bis Bhf. ...
zu benutzen.
6. Dienstgrad, Vor- und Zuname des Reisenden: Uffz. Johl Müller
(bei mehreren des Transportführers)
7. Zweck und Veranlassung der Reise: Rückfahrt zur Truppe
8. Dieser Fahrausweis ist bei der Fahrkartenprüfung durch die Eisenbahn und bei der Zugkontrolle durch die Organe der Wehrmacht vorzuzeigen.

D

Figure 2-100. Although many clerks used carbon paper to fill out the Wehrmachtfahrschein, this is an example of how it was supposed to be filled out. Teil 1 (page 1) is filled out showing the trip from Bahnhof Stettin to Berlin, through Angermünde. On the back of page 1, the purpose of travel is listed as Dienstreise; Service Travel (image B). On Teil 2, page 2 (image C), the route shows Unteroffizier Johann Müller returning from Berlin to Stettin through Eberswalde to rejoin his unit (Rückfahrt zur Truppe, image D). (A6)

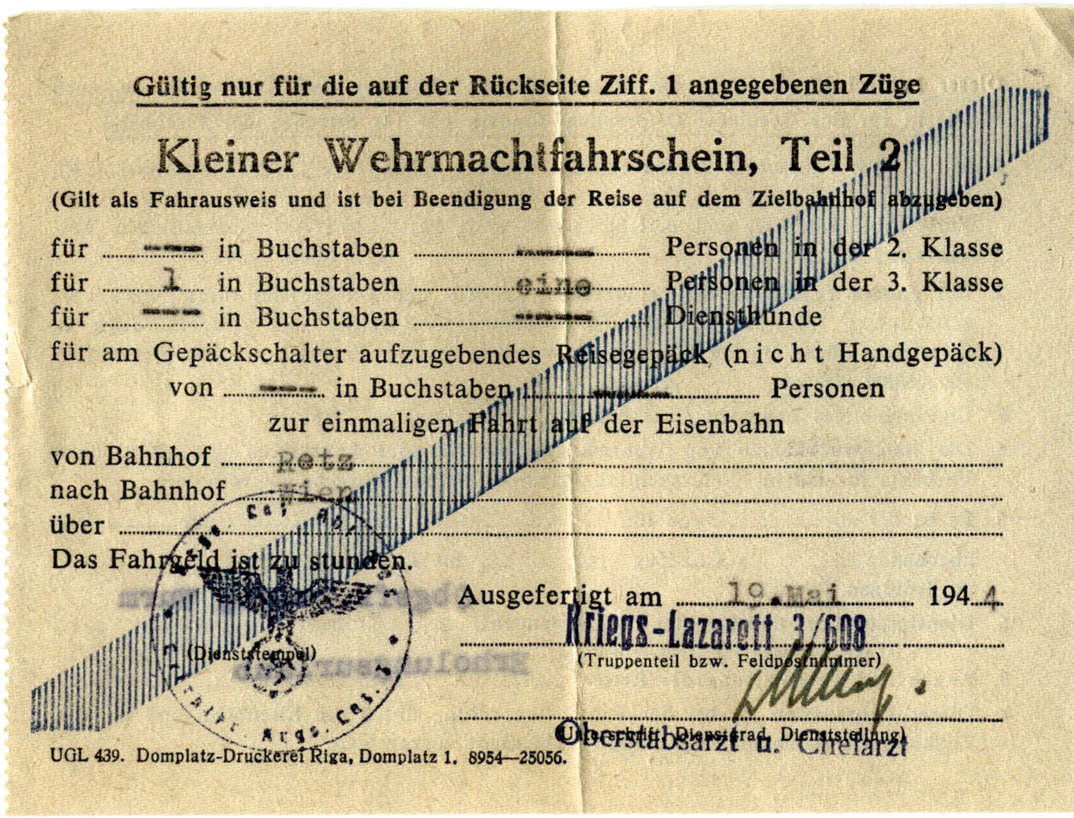

Gültig nur für die auf der Rückseite Ziff. 1 angegebenen Züge

Kleiner Wehrmachtfahrschein, Teil 2

(Gilt als Fahrausweis und ist bei Beendigung der Reise auf dem Zielbahnhof abzugeben)

für ---- in Buchstaben ---- Personen in der 2. Klasse
für 1 in Buchstaben eine Personen in der 3. Klasse
für ---- in Buchstaben ---- Diensthunde
für am Gepäckschalter aufzugebendes Reisegepäck (nicht Handgepäck)
von ---- in Buchstaben ---- Personen
zur einmaligen Fahrt auf der Eisenbahn
von Bahnhof Retz
nach Bahnhof Wien
über
Das Fahrgeld ist zu stunden.

Ausgefertigt am 19. Mai 1944

Kriegs-Lazarett 3/608
(Truppenteil bzw. Feldpostnummer)

(Dienststempel)

(Unterschrift, Dienstgrad, Dienststellung)
Oberstabsarzt u. Chefarzt

UGL 439. Domplatz-Druckerei Riga, Domplatz 1. 8954—25056.

Figure 2-101. This Fahrschein was issued to Obergefreiter Ludwig Wurm by Kriegs-Lazarett 3/608 (War Hospital 3/608) in Retz, Austria, on the Czech-Austrian border. Head Doctors (or rather, their offices) were permitted not only to care for the sick and wounded, but were required to authorize leave as well (the Oberstabsarzt und Chefarzt, Head Staff Doctor and Chief Doctor, was roughly the equivalent to a Director of a hospital today).

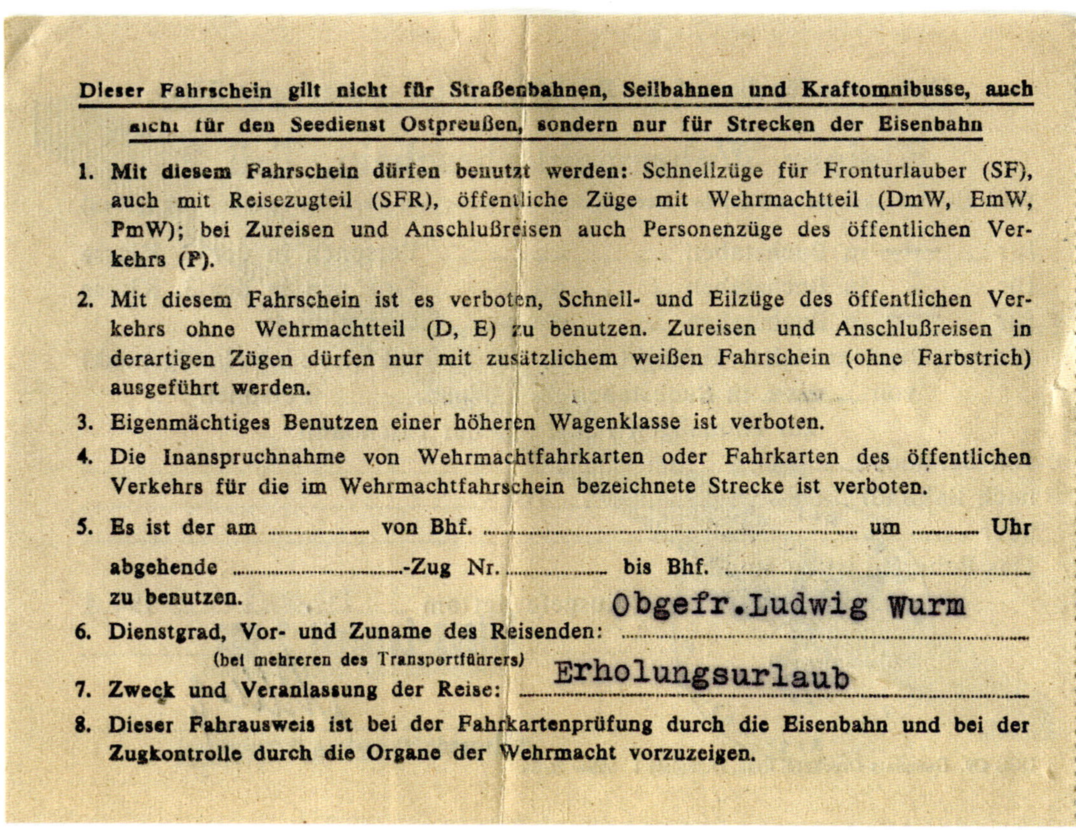

Dieser Fahrschein gilt nicht für Straßenbahnen, Seilbahnen und Kraftomnibusse, auch nicht für den Seedienst Ostpreußen, sondern nur für Strecken der Eisenbahn

1. **Mit diesem Fahrschein dürfen benutzt werden:** Schnellzüge für Fronturlauber (SF), auch mit Reisezugteil (SFR), öffentliche Züge mit Wehrmachtteil (DmW, EmW, PmW); bei Zureisen und Anschlußreisen auch Personenzüge des öffentlichen Verkehrs (P).
2. Mit diesem Fahrschein ist es verboten, Schnell- und Eilzüge des öffentlichen Verkehrs ohne Wehrmachtteil (D, E) zu benutzen. Zureisen und Anschlußreisen in derartigen Zügen dürfen nur mit zusätzlichem weißen Fahrschein (ohne Farbstrich) ausgeführt werden.
3. Eigenmächtiges Benutzen einer höheren Wagenklasse ist verboten.
4. Die Inanspruchnahme von Wehrmachtfahrkarten oder Fahrkarten des öffentlichen Verkehrs für die im Wehrmachtfahrschein bezeichnete Strecke ist verboten.
5. Es ist der am .... von Bhf. .... um .... Uhr abgehende ....-Zug Nr. .... bis Bhf. .... zu benutzen.
6. Dienstgrad, Vor- und Zuname des Reisenden: Obgefr. Ludwig Wurm
(bei mehreren des Transportführers)
7. Zweck und Veranlassung der Reise: Erholungsurlaub
8. Dieser Fahrausweis ist bei der Fahrkartenprüfung durch die Eisenbahn und bei der Zugkontrolle durch die Organe der Wehrmacht vorzuzeigen.

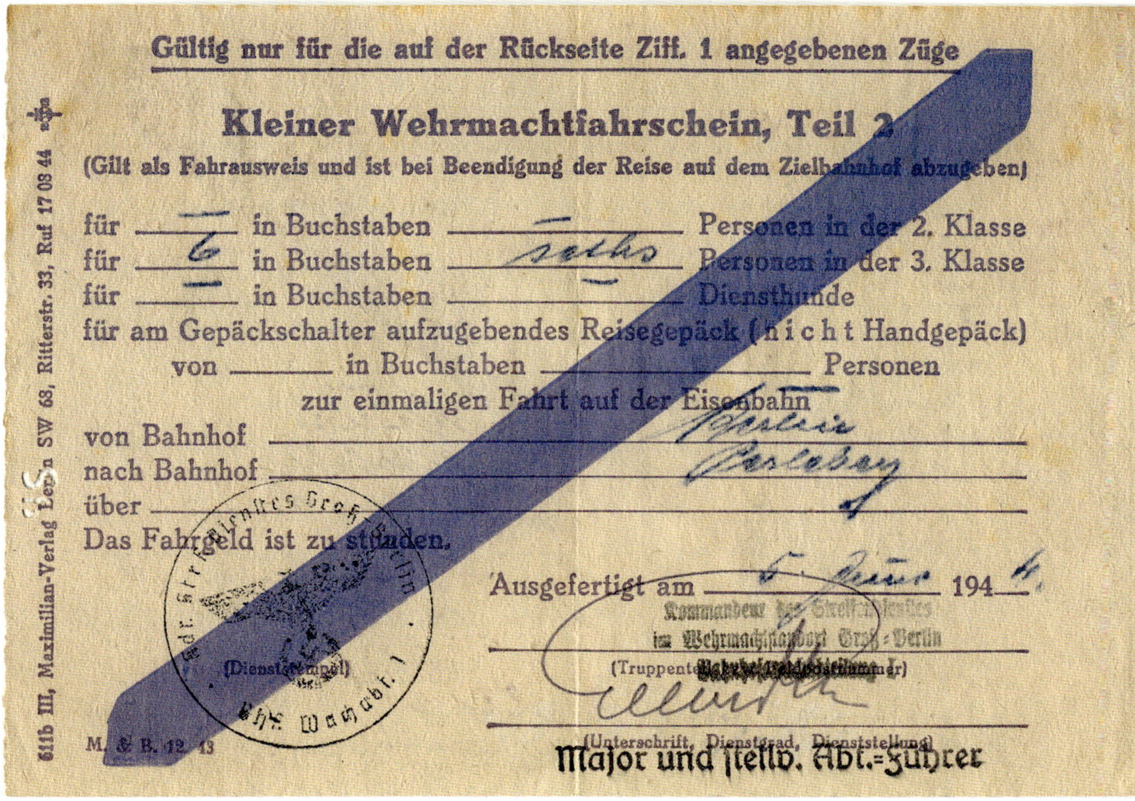

Gültig nur für die auf der Rückseite Ziff. 1 angegebenen Züge

Kleiner Wehrmachtfahrschein, Teil 2

(Gilt als Fahrausweis und ist bei Beendigung der Reise auf dem Zielbahnhof abzugeben)

für — in Buchstaben — Personen in der 2. Klasse
für 6 in Buchstaben sechs Personen in der 3. Klasse
für — in Buchstaben — Diensthunde
für am Gepäckschalter aufzugebendes Reisegepäck (nicht Handgepäck)
von ______ in Buchstaben ______ Personen
zur einmaligen Fahrt auf der Eisenbahn
von Bahnhof ______
nach Bahnhof ______
über ______
Das Fahrgeld ist zu stunden.

Ausgefertigt am ______ 194 4.

Kommandeur des Streifendienstes im Wehrmachtstandort Groß-Berlin

(Dienststempel)

(Truppenteil, Feldpostnummer)

(Unterschrift, Dienstgrad, Dienststellung)

Major und stellv. Abt.-Führer

M. & B. 12. 43

Stilb III, Maximilian-Verlag Berlin SW 68, Ritterstr. 33, Ruf 17 08 44

Figure 2-102. Not everyone received their own Fahrschein; it was just as common to have one ticket for a number of soldiers. This one Ticket permitted six Soldaten to ride in 3rd class.

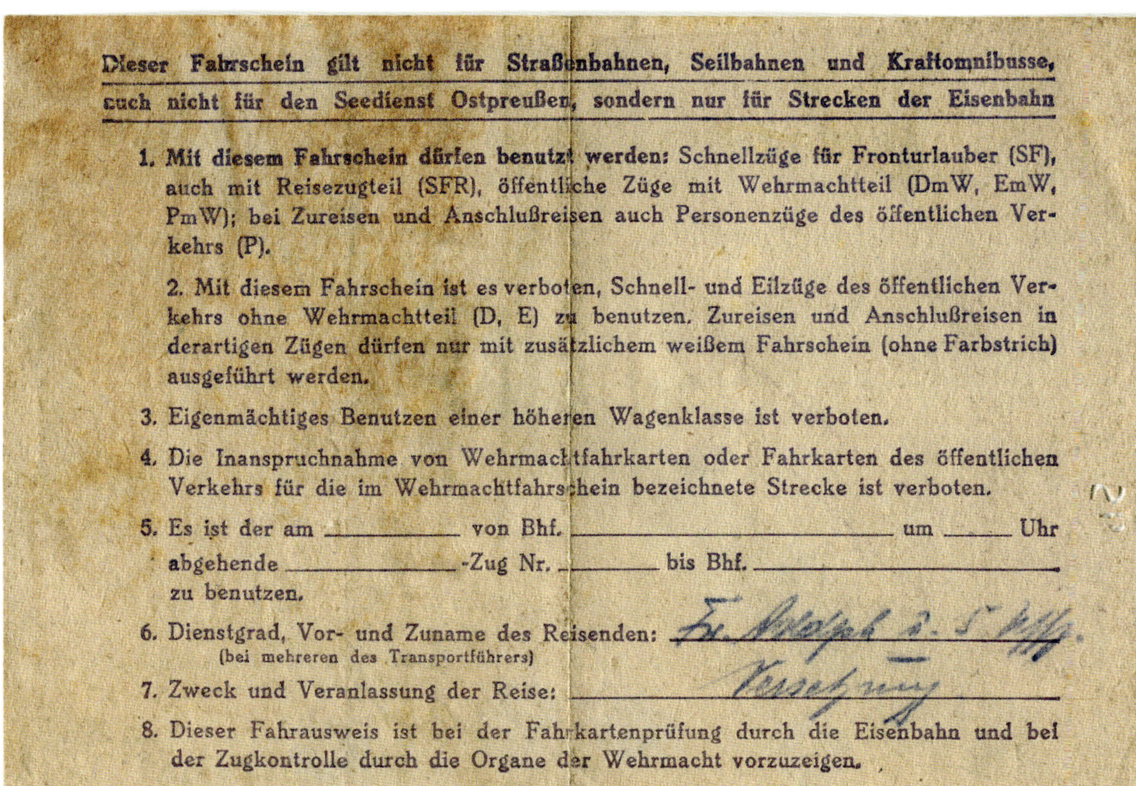

Dieser Fahrschein gilt nicht für Straßenbahnen, Seilbahnen und Kraftomnibusse, auch nicht für den Seedienst Ostpreußen, sondern nur für Strecken der Eisenbahn

1. Mit diesem Fahrschein dürfen benutzt werden: Schnellzüge für Fronturlauber (SF), auch mit Reisezugteil (SFR), öffentliche Züge mit Wehrmachtteil (DmW, EmW, PmW); bei Zureisen und Anschlußreisen auch Personenzüge des öffentlichen Verkehrs (P).

2. Mit diesem Fahrschein ist es verboten, Schnell- und Eilzüge des öffentlichen Verkehrs ohne Wehrmachtteil (D, E) zu benutzen. Zureisen und Anschlußreisen in derartigen Zügen dürfen nur mit zusätzlichem weißem Fahrschein (ohne Farbstrich) ausgeführt werden.

3. Eigenmächtiges Benutzen einer höheren Wagenklasse ist verboten.

4. Die Inanspruchnahme von Wehrmachtfahrkarten oder Fahrkarten des öffentlichen Verkehrs für die im Wehrmachtfahrschein bezeichnete Strecke ist verboten.

5. Es ist der am ______ von Bhf. ______ um ______ Uhr abgehende ______-Zug Nr. ______ bis Bhf. ______ zu benutzen.

6. Dienstgrad, Vor- und Zuname des Reisenden: ______
(bei mehreren des Transportführers)

7. Zweck und Veranlassung der Reise: ______

8. Dieser Fahrausweis ist bei der Fahrkartenprüfung durch die Eisenbahn und bei der Zugkontrolle durch die Organe der Wehrmacht vorzuzeigen.

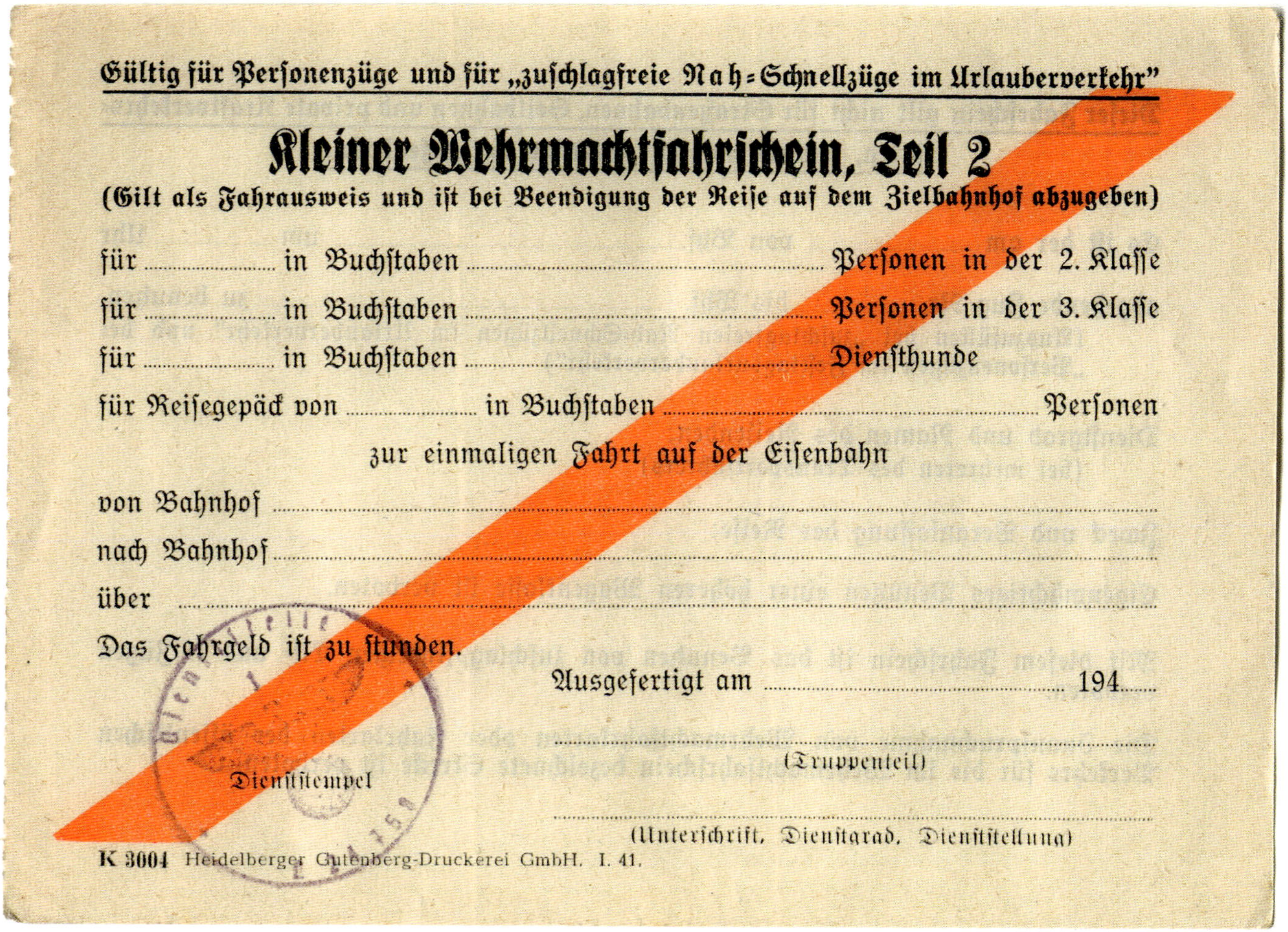
Gültig für Personenzüge und für „zuschlagfreie Nah-Schnellzüge im Urlauberverkehr"

Kleiner Wehrmachtfahrschein, Teil 2

(Gilt als Fahrausweis und ist bei Beendigung der Reise auf dem Zielbahnhof abzugeben)

für .... in Buchstaben .... Personen in der 2. Klasse

für .... in Buchstaben .... Personen in der 3. Klasse

für .... in Buchstaben .... Diensthunde

für Reisegepäck von .... in Buchstaben .... Personen

zur einmaligen Fahrt auf der Eisenbahn

von Bahnhof ....

nach Bahnhof ....

über ....

Das Fahrgeld ist zu stunden.

Ausgefertigt am .... 194....

....
(Truppenteil)

Dienststempel

....
(Unterschrift, Dienstgrad, Dienststellung)

K 3004 Heidelberger Gutenberg-Druckerei GmbH. I. 41.

Figure 2-104. A red-striped Kleiner Wehrmachtfahrschein, valid for shorter distances and travel on slower trains with more frequent stops.

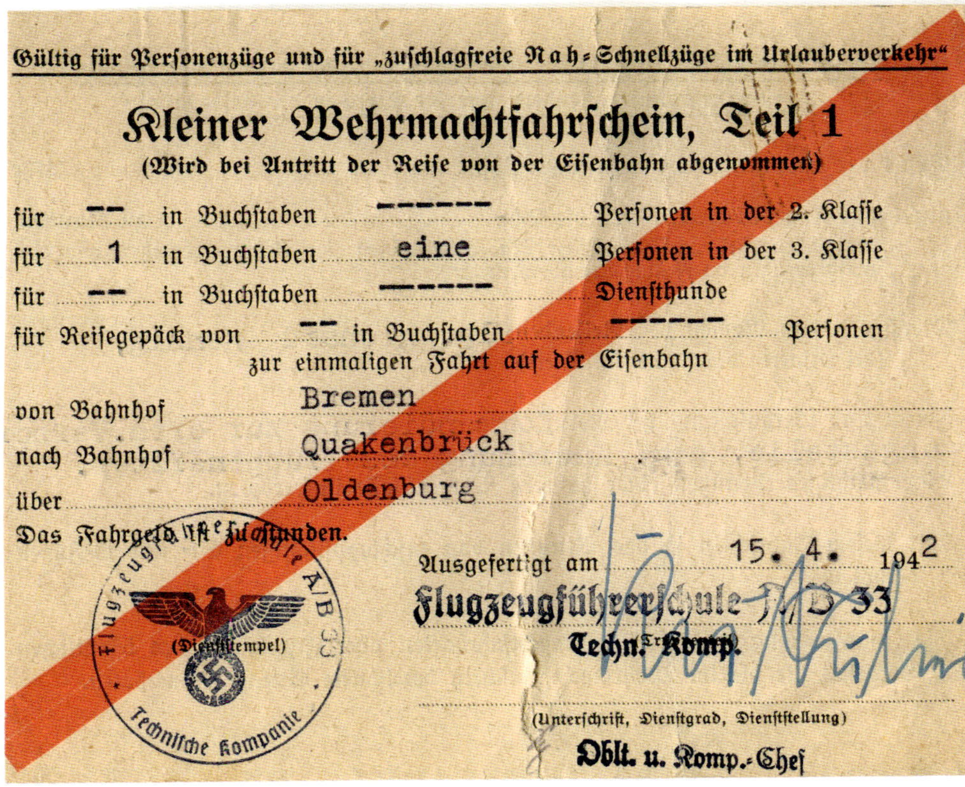

Gültig für Personenzüge und für „zuschlagfreie Nah-Schnellzüge im Urlauberverkehr"

Kleiner Wehrmachtfahrschein, Teil 1

(Wird bei Antritt der Reise von der Eisenbahn abgenommen)

für -- in Buchstaben ------ Personen in der 2. Klasse
für 1 in Buchstaben eine Personen in der 3. Klasse
für -- in Buchstaben ------ Diensthunde
für Reisegepäck von -- in Buchstaben ------ Personen
zur einmaligen Fahrt auf der Eisenbahn
von Bahnhof Bremen
nach Bahnhof Quakenbrück
über Oldenburg
Das Fahrgeld ist zu stunden.

Ausgefertigt am 15. 4. 1942
Flugzeugführerschule A/B 33
Techn. Komp.
(Dienststempel)
(Unterschrift, Dienstgrad, Dienststellung)
Oblt. u. Komp.-Chef

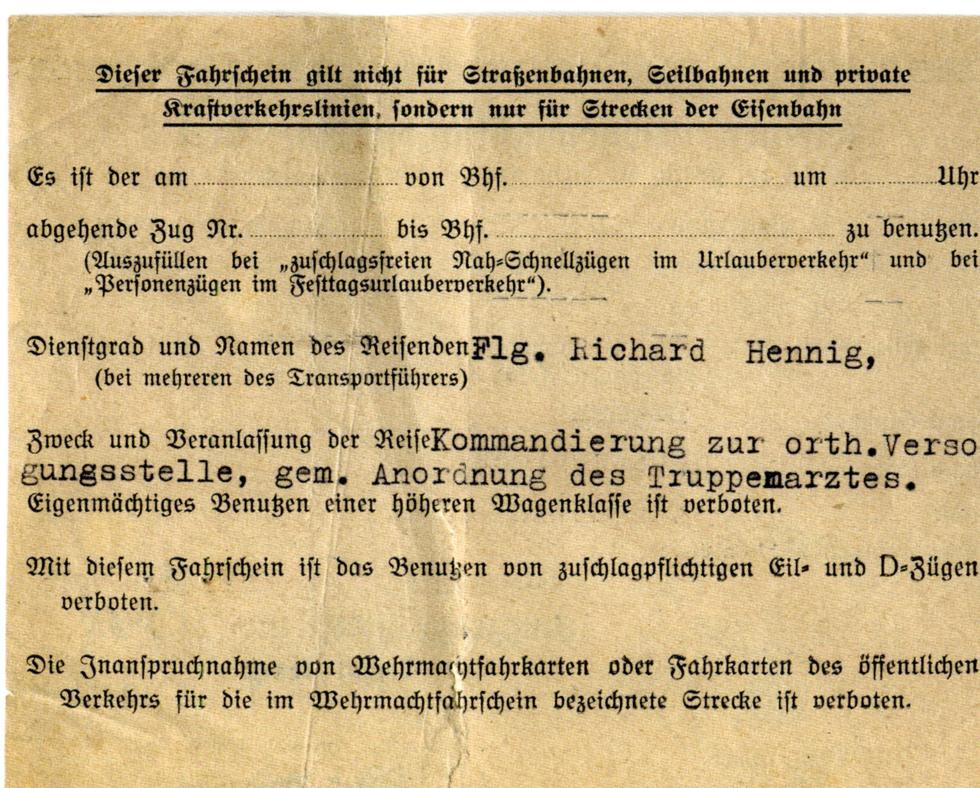

Dieser Fahrschein gilt nicht für Straßenbahnen, Seilbahnen und private Kraftverkehrslinien, sondern nur für Strecken der Eisenbahn

Es ist der am .... von Bhf. .... um .... Uhr
abgehende Zug Nr. .... bis Bhf. .... zu benutzen.
(Auszufüllen bei „zuschlagsfreien Nah-Schnellzügen im Urlauberverkehr" und bei „Personenzügen im Festtagsurlauberverkehr").

Dienstgrad und Namen des Reisenden Flg. Richard Hennig,
(bei mehreren des Transportführers)

Zweck und Veranlassung der Reise Kommandierung zur orth.Versorgungsstelle, gem. Anordnung des Truppenarztes.
Eigenmächtiges Benutzen einer höheren Wagenklasse ist verboten.

Mit diesem Fahrschein ist das Benutzen von zuschlagpflichtigen Eil- und D-Zügen verboten.

Die Inanspruchnahme von Wehrmachtfahrkarten oder Fahrkarten des öffentlichen Verkehrs für die im Wehrmachtfahrschein bezeichnete Strecke ist verboten.

Figure 2-105. This Fahrschein issued by the Technical Company of Pilots' School A/B 33 allowed Flieger Richard Hennig to travel from Bremen to Quakenbrück at the order of the unit's doctor. (Trimmed to $4^1/_4$" x $5^7/_8$")

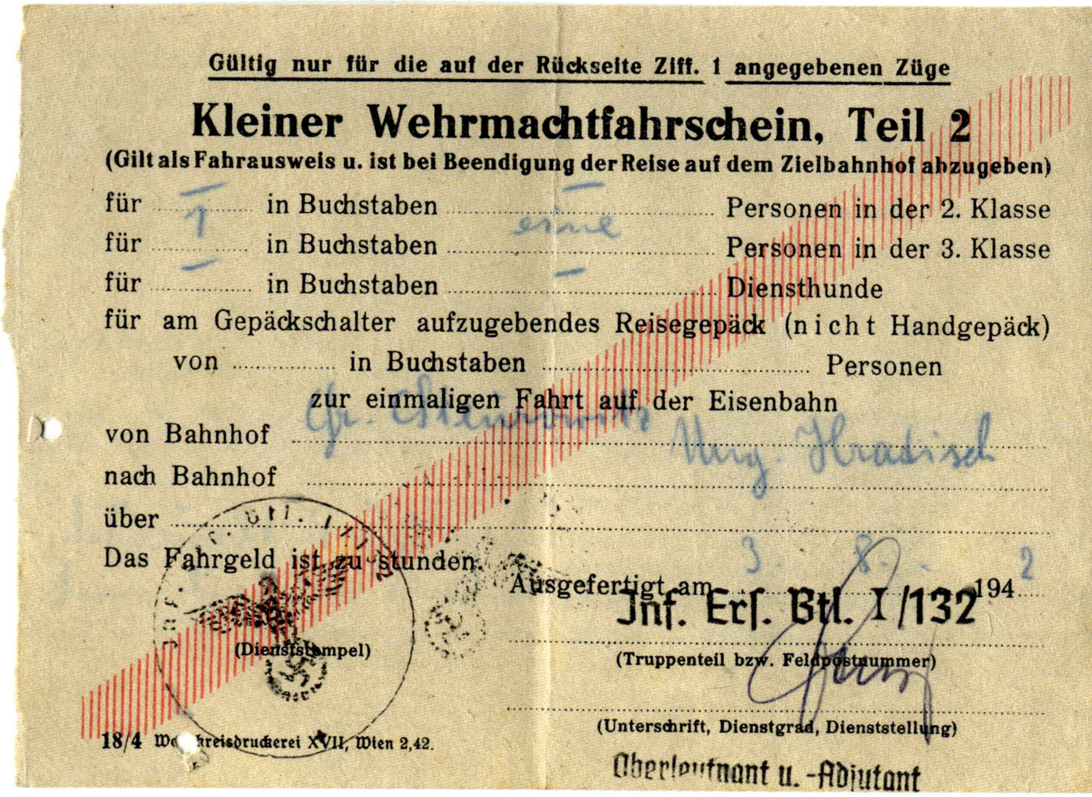
Gültig nur für die auf der Rückseite Ziff. 1 angegebenen Züge

Kleiner Wehrmachtfahrschein, Teil 2

(Gilt als Fahrausweis u. ist bei Beendigung der Reise auf dem Zielbahnhof abzugeben)

für ...... in Buchstaben ...... Personen in der 2. Klasse

für ...1... in Buchstaben ...eine... Personen in der 3. Klasse

für ...... in Buchstaben ...... Diensthunde

für am Gepäckschalter aufzugebendes Reisegepäck (nicht Handgepäck)

von ...... in Buchstaben ...... Personen

zur einmaligen Fahrt auf der Eisenbahn

von Bahnhof ......

nach Bahnhof ...Ung. Hradisch...

über ......

Das Fahrgeld ist zu stunden.

(Dienststempel)

Ausgefertigt am 3. 8. 1942

Inf. Ers. Btl. I/132

(Truppenteil bzw. Feldpostnummer)

(Unterschrift, Dienstgrad, Dienststellung)

Oberleutnant u. -Adjutant

18/4 Wehrkreisdruckerei XVII, Wien 2,42.

Figure 2-106. Gefreiter Johann Reitbauer, returned from the harvest (Rückreise von Ernteeinsatz) using this red-striped Fahrschein. Again, the printer misinterpreted the regulation similarly to that in figure 2-77. (A6)

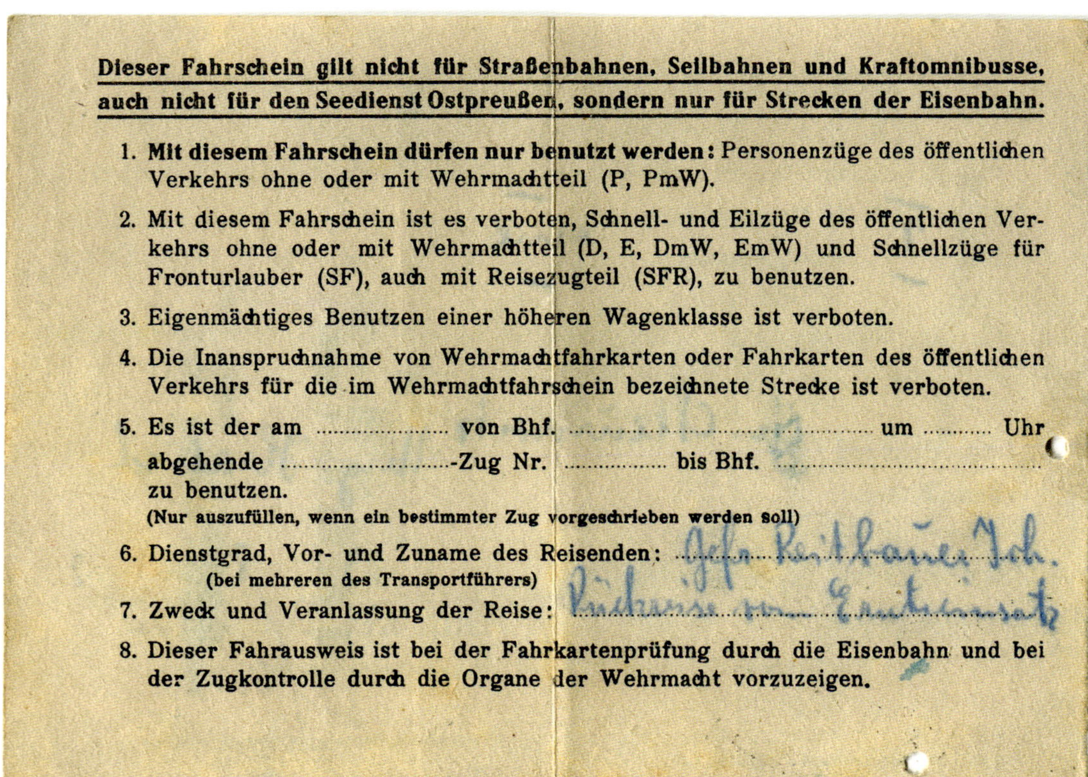
Dieser Fahrschein gilt nicht für Straßenbahnen, Seilbahnen und Kraftomnibusse, auch nicht für den Seedienst Ostpreußen, sondern nur für Strecken der Eisenbahn.

1. **Mit diesem Fahrschein dürfen nur benutzt werden:** Personenzüge des öffentlichen Verkehrs ohne oder mit Wehrmachtteil (P, PmW).
2. Mit diesem Fahrschein ist es verboten, Schnell- und Eilzüge des öffentlichen Verkehrs ohne oder mit Wehrmachtteil (D, E, DmW, EmW) und Schnellzüge für Fronturlauber (SF), auch mit Reisezugteil (SFR), zu benutzen.
3. Eigenmächtiges Benutzen einer höheren Wagenklasse ist verboten.
4. Die Inanspruchnahme von Wehrmachtfahrkarten oder Fahrkarten des öffentlichen Verkehrs für die im Wehrmachtfahrschein bezeichnete Strecke ist verboten.
5. Es ist der am ...... von Bhf. ...... um ...... Uhr abgehende ......-Zug Nr. ...... bis Bhf. ...... zu benutzen.
(Nur auszufüllen, wenn ein bestimmter Zug vorgeschrieben werden soll)
6. Dienstgrad, Vor- und Zuname des Reisenden: Gefr. Reitbauer Joh.
(bei mehreren des Transportführers)
7. Zweck und Veranlassung der Reise: Rückreise von Ernteeinsatz
8. Dieser Fahrausweis ist bei der Fahrkartenprüfung durch die Eisenbahn und bei der Zugkontrolle durch die Organe der Wehrmacht vorzuzeigen.

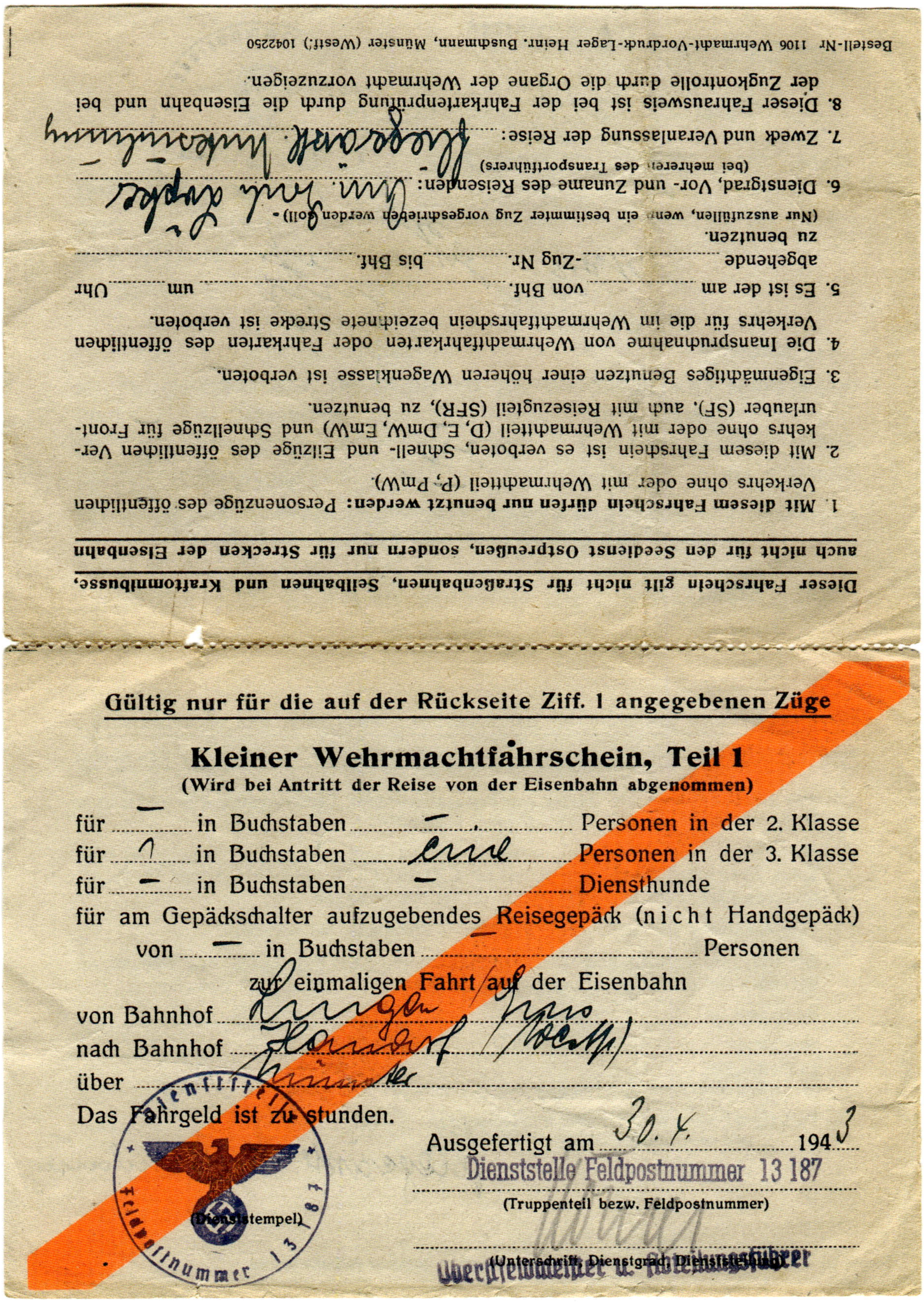

Dieser Fahrschein gilt nicht für Straßenbahnen, Seilbahnen und Kraftomnibusse, auch nicht für den Seedienst Ostpreußen, sondern nur für Strecken der Eisenbahn

1. **Mit diesem Fahrschein dürfen nur benutzt werden:** Personenzüge des öffentlichen Verkehrs ohne oder mit Wehrmachtteil (P, PmW).
2. Mit diesem Fahrschein ist es verboten, Schnell- und Eilzüge des öffentlichen Verkehrs ohne oder mit Wehrmachtteil (D, E, DmW, EmW) und Schnellzüge für Fronturlauber (SF), auch mit Reisezugteil (SFR), zu benutzen.
3. Eigenmächtiges Benutzen einer höheren Wagenklasse ist verboten.
4. Die Inanspruchnahme von Wehrmachtfahrkarten oder Fahrkarten des öffentlichen Verkehrs für die im Wehrmachtfahrschein bezeichnete Strecke ist verboten.
5. Es ist der am .... von Bhf. .... um .... Uhr abgehende ....-Zug Nr. .... bis Bhf. .... zu benutzen.
(Nur auszufüllen, wenn ein bestimmter Zug vorgeschrieben werden soll) -
6. Dienstgrad, Vor- und Zuname des Reisenden: Arm. Erich Löpker
(bei mehreren des Transportführers)
7. Zweck und Veranlassung der Reise: Fliegerärztl. Untersuchung
8. Dieser Fahrausweis ist bei der Fahrkartenprüfung durch die Eisenbahn und bei der Zugkontrolle durch die Organe der Wehrmacht vorzuzeigen.

Bestell-Nr. 1106 Wehrmacht-Vordruck-Lager Heinr. Buschmann, Münster (Westf.) 104250

Gültig nur für die auf der Rückseite Ziff. 1 angegebenen Züge

Kleiner Wehrmachtfahrschein, Teil 1
(Wird bei Antritt der Reise von der Eisenbahn abgenommen)

für – in Buchstaben – Personen in der 2. Klasse
für 1 in Buchstaben eine Personen in der 3. Klasse
für – in Buchstaben – Diensthunde
für am Gepäckschalter aufzugebendes Reisegepäck (nicht Handgepäck)
von – in Buchstaben – Personen
zur einmaligen Fahrt auf der Eisenbahn
von Bahnhof Lingen (Ems)
nach Bahnhof Handorf (Westf.)
über Münster
Das Fahrgeld ist zu stunden.

Ausgefertigt am 30.4. 1943
Dienststelle Feldpostnummer 13 187
(Truppenteil bezw. Feldpostnummer)

(Dienststempel) Dienststelle Feldpostnummer 13 187

(Unterschrift, Dienstgrad, Dienststellung)
Oberstfeldmeister u. Abteilungsführer

Figure 2-107. One of the issues with forms filled out by hand is often legibility, however we can read (barely) that Erich Löpker of Reichsarbeitsdienst (RAD) Abteilung 3/163 (Reich Work Service Section 3/163) used this Fahrschein to travel to take a flight examination (Flieger-Untersuchung) of some sort. (A5)

Dieser Fahrschein gilt nicht für Straßenbahnen, Seilbahnen und Kraftomnibusse, auch nicht für den Seedienst Ostpreußen, sondern nur für Strecken der Eisenbahn

1. **Mit diesem Fahrschein dürfen nur benutzt werden:** Personenzüge des öffentlichen Verkehrs ohne oder mit Wehrmachtteil (P, PmW).
2. Mit diesem Fahrschein ist es verboten, Schnell- und Eilzüge des öffentlichen Verkehrs ohne oder mit Wehrmachteil (D, E, DmW, EmW) und Schnellzüge für Fronturlauber (SF), auch mit Reisezugteil (SFR), zu benutzen.
3. Eigenmächtiges Benutzen einer höheren Wagenklasse ist verboten.
4. Die Inanspruchnahme von Wehrmachtfahrkarten oder Fahrkarten des öffentlichen Verkehrs für die im Wehrmachtfahrschein bezeichnete Strecke ist verboten.
5. Es ist der am .... von Bhf. .... um .... Uhr abgehende ....-Zug Nr. .... bis Bhf. .... zu benutzen.
Nur auszufüllen, wenn ein bestimmter Zug vorgeschrieben werden soll.
6. Dienstgrad, Vor- und Zuname des Reisenden: ....
bei mehreren des Transportführers.
7. Zweck und Veranlassung der Reise: Leutnant Dichlinger
8. Dieser Fahrausweis ist bei der Fahrkartenprüfung durch die Eisenbahn und bei der Zugkontrolle durch die Organe der Wehrmacht vorzuzeigen.

Gültig nur für die auf der Rückseite Ziff. 1 angegebenen Züge

Kleiner Wehrmachtfahrschein, Teil 1

(Wird bei Antritt der Reise von der Eisenbahn abgenommen)

für 1 in Buchstaben eine Personen in der 2. Klasse
für .... in Buchstaben .... Personen in der 3. Klasse
für .... in Buchstaben .... Diensthunde
für am Gepäckschalter aufzugebendes Reisegepäck (nicht Handgepäck)
von .... in Buchstaben .... Personen
zur einmaligen Fahrt auf der Eisenbahn
von Bahnhof Groß-Born/Westfalenhof
nach Bahnhof Wien
über München
Das Fahrgeld ist zu stunden.

Ausgefertigt am 7.10. 1944

Dienststempel

Schule f. Fhj. d. Art. Lg. III
Truppenteil bzw. Feldpostnummer

Lt. u. Adjutant
Unterschrift, Dienstgrad, Dienststellung

Wehrkreisdruckerei XX, Danzig

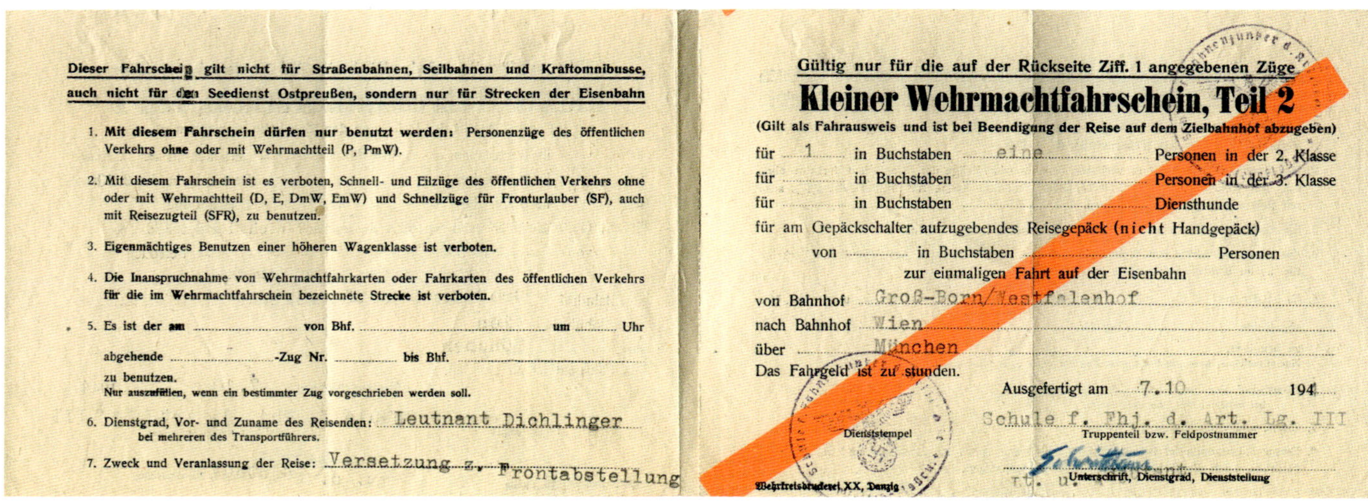

Dieser Fahrschein gilt nicht für Straßenbahnen, Seilbahnen und Kraftomnibusse, auch nicht für den Seedienst Ostpreußen, sondern nur für Strecken der Eisenbahn

1. **Mit diesem Fahrschein dürfen nur benutzt werden:** Personenzüge des öffentlichen Verkehrs ohne oder mit Wehrmachtteil (P, PmW).
2. Mit diesem Fahrschein ist es verboten, Schnell- und Eilzüge des öffentlichen Verkehrs ohne oder mit Wehrmachtteil (D, E, DmW, EmW) und Schnellzüge für Fronturlauber (SF), auch mit Reisezugteil (SFR), zu benutzen.
3. Eigenmächtiges Benutzen einer höheren Wagenklasse ist verboten.
4. Die Inanspruchnahme von Wehrmachtfahrkarten oder Fahrkarten des öffentlichen Verkehrs für die im Wehrmachtfahrschein bezeichnete Strecke ist verboten.
5. Es ist der am .... von Bhf. .... um .... Uhr abgehende ....-Zug Nr. .... bis Bhf. .... zu benutzen.
Nur auszufüllen, wenn ein bestimmter Zug vorgeschrieben werden soll.
6. Dienstgrad, Vor- und Zuname des Reisenden: Leutnant Dichlinger
bei mehreren des Transportführers.
7. Zweck und Veranlassung der Reise: Versetzung z. Frontabstellung

Gültig nur für die auf der Rückseite Ziff. 1 angegebenen Züge

Kleiner Wehrmachtfahrschein, Teil 2

(Gilt als Fahrausweis und ist bei Beendigung der Reise auf dem Zielbahnhof abzugeben)

für 1 in Buchstaben eine Personen in der 2. Klasse
für .... in Buchstaben .... Personen in der 3. Klasse
für .... in Buchstaben .... Diensthunde
für am Gepäckschalter aufzugebendes Reisegepäck (nicht Handgepäck)
von .... in Buchstaben .... Personen
zur einmaligen Fahrt auf der Eisenbahn
von Bahnhof Groß-Born/Westfalenhof
nach Bahnhof Wien
über München
Das Fahrgeld ist zu stunden.

Ausgefertigt am 7.10. 194

Dienststempel

Schule f. Fhj. d. Art. Lg. III
Truppenteil bzw. Feldpostnummer

Lt. u.
Unterschrift, Dienstgrad, Dienststellung

Wehrkreisdruckerei XX, Danzig

Figure 2-108. This is the ticket that newly commissioned Leutnant Dichlinger presumably used after graduating from Schule für Fahnenjunker der Artillerie (School for Officer Candidates of Artillery) in the Wehrmacht garrison and training facility of Gross-Born/Westfalenhof (which is now the ghost town of Klomino, near Szczecinek) for a front line transfer in Vienna, Austria. See also figure 2-131.

(Special Form for Service Travel; more on that later), and the *Wehrmachtfahrschein*, into a single document.

This *kombinierte Fahrschein* (Combined Travel Pass - not the official designation) was a watermarked A4 sheet printed front and back in two parts. The top section was reserved for the information normally contained on the *Kleiner Wehrmachtfahrschein*; it, in turn, was divided into two large and two small blocks. The two largest served the same purpose as pages one and two of the *Kleiner Wehrmachtfahrschein*, namely, departure travel and return travel. The two smaller sections to the right were reserved for the date and *Dienststempeln* of the unit issuing the form. At the top of these two smaller sections, it notes that train travel had become restricted to *Durchgangs-* and *Eilzüge*. Allied aircraft were pummeling anything that moved and these were some of the few trains that succeeded in getting through.

In theory, if travel was authorized, but not service related or for leave, the form could be separated into its two components and the soldier would only use the upper portion, just like the *Kleiner Wehrmachtfahrschein*. In theory. There were, after all, few occasions that travel would be permitted when not leave or service related, so situations in which the forms might be separated were quite rare. Still, it was provided for.

The lower section, about two-thirds of the form and separable from the top by a perforation, was reserved for information normally recorded on the *Kriegsurlaubsschein* and/or the *Sonderausweis* (noted on the combined form as *Dienstreiseschein*, or Service Travel Pass).

The top half of the lower section held the details often required to justify travel: the rank and name of the *Soldat*, grounds for travel, approved departure and destination stations, and the dates.

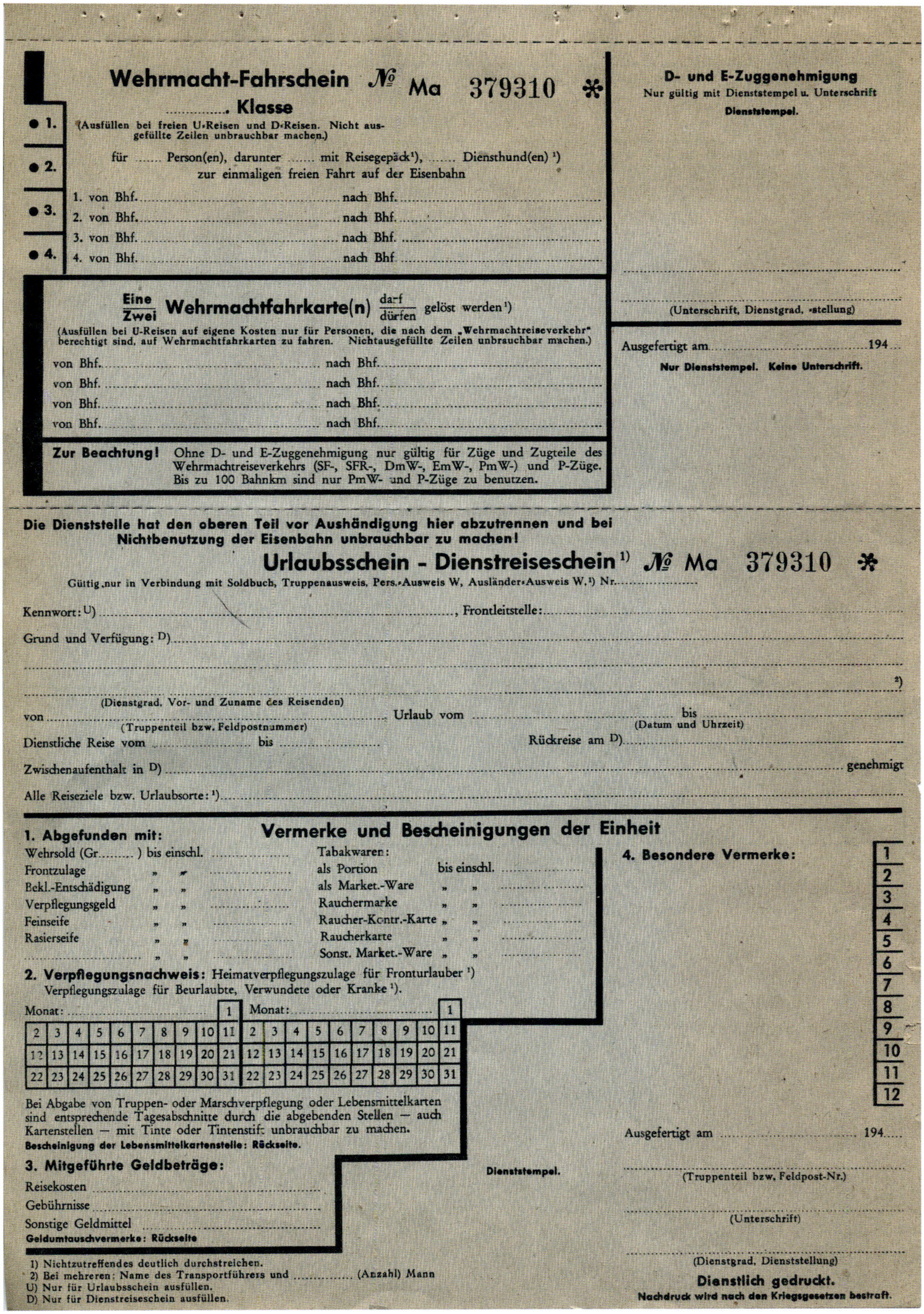

Wehrmacht-Fahrschein № Ma 379310 *

.... **Klasse**

(Ausfüllen bei freien U-Reisen und D-Reisen. Nicht ausgefüllte Zeilen unbrauchbar machen.)

● 1.
● 2.
● 3.
● 4.

für .... Person(en), darunter .... mit Reisegepäck¹), ... Diensthund(en) ¹) zur einmaligen freien Fahrt auf der Eisenbahn

1. von Bhf. .... nach Bhf. ....
2. von Bhf. .... nach Bhf. ....
3. von Bhf. .... nach Bhf. ....
4. von Bhf. .... nach Bhf. ....

D- und E-Zuggenehmigung
Nur gültig mit Dienststempel u. Unterschrift
Dienststempel.

....
(Unterschrift, Dienstgrad, -stellung)

Ausgefertigt am .... 194...
Nur Dienststempel. Keine Unterschrift.

Eine/Zwei Wehrmachtfahrkarte(n) darf/dürfen gelöst werden¹)

(Ausfüllen bei U-Reisen auf eigene Kosten nur für Personen, die nach dem „Wehrmachtreiseverkehr" berechtigt sind, auf Wehrmachtfahrkarten zu fahren. Nichtausgefüllte Zeilen unbrauchbar machen.)

von Bhf. .... nach Bhf. ....
von Bhf. .... nach Bhf. ....
von Bhf. .... nach Bhf. ....
von Bhf. .... nach Bhf. ....

Zur Beachtung! Ohne D- und E-Zuggenehmigung nur gültig für Züge und Zugteile des Wehrmachtreiseverkehrs (SF-, SFR-, DmW-, EmW-, PmW-) und P-Züge. Bis zu 100 Bahnkm sind nur PmW- und P-Züge zu benutzen.

Die Dienststelle hat den oberen Teil vor Aushändigung hier abzutrennen und bei Nichtbenutzung der Eisenbahn unbrauchbar zu machen!

Urlaubsschein - Dienstreiseschein ¹) № Ma 379310 *

Gültig nur in Verbindung mit Soldbuch, Truppenausweis, Pers.-Ausweis W, Ausländer-Ausweis W.¹) Nr. ....

Kennwort: U) ...., Frontleitstelle: ....

Grund und Verfügung: D) ....

....

.... ²)
(Dienstgrad, Vor- und Zuname des Reisenden)

von .... Urlaub vom .... bis ....
(Truppenteil bzw. Feldpostnummer) (Datum und Uhrzeit)

Dienstliche Reise vom .... bis .... Rückreise am D) ....

Zwischenaufenthalt in D) .... genehmigt

Alle Reiseziele bzw. Urlaubsorte: ¹) ....

Vermerke und Bescheinigungen der Einheit

1. Abgefunden mit:

Wehrsold (Gr........) bis einschl. ....
Frontzulage „ „ ....
Bekl.-Entschädigung „ „ ....
Verpflegungsgeld „ „ ....
Feinseife „ „ ....
Rasierseife „ „ ....
.... „ „ ....

Tabakwaren:
als Portion bis einschl. ....
als Market.-Ware „ „ ....
Rauchermarke „ „ ....
Raucher-Kontr.-Karte „ „ ....
Raucherkarte „ „ ....
Sonst. Market.-Ware „ „ ....

2. Verpflegungsnachweis: Heimatverpflegungszulage für Fronturlauber ¹)
Verpflegungszulage für Beurlaubte, Verwundete oder Kranke ¹).

Monat:									1	Monat:									1
2	3	4	5	6	7	8	9	10	11	2	3	4	5	6	7	8	9	10	11
12	13	14	15	16	17	18	19	20	21	12	13	14	15	16	17	18	19	20	21
22	23	24	25	26	27	28	29	30	31	22	23	24	25	26	27	28	29	30	31

Bei Abgabe von Truppen- oder Marschverpflegung oder Lebensmittelkarten sind entsprechende Tagesabschnitte durch die abgebenden Stellen — auch Kartenstellen — mit Tinte oder Tintenstift unbrauchbar zu machen.
Bescheinigung der Lebensmittelkartenstelle: Rückseite.

3. Mitgeführte Geldbeträge:

Reisekosten ....
Gebührnisse ....
Sonstige Geldmittel ....
Geldumtauschvermerke: Rückseite

Dienststempel.

4. Besondere Vermerke:

1
2
3
4
5
6
7
8
9
10
11
12

Ausgefertigt am .... 194.....

....
(Truppenteil bzw. Feldpost-Nr.)

....
(Unterschrift)

....
(Dienstgrad, Dienststellung)

1) Nichtzutreffendes deutlich durchstreichen.
2) Bei mehreren: Name des Transportführers und .... (Anzahl) Mann
U) Nur für Urlaubsschein ausfüllen.
D) Nur für Dienstreiseschein ausfüllen.

Dienstlich gedruckt.
Nachdruck wird nach den Kriegsgesetzen bestraft.

Figure 2-109. A well-preserved example of a late-war combined Wehrmachtfahrschein-Urlaubsschein-Dienstresieschein (Wehrmacht Ticket-Leave Pass-Service Travel Pass). (A4)

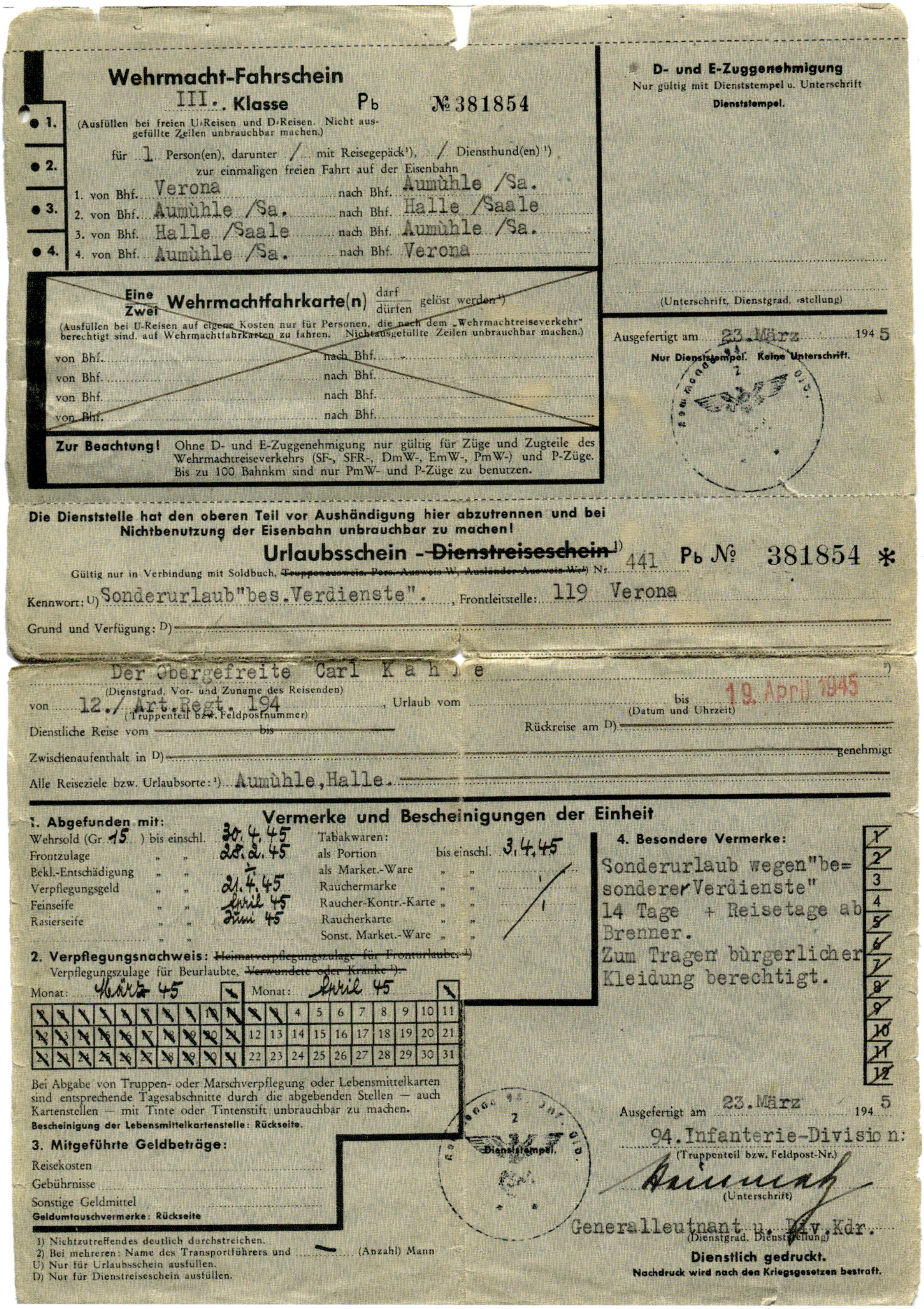

Wehrmacht-Fahrschein

III. Klasse Pb № 381854

1. (Ausfüllen bei freien U-Reisen und D-Reisen. Nicht ausgefüllte Zeilen unbrauchbar machen.)

2. für 1 Person(en), darunter / mit Reisegepäck[1]), / Diensthund(en)[1])
zur einmaligen freien Fahrt auf der Eisenbahn

3.
1. von Bhf. Verona nach Bhf. Aumühle /Sa.
2. von Bhf. Aumühle /Sa. nach Bhf. Halle /Saale
3. von Bhf. Halle /Saale nach Bhf. Aumühle /Sa.
4. 4. von Bhf. Aumühle /Sa. nach Bhf. Verona

D- und E-Zuggenehmigung
Nur gültig mit Dienststempel u. Unterschrift
Dienststempel.

(Unterschrift, Dienstgrad, -stellung)

~~Eine~~ Zwei **Wehrmachtfahrkarte(n)** darf/dürfen gelöst werden[1])
(Ausfüllen bei U-Reisen auf eigene Kosten nur für Personen, die nach dem „Wehrmachtreiseverkehr" berechtigt sind, auf Wehrmachtfahrkarten zu fahren. Nichtausgefüllte Zeilen unbrauchbar machen.)
von Bhf. nach Bhf.
von Bhf. nach Bhf.
von Bhf. nach Bhf.
von Bhf. nach Bhf.

Ausgefertigt am 23. März 1945
Nur Dienststempel. Keine Unterschrift.

Zur Beachtung! Ohne D- und E-Zuggenehmigung nur gültig für Züge und Zugteile des Wehrmachtreiseverkehrs (SF-, SFR-, DmW-, EmW-, PmW-) und P-Züge. Bis zu 100 Bahnkm sind nur PmW- und P-Züge zu benutzen.

Die Dienststelle hat den oberen Teil vor Aushändigung hier abzutrennen und bei Nichtbenutzung der Eisenbahn unbrauchbar zu machen!

Urlaubsschein - ~~Dienstreiseschein~~[1]) 441 Pb № 381854 *
Gültig nur in Verbindung mit Soldbuch, ~~Truppenausweis, Pers.-Ausweis W, Ausländer-Ausweis W~~[1]) Nr.
Kennwort: U) Sonderurlaub"bes.Verdienste". , Frontleitstelle: 119 Verona
Grund und Verfügung: D)

Der Obergefreite Carl Kahle
(Dienstgrad, Vor- und Zuname des Reisenden)
von 12./Art.Regt. 194 (Truppenteil bzw. Feldpostnummer), Urlaub vom bis 19. April 1945 (Datum und Uhrzeit)
Dienstliche Reise vom bis Rückreise am D)
Zwischenaufenthalt in D) genehmigt
Alle Reiseziele bzw. Urlaubsorte:[1]) Aumühle, Halle.

Vermerke und Bescheinigungen der Einheit

1. Abgefunden mit:

Wehrsold (Gr. 15) bis einschl.	30.4.45	Tabakwaren:		
Frontzulage „ „	28.2.45	als Portion	bis einschl.	3.4.45
Bekl.-Entschädigung „ „		als Market.-Ware	„ „	
Verpflegungsgeld „ „	21.4.45	Rauchermarke	„ „	
Feinseife „ „	April 45	Raucher-Kontr.-Karte	„ „	
Rasierseife „ „	Juni 45	Raucherkarte	„ „	
„ „		Sonst. Market.-Ware	„ „	

4. Besondere Vermerke:
Sonderurlaub wegen"besonderer Verdienste"
14 Tage + Reisetage ab Brenner.
Zum Tragen bürgerlicher Kleidung berechtigt.

2. Verpflegungsnachweis: ~~Heimatverpflegungszulage für Fronturlauber~~[1])
Verpflegungszulage für Beurlaubte, ~~Verwundete oder Kranke~~[1])
Monat: März 45 Monat: April 45

Bei Abgabe von Truppen- oder Marschverpflegung oder Lebensmittelkarten sind entsprechende Tagesabschnitte durch die abgebenden Stellen — auch Kartenstellen — mit Tinte oder Tintenstift unbrauchbar zu machen.
Bescheinigung der Lebensmittelkartenstelle: Rückseite.

3. Mitgeführte Geldbeträge:
Reisekosten
Gebührnisse
Sonstige Geldmittel
Geldumtauschvermerke: Rückseite

Ausgefertigt am 23. März 1945
94. Infanterie-Division
(Truppenteil bzw. Feldpost-Nr.)
(Unterschrift)
Generalleutnant u. Div.Kdr.
(Dienstgrad, Dienststellung)
Dienstlich gedruckt.
Nachdruck wird nach den Kriegsgesetzen bestraft.

1) Nichtzutreffendes deutlich durchstreichen.
2) Bei mehreren: Name des Transportführers und — (Anzahl) Mann
U) Nur für Urlaubsschein ausfüllen.
D) Nur für Dienstreiseschein ausfüllen.

Figure 2-110. An interesting example of travel at the close of the war using a late-war combined form. Obergefreite (sic) Carl Kahle was sent on Sonderurlaub wegen "besondere Verdienste" (Special Leave for special merit) from Verona, Italy through the Brenner Pass to Halle and return on April 19, 1945, just in time to surrender with the rest of his division on April 22, 1945. It must have been a special merit indeed: Division Commander, Generalleutnant Bernhard Steinmetz, signed the pass personally. (A4)

Gepäckabfertigung (Hier abstempeln!)

D- und E-Zuggenehmigung:

Zur Beachtung für den reisenden Soldaten!

1. **Bei freier Fahrt** ist dem Eisenbahnpersonal **nur der** Wehrmachtfahrschein, **bei Reisen auf Wehrmachtfahrkarten** ist dem **deutschen** Eisenbahnpersonal außerdem der Urlaubschein vorzuzeigen.
2. **Reisegepäck** ist bei freier Fahrt bis zu 75 kg gebührenfrei. Bei mehr als 75 kg für eine Person ist für das Gesamtgewicht die tarifmäßige Gebühr zu bezahlen.
3. **Urlaubsschein** und **Dienstreiseschein** nur Wehrmachtstreifendienst und Dienststellen der Wehrmacht vorzeigen! (Ausnahmen: Polizeibehörde am Aufenthaltsort, Lebensmittelkartenstelle, Geldumtauschstelle, Polizeiorgane und deutsches Eisenbahnpersonal gem. Ziff. 1). Urlaubschein-Dienstreiseschein nur gültig für einmalige Beurlaubung oder dienstliche Reise. Dieser ist mit dem Fahrschein nach Beendigung der Reise an die zuständige Dienststelle zurückzugeben.
4. **Die im Wehrmachtstreifendienst eingesetzten Soldaten gelten als militärische Wache;** sie haben Befehlsbefugnis innerhalb ihres Aufgabenbereichs gegenüber allen Angehörigen der Wehrmacht und der Waffen-ϟϟ und gegenüber allen mit diesem Urlaubschein-Dienstreiseschein Reisenden.
5. Eigenmächtige Benutzung einer **höheren Wagenklasse** und **Umwege** sind verboten. Eigenmächtiges Abweichen von der vorgeschriebenen Reisestrecke oder **Überschreitungen der Urlaubszeit** können als „unerlaubte Entfernung" verfolgt werden. Dasselbe gilt für **Zwischenaufenthalt** bei **dienstlichen Reisen**, der nicht vom zuständigen Disziplinarvorgesetzten genehmigt ist.
6. Bei **Urlaub** und **dienstlichen Reisen** besteht **Meldepflicht**, wenn der Aufenthalt am Zielort über **48 Stunden** dauert. Die Meldung hat innerhalb von 48 Stunden bei der Wehrmachtkommandantur (Wehrmachtstandortältesten) oder in Orten, die nicht Standort sind, bei der Ortspolizei zu erfolgen. Bei Beurlaubung **über 4 Wochen** stets persönliche Meldung bei dem für den Urlaubsort zuständigen Wehrmachtstandortältesten. Meldepflicht bei **Kurzurlaub** entfällt.
7. Bei **Erkrankung** sofort den nächsten Wehrmachtarzt (Standortarzt, Lazarett) aufsuchen und der vorgesetzten Dienststelle Meldung erstatten. Zivilarzt nur in Notfällen aufsuchen.
8. Bei **Fliegeralarm** hat sich jeder Urlauber und dienstlich Reisende unaufgefordert dem örtlichen Luftschutzdienst zur Verfügung zu stellen. Gasmaske ist mitzunehmen.
9. **Schußwaffen u. Munition** dürfen nur bei wehrmachteigenen Gepäckaufbewahrungen abgegeben werden.
10. Erforderliche **Auskunft** nur bei Wehrmachtdienststellen einholen.
11. Bei Überschreiten der **Devisengrenze** dürfen **Reichsbanknoten** nicht mitgenommen werden. **Rentenbankscheine** und **Hartgeld** bis zu 10,— RM (Reisefreigrenze). **RKK-Scheine** und **ausländische Zahlungsmittel** nur in zugelassener Höhe laut Bescheinigung der Truppe. Zuwiderhandlungen werden kriegsgerichtlich bestraft.

Feind hört mit! Verschwiegenheit und Zurückhaltung bei Gesprächen!

D- und E-Zuggenehmigung:

PLATZKARTE NR. 118 SF
Gultig: 20.III.45
Das Gültigkeitsdatum bezieht sich auf den Tag der Abfahrt des *SF-Zuges* vom *Ausgangsbahnhof*. Nur gültig in Verbindung mit dem mit der Nummer der Platzkarte versehenen Urlaubschein

Urlaubsdauer
ab Hauptumsteigebahnhof, Grenzübergang oder Frontleitstelle
14 Tage Sonderurlaub + Reisetage ab Brenner.
Oberleutnant u. Battr. Chef

Meldung am Zielort
Kdt. d. Wehrmachtreiseverkehrs Brenner
Abfahrtstag: 1. April 1945
Wiedereintrefftag: 19. April 1945

Geldumtauschvermerke

Lebensmittelkartenstelle
v. 4. 4. –19. 4. 45

Truppenarzt bzw. E-Anstalt
Frei von ansteckenden Krankheiten und Ungeziefer. Wäsche imprägniert.
Oberarzt u. Abt. Arzt

Stempel und sonstige Eintragungen (von links nach rechts!)

1) Ortskommandantur Mirandola 29. MAR
2) Weitergeleitet am 30. MAR. 1945 um 0⁰⁰–6⁰⁰ um 12⁰⁰–18⁰⁰ um 6⁰⁰–12⁰⁰ um 18⁰⁰–24⁰⁰
3) Trient Kdt. d. Wehrm. Reiseverk. 31. 3. 45
4) Urlauberpaket erhalten. B. u. V.-Stelle Brenner 1. IV
5)
6)
7)
8)
9)
10)
11)
12)

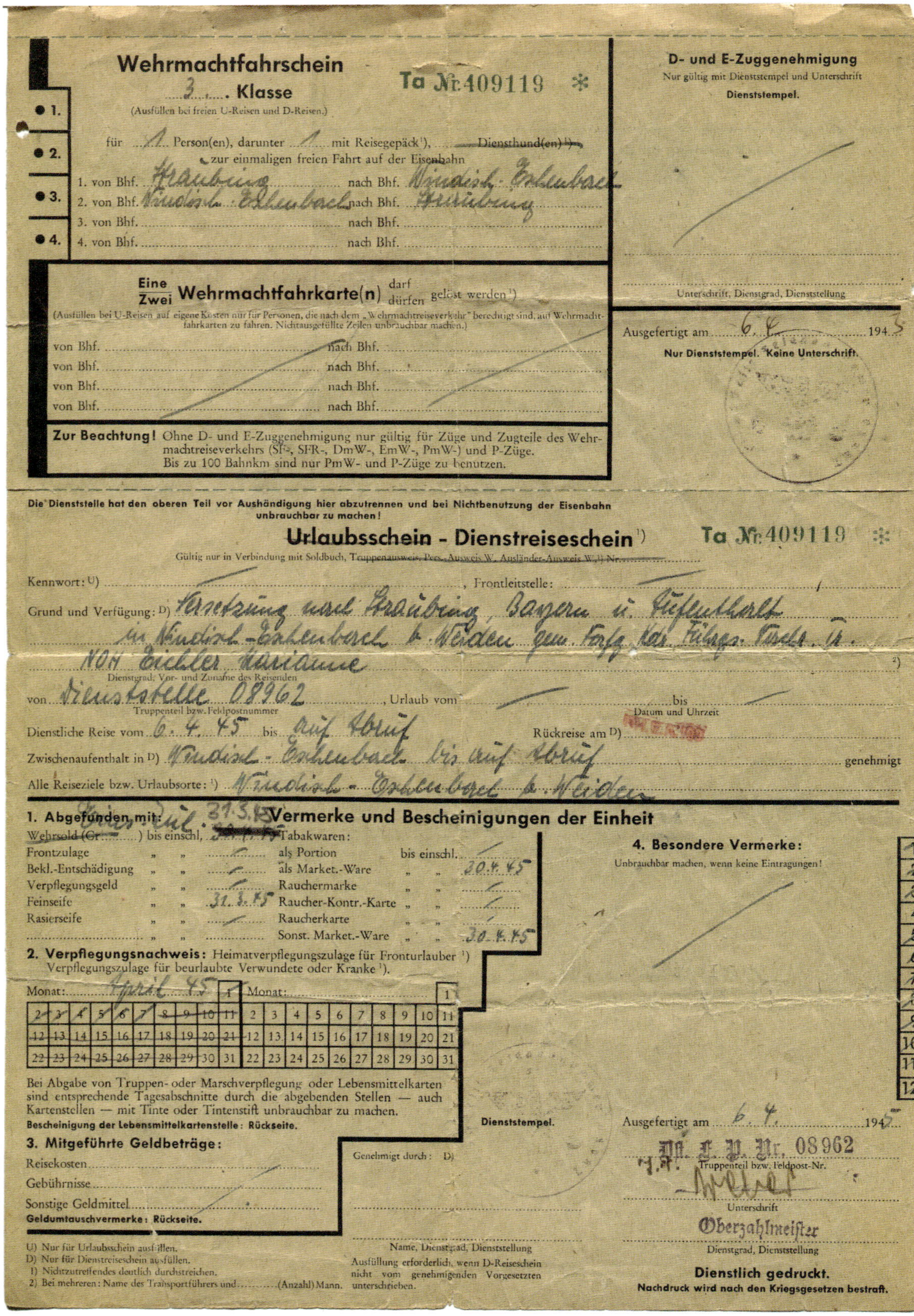
Wehrmachtfahrschein

3. Klasse

(Ausfüllen bei freien U-Reisen und D-Reisen.)

Ta Nr. 409119 *

für 1 Person(en), darunter 1 mit Reisegepäck[1]), ~~Diensthund(en)~~[1])

zur einmaligen freien Fahrt auf der Eisenbahn

1. von Bhf. Straubing nach Bhf. Windisch-Eschenbach
2. von Bhf. Windisch-Eschenbach nach Bhf. Straubing
3. von Bhf. .... nach Bhf. ....
4. von Bhf. .... nach Bhf. ....

D- und E-Zuggenehmigung

Nur gültig mit Dienststempel und Unterschrift

Dienststempel.

Unterschrift, Dienstgrad, Dienststellung

Eine / Zwei Wehrmachtfahrkarte(n) darf / dürfen gelöst werden[1])

(Ausfüllen bei U-Reisen auf eigene Kosten nur für Personen, die nach dem „Wehrmachtreiseverkehr" berechtigt sind, auf Wehrmachtfahrkarten zu fahren. Nichtausgefüllte Zeilen unbrauchbar machen.)

von Bhf. .... nach Bhf. ....

von Bhf. .... nach Bhf. ....

von Bhf. .... nach Bhf. ....

von Bhf. .... nach Bhf. ....

Ausgefertigt am 6.4. 1945

Nur Dienststempel. Keine Unterschrift.

Zur Beachtung! Ohne D- und E-Zuggenehmigung nur gültig für Züge und Zugteile des Wehrmachtreiseverkehrs (SF-, SFR-, DmW-, EmW-, PmW-) und P-Züge. Bis zu 100 Bahnkm sind nur PmW- und P-Züge zu benutzen.

Die Dienststelle hat den oberen Teil vor Aushändigung hier abzutrennen und bei Nichtbenutzung der Eisenbahn unbrauchbar zu machen!

Urlaubsschein - Dienstreiseschein[1])

Ta Nr. 409119 *

Gültig nur in Verbindung mit Soldbuch, ~~Truppenausweis, Pers.-Ausweis W, Ausländer-Ausweis W~~[1]) Nr. ....

Kennwort:[U]) .... , Frontleitstelle: ....

Grund und Verfügung:[D]) Versetzung nach Straubing, Bayern u. Aufenthalt in Windisch-Eschenbach b. Weiden gem. Verfg. Kdr. Fhrgs. Stelle ..

NH Eichler Marianne[2])

Dienstgrad, Vor- und Zuname des Reisenden

von Dienststelle 08962 , Urlaub vom .... bis ....

Truppenteil bzw. Feldpostnummer — Datum und Uhrzeit

Dienstliche Reise vom 6.4.45 bis auf Abruf — Rückreise am[D]) ....

Zwischenaufenthalt in[D]) Windisch-Eschenbach bis auf Abruf .... genehmigt

Alle Reiseziele bzw. Urlaubsorte:[1]) Windisch-Eschenbach b. Weiden

1. Abgefunden mit: — Vermerke und Bescheinigungen der Einheit

			bis einschl.			bis einschl.
~~Wehrsold (Gr ....)~~	) bis einschl.		31.3.45	Tabakwaren:		
Frontzulage	„	„	—	als Portion	bis einschl.	—
Bekl.-Entschädigung	„	„	—	als Market.-Ware	„ „	30.4.45
Verpflegungsgeld	„	„	—	Rauchermarke	„ „	—
Feinseife	„	„	31.3.45	Raucher-Kontr.-Karte	„ „	—
Rasierseife	„	„	—	Raucherkarte	„ „	—
....	„	„	....	Sonst. Market.-Ware	„ „	30.4.45

2. Verpflegungsnachweis: Heimatverpflegungszulage für Fronturlauber[1]) / Verpflegungszulage für beurlaubte Verwundete oder Kranke[1]).

Monat: April 45 — Monat: ....

1										1
2	3	4	5	6	7	8	9	10	11	2	3	4	5	6	7	8	9	10	11
12	13	14	15	16	17	18	19	20	21	12	13	14	15	16	17	18	19	20	21
22	23	24	25	26	27	28	29	30	31	22	23	24	25	26	27	28	29	30	31

Bei Abgabe von Truppen- oder Marschverpflegung oder Lebensmittelkarten sind entsprechende Tagesabschnitte durch die abgebenden Stellen — auch Kartenstellen — mit Tinte oder Tintenstift unbrauchbar zu machen.

Bescheinigung der Lebensmittelkartenstelle: Rückseite.

4. Besondere Vermerke:

Unbrauchbar machen, wenn keine Eintragungen!

1 2 3 4 5 6 7 8 9 10 11 12

3. Mitgeführte Geldbeträge:

Reisekosten ....

Gebührnisse ....

Sonstige Geldmittel ....

Geldumtauschvermerke: Rückseite.

Dienststempel.

Genehmigt durch:[D])

Name, Dienstgrad, Dienststellung

Ausfüllung erforderlich, wenn D-Reiseschein nicht vom genehmigenden Vorgesetzten unterschrieben.

Ausgefertigt am 6.4. 1945

Dst. F. P. Nr. 08962

Truppenteil bzw. Feldpost-Nr.

Unterschrift

Oberzahlmeister

Dienstgrad, Dienststellung

U) Nur für Urlaubsschein ausfüllen.
D) Nur für Dienstreiseschein ausfüllen.
1) Nichtzutreffendes deutlich durchstreichen.
2) Bei mehreren: Name des Transportführers und .... (Anzahl) Mann.

Dienstlich gedruckt.
Nachdruck wird nach den Kriegsgesetzen bestraft.

Figure 2-111. This pass was issued on April 6, 1945, directing Nachrichten-Helferin (Communications Helper) Marianne Eichler to transfer to the Windisch-Eschenbach Airfield in Straubing, Bavaria. The trip was to last from April 6 "bis auf Abruf;" until called back. This was close enough to the end of the war that it's entirely possible that she was sent there to protect her from advancing Russian troops. Note on the back that they still took the time to issue her ration cards, including tobacco rations, and have her checked by the Truppenarzt (Unit Doctor) prior to her departure.(A4)

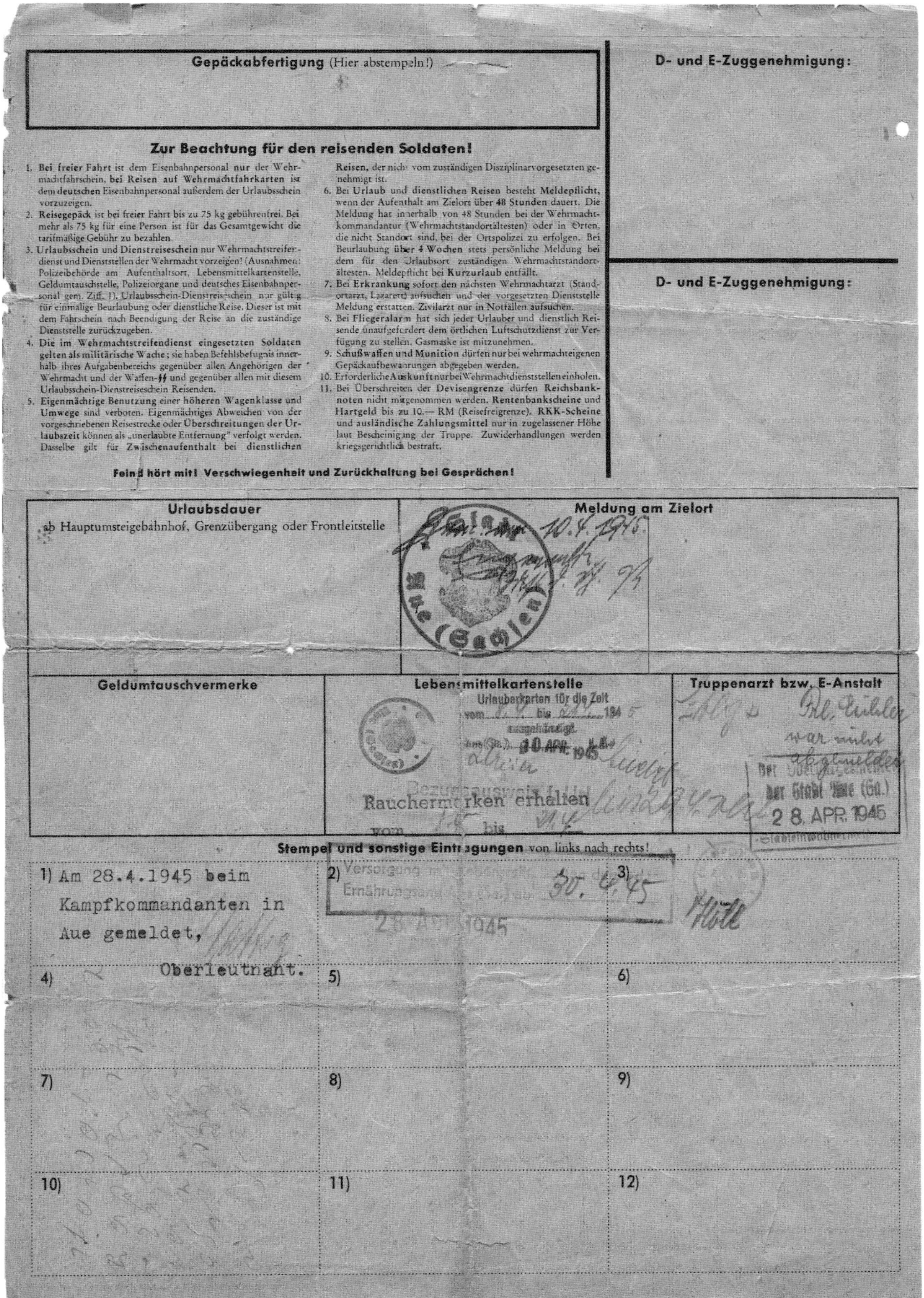

Gepäckabfertigung (Hier abstempeln!)

D- und E-Zuggenehmigung:

D- und E-Zuggenehmigung:

Zur Beachtung für den reisenden Soldaten!

1. **Bei freier Fahrt** ist dem Eisenbahnpersonal nur der Wehrmachtfahrschein, **bei Reisen auf Wehrmachtfahrkarten** ist dem **deutschen** Eisenbahnpersonal außerdem der Urlaubsschein vorzuzeigen.
2. **Reisegepäck** ist bei freier Fahrt bis zu 75 kg gebührenfrei. Bei mehr als 75 kg für eine Person ist für das Gesamtgewicht die tarifmäßige Gebühr zu bezahlen.
3. **Urlaubsschein und Dienstreiseschein** nur Wehrmachtstreifendienst und Dienststellen der Wehrmacht vorzeigen! (Ausnahmen: Polizeibehörde am Aufenthaltsort, Lebensmittelkartenstelle, Geldumtauschstelle, Polizeiorgane und deutsches Eisenbahnpersonal gem. Ziff. 1). Urlaubsschein-Dienstreiseschein nur gültig für einmalige Beurlaubung oder dienstliche Reise. Dieser ist mit dem Fahrschein nach Beendigung der Reise an die zuständige Dienststelle zurückzugeben.
4. **Die im Wehrmachtstreifendienst eingesetzten Soldaten gelten als militärische Wache**; sie haben Befehlsbefugnis innerhalb ihres Aufgabenbereichs gegenüber allen Angehörigen der Wehrmacht und der Waffen-SS und gegenüber allen mit diesem Urlaubsschein-Dienstreiseschein Reisenden.
5. **Eigenmächtige Benutzung** einer **höheren Wagenklasse** und **Umwege** sind verboten. Eigenmächtiges Abweichen von der vorgeschriebenen Reisestrecke oder **Überschreitungen der Urlaubszeit** können als „unerlaubte Entfernung" verfolgt werden. Dasselbe gilt für **Zwischenaufenthalt** bei dienstlichen Reisen, der nicht vom zuständigen Disziplinarvorgesetzten genehmigt ist.
6. Bei **Urlaub** und **dienstlichen Reisen** besteht **Meldepflicht**, wenn der Aufenthalt am Zielort über **48 Stunden** dauert. Die Meldung hat innerhalb von 48 Stunden bei der Wehrmachtkommandantur (Wehrmachtstandortältesten) oder in Orten, die nicht Standort sind, bei der Ortspolizei zu erfolgen. Bei Beurlaubung **über 4 Wochen** stets persönliche Meldung bei dem für den Urlaubsort zuständigen Wehrmachtstandortältesten. Meldepflicht bei **Kurzurlaub** entfällt.
7. Bei **Erkrankung** sofort den nächsten Wehrmachtarzt (Standortarzt, Lazarett) aufsuchen und der vorgesetzten Dienststelle Meldung erstatten. Zivilarzt nur in Notfällen aufsuchen.
8. Bei **Fliegeralarm** hat sich jeder Urlauber und dienstlich Reisende unaufgefordert dem örtlichen Luftschutzdienst zur Verfügung zu stellen. Gasmaske ist mitzunehmen.
9. **Schußwaffen und Munition** dürfen nur bei wehrmachteigenen Gepäckaufbewahrungen abgegeben werden.
10. Erforderliche **Auskunft** nur bei Wehrmachtdienststellen einholen.
11. Bei Überschreiten der **Devisengrenze** dürfen **Reichsbanknoten** nicht mitgenommen werden. **Rentenbankscheine** und **Hartgeld** bis zu 10.— RM (Reisefreigrenze). **RKK-Scheine** und **ausländische Zahlungsmittel** nur in zugelassener Höhe laut Bescheinigung der Truppe. Zuwiderhandlungen werden kriegsgerichtlich bestraft.

Feind hört mit! Verschwiegenheit und Zurückhaltung bei Gesprächen!

Urlaubsdauer ab Hauptumsteigebahnhof, Grenzübergang oder Frontleitstelle	**Meldung am Zielort**
	10.4.1945

Geldumtauschvermerke	**Lebensmittelkartenstelle**	**Truppenarzt bzw. E-Anstalt**
	Urlauberkarten für die Zeit vom … bis … 1945 ausgehändigt. 30 APR. 1945 Rauchermarken erhalten vom … bis …	Der Oberbürgermeister der Stadt Aue (Sa.) 28. APR. 1945

Stempel und sonstige Eintragungen von links nach rechts!

1) Am 28.4.1945 beim Kampfkommandanten in Aue gemeldet, Oberleutnant.	2) Versorgung … Ernährungsamt … 30. 4. 45 28. APR. 1945	3)
4)	5)	6)
7)	8)	9)
10)	11)	12)

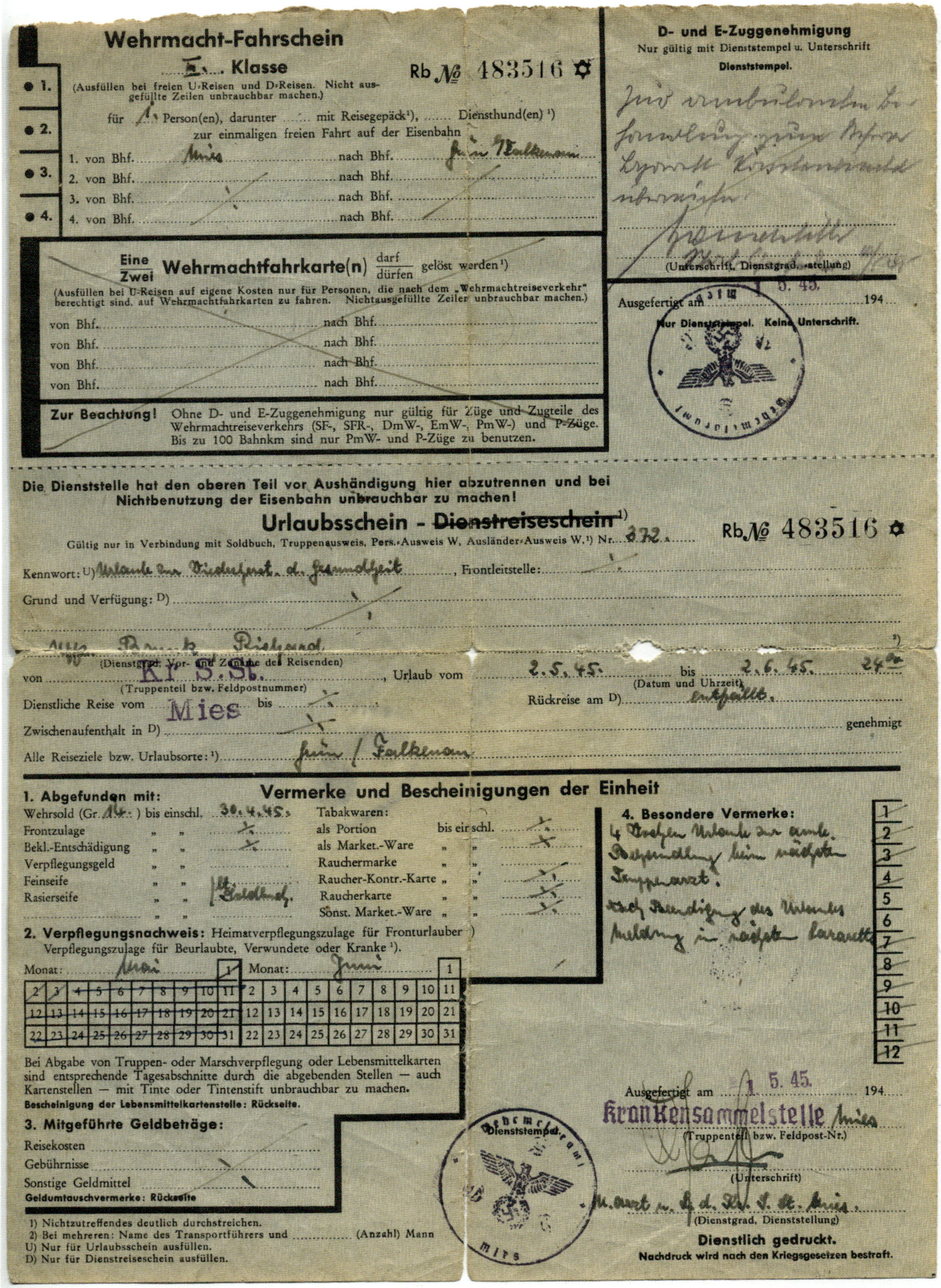

Wehrmacht-Fahrschein

.....I..... Klasse Rb № 483516 ✡

(Ausfüllen bei freien U-Reisen und D-Reisen. Nicht ausgefüllte Zeilen unbrauchbar machen.)

für 1 Person(en), darunter ...... mit Reisegepäck¹), ... Diensthund(en) ¹) zur einmaligen freien Fahrt auf der Eisenbahn

1. von Bhf. Mies nach Bhf. ... Falkenau
2. von Bhf. ... nach Bhf. ...
3. von Bhf. ... nach Bhf. ...
4. von Bhf. ... nach Bhf. ...

Eine / Zwei Wehrmachtfahrkarte(n) darf / dürfen gelöst werden ¹)

(Ausfüllen bei U-Reisen auf eigene Kosten nur für Personen, die nach dem „Wehrmachtreiseverkehr" berechtigt sind, auf Wehrmachtfahrkarten zu fahren. Nichtausgefüllte Zeilen unbrauchbar machen.)

von Bhf. ... nach Bhf. ...
von Bhf. ... nach Bhf. ...
von Bhf. ... nach Bhf. ...
von Bhf. ... nach Bhf. ...

Zur Beachtung! Ohne D- und E-Zuggenehmigung nur gültig für Züge und Zugteile des Wehrmachtreiseverkehrs (SF-, SFR-, DmW-, EmW-, PmW-) und P-Züge. Bis zu 100 Bahnkm sind nur PmW- und P-Züge zu benutzen.

D- und E-Zuggenehmigung
Nur gültig mit Dienststempel u. Unterschrift
Dienststempel.

(Unterschrift, Dienstgrad, -stellung)

Ausgefertigt am 1. 5. 45. 194...

Nur Dienststempel. Keine Unterschrift.

Die Dienststelle hat den oberen Teil vor Aushändigung hier abzutrennen und bei Nichtbenutzung der Eisenbahn unbrauchbar zu machen!

Urlaubsschein - ~~Dienstreiseschein~~ ¹) Rb № 483516 ✡

Gültig nur in Verbindung mit Soldbuch, Truppenausweis, Pers.-Ausweis W, Ausländer-Ausweis W. ¹) Nr. 372

Kennwort: U) ... Frontleitstelle: ...

Grund und Verfügung: D) ...

(Dienstgrad, Vor- und Zuname des Reisenden) Uffz. Brank Richard

von Kr. S. St. (Truppenteil bzw. Feldpostnummer), Urlaub vom 2. 5. 45. bis 2. 6. 45. 24⁰⁰ (Datum und Uhrzeit)

Dienstliche Reise vom Mies bis ... Rückreise am D) entfällt.

Zwischenaufenthalt in D) ... genehmigt

Alle Reiseziele bzw. Urlaubsorte: ¹) ... / Falkenau

Vermerke und Bescheinigungen der Einheit

1. Abgefunden mit:
Wehrsold (Gr. ...) bis einschl. 30. 4. 45.
Frontzulage
Bekl.-Entschädigung
Verpflegungsgeld
Feinseife
Rasierseife

Tabakwaren: als Portion bis einschl. / als Market.-Ware / Rauchermarke / Raucher-Kontr.-Karte / Raucherkarte / Sonst. Market.-Ware

2. Verpflegungsnachweis: Heimatverpflegungszulage für Fronturlauber / Verpflegungszulage für Beurlaubte, Verwundete oder Kranke ¹).

Monat: Mai — Monat: Juni

1	2	3	4	5	6	7	8	9	10	11	1	2	3	4	5	6	7	8	9	10	11
12	13	14	15	16	17	18	19	20	21		12	13	14	15	16	17	18	19	20	21	
22	23	24	25	26	27	28	29	30	31		22	23	24	25	26	27	28	29	30	31	

Bei Abgabe von Truppen- oder Marschverpflegung oder Lebensmittelkarten sind entsprechende Tagesabschnitte durch die abgebenden Stellen — auch Kartenstellen — mit Tinte oder Tintenstift unbrauchbar zu machen.
Bescheinigung der Lebensmittelkartenstelle: Rückseite.

3. Mitgeführte Geldbeträge:
Reisekosten
Gebührnisse
Sonstige Geldmittel
Geldumtauschvermerke: Rückseite

4. Besondere Vermerke: 1–12

Ausgefertigt am 1. 5. 45. 194...
Krankensammelstelle Mies
(Truppenteil bzw. Feldpost-Nr.)
Dienststempel
(Unterschrift)
(Dienstgrad, Dienststellung)

Dienstlich gedruckt.
Nachdruck wird nach den Kriegsgesetzen bestraft.

1) Nichtzutreffendes deutlich durchstreichen.
2) Bei mehreren: Name des Transportführers und ...... (Anzahl) Mann
U) Nur für Urlaubsschein ausfüllen.
D) Nur für Dienstreiseschein ausfüllen.

Figure 2-112. Departing Mies, Germany on "leave." Unteroffizier Richard Brank was transferred to Falkenau on May 2, 1945 by the Krankensammelstelle Mies (Medical Collection Station, Mies). Both Mies and Falkenau had been under Allied control by then, but since even in defeat German authorities did maintain some administrative duties (medical, rations, and the like), it is quite possible that this is not a faked document, even though the stamps have yet to be "de-Nazified."(A4)

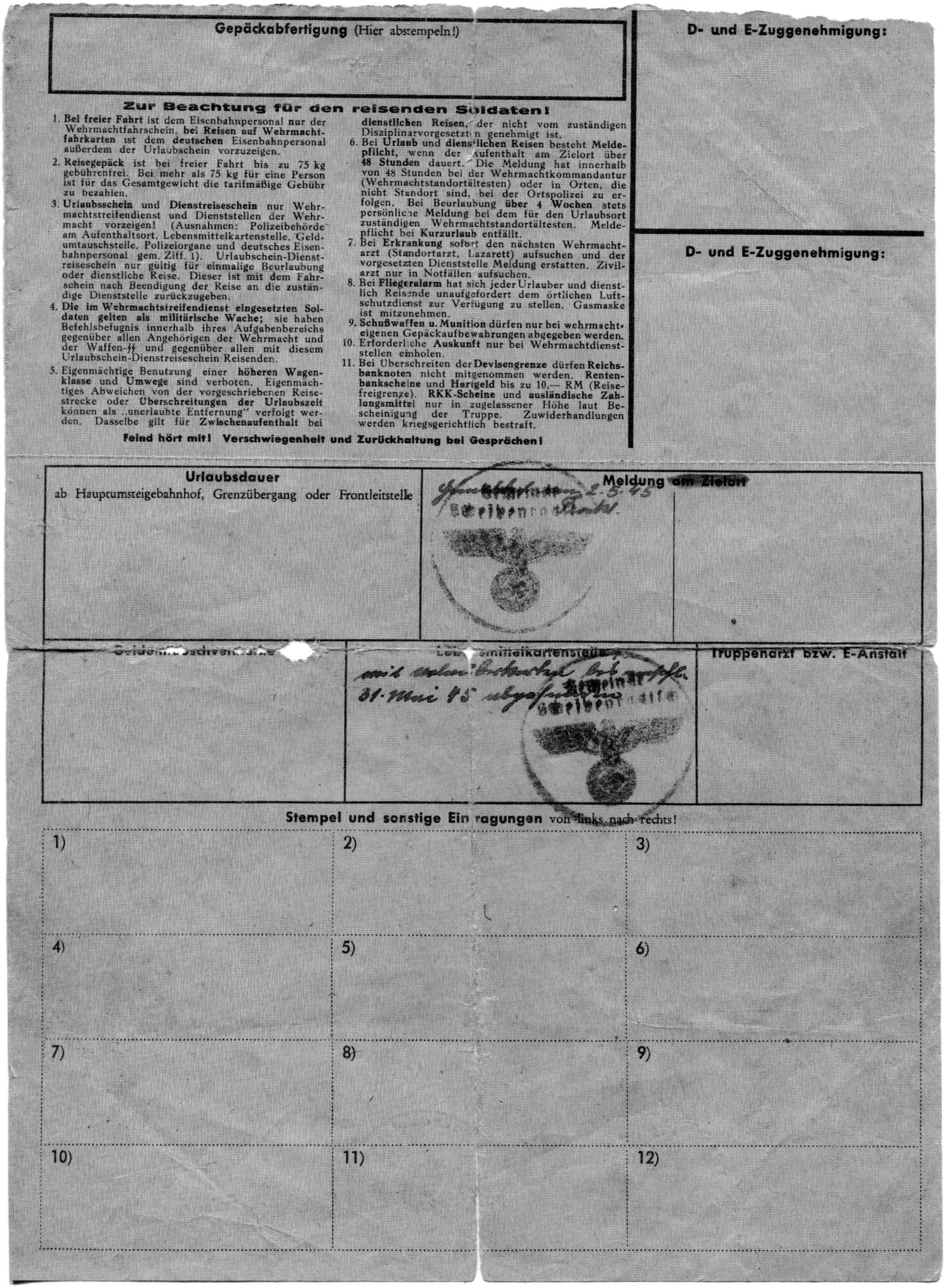

Gepäckabfertigung (Hier abstempeln!)

D- und E-Zuggenehmigung:

D- und E-Zuggenehmigung:

Zur Beachtung für den reisenden Soldaten!

1. **Bei freier Fahrt** ist dem Eisenbahnpersonal **nur** der Wehrmachtfahrschein, **bei Reisen auf Wehrmachtfahrkarten** ist dem **deutschen** Eisenbahnpersonal außerdem der Urlaubschein vorzuzeigen.
2. **Reisegepäck** ist bei freier Fahrt bis zu 75 kg gebührenfrei. Bei mehr als 75 kg für eine Person ist für das Gesamtgewicht die tarifmäßige Gebühr zu bezahlen.
3. **Urlaubsschein** und **Dienstreiseschein** nur Wehrmachtstreifendienst und Dienststellen der Wehrmacht vorzeigen! (Ausnahmen: Polizeibehörde am Aufenthaltsort, Lebensmittelkartenstelle, Geldumtauschstelle, Polizeiorgane und deutsches Eisenbahnpersonal gem. Ziff. 1). Urlaubschein-Dienstreiseschein nur gültig für einmalige Beurlaubung oder dienstliche Reise. Dieser ist mit dem Fahrschein nach Beendigung der Reise an die zuständige Dienststelle zurückzugeben.
4. **Die im Wehrmachtstreifendienst eingesetzten Soldaten gelten als militärische Wache;** sie haben Befehlsbefugnis innerhalb ihres Aufgabenbereichs gegenüber allen Angehörigen der Wehrmacht und der Waffen-SS und gegenüber allen mit diesem Urlaubschein-Dienstreiseschein Reisenden.
5. Eigenmächtige Benutzung einer **höheren Wagenklasse** und **Umwege** sind verboten. Eigenmächtiges Abweichen von der vorgeschriebenen Reisestrecke oder **Überschreitungen der Urlaubszeit** können als „unerlaubte Entfernung" verfolgt werden. Dasselbe gilt für **Zwischenaufenthalt** bei **dienstlichen Reisen,** der nicht vom zuständigen Disziplinarvorgesetzten genehmigt ist.
6. Bei **Urlaub** und **dienstlichen Reisen** besteht **Meldepflicht,** wenn der Aufenthalt am Zielort über **48 Stunden** dauert. Die Meldung hat innerhalb von 48 Stunden bei der Wehrmachtkommandantur (Wehrmachtstandortältesten) oder in Orten, die nicht Standort sind, bei der Ortspolizei zu erfolgen. Bei Beurlaubung **über 4 Wochen** stets persönliche Meldung bei dem für den Urlaubsort zuständigen Wehrmachtstandortältesten. Meldepflicht bei **Kurzurlaub** entfällt.
7. Bei **Erkrankung** sofort den nächsten Wehrmachtarzt (Standortarzt, Lazarett) aufsuchen und der vorgesetzten Dienststelle Meldung erstatten. Zivilarzt nur in Notfällen aufsuchen.
8. Bei **Fliegeralarm** hat sich jeder Urlauber und dienstlich Reisende unaufgefordert dem örtlichen Luftschutzdienst zur Verfügung zu stellen. Gasmaske ist mitzunehmen.
9. **Schußwaffen u. Munition** dürfen nur bei wehrmachteigenen Gepäckaufbewahrungen abgegeben werden.
10. Erforderliche **Auskunft** nur bei Wehrmachtdienststellen einholen.
11. Bei Überschreiten der **Devisengrenze** dürfen **Reichsbanknoten** nicht mitgenommen werden. **Rentenbankscheine** und **Hartgeld** bis zu 10,— RM (Reisefreigrenze). **RKK-Scheine** und **ausländische Zahlungsmittel** nur in zugelassener Höhe laut Bescheinigung der Truppe. Zuwiderhandlungen werden kriegsgerichtlich bestraft.

Feind hört mit! Verschwiegenheit und Zurückhaltung bei Gesprächen!

Urlaubsdauer
ab Hauptumsteigebahnhof, Grenzübergang oder Frontleitstelle

Meldung am Zielort

Truppenarzt bzw. E-Anstalt

Stempel und sonstige Eintragungen von links nach rechts!

1)	2)	3)
4)	5)	6)
7)	8)	9)
10)	11)	12)

The bottom half of the lower section was reserved for *Vermerke und Bescheinigung* (Notices and Certifications). The *Vermerken* segment held all the information that would have otherwise been included by *Sonderstempel* on either the *Kriegsurlaubsschein* or the *Sonderausweis*: verification of the payment of a *Wehrsold*, the issuance of tobacco rations, food rations, soap, shaving soap, and so on.

The form also served as a *Verpflegungsnachweis* (Travel Ration Card); blocks representing the days of the week were marked through or left blank to note the approved days that rations were available while traveling. When the soldier collected rations, the date was crossed off by the issuing authority.

The area to the lower right, normally set aside for the *Truppenteil*, *Dienststempel*, and commanding officer's signature, also had space for additional stamps, marks, notes, or conditions for travel.

The back of the form, again in two sections, one above the perforation and the other below it, contained the rules, regulations, and stipulations for traveling soldiers. Below the rules, themselves neatly tucked into the upper section, was the ever-present warning in late war Germany: "*Feind hört mit! Verschwiegenheit und Zurückhaltung bei Gesprächen!*" (The enemy is listening! Maintain discretion and restraint in conversations!). This was the German equivalent of the United States' counterespionage slogan: "Loose Lips Sink Ships."

The lower portion was divided into a series of blocks for the *Dienststempel* of the officials and bureaus issuing pay and rations, and a special block for the *Truppenarzt*, or military doctor, to indicate whether the *Soldat* in question was healthy enough for travel (i.e. not contagious).

It was subdivided into a grid for additional *Stempel*, specifications, and comments, such as passage through a delousing station, layovers in train stations, and so forth. For the most part, there was little cause to use this section; most of the conditions of travel were already well accounted for by the thoroughness of the other portions of this form.

Service-Related Travel

There are always situations in which a soldier might be required to be away from his unit and not be on leave. This service-related travel required special paperwork to prevent the temptation of desertion, and so the *Sonderausweis* (Special Identity Form) was created.

There are three different *Sonderausweis*, the *Sonderausweis-D* valid only for *Dienstreisen* (Service Travel), the *Sonderausweis-I* for travel in and through Italy, and the *Sonderausweis-SO* for travel in and out of the *Süd-Ost*, the Southeast, namely from the Balkans to the Caucasus Mountains.

Collectors are most familiar with the *Sonderausweis-D*. As with the *Kleiner Wehrmachtfahrschein*, this form was extensively used, so there are a number of them available.

Among the many pieces of paperwork a soldier often carried, the *Sonderausweis-D* was difficult to miss. Not only was the legend, "*Gültig nur bei Dienstreisen!*," or valid only for service travel, printed above or below the title of the form, each corner was marked with a large capital letter "D," often in either an extra bold font or in excess of 48-points in size.

The front of the page required the expected information: rank and name, *Dienststelle*, travel dates, and where the soldier was traveling to. It also had a line for "*Grund*," grounds for travel, the specific reason why one was traveling to the listed location and not with one's unit.

The purpose for travel might be simple, such as transfer to a new duty station or to a hospital due to injury or illness. Other situations requiring the use of a *Sonderausweis* might include driving a transport of food or fuel, in which case the *Fahrbefehl*, or Travel Order, might also be issued to identify the vehicle and itinerary. Another reason might be to conduct an inspection tour. Yes, officers and even high-ranking officers required a *Sonderausweis* to be away from their post.

The last line before the usual date and signature information states the date that a return trip, the *Rückreise*, was expected. It might be the same date the document was issued if the ground for travel was to simply deliver a message. It might not be a specific date at all, but rather, pending the outcome of a situation or condition, such as successful graduation from Radio Operator's School.

At the very bottom of the *Sonderausweis-D* was an often large, often bolded line of text that says: "*Etwa erforderliche Angaben über Abfindungen mit Verpflegung usw. Nur mit Dienststempel und Unterschrift des Kompanie- usw. Führers gültig – Siehe Rückseite*." It translates as: "Various provisions and settlements are only granted and valid with the signature and *Dienststempel* of the commanding officer. See reverse." Following the recommendation of the bolded text, conditions of and provisions for the bearer in the event of extended travel can be found. The first of which is that this form is only to be used for official purposes of service-related travel, and that it is not valid as a travel pass; it does not provide for the cost of travel.

The list also states that since this is service-related, one must be cautious about what one says. Other rules

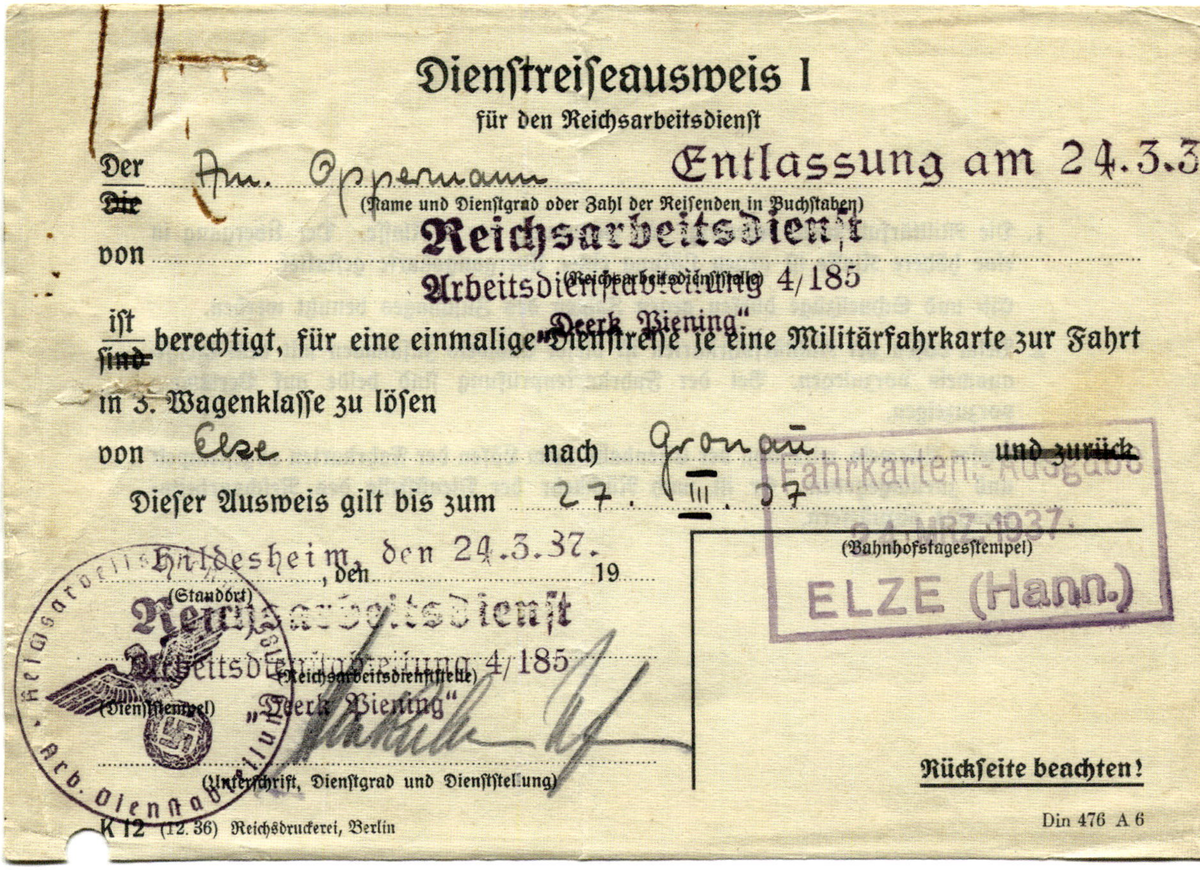

Dienstreiseausweis I

für den Reichsarbeitsdienst

Der ~~Die~~ Am. Oppermann Entlassung am 24.3.37

(Name und Dienstgrad oder Zahl der Reisenden in Buchstaben)

von Reichsarbeitsdienst Arbeitsdienstabteilung 4/185 „Deerk Piening"

(Reichsarbeitsdienststelle)

ist ~~sind~~ berechtigt, für eine einmalige Dienstreise je eine Militärfahrkarte zur Fahrt in 3. Wagenklasse zu lösen

von Elze nach Gronau ~~und zurück~~

Dieser Ausweis gilt bis zum 27. III. 37

Hildesheim, den 24.3.37. 19

(Standort)

Reichsarbeitsdienst Arbeitsdienstabteilung 4/185 „Deerk Piening"

(Reichsarbeitsdienststelle)

(Dienststempel)

(Unterschrift, Dienstgrad und Dienststellung)

Fahrkarten-Ausgabe 24.MRZ.1937 ELZE (Hann.)

(Bahnhofstagesstempel)

Rückseite beachten!

K12 (12.36) Reichsdruckerei, Berlin

Din 476 A 6

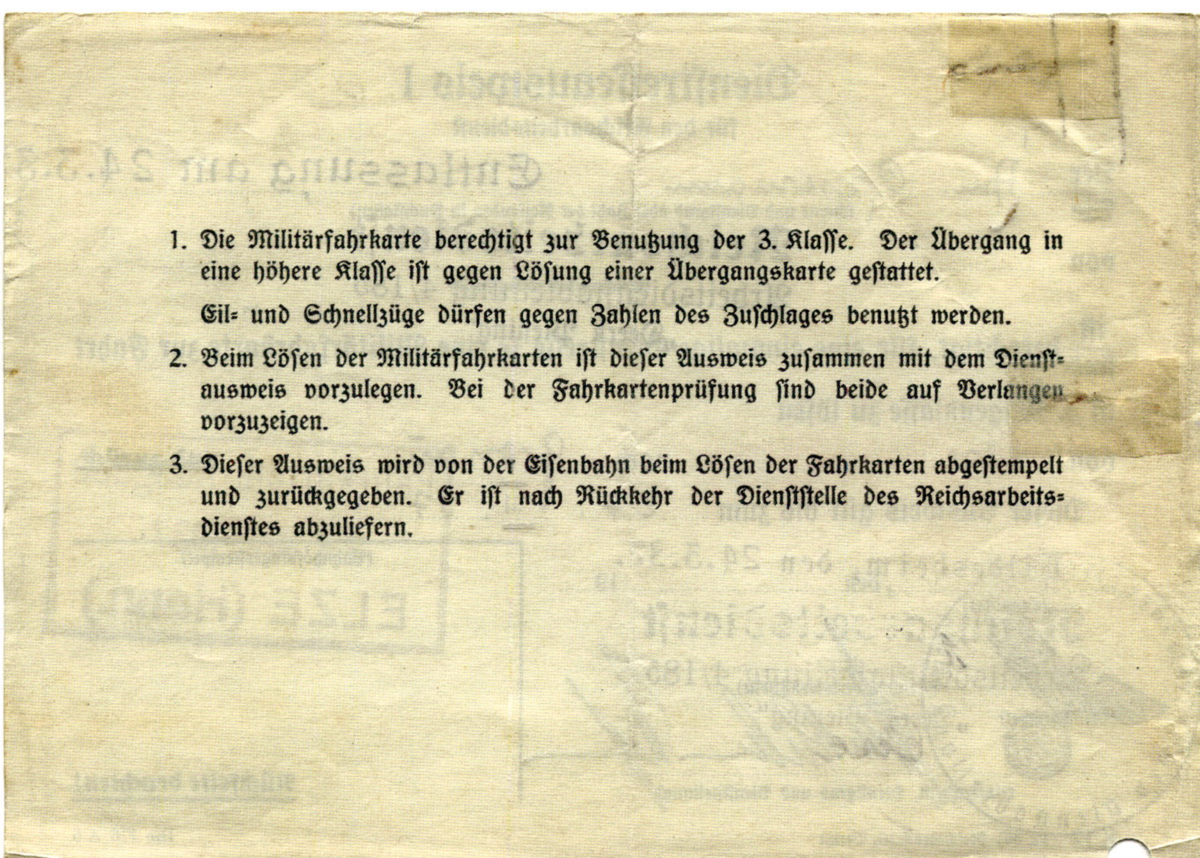

1. Die Militärfahrkarte berechtigt zur Benutzung der 3. Klasse. Der Übergang in eine höhere Klasse ist gegen Lösung einer Übergangskarte gestattet.

   Eil- und Schnellzüge dürfen gegen Zahlen des Zuschlages benutzt werden.

2. Beim Lösen der Militärfahrkarten ist dieser Ausweis zusammen mit dem Dienstausweis vorzulegen. Bei der Fahrkartenprüfung sind beide auf Verlangen vorzuzeigen.

3. Dieser Ausweis wird von der Eisenbahn beim Lösen der Fahrkarten abgestempelt und zurückgegeben. Er ist nach Rückkehr der Dienststelle des Reichsarbeitsdienstes abzuliefern.

Figure 2-113. A prewar Reichsarbeitsdienst (RAD) Dienstreiseausweis (Reich Work Service Service-Travel Identification) from 1937; this was a precursor to the Sonderausweis for service-related travel. (A5)

regarding the proper use of the form include instructions if one should fall ill while traveling, warnings against unnecessary stays and detours (*unnötigen Aufenthalt und Umwege*), and that once the trip is completed that the soldier is required to turn the form in.

Line-7 of the *Sonderausweis-D* lists *Abgefunden*, items and provisions issued to the soldier for travel. These items include the *Wehrsold*, the *Frontzulage*, or hazardous duty pay above and beyond the *Wehrsold*, an *Afrikazulage*, hazardous duty pay beyond both the *Wehrsold* and the *Frontzulage* for those stationed in North Africa and the Mediterranean, various forms of ration cards, tobacco ration cards, bread, soap, and shaving soap. Any items issued to the *Soldat* would be noted in this space, rather than by the use of a *Sonderstempel*. Of course, at times an overzealous or overworked clerk might get carried away and stamp the form, then fill that out instead. Either way, the certification that such items had been issued would be noted.

Finally, spaces were provided for additional instructions or notations by officers, doctors (upon inspection of a soldier's travel-worthiness), train stations, and so on, as needed, often dated and accompanied by a *Dienststempel*.

The *Sonderausweis-I* (in Italian, *Lasciapassare Speciale "I"* or Special Pass for Through-Travel) was a bilingual, German and Italian, A4 document created for *Wehrmacht* personnel traveling on official *Wehrmacht* business (still noted at the top left of the page: *Gültig nur bei Dienstreisen!*) to pass through Italy with a minimum of difficulty.

The pass is printed only on the front of the page; the back is blank. The notation restricting the pass to service travel is joined by a line (two lines, if one counts the Italian translation) that reads "*Den italienischen Behörden unaufgefordert vorzuzeigen*," meaning that the Soldat should be prepared to show this pass to Italian authorities without being asked. Naturally, the *Soldat* understood this to mean "You're in someone else's country; don't be a pain."

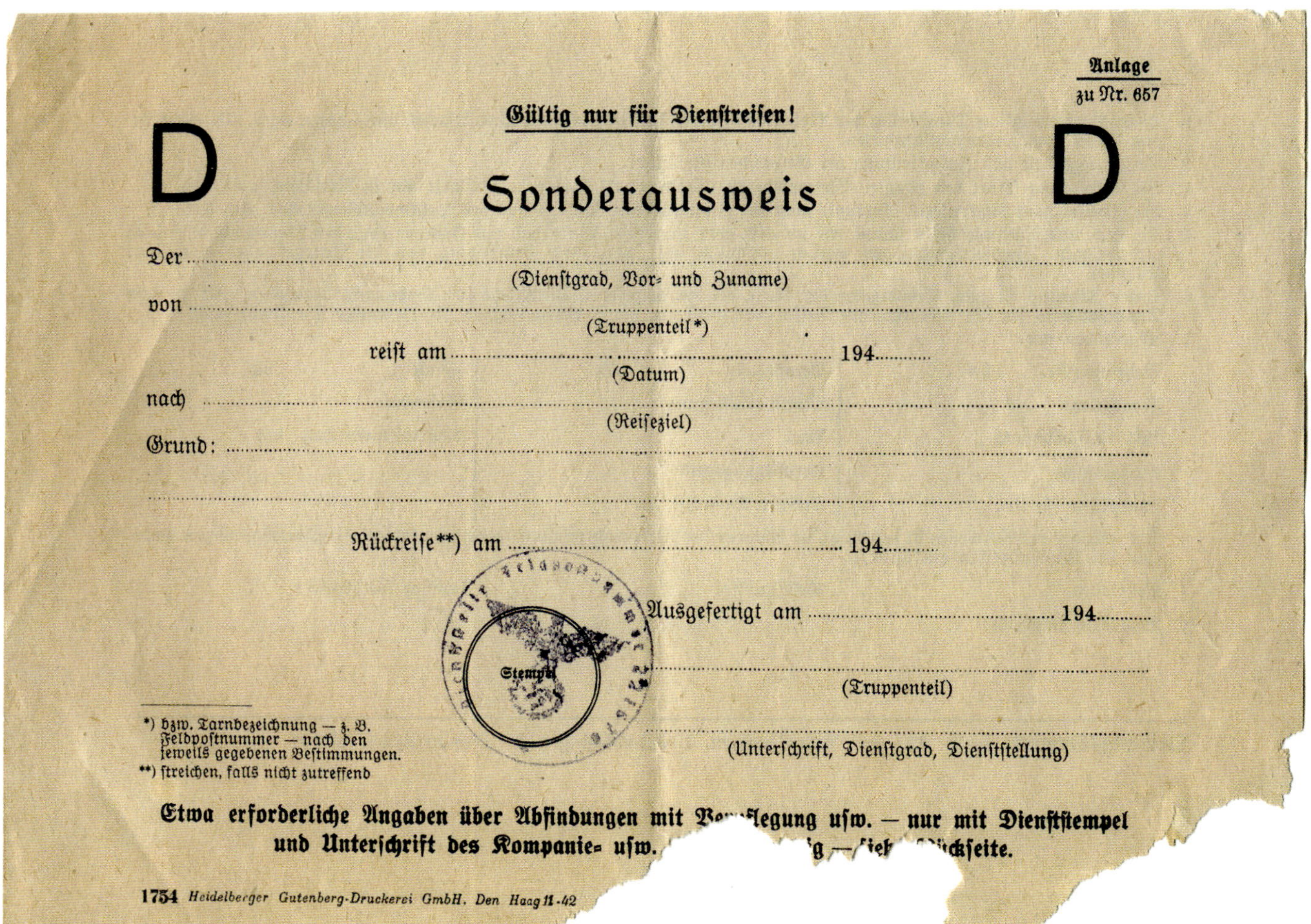
Anlage
zu Nr. 657

Gültig nur für Dienstreisen!

D Sonderausweis D

Der ....
(Dienstgrad, Vor- und Zuname)

von ....
(Truppenteil*)

reist am .... 194.....
(Datum)

nach ....
(Reiseziel)

Grund: ....

....

Rückreise**) am .... 194.....

Stempel

Ausgefertigt am .... 194.....

....
(Truppenteil)

....
(Unterschrift, Dienstgrad, Dienststellung)

*) bzw. Tarnbezeichnung — z. B. Feldpostnummer — nach den jeweils gegebenen Bestimmungen.
**) streichen, falls nicht zutreffend

Etwa erforderliche Angaben über Abfindungen mit Be[illegible]legung usw. — nur mit Dienststempel und Unterschrift des Kompanie- usw. [illegible]g — sie[illegible]ckseite.

1754 *Heidelberger Gutenberg-Druckerei GmbH. Den Haag 11-42*

Figure 2-114. The Sonderausweis D ("D" for Dienstreise or Service Travel), which authorized Soldaten to be away from their unit for official purposes. This version used a Fraktur typeface. (A5)

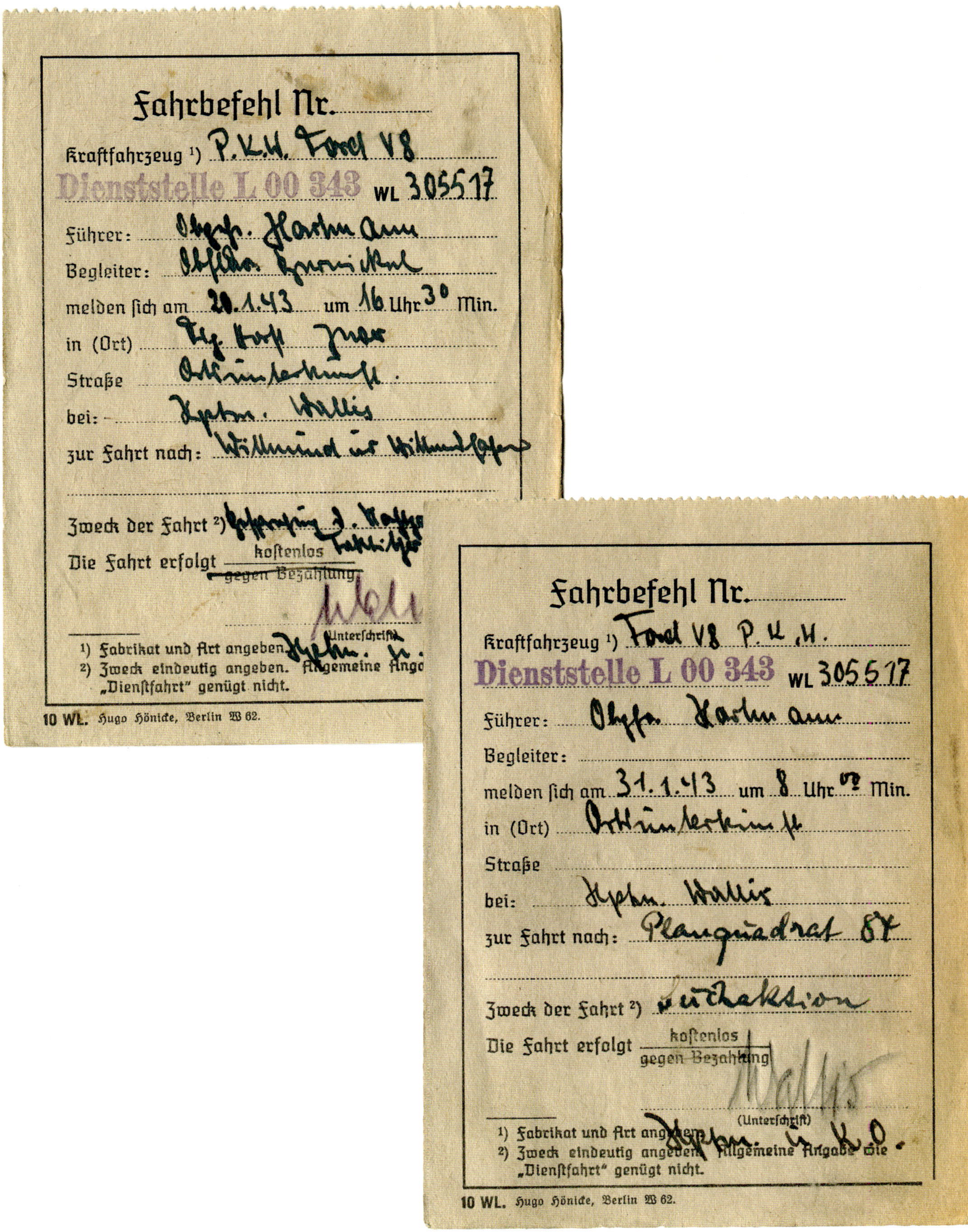

Fahrbefehl Nr.

Kraftfahrzeug 1) P.K.W. Ford V8

Dienststelle L 00 343 WL 305517

Führer:

Begleiter:

melden sich am 20.1.43 um 16 Uhr 30 Min.

in (Ort)

Straße

bei:

zur Fahrt nach:

Zweck der Fahrt 2)

Die Fahrt erfolgt kostenlos / gegen Bezahlung

(Unterschrift)

1) Fabrikat und Art angeben.

2) Zweck eindeutig angeben. Allgemeine Angabe wie „Dienstfahrt" genügt nicht.

10 WL. Hugo Hönicke, Berlin W 62.

Fahrbefehl Nr.

Kraftfahrzeug 1) Ford V8 P.K.W.

Dienststelle L 00 343 WL 305517

Führer:

Begleiter:

melden sich am 31.1.43 um 8 Uhr Min.

in (Ort)

Straße

bei:

zur Fahrt nach: Planquadrat 84

Zweck der Fahrt 2)

Die Fahrt erfolgt kostenlos / gegen Bezahlung

(Unterschrift)

1) Fabrikat und Art angeben.

2) Zweck eindeutig angeben. Allgemeine Angabe wie „Dienstfahrt" genügt nicht.

10 WL. Hugo Hönicke, Berlin W 62.

Figure 2-115. The Sonderausweis was not to be confused with the Fahrbefehl; the latter was used whenever a Soldat was away from his unit while performing duties associated with that unit, such as part of a military transport company.

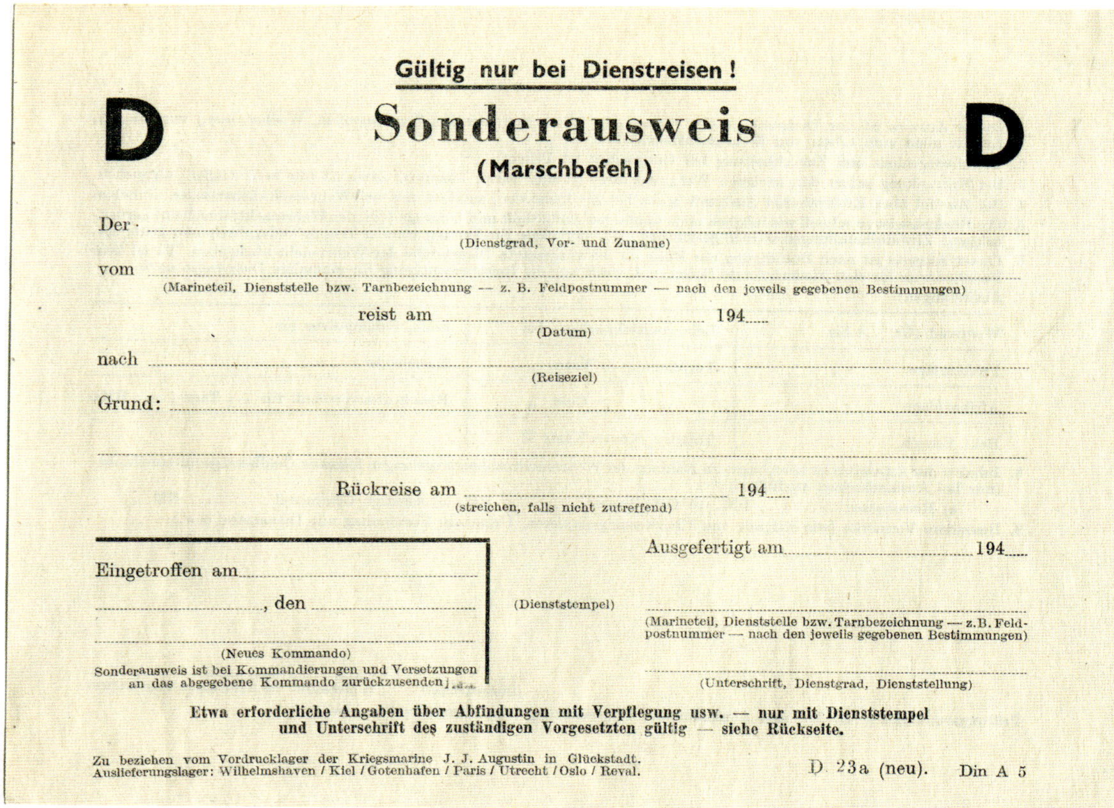

Gültig nur bei Dienstreisen!

D **Sonderausweis** D

(Marschbefehl)

Der ....
(Dienstgrad, Vor- und Zuname)

vom ....
(Marineteil, Dienststelle bzw. Tarnbezeichnung — z. B. Feldpostnummer — nach den jeweils gegebenen Bestimmungen)

reist am .... 194.....
(Datum)

nach ....
(Reiseziel)

Grund: ....

....

Rückreise am .... 194.....
(streichen, falls nicht zutreffend)

Eingetroffen am ....

.............................., den ....

....
(Neues Kommando)
Sonderausweis ist bei Kommandierungen und Versetzungen an das abgegebene Kommando zurückzusenden!

(Dienststempel)

Ausgefertigt am .... 194.....

....
(Marineteil, Dienststelle bzw. Tarnbezeichnung — z.B. Feldpostnummer — nach den jeweils gegebenen Bestimmungen)

....
(Unterschrift, Dienstgrad, Dienststellung)

Etwa erforderliche Angaben über Abfindungen mit Verpflegung usw. — nur mit Dienststempel und Unterschrift des zuständigen Vorgesetzten gültig — siehe Rückseite.

Zu beziehen vom Vordrucklager der Kriegsmarine J. J. Augustin in Glückstadt.
Auslieferungslager: Wilhelmshaven / Kiel / Gotenhafen / Paris / Utrecht / Oslo / Reval.

D. 23a (neu). Din A 5

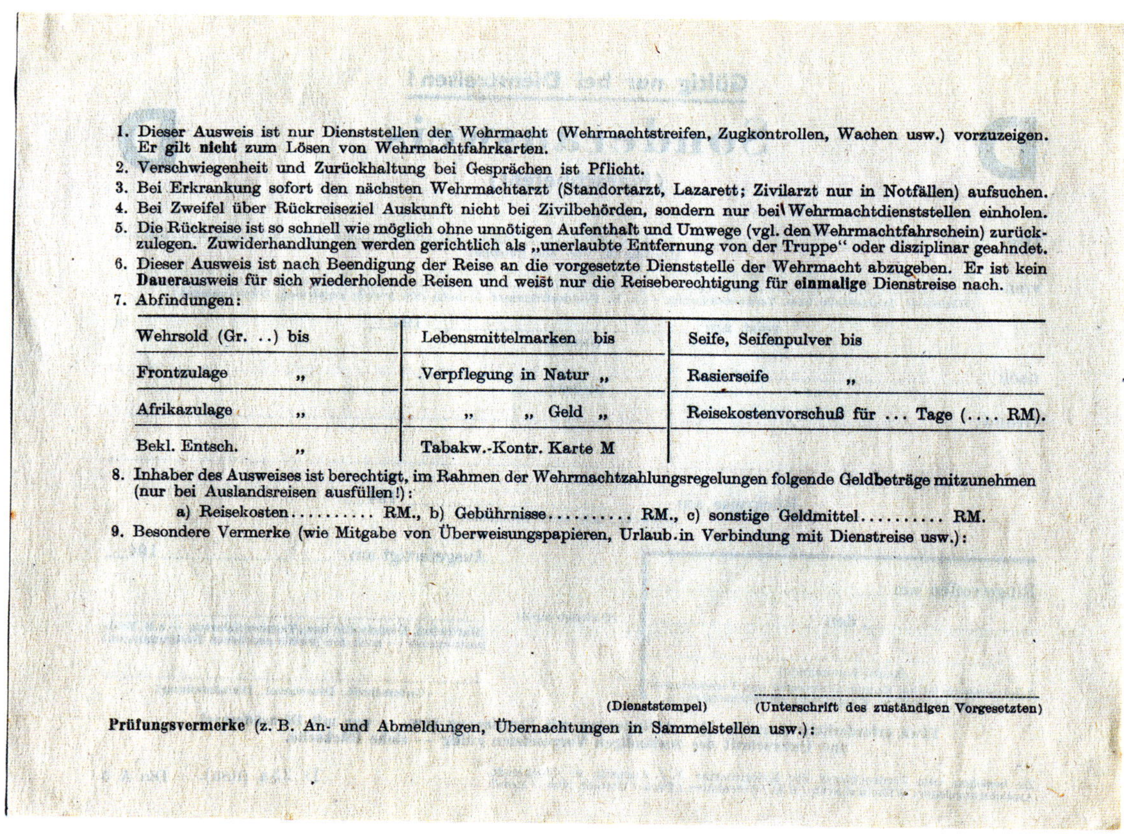

1. **Dieser Ausweis ist nur Dienststellen der Wehrmacht (Wehrmachtstreifen, Zugkontrollen, Wachen usw.) vorzuzeigen. Er gilt nicht zum Lösen von Wehrmachtfahrkarten.**
2. **Verschwiegenheit und Zurückhaltung bei Gesprächen ist Pflicht.**
3. **Bei Erkrankung sofort den nächsten Wehrmachtarzt (Standortarzt, Lazarett; Zivilarzt nur in Notfällen) aufsuchen.**
4. **Bei Zweifel über Rückreiseziel Auskunft nicht bei Zivilbehörden, sondern nur bei Wehrmachtdienststellen einholen.**
5. **Die Rückreise ist so schnell wie möglich ohne unnötigen Aufenthalt und Umwege (vgl. den Wehrmachtfahrschein) zurückzulegen. Zuwiderhandlungen werden gerichtlich als „unerlaubte Entfernung von der Truppe" oder disziplinar geahndet.**
6. **Dieser Ausweis ist nach Beendigung der Reise an die vorgesetzte Dienststelle der Wehrmacht abzugeben. Er ist kein Dauerausweis für sich wiederholende Reisen und weist nur die Reiseberechtigung für einmalige Dienstreise nach.**
7. **Abfindungen:**

Wehrsold (Gr. ..) bis	Lebensmittelmarken bis	Seife, Seifenpulver bis
Frontzulage „	Verpflegung in Natur „	Rasierseife „
Afrikazulage „	„ „ Geld „	Reisekostenvorschuß für ... Tage (.... RM).
Bekl. Entsch. „	Tabakw.-Kontr. Karte M	

8. **Inhaber des Ausweises ist berechtigt, im Rahmen der Wehrmachtzahlungsregelungen folgende Geldbeträge mitzunehmen (nur bei Auslandsreisen ausfüllen!):**
   a) Reisekosten.......... RM., b) Gebührnisse.......... RM., c) sonstige Geldmittel.......... RM.
9. **Besondere Vermerke (wie Mitgabe von Überweisungspapieren, Urlaub in Verbindung mit Dienstreise usw.):**

(Dienststempel) .... (Unterschrift des zuständigen Vorgesetzten)

Prüfungsvermerke (z. B. An- und Abmeldungen, Übernachtungen in Sammelstellen usw.):

Figure 2-116. Another Sonderausweis, this time set in a serif typeface, printed for the Kriegsmarine. (A5)

Gültig nur bei Dienstreisen!

D **Sonderausweis** D

Der Gefr. Johann Hassler (Dienstgrad, Vor- und Zuname)

von Feldpost Nr. 24077 (Truppenteil*)

reist am 24. Januar (Datum) 1941

nach Czersk (Reiseziel)

Grund: Kommandierung

Rückreise**) am — 194

Ausgefertigt am 24. Januar 1941

Feldpost Nr. 24077 (Truppenteil*)

(Dienststempel)

(Unterschrift, Dienstgrad, Dienststellung)

*) bzw. Tarnbezeichnung — z. B. Feldpostnummer — nach den jeweils gegebenen Bestimmungen.

**) streichen, falls nicht zutreffend.

Etwa erforderliche Angaben über Abfindungen mit Verpflegung usw. — nur mit Dienststempel und Unterschrift des Kompanie- usw. Führers gültig — siehe Rückseite.

Wehrkreisdruckerei XX

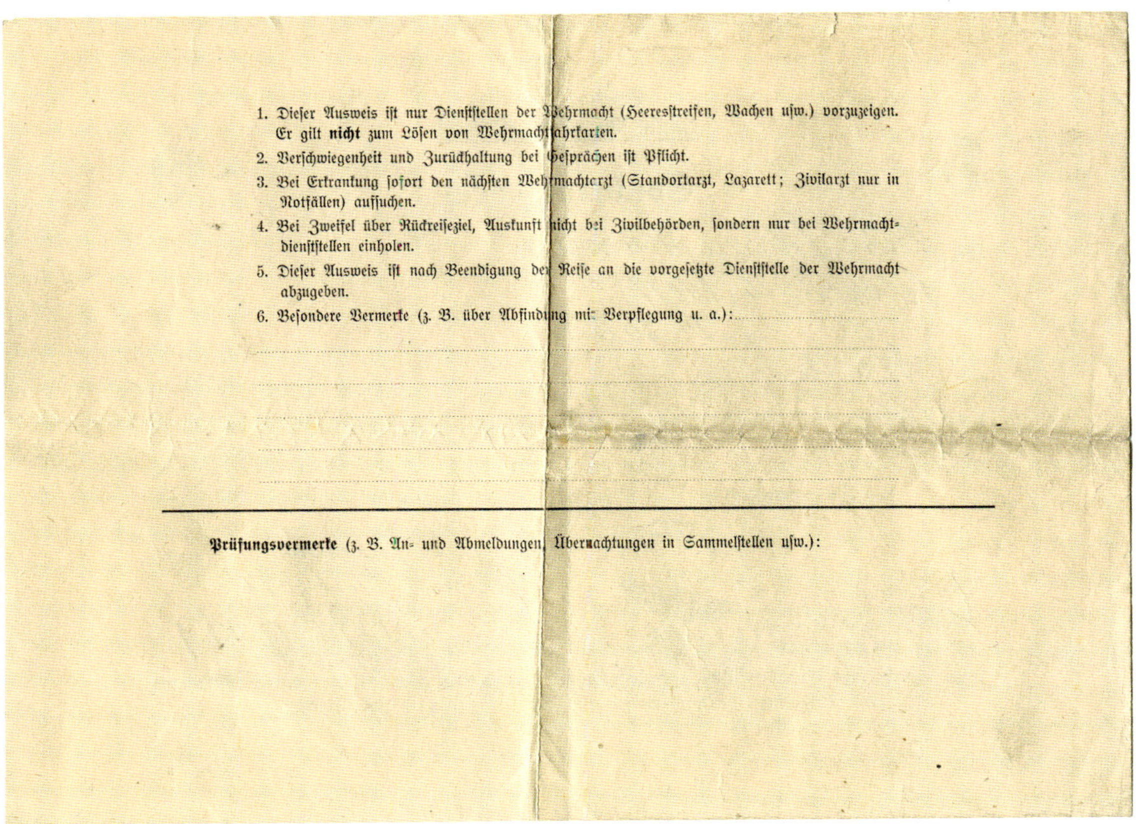

1. Dieser Ausweis ist nur Dienststellen der Wehrmacht (Heeresstreifen, Wachen usw.) vorzuzeigen. Er gilt **nicht** zum Lösen von Wehrmachtfahrkarten.
2. Verschwiegenheit und Zurückhaltung bei Gesprächen ist Pflicht.
3. Bei Erkrankung sofort den nächsten Wehrmachtarzt (Standortarzt, Lazarett; Zivilarzt nur in Notfällen) aufsuchen.
4. Bei Zweifel über Rückreiseziel, Auskunft nicht bei Zivilbehörden, sondern nur bei Wehrmachtdienststellen einholen.
5. Dieser Ausweis ist nach Beendigung der Reise an die vorgesetzte Dienststelle der Wehrmacht abzugeben.
6. Besondere Vermerke (z. B. über Abfindung mit Verpflegung u. a.):

Prüfungsvermerke (z. B. An- und Abmeldungen, Übernachtungen in Sammelstellen usw.):

Figure 2-117. Gefreiter Johann Hassler was directed to proceed to Czersk as part of the 2. Kompanie Eisenbahn-Bau-Pionier-Bataillon 106, Railroad Construction Pioniere Battalion 106. This is a prewar version of the form that was used shortly after the war started; note that the back doesn't have the spaces for rations issued like the previous examples. (A5)

Gültig nur für Dienstreisen!

Die Dringlichkeit der Reise wird bescheinigt.

D **Sonderausweis** D

Der Carol Härtig
(Dienstgrad, Vor- und Zuname)

von der Frontbühne "Niedersächsische Landesbühne"
(Truppenteil*)

reist am 11.8.1941 194
(Datum)

nach Leipzig
(Reiseziel)

Grund: Beendigung der Tournee

Rückreise**) am 194

*) bzw. Tarnbezeichnung — z. B. Feldpostnummer — nach den jeweils gegebenen Bestimmungen.
**) streichen, falls nicht zutreffend.

Dienststempel

Ausgefertigt am 6.8.1941 194
Aussenstelle O. K. W./I=Ost
(Truppenteil*)

I.V. [signature] Oberleutnant.
(Unterschrift, Dienstgrad, Dienststellung)
Leiter der Aussenstelle

Etwa erforderliche Angaben über Abfindungen mit Verpflegung usw. — nur mit Dienststempel und Unterschrift des Kompanie- usw. Führers gültig — siehe Rückseite.

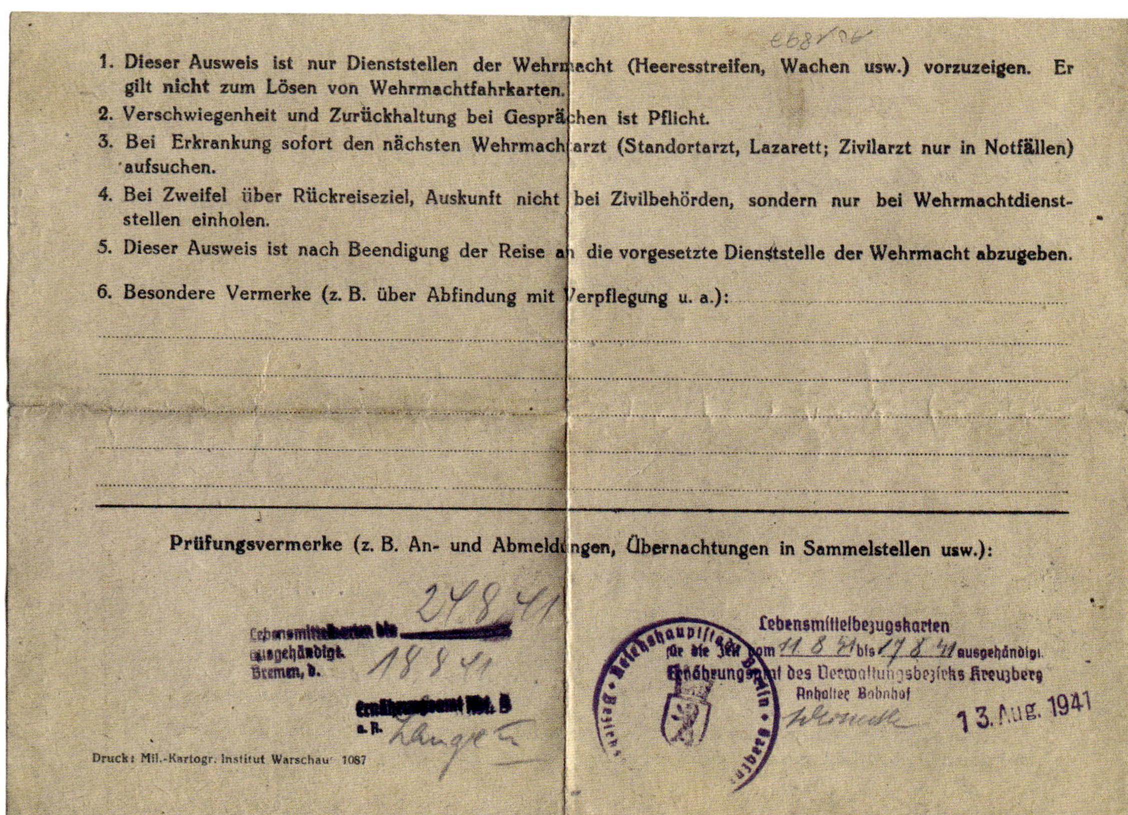

1. Dieser Ausweis ist nur Dienststellen der Wehrmacht (Heeresstreifen, Wachen usw.) vorzuzeigen. Er gilt nicht zum Lösen von Wehrmachtfahrkarten.
2. Verschwiegenheit und Zurückhaltung bei Gesprächen ist Pflicht.
3. Bei Erkrankung sofort den nächsten Wehrmachtarzt (Standortarzt, Lazarett; Zivilarzt nur in Notfällen) aufsuchen.
4. Bei Zweifel über Rückreiseziel, Auskunft nicht bei Zivilbehörden, sondern nur bei Wehrmachtdienststellen einholen.
5. Dieser Ausweis ist nach Beendigung der Reise an die vorgesetzte Dienststelle der Wehrmacht abzugeben.
6. Besondere Vermerke (z. B. über Abfindung mit Verpflegung u. a.):

Prüfungsvermerke (z. B. An- und Abmeldungen, Übernachtungen in Sammelstellen usw.):

Lebensmittelkarten bis 24.8.41 ausgehändigt. Bremen, d. 18.8.41
Ernährungsamt Abt. B
a. B. Lange

Lebensmittelbezugskarten für die Zeit vom 11.8.41 bis 17.8.41 ausgehändigt.
Ernährungsamt des Verwaltungsbezirks Kreuzberg
Anhalter Bahnhof
13. Aug. 1941

Druck: Mil.-Kartogr. Institut Warschau 1087

Figure 2-118. The top of this service-related travel form is marked "The urgency of the trip is certified," though why a civilian member of the Lower Saxony State Theater would be certified for "urgent travel" is not mentioned, though she has completed her tour, as noted in the entry "Grund" (Grounds for travel). (A5)

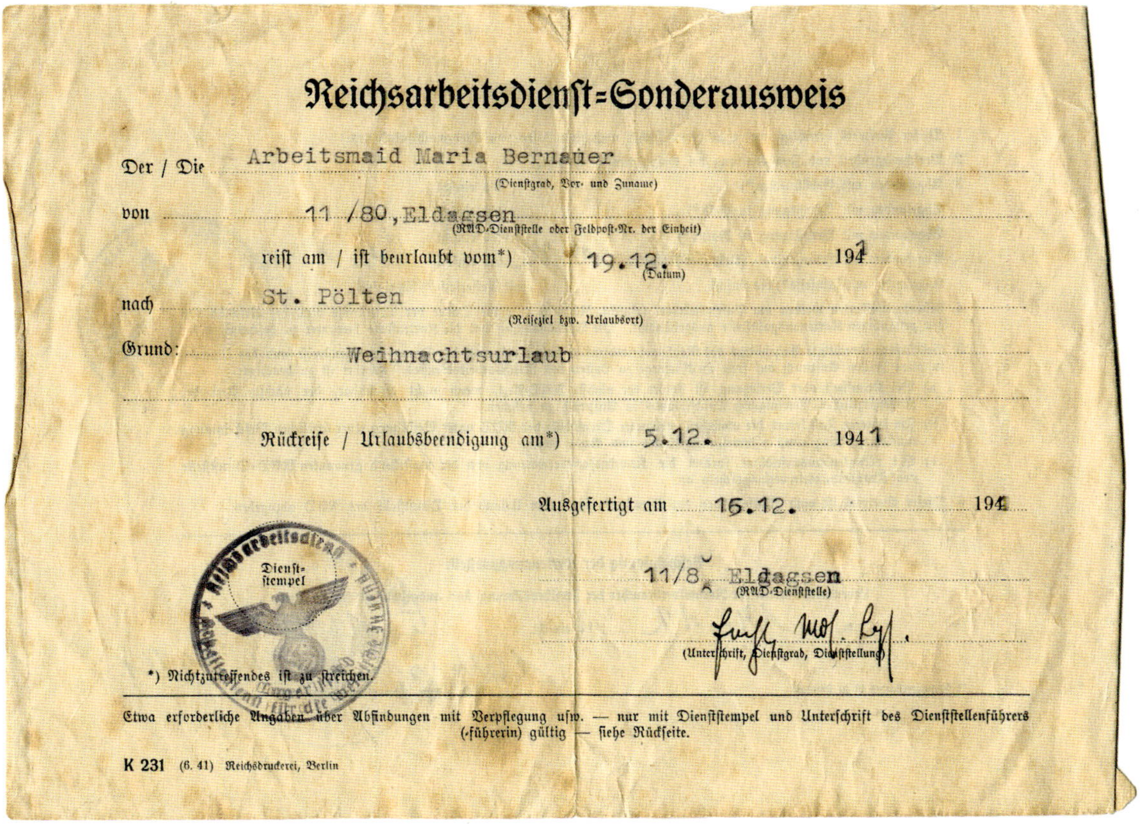

Reichsarbeitsdienst=Sonderausweis

Der / Die Arbeitsmaid Maria Bernauer
(Dienstgrad, Vor- und Zuname)

von 11/80, Eldagsen
(RAD-Dienststelle oder Feldpost-Nr. der Einheit)

reist am / ist beurlaubt vom*) 19.12. (Datum) 1941

nach St. Pölten
(Reiseziel bzw. Urlaubsort)

Grund: Weihnachtsurlaub

Rückreise / Urlaubsbeendigung am*) 5.12. 1941

Ausgefertigt am 16.12. 1941

Dienst-stempel

11/8 Eldagsen
(RAD-Dienststelle)

(Unterschrift, Dienstgrad, Dienststellung)

*) Nichtzutreffendes ist zu streichen.

Etwa erforderliche Angaben über Abfindungen mit Verpflegung usw. — nur mit Dienststempel und Unterschrift des Dienststellenführers (-führerin) gültig — siehe Rückseite.

K 231 (6. 41) Reichsdruckerei, Berlin

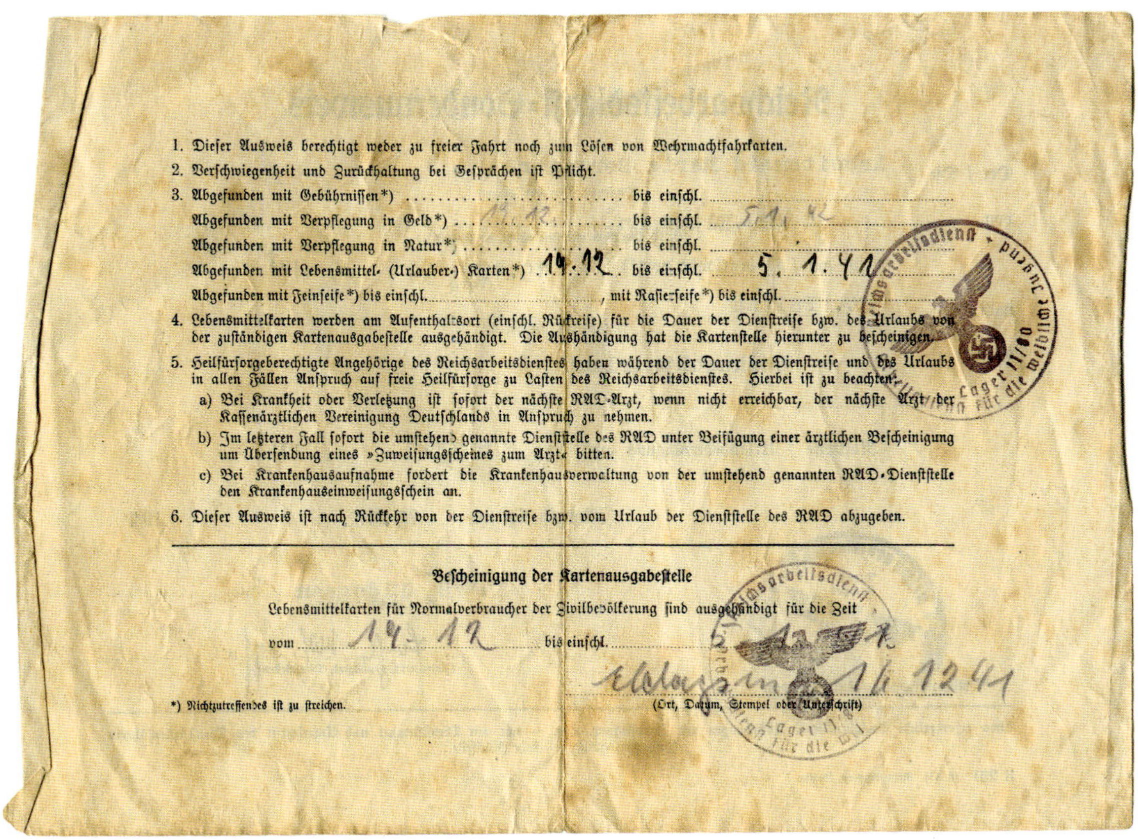

1. Dieser Ausweis berechtigt weder zu freier Fahrt noch zum Lösen von Wehrmachtfahrkarten.
2. Verschwiegenheit und Zurückhaltung bei Gesprächen ist Pflicht.
3. Abgefunden mit Gebührnissen*) .... bis einschl. ....
   Abgefunden mit Verpflegung in Geld*) .... bis einschl. ....
   Abgefunden mit Verpflegung in Natur*) .... bis einschl. ....
   Abgefunden mit Lebensmittel- (Urlauber-) Karten*) 14.12. bis einschl. 5. 1. 42
   Abgefunden mit Feinseife*) bis einschl. ...., mit Rasierseife*) bis einschl. ....
4. Lebensmittelkarten werden am Aufenthaltsort (einschl. Rückreise) für die Dauer der Dienstreise bzw. des Urlaubs von der zuständigen Kartenausgabestelle ausgehändigt. Die Aushändigung hat die Kartenstelle hierunter zu bescheinigen.
5. Heilfürsorgeberechtigte Angehörige des Reichsarbeitsdienstes haben während der Dauer der Dienstreise und des Urlaubs in allen Fällen Anspruch auf freie Heilfürsorge zu Lasten des Reichsarbeitsdienstes. Hierbei ist zu beachten:
   a) Bei Krankheit oder Verletzung ist sofort der nächste RAD-Arzt, wenn nicht erreichbar, der nächste Arzt der Kassenärztlichen Vereinigung Deutschlands in Anspruch zu nehmen.
   b) Im letzteren Fall sofort die umstehend genannte Dienststelle des RAD unter Beifügung einer ärztlichen Bescheinigung um Übersendung eines »Zuweisungsscheines zum Arzt« bitten.
   c) Bei Krankenhausaufnahme fordert die Krankenhausverwaltung von der umstehend genannten RAD-Dienststelle den Krankenhauseinweisungsschein an.
6. Dieser Ausweis ist nach Rückkehr von der Dienstreise bzw. vom Urlaub der Dienststelle des RAD abzugeben.

Bescheinigung der Kartenausgabestelle

Lebensmittelkarten für Normalverbraucher der Zivilbevölkerung sind ausgehändigt für die Zeit

vom 14. 12 bis einschl. 5. 1. 42

Eldagsen 1/12 41

(Ort, Datum, Stempel oder Unterschrift)

*) Nichtzutreffendes ist zu streichen.

Figure 2-119. Another civilian, RAD Arbeitsmaid (Female Worker) Maria Bernauer, was issued this Sonderausweis to travel to St. Pölten for Weihnachtsurlaub (Christmas Leave). (A5)

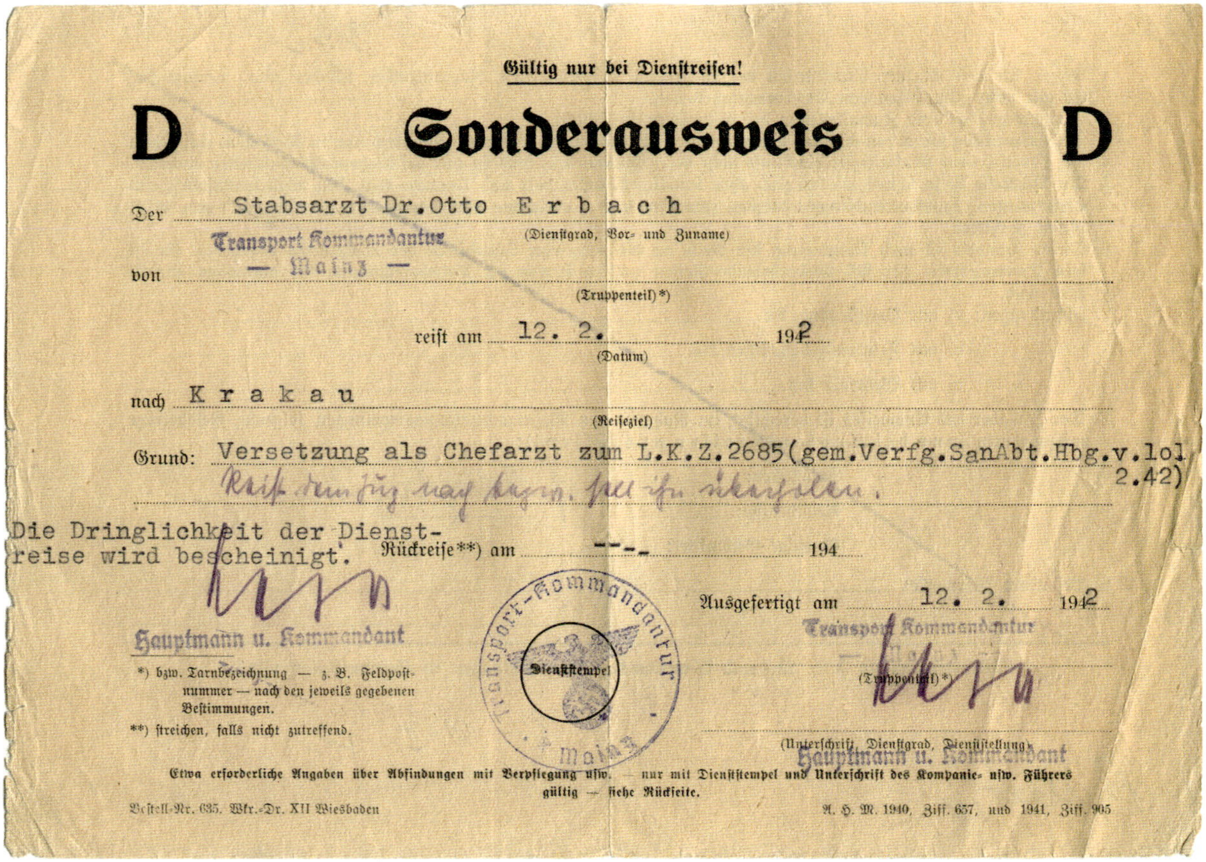

Gültig nur bei Dienstreisen!

D **Sonderausweis** D

Der Stabsarzt Dr.Otto Erbach
(Dienstgrad, Vor- und Zuname)

von Transport Kommandantur — Mainz —
(Truppenteil)*)

reist am 12. 2. 1942
(Datum)

nach Krakau
(Reiseziel)

Grund: Versetzung als Chefarzt zum L.K.Z.2685(gem.Verfg.SanAbt.Hbg.v.10.2.42)

Die Dringlichkeit der Dienstreise wird bescheinigt.

Rückreise**) am --.- 194

Hauptmann u. Kommandant

*) bzw. Tarnbezeichnung — z. B. Feldpostnummer — nach den jeweils gegebenen Bestimmungen.

**) streichen, falls nicht zutreffend.

Transport-Kommandantur Mainz — Dienststempel

Ausgefertigt am 12. 2. 1942

Transport Kommandantur
(Truppenteil)*)

(Unterschrift, Dienstgrad, Dienststellung)
Hauptmann u. Kommandant

Etwa erforderliche Angaben über Abfindungen mit Verpflegung usw. — nur mit Dienststempel und Unterschrift des Kompanie- usw. Führers gültig — siehe Rückseite.

Bestell-Nr. 635. Wkr.-Dr. XII Wiesbaden — A. H. M. 1940, Ziff. 657, und 1941, Ziff. 905

Figure 2-120. Staff Doctor Otto Erbach transferred from Mainz to become the Chefarzt (Head Doctor) of the medical department in the Kriegslazarett Heidelberg. (A5)

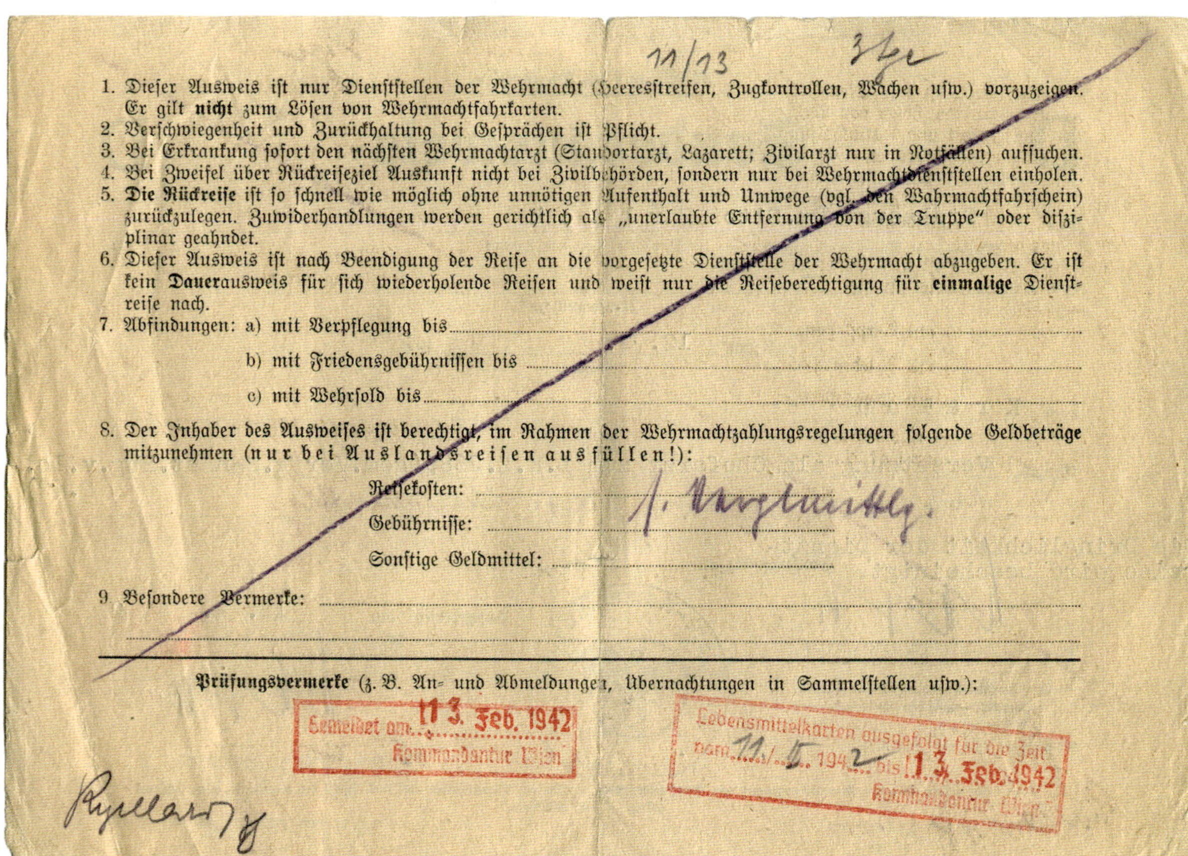

1. Dieser Ausweis ist nur Dienststellen der Wehrmacht (Heeresstreifen, Zugkontrollen, Wachen usw.) vorzuzeigen. Er gilt **nicht** zum Lösen von Wehrmachtfahrkarten.
2. Verschwiegenheit und Zurückhaltung bei Gesprächen ist Pflicht.
3. Bei Erkrankung sofort den nächsten Wehrmachtarzt (Standortarzt, Lazarett; Zivilarzt nur in Notfällen) aufsuchen.
4. Bei Zweifel über Rückreiseziel Auskunft nicht bei Zivilbehörden, sondern nur bei Wehrmachtdienststellen einholen.
5. **Die Rückreise** ist so schnell wie möglich ohne unnötigen Aufenthalt und Umwege (vgl. den Wahrmachtfahrschein) zurückzulegen. Zuwiderhandlungen werden gerichtlich als „unerlaubte Entfernung von der Truppe" oder disziplinar geahndet.
6. Dieser Ausweis ist nach Beendigung der Reise an die vorgesetzte Dienststelle der Wehrmacht abzugeben. Er ist kein **Dauerausweis** für sich wiederholende Reisen und weist nur die Reiseberechtigung für **einmalige** Dienstreise nach.
7. Abfindungen: a) mit Verpflegung bis
   b) mit Friedensgebührnissen bis
   c) mit Wehrsold bis
8. Der Inhaber des Ausweises ist berechtigt, im Rahmen der Wehrmachtzahlungsregelungen folgende Geldbeträge mitzunehmen (nur bei Auslandsreisen ausfüllen!):
   Reisekosten:
   Gebührnisse:
   Sonstige Geldmittel:
9. Besondere Vermerke:

Prüfungsvermerke (z. B. An- und Abmeldungen, Übernachtungen in Sammelstellen usw.):

Gemeldet am: 13. Feb. 1942 Kommandantur Wien

Lebensmittelkarten ausgefolgt für die Zeit vom 11./5. 1942 bis 13. Feb. 1942 Kommandantur Wien

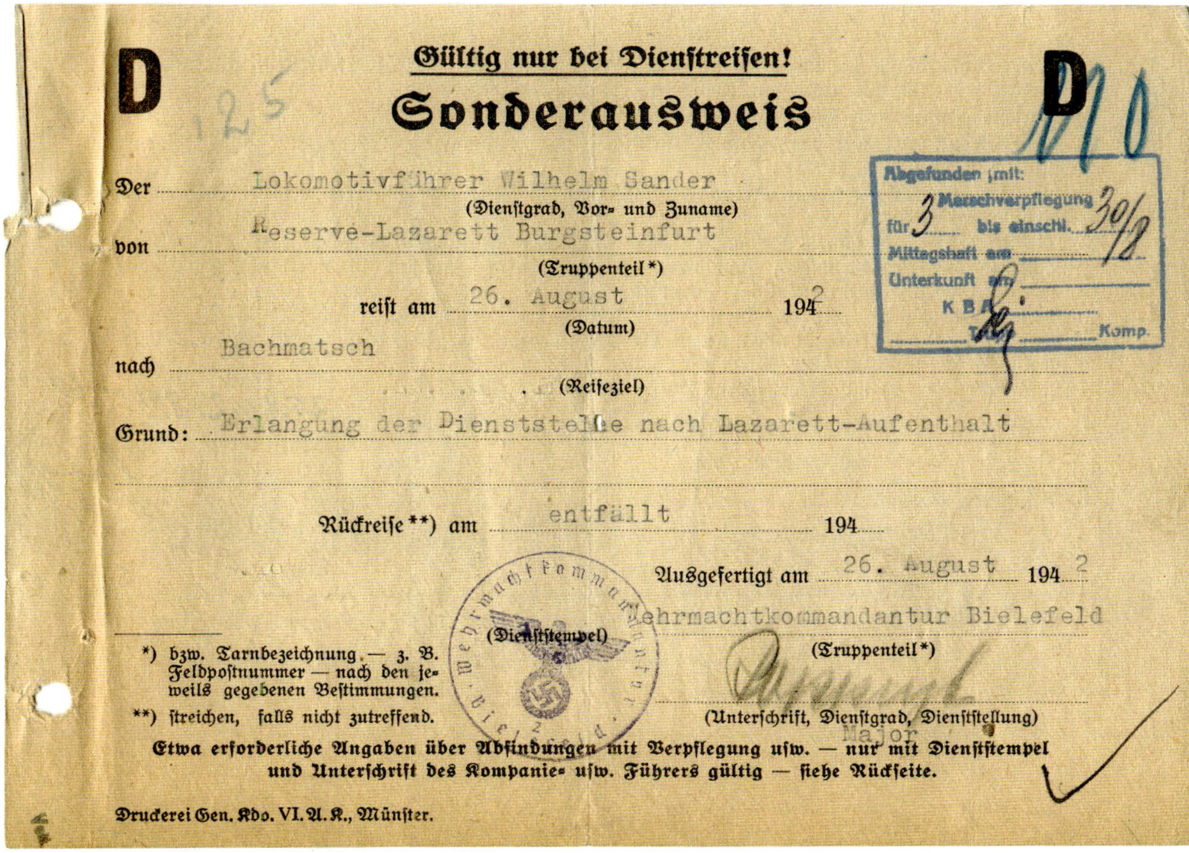

D Gültig nur bei Dienstreisen! D

Sonderausweis

Der Lokomotivführer Wilhelm Sander
(Dienstgrad, Vor- und Zuname)

von Reserve-Lazarett Burgsteinfurt
(Truppenteil*)

reist am 26. August 1942
(Datum)

nach Bachmatsch
(Reiseziel)

Grund: Erlangung der Dienststelle nach Lazarett-Aufenthalt

Rückreise**) am entfällt 194..

Ausgefertigt am 26. August 1942

Wehrmachtkommandantur Bielefeld
(Truppenteil*)

(Dienststempel)

(Unterschrift, Dienstgrad, Dienststellung)
Major

*) bzw. Tarnbezeichnung. — z. B. Feldpostnummer — nach den jeweils gegebenen Bestimmungen.

**) streichen, falls nicht zutreffend.

Etwa erforderliche Angaben über Abfindungen mit Verpflegung usw. — nur mit Dienststempel und Unterschrift des Kompanie- usw. Führers gültig — siehe Rückseite.

Druckerei Gen. Kdo. VI. A. K., Münster.

Abgefunden mit:
3 Marschverpflegung
für ... bis einschl. 30/8
Mittagskost am
Unterkunft am
KBA
Komp.

Figure 2-121. Reichsbahn Engineer Wilhelm Sander transferred from the Burgsteinfurt reserve hospital to resume his service following a prolonged hospital stay. On the reverse, he has been issued marching rations (Marschverpflegung) at the Reichsbahndurchgangslager, the Railroad Transfer Camp. (A5)

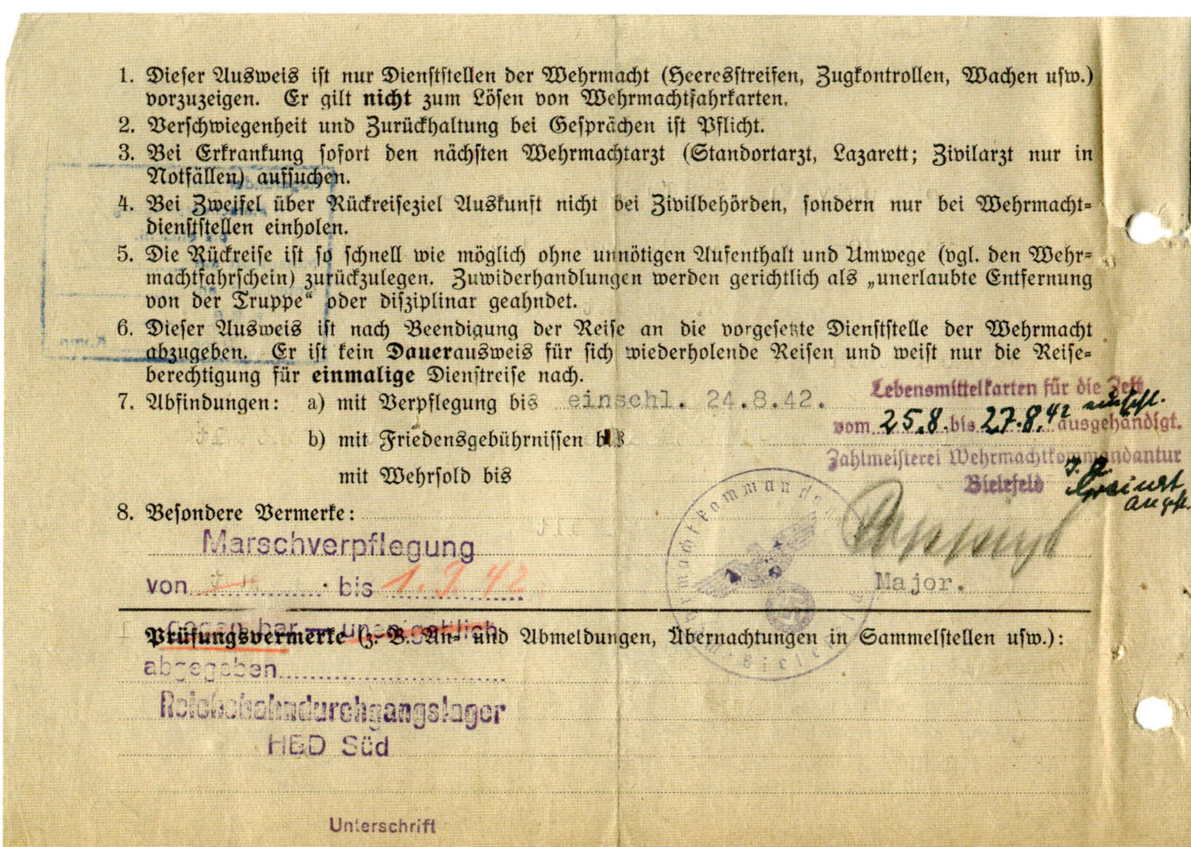

1. Dieser Ausweis ist nur Dienststellen der Wehrmacht (Heeresstreifen, Zugkontrollen, Wachen usw.) vorzuzeigen. Er gilt **nicht** zum Lösen von Wehrmachtfahrkarten.
2. Verschwiegenheit und Zurückhaltung bei Gesprächen ist Pflicht.
3. Bei Erkrankung sofort den nächsten Wehrmachtarzt (Standortarzt, Lazarett; Zivilarzt nur in Notfällen) aufsuchen.
4. Bei Zweifel über Rückreiseziel Auskunft nicht bei Zivilbehörden, sondern nur bei Wehrmachtdienststellen einholen.
5. Die Rückreise ist so schnell wie möglich ohne unnötigen Aufenthalt und Umwege (vgl. den Wehrmachtfahrschein) zurückzulegen. Zuwiderhandlungen werden gerichtlich als „unerlaubte Entfernung von der Truppe" oder disziplinar geahndet.
6. Dieser Ausweis ist nach Beendigung der Reise an die vorgesetzte Dienststelle der Wehrmacht abzugeben. Er ist kein **Dauer**ausweis für sich wiederholende Reisen und weist nur die Reiseberechtigung für **einmalige** Dienstreise nach.
7. Abfindungen: a) mit Verpflegung bis einschl. 24.8.42.
   b) mit Friedensgebührnissen bis
   mit Wehrsold bis
8. Besondere Vermerke:
   Marschverpflegung
   von ... bis 1.9.42.

Lebensmittelkarten für die Zeit vom 25.8. bis 27.8.42 ausgehändigt.
Zahlmeisterei Wehrmachtkommandantur Bielefeld

Major.

Prüfungsvermerke (z. B. An- und Abmeldungen, Übernachtungen in Sammelstellen usw.):

abgegeben

Reichsbahndurchgangslager
HBD Süd

Unterschrift

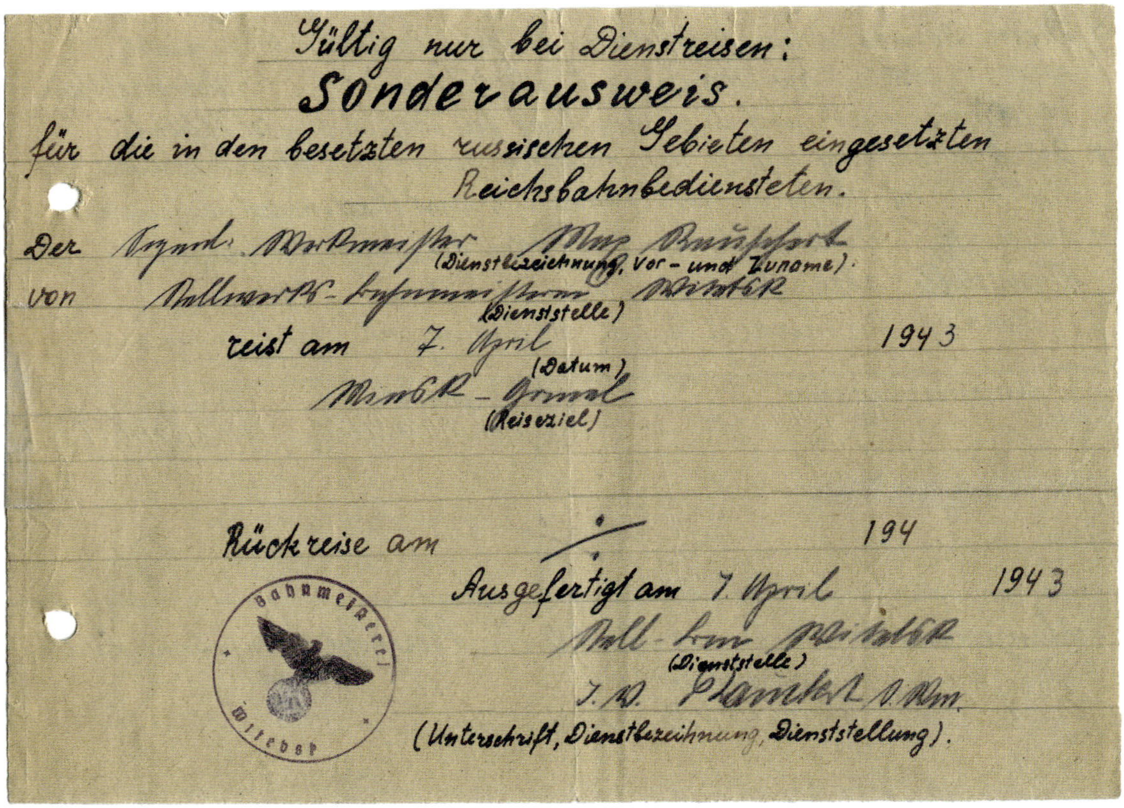
Gültig nur bei Dienstreisen:
Sonderausweis.
für die in den besetzten russischen Gebieten eingesetzten Reichsbahnbediensteten.
Der [illegible] (Dienstbezeichnung, Vor- und Zuname).
von [illegible] (Dienststelle)
reist am 7. April 1943 (Datum)
Minsk - Grmel (Reiseziel)
Rückreise am ./. 194
Ausgefertigt am 7. April 1943
[illegible] (Dienststelle)
I.V. [illegible] (Unterschrift, Dienstbezeichnung, Dienststellung).
Bahnmeisterei Witebsk

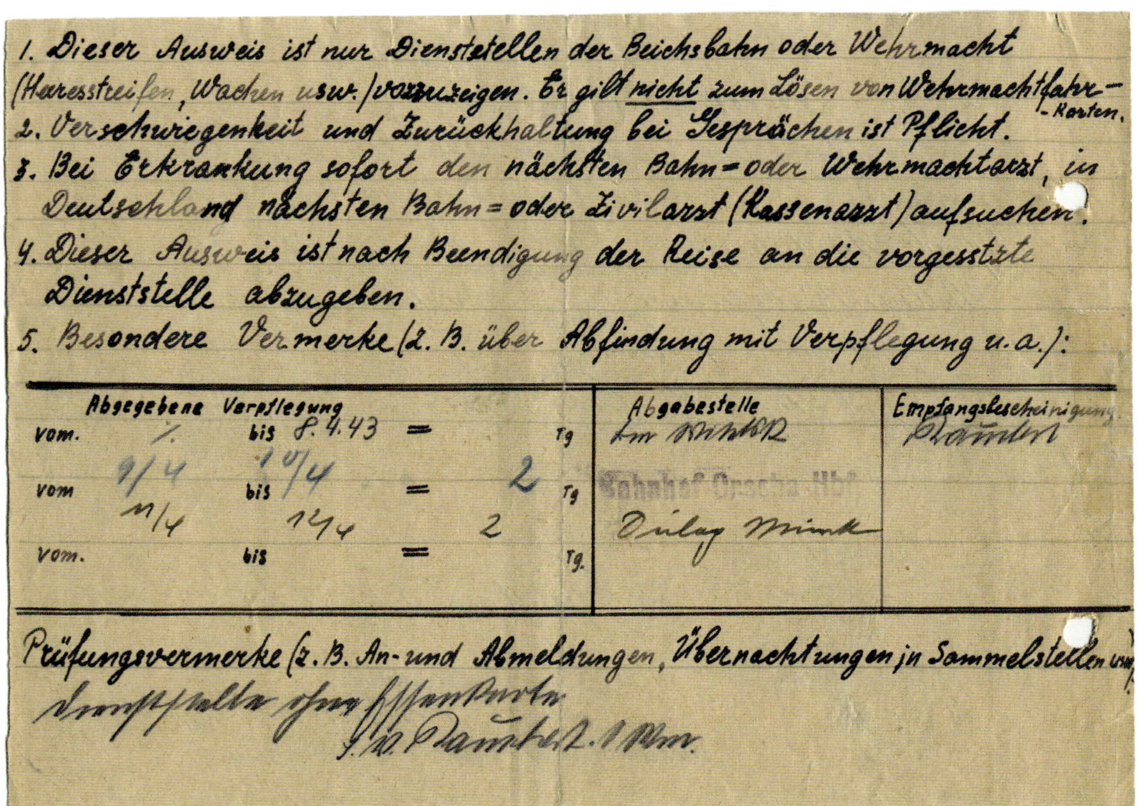
1. Dieser Ausweis ist nur Dienststellen der Reichsbahn oder Wehrmacht (Heeresstreifen, Wachen usw.) vorzuzeigen. Er gilt nicht zum Lösen von Wehrmachtfahr-Karten.
2. Verschwiegenheit und Zurückhaltung bei Gesprächen ist Pflicht.
3. Bei Erkrankung sofort den nächsten Bahn- oder Wehrmachtarzt, in Deutschland nächsten Bahn= oder Zivilarzt (Kassenarzt) aufsuchen.
4. Dieser Ausweis ist nach Beendigung der Reise an die vorgesetzte Dienststelle abzugeben.
5. Besondere Vermerke (z. B. über Abfindung mit Verpflegung u.a.):

Abgegebene Verpflegung	Abgabestelle	Empfangsbescheinigung
vom. ./. bis 8.4.43 = Tg	[illegible]	[illegible]
vom 9/4 bis 10/4 = 2 Tg	Bahnhof Orscha Hbf	
11/4 12/4 2	Dulag Minsk	
vom. bis = Tg.		

Prüfungsvermerke (z. B. An- und Abmeldungen, Übernachtungen in Sammelstellen usw.)
[illegible]
I.V. [illegible]

Figure 2-122. Clerks were permitted a degree of leeway when the proper forms were not available, so long as the correct format was followed. This Reischsbahn Ersatzsonderausweis (Railroad Temporary Special Identity) prepared for railroad personnel in the occupied Russian territories. Werkmeister (Supervisor) Reuschort transferred from Bahnmeisterei (Main Railroad Office) Vitebsk to Minsk-Grmel in April 7, 1943; no return trip (Rückreise) was necessary. (A5)

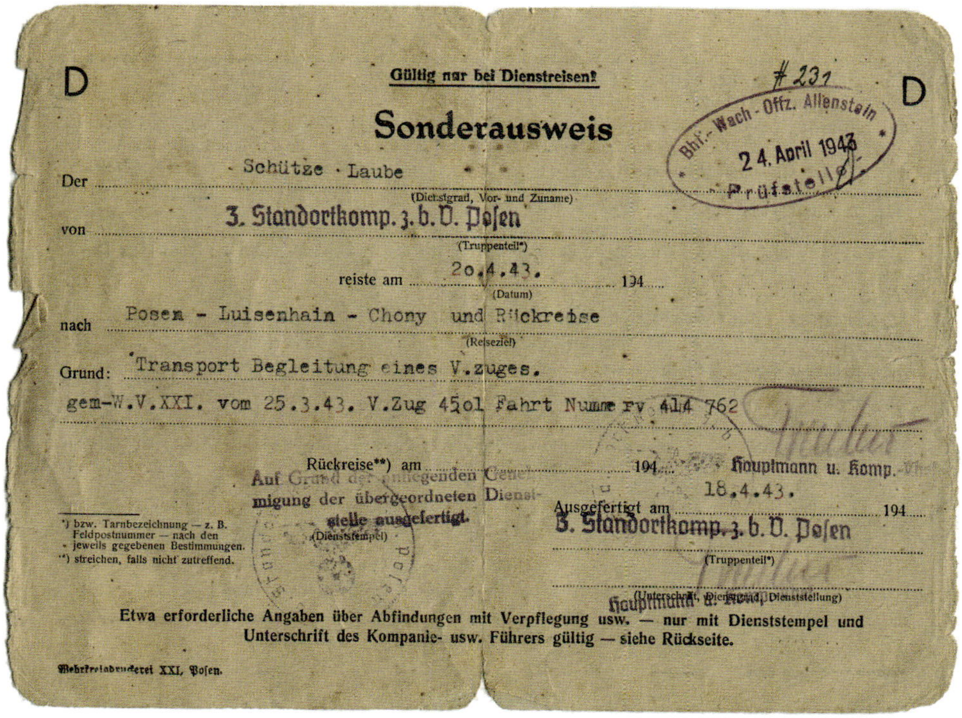
D

Gültig nur bei Dienstreisen!

#231

Bhf.-Wach-Offz. Allenstein
24. April 1943
Prüfstelle

D

Sonderausweis

Der Schütze Laube
(Dienstgrad, Vor- und Zuname)

von 3. Standortkomp. z. b. V. Posen
(Truppenteil*)

reiste am 20.4.43. 194
(Datum)

nach Posen - Luisenhain - Chony und Rückreise
(Reiseziel)

Grund: Transport Begleitung eines V.zuges.
gem-W.V.XXI. vom 25.3.43. V.Zug 45ol Fahrt Numme rv 414 762

Rückreise**) am 194

Auf Grund der vorliegenden Genehmigung der übergeordneten Dienststelle ausgefertigt.
(Dienststempel)

Hauptmann u. Komp.-Chef
18.4.43.

Ausgefertigt am 194

3. Standortkomp. z. b. V. Posen
(Truppenteil*)

(Unterschrift, Dienstgrad, Dienststellung)

*) bzw. Tarnbezeichnung — z. B. Feldpostnummer — nach den jeweils gegebenen Bestimmungen.
**) streichen, falls nicht zutreffend.

Etwa erforderliche Angaben über Abfindungen mit Verpflegung usw. — nur mit Dienststempel und Unterschrift des Kompanie- usw. Führers gültig — siehe Rückseite.

Wehrkreisdruckerei XXI, Posen.

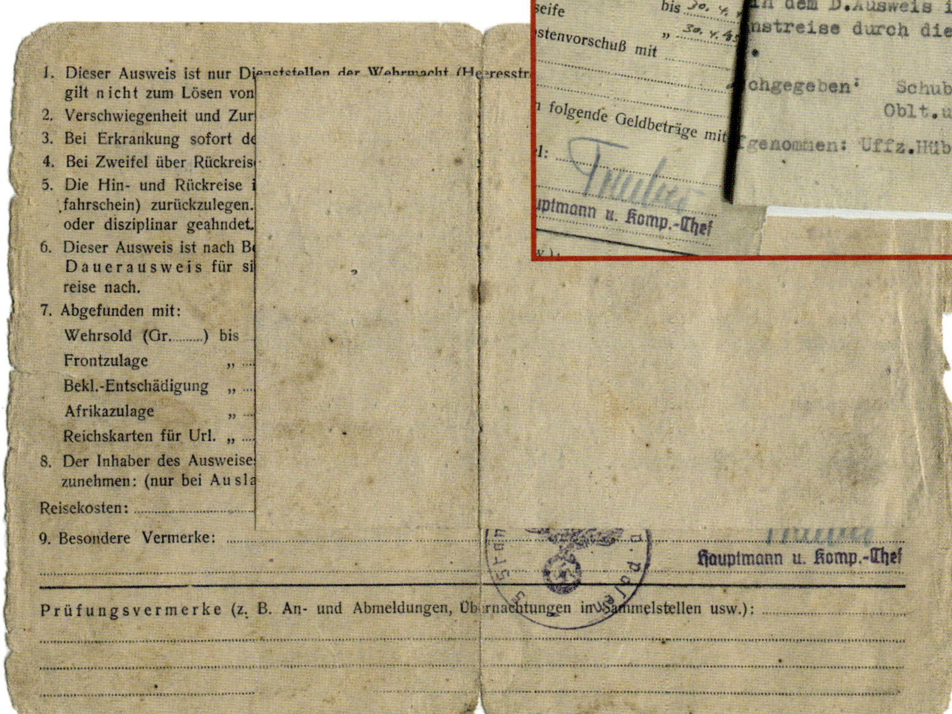
1. Dieser Ausweis ist nur Dienststellen der Wehrmacht (H... gilt nicht zum Lösen von...
2. Verschwiegenheit und Zur...
3. Bei Erkrankung sofort d...
4. Bei Zweifel über Rückreis...
5. Die Hin- und Rückreise i... fahrschein) zurückzulegen. ... oder disziplinar geahndet.
6. Dieser Ausweis ist nach B... Dauerausweis für si... reise nach.
7. Abgefunden mit:
   Wehrsold (Gr.......) bis
   Frontzulage „
   Bekl.-Entschädigung „
   Afrikazulage „
   Reichskarten für Url. „
8. Der Inhaber des Ausweise... zunehmen: (nur bei Ausla...

Reisekosten:

9. Besondere Vermerke:

Hauptmann u. Komp.-Chef

Prüfungsvermerke (z. B. An- und Abmeldungen, Übernachtungen in Sammelstellen usw.):

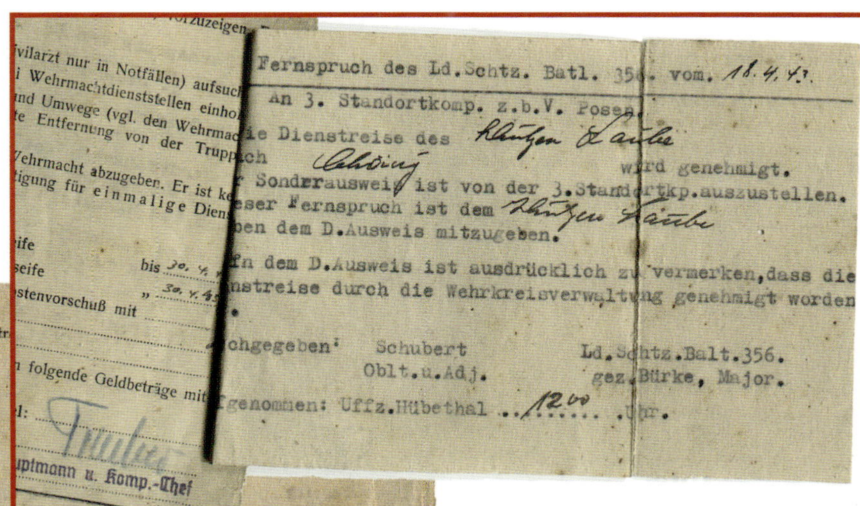
Fernspruch des Ld.Schtz. Batl. 356. vom. 18.4.43.
An 3. Standortkomp. z.b.V. Posen.
...ie Dienstreise des Schützen Laube
...ch Chony wird genehmigt.
...Sonderausweis ist von der 3.Standortkp.auszustellen.
...eser Fernspruch ist dem Schützen Laube
...ben dem D.Ausweis mitzugeben.
...n dem D.Ausweis ist ausdrücklich zu vermerken,dass die ...nstreise durch die Wehrkreisverwaltung genehmigt worden.

...chgegeben: Schubert Oblt.u.Adj. Ld.Schtz.Balt.356. gez.Bürke, Major.
...genommen: Uffz.Hübethal ..12.00... Uhr.

Figure 2-123. Nothing in regulations prohibited lengthy explanations for reasons of travel. A piece of paper has been attached to this Sonderausweis that gives a rather detailed account of a telephone conversation permitting Schütze (Private) Laube to travel through the military district. (A5)

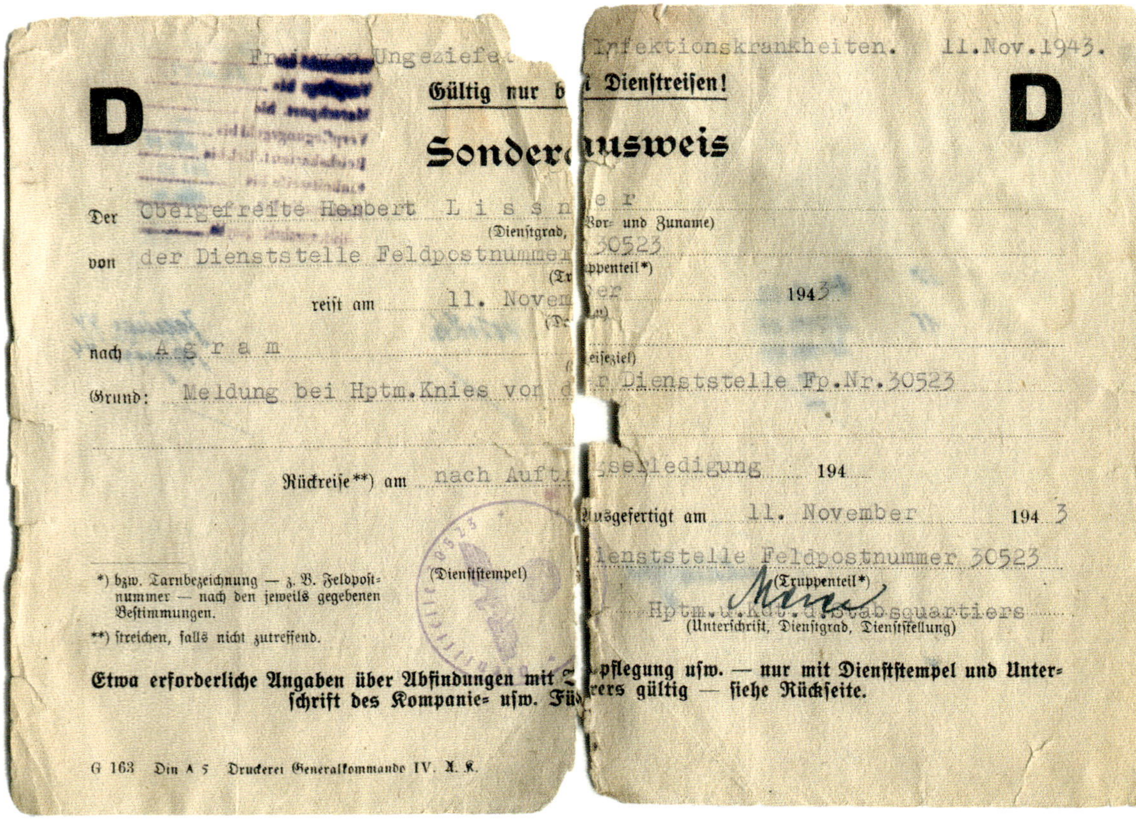

Frei von Ungeziefer und Infektionskrankheiten. 11.Nov.1943.

D **Gültig nur bei Dienstreisen!** D

Sonderausweis

Der Obergefreite Herbert Lissner (Dienstgrad, Vor- und Zuname)

von der Dienststelle Feldpostnummer 30523 (Truppenteil*)

reist am 11. November 1943

nach Agram (Reiseziel)

Grund: Meldung bei Hptm.Knies von der Dienststelle Fp.Nr.30523

Rückreise**) am nach Auftragserledigung 194

Ausgefertigt am 11. November 1943

(Dienststempel) Dienststelle Feldpostnummer 30523 (Truppenteil*)

Hptm.u.Kdt.d.Stabsquartiers (Unterschrift, Dienstgrad, Dienststellung)

*) bzw. Tarnbezeichnung — z. B. Feldpostnummer — nach den jeweils gegebenen Bestimmungen.

**) streichen, falls nicht zutreffend.

Etwa erforderliche Angaben über Abfindungen mit Verpflegung usw. — nur mit Dienststempel und Unterschrift des Kompanie- usw. Führers gültig — siehe Rückseite.

G 163 Din A 5 Druckerei Generalkommando IV. A. K.

Figure 2-124. This very worn example was carried by Obergefreite (sic) Lissner to deliver a message to Captain Knies of the Commandant of the Rear Area Army Area 582 (Kommandant rückwärtiges Armeegebiet 582, FPN 30523) and return once that message had been delivered. (A5)

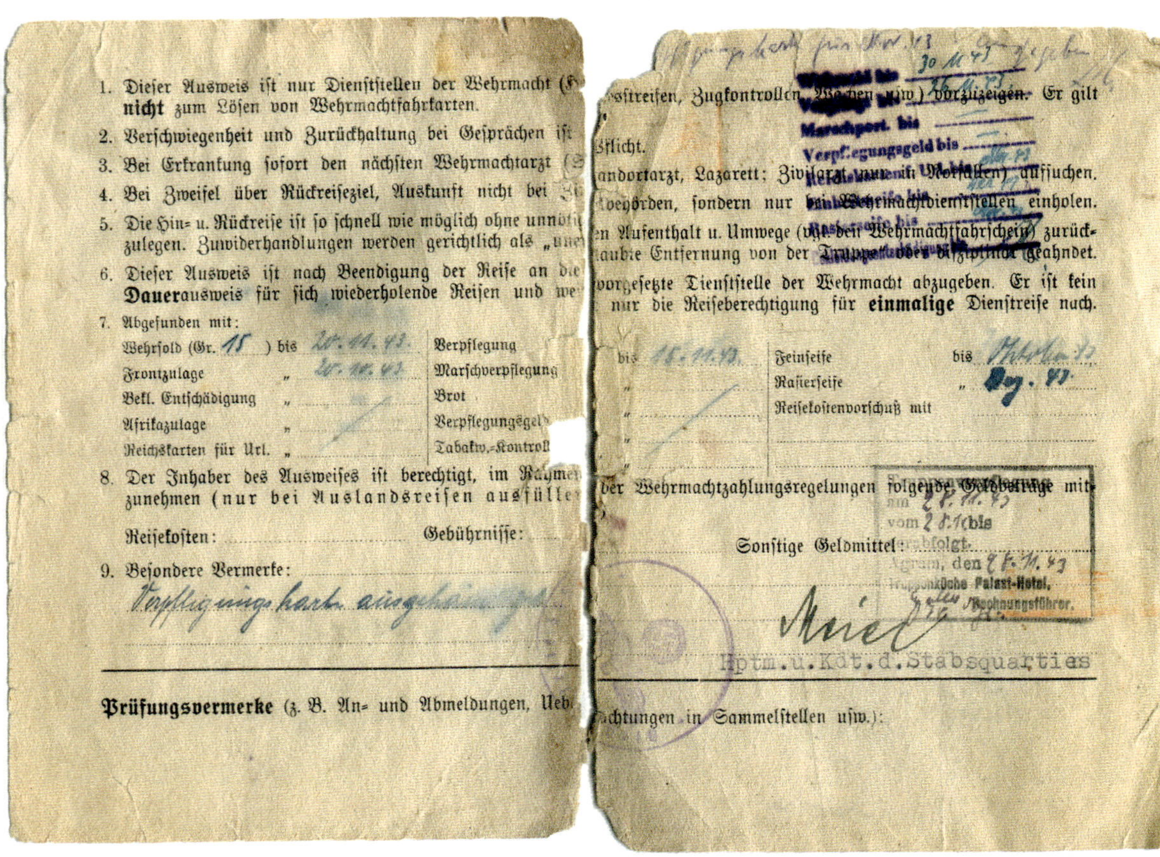

1. Dieser Ausweis ist nur Dienststellen der Wehrmacht ... Dienstreisen, Zugkontrollen ... vorzuzeigen. Er gilt **nicht** zum Lösen von Wehrmachtfahrkarten.
2. Verschwiegenheit und Zurückhaltung bei Gesprächen ist ... Pflicht.
3. Bei Erkrankung sofort den nächsten Wehrmachtarzt ... Standortarzt, Lazarett; Zivilarzt nur in Notfällen) aufsuchen.
4. Bei Zweifel über Rückreiseziel, Auskunft nicht bei ... Behörden, sondern nur bei Wehrmachtdienststellen einholen.
5. Die Hin- u. Rückreise ist so schnell wie möglich ohne unnötigen Aufenthalt u. Umwege (vgl. den Wehrmachtfahrschein) zurückzulegen. Zuwiderhandlungen werden gerichtlich als „unerlaubte Entfernung von der Truppe" ... geahndet.
6. Dieser Ausweis ist nach Beendigung der Reise an die vorgesetzte Dienststelle der Wehrmacht abzugeben. Er ist kein **Dauer**ausweis für sich wiederholende Reisen und ... nur die Reiseberechtigung für **einmalige** Dienstreise nach.
7. Abgefunden mit:

Wehrsold (Gr. 15)	bis 20.11.43	Verpflegung	bis 15.11.43	Feinseife	bis Okt./Nov. 43
Frontzulage	„ 20.11.43	Marschverpflegung	„	Rasierseife	„ Aug. 43
Bekl. Entschädigung	„	Brot	„	Reisekostenvorschuß mit	
Afrikazulage	„	Verpflegungsgeld	„		
Reichskarten für Url.	„	Tabakw.-Kontroll...	„		

8. Der Inhaber des Ausweises ist berechtigt, im Rahmen der Wehrmachtzahlungsregelungen folgende Geldbeträge mitzunehmen (nur bei Auslandsreisen ausfüllen):

Reisekosten: Gebührnisse: Sonstige Geldmittel:

9. Besondere Vermerke: Verpflegungskarte ausgehändigt

Hptm.u.Kdt.d.Stabsquarties

Prüfungsvermerke (z. B. An- und Abmeldungen, Uebernachtungen in Sammelstellen usw.):

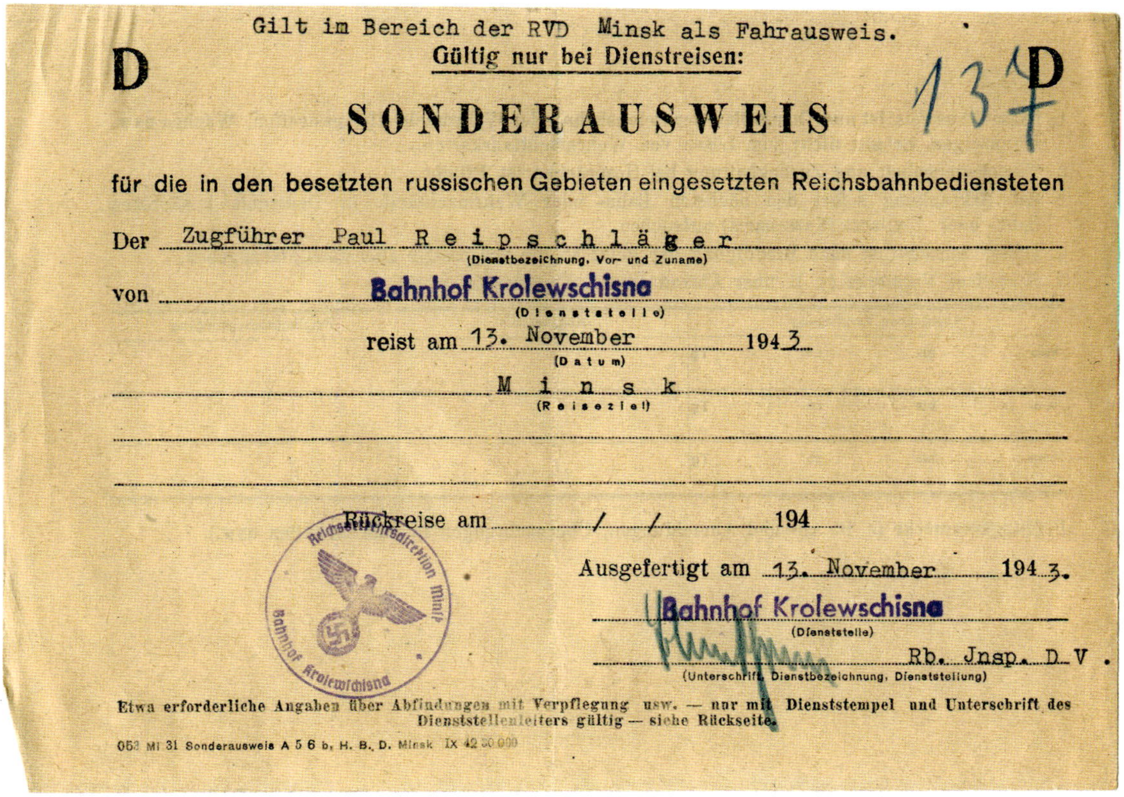

D Gilt im Bereich der RVD Minsk als Fahrausweis. D

Gültig nur bei Dienstreisen:

137

SONDERAUSWEIS

für die in den besetzten russischen Gebieten eingesetzten Reichsbahnbediensteten

Der Zugführer Paul Reipschläger
(Dienstbezeichnung, Vor- und Zuname)

von Bahnhof Krolewschisna
(Dienststelle)

reist am 13. November 1943
(Datum)

Minsk
(Reiseziel)

Rückreise am / / 194

Ausgefertigt am 13. November 1943.

Bahnhof Krolewschisna
(Dienststelle)

Rb. Jnsp. D V.
(Unterschrift, Dienstbezeichnung, Dienststellung)

Reichsbahndirektion Minsk Bahnhof Krolewschisna

Etwa erforderliche Angaben über Abfindungen mit Verpflegung usw. — nur mit Dienststempel und Unterschrift des Dienststellenleiters gültig — siehe Rückseite.

053 Mi 31 Sonderausweis A 5 6 b, H. B. D. Minsk IX 42

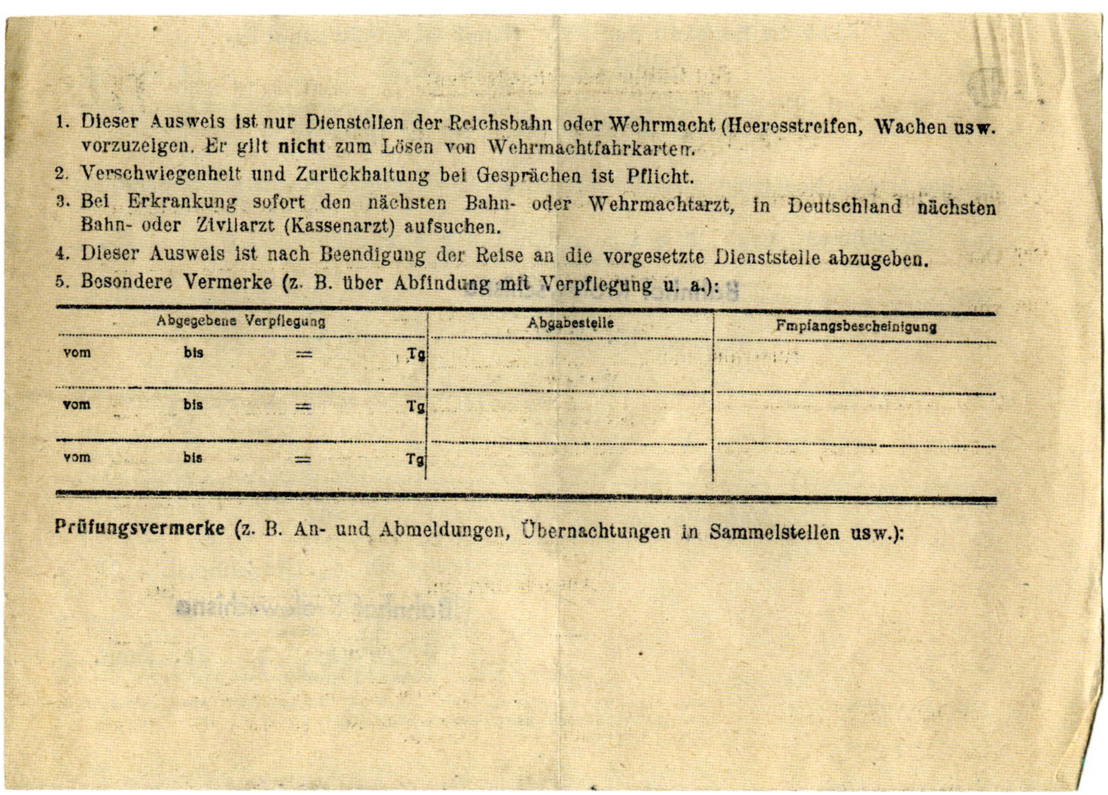

1. Dieser Ausweis ist nur Dienstellen der Reichsbahn oder Wehrmacht (Heeresstreifen, Wachen usw. vorzuzeigen. Er gilt **nicht** zum Lösen von Wehrmachtfahrkarten.
2. Verschwiegenheit und Zurückhaltung bei Gesprächen ist Pflicht.
3. Bei Erkrankung sofort den nächsten Bahn- oder Wehrmachtarzt, in Deutschland nächsten Bahn- oder Zivilarzt (Kassenarzt) aufsuchen.
4. Dieser Ausweis ist nach Beendigung der Reise an die vorgesetzte Dienststelle abzugeben.
5. Besondere Vermerke (z. B. über Abfindung mit Verpflegung u. a.):

Abgegebene Verpflegung				Abgabestelle	Empfangsbescheinigung
vom	bis	=	Tg		
vom	bis	=	Tg		
vom	bis	=	Tg		

Prüfungsvermerke (z. B. An- und Abmeldungen, Übernachtungen in Sammelstellen usw.):

Figure 2-124. This Reichsbahn version of a Sonderausweis permitted Engineer Reipschläger to travel from Krolewskie, Poland to Minsk on November 13, 1943, though no details as to why have been included. It's presumed he had been transferred there, as no return date was authorized. (A5)

Gültig nur bei Dienstreisen!

Anlage
zu Nr. 657
A. H. M. Bl. 12 v. 21. 5. 40

D **Sonderausweis** D

Der Obergefreite Herbert Lissner
(Dienstgrad, Vor- und Zuname)

von der Dienststelle Feldpostnummer 30523
(Truppenteil) *)

reist am 5. Januar 1944 nach Agram
(Datum) (Reiseziel)

Grund: Meldung beim Verbindungsoffizier des Inspekteurs der Eisenbahnsicherung für Kroatien in Agram, Major Heuser, lt. Befehl des IIa des Inspekteurs der Eisenbahnsicherung für Kroatien.

Rückreise**) am ./. 194 Ausgefertigt am 5. Januar 1944

(Dienststempel)

Dienststelle Feldpostnummer 30523
(Truppenteil)
I.A.
Lt.u.stellv.Kdt.d.Stabsquartiers.
(Unterschrift)

*) bzw. Tarnbezeichnung — z. B. Feldpostnummer — nach den jeweils gegebenen Bestimmungen.
**) streichen, falls nicht zutreffend.

Etwa erforderliche Angaben über Abfindungen mit Verpflegung usw. — nur mit Dienststempel und Unterschrift des Kompanie- usw. Führers gültig — siehe Rückseite.

6121. W. B. A

Wehrsold ausgezahlt am 10.5.
für die Zeit vom 1. **bis** 10.5.44

Wehrsold ausgezahlt am 11.5.
für die Zeit vom 11. **bis** 20.5.44

Zahlmeisterei Frontleitstelle 56

1. Dieser Ausweis ist nur Dienststellen der Wehrmacht (Heeresstreifen, Zugkontrollen, Wachen usw.) vorzuzeigen. Er gilt nicht zum Lösen von Wehrmachtfahrkarten.
2. Verschwiegenheit und Zurückhaltung bei Gesprächen ist Pflicht.
3. Bei Erkrankung sofort den nächsten Wehrmachtarzt (Standortarzt, Lazarett; Zivilarzt nur in Notfällen) aufsuchen.
4. Bei Zweifel über Rückreiseziel Auskunft nicht bei Zivilbehörden, sondern nur bei Wehrmachtdienststellen einholen.
5. Die Hin- und Rückreise ist so schnell wie möglich ohne unnötigen Aufenthalt und Umwege (vgl. den Wehrmachtfahrschein) zurückzulegen. Zuwiderhandlungen werden gerichtlich „als unerlaubte Entfernung von der Truppe" oder disziplinar geahndet.
6. Dieser Ausweis ist nach Beendigung der Reise an die vorgesetzte Dienststelle der Wehrmacht abzugeben. Er ist kein Dauerausweis für sich wiederholende Reisen und weist nur die Reiseberechtigung für einmalige Dienstreise nach.
7. Abgefunden mit:

Wehrsold (Gr. 15)	bis 31.12.43	Verpflegung	bis 5.1.44	Feinseife	bis Januar 44
Frontzulage	„ —	Marschverpflegung	„ —	Rasierseife	„ Januar 44
Bekl.-Entschädigung	„ —	Brot	„ —	Reisekostenvorschuß mit	
Afrikazulage	„ —	Verpflegungsgeld	„ —		
Reichskarten für Url.	„ —	Tabakw.-Kontrollk.	„ —		

8. Der Inhaber des Ausweises ist berechtigt, im Rahmen der Wehrmachtzahlungsregelungen folgende Geldbeträge mitzunehmen: (Nur bei Auslandsreisen ausfüllen!)
Reisekosten: Gebührnisse: Sonstige Geldmittel:
9. Besondere Vermerke:

Lt.u.stellv.Kdt.d.Stabsquartiers.

Prüfungsvermerke (z. B. An- und Abmeldungen, Übernachtungen in Sammelstellen usw.)

Truppenverpflegung ... vom 6.1.44 11.1.44. verabfolgt. Agram, den 6.1.44

Figure 2-125. Obergefreite (sic) Lissner used this Sonderausweis to deliver a message to the Liaison Officer to the Inspector for Railway Defense for Croatia in Agram (Zagreb). Interestingly, no return date has been specified. (A5)

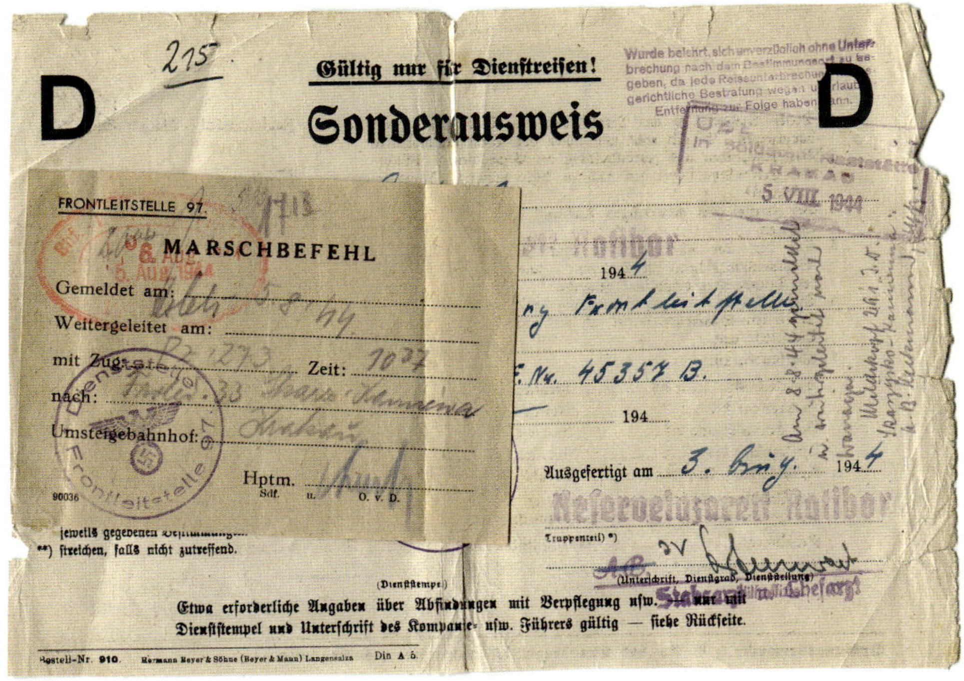

D

Gültig nur für Dienstreisen!

Sonderausweis

D

Würde belehrt, sich unverzüglich ohne Unterbrechung nach dem Bestimmungsort zu begeben, da jede Reiseunterbrechung ... gerichtliche Bestrafung wegen ... Entfernung zur Folge haben kann.

FRONTLEITSTELLE 97

MARSCHBEFEHL

Gemeldet am: 5.8.44

Weitergeleitet am:

mit Zug: 1273 Zeit: 1037

nach:

Umsteigebahnhof:

Hptm.

Sdf. u. O. v. D.

90036

Ausgefertigt am 3. Aug. 1944

Reservelazarett Ratibor

(Truppenteil) *)

(Dienststempel)

(Unterschrift, Dienstgrad, Dienststellung)

Stabsarzt u. Chefarzt

jeweils gegebenen Bestimmungen.

**) streichen, falls nicht zutreffend.

Etwa erforderliche Angaben über Abfindungen mit Verpflegung usw. sind nur mit Dienststempel und Unterschrift des Kompanie- usw. Führers gültig — siehe Rückseite.

Bestell-Nr. 910. Hermann Beyer & Söhne (Beyer & Mann) Langensalza Din A 6

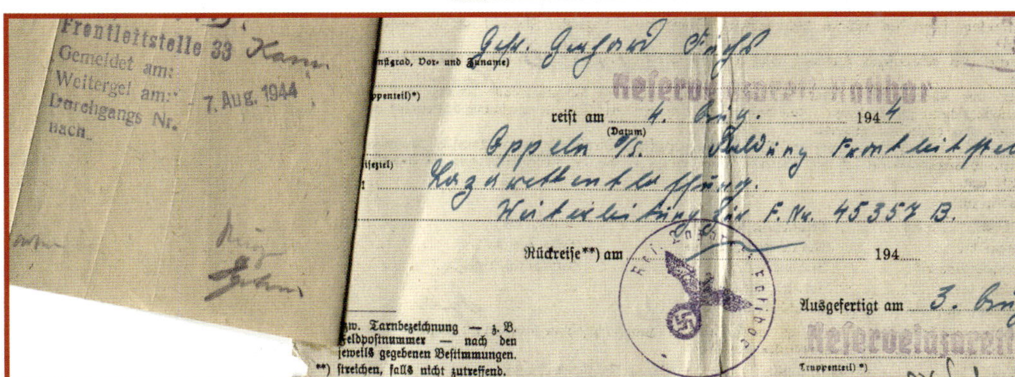

Frontleitstelle 33

Gemeldet am:

Weitergel. am: 7. Aug. 1944

Durchgangs Nr.

nach

(Dienstgrad, Vor- und Zuname) Gefr. Gerhard Fuchs

(Truppenteil) *) Reservelazarett Ratibor

reist am 4. Aug. 1944 (Datum)

Oppeln ... Frontleitstelle

Lazarettentlassung.

Weiterleitung für F. Nr. 45357 B.

Rückreise**) am 194

Ausgefertigt am 3. Aug.

Reservelazarett

(Truppenteil) *)

zw. Tarnbezeichnung — z. B. Feldpostnummer — nach den jeweils gegebenen Bestimmungen.

**) streichen, falls nicht zutreffend.

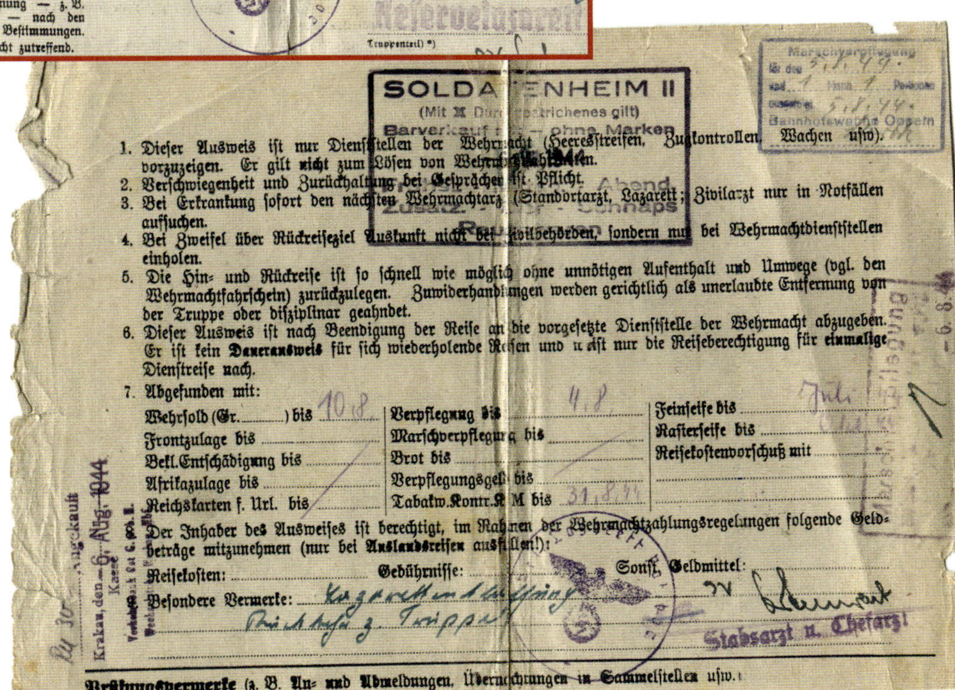

SOLDATENHEIM II

(Mit X Durchgestrichenes gilt)

Barverkauf ... ohne Marken

Abend

Zusatz ... Schnaps

Marschverpflegung für die 5.8.44 ... Bahnhofswache Oppeln

1. Dieser Ausweis ist nur Dienststellen der Wehrmacht (Heeresstreifen, Zugkontrollen, Wachen usw.) vorzuzeigen. Er gilt nicht zum Lösen von Wehrmachtfahrkarten.
2. Verschwiegenheit und Zurückhaltung bei Gesprächen ist Pflicht.
3. Bei Erkrankung sofort den nächsten Wehrmachtarzt (Standortarzt, Lazarett; Zivilarzt nur in Notfällen aufsuchen.
4. Bei Zweifel über Rückreiseziel Auskunft nicht bei Zivilbehörden, sondern nur bei Wehrmachtdienststellen einholen.
5. Die Hin- und Rückreise ist so schnell wie möglich ohne unnötigen Aufenthalt und Umwege (vgl. den Wehrmachtfahrschein) zurückzulegen. Zuwiderhandlungen werden gerichtlich als unerlaubte Entfernung von der Truppe oder disziplinar geahndet.
6. Dieser Ausweis ist nach Beendigung der Reise an die vorgesetzte Dienststelle der Wehrmacht abzugeben. Er ist kein Dauerausweis für sich wiederholende Reisen und gilt nur die Reiseberechtigung für einmalige Dienstreise nach.
7. Abgefunden mit:

Wehrsold (Gr. ...) bis 10.8.	Verpflegung bis 4.8.	Feinseife bis Juli
Frontzulage bis	Marschverpflegung bis	Rasierseife bis
Bekl.Entschädigung bis	Brot bis	Reisekostenvorschuß mit
Afrikazulage bis	Verpflegungsgeld bis	
Reichskarten f. Url. bis	Tabakw.Kontr.K.M. bis 31.8.	

Der Inhaber des Ausweises ist berechtigt, im Rahmen der Wehrmachtzahlungsregelungen folgende Geldbeträge mitzunehmen (nur bei Auslandsreisen ausfüllen!):

Reisekosten: Gebührnisse: Sonst. Geldmittel:

Besondere Vermerke: Lazarettentlassung

Stabsarzt u. Chefarzt

Krakau, den 6. Aug. 1944

Prüfungsvermerke (z. B. An- und Abmeldungen, Übernachtungen in Sammelstellen usw.)

Figure 2-126. When Gefreiter Gerhard Fuchs was discharged from the Reservelazarett in Ratibor, Poland, this form authorized him to return to his unit, the 5th Squadron of Nacht-Jagdgeschwader 6 (Night Fighter Wing 6). (A5)

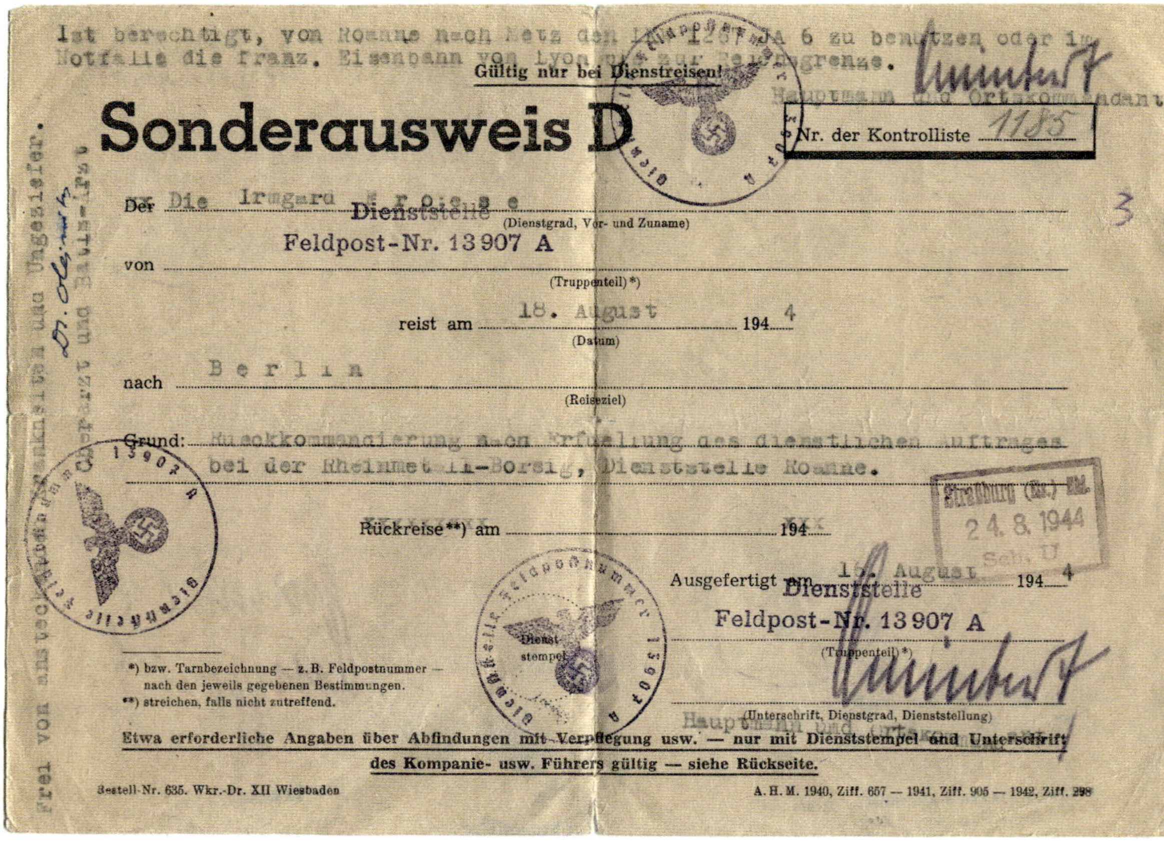
Ist berechtigt, von Rouen nach Metz den ... A 6 zu benutzen oder im Notfalle die franz. Eisenbahn von Lyon ... zur Reichsgrenze.

Gültig nur bei Dienstreisen!

Hauptmann und Ortskommandant

Sonderausweis D

Nr. der Kontrolliste 1185

Der Die Irmgard Erösse Dienststelle (Dienstgrad, Vor- und Zuname)

Feldpost-Nr. 13907 A

von .... (Truppenteil)*)

reist am 18. August 1944 (Datum)

nach Berlin (Reiseziel)

Grund: Rückkommandierung nach Erfüllung des dienstlichen Auftrages bei der Rheinmetall-Borsig, Dienststelle Rouen.

Rückreise**) am .... 194..

Strassburg (Els.) Hbf. 24. 8. 1944

Ausgefertigt am 16. August 1944

Dienststelle Feldpost-Nr. 13907 A (Truppenteil)*)

Hauptmann und Ortskommandant (Unterschrift, Dienstgrad, Dienststellung)

Dienststempel

*) bzw. Tarnbezeichnung — z. B. Feldpostnummer — nach den jeweils gegebenen Bestimmungen.
**) streichen, falls nicht zutreffend.

Frei von ansteckenden Krankheiten und Ungeziefer. Oberarzt und Bataillonsarzt

Etwa erforderliche Angaben über Abfindungen mit Verpflegung usw. — nur mit Dienststempel und Unterschrift des Kompanie- usw. Führers gültig — siehe Rückseite.

Bestell-Nr. 635. Wkr.-Dr. XII Wiesbaden

A. H. M. 1940, Ziff. 657 — 1941, Ziff. 905 — 1942, Ziff. 298

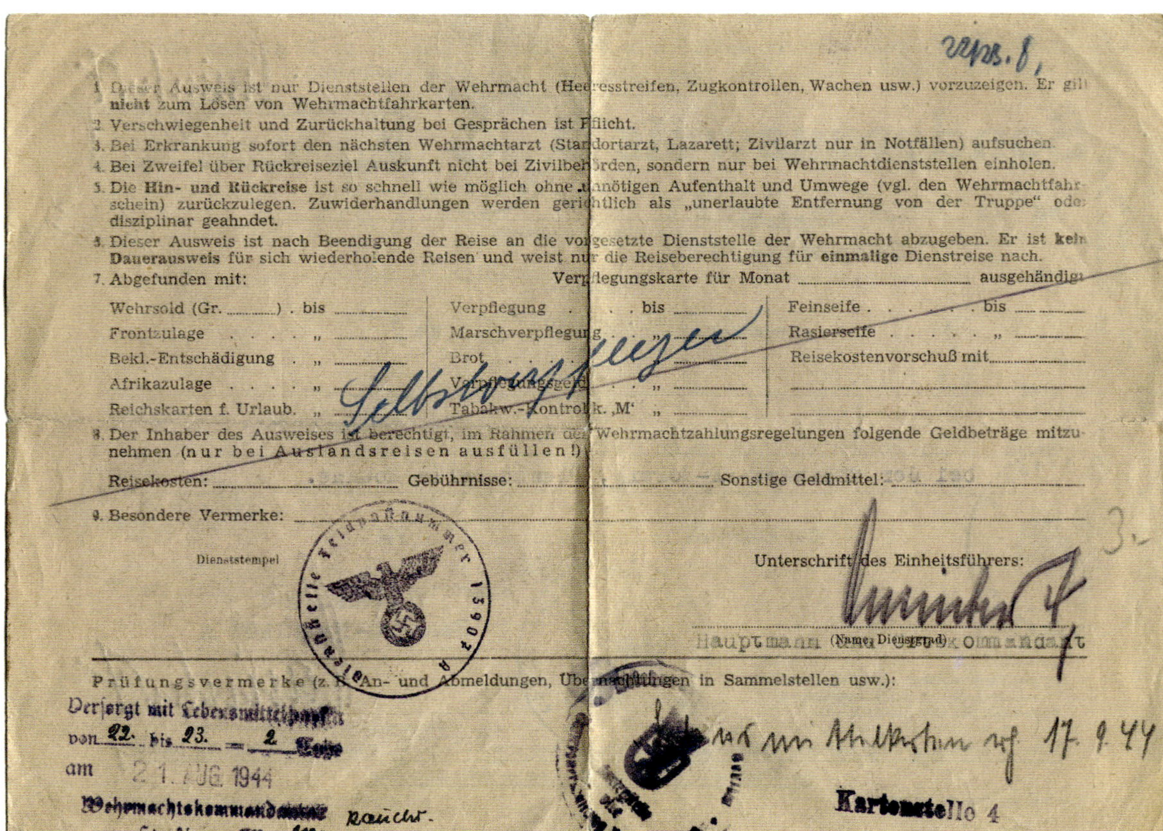
1. Dieser Ausweis ist nur Dienststellen der Wehrmacht (Heeresstreifen, Zugkontrollen, Wachen usw.) vorzuzeigen. Er gilt nicht zum Lösen von Wehrmachtfahrkarten.
2. Verschwiegenheit und Zurückhaltung bei Gesprächen ist Pflicht.
3. Bei Erkrankung sofort den nächsten Wehrmachtarzt (Standortarzt, Lazarett; Zivilarzt nur in Notfällen) aufsuchen.
4. Bei Zweifel über Rückreiseziel Auskunft nicht bei Zivilbehörden, sondern nur bei Wehrmachtdienststellen einholen.
5. Die Hin- und Rückreise ist so schnell wie möglich ohne unnötigen Aufenthalt und Umwege (vgl. den Wehrmachtfahrschein) zurückzulegen. Zuwiderhandlungen werden gerichtlich als „unerlaubte Entfernung von der Truppe" oder disziplinar geahndet.
6. Dieser Ausweis ist nach Beendigung der Reise an die vorgesetzte Dienststelle der Wehrmacht abzugeben. Er ist kein Dauerausweis für sich wiederholende Reisen und weist nur die Reiseberechtigung für einmalige Dienstreise nach.
7. Abgefunden mit: Verpflegungskarte für Monat .... ausgehändigt

Wehrsold (Gr. ....) . bis	Verpflegung . . bis	Feinseife . . . . bis
Frontzulage . . . . „	Marschverpflegung . „	Rasierseife . . . . „
Bekl.-Entschädigung . „	Brot . . . „	Reisekostenvorschuß mit
Afrikazulage . . . . „	Verpflegungsgeld „	
Reichskarten f. Urlaub . „	Tabakw.-Kontrollk. „M" „	

Selbstverpflegen

8. Der Inhaber des Ausweises ist berechtigt, im Rahmen der Wehrmachtzahlungsregelungen folgende Geldbeträge mitzunehmen (nur bei Auslandsreisen ausfüllen!):

Reisekosten: .... Gebührnisse: .... Sonstige Geldmittel: ....

9. Besondere Vermerke:

Dienststempel

Unterschrift des Einheitsführers:

Hauptmann und Ortskommandant (Name, Dienstgrad)

Prüfungsvermerke (z. B. An- und Abmeldungen, Übernachtungen in Sammelstellen usw.):

Versorgt mit Lebensmittelkarten von 22. bis 23. = 2 Tage am 21. AUG. 1944 Wehrmachtskommandantur Straßburg/Els.

... mit Lebensmitteln ... 17. 9. 44

Kartenstelle 4

Figure 2-127. Irmgard Eröse, a civilian worker on official business for Reinmetall-Borsig in Rouen, fled the city just two weeks prior to its liberation by Canadian troops on August 30, 1944. The Reichsbahn date stamp for Strassbourg on August 24 indicates that she at least got out of France. (A5)

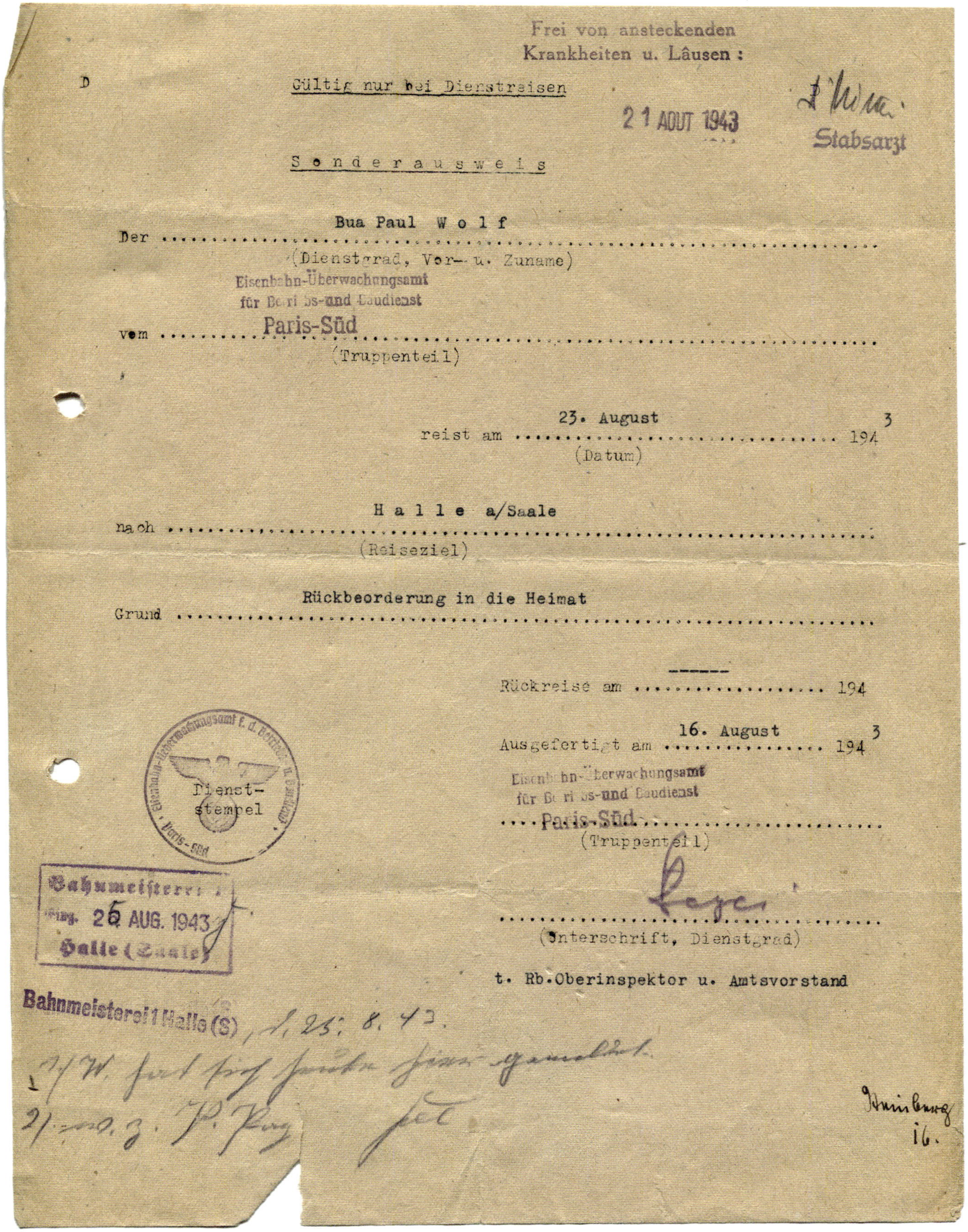

Frei von ansteckenden
Krankheiten u. Läusen :

D

Gültig nur bei Dienstreisen

21 AOUT 1943

Stabsarzt

Sonderausweis

Der Bua Paul Wolf
(Dienstgrad, Vor- u. Zuname)

vom Eisenbahn-Überwachungsamt für Betriebs-und Baudienst Paris-Süd
(Truppenteil)

reist am 23. August 1943
(Datum)

nach Halle a/Saale
(Reiseziel)

Grund Rückbeorderung in die Heimat

Rückreise am ------ 194

Ausgefertigt am 16. August 1943

Eisenbahn-Überwachungsamt für Betriebs-und Baudienst Paris-Süd
(Truppenteil)

Dienst-
stempel

(Unterschrift, Dienstgrad)

t. Rb.Oberinspektor u. Amtsvorstand

Bahnmeisterei 1
Eing. 25 AUG. 1943
Halle (Saale)

Bahnmeisterei 1 Halle (S), d. 25. 8. 43.

Figure 2-128. Prepared on August 16, 1944, this Ersatzsonderausweis (Replacement Special Identity Pass) was hastily drawn up for Bahnunterhaltungsarbeiter (abbreviated BUA, Railroad Maintenance Worker) Paul Wolf, who was authorized to leave Paris just two days before German forces surrendered the city to the Allies. We have no idea whether or not he made it; the Free French Resistance's uprising began on the August 19th and lasted until the day he was supposed to depart. (A4)

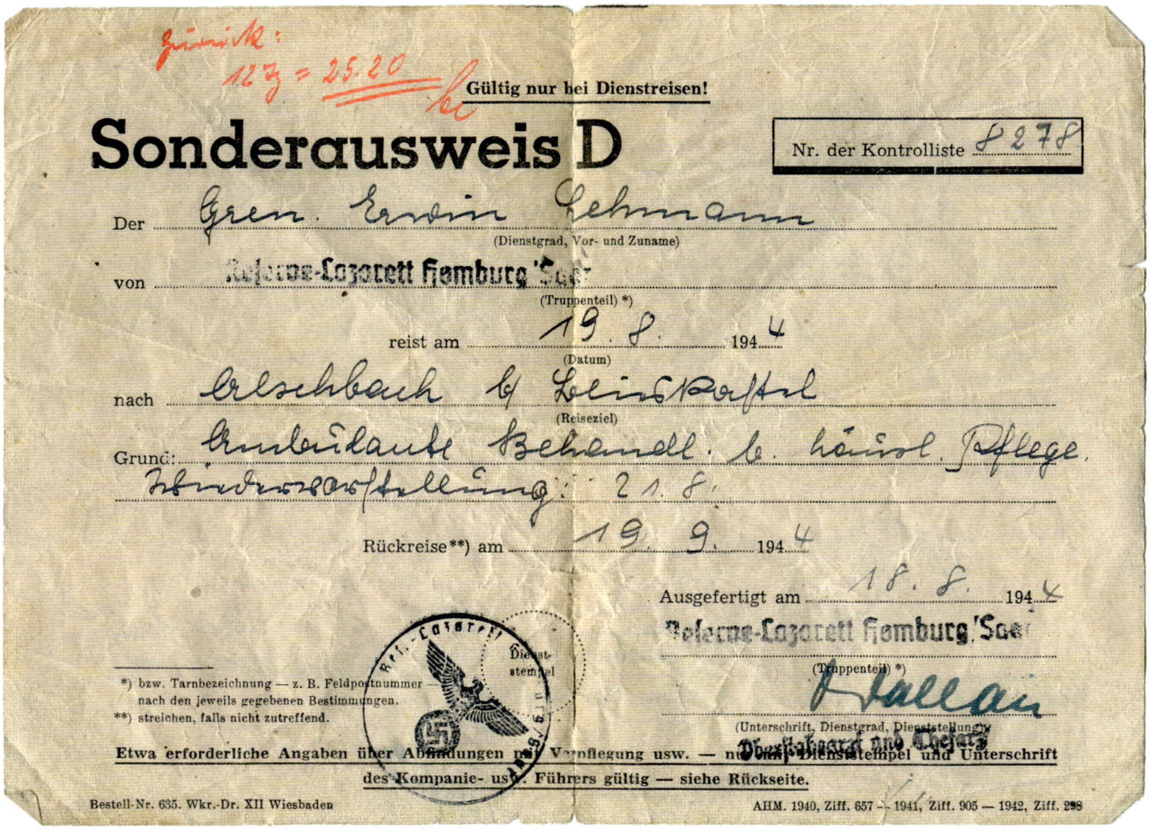

Gültig nur bei Dienstreisen!

Sonderausweis D

Nr. der Kontrolliste 8278

Der Gren. Erwin Lehmann
(Dienstgrad, Vor- und Zuname)

von Reserve-Lazarett Homburg/Saar
(Truppenteil) *)

reist am 19. 8. 1944
(Datum)

nach Webenheim b/ Blieskastel
(Reiseziel)

Grund: Ambulante Behandl. b. häusl. Pflege. Wiedervorstellung: 21. 8.

Rückreise**) am 19. 9. 1944

Ausgefertigt am 18. 8. 1944

Reserve-Lazarett Homburg/Saar
(Truppenteil) *)

(Unterschrift, Dienstgrad, Dienststellung)
Oberstabsarzt und Chefarzt

Dienststempel

*) bzw. Tarnbezeichnung — z. B. Feldpostnummer — nach den jeweils gegebenen Bestimmungen.
**) streichen, falls nicht zutreffend.

Etwa erforderliche Angaben über Abfindungen mit Verpflegung usw. — nur mit Dienststempel und Unterschrift des Kompanie- usw. Führers gültig — siehe Rückseite.

Bestell-Nr. 635. Wkr.-Dr. XII Wiesbaden — AHM. 1940, Ziff. 657 — 1941, Ziff. 905 — 1942, Ziff. 298

Figure 2-129. Grenadier Erwin Lehmann, discharged from Reserve-Lazarett (Reserve Hospital) Hamburg to Blieskastel, Germany for further deployment on August 21, 1944. (A5)

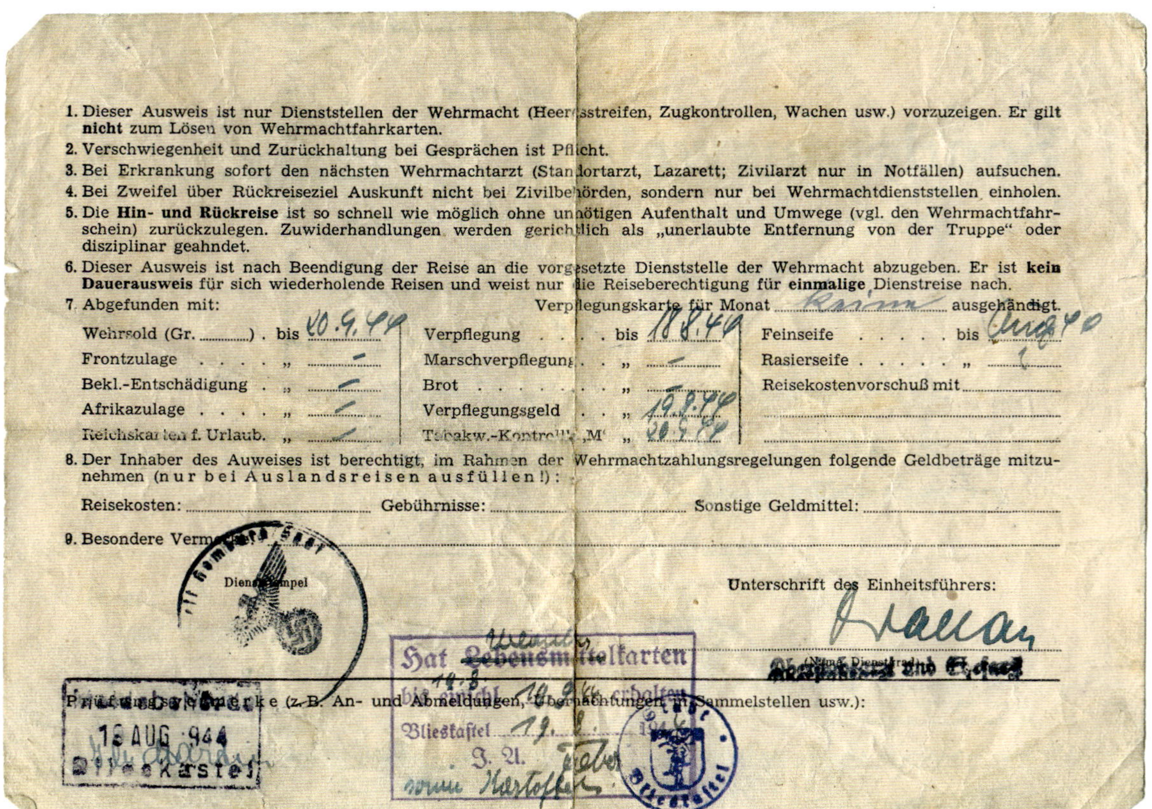

1. Dieser Ausweis ist nur Dienststellen der Wehrmacht (Heeresstreifen, Zugkontrollen, Wachen usw.) vorzuzeigen. Er gilt **nicht** zum Lösen von Wehrmachtfahrkarten.
2. Verschwiegenheit und Zurückhaltung bei Gesprächen ist Pflicht.
3. Bei Erkrankung sofort den nächsten Wehrmachtarzt (Standortarzt, Lazarett; Zivilarzt nur in Notfällen) aufsuchen.
4. Bei Zweifel über Rückreiseziel Auskunft nicht bei Zivilbehörden, sondern nur bei Wehrmachtdienststellen einholen.
5. Die **Hin- und Rückreise** ist so schnell wie möglich ohne unnötigen Aufenthalt und Umwege (vgl. den Wehrmachtfahrschein) zurückzulegen. Zuwiderhandlungen werden gerichtlich als „unerlaubte Entfernung von der Truppe" oder disziplinar geahndet.
6. Dieser Ausweis ist nach Beendigung der Reise an die vorgesetzte Dienststelle der Wehrmacht abzugeben. Er ist **kein Dauerausweis** für sich wiederholende Reisen und weist nur die Reiseberechtigung für **einmalige** Dienstreise nach.
7. Abgefunden mit: Verpflegungskarte für Monat keine ausgehändigt.

Wehrsold (Gr. ....) . bis	10.9.44	Verpflegung . . . . bis	18.8.44	Feinseife . . . . . bis	Aug. 44
Frontzulage . . . . „	—	Marschverpflegung . . „	—	Rasierseife . . . . . „	—
Bekl.-Entschädigung . „	—	Brot . . . . „	—	Reisekostenvorschuß mit	
Afrikazulage . . . . „	—	Verpflegungsgeld . . „	19.8.44		
Reichskarten f. Urlaub. „	—	Tabakw.-Kontrollk. M. „	20.9.44		

8. Der Inhaber des Ausweises ist berechtigt, im Rahmen der Wehrmachtzahlungsregelungen folgende Geldbeträge mitzunehmen (nur bei Auslandsreisen ausfüllen!):

Reisekosten: .... Gebührnisse: .... Sonstige Geldmittel: ....

9. Besondere Vermerke:

Unterschrift des Einheitsführers:
(Name, Dienstgrad)
Oberstabsarzt und Chefarzt

Dienststempel

Prüfungsvermerke (z. B. An- und Abmeldungen, Übernachtungen in Sammelstellen usw.):

16 AUG 1944 Blieskastel

Hat Lebensmittelkarten bis 19. 8. 44 erhalten
Blieskastel 19. 8.

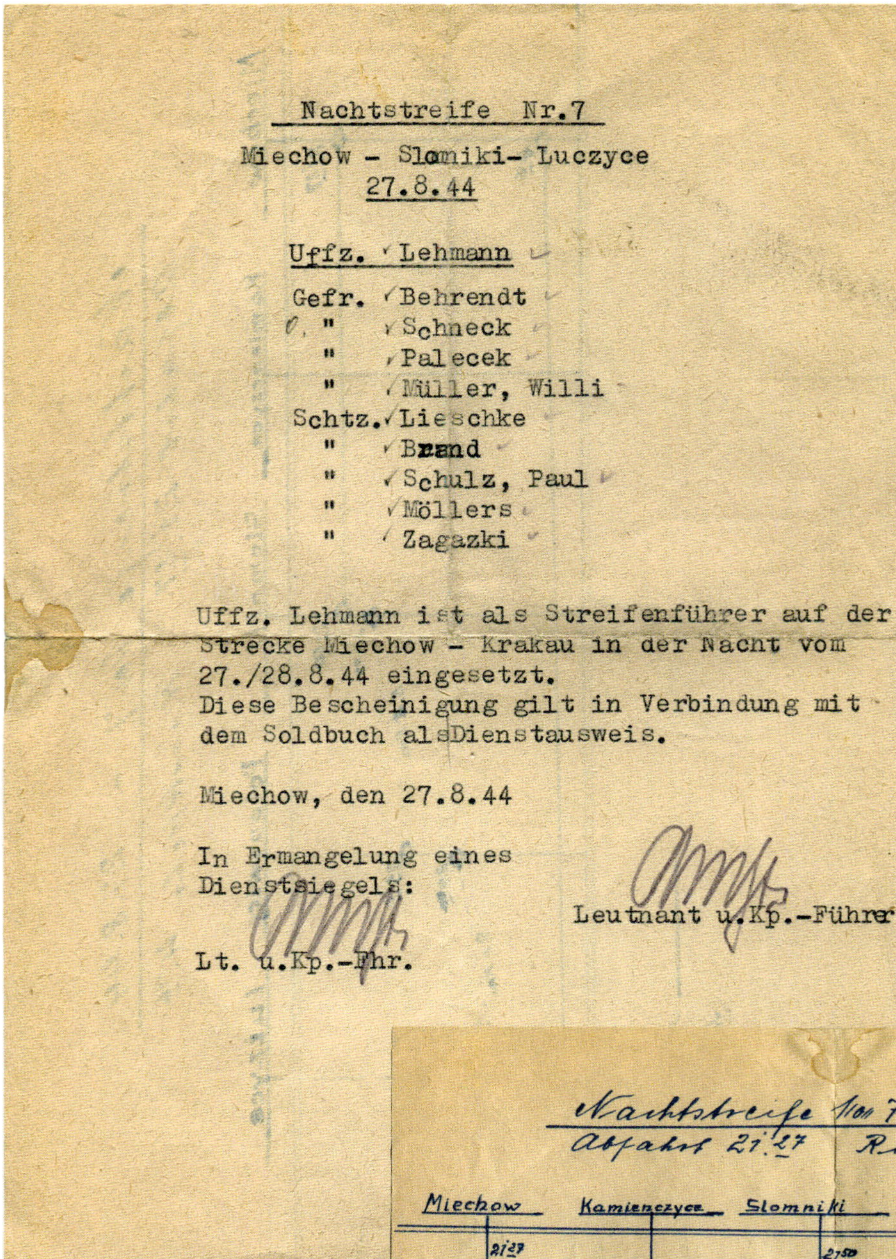

Nachtstreife Nr.7

Miechow - Slomiki- Luczyce
27.8.44

Uffz. Lehmann

Gefr. Behrendt
" Schneck
" Palecek
" Müller, Willi
Schtz. Lieschke
" Brand
" Schulz, Paul
" Möllers
" Zagazki

Uffz. Lehmann ist als Streifenführer auf der Strecke Miechow - Krakau in der Nacht vom 27./28.8.44 eingesetzt.
Diese Bescheinigung gilt in Verbindung mit dem Soldbuch alsDienstausweis.

Miechow, den 27.8.44

In Ermangelung eines Dienstsiegels:

Lt. u.Kp.-Fhr.

Leutnant u.Kp.-Führer

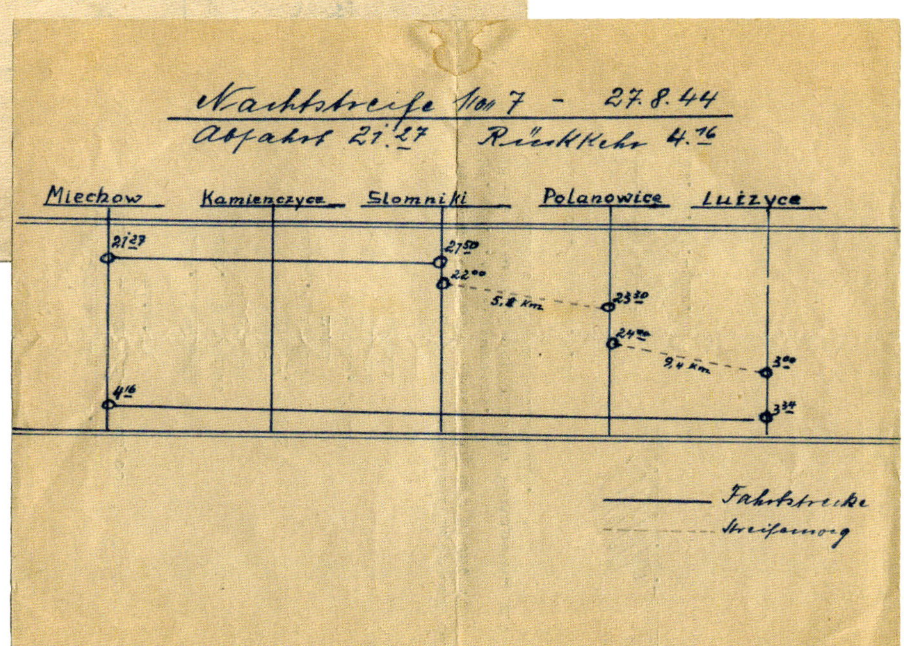

Figure 2-130. This Nachtstreife or "Night Strip" (see the back) of the route that freshly promoted Unteroffizier Lehmann led his nine charges on a night train from Miechow to Krakow on August 27, 1944. Unteroffizier Lehmann's son informed the author that his father was wounded shortly after this trip, which as it happened was most fortuitous, as his evacuation to a hospital in the west prevented his capture by the advancing Russians. (roughly 6" x 8¼")

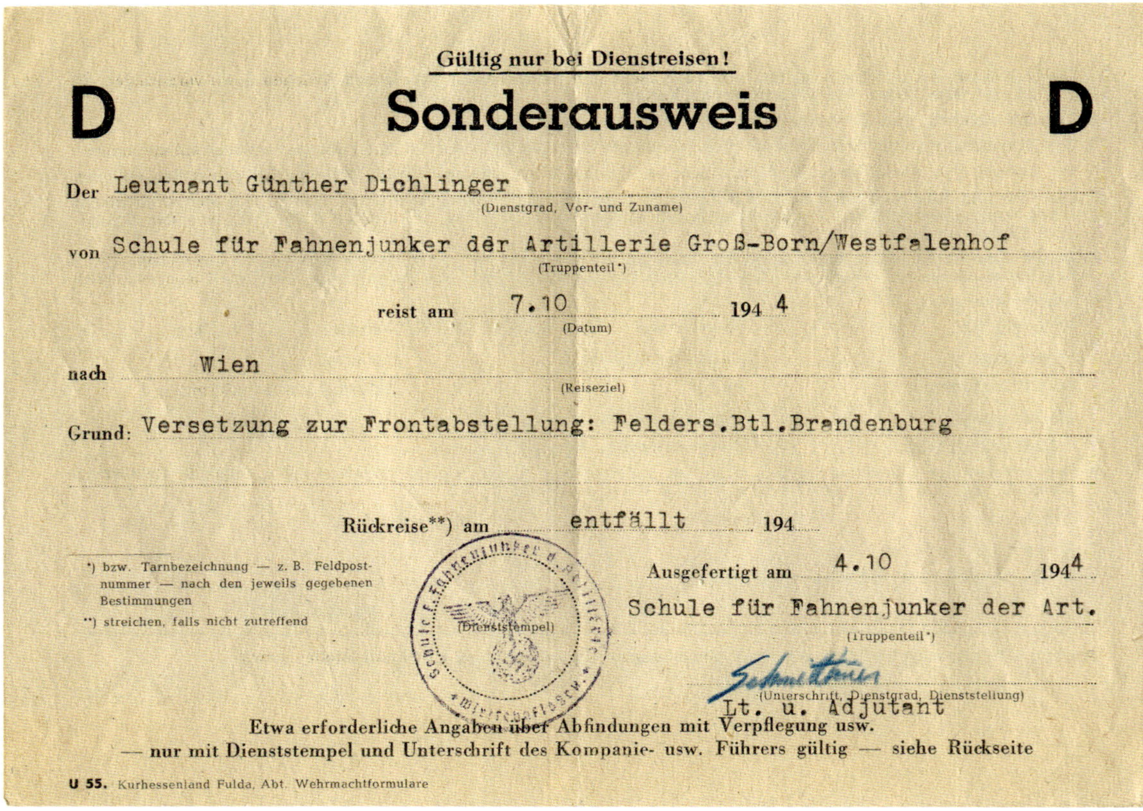

Gültig nur bei Dienstreisen!

D **Sonderausweis** D

Der Leutnant Günther Dichlinger
(Dienstgrad, Vor- und Zuname)

von Schule für Fahnenjunker der Artillerie Groß-Born/Westfalenhof
(Truppenteil *)

reist am 7.10 1944
(Datum)

nach Wien
(Reiseziel)

Grund: Versetzung zur Frontabstellung: Felders.Btl.Brandenburg

Rückreise**) am entfällt 194

*) bzw. Tarnbezeichnung — z. B. Feldpostnummer — nach den jeweils gegebenen Bestimmungen
**) streichen, falls nicht zutreffend

(Dienststempel)

Ausgefertigt am 4.10 1944

Schule für Fahnenjunker der Art.
(Truppenteil *)

(Unterschrift, Dienstgrad, Dienststellung)
Lt. u. Adjutant

Etwa erforderliche Angaben über Abfindungen mit Verpflegung usw.
— nur mit Dienststempel und Unterschrift des Kompanie- usw. Führers gültig — siehe Rückseite

U 55. Kurhessenland Fulda, Abt. Wehrmachtformulare

Figure 2-131. This Sonderausweis accompanied the Kleiner Wehrmachtfahrschein in figure 2-108 for Leutnant Dichlinger's transfer to the Feldersatz Bataillon (Field Replacement Battalion) Brandenburg, the famous Abwehr special operations unit, but well after the Abwehr had lost control of it. (A5)

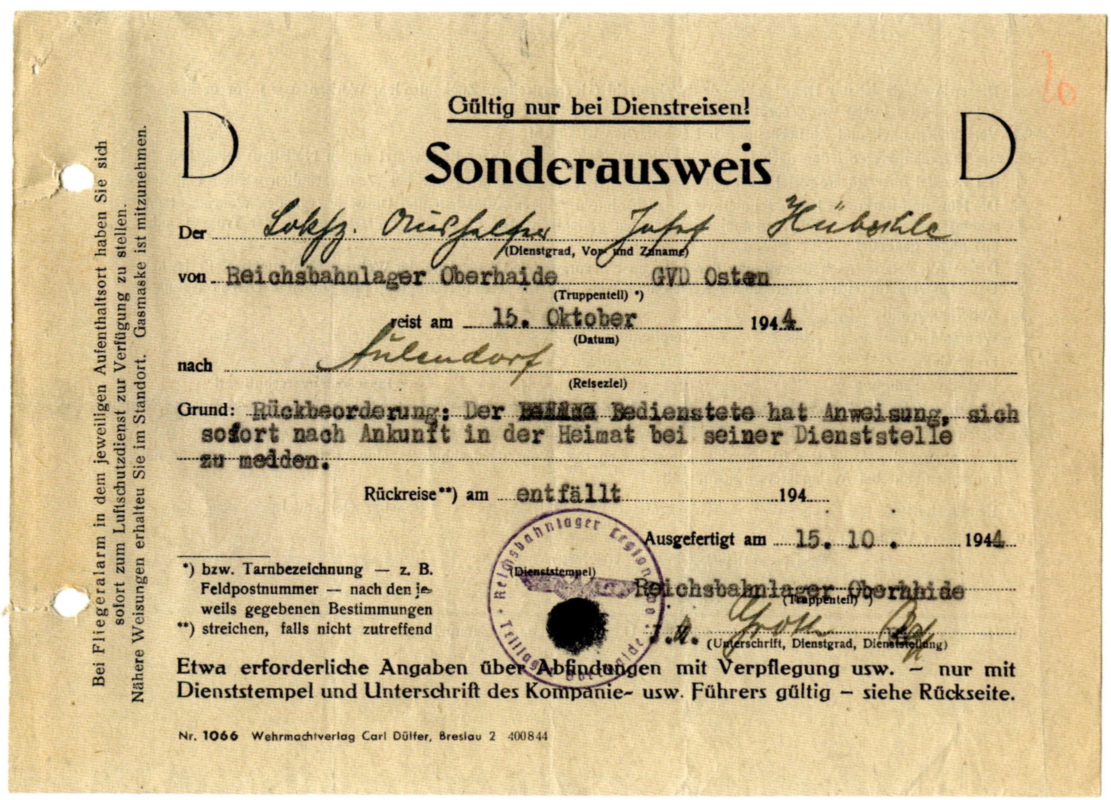

Bei Fliegeralarm in dem jeweiligen Aufenthaltsort haben Sie sich sofort zum Luftschutzdienst zur Verfügung zu stellen. Nähere Weisungen erhalten Sie im Standort. Gasmaske ist mitzunehmen.

Gültig nur bei Dienstreisen!

D **Sonderausweis** D

Der Lokhzg. Aushelfer Josef Hübschle
(Dienstgrad, Vor- und Zuname)

von Reichsbahnlager Oberhaide GVD Osten
(Truppenteil) *)

reist am 15. Oktober 1944
(Datum)

nach Stulendorf
(Reiseziel)

Grund: Rückbeorderung: Der Bedienstete hat Anweisung, sich sofort nach Ankunft in der Heimat bei seiner Dienststelle zu melden.

Rückreise**) am entfällt 194

Ausgefertigt am 15. 10. 1944

*) bzw. Tarnbezeichnung — z. B. Feldpostnummer — nach den jeweils gegebenen Bestimmungen
**) streichen, falls nicht zutreffend

(Dienststempel)

Reichsbahnlager Oberhaide
(Truppenteil) *)

I.A.
(Unterschrift, Dienstgrad, Dienststellung)

Etwa erforderliche Angaben über Abfindungen mit Verpflegung usw. – nur mit Dienststempel und Unterschrift des Kompanie- usw. Führers gültig – siehe Rückseite.

Nr. 1066 Wehrmachtverlag Carl Dülfer, Breslau 2 400844

Figure 2-132. Lokomotivheizer (Stoker) Josef Hübschle transferred from Legionovo-Oberhaide on the Eastern Front to Stulendorf, with direct orders to report immediately upon arrival home to his new station. (A5)

Gültig nur bei Dienstreisen!

D **Sonderausweis** D

(Marschbefehl)

Der Einberufene Friedrich Kleinfartmann
(Dienstgrad, Vor- und Zuname)

vom 14. M.E.A. 14. M.E.A.
(Marineteil, Dienststelle bzw. Tarnbezeichnung — z. B. Feldpostnummer — nach den jeweils gegebenen Bestimmungen)

reist am 20. Okt. 1944.
(Datum)

nach Essen Hbf. Rubenstr. Nr. 5
(Reiseziel)

Grund: Entlassung

Rückreise am erfolgt nicht 194
(streichen, falls nicht zutreffend)

Ausgefertigt am 20. Okt. 1944.

Eingetroffen am ..., den ...
(Neues Kommando)
Sonderausweis ist bei Kommandierungen und Versetzungen an das abgegebene Kommando zurückzusenden

(Dienststempel) 14. M.E.A.
(Marineteil, Dienststelle bzw. Tarnbezeichnung — z. B. Feldpostnummer — nach den jeweils gegebenen Bestimmungen)
(Unterschrift, Dienstgrad, Dienststellung)

Etwa erforderliche Angaben über Abfindungen mit Verpflegung usw. — nur mit Dienststempel und Unterschrift des zuständigen Vorgesetzten gültig — siehe Rückseite.

D. 23a (neu). Zu beziehen vom Vordrucklager der Kriegsmarine J. J. Augustin in Glückstadt. Auslieferungslager: Wilhelmshaven / Kiel / Gotenhafen / Paris / Utrecht / Oslo / Reval. Din A 5

Figure 2-133. Einberufene (Conscript) Friedrich Kleinfartmann's Sonderausweis to return to Essen after being discharged from 14. Marine-Ersatz-Abteilung (14th Naval Replacement Section) was stamped by the Marineaustrüstungsstelle 20 (Naval Equipment Station 20). There are two different styles of handwriting, indicating that numerous forms were filled out with the basic information by one clerk and other clerks added specific information for each dischargee. (A5)

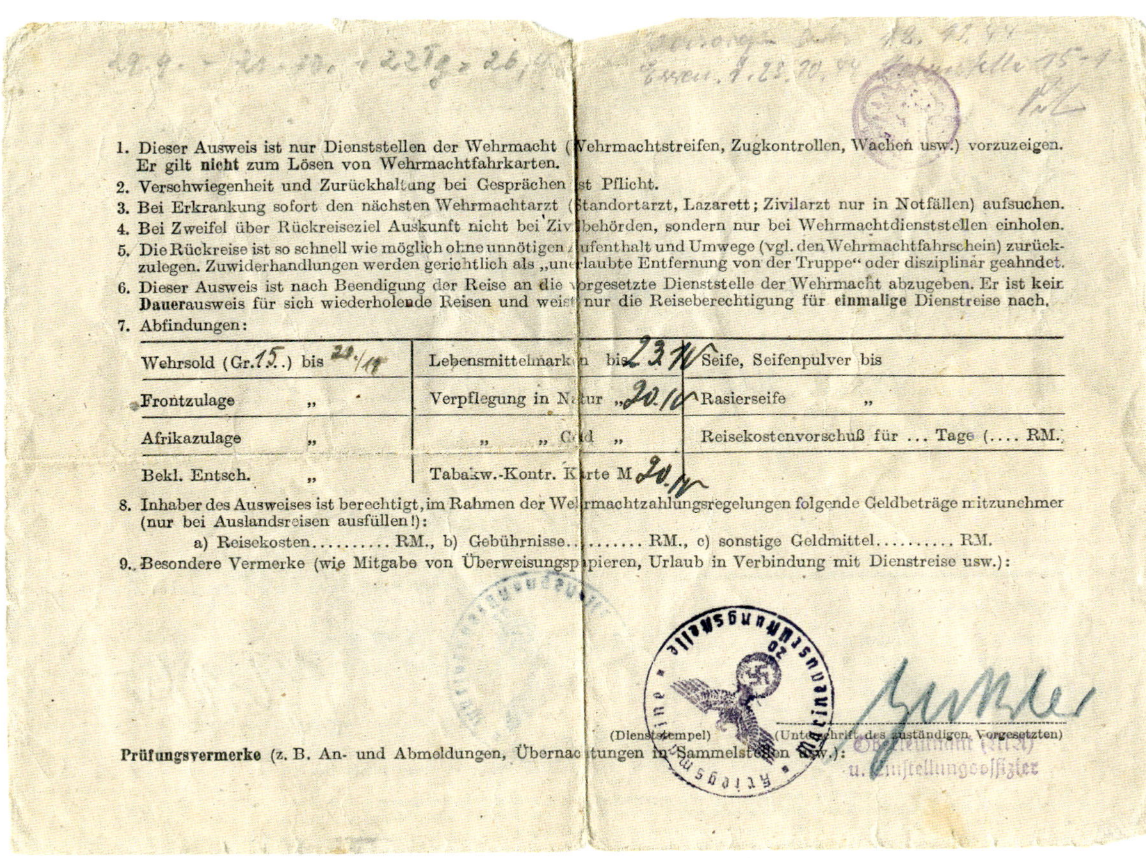

1. Dieser Ausweis ist nur Dienststellen der Wehrmacht (Wehrmachtstreifen, Zugkontrollen, Wachen usw.) vorzuzeigen. Er gilt **nicht** zum Lösen von Wehrmachtfahrkarten.
2. Verschwiegenheit und Zurückhaltung bei Gesprächen ist Pflicht.
3. Bei Erkrankung sofort den nächsten Wehrmachtarzt (Standortarzt, Lazarett; Zivilarzt nur in Notfällen) aufsuchen.
4. Bei Zweifel über Rückreiseziel Auskunft nicht bei Zivilbehörden, sondern nur bei Wehrmachtdienststellen einholen.
5. Die Rückreise ist so schnell wie möglich ohne unnötigen Aufenthalt und Umwege (vgl. den Wehrmachtfahrschein) zurückzulegen. Zuwiderhandlungen werden gerichtlich als „unerlaubte Entfernung von der Truppe" oder disziplinär geahndet.
6. Dieser Ausweis ist nach Beendigung der Reise an die vorgesetzte Dienststelle der Wehrmacht abzugeben. Er ist kein **Dauer**ausweis für sich wiederholende Reisen und weist nur die Reiseberechtigung für **einmalige** Dienstreise nach.
7. Abfindungen:

Wehrsold (Gr. 15.) bis 20/10	Lebensmittelmarken bis 23/10	Seife, Seifenpulver bis
Frontzulage „	Verpflegung in Natur „ 20/10	Rasierseife „
Afrikazulage „	„ „ Geld „	Reisekostenvorschuß für ... Tage (.... RM.)
Bekl. Entsch. „	Tabakw.-Kontr. Karte M 20/10	

8. Inhaber des Ausweises ist berechtigt, im Rahmen der Wehrmachtzahlungsregelungen folgende Geldbeträge mitzunehmer (nur bei Auslandsreisen ausfüllen!):
   a) Reisekosten.......... RM., b) Gebührnisse.......... RM., c) sonstige Geldmittel.......... RM.
9. Besondere Vermerke (wie Mitgabe von Überweisungspapieren, Urlaub in Verbindung mit Dienstreise usw.):

(Dienststempel) (Unterschrift des zuständigen Vorgesetzten)

Prüfungsvermerke (z. B. An- und Abmeldungen, Übernachtungen in Sammelstellen usw.):

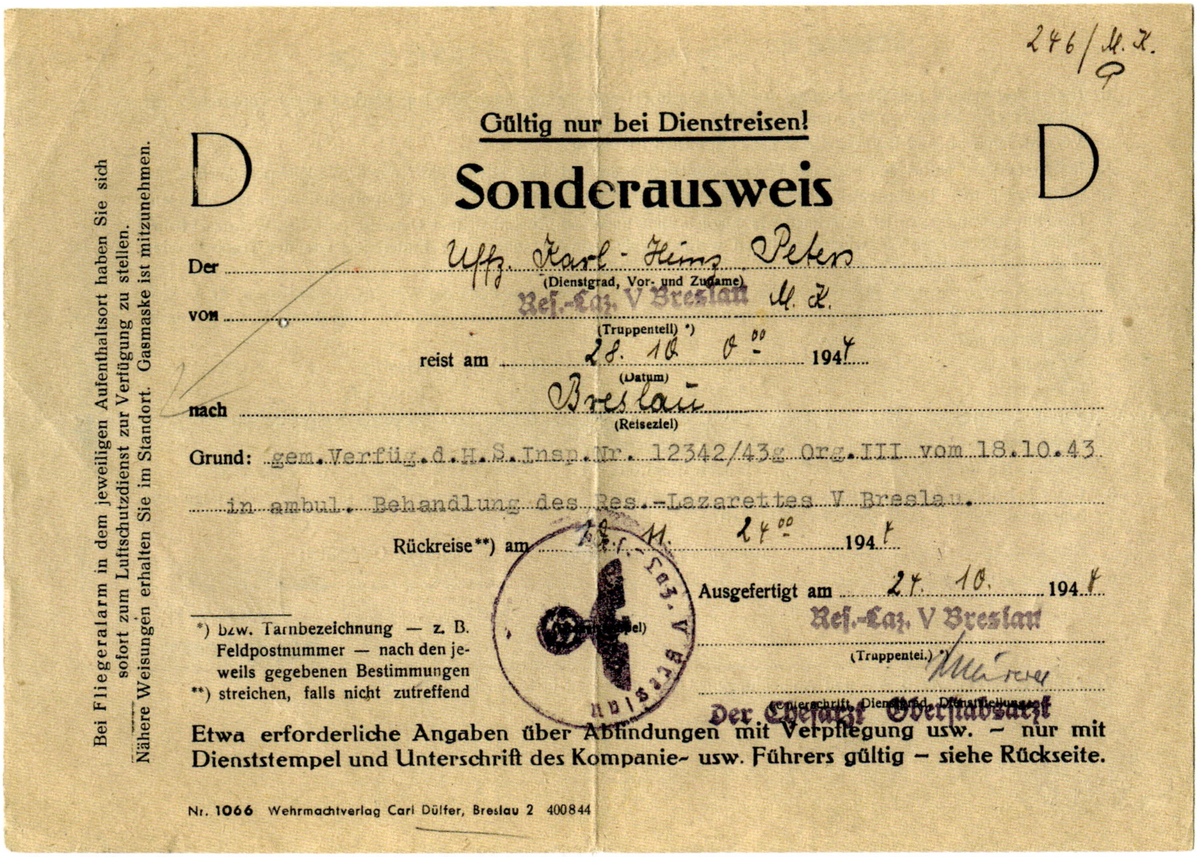

246/M.K.
9

Gültig nur bei Dienstreisen!

D **Sonderausweis** D

Der Uffz. Karl-Heinz Peters
(Dienstgrad, Vor- und Zuname)

von Res.-Laz. V Breslau M.K.
(Truppenteil) *)

reist am 28.10. 8[00] 1944
(Datum)

nach Breslau
(Reiseziel)

Grund: gem. Verfüg. d. H. S. Insp. Nr. 12342/43g Org. III vom 18.10.43
in ambul. Behandlung des Res.-Lazarettes V Breslau.

Rückreise**) am 28. 11. 24[00] 1944

Ausgefertigt am 24. 10. 1944

Res.-Laz. V Breslau
(Truppenteil)

Der Chefarzt Oberstabsarzt
(Unterschrift, Dienstgrad, Dienststellung)

*) bzw. Tarnbezeichnung — z. B. Feldpostnummer — nach den jeweils gegebenen Bestimmungen
**) streichen, falls nicht zutreffend

Etwa erforderliche Angaben über Abfindungen mit Verpflegung usw. — nur mit Dienststempel und Unterschrift des Kompanie- usw. Führers gültig — siehe Rückseite.

Bei Fliegeralarm in dem jeweiligen Aufenthaltsort haben Sie sich sofort zum Luftschutzdienst zur Verfügung zu stellen.
Nähere Weisungen erhalten Sie im Standort. Gasmaske ist mitzunehmen.

Nr. 1066 Wehrmachtverlag Carl Dülfer, Breslau 2 400844

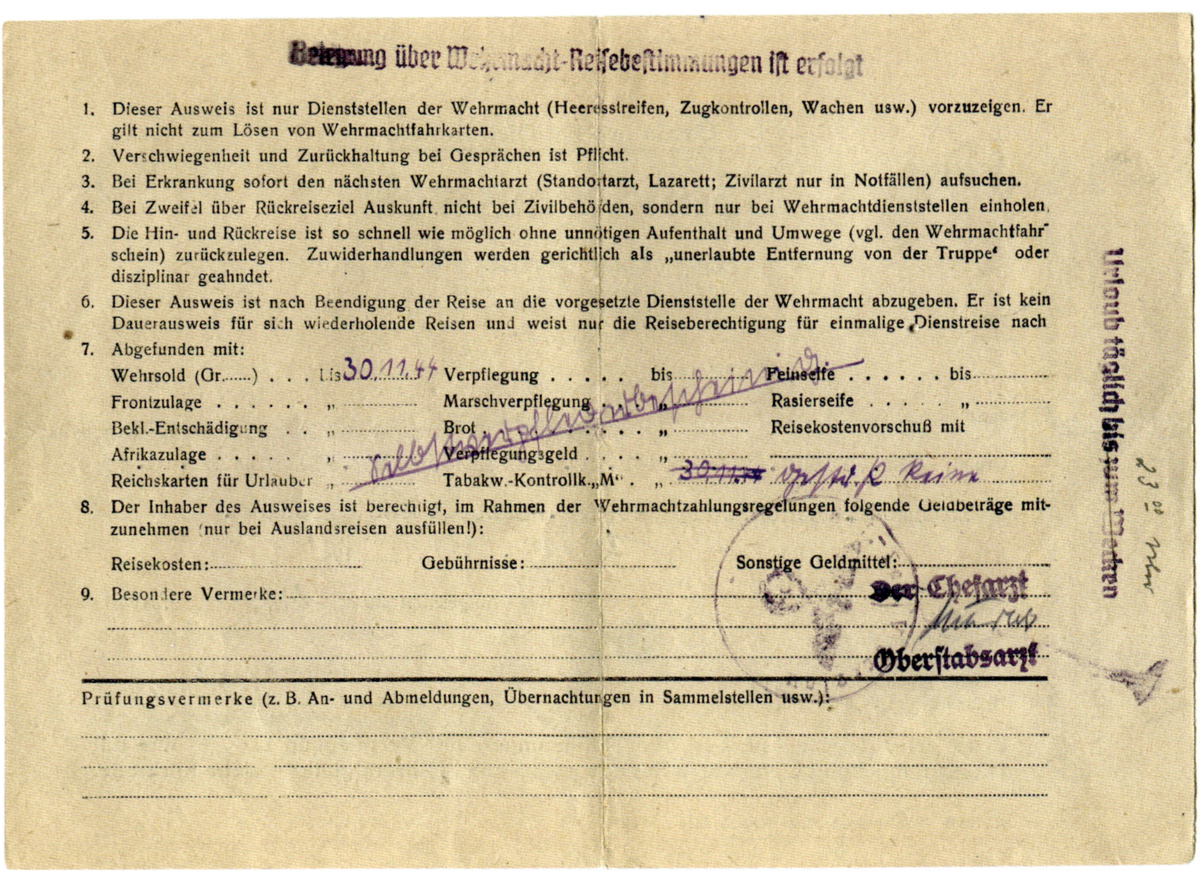

Belehrung über Wehrmacht-Reisebestimmungen ist erfolgt

1. Dieser Ausweis ist nur Dienststellen der Wehrmacht (Heeresstreifen, Zugkontrollen, Wachen usw.) vorzuzeigen. Er gilt nicht zum Lösen von Wehrmachtfahrkarten.
2. Verschwiegenheit und Zurückhaltung bei Gesprächen ist Pflicht.
3. Bei Erkrankung sofort den nächsten Wehrmachtarzt (Standortarzt, Lazarett; Zivilarzt nur in Notfällen) aufsuchen.
4. Bei Zweifel über Rückreiseziel Auskunft nicht bei Zivilbehörden, sondern nur bei Wehrmachtdienststellen einholen.
5. Die Hin- und Rückreise ist so schnell wie möglich ohne unnötigen Aufenthalt und Umwege (vgl. den Wehrmachtfahrschein) zurückzulegen. Zuwiderhandlungen werden gerichtlich als „unerlaubte Entfernung von der Truppe" oder disziplinar geahndet.
6. Dieser Ausweis ist nach Beendigung der Reise an die vorgesetzte Dienststelle der Wehrmacht abzugeben. Er ist kein Dauerausweis für sich wiederholende Reisen und weist nur die Reiseberechtigung für einmalige Dienstreise nach.
7. Abgefunden mit:
Wehrsold (Gr.......) . . . bis 30.11.44 Verpflegung . . . . . bis .... Feinseife . . . . . . bis ....
Frontzulage . . . . . . „ .... Marschverpflegung . . „ .... Rasierseife . . . . . „ ....
Bekl.-Entschädigung . . „ .... Brot . . . . „ .... Reisekostenvorschuß mit ....
Afrikazulage . . . . . „ .... Verpflegungsgeld . . . . „ ....
Reichskarten für Urlauber „ .... Tabakw.-Kontrollk. „M" . „ 30.11.44
8. Der Inhaber des Ausweises ist berechtigt, im Rahmen der Wehrmachtzahlungsregelungen folgende Geldbeträge mitzunehmen (nur bei Auslandsreisen ausfüllen!):
Reisekosten: .... Gebührnisse: .... Sonstige Geldmittel: ....
9. Besondere Vermerke: ....

Der Chefarzt
Oberstabsarzt

Urlaub täglich bis zum 23[00] Uhr
Werden

Prüfungsvermerke (z. B. An- und Abmeldungen, Übernachtungen in Sammelstellen usw.):

Figure 2-134. Unteroffizier Karl-Heinz Peters with Reserve-Lazarett V. Breslau, an outpatient since October 18, 1943 remains under the care of the hospital. On the back is a stamp permitting him to be out on "Urlaub täglich bis zum 23 Uhr," daily leave until 11:00 pm. (A5)

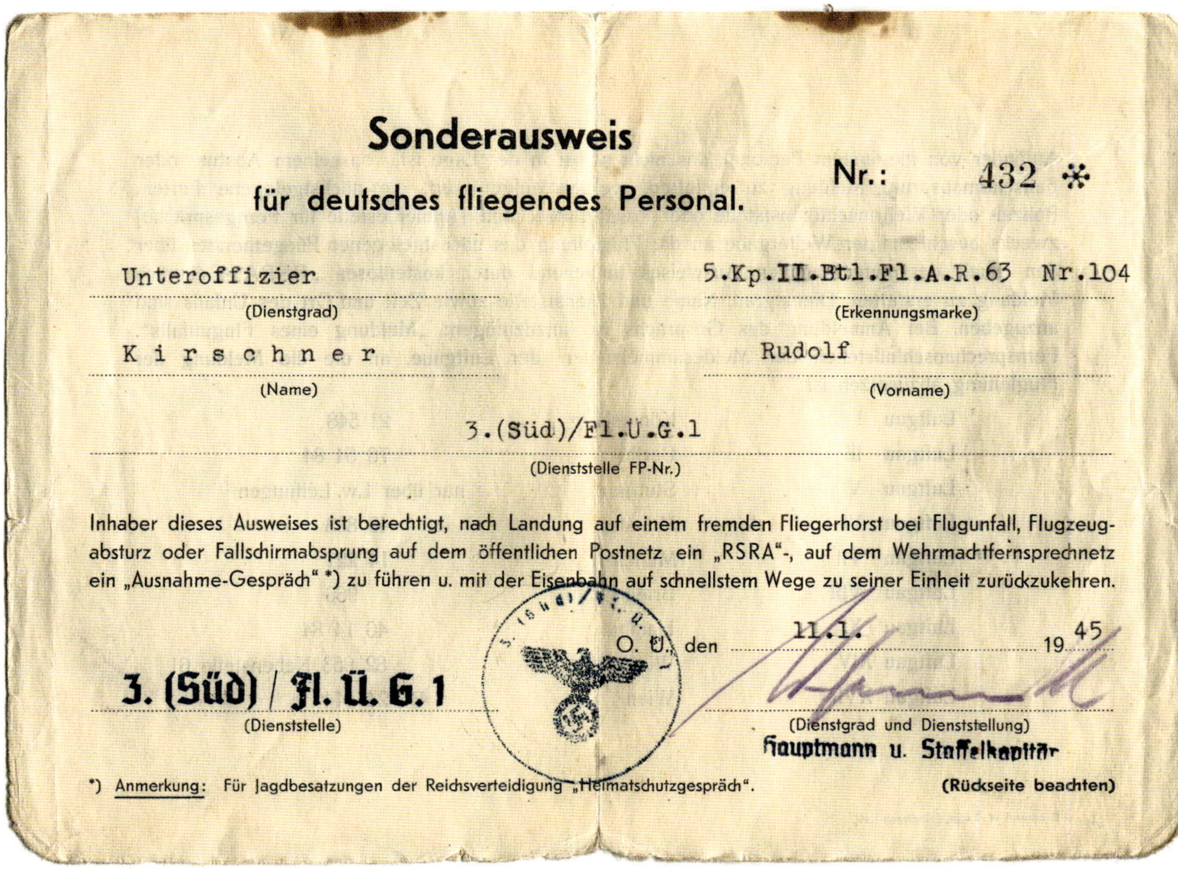

Sonderausweis

für deutsches fliegendes Personal.

Nr.: 432 *

Unteroffizier (Dienstgrad) 5.Kp.II.Btl.Fl.A.R.63 Nr.104 (Erkennungsmarke)

K i r s c h n e r (Name) Rudolf (Vorname)

3.(Süd)/Fl.Ü.G.1 (Dienststelle FP-Nr.)

Inhaber dieses Ausweises ist berechtigt, nach Landung auf einem fremden Fliegerhorst bei Flugunfall, Flugzeugabsturz oder Fallschirmabsprung auf dem öffentlichen Postnetz ein „RSRA"-, auf dem Wehrmachtfernsprechnetz ein „Ausnahme-Gespräch" *) zu führen u. mit der Eisenbahn auf schnellstem Wege zu seiner Einheit zurückzukehren.

O. U., den 11.1. 1945

3. (Süd) / Fl. Ü. G. 1 (Dienststelle)

(Dienstgrad und Dienststellung) Hauptmann u. Staffelkapitän

*) Anmerkung: Für Jagdbesatzungen der Reichsverteidigung „Heimatschutzgespräch".

(Rückseite beachten)

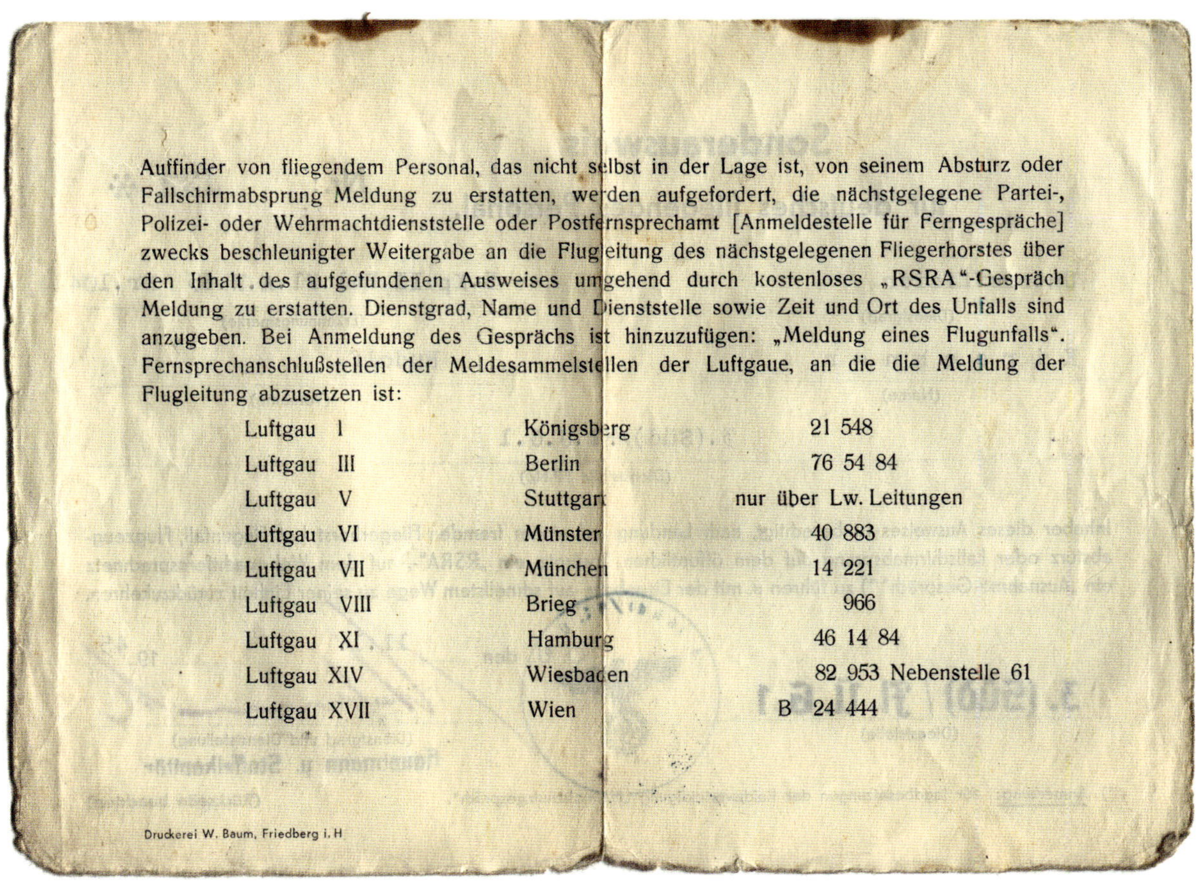

Auffinder von fliegendem Personal, das nicht selbst in der Lage ist, von seinem Absturz oder Fallschirmabsprung Meldung zu erstatten, werden aufgefordert, die nächstgelegene Partei-, Polizei- oder Wehrmachtdienststelle oder Postfernsprechamt [Anmeldestelle für Ferngespräche] zwecks beschleunigter Weitergabe an die Flugleitung des nächstgelegenen Fliegerhorstes über den Inhalt des aufgefundenen Ausweises umgehend durch kostenloses „RSRA"-Gespräch Meldung zu erstatten. Dienstgrad, Name und Dienststelle sowie Zeit und Ort des Unfalls sind anzugeben. Bei Anmeldung des Gesprächs ist hinzuzufügen: „Meldung eines Flugunfalls". Fernsprechanschlußstellen der Meldesammelstellen der Luftgaue, an die die Meldung der Flugleitung abzusetzen ist:

Luftgau I	Königsberg	21 548
Luftgau III	Berlin	76 54 84
Luftgau V	Stuttgart	nur über Lw. Leitungen
Luftgau VI	Münster	40 883
Luftgau VII	München	14 221
Luftgau VIII	Brieg	966
Luftgau XI	Hamburg	46 14 84
Luftgau XIV	Wiesbaden	82 953 Nebenstelle 61
Luftgau XVII	Wien	B 24 444

Druckerei W. Baum, Friedberg i. H

Figure 2-135. This example of a Luftwaffe-specific Sonderausweis is for a Luftwaffe pilot who has landed at an airfield that is normally not his own. One might think that landing at the wrong airfield could get one in trouble, however in this case, it's not; Unteroffizier Rudolf Kirschner flew for Flugzeugüberführungsgeschwader 1, Aircraft Transfer Wing 1, out of Erding.(A5)

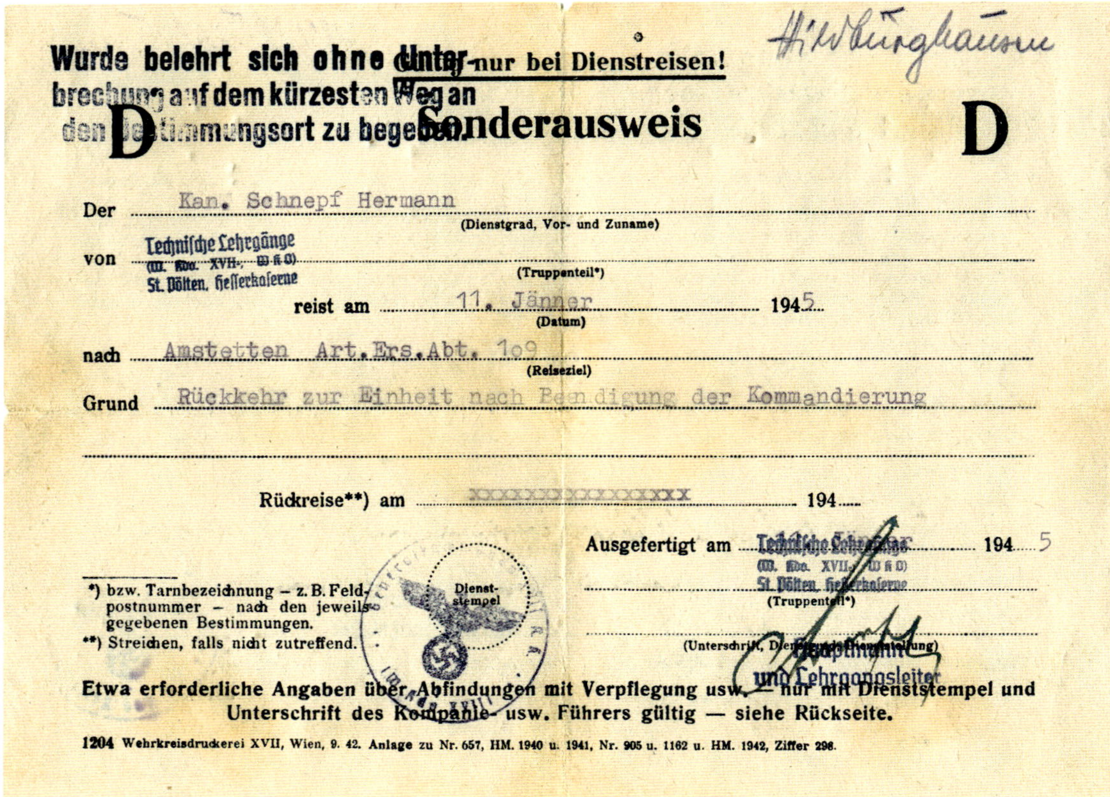

Wurde belehrt sich ohne Unter- nur bei Dienstreisen!
brechung auf dem kürzesten Weg an
den Bestimmungsort zu begeben.

D **Sonderausweis** D

Hildburghausen

Der Kan. Schnepf Hermann
(Dienstgrad, Vor- und Zuname)

von Technische Lehrgänge (III. Kdo. XVII. W.K.O.) St. Pölten, Hesserkaserne
(Truppenteil*)

reist am 11. Jänner 1945
(Datum)

nach Amstetten Art.Ers.Abt. 109
(Reiseziel)

Grund Rückkehr zur Einheit nach Beendigung der Kommandierung

Rückreise**) am xxxxxxxxxxxxxxxx 194..

Ausgefertigt am Technische Lehrgänge (III. Kdo. XVII. W.K.O.) St. Pölten, Hesserkaserne 1945
(Truppenteil*)

Dienst-stempel

(Unterschrift, Dienststellung)
Hauptmann und Lehrgangsleiter

*) bzw. Tarnbezeichnung – z. B. Feldpostnummer – nach den jeweils gegebenen Bestimmungen.
**) Streichen, falls nicht zutreffend.

Etwa erforderliche Angaben über Abfindungen mit Verpflegung usw. — nur mit Dienststempel und Unterschrift des Kompanie- usw. Führers gültig — siehe Rückseite.

1204 Wehrkreisdruckerei XVII, Wien, 9. 42. Anlage zu Nr. 657, HM. 1940 u. 1941, Nr. 905 u. 1162 u. HM. 1942, Ziffer 298.

Figure 2-136. Dated January 11, 1945, Kanonier (Canoneer) Hermann Schnepf was transferred from Technical Instruction at the Hessekaserne (Hesse Barracks) in St. Pölten Artillery Training Section 109. Special instructions direct him to "...proceed on the shortest route without interruption" (Wurde belehrt sich...) and to "Return to your unit after the end of this assignment." (A5)

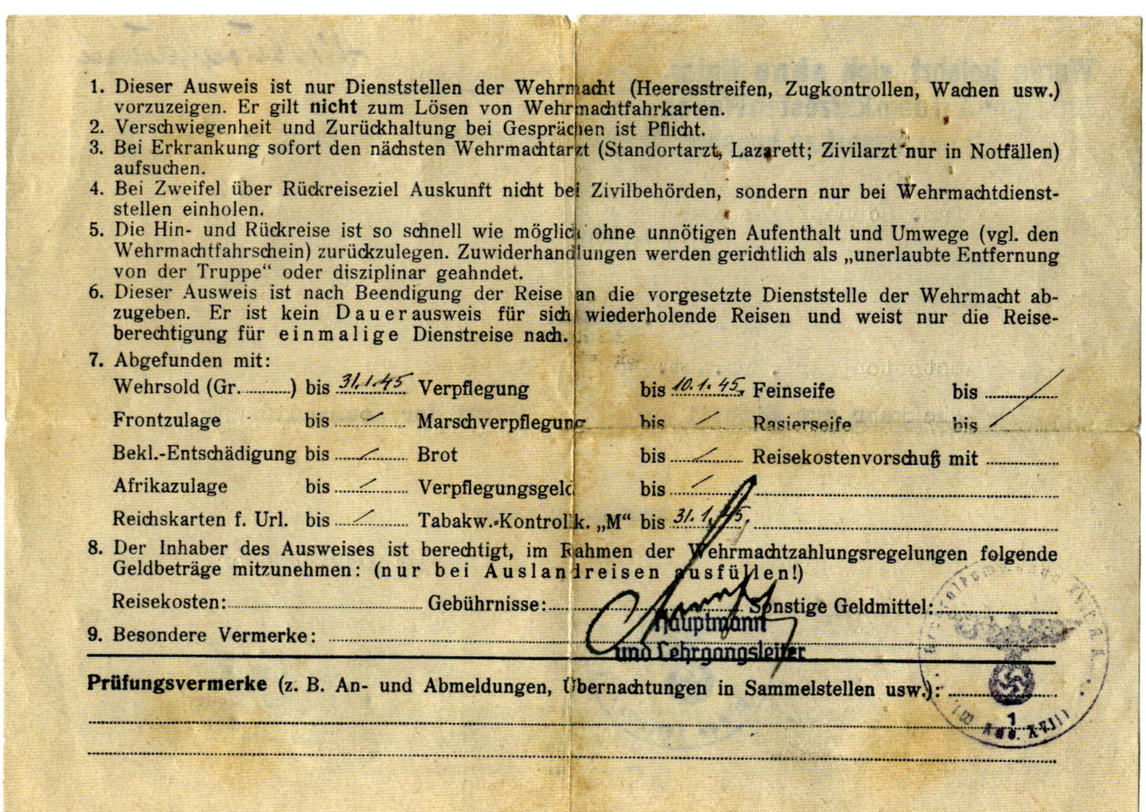

1. Dieser Ausweis ist nur Dienststellen der Wehrmacht (Heeresstreifen, Zugkontrollen, Wachen usw.) vorzuzeigen. Er gilt **nicht** zum Lösen von Wehrmachtfahrkarten.
2. Verschwiegenheit und Zurückhaltung bei Gesprächen ist Pflicht.
3. Bei Erkrankung sofort den nächsten Wehrmachtarzt (Standortarzt, Lazarett; Zivilarzt nur in Notfällen) aufsuchen.
4. Bei Zweifel über Rückreiseziel Auskunft nicht bei Zivilbehörden, sondern nur bei Wehrmachtdienststellen einholen.
5. Die Hin- und Rückreise ist so schnell wie möglich ohne unnötigen Aufenthalt und Umwege (vgl. den Wehrmachtfahrschein) zurückzulegen. Zuwiderhandlungen werden gerichtlich als „unerlaubte Entfernung von der Truppe" oder disziplinar geahndet.
6. Dieser Ausweis ist nach Beendigung der Reise an die vorgesetzte Dienststelle der Wehrmacht abzugeben. Er ist kein Dauerausweis für sich wiederholende Reisen und weist nur die Reiseberechtigung für einmalige Dienstreise nach.
7. Abgefunden mit:

Wehrsold (Gr. ......)	bis 31.1.45	Verpflegung	bis 10.1.45	Feinseife	bis /
Frontzulage	bis /	Marschverpflegung	bis /	Rasierseife	bis /
Bekl.-Entschädigung	bis /	Brot	bis /	Reisekostenvorschuß mit	
Afrikazulage	bis /	Verpflegungsgeld	bis /		
Reichskarten f. Url.	bis /	Tabakw.-Kontrollk. „M"	bis 31.1.45		

8. Der Inhaber des Ausweises ist berechtigt, im Rahmen der Wehrmachtzahlungsregelungen folgende Geldbeträge mitzunehmen: (nur bei Auslandreisen ausfüllen!)

Reisekosten: .... Gebührnisse: .... Sonstige Geldmittel: ....

9. Besondere Vermerke: .... Hauptmann und Lehrgangsleiter

Prüfungsvermerke (z. B. An- und Abmeldungen, Übernachtungen in Sammelstellen usw.):

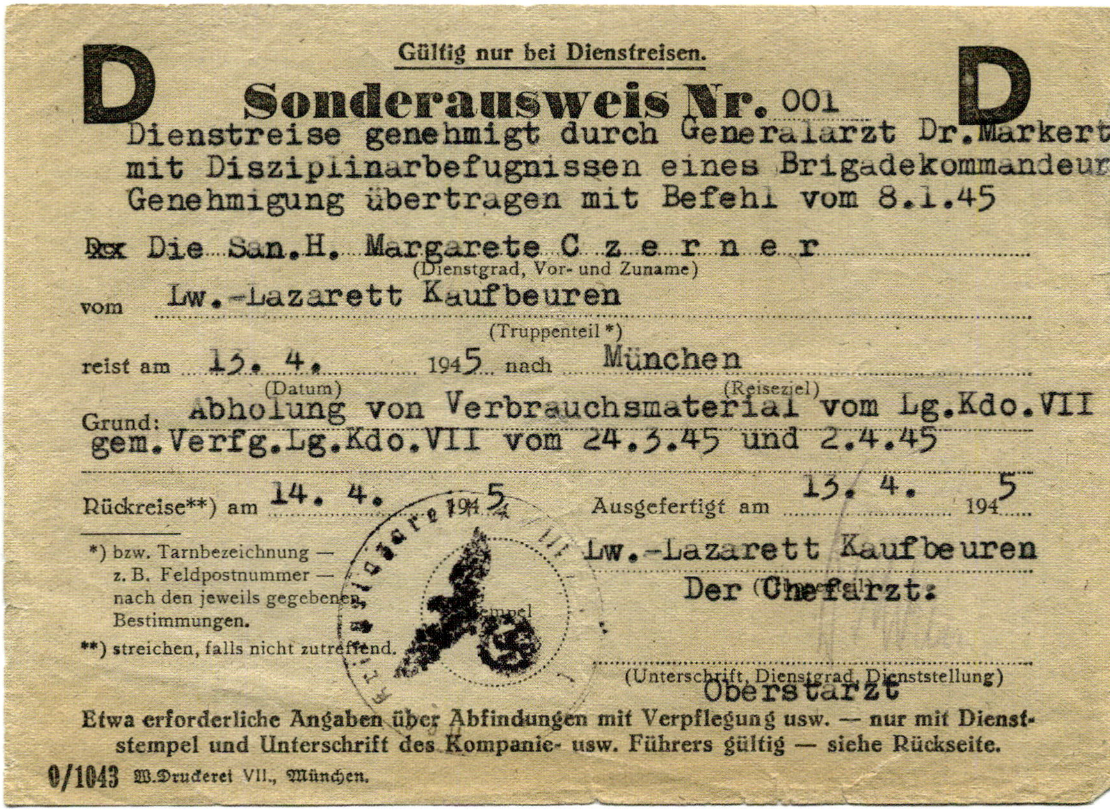

D Gültig nur bei Dienstreisen. D

Sonderausweis Nr. 001

Dienstreise genehmigt durch Generalarzt Dr.Markert mit Disziplinarbefugnissen eines Brigadekommandeur Genehmigung übertragen mit Befehl vom 8.1.45

Der Die San.H. Margarete C z e r n e r
(Dienstgrad, Vor- und Zuname)

vom Lw.-Lazarett Kaufbeuren
(Truppenteil *)

reist am 13. 4. 1945 nach München
(Datum) (Reiseziel)

Grund: Abholung von Verbrauchsmaterial vom Lg.Kdo.VII gem.Verfg.Lg.Kdo.VII vom 24.3.45 und 2.4.45

Rückreise**) am 14. 4. 1945 Ausgefertigt am 13. 4. 1945

Lw.-Lazarett Kaufbeuren
Der Chefarzt:

*) bzw. Tarnbezeichnung — z. B. Feldpostnummer — nach den jeweils gegebenen Bestimmungen.

**) streichen, falls nicht zutreffend.

(Unterschrift, Dienstgrad, Dienststellung)
Oberstarzt

Etwa erforderliche Angaben über Abfindungen mit Verpflegung usw. — nur mit Dienststempel und Unterschrift des Kompanie- usw. Führers gültig — siehe Rückseite.

0/1043 W.Druckerei VII., München.

Figure 2-137. As the war drew to a close, many found themselves pressed into roles they had never trained for. Here, Sanitäts-Helferin (Female Medical Assistant) Margarete Czerner, acting under the orders of General Doctor Merkt who, it notes, has the disciplinary authority of a Brigade Commander (in the event an overzealous Feldgendarmerie may have asked), has been ordered to transport "consumables" (blood supplies?) from Luftwaffe Lazarett Kaufbeuren (where there remains an active airfield today). (A6)

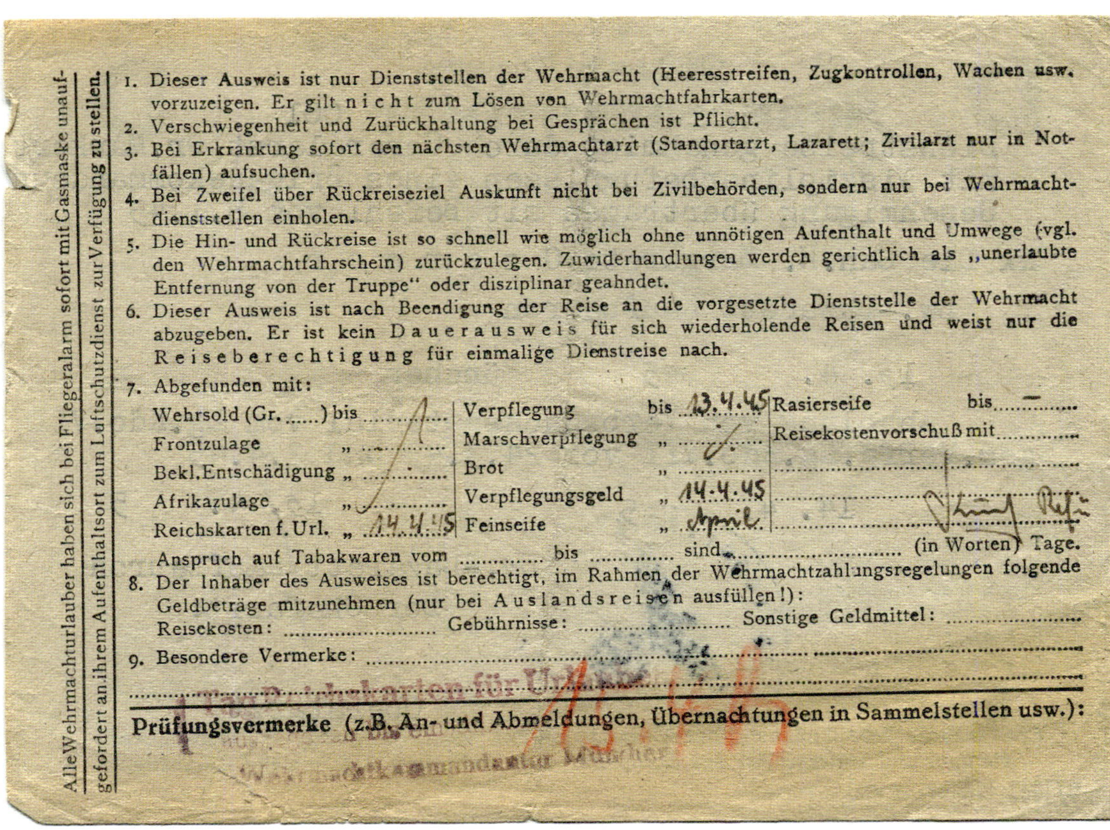

Alle Wehrmachturlauber haben sich bei Fliegeralarm sofort mit Gasmaske unaufgefordert an ihrem Aufenthaltsort zum Luftschutzdienst zur Verfügung zu stellen.

1. Dieser Ausweis ist nur Dienststellen der Wehrmacht (Heeresstreifen, Zugkontrollen, Wachen usw. vorzuzeigen. Er gilt n i c h t zum Lösen von Wehrmachtfahrkarten.
2. Verschwiegenheit und Zurückhaltung bei Gesprächen ist Pflicht.
3. Bei Erkrankung sofort den nächsten Wehrmachtarzt (Standortarzt, Lazarett; Zivilarzt nur in Notfällen) aufsuchen.
4. Bei Zweifel über Rückreiseziel Auskunft nicht bei Zivilbehörden, sondern nur bei Wehrmachtdienststellen einholen.
5. Die Hin- und Rückreise ist so schnell wie möglich ohne unnötigen Aufenthalt und Umwege (vgl. den Wehrmachtfahrschein) zurückzulegen. Zuwiderhandlungen werden gerichtlich als „unerlaubte Entfernung von der Truppe" oder disziplinar geahndet.
6. Dieser Ausweis ist nach Beendigung der Reise an die vorgesetzte Dienststelle der Wehrmacht abzugeben. Er ist kein D a u e r a u s w e i s für sich wiederholende Reisen und weist nur die R e i s e b e r e c h t i g u n g für einmalige Dienstreise nach.
7. Abgefunden mit:

Wehrsold (Gr. ......) bis	/	Verpflegung bis	13.4.45	Rasierseife bis	—
Frontzulage „	/	Marschverpflegung „	/	Reisekostenvorschuß mit	
Bekl.Entschädigung „	/	Brot „			
Afrikazulage „	/	Verpflegungsgeld „	14.4.45		
Reichskarten f. Url. „	14.4.45	Feinseife „	April		

Anspruch auf Tabakwaren vom .... bis .... sind .... (in Worten) Tage.

8. Der Inhaber des Ausweises ist berechtigt, im Rahmen der Wehrmachtzahlungsregelungen folgende Geldbeträge mitzunehmen (nur bei A u s l a n d s r e i s e n ausfüllen!):
Reisekosten: .... Gebührnisse: .... Sonstige Geldmittel: ....
9. Besondere Vermerke: ....

Prüfungsvermerke (z.B. An- und Abmeldungen, Übernachtungen in Sammelstellen usw.):

Wehrmachtkommandantur München

The expected information is required: rank, name, and travel dates, as well as which sanctioned *Grenzübertritt* (Border Crossing) the soldier is required to utilize: the Brenner Pass, Tarviso, or the airports of Munich or Monaco. Once one returns from travel, the pass is to be returned to the issuing office.

An interesting feature to the *Sonderausweis-I* is the requirement of Italian stamps upon entering or leaving the country, much like a passport, with a stamp noting either the *Entrata* (Entrance) or *Uscita* (Departure) date. Of particular interest are the Roman numerals behind the dates on these stamps. The *Fascisti* came to power in Italy in 1922 with the appointment of Benito Mussolini as Prime Minister. Just like the reigns of Roman Emperors, the *Fascisti* noted the number of years of their administration by placing Roman numerals behind the date, counting up from October of 1922. This was a fiscal dating system, not calendar; December of 1940 and January of 1941 both bore the Roman numeral XVIII.

Like all cooperative organizations of the two Axis countries, the form fell into disfavor following the capitulation of Italy in September of 1943. Although Northern Italy remained under Fascist control, it was treated much more like a conquered territory than an ally.

The *Sonderausweis-SO* (*Süd-Ost*, hence SO), on the other hand, is a form meant to be used throughout the Southeast of "Greater" Germany and its conquered territories, from Italy to the Balkans to the Caucasus, though the Southeast swiftly started decreasing in area following the disastrous Stalingrad campaign. Like the *Sonderausweis-I*, it was a multilingual A4 form printed on one side only, but in seven different languages: German, Bulgarian, Italian, Slovenian, Romanian, Slovak, and Hungarian, with a 15mm green stripe down the center.

It had the same two lines at the top as the *Sonderausweis-I*, that the pass was only valid for service-related travel and that one should obey the local authorities. The form was used by soldiers traveling through not just conquered territory, but also permitted passage throughout the borders of Germany's Balkan allies. Smooth relations were vital among those nations to prevent the creation of another front; Germany already had its hands full in Russia and North Africa. The document required much the same information as other forms, rank and name, valid dates for travel, departure and arrival stations, grounds for travel, and special circumstances and conditions; it just took longer to read.

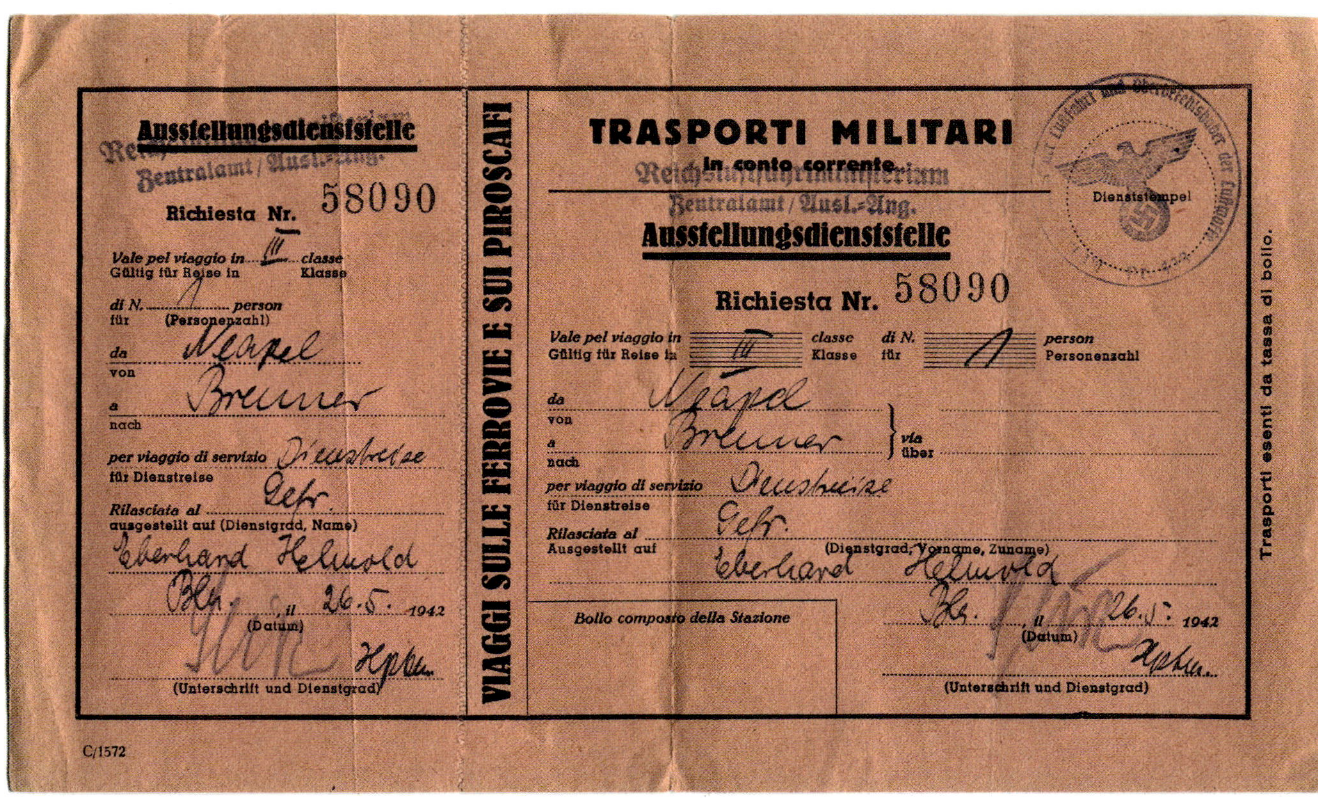

Ausstellungsdienststelle
Reichsluftfahrtministerium
Zentralamt / Ausl.-Ang.
Richiesta Nr. 58090
Vale pel viaggio in III classe
Gültig für Reise in Klasse
di N. 1 person
für (Personenzahl)
da Neapel
von
a Brenner
nach
per viaggio di servizio Dienstreise
für Dienstreise
Rilasciata al Gefr.
ausgestellt auf (Dienstgrad, Name)
Eberhard Helmold
Bln., il 26.5. 1942
(Datum)
(Unterschrift und Dienstgrad)
C/1572

VIAGGI SULLE FERROVIE E SUI PIROSCAFI

TRASPORTI MILITARI
in conto corrente
Reichsluftfahrtministerium
Zentralamt / Ausl.-Ang.
Ausstellungsdienststelle
Dienststempel
Richiesta Nr. 58090
Vale pel viaggio in III classe di N. 1 person
Gültig für Reise in Klasse für Personenzahl
da Neapel
von
a Brenner via
nach über
per viaggio di servizio Dienstreise
für Dienstreise
Rilasciata al Gefr.
Ausgestellt auf (Dienstgrad, Vorname, Zuname)
Eberhard Helmold
Bollo composto della Stazione
Bln., il 26.5. 1942
(Datum)
(Unterschrift und Dienstgrad)
Trasporti esenti da tassa di bollo.

Figure 2-138. This German-Italian military train ticket from Naples to the Brenner Pass would probably have been used in conjunction with the Sonderausweis-I, like the one on the following page. (4 7/8" x 8 3/8")

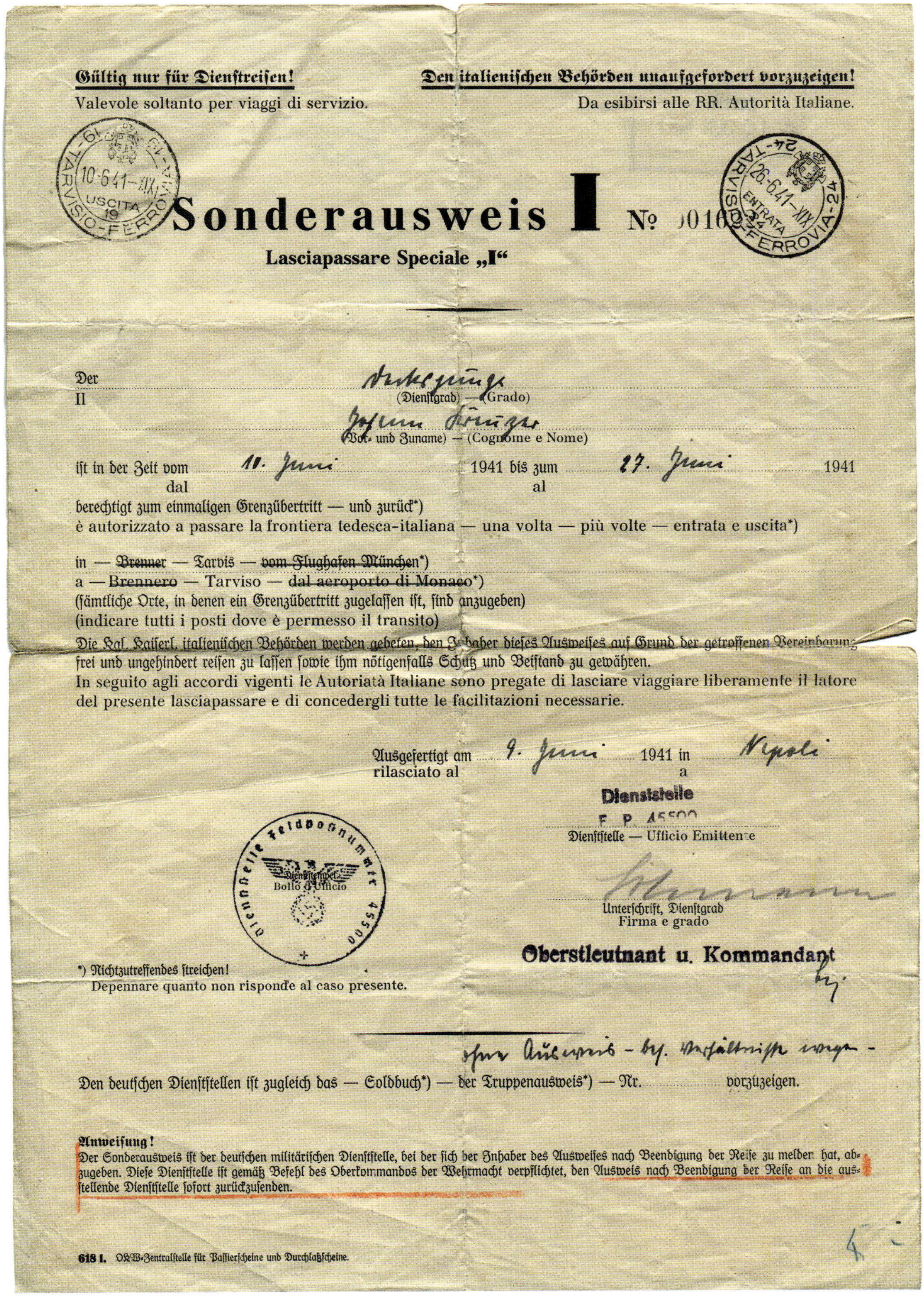

Gültig nur für Dienstreisen!
Valevole soltanto per viaggi di servizio.

Den italienischen Behörden unaufgefordert vorzuzeigen!
Da esibirsi alle RR. Autorità Italiane.

TARVISIO-FERROVIA 19 — 10-6-41-XIX — USCITA

TARVISIO-FERROVIA 24 — 26-6-41-XIX — ENTRATA

Sonderausweis I

№ 00162

Lasciapassare Speciale „I"

Der
Il .... (Dienstgrad) — (Grado)

.... (Vor- und Zuname) — (Cognome e Nome)

ist in der Zeit vom ...... 1941 bis zum 1941
dal ...... al

berechtigt zum einmaligen Grenzübertritt — und zurück*)
è autorizzato a passare la frontiera tedesca-italiana — una volta — più volte — entrata e uscita*)

in — ~~Brenner~~ — Tarvis — ~~vom Flughafen München~~*)
a — ~~Brennero~~ — Tarviso — ~~dal aeroporto di Monaco~~*)
(sämtliche Orte, in denen ein Grenzübertritt zugelassen ist, sind anzugeben)
(indicare tutti i posti dove è permesso il transito)

Die Kgl. Kaiserl. italienischen Behörden werden gebeten, den Inhaber dieses Ausweises auf Grund der getroffenen Vereinbarung frei und ungehindert reisen zu lassen sowie ihm nötigenfalls Schutz und Beistand zu gewähren.
In seguito agli accordi vigenti le Autoriatà Italiane sono pregate di lasciare viaggiare liberamente il latore del presente lasciapassare e di concedergli tutte le facilitazioni necessarie.

Ausgefertigt am ...... 1941 in ......
rilasciato al ...... a ......

Dienststelle
F. P. 45500
Dienststelle — Ufficio Emittente

Dienststempel
Bollo d'Ufficio

Dienststelle Feldpostnummer 45500

Unterschrift, Dienstgrad
Firma e grado

Oberstleutnant u. Kommandant

*) Nichtzutreffendes streichen!
Depennare quanto non risponde al caso presente.

Den deutschen Dienststellen ist zugleich das — Soldbuch*) — der Truppenausweis*) — Nr. ...... vorzuzeigen.

Anweisung!
Der Sonderausweis ist der deutschen militärischen Dienststelle, bei der sich der Inhaber des Ausweises nach Beendigung der Reise zu melden hat, abzugeben. Diese Dienststelle ist gemäß Befehl des Oberkommandos der Wehrmacht verpflichtet, den Ausweis nach Beendigung der Reise an die ausstellende Dienststelle sofort zurückzusenden.

618 I. OKW-Zentralstelle für Passierscheine und Durchlaßscheine.

Figure 2-139. The Sonderausweis-I, a specialized travel pass for personnel between Germany and Italy, is a bilingual form and is often stamped by both German and Italian authorities. Note the Italian date stamps with the Roman numerals, the number of years the Fascists have reigned since 1922.(A4)

Nr. 02589 * Grenzübertrittsausweis (Weiß-Grün) für Angehörige der deutschen Wehrmacht
Sammel -
Lasciapassare di frontiera (bianco-verde) per appartenenti alle forze armate tedesche
Granična propustnica (bielo-zelena) za pripadnike njemačke oružane sile
Legitimaţie de trecere a frontierei (alb-verde) pentru persoanele din cadrele armatei germane
Preukaz ku prestúpeniu hraníc (bielo-zelený) pre príslušníkov nemeckej brannej moci
Határátlépési igazolvány (fehér-zöld) a német véderő tagjai számára
Разрешително за преминаване границата (бѣло-зелено) за чиноветѣ отъ германскитѣ въоржжени сили

Der — Il — D — Господинъ: Obergefreite Herbert Lissner und ein Mann siehe Rückseite
(Dienstgrad, Vor- und Zuname sowie Dienststelle) — (Grado, nome e cognome, ufficio di appartenenza) — (Čin, ime i prezime, službeno mjesto) — (Gradul, prenumele şi numele de familie, autoritatea) — (Vojenská hodnosť, krstné a rodinné meno a služobné miesto) — (Szolgálati rangfokozat, vezeték-és keresztnév, szolgálati hatóság) — (Чинъ, име и презиме, както и служба)

reist in der Zeit vom 13. September 1943 bis 20. September 1943
viaggia dal ..1943 al ..1943 — putuje za vrijeme od ..1943 do ..1943 — călătoreşte în intervalul dela ..1943 până la ..1943 — cestuje od ..1943 do ..1943 — utazik 1943 ..tól, 1943 ..ig terjedő időben — време на пжтуването - отъ ..1943 до ..1943

einmal — und zurück — wiederholt*)
una volta - e ritorno - ripetutamente*) — jedamput - i natrag - opetovano*) — dus - şi întors - de repetate ori*) — jednorázove - a zpäť - opätovne*) — egyszer - és vissza - ismételten*) — единъ пжть - и обратно - повторно*)

von Reichsgebiet
da — iz — din — z — отъ (Gebiet) — (Zona) — (Područje) — (Teritoriu) — (Územie) — (Terület) — (Страна) (ból)

durch Ungarn - Kroatien
attraversando — kroz — prin — cez — презъ (Durchreisegebiete) — (Territori di transito) — (Područja proputovanja) — (Tările de tranzit) — (Územia, ktorými sa precestuje) — (Atutazó terület) — (Страна на преминаването) keresztül

über Sauerbrunn
passando da — preko — prin — cez — презъ (Deutsche Grenzübergangsstelle) — (Posto di passaggio della frontiera tedesca) — (Njemačke granične prijelazne stanice) — (Locul de frontieră german) — (Nemecká pasová kontrola) — (A német határátlépési kirendeltségen át) — (Германски граниченъ пропускателенъ пунктъ)

nach Belgrad - Serbien
a — u — la — do — за ba

im — Eisenbahnzug — Flugzeug — Kraftfahrzeug Nr.
in ferrovia - velivolo - automezzo N... — vlakom - zrakoplovom - samovozom br... — cu trenul - avionul - automobilul No... — železnicou - lietadlom - motorovým vozidlom č... — vonaton, repülőgépen, teherkocsin ...sz. — съ желѣзница - самолетъ - моторна кола №.

Die Fahrt darf in den Durchreisegebieten nicht ohne zwingenden Grund unterbrochen werden.
Il viaggio non può venire interrotto senza motivi di forza maggiore nei territori di transito. — Putovanje se bez nužnih razloga ne smije prekidati u područjima proputovanja. — Călătoria nu poate fi întreruptă în ţările de tranzit fără un motiv bine întemeiat. — Na územiach, cez ktoré sa precestuje, nesmie byť cesta bez nutných príčin prerušená. — Az utazás az átmenő területeken kényszerítő ok nélkül nem szakítható félbe. — Пжтуването не бива да бжде прекжснато въ страната на преминаването безъ принудителни причини.

Bemerkungen: Reise darf nur in Uniform erfolgen
Osservazioni — Opaske — Observaţiuni — Poznámky — Jegyzetek — Забележки

Wien, den 13. September 1943
il — dne — dňa —
194.. ..hó ..n

Durchlaßscheinstelle der Wehrmacht

(Eigenhändige Unterschrift des Ausweisinhabers)
(Firma autografa del titolare)
(Vlastoručni potpis vlasnika iskaznice)
(Semnătura proprie a deţinătorului legitimaţiei)
(Vlastnoručný podpis majiteľa preukazu)
(Az igazolvány tulajdonosának sajátkezű aláírása)
(Собственоржченъ подписъ на притежателя на личната карта)

(Unterschrift, Dienstgrad) — (Firma e grado) — (Potpis, čin) — (Semnătura, gradul) — (Podpis, hodnosť) — (Aláírás rangfokozat) — (Подписъ, служебенъ чинъ)
Hauptmann

*) Nichtzutreffendes streichen. — *) Cancellare ciò che non interessa. — *) Nevažeće precrtati. — *) A se şterge ceeace nu este valabil. — *) Čo sa nehodí, škrtnúť. — *) A meg nem felelő törlendő. — *) Излишното се зачерква.

Nur gültig in Verbindung mit — Soldbuch — Truppenausweis — Nr. 717 — Soldbuch oder Truppenausweis ist nur deutschen Dienststellen vorzuzeigen. Dieser Sonderausweis ist nach Beendigung der Reise an die deutsche militärische Dienststelle, bei der sich der Ausweisinhaber zu melden hat, abzugeben.

OKW-Zentralstelle für Durchlaßscheine, Berlin W 35, Großadmiral-Prinz-Heinrich-Str. 1

2463 43 2B

Figure 2-140. With German losses in the Southeast throughout 1943, the Sonderausweis SO was discontinued in favor of the Grenzübertrittsauweis (Border Crossing Identity Pass). If one examines the document, the bearer's name may seem familiar (see figures 2-44, 2-64, 2-68, 2-93, 2-129, 2-131, and 2-166). Remarkably, the author acquired these documents years apart.(A4)

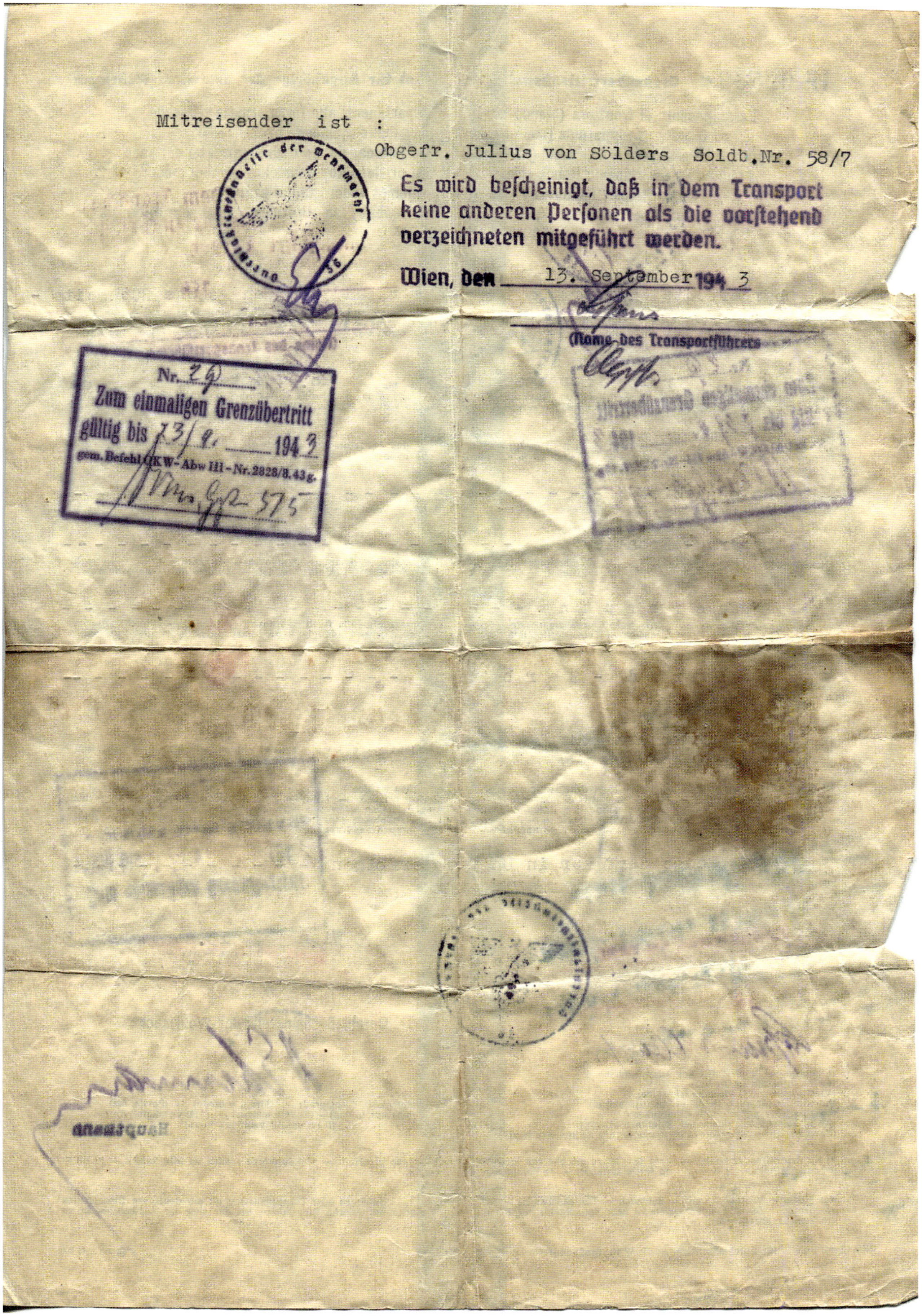

Mitreisender ist :

Obgefr. Julius von Sölders Soldb.Nr. 58/7

Es wird bescheinigt, daß in dem Transport keine anderen Personen als die vorstehend verzeichneten mitgeführt werden.

Wien, den 13. September 1943

(Name des Transportführers)

Nr. 29
Zum einmaligen Grenzübertritt
gültig bis 13/9. 1943
gem. Befehl OKW-Abw III-Nr. 2828/8.43 g.

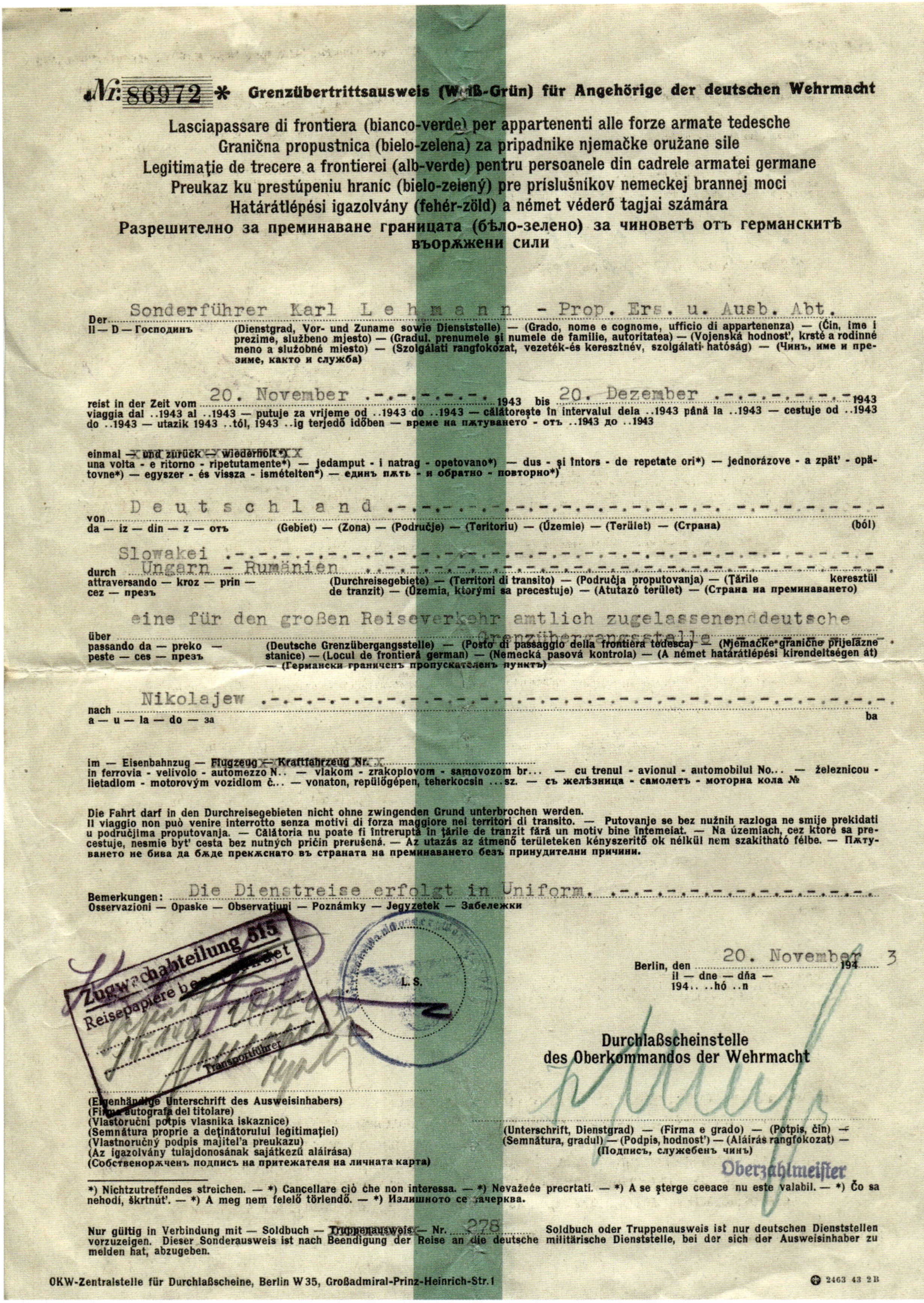

Nr. 86972 * Grenzübertrittsausweis (Weiß-Grün) für Angehörige der deutschen Wehrmacht
Lasciapassare di frontiera (bianco-verde) per appartenenti alle forze armate tedesche
Granična propusnica (bielo-zelena) za pripadnike njemačke oružane sile
Legitimaţie de trecere a frontierei (alb-verde) pentru persoanele din cadrele armatei germane
Preukaz ku prestúpeniu hraníc (bielo-zelený) pre príslušníkov nemeckej brannej moci
Határátlépési igazolvány (fehér-zöld) a német véderő tagjai számára
Разрешително за преминаване границата (бѣло-зелено) за чиноветѣ отъ германскитѣ въоржжени сили

Der Sonderführer Karl Lehmann - Prop. Ers. u. Ausb. Abt.
Il — D — Господинъ (Dienstgrad, Vor- und Zuname sowie Dienststelle) — (Grado, nome e cognome, ufficio di appartenenza) — (Čin, ime i prezime, službeno mjesto) — (Gradul, prenumele şi numele de familie, autoritatea) — (Vojenská hodnosť, krstné a rodinné meno a služobné miesto) — (Szolgálati rangfokozat, vezeték-és keresztnév, szolgálati hatóság) — (Чинъ, име и презиме, както и служба)

reist in der Zeit vom 20. November 1943 bis 20. Dezember 1943
viaggia dal ..1943 al ..1943 — putuje za vrijeme od ..1943 do ..1943 — călătoreşte în intervalul dela ..1943 până la ..1943 — cestuje od ..1943 do ..1943 — utazik 1943 ..tól, 1943 ..ig terjedő időben — време на пжтуването - отъ ..1943 до ..1943

einmal — und zurück — wiederholt*) X
una volta - e ritorno - ripetutamente*) — jedamput - i natrag - opetovano*) — dus - şi întors - de repetate ori*) — jednorázove - a zpäť - opätovne*) — egyszer - és vissza - ismételten*) — единъ пжть - и обратно - повторно*)

von Deutschland
da — iz — din — z — отъ (Gebiet) — (Zona) — (Područje) — (Teritoriu) — (Územie) — (Terület) — (Страна) (ból)

durch Slowakei Ungarn - Rumänien
attraversando — kroz — prin — cez — презъ (Durchreisegebiete) — (Territori di transito) — (Područja proputovanja) — (Ţările de tranzit) — (Územia, ktorými sa precestuje) — (Átutazó terület) — (Страна на преминаването) keresztül

über eine für den großen Reiseverkehr amtlich zugelassene deutsche Grenzübergangsstelle
passando da — preko — peste — ces — презъ (Deutsche Grenzübergangsstelle) — (Posto di passaggio della frontiera tedesca) — (Njemačke granične prijelazne stanice) — (Locul de frontieră german) — (Nemecká pasová kontrola) — (A német határátlépési kirendeltségen át) — (Германски граниченъ пропускателенъ пунктъ)

nach Nikolajew
a — u — la — do — за ba

im — Eisenbahnzug — Flugzeug — Kraftfahrzeug Nr. X
in ferrovia - velivolo - automezzo N.. — vlakom - zrakoplovom - samovozom br... — cu trenul - avionul - automobilul No... — železnicou - lietadlom - motorovým vozidlom č... — vonaton, repülőgépen, teherkocsin ...sz. — съ желѣзница - самолетъ - моторна кола №

Die Fahrt darf in den Durchreisegebieten nicht ohne zwingenden Grund unterbrochen werden.
Il viaggio non può venire interrotto senza motivi di forza maggiore nei territori di transito. — Putovanje se bez nužnih razloga ne smije prekidati u područjima proputovanja. — Călătoria nu poate fi întreruptă în ţările de tranzit fără un motiv bine întemeiat. — Na územiach, cez ktoré sa precestuje, nesmie byť cesta bez nutných príčin prerušená. — Az utazás az átmenő területeken kényszerítő ok nélkül nem szakítható félbe. — Пжтуването не бива да бжде прекжснато въ страната на преминаването безъ принудителни причини.

Bemerkungen: Die Dienstreise erfolgt in Uniform.
Osservazioni — Opaske — Observaţiuni — Poznámky — Jegyzetek — Забележки

Zugwachabteilung 515
Reisepapiere bearbeitet
Transportführer

L. S.

Berlin, den 20. November 1943
il — dne — dňa —
194.. ..hó ..n

Durchlaßscheinstelle
des Oberkommandos der Wehrmacht

(Eigenhändige Unterschrift des Ausweisinhabers)
(Firma autografa del titolare)
(Vlastoručni potpis vlasnika iskaznice)
(Semnătura proprie a deţinătorului legitimaţiei)
(Vlastnoručný podpis majiteľa preukazu)
(Az igazolvány tulajdonosának sajátkezű aláírása)
(Собственоржченъ подписъ на притежателя на личната карта)

(Unterschrift, Dienstgrad) — (Firma e grado) — (Potpis, čin) — (Semnătura, gradul) — (Podpis, hodnosť) — (Aláírás rangfokozat) — (Подписъ, служебенъ чинъ)

Oberzahlmeister

*) Nichtzutreffendes streichen. — *) Cancellare ciò che non interessa. — *) Nevažeće precrtati. — *) A se şterge ceeace nu este valabil. — *) Čo sa nehodí, škrtnúť. — *) A meg nem felelő törlendő. — *) Излишното се зачерква.

Nur gültig in Verbindung mit — Soldbuch — Truppenausweis — Nr. 278 Soldbuch oder Truppenausweis ist nur deutschen Dienststellen vorzuzeigen. Dieser Sonderausweis ist nach Beendigung der Reise an die deutsche militärische Dienststelle, bei der sich der Ausweisinhaber zu melden hat, abzugeben.

OKW-Zentralstelle für Durchlaßscheine, Berlin W 35, Großadmiral-Prinz-Heinrich-Str. 1 2463 43 2B

Figure 2-141. Sonderführer (Specialist Leader) Karl Lehmann (no relation – see figures 2-129 and 2-130) of the Propaganda Training and Replacement Detachment travelled from Germany, through Slovakia, Hungary, and Romania to Nikolayev in the Ukraine, just north of the Crimea. Note under Bemerkungen that he was required to travel in uniform. (A4)

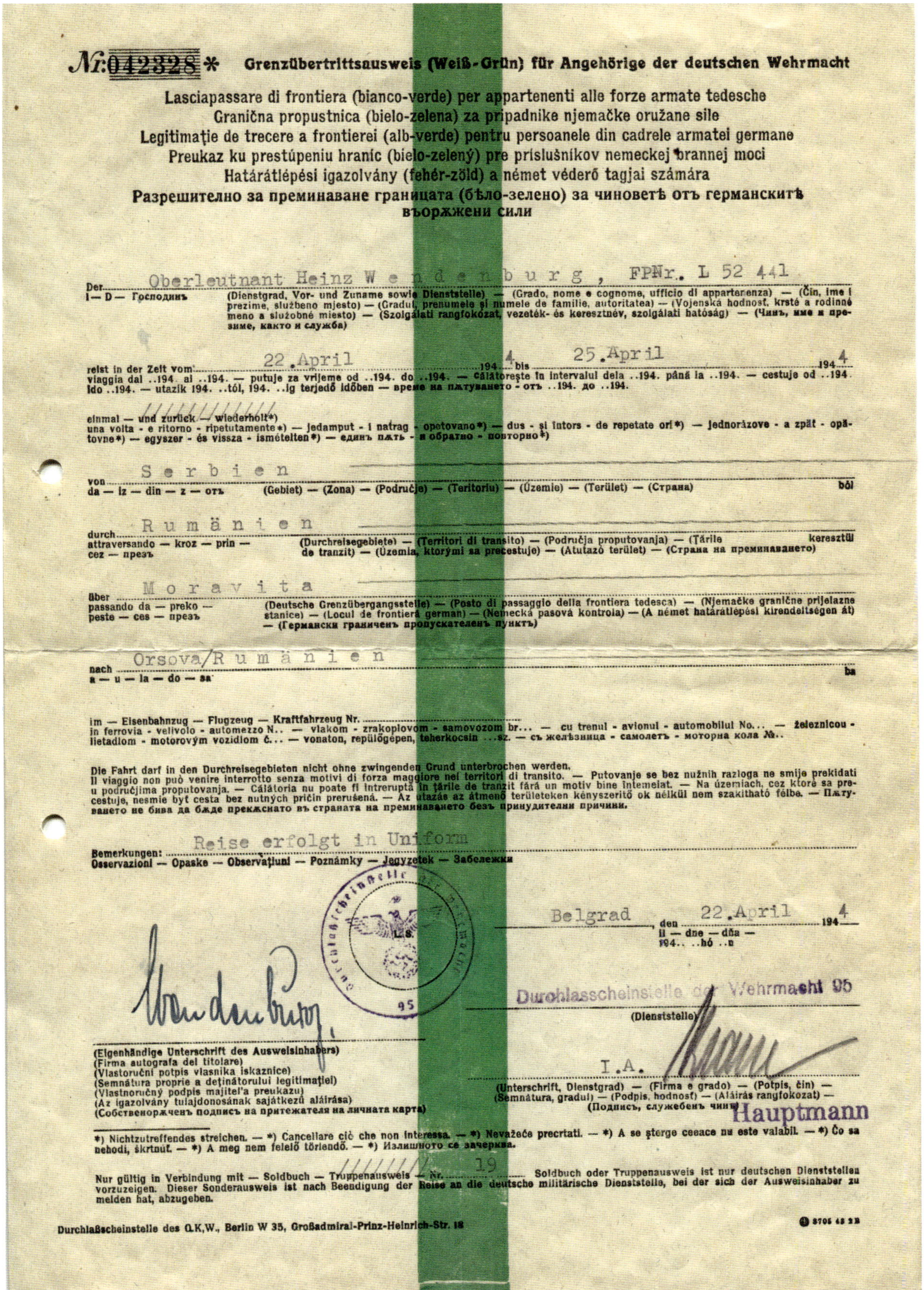

Nr. 042328 * **Grenzübertrittsausweis (Weiß-Grün) für Angehörige der deutschen Wehrmacht**

Lasciapassare di frontiera (bianco-verde) per appartenenti alle forze armate tedesche
Granična propustnica (bielo-zelena) za pripadnike njemačke oružane sile
Legitimaţie de trecere a frontierei (alb-verde) pentru persoanele din cadrele armatei germane
Preukaz ku prestúpeniu hraníc (bielo-zelený) pre príslušníkov nemeckej brannej moci
Határátlépési igazolvány (fehér-zöld) a német véderő tagjai számára
Разрешително за преминаване границата (бѣло-зелено) за чиноветѣ отъ германскитѣ въоржжени сили

Der — I — D — Господинъ: Oberleutnant Heinz Wendenburg, FPNr. L 52 441
(Dienstgrad, Vor- und Zuname sowie Dienststelle) — (Grado, nome e cognome, ufficio di appartenenza) — (Čin, ime i prezime, službeno mjesto) — (Gradul, prenumele şi numele de familie, autoritatea) — (Vojenská hodnosť, krstné a rodinné meno a služobné miesto) — (Szolgálati rangfokozat, vezeték- és keresztnév, szolgálati hatóság) — (Чинъ, име и презиме, както и служба)

reist in der Zeit vom 22. April 1944 bis 25. April 1944
viaggia dal ..194. al ..194. — putuje za vrijeme od ..194. do ..194. — călătoreşte în intervalul dela ..194. până la ..194. — cestuje od ..194. do ..194. — utazik 194. ..tól, 194. ..ig terjedő időben — време на пжтуването - отъ ..194. до ..194.

einmal — und zurück — wiederholt*)
una volta - e ritorno - ripetutamente*) — jedamput - i natrag - opetovano*) — dus - şi întors - de repetate ori*) — jednorázove - a zpät - opätovne*) — egyszer - és vissza - ismételten*) — единъ пжть - и обратно - повторно*)

von — da — iz — din — z — отъ: Serbien — ből
(Gebiet) — (Zona) — (Područje) — (Teritoriu) — (Územie) — (Terület) — (Страна)

durch — attraversando — kroz — prin — cez — презъ: Rumänien — keresztül
(Durchreisegebiete) — (Territori di transito) — (Područja proputovanja) — (Ţările de tranzit) — (Územia, ktorými sa precestuje) — (Atutazó terület) — (Страна на преминаването)

über — passando da — preko — peste — ces — презъ: Moravita
(Deutsche Grenzübergangsstelle) — (Posto di passaggio della frontiera tedesca) — (Njemačke granične prijelazne stanice) — (Locul de frontieră german) — (Nemecká pasová kontrola) — (A német határátlépési kirendeltségen át) — (Германски граниченъ пропускателенъ пунктъ)

nach — a — u — la — do — sa: Orsova/Rumänien — ba

im — Eisenbahnzug — Flugzeug — Kraftfahrzeug Nr. ....
in ferrovia - velivolo - automezzo N.. — vlakom - zrakoplovom - samovozom br... — cu trenul - avionul - automobilul No... — železnicou - lietadlom - motorovým vozidlom č... — vonaton, repülőgépen, teherkocsin ...sz. — съ желѣзница - самолетъ - моторна кола №..

Die Fahrt darf in den Durchreisegebieten nicht ohne zwingenden Grund unterbrochen werden.
Il viaggio non può venire interrotto senza motivi di forza maggiore nei territori di transito. — Putovanje se bez nužnih razloga ne smije prekidati u područjima proputovanja. — Călătoria nu poate fi întreruptă în ţările de tranzit fără un motiv bine întemeiat. — Na územiach, cez ktoré sa precestuje, nesmie byť cesta bez nutných príčin prerušená. — Az utazás az átmenő területeken kényszerítő ok nélkül nem szakitható félbe. — Пжтуването не бива да бжде прекжснато въ страната на преминаването безъ принудителни причини.

Bemerkungen: Reise erfolgt in Uniform
Osservazioni — Opaske — Observaţiuni — Poznámky — Jegyzetek — Забележки

Belgrad, den 22. April 1944
li — dne — dňa — 194.. ..hó ..n

Durchlasscheinstelle der Wehrmacht 95
(Dienststelle)

(Eigenhändige Unterschrift des Ausweisinhabers)
(Firma autografa del titolare)
(Vlastoručni potpis vlasnika iskaznice)
(Semnătura proprie a deţinătorului legitimaţiei)
(Vlastnoručný podpis majiteľa preukazu)
(Az igazolvány tulajdonosának sajátkezű aláírása)
(Собственоржчень подписъ на притежателя на личната карта)

I.A.
(Unterschrift, Dienstgrad) — (Firma e grado) — (Potpis, čin) — (Semnătura, gradul) — (Podpis, hodnosť) — (Aláírás rangfokozat) — (Подписъ, служебенъ чинъ)
Hauptmann

*) Nichtzutreffendes streichen. — *) Cancellare ciò che non interessa. — *) Nevažeće precrtati. — *) A se şterge ceeace nu este valabil. — *) Čo sa nehodi, škrtnúť. — *) A meg nem felelő törlendő. — *) Излишното се зачерква.

Nur gültig in Verbindung mit — Soldbuch — Truppenausweis — Nr. 19 Soldbuch oder Truppenausweis ist nur deutschen Dienststellen vorzuzeigen. Dieser Sonderausweis ist nach Beendigung der Reise an die deutsche militärische Dienststelle, bei der sich der Ausweisinhaber zu melden hat, abzugeben.

Durchlaßscheinstelle des O.K.W., Berlin W 35, Großadmiral-Prinz-Heinrich-Str. 18

8705 43 2B

Figure 2-142. Luftwaffe Oberleutnant (Senior Lieutenant) Heinz Wendenburg of Flak-Regimentsstab 38 (mot.) (Staff of Motorized Flak Regiment 38) transferred from Belgrade to Orsova, Romania, between American airfields in Italy and the Ploesti oil fields. (A4)

As Russian territories diminished, the *Sonderausweis-SO* was replaced in 1943 by a specialized border passage form exclusively for the *Wehrmacht* called the *Grenzübertrittsausweis*. Printed in the same seven languages with an identical green stripe down the middle, this was an abbreviated *Sonderausweis*, one that did not require grounds for travel, and only identified the bearer and his itinerary, along with provided space to include any added conditions.

In the middle of the form was a block of information, one sentence translated six times, that reads *Die Fahrt darf in den Durchreisegebieten nicht ohne zwingenden Grund unterbrochen werden*, namely that this trip should not be interrupted without compelling reason. Wise advice in potentially hostile territories!

By late 1943, all three *Sonderausweis* were superceded by its addition into the combined version of *Wehrmachtfahrschein*, but individual forms continued to be used until the end of the war. Frugal clerks, who had more often than not stockpiled forms, used their stocks before succumbing to the expense of ordering the larger, more inclusive documents. As such, there are almost as many *Sonderausweis* from the beginning of the war as there are at the end.

Marching Orders

A soldier's primary duty, at least in the eyes of his Sergeant, is to do what he's told, and that entails the issuance and following of orders. Travel or marching orders are given and followed easiest when they are presented in writing, leaving little to be misunderstood.

The last of the primary travel forms, the *Marschbefehl* (literally "Marching Order"), was presented upon arrival to a new duty station to verify a soldier's transfer. Like the *Sonderausweis-D* that normally accompanied it, the *Marschbefehl* was valid only for service-related travel, and further explained why a soldier was away from his duty station.

The soldier and destination was identified on the front of the form as usual, but includes an explanation to anyone stopping him: "*(Er) hat Befehl, die Reise ohne Verzug auszuführen.*" This translates to indicate that the soldier listed has orders, and that he should not be detained or delayed in its fulfillment. This served to speed a *Soldat* on his way, especially later in the war, when the search for deserting or shirking soldiers often meant long lines at checkpoints and train stations.

In the center of the page are the grounds for the orders. Normal grounds for this form would be a transfer from one duty station to another, as I mentioned, but it could be for any official purpose including discharge; one of the *Marschbefehl* in this collection is actually an order to go home and await further orders.

The reverse of the form contains rules and conditions for travel, primarily that the form is for service use only, and that it is not valid as a travel pass. The back also directs the bearer to makes trips as swiftly as possible, to be cautious about what one says while traveling, to use only valid medical stations in the event of accident or sickness, and to return the form to authorities when finished. There is also a small section to note the distribution of rations, *Wehrsold*, and other items, similar to what was listed on the back of the *Sonderausweis-D*, which usually accompanied the *Marschausweis*, so items granted are rarely noted here.

Later in the war, again in an attempt to minimize work required to fill out and maintain a stock of multiple forms, the OKW introduced a new form, the *Wehrmacht-Marschausweis*. It was an A6 form, the front side of which contained the same information as the *Marschbefehl*, but combined the *Wehrmacht-Fahrschein* and the *Wehrmacht-Fahrkarte* (*Wehrmacht* Ticket) on the back. One or the other would be used, depending on whether travel was paid for by *Wehrmacht* or not. These forms are difficult at best to find, primarily because so few of them were used. As a result, there are few available to collectors, especially when compared to the availability of the *Marschbefehl*.

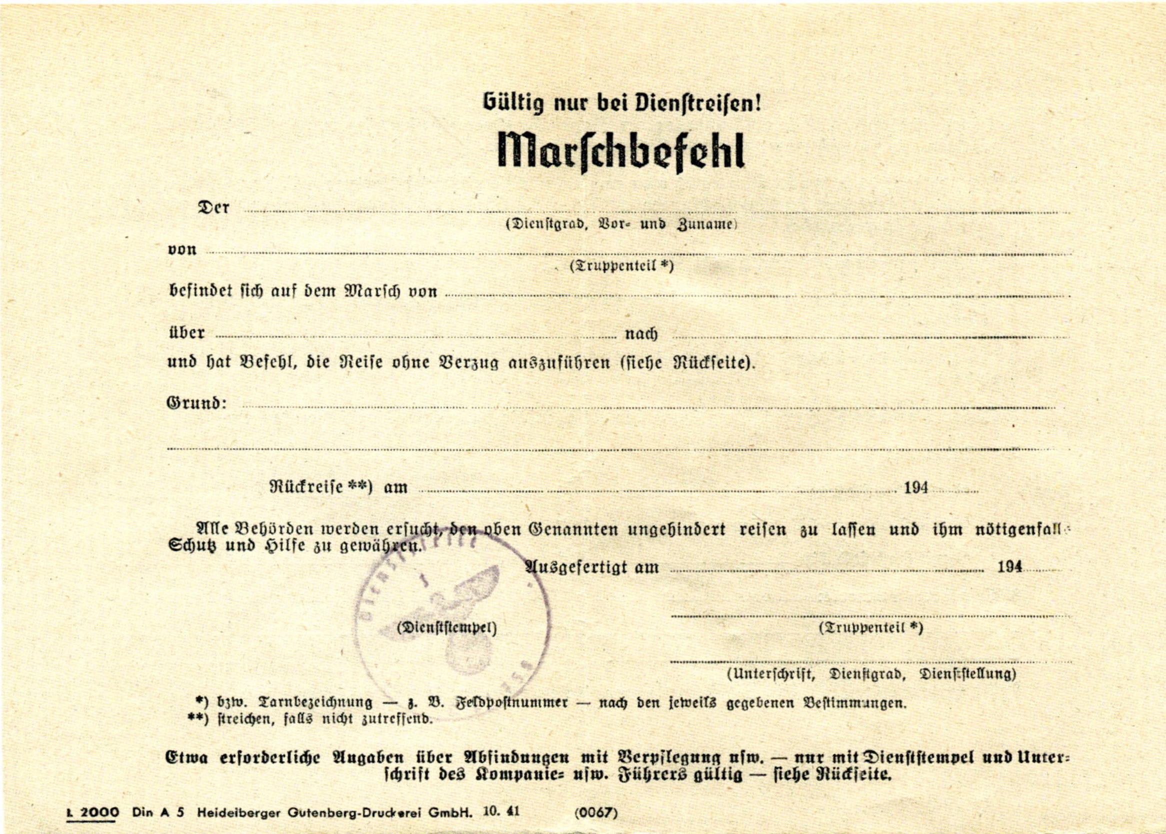

Gültig nur bei Dienstreisen!

Marschbefehl

Der ....
(Dienstgrad, Vor- und Zuname)

von ....
(Truppenteil *)

befindet sich auf dem Marsch von ....

über .... nach ....

und hat Befehl, die Reise ohne Verzug auszuführen (siehe Rückseite).

Grund: ....

Rückreise **) am .... 194......

Alle Behörden werden ersucht, den oben Genannten ungehindert reisen zu lassen und ihm nötigenfalls Schutz und Hilfe zu gewähren.

Ausgefertigt am .... 194......

(Dienststempel)

(Truppenteil *)

(Unterschrift, Dienstgrad, Dienststellung)

*) bzw. Tarnbezeichnung — z. B. Feldpostnummer — nach den jeweils gegebenen Bestimmungen.
**) streichen, falls nicht zutreffend.

Etwa erforderliche Angaben über Abfindungen mit Verpflegung usw. — nur mit Dienststempel und Unterschrift des Kompanie- usw. Führers gültig — siehe Rückseite.

L 2000 Din A 5 Heidelberger Gutenberg-Druckerei GmbH. 10. 41 (0067)

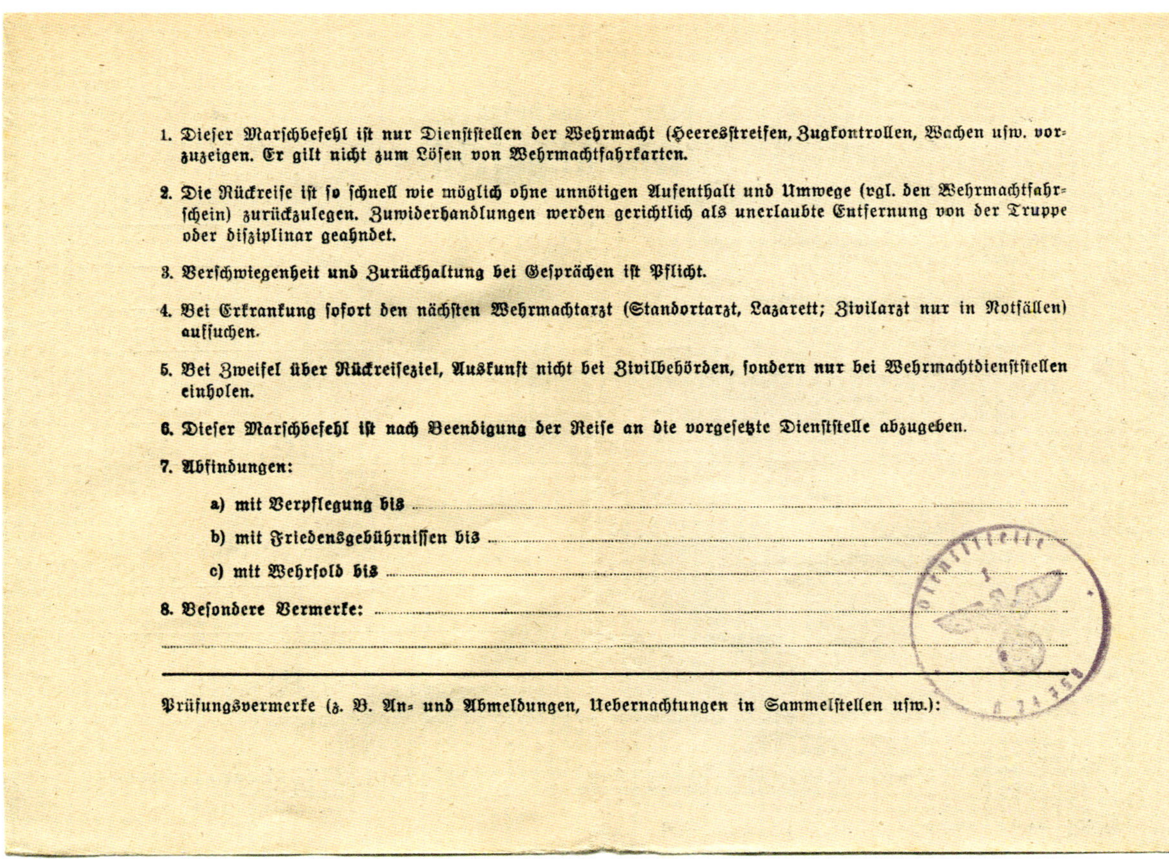

1. Dieser Marschbefehl ist nur Dienststellen der Wehrmacht (Heeresstreifen, Zugkontrollen, Wachen usw. vorzuzeigen. Er gilt nicht zum Lösen von Wehrmachtfahrkarten.
2. Die Rückreise ist so schnell wie möglich ohne unnötigen Aufenthalt und Umwege (vgl. den Wehrmachtfahrschein) zurückzulegen. Zuwiderhandlungen werden gerichtlich als unerlaubte Entfernung von der Truppe oder disziplinar geahndet.
3. Verschwiegenheit und Zurückhaltung bei Gesprächen ist Pflicht.
4. Bei Erkrankung sofort den nächsten Wehrmachtarzt (Standortarzt, Lazarett; Zivilarzt nur in Notfällen) aufsuchen.
5. Bei Zweifel über Rückreiseziel, Auskunft nicht bei Zivilbehörden, sondern nur bei Wehrmachtdienststellen einholen.
6. Dieser Marschbefehl ist nach Beendigung der Reise an die vorgesetzte Dienststelle abzugeben.
7. Abfindungen:
   a) mit Verpflegung bis ....
   b) mit Friedensgebührnissen bis ....
   c) mit Wehrsold bis ....
8. Besondere Vermerke: ....

Prüfungsvermerke (z. B. An- und Abmeldungen, Uebernachtungen in Sammelstellen usw.):

Figure 2-143. A Marschbefehl (Marching Orders) nearly always accompanied the Sonderausweis D to prove that the Soldat bearing the two documents was indeed away from his unit for legitimate reasons.(A5)

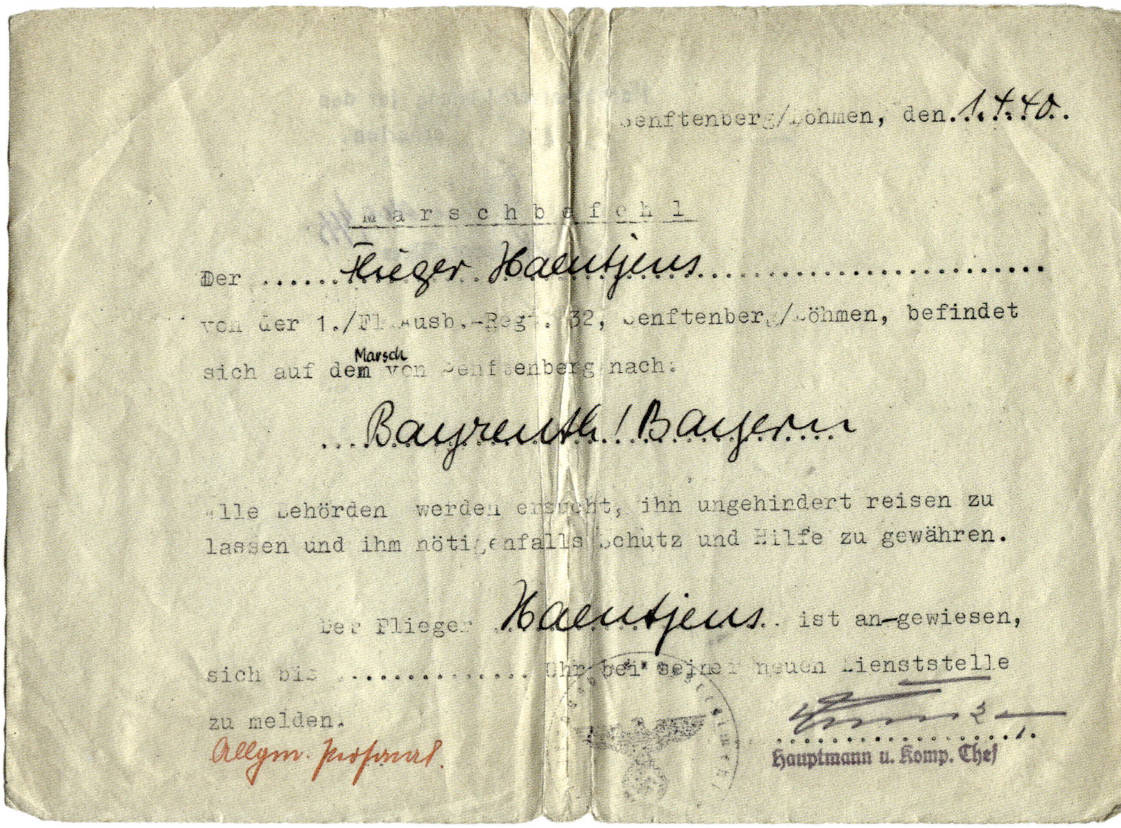

Senftenberg/Böhmen, den. 1.4.40.

Marschbefehl

Der ......Flieger Haeutjens..........................

von der 1./Fl.Ausb.-Regt. 32, Senftenberg/Böhmen, befindet sich auf dem Marsch von Senftenberg nach:

...Bayreuth/Bayern...

Alle Behörden werden ersucht, ihn ungehindert reisen zu lassen und ihm nötigenfalls Schutz und Hilfe zu gewähren.

Der Flieger Haeutjens ist an-gewiesen, sich bis .... Uhr bei seiner neuen Dienststelle zu melden.

Allgm. [illegible]

Hauptmann u. Komp. Chef

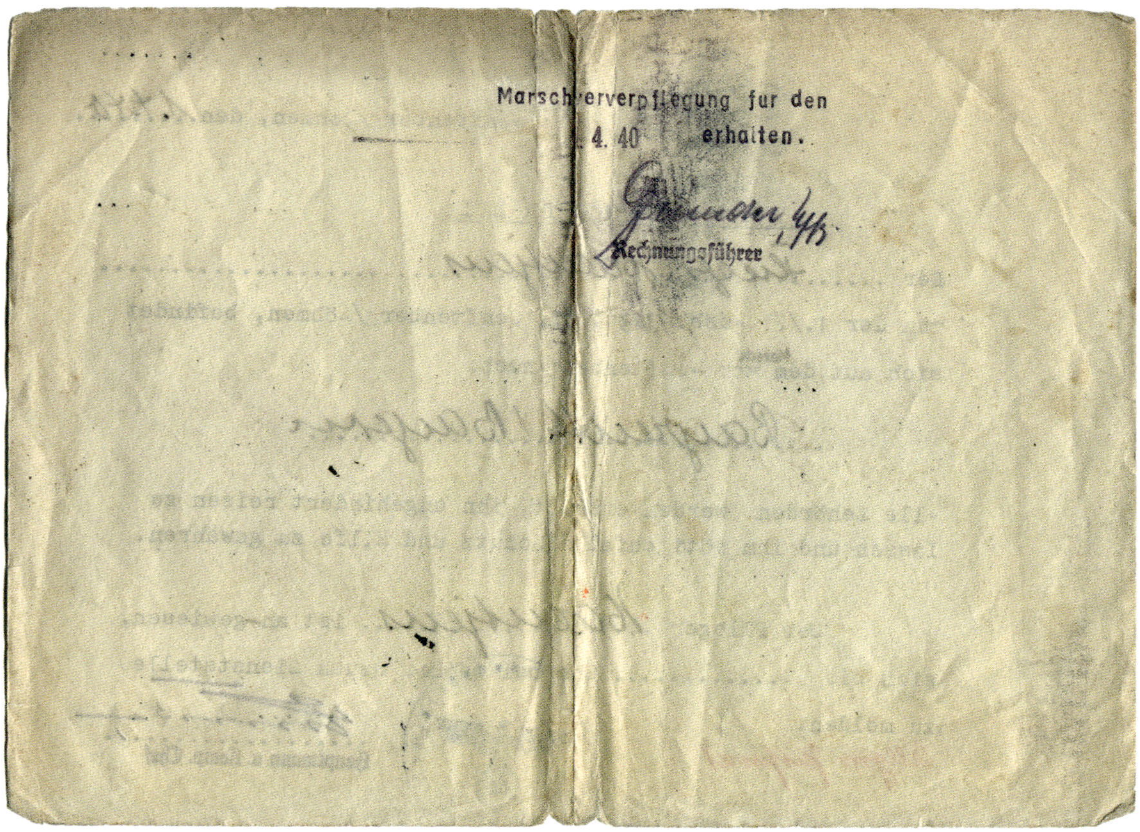

Marschverpflegung für den

4. 40 erhalten.

Rechnungsführer

Figure 2-144. A mimeographed Ersatzmarschbefehl, or Replacement Marching Order, for Airman Häutjens to proceed from Flieger Ausbildungs-Regiment 32 (Flight Training Regiment 32) in Senftenberg, Bohemia to Bayreuth in Bavaria. (5 7/8" x 8 1/8")

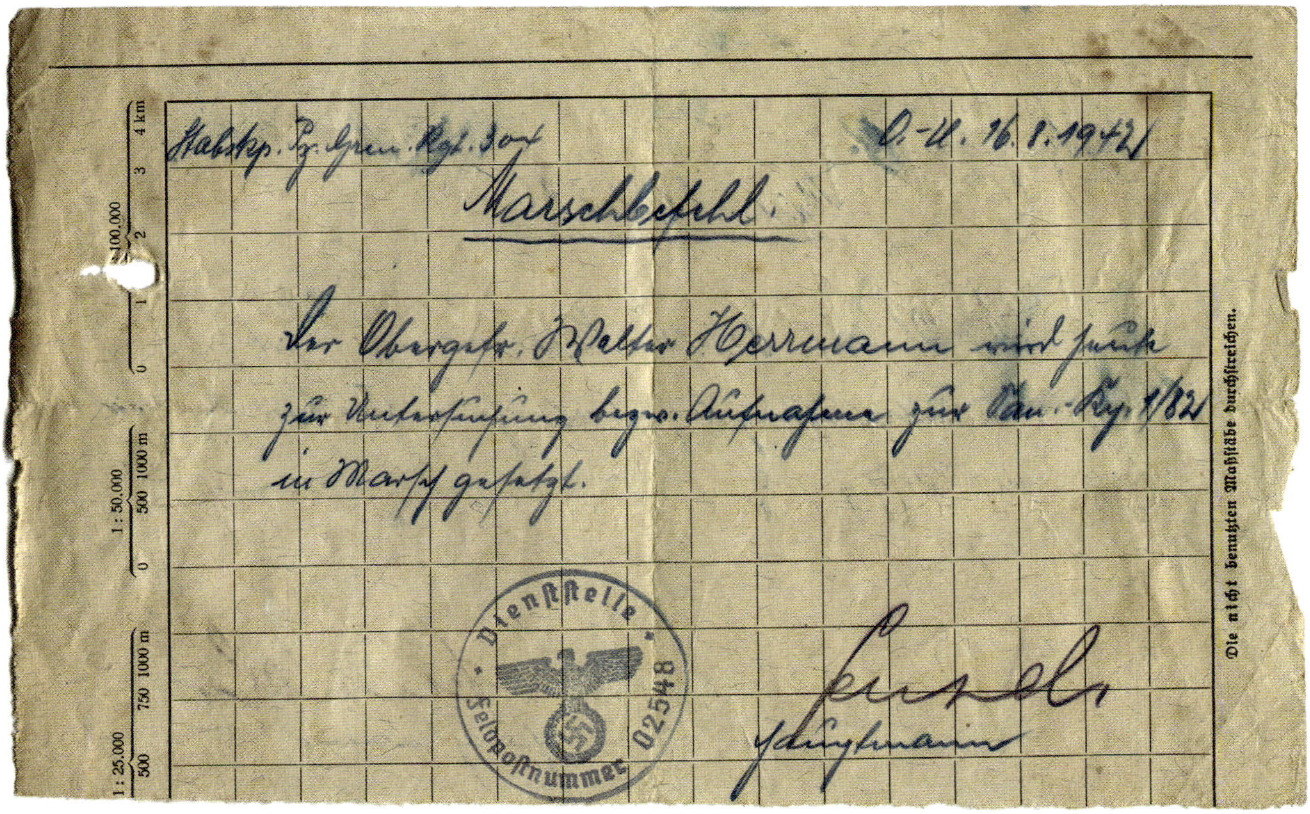
Stabskp. Pz. Gren. Rgt. 304 O.-U. 16.1.1942

Marschbefehl.

Der Obergefr. Walter Herrmann wird heute zur Untersuchung bezw. Aufnahme zur San.-Kp. 1/821 in Marsch gesetzt.

Dienststelle Feldpostnummer 02548

Hauptmann

Die nicht benutzten Maßstäbe durchstreichen.

1 : 100,000 1 : 50,000 1 : 25,000

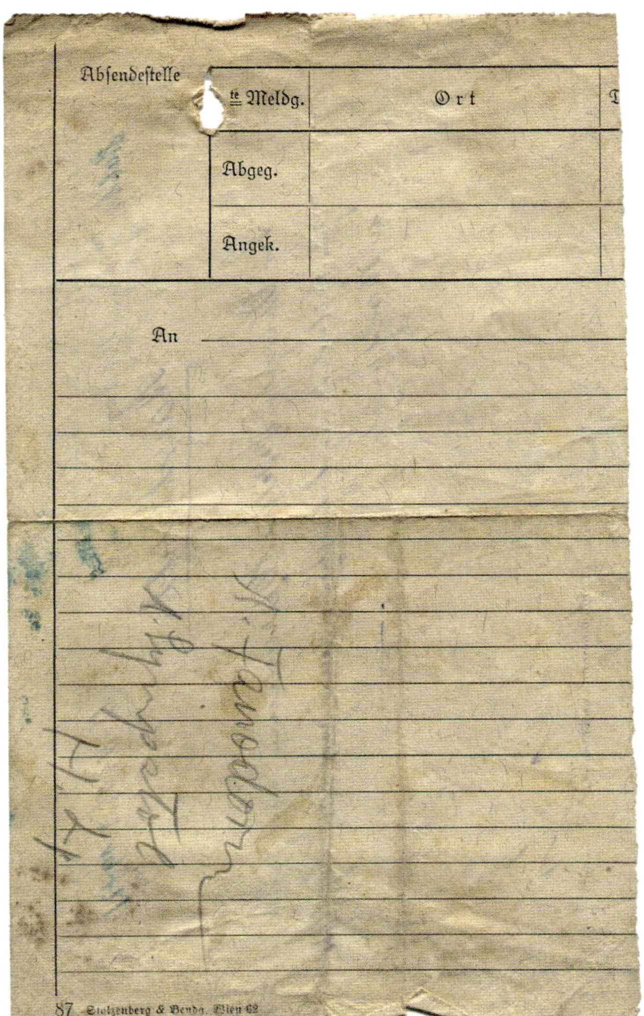
Absendestelle

Nr. d. Meldg. | Ort

Abgeg.

Angek.

An

87 Stolzenberg & Bendy, Wien 62

Figure 2-145. Once again, when the proper forms are unavailable, never doubt the resourcefulness of a Soldat. This Marschbefehl was almost certainly issued in the field (the paper is a torn Skizzeseite from a Meldeblock – a page from a message notebook) to Obergefreiter Walter Herrmann of Panzergrenadier-Regiment 304. (4 5/8" x 7 1/2")

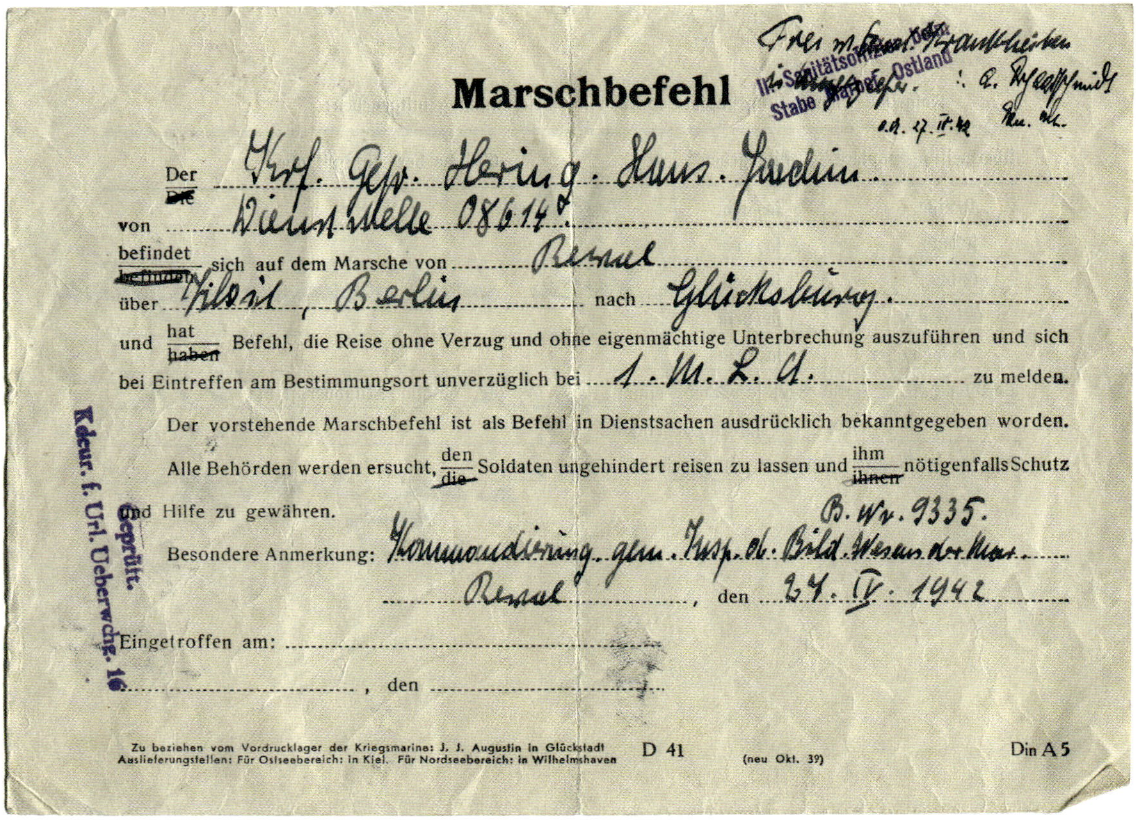

Marschbefehl

Der ~~Die~~ Krf. Gefr. Hering. Hans. Joachim

von Dienststelle 08614

befindet ~~befinden~~ sich auf dem Marsche von Reval

über Tilsit, Berlin nach Glücksburg.

und hat ~~haben~~ Befehl, die Reise ohne Verzug und ohne eigenmächtige Unterbrechung auszuführen und sich bei Eintreffen am Bestimmungsort unverzüglich bei 1. M. L. A. zu melden.

Der vorstehende Marschbefehl ist als Befehl in Dienstsachen ausdrücklich bekanntgegeben worden.

Alle Behörden werden ersucht, den ~~die~~ Soldaten ungehindert reisen zu lassen und ihm ~~ihnen~~ nötigenfalls Schutz und Hilfe zu gewähren.

B. Nr. 9335.

Besondere Anmerkung: Kommandierung gem. Insp. d. Bild. Wesens d. Mar.

Reval, den 24. IV. 1942

Eingetroffen am:

, den

Geprüft. Kdeur. f. Url. Ueberwchg. 16

Stabe ... Ostland

Zu beziehen vom Vordrucklager der Kriegsmarine: J. J. Augustin in Glückstadt
Auslieferungsstellen: Für Ostseebereich: in Kiel. Für Nordseebereich: in Wilhelmshaven

D 41 (neu Okt. 39) Din A 5

Figure 2-146. This Marschbefehl was printed for the Kriegsmarine (Navy), which is one reason why the reverse appears so radically different from other versions. Krf (Kraftfahrer? Driver) Gefreiter Hans Hering of Marine-Artillerie-Abteilung 531 (Naval Artillery Section 531) was ordered from Revel, France to Glücksburg, north of Kiel on the Danish border as part of an inspection detail. (A5)

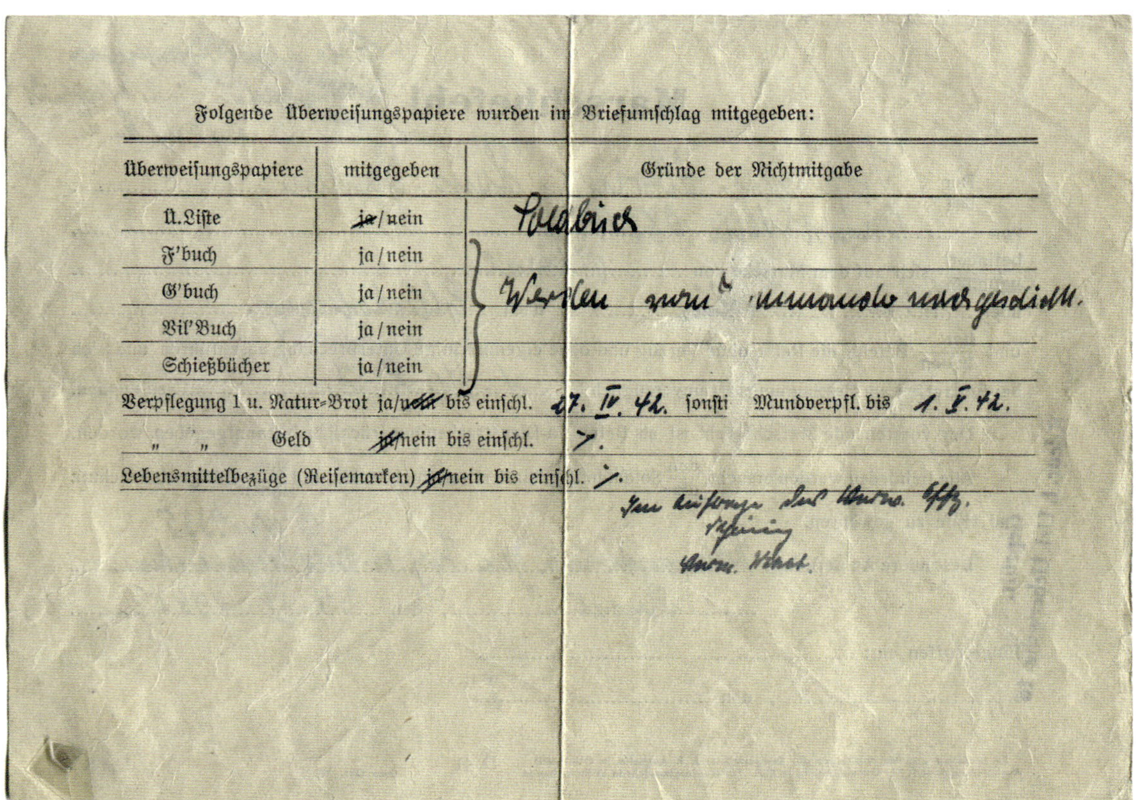

Folgende Überweisungspapiere wurden im Briefumschlag mitgegeben:

Überweisungspapiere	mitgegeben	Gründe der Nichtmitgabe
U. Liste	~~ja~~/nein	
F'buch	ja/nein	
G'buch	ja/nein	
Bil'Buch	ja/nein	
Schießbücher	ja/nein	

Verpflegung 1 u. Natur-Brot ja/~~nein~~ bis einschl. 27. IV. 42. sonst Mundverpfl. bis 1. V. 42.

„ „ Geld ~~ja~~/nein bis einschl. ./.

Lebensmittelbezüge (Reisemarken) ~~ja~~/nein bis einschl. ./.

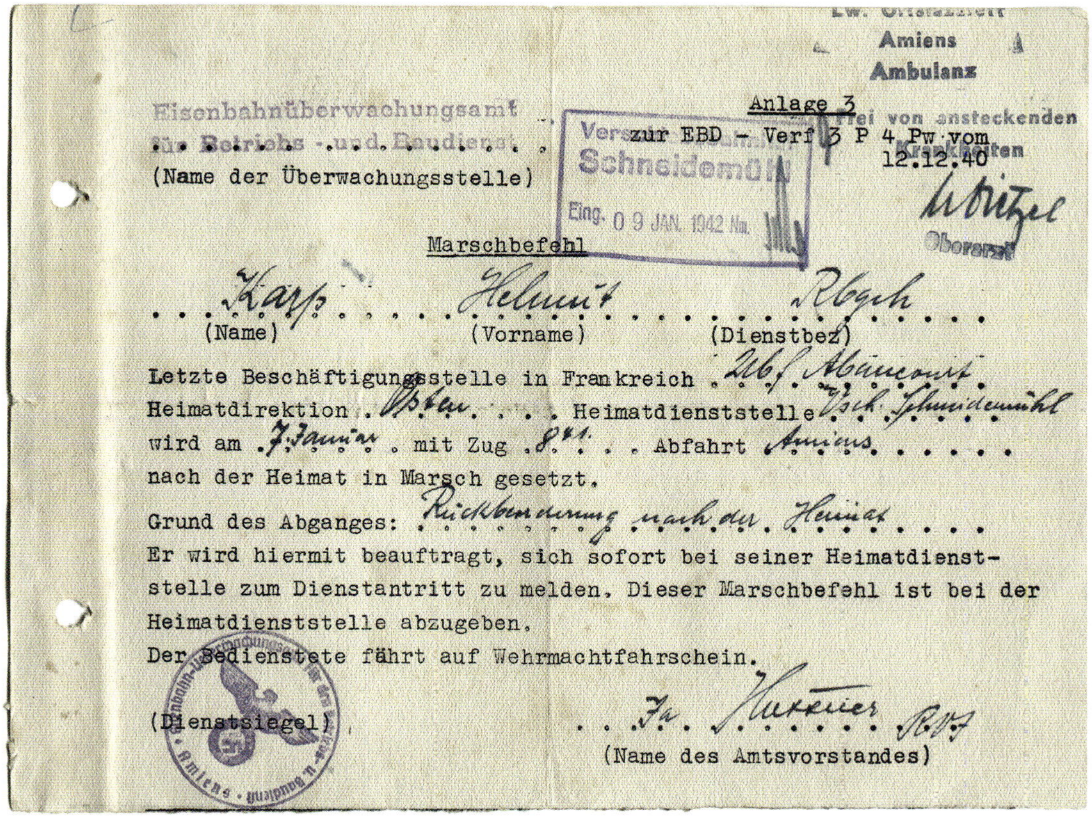

Eisenbahnüberwachungsamt für Betriebs- und Baudienst
(Name der Überwachungsstelle)

Anlage 3 zur EBD - Verf 3 P 4 Pw vom 12.12.40

Lw. [illegible] Amiens Ambulanz [illegible] frei von ansteckenden Krankheiten
Oberarzt

Verschiebebahnhof Schneidemühl
Eing. 09 JAN. 1942 Nr.

Marschbefehl

Karp (Name) Helmut (Vorname) Rbgeh (Dienstbez)

Letzte Beschäftigungsstelle in Frankreich Ubf. Abancourt
Heimatdirektion Osten . . . Heimatdienststelle Vsch. Schneidemühl
wird am 7. Januar mit Zug 8[illegible] Abfahrt Amiens
nach der Heimat in Marsch gesetzt.
Grund des Abganges: Rückbeorderung nach der Heimat
Er wird hiermit beauftragt, sich sofort bei seiner Heimatdienststelle zum Dienstantritt zu melden. Dieser Marschbefehl ist bei der Heimatdienststelle abzugeben.
Der Bedienstete fährt auf Wehrmachtfahrschein.

(Dienstsiegel) Amiens

I.A. [illegible]
(Name des Amtsvorstandes)

Figure 2-147. His tour of duty in France completed, this Ersatzmarschbefehl directed Helmut Karp of the Reichsbahn from his station in Amiens to Karp's home in Schneidumühl in January of 1942. (6 1/8" x 8 1/4")

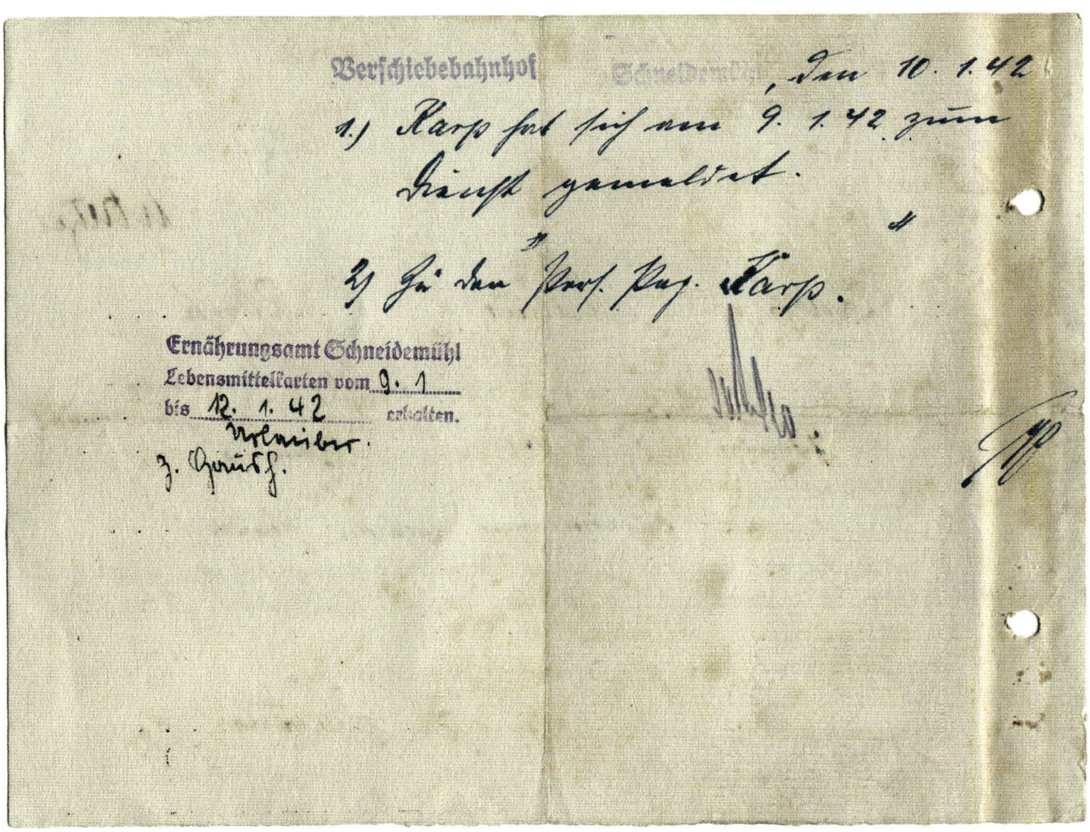

Verschiebebahnhof Schneidemühl, den 10.1.42

1.) Karp hat sich am 9.1.42 zum Dienst gemeldet.

2.) Zu den Pers. Akt. Karp.

Ernährungsamt Schneidemühl
Lebensmittelkarten vom 9.1
bis 12.1.42 erhalten.

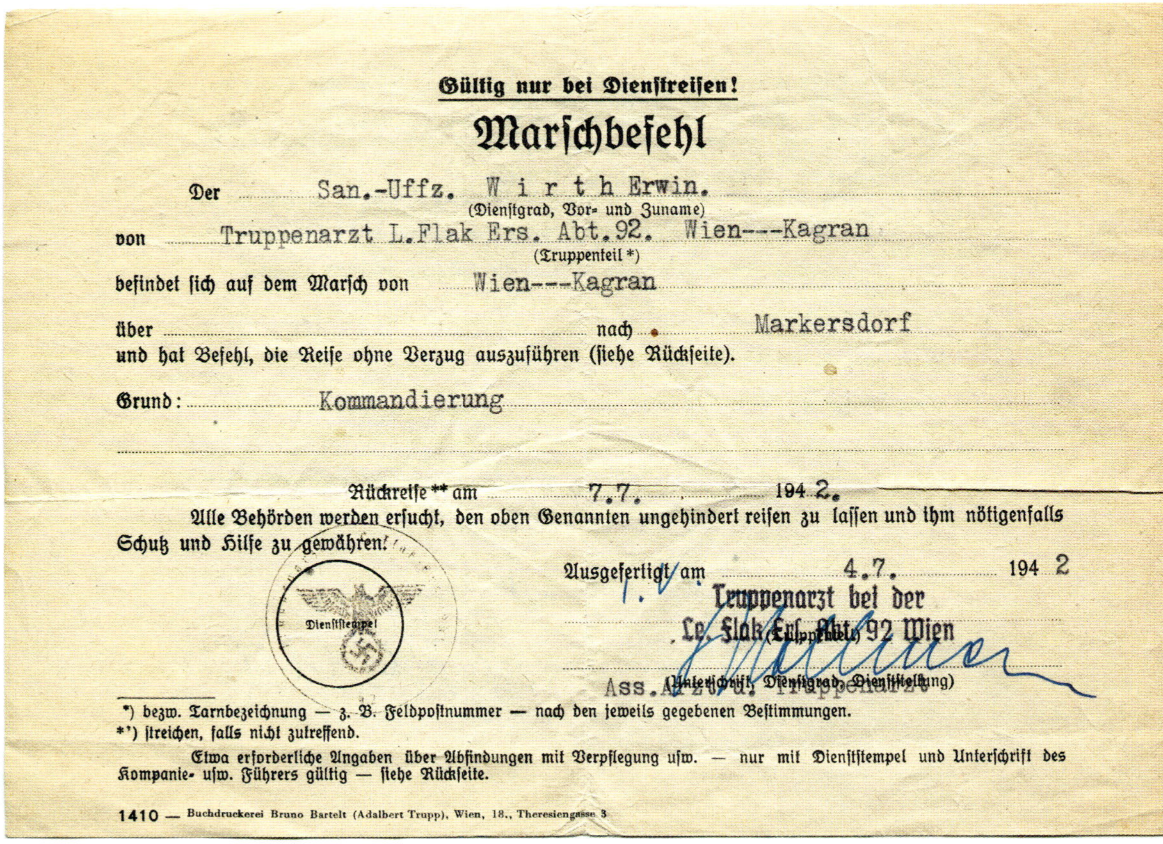

Gültig nur bei Dienstreisen!

Marschbefehl

Der San.-Uffz. W i r t h Erwin.
(Dienstgrad, Vor- und Zuname)

von Truppenarzt L.Flak Ers. Abt.92. Wien---Kagran
(Truppenteil *)

befindet sich auf dem Marsch von Wien---Kagran

über .... nach Markersdorf

und hat Befehl, die Reise ohne Verzug auszuführen (siehe Rückseite).

Grund: Kommandierung

Rückreise ** am 7.7. 194 2.

Alle Behörden werden ersucht, den oben Genannten ungehindert reisen zu lassen und ihm nötigenfalls Schutz und Hilfe zu gewähren!

Dienststempel

Ausgefertigt am 4.7. 194 2

I.V. Truppenarzt bei der Le. Flak Ers. Abt. 92 Wien
(Truppenteil)

Ass.Arzt u. Truppenarzt
(Unterschrift, Dienstgrad, Dienststellung)

*) bezw. Tarnbezeichnung — z. B. Feldpostnummer — nach den jeweils gegebenen Bestimmungen.
**) streichen, falls nicht zutreffend.

Etwa erforderliche Angaben über Abfindungen mit Verpflegung usw. — nur mit Dienststempel und Unterschrift des Kompanie- usw. Führers gültig — siehe Rückseite.

1410 — Buchdruckerei Bruno Bartelt (Adalbert Trupp), Wien, 18., Theresiengasse 3

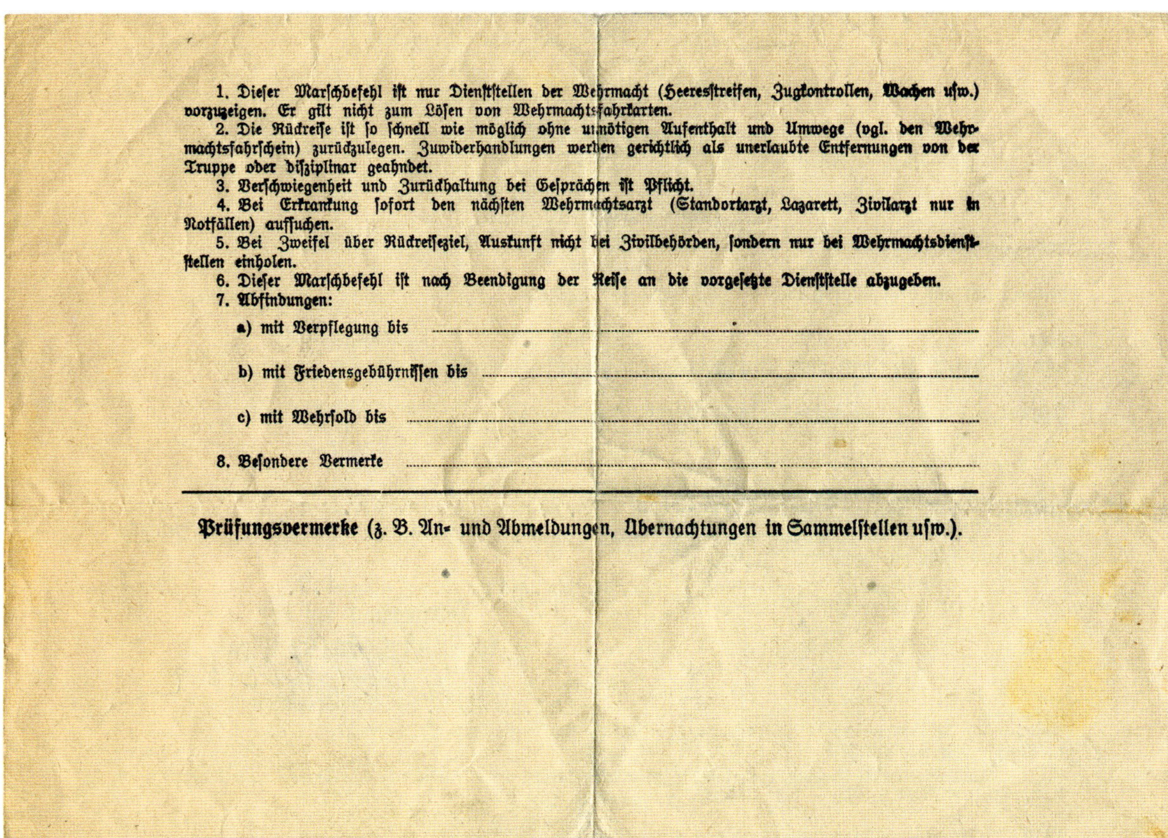

1. Dieser Marschbefehl ist nur Dienststellen der Wehrmacht (Heeresstreifen, Zugkontrollen, Wachen usw.) vorzuzeigen. Er gilt nicht zum Lösen von Wehrmachtsfahrkarten.
2. Die Rückreise ist so schnell wie möglich ohne unnötigen Aufenthalt und Umwege (vgl. den Wehrmachtsfahrschein) zurückzulegen. Zuwiderhandlungen werden gerichtlich als unerlaubte Entfernungen von der Truppe oder disziplinar geahndet.
3. Verschwiegenheit und Zurückhaltung bei Gesprächen ist Pflicht.
4. Bei Erkrankung sofort den nächsten Wehrmachtsarzt (Standortarzt, Lazarett, Zivilarzt nur in Notfällen) aufsuchen.
5. Bei Zweifel über Rückreiseziel, Auskunft nicht bei Zivilbehörden, sondern nur bei Wehrmachtsdienststellen einholen.
6. Dieser Marschbefehl ist nach Beendigung der Reise an die vorgesetzte Dienststelle abzugeben.
7. Abfindungen:
   a) mit Verpflegung bis ....
   b) mit Friedensgebührnissen bis ....
   c) mit Wehrsold bis ....
8. Besondere Vermerke ....

Prüfungsvermerke (z. B. An- und Abmeldungen, Übernachtungen in Sammelstellen usw.).

Figure 2-148. Sanitäts-Unteroffizier (Medical Corporal) Erwin Wirth serving with the Truppenarzt or Unit Doctor of Leichte Flak Ersatz Abteilung 92 (Light Anti-Aircraft Replacement Section 92) in Vienna, Austria to Markersdorf. The only reason given was that he had been commanded to (Kommandierung). (A5)

Figures 2-149 & 2-150. It's possible that one of these Viennese towers might have been Sanitäts-Unteroffizier Wirth's duty station; the Augarten Flaktürmer are the closest Flak Towers to Kagran, the suburb of Vienna from which he was directed. These photographs of the structures are deceptive; the massive constructs are each twelve to fourteen stories in height.

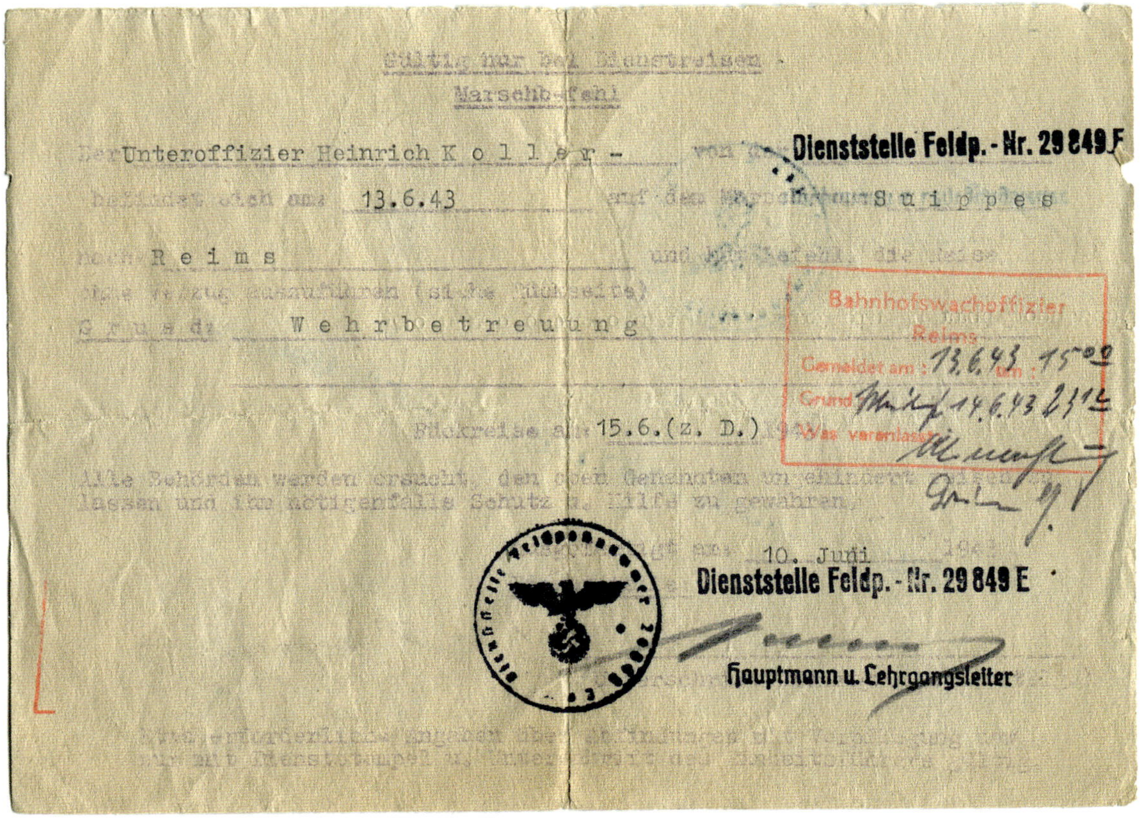

Gültig nur bei Dienstreisen

Marschbefehl

Der Unteroffizier Heinrich K o l l e r - von Dienststelle Feldp.-Nr. 29 849 E

befindet sich am: 13.6.43 auf dem Marsch von S u i p p e s

nach R e i m s und hat Befehl, die Reise ohne Verzug auszuführen (siehe Rückseite)

Grund: W e h r b e t r e u u n g

Rückreise am 15.6.(z. D.) 1943

Alle Behörden werden ersucht, den oben Genannten ungehindert reisen zu lassen und ihm nötigenfalls Schutz u. Hilfe zu gewähren.

den 10. Juni 1943

Dienststelle Feldp.-Nr. 29 849 E

Hauptmann u. Lehrgangsleiter

Bahnhofswachoffizier Reims

Gemeldet am: 13.6.43 um: 15⁰⁰

Grund:

Was veranlasst:

Figure 2-151. An Ersatzmarschbefehl directing Unteroffizier (Corporal) Heinrich Koller of the Lehrstab, Artillerie-Schule III (Instructional Staff, Artillery School III) from Suippes, France to Reims to care for the weaponry there (Wehrbetreuung) on June 13, 1943; a year later, doing so would be decidedly more dangerous. (A5)

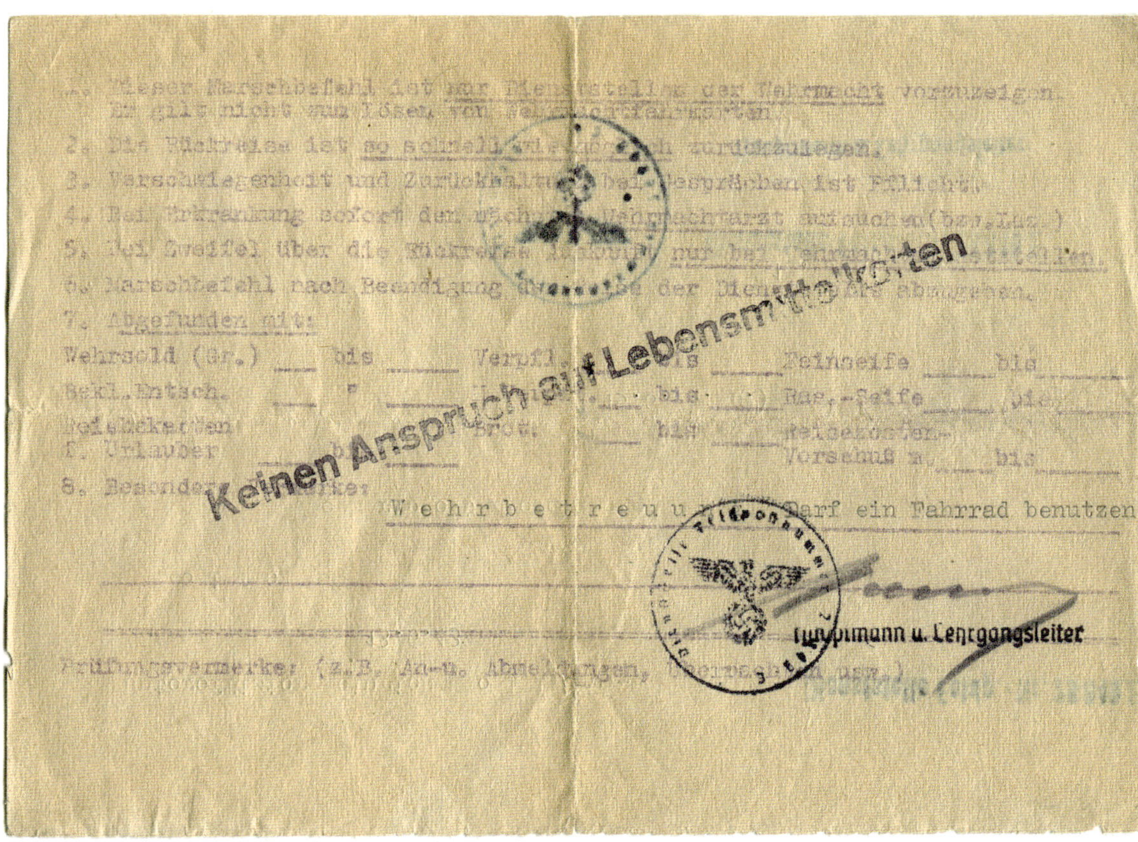

1. Dieser Marschbefehl ist nur Dienststellen der Wehrmacht vorzuzeigen. Er gilt nicht zum Lösen von Wehrmachtfahrkarten.
2. Die Rückreise ist so schnell wie möglich zurückzulegen.
3. Verschwiegenheit und Zurückhaltung bei Gesprächen ist Pflicht.
4. Bei Erkrankung sofort den nächsten Wehrmachtarzt aufsuchen (bzw. Lkz.)
5. Bei Zweifel über die Rückreise Auskunft nur bei Wehrmachtdienststellen einholen.
6. Marschbefehl nach Beendigung der Reise der Dienststelle abzugeben.
7. Abgefunden mit:

Wehrsold (Gr.) bis Verpfl. bis Feinseife bis

Bekl.Entsch. bis Ras.-Seife bis

Reisemarken f. Urlauber bis Brot bis Reisekosten-Vorschuß bis

8. Besondere Vermerke: W e h r b e t r e u u n g Darf ein Fahrrad benutzen

Keinen Anspruch auf Lebensmittelkarten

Hauptmann u. Lehrgangsleiter

Prüfungsvermerke: (z.B. An-u. Abmeldungen, Übernachtung usw.)

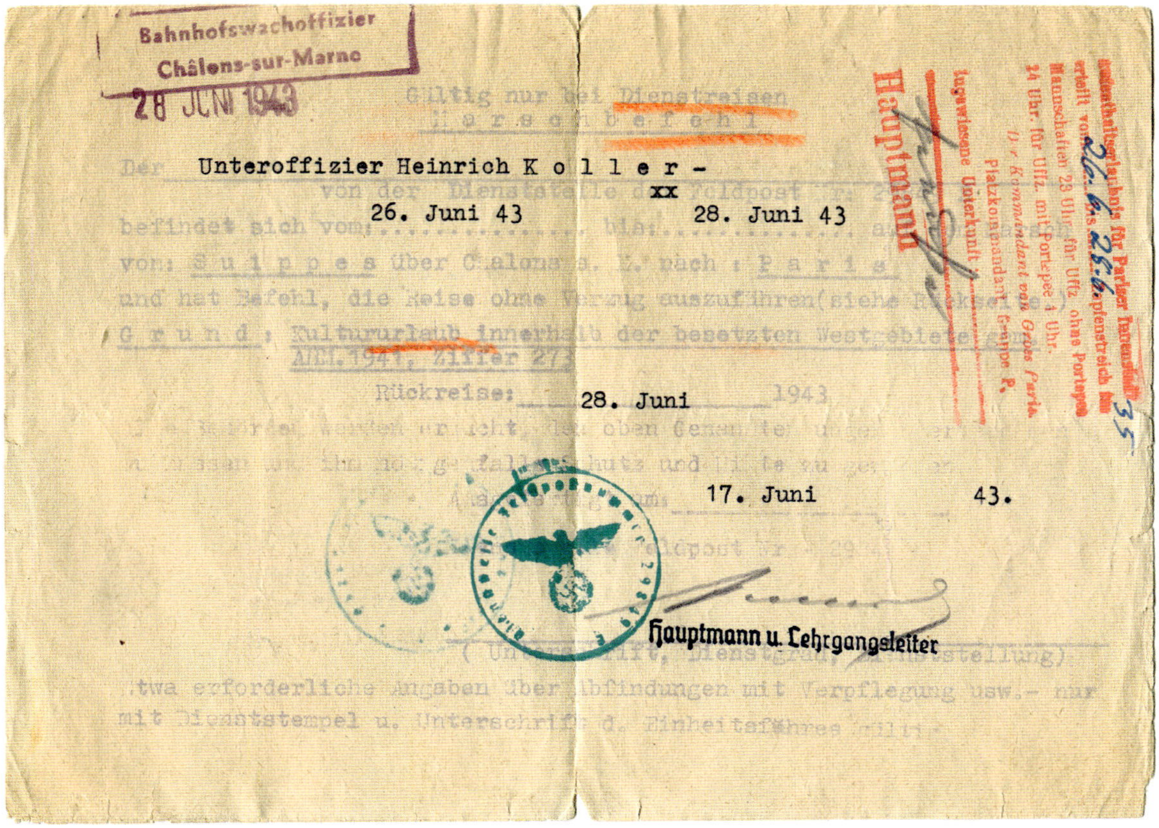
Bahnhofswachoffizier
Châlons-sur-Marne
28 JUNI 1943
Gültig nur bei Dienstreisen
Marschbefehl
Der Unteroffizier Heinrich K o l l e r -
von der Dienststelle d. Feldpost Nr. 2
befindet sich vom: 26. Juni 43 bis: 28. Juni 43
von: Suippes über Chalons s. M. nach: Paris
und hat Befehl, die Reise ohne Verzug auszuführen (siehe Rückseite.)
Grund: Kultururlaub innerhalb der besetzten Westgebiete gem. AVBl.1941, Ziffer 273
Rückreise: 28. Juni 1943
Alle Dienststellen werden ersucht, den oben Genannten ungehindert reisen zu lassen und ihm nötigenfalls Schutz und Hilfe zu gewähren.
17. Juni 43.
Feldpost Nr. 29
Hauptmann u. Lehrgangsleiter
(Unterschrift, Dienstgrad, Dienststellung)
Etwa erforderliche Angaben über Abfindungen mit Verpflegung usw. nur mit Dienststempel u. Unterschrift d. Einheitsführers gültig.
erteilt vom 26.6. bis 28.6.
Mannschaften 23 Uhr für Uffz. ohne Portepee
24 Uhr für Uffz. mit Portepee 1 Uhr.
Der Kommandant von Gross Paris
Platzkommandant Gruppe P.
Zugewiesene Unterkunft
Hauptmann
35

Figure 2-152. Another Ersatzmarschbefehl for Unteroffizier Koller, this time directing him from Suippes to Paris for Kultururlaub, or Cultural Leave. Note that the backs of both of these are marked on "Keinen Anspruch auf Lebensmittelkarten," meaning that Koller was not eligible for ration cards. (A5)

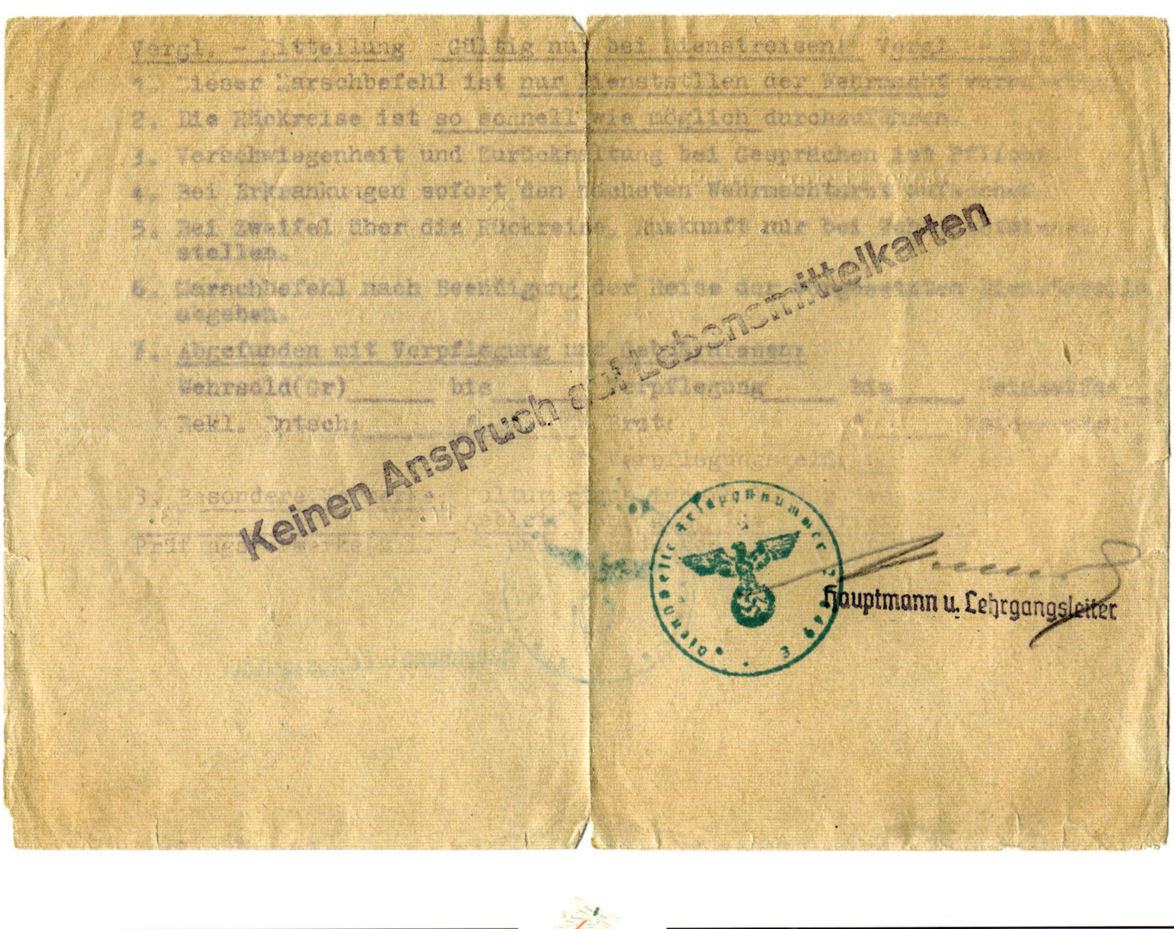
Vergl. - Mitteilung Gültig nur bei Dienstreisen!
1. Dieser Marschbefehl ist nur Dienststellen der Wehrmacht vorzuzeigen.
2. Die Rückreise ist so schnell wie möglich durchzuführen.
3. Verschwiegenheit und Zurückhaltung bei Gesprächen ist Pflicht.
4. Bei Erkrankungen sofort den nächsten Wehrmachtarzt aufsuchen.
5. Bei Zweifel über die Rückreise, Auskunft nur bei Wehrmachtdienststellen.
6. Marschbefehl nach Beendigung der Reise der ausstellenden Dienststelle abgeben.
7. Abgefunden mit Verpflegung und Gebührnissen:
Wehrsold(Gr) ___ bis ___ Verpflegung ___ bis ___
Keinen Anspruch auf Lebensmittelkarten
Hauptmann u. Lehrgangsleiter

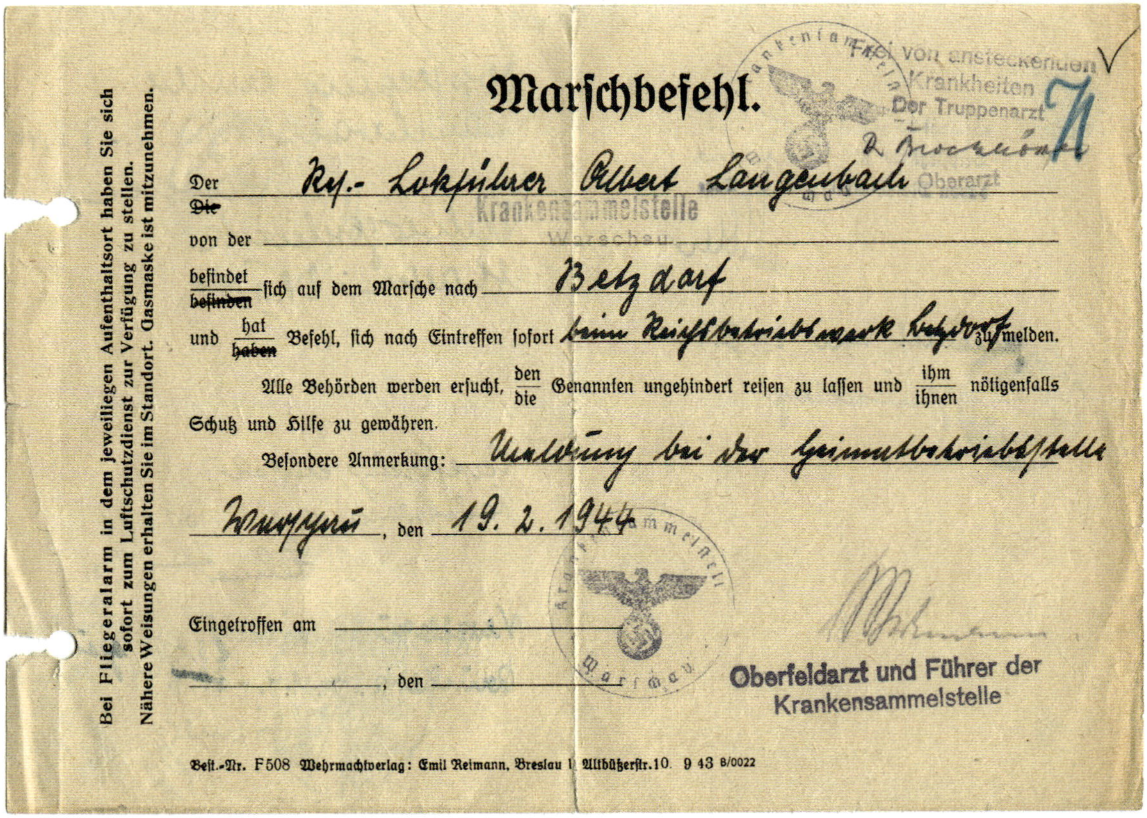

Figure 2-153. February 2, 1944 found Reserve Lokomtiveführer (Reserve Engineer) Albert Langenbach travelling from the Krankensammelstelle Warschau to Belzdorf, Germany. This Marschbefehl gives the reason for his transfer as an assignment to the Heimatbetriebsstelle (Home Place of Business). (A5)

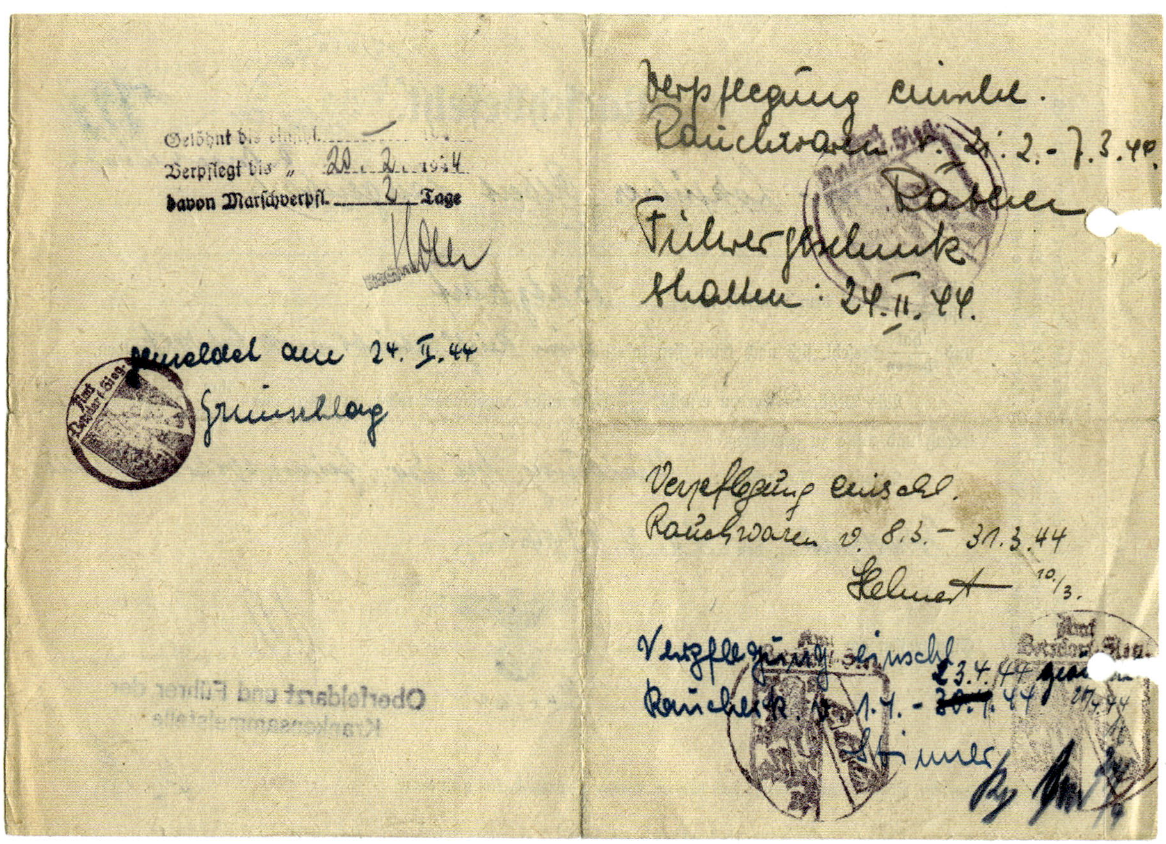

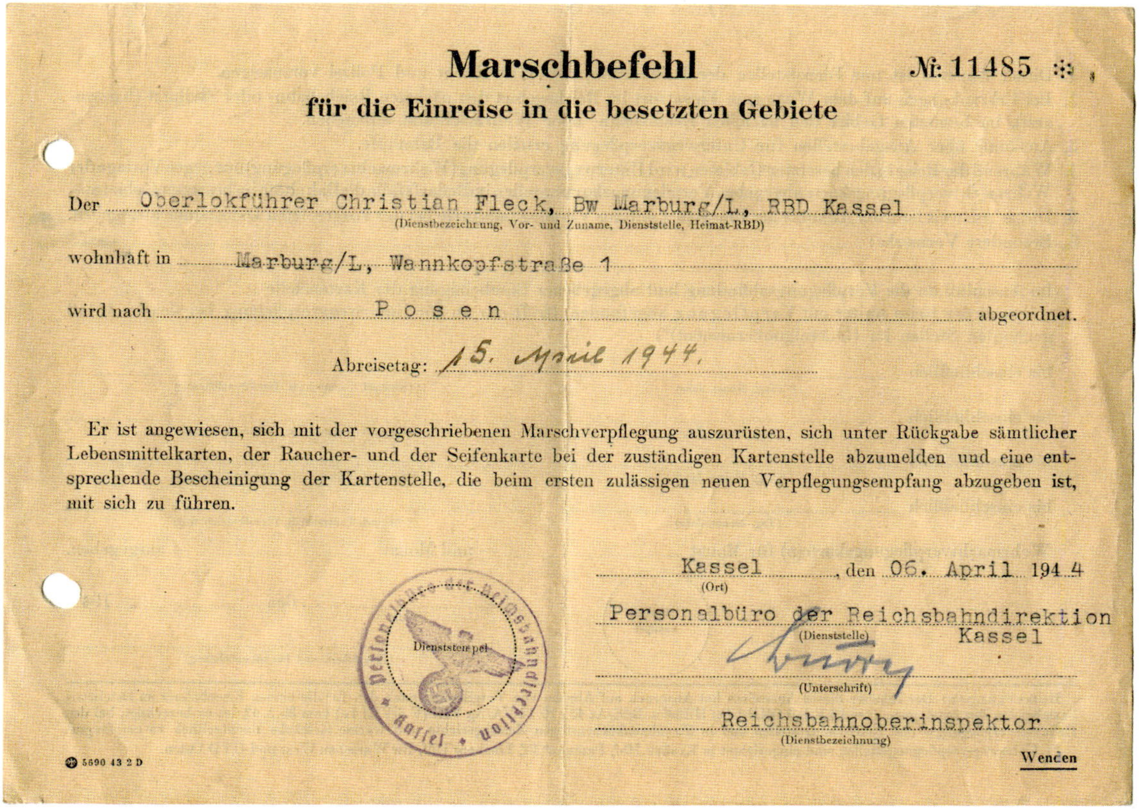

Marschbefehl №: 11485

für die Einreise in die besetzten Gebiete

Der Oberlokführer Christian Fleck, Bw Marburg/L, RBD Kassel
(Dienstbezeichnung, Vor- und Zuname, Dienststelle, Heimat-RBD)

wohnhaft in Marburg/L, Wannkopfstraße 1

wird nach Posen abgeordnet.

Abreisetag: 15. April 1944.

Er ist angewiesen, sich mit der vorgeschriebenen Marschverpflegung auszurüsten, sich unter Rückgabe sämtlicher Lebensmittelkarten, der Raucher- und der Seifenkarte bei der zuständigen Kartenstelle abzumelden und eine entsprechende Bescheinigung der Kartenstelle, die beim ersten zulässigen neuen Verpflegungsempfang abzugeben ist, mit sich zu führen.

Kassel, den 06. April 1944
(Ort)

Personalbüro der Reichsbahndirektion Kassel
(Dienststelle)

(Unterschrift)

Reichsbahnoberinspektor
(Dienstbezeichnung)

Dienststempel

5590 43 2 D

Wencen

Figure 2-154. This Marschbefehl from the Personalbüro der Reichbahndirektion Kassel (Personnel Bureau of Railroad Directorate Kassel) transferred Oberlokomotivführer Christian Fleck east to Posen (now Poznan, Poland) in April, 1944, the exact opposite direction everyone else seemed to be going. The top of the form states that this particular Marschbefehl is to be used "for entry into the occupied territories." (A5)

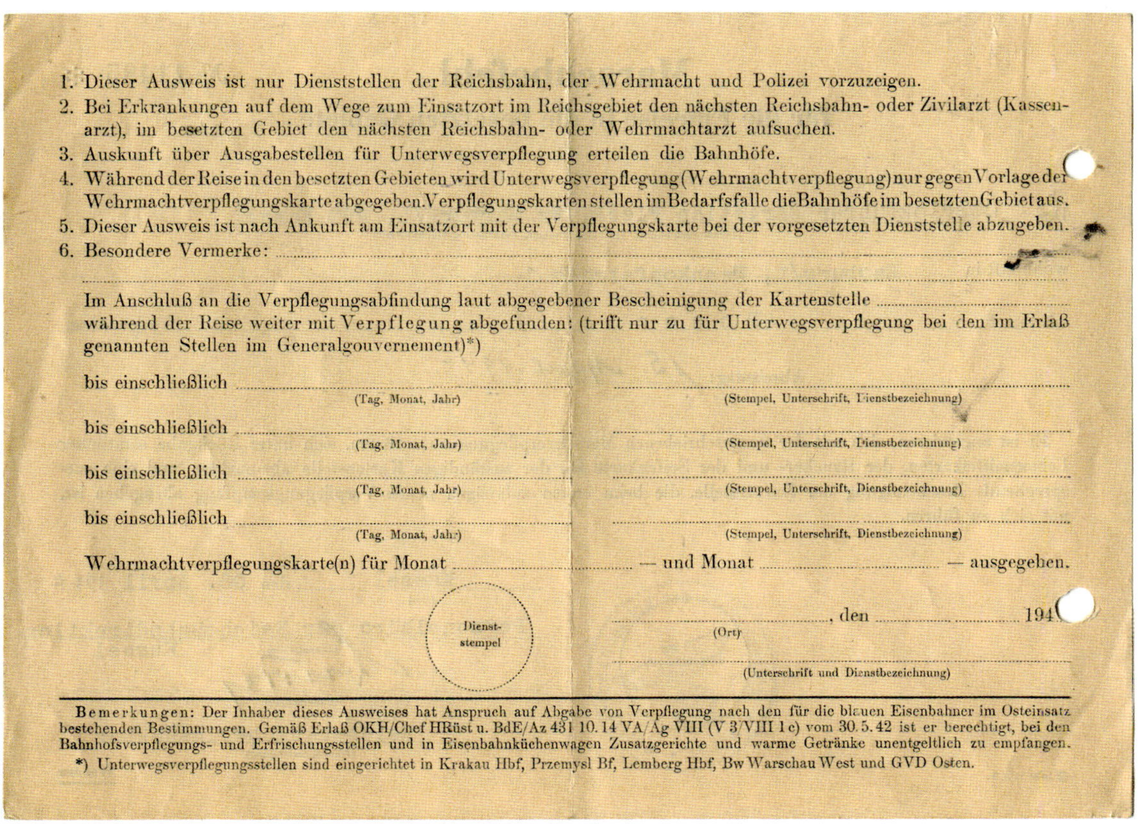

1. Dieser Ausweis ist nur Dienststellen der Reichsbahn, der Wehrmacht und Polizei vorzuzeigen.
2. Bei Erkrankungen auf dem Wege zum Einsatzort im Reichsgebiet den nächsten Reichsbahn- oder Zivilarzt (Kassenarzt), im besetzten Gebiet den nächsten Reichsbahn- oder Wehrmachtarzt aufsuchen.
3. Auskunft über Ausgabestellen für Unterwegsverpflegung erteilen die Bahnhöfe.
4. Während der Reise in den besetzten Gebieten wird Unterwegsverpflegung (Wehrmachtverpflegung) nur gegen Vorlage der Wehrmachtverpflegungskarte abgegeben. Verpflegungskarten stellen im Bedarfsfalle die Bahnhöfe im besetzten Gebiet aus.
5. Dieser Ausweis ist nach Ankunft am Einsatzort mit der Verpflegungskarte bei der vorgesetzten Dienststelle abzugeben.
6. Besondere Vermerke:

Im Anschluß an die Verpflegungsabfindung laut abgegebener Bescheinigung der Kartenstelle während der Reise weiter mit Verpflegung abgefunden: (trifft nur zu für Unterwegsverpflegung bei den im Erlaß genannten Stellen im Generalgouvernement)*)

bis einschließlich (Tag, Monat, Jahr) (Stempel, Unterschrift, Dienstbezeichnung)

bis einschließlich (Tag, Monat, Jahr) (Stempel, Unterschrift, Dienstbezeichnung)

bis einschließlich (Tag, Monat, Jahr) (Stempel, Unterschrift, Dienstbezeichnung)

bis einschließlich (Tag, Monat, Jahr) (Stempel, Unterschrift, Dienstbezeichnung)

Wehrmachtverpflegungskarte(n) für Monat — und Monat — ausgegeben.

Dienst-stempel

, den 194
(Ort)

(Unterschrift und Dienstbezeichnung)

Bemerkungen: Der Inhaber dieses Ausweises hat Anspruch auf Abgabe von Verpflegung nach den für die blauen Eisenbahner im Osteinsatz bestehenden Bestimmungen. Gemäß Erlaß OKH/Chef HRüst u. BdE/Az 431 10.14 VA/Ag VIII (V 3/VIII 1 c) vom 30.5.42 ist er berechtigt, bei den Bahnhofsverpflegungs- und Erfrischungsstellen und in Eisenbahnküchenwagen Zusatzgerichte und warme Getränke unentgeltlich zu empfangen.

*) Unterwegsverpflegungsstellen sind eingerichtet in Krakau Hbf, Przemysl Bf, Lemberg Hbf, Bw Warschau West und GVD Osten.

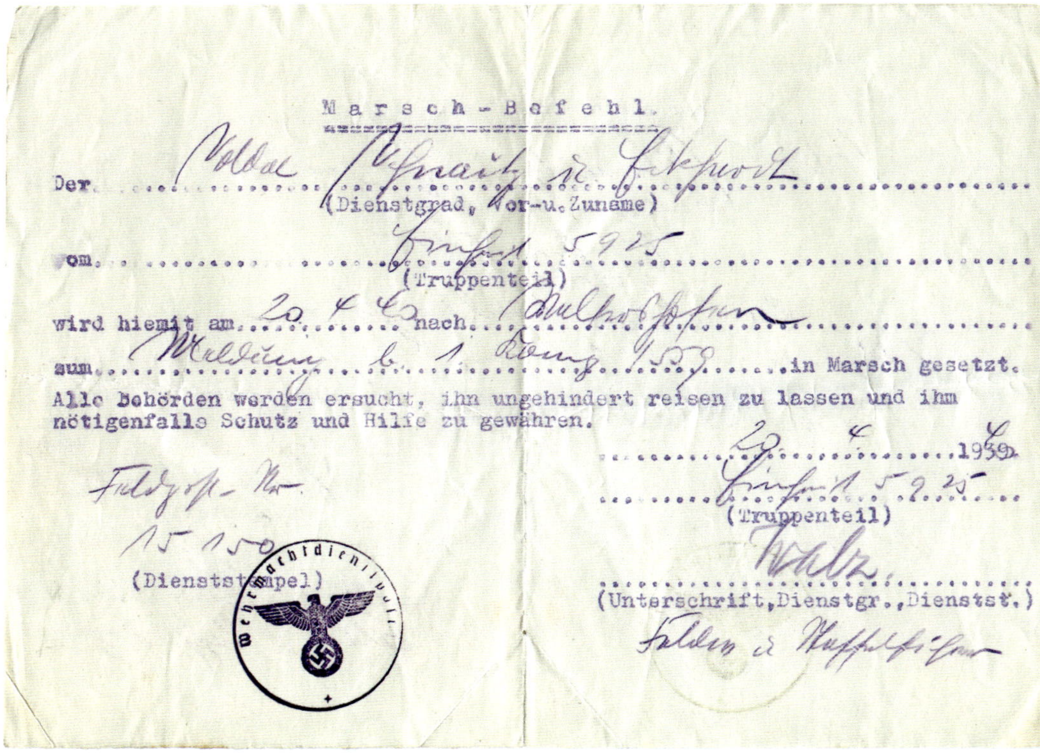

Marsch-Befehl.

Der ....
(Dienstgrad, Vor-u. Zuname)

vom ....
(Truppenteil)

wird hiemit am.............nach...............................
zum.......................................in Marsch gesetzt.
Alle Behörden werden ersucht, ihn ungehindert reisen zu lassen und ihm nötigenfalls Schutz und Hilfe zu gewähren.

.....................1939
....
(Truppenteil)

(Dienststempel)

....
(Unterschrift, Dienstgr., Dienstst.)

Figure 2-155. A mimeographed Ersatzmarschbefehl transferring Soldaten Pfnaitz and Fikpodt to the first company of Bau-Pionier-Bataillon 559 (Construction Pioneer Battalion 559). Often reserved for officers to authorize, this form was signed by Feldwebel und Truppenführer (Sergeant and Troop Leader) Walz. (A5)

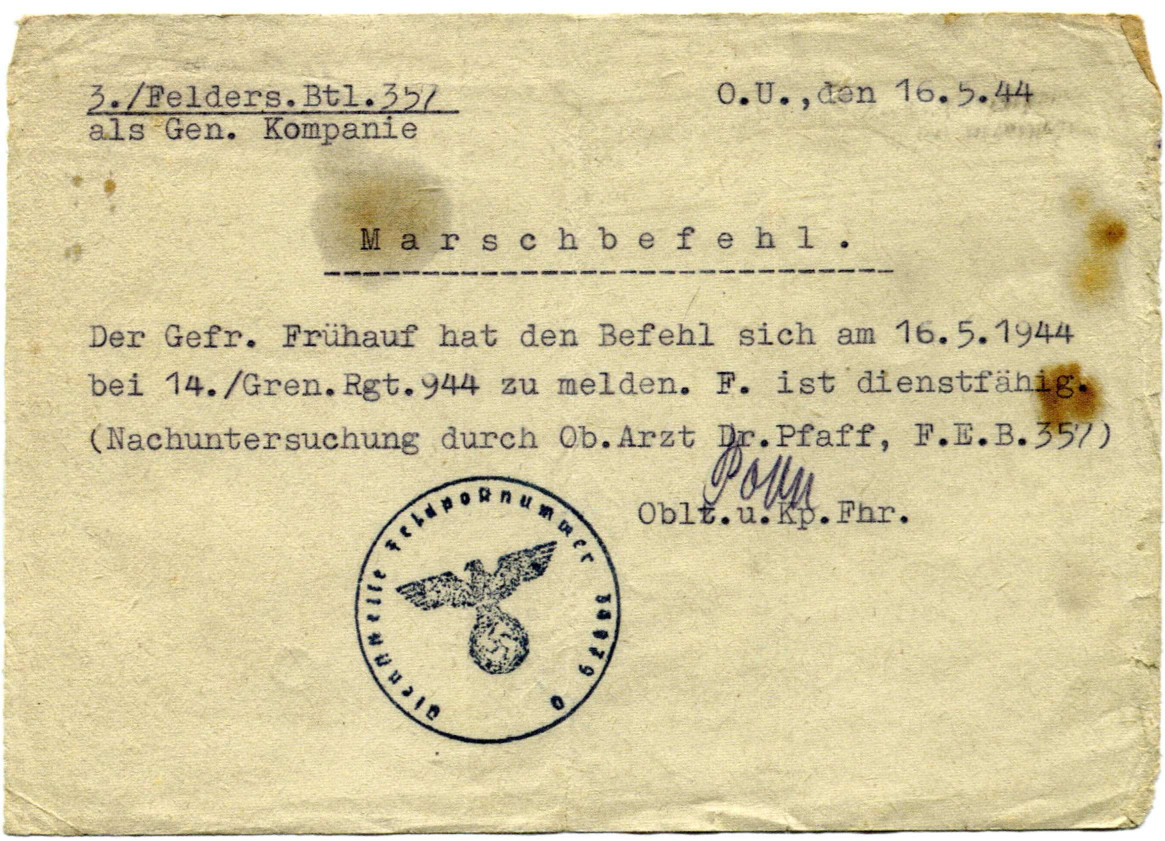

3./Felders.Btl.357
als Gen. Kompanie

O.U., den 16.5.44

Marschbefehl.

Der Gefr. Frühauf hat den Befehl sich am 16.5.1944 bei 14./Gren.Rgt.944 zu melden. F. ist dienstfähig. (Nachuntersuchung durch Ob.Arzt Dr.Pfaff, F.E.B.357)

Oblt.u.Kp.Fhr.

Figure 2-156. Another Ersatzmarschbefehl, this time typed, that authorized Gefreiter Frühauf, who has orders to return to his unit, 14. Kompanie/Grenadier Regiment 944. He is now dienstfähig (fit for duty) after being under Oberarzt Dr. Pfaff's care.

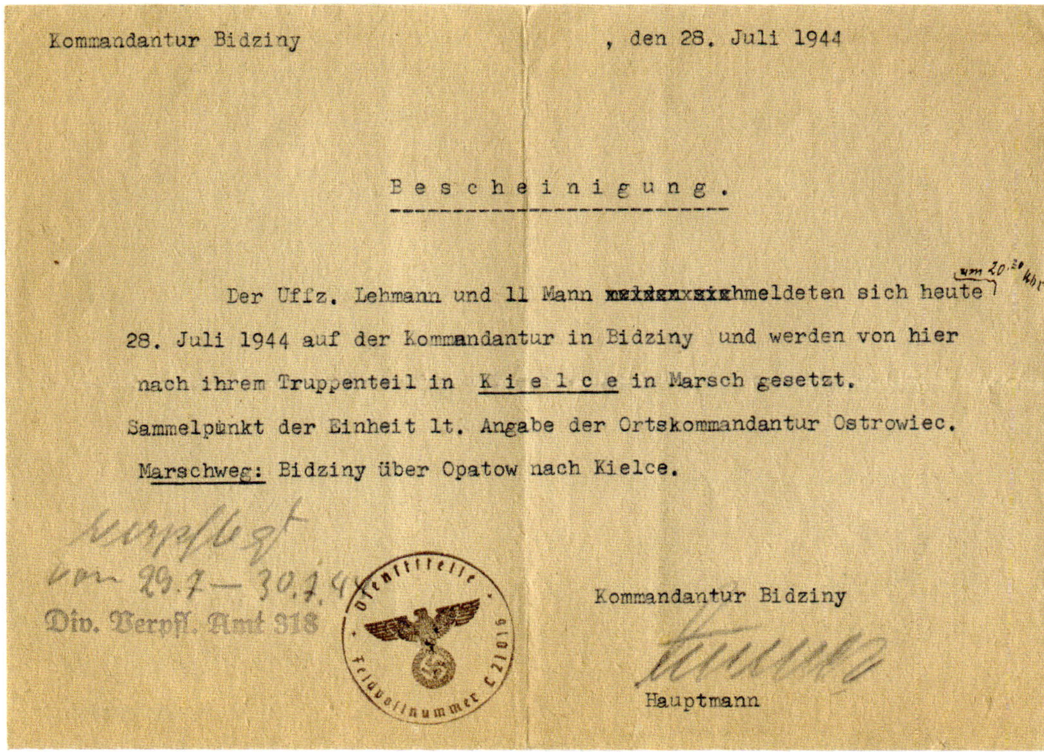

Kommandantur Bidziny , den 28. Juli 1944

Bescheinigung.

Der Uffz. Lehmann und 11 Mann meldeten sich heute (um 20.30 Uhr) 28. Juli 1944 auf der Kommandantur in Bidziny und werden von hier nach ihrem Truppenteil in Kielce in Marsch gesetzt.
Sammelpunkt der Einheit lt. Angabe der Ortskommandantur Ostrowiec.
Marschweg: Bidziny über Opatow nach Kielce.

verpflegt vom 29.7–30.7.44
Div. Verpfl. Amt 318

Dienststelle Feldpostnummer L 21016

Kommandantur Bidziny
Hauptmann

Figure 2-157. This is the Bescheinigung (Attestation) used in place of a Marschbefehl directing Unteroffizier Lehmann and his 11 charges on his fateful trip (see figures 2-129, and 2-130). (A5)

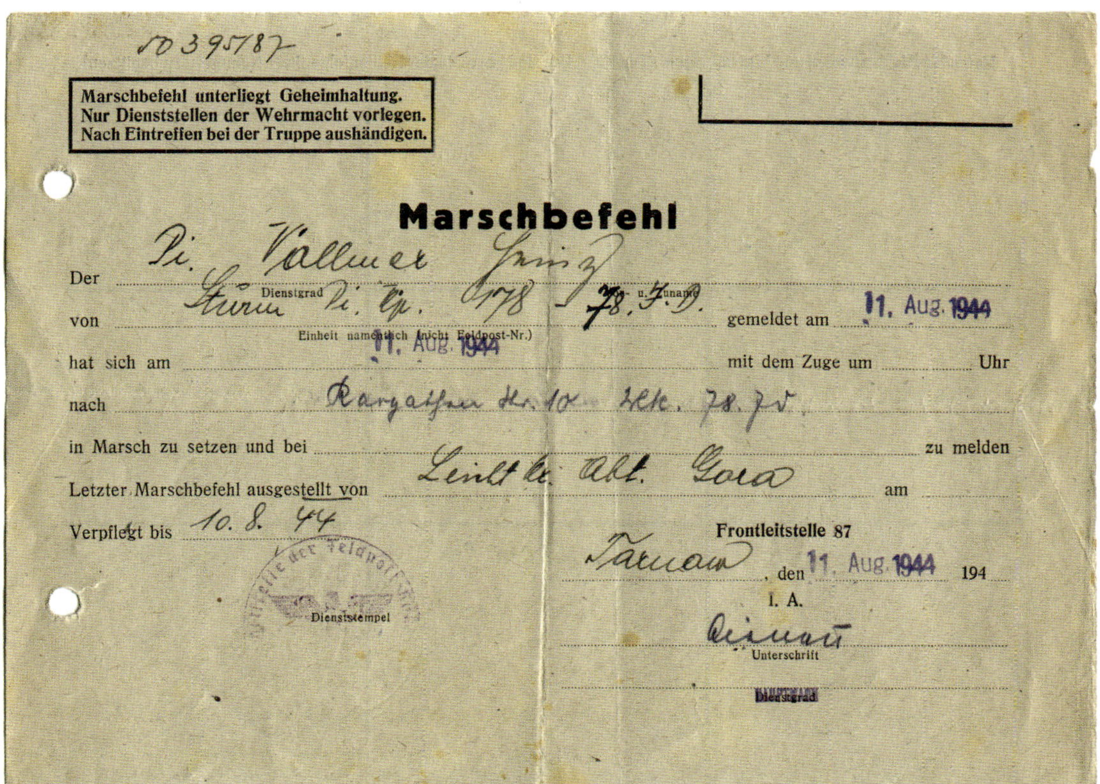

10 39787

Marschbefehl unterliegt Geheimhaltung.
Nur Dienststellen der Wehrmacht vorlegen.
Nach Eintreffen bei der Truppe aushändigen.

Marschbefehl

Der Pi. Vallmer Heinz (Dienstgrad u. Zuname)
von Sturm Pi. Bt. 178 – 78. J. D. (Einheit namentlich (nicht Feldpost-Nr.)) gemeldet am 11. Aug. 1944
hat sich am 11. Aug. 1944 mit dem Zuge um .... Uhr
nach Kargathen Nr. 10 Whk. 78. J. D.
in Marsch zu setzen und bei .... zu melden
Letzter Marschbefehl ausgestellt von Leitstelle Abt. Gora am
Verpflegt bis 10. 8. 44

Frontleitstelle 87
Tarnow, den 11. Aug. 1944
I. A.
Unterschrift
Dienstgrad
Dienststempel

Figure 2-158. Here is an interesting version of the Marschbefehl, quite possibly rushed through a Polish printer's shop, as the layout of the form is very different from previous examples. Pioniere Heinz Viallmer of Sturm-Pioniere-Bataillon 178 (Assault Pioneer Battalion 178) of 78. Infanterie-Division used this form in August of 1944. Note on the back that he passed through the Soldatenheim in Tarnow. (For more information on Soldatenheim, see figures 4-20 through 4-31.) (A5)

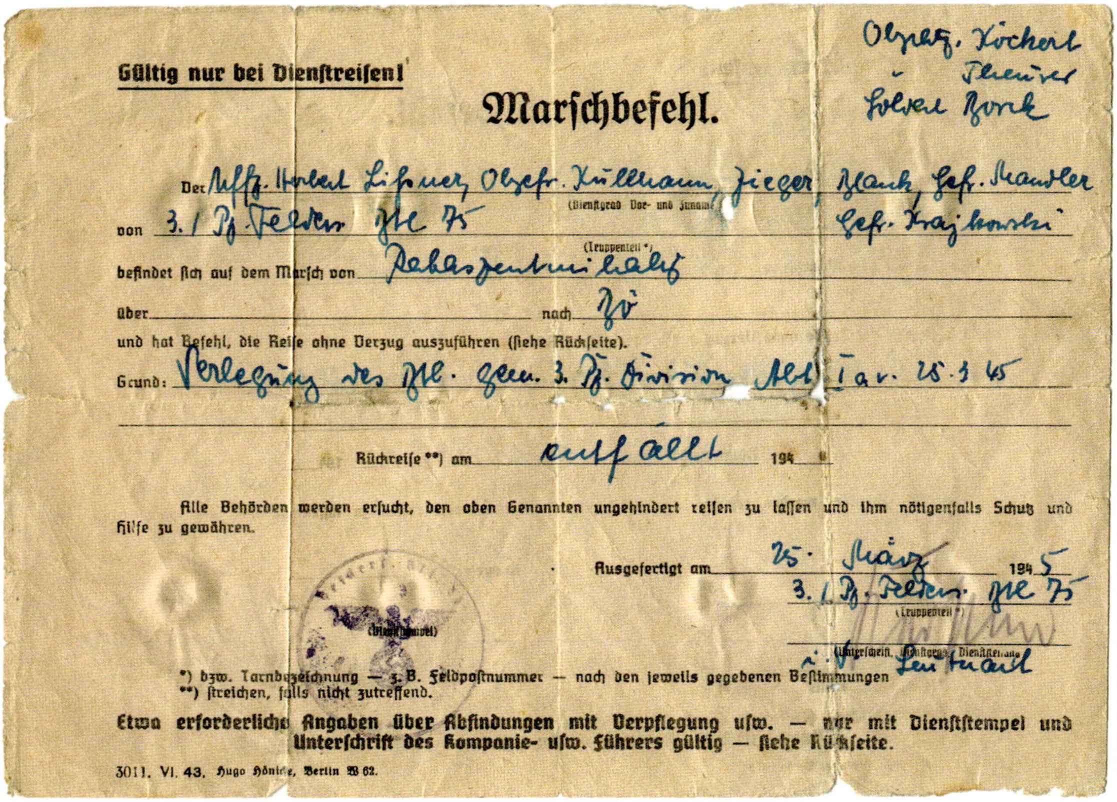

Gültig nur bei Dienstreisen!

Marschbefehl.

Der Uffz. Herbert Lißner, Obgefr. Kullmann, Flieger Blank, Gefr. Mandler (Dienstgrad Vor- und Zuname)
von 3./Pz.Felders.Abt.75 Gefr. Krajkowski (Truppenteil *)
befindet sich auf dem Marsch von
über nach
und hat Befehl, die Reise ohne Verzug auszuführen (siehe Rückseite).
Grund: Verlegung des Btl. gem. 3. Pz. Division Abt. Ia v. 25.3.45

Rückreise **) am entfällt 194

Alle Behörden werden ersucht, den oben Genannten ungehindert reisen zu lassen und ihm nötigenfalls Schutz und Hilfe zu gewähren.

Ausgefertigt am 25. März 1945
3./Pz.Felders.Abt.75 (Truppenteil *)
(Dienststempel) (Unterschrift, Dienstgrad, Dienststellung) Leutnant

*) bzw. Tarnbezeichnung — z. B. Feldpostnummer — nach den jeweils gegebenen Bestimmungen
**) streichen, falls nicht zutreffend.

Etwa erforderliche Angaben über Abfindungen mit Verpflegung usw. — nur mit Dienststempel und Unterschrift des Kompanie- usw. Führers gültig — siehe Rückseite.

3011. VI. 43. Hugo Hönicke, Berlin W 62.

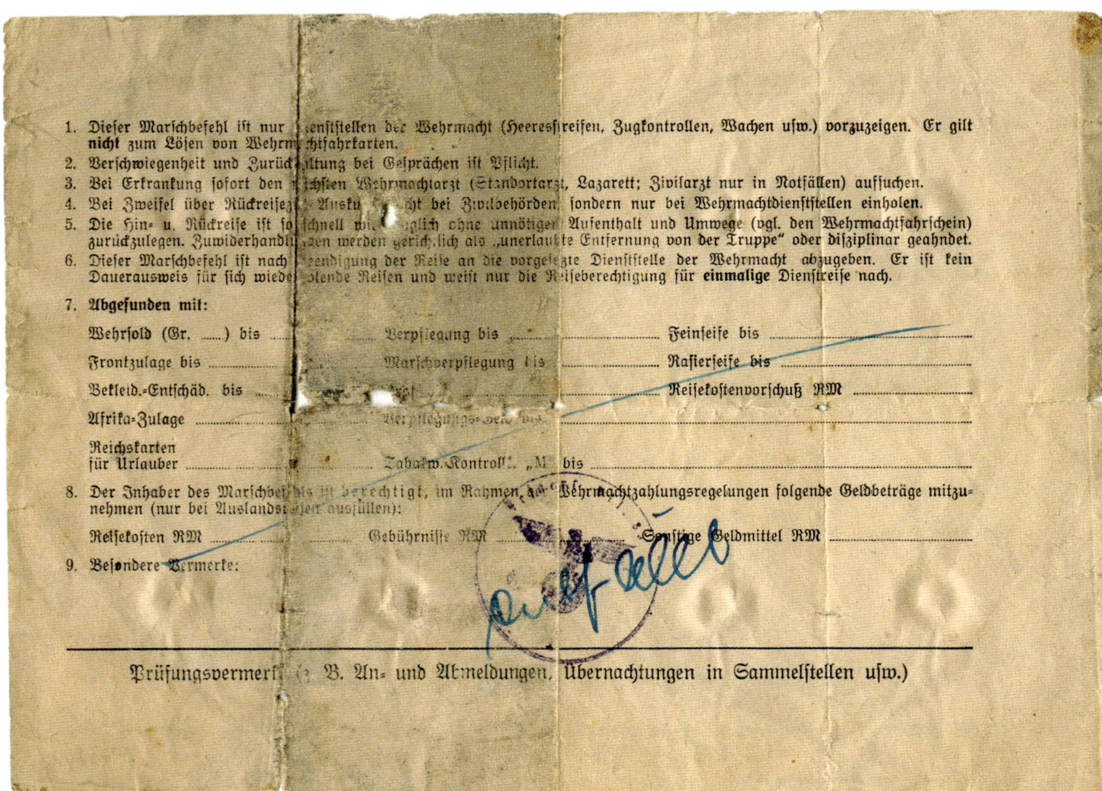

1. Dieser Marschbefehl ist nur Dienststellen der Wehrmacht (Heeresstreifen, Zugkontrollen, Wachen usw.) vorzuzeigen. Er gilt nicht zum Lösen von Wehrmachtfahrkarten.
2. Verschwiegenheit und Zurückhaltung bei Gesprächen ist Pflicht.
3. Bei Erkrankung sofort den nächsten Wehrmachtarzt (Standortarzt, Lazarett; Zivilarzt nur in Notfällen) aufsuchen.
4. Bei Zweifel über Rückreise Auskunft nicht bei Zivilbehörden, sondern nur bei Wehrmachtdienststellen einholen.
5. Die Hin- u. Rückreise ist so schnell wie möglich ohne unnötigen Aufenthalt und Umwege (vgl. den Wehrmachtfahrschein) zurückzulegen. Zuwiderhandlungen werden gerichtlich als „unerlaubte Entfernung von der Truppe" oder disziplinar geahndet.
6. Dieser Marschbefehl ist nach Beendigung der Reise an die vorgesetzte Dienststelle der Wehrmacht abzugeben. Er ist kein Dauerausweis für sich wiederholende Reisen und weist nur die Reiseberechtigung für **einmalige** Dienstreise nach.
7. **Abgefunden mit:**

Wehrsold (Gr. ....) bis ... Verpflegung bis ... Feinseife bis ...
Frontzulage bis ... Marschverpflegung bis ... Rasierseife bis ...
Bekleid.-Entschäd. bis ... ... Reisekostenvorschuß RM ...
Afrika-Zulage ... Verpflegungsgeld bis ...
Reichskarten für Urlauber ... Tabakw.-Kontroll. „M" bis ...

8. Der Inhaber des Marschbefehls ist berechtigt, im Rahmen der Wehrmachtzahlungsregelungen folgende Geldbeträge mitzunehmen (nur bei Auslandsreisen ausfüllen):
Reisekosten RM ... Gebührnisse RM ... Sonstige Geldmittel RM ...
9. Besondere Vermerke:

entfällt

Prüfungsvermerk (z. B. An- und Abmeldungen, Übernachtungen in Sammelstellen usw.)

Figure 2-159. A single Marschbefehl could be used for a number of Soldaten at once: Unteroffizier Herbert Lissner, accompanied by Obergefreiter Kullmann, Flieger (Airman) Blank, Gefreiter Mandler, Gefreiter Krajkowski, Soldat Bonk, and Ober---(?)s Köchert and Theuver all transferred from the 3rd Company of Panzer-Feldersatz-Bataillon 75 (Armored Field Training Battalion 75) to the 3. Panzer-Division. The reverse, where ration issue would have been listed, is merely marked entfället (not applicable). (A5)

Wehrmacht-Marschausweis 1) Nr.

Gültig bis ....

Gültig nur in Verbindung mit Soldbuch, Truppenausweis, Pers.-Ausweis W, Ausländer-Ausweis W 2) Nr.......................... Die Gültigkeit ist zu beschränken, sie ist höchstens bis zum Ende des auf die Ausstellung folgenden Monats zulässig.

Dienstgrad, Vor- und Zuname: ....

Truppenteil bzw. Feldpostnummer: ....

ist berechtigt, sich innerhalb der Gültigkeitsdauer dieses Ausweises mehrmals

von .... nach .... und zurück zu bewegen.

Fahrten werden ausgeführt:
a) auf Kosten der Wehrmacht mit umseitigem Wehrmacht-Fahrschein 2)
b) auf eigene Kosten mit Wehrmachtfahrkarte(n) 2)
c) auf eigene Kosten mit Fahrkarten des öffentlichen Verkehrs 2)

Inhaber wird mit allen Gebührnissen durch den Truppenteil abgefunden. Verpflegung, Lebensmittelkarten oder irgendwelche andere Gebührnisse dürfen von anderer Stelle nicht empfangen werden. Der Ausweis ist nach Ablauf der Gültigkeitsdauer der Einheit zurückzugeben. Für tägliche Fahrten zwischen Wohnung und Dienststätte ist die Benutzung von Wehrmachtfahrkarten unzulässig.

Ausgefertigt am .... 194..... ....
Unterschrift

Dienststempel

....
Truppenteil bzw. Feldpost-Nr. Dienstgrad und Dienststellung

1) Bei Nichtbenutzung der Eisenbahn oder Lösung von Zivil-Fahrkarten (auch Monatskarten usw.) Rückseite mit Tinte durchkreuzen.
2) Nichtzutreffendes durchstreichen.

Dienstlich gedruckt. Nachdruck wird nach den Kriegsgesetzen bestraft.

Figure 2-160. Late in the war, after the Wehrmachtfahrschein and Kriegsurlaubsschein were combined with the Sonderausweis to create a single form, the Marschbefehl, Fahrschein, and Fahrkarte were also combined into a single form. Much more rare than its earlier counterpart, this form came out so late in the war that one almost never finds examples that have been used.

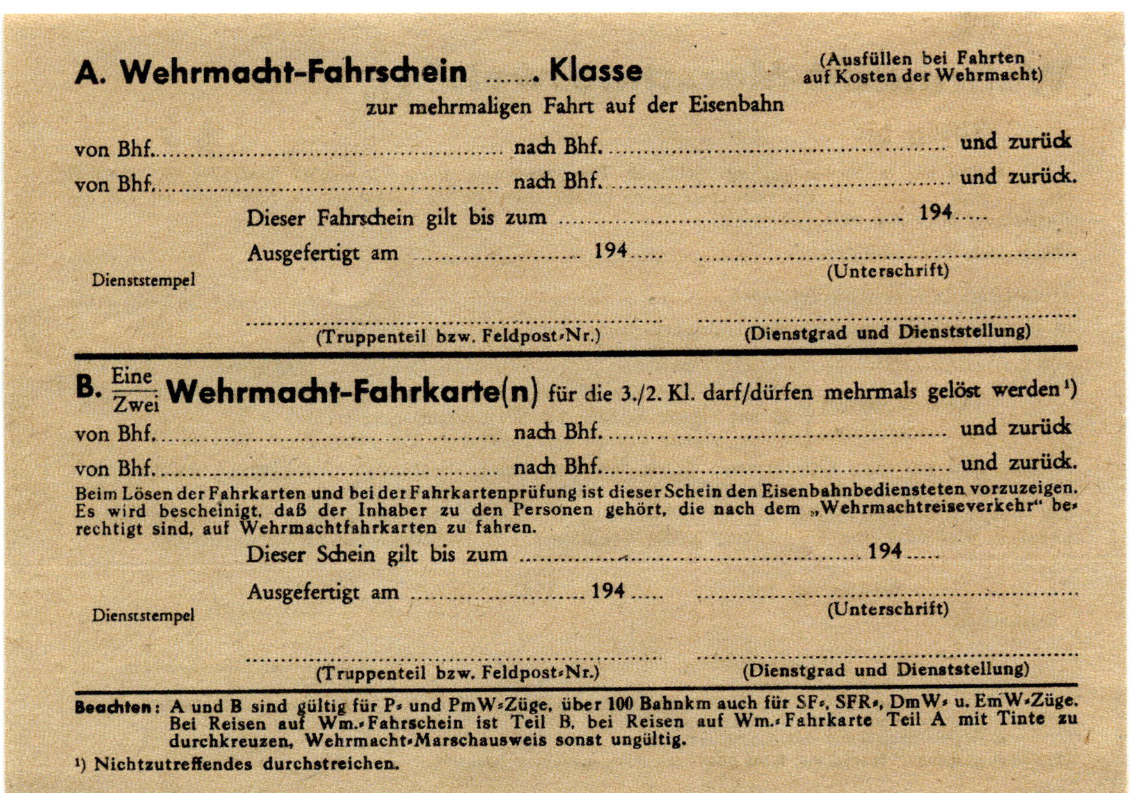

A. Wehrmacht-Fahrschein .... Klasse (Ausfüllen bei Fahrten auf Kosten der Wehrmacht)

zur mehrmaligen Fahrt auf der Eisenbahn

von Bhf.............................. nach Bhf.............................. und zurück

von Bhf.............................. nach Bhf.............................. und zurück.

Dieser Fahrschein gilt bis zum .... 194.....

Ausgefertigt am .... 194..... ....
(Unterschrift)

Dienststempel

....
(Truppenteil bzw. Feldpost-Nr.) (Dienstgrad und Dienststellung)

B. Eine/Zwei **Wehrmacht-Fahrkarte(n)** für die 3./2. Kl. darf/dürfen mehrmals gelöst werden 1)

von Bhf.............................. nach Bhf.............................. und zurück

von Bhf.............................. nach Bhf.............................. und zurück.

Beim Lösen der Fahrkarten und bei der Fahrkartenprüfung ist dieser Schein den Eisenbahnbediensteten vorzuzeigen. Es wird bescheinigt, daß der Inhaber zu den Personen gehört, die nach dem „Wehrmachtreiseverkehr" berechtigt sind, auf Wehrmachtfahrkarten zu fahren.

Dieser Schein gilt bis zum .... 194.....

Ausgefertigt am .... 194..... ....
(Unterschrift)

Dienststempel

....
(Truppenteil bzw. Feldpost-Nr.) (Dienstgrad und Dienststellung)

Beachten: A und B sind gültig für P- und PmW-Züge, über 100 Bahnkm auch für SF-, SFR-, DmW- u. EmW-Züge. Bei Reisen auf Wm.-Fahrschein ist Teil B, bei Reisen auf Wm.-Fahrkarte Teil A mit Tinte zu durchkreuzen, Wehrmacht-Marschausweis sonst ungültig.

1) Nichtzutreffendes durchstreichen.

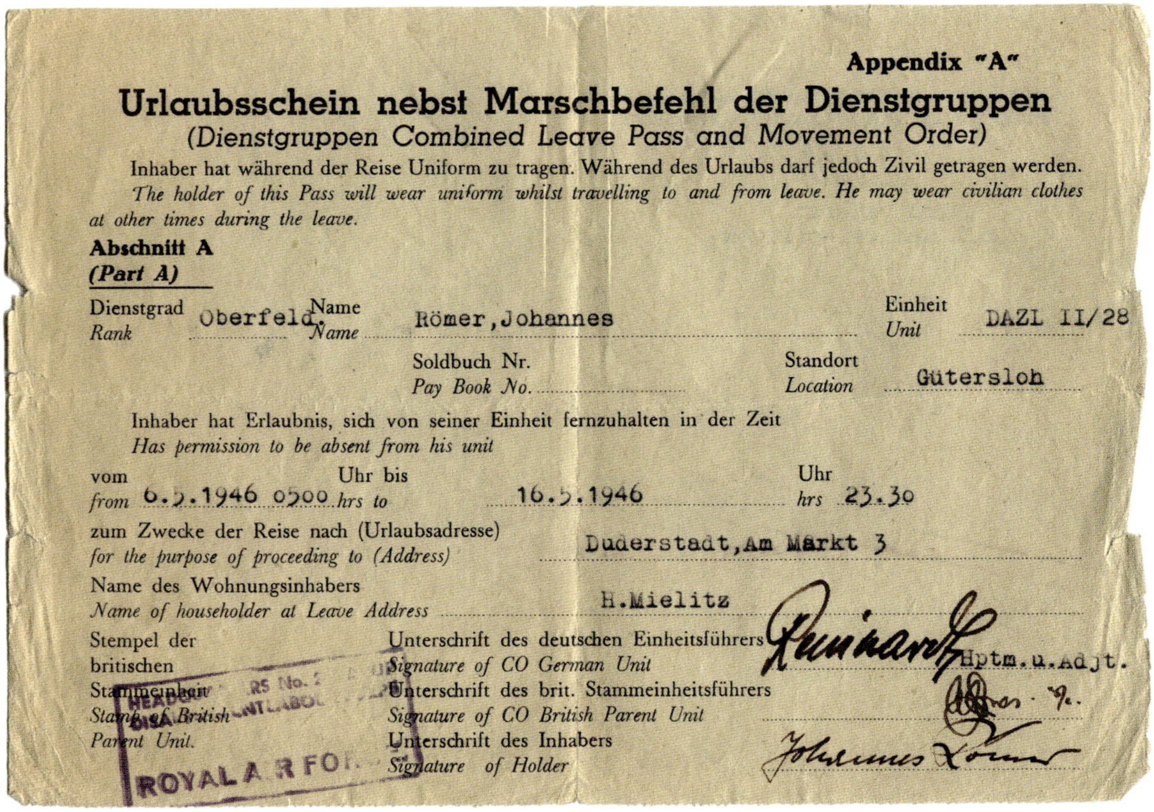

Appendix "A"

Urlaubsschein nebst Marschbefehl der Dienstgruppen

(Dienstgruppen Combined Leave Pass and Movement Order)

Inhaber hat während der Reise Uniform zu tragen. Während des Urlaubs darf jedoch Zivil getragen werden.
The holder of this Pass will wear uniform whilst travelling to and from leave. He may wear civilian clothes at other times during the leave.

Abschnitt A
(Part A)

Dienstgrad / *Rank* Oberfeld. Name / *Name* Römer, Johannes Einheit / *Unit* DAZL II/28

Soldbuch Nr. / *Pay Book No.* Standort / *Location* Gütersloh

Inhaber hat Erlaubnis, sich von seiner Einheit fernzuhalten in der Zeit
Has permission to be absent from his unit

vom / *from* 6.5.1946 0500 Uhr bis / *hrs to* 16.5.1946 Uhr / *hrs* 23.30

zum Zwecke der Reise nach (Urlaubsadresse) / *for the purpose of proceeding to (Address)* Duderstadt, Am Markt 3

Name des Wohnungsinhabers / *Name of householder at Leave Address* H.Mielitz

Stempel der britischen Stammeinheit / *Stamp British Parent Unit.* ROYAL A R FO

Unterschrift des deutschen Einheitsführers / *Signature of CO German Unit* Hptm.u.Adjt.

Unterschrift des brit. Stammeinheitsführers / *Signature of CO British Parent Unit*

Unterschrift des Inhabers / *Signature of Holder* Johannes Römer

Frei von ansteckenden Krankheiten
Free from infectioues deseases

Truppenarzt
Unit Medical-Officer

Figure 2-161. Old habits die hard; here is proof. Oberfedlwebel (Master Sergeant) Johannes Römer used this bilingual Royal Air Force Urlaubsschein-Marschbefehl to transfer from a DAZL unit (a British-controlled semi-military specialist unit of POWs) in the RAF POW camp in Gütersloh to Duderstadt and back, over a full year following the end of the war. The common wartime practice for travel papers is still used; the back is even marked "Free from infectious diseases."(A5)

Figure 2-162. An Ersatz Feldverwaltungsstelle, or temporary field administrative station in November of 1939, complete with desk and straw chair, though sadly lacking in other amenities. The truck in the background is marked NS-Flieger(korps), a civilian flight organization, so it's presumed that this was during maneuvers somewhere in Germany.

Figure 3-1. The entrance of railroad cars displayed signs such as this one, showing the route from Frankfurt am Main to the Paris-East train station. Once the train arrived at its destination, the sign was flipped over for the return trip to display the same route in reverse order. (8¼" x 13¾")

3

Other Wehrmacht Papers Related to or Required for Travel

As anyone who has traveled knows, there are some documents that are required to travel, and some documents that are required *for* travel; the *Soldat* was no different. Thus far, we have examined the forms and papers necessary for a German soldier to leave his unit for leave or service, but not the items he would have picked up along the way. Once approved to depart, some of these would have been vital to keep with him. Other items and sundry "pocket trash" would have been accumulated as a course of his excursion.

The following section contains paperwork and documents associated with the German soldier's journey. Few of these were required, but almost all would be encountered in one form or another; each would become a souvenir as precious as any other.

Required to Leave the Front

Many believe that the worst enemy a soldier faced was the soldier across the field from him. Although that man was often considerably more lethal, many veterans will tell you that their worst enemy was the elements. For those who had spent any length of time at the front, there were two nuisances that the elements presented beyond weather, though often that was grief enough: pests and disease.

During the American Civil War, 1861-65, more soldiers died of disease than in combat. By World War I, that statistic had started to turn around, but because of the static conditions of that conflict, disease remained rife among troops. Although sickness did not kill more than combat, it continued to level vast percentages, depending on which army, the conditions, and the availability of medical technology.

Germany fielded many World War I veterans between 1939 and 1945, many of whom had experienced the complications of illnesses in the trenches. *Soldaten* and the *Wehrmacht* both took measures to prevent the spread of diseases of all kinds. That became especially important when soldiers requested leave to visit their families back home.

In order to prevent mass contagion of the home front, troops of all nations were regularly immunized against some of history's greatest killers: Cholera, Diphtheria, and Typhus. These immunizations would have been noted in the German soldier's *Soldbuch*, which is about all the soldier himself would have seen; it would also have been noted on a series of different documents, all of which would have been kept in medical and military records.

Although not handled by the soldier, *Ärztlicher Befundscheinen* (Doctor's Condition Certificates), *Gesundheitsblätter* (Health Leaflets), *Krankenblätter* (Sickness Reports), and many other medical reports and transcripts would have recorded whether a soldier was healthy enough to travel.

In addition to prevention via immunization, the *Wehrmacht* spent much effort to prevent the spread of disease by way of education. The *Merkblatt*, an informational leaflet, was often the method of choice, but those were only useful if a soldier read it, so hygiene classes taught by doctors, the *Hauptfeldwebel* ("*Spiess*" or Sergeant Major), and other knowledgeable individuals often attempted to fill the void left by an unread *Merkblatt*.

One contagion that a soldier did have to carry proof of eradication from was *Pediculus humanus humans*, the body louse.

Lice are common insect pests that infect clothing, hair, and skin due to unhygienic surroundings. Frequent bathing and changing or washing of clothes can prevent infection, but soldiers may go weeks without bathing during combat conditions. As a result, these insects thrived on soldiers in the field.

A louse-ridden soldier on a train to the Fatherland is the last thing the Third Reich could afford to allow, and so the *Wehrmacht* set up a number of *Entlausungsstelle*, or Delousing Stations, along the front. Soldiers due to receive leave would be directed to these stations before being permitted to return home.

Once they had been deloused, either by thorough scrubbing or by copious applications of insecticides (often both), they would be issued a certificate that was almost as valuable as the leave papers themselves, an *Entlausungsschein,* or *E-schein* for short, a Delousing Certificate. This small A7 piece of paper documented that the soldier had been deloused, and where and when

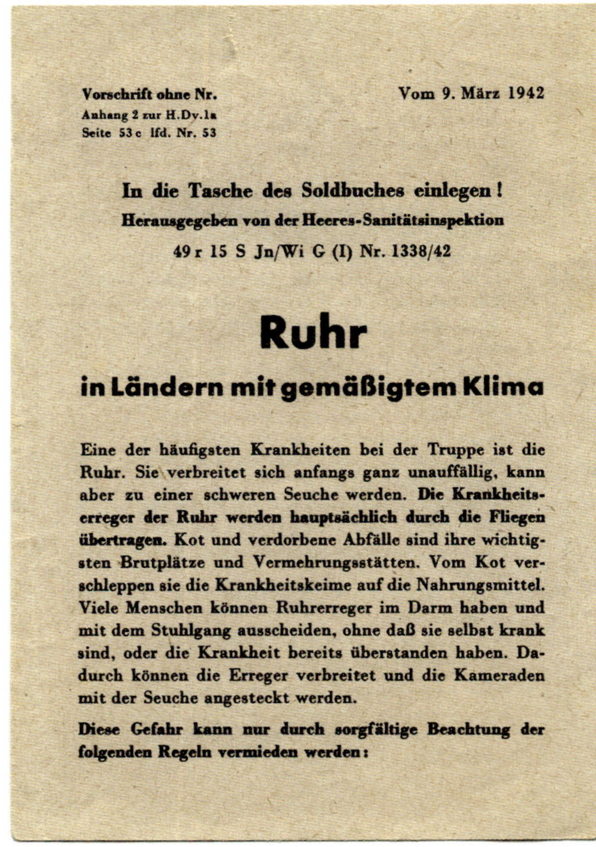

Vorschrift ohne Nr. Vom 9. März 1942
Anhang 2 zur H.Dv.1a
Seite 53c lfd. Nr. 53

In die Tasche des Soldbuches einlegen!
Herausgegeben von der Heeres-Sanitätsinspektion
49 r 15 S Jn/Wi G (I) Nr. 1338/42

Ruhr
in Ländern mit gemäßigtem Klima

Eine der häufigsten Krankheiten bei der Truppe ist die Ruhr. Sie verbreitet sich anfangs ganz unauffällig, kann aber zu einer schweren Seuche werden. Die Krankheitserreger der Ruhr werden hauptsächlich durch die Fliegen übertragen. Kot und verdorbene Abfälle sind ihre wichtigsten Brutplätze und Vermehrungsstätten. Vom Kot verschleppen sie die Krankheitskeime auf die Nahrungsmittel. Viele Menschen können Ruhrerreger im Darm haben und mit dem Stuhlgang ausscheiden, ohne daß sie selbst krank sind, oder die Krankheit bereits überstanden haben. Dadurch können die Erreger verbreitet und die Kameraden mit der Seuche angesteckt werden.

Diese Gefahr kann nur durch sorgfältige Beachtung der folgenden Regeln vermieden werden:

Figure 3-3. This informative document warns Soldaten about the danger of dysentery in countries with "difficult" climates. (A6 folded to A7)

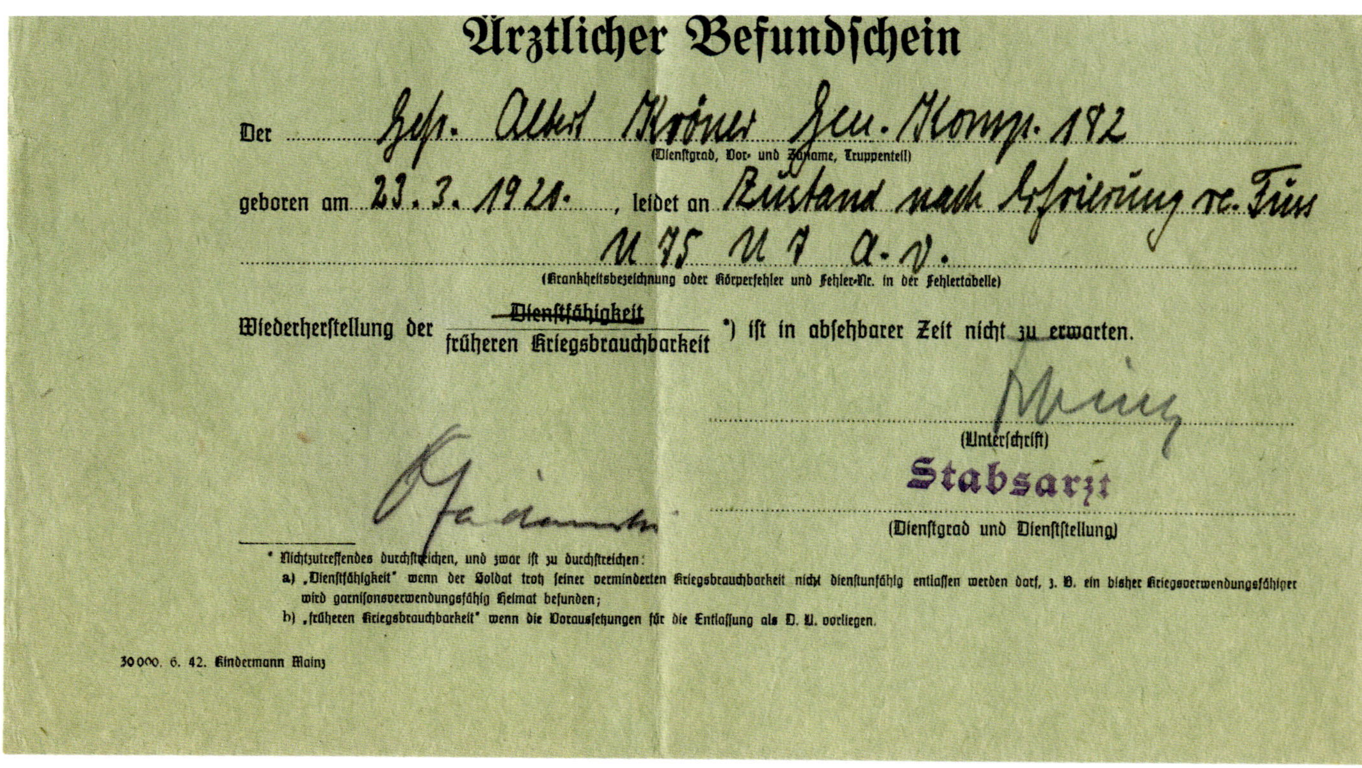

Ärztlicher Befundschein

Der ....
(Dienstgrad, Vor- und Zuname, Truppenteil)

geboren am 23. 3. 1921. , leidet an ....
(Krankheitsbezeichnung oder Körperfehler und Fehler-Nr. in der Fehlertabelle)

Wiederherstellung der ~~Dienstfähigkeit~~ / früheren Kriegsbrauchbarkeit *) ist in absehbarer Zeit nicht zu erwarten.

....
(Unterschrift)

Stabsarzt
....
(Dienstgrad und Dienststellung)

* Nichtzutreffendes durchstreichen, und zwar ist zu durchstreichen:
a) „Dienstfähigkeit" wenn der Soldat trotz seiner verminderten Kriegsbrauchbarkeit nicht dienstunfähig entlassen werden darf, z. B. ein bisher kriegsverwendungsfähiger wird garnisonsverwendungsfähig Heimat befunden;
b) „früheren Kriegsbrauchbarkeit" wenn die Voraussetzungen für die Entlassung als D. U. vorliegen.

30000. 6. 42. Kindermann Mainz

Figure 3-2. Documents about a Soldat such as this Ärztlicher Befundschein (Certificate of Doctor's Findings), Krankenblätter (Sickness Reports), etc., which the Soldat himself rarely if ever saw, attested to whether he was fit to travel. (A5)

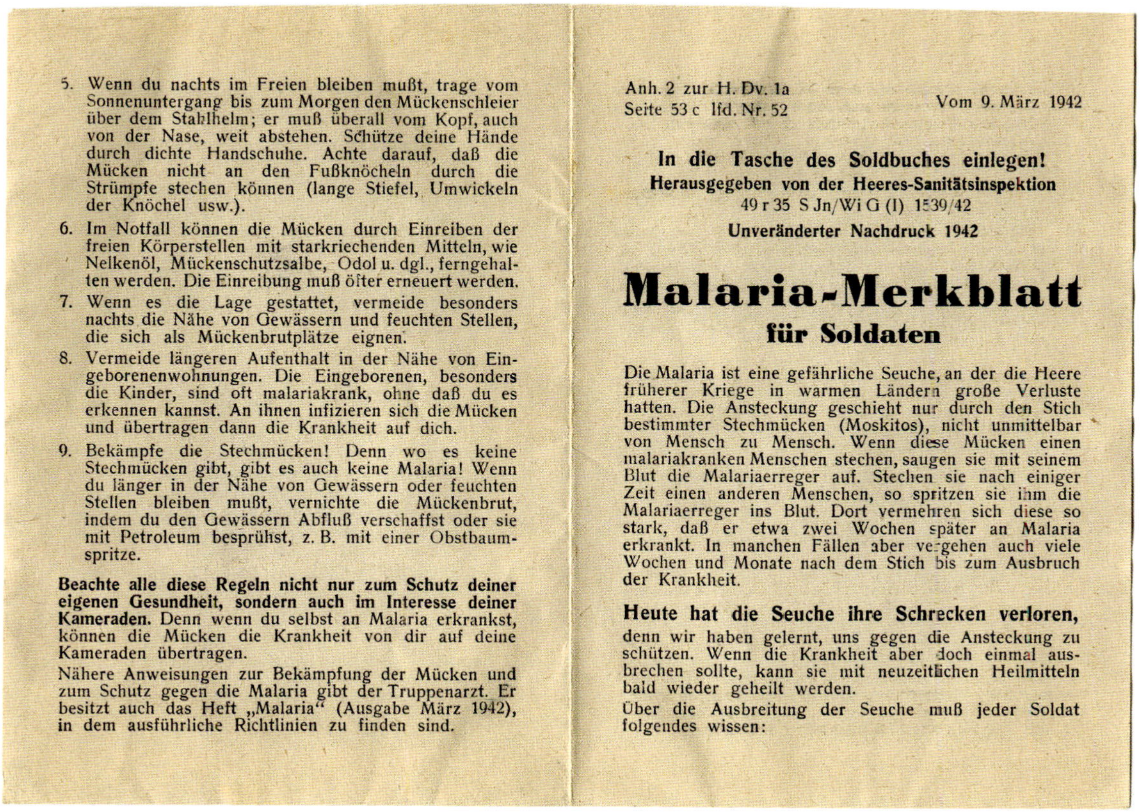

5. Wenn du nachts im Freien bleiben mußt, trage vom Sonnenuntergang bis zum Morgen den Mückenschleier über dem Stahlhelm; er muß überall vom Kopf, auch von der Nase, weit abstehen. Schütze deine Hände durch dichte Handschuhe. Achte darauf, daß die Mücken nicht an den Fußknöcheln durch die Strümpfe stechen können (lange Stiefel, Umwickeln der Knöchel usw.).
6. Im Notfall können die Mücken durch Einreiben der freien Körperstellen mit starkriechenden Mitteln, wie Nelkenöl, Mückenschutzsalbe, Odol u. dgl., ferngehalten werden. Die Einreibung muß öfter erneuert werden.
7. Wenn es die Lage gestattet, vermeide besonders nachts die Nähe von Gewässern und feuchten Stellen, die sich als Mückenbrutplätze eignen.
8. Vermeide längeren Aufenthalt in der Nähe von Eingeborenenwohnungen. Die Eingeborenen, besonders die Kinder, sind oft malariakrank, ohne daß du es erkennen kannst. An ihnen infizieren sich die Mücken und übertragen dann die Krankheit auf dich.
9. Bekämpfe die Stechmücken! Denn wo es keine Stechmücken gibt, gibt es auch keine Malaria! Wenn du länger in der Nähe von Gewässern oder feuchten Stellen bleiben mußt, vernichte die Mückenbrut, indem du den Gewässern Abfluß verschaffst oder sie mit Petroleum besprühst, z. B. mit einer Obstbaumspritze.

Beachte alle diese Regeln nicht nur zum Schutz deiner eigenen Gesundheit, sondern auch im Interesse deiner Kameraden. Denn wenn du selbst an Malaria erkrankst, können die Mücken die Krankheit von dir auf deine Kameraden übertragen.

Nähere Anweisungen zur Bekämpfung der Mücken und zum Schutz gegen die Malaria gibt der Truppenarzt. Er besitzt auch das Heft „Malaria" (Ausgabe März 1942), in dem ausführliche Richtlinien zu finden sind.

Anh. 2 zur H. Dv. 1a
Seite 53 c lfd. Nr. 52

Vom 9. März 1942

In die Tasche des Soldbuches einlegen!
Herausgegeben von der Heeres-Sanitätsinspektion
49 r 35 S Jn/Wi G (I) 1539/42
Unveränderter Nachdruck 1942

Malaria-Merkblatt
für Soldaten

Die Malaria ist eine gefährliche Seuche, an der die Heere früherer Kriege in warmen Ländern große Verluste hatten. Die Ansteckung geschieht nur durch den Stich bestimmter Stechmücken (Moskitos), nicht unmittelbar von Mensch zu Mensch. Wenn diese Mücken einen malariakranken Menschen stechen, saugen sie mit seinem Blut die Malariaerreger auf. Stechen sie nach einiger Zeit einen anderen Menschen, so spritzen sie ihm die Malariaerreger ins Blut. Dort vermehren sich diese so stark, daß er etwa zwei Wochen später an Malaria erkrankt. In manchen Fällen aber vergehen auch viele Wochen und Monate nach dem Stich bis zum Ausbruch der Krankheit.

Heute hat die Seuche ihre Schrecken verloren,
denn wir haben gelernt, uns gegen die Ansteckung zu schützen. Wenn die Krankheit aber doch einmal ausbrechen sollte, kann sie mit neuzeitlichen Heilmitteln bald wieder geheilt werden.

Über die Ausbreitung der Seuche muß jeder Soldat folgendes wissen:

Figure 3-4. Merkblätter, information pamphlets, were distributed among both troops and civilians to provide information. This Merkblatt educated Soldaten in the prevention of malaria. Troops were expected to keep this as the bold line at the top of the front page implies: "In die Tasche des Soldbuches einlegen!" Place in the pocket of one's Soldbuch! (A6)

20. **Personalfahrpreise**
gültig vom 15. Juni 1938 an

Entfernung	Personenzug			Schnellzug		
	3.	2.	1.	3.	2.	1.
	Klasse					
km	Reichsmark					
1— 16	-.10	-.20	-.40	-.15	-.30	—.60
17— 25	-.20	-.40	-.80	-.30	-.60	1.20
26— 50	-.30	-.60	1.20	-.45	-.90	1.80
51— 80	-.50	1.00	2.00	-.75	1.50	3.00
81—110	-.70	1.40	2.80	1.05	2.10	4.20
111—140	-.90	1.80	3.60	1.35	2.70	5.40
141—160	1.10	2.20	4.40	1.65	3.30	6.60
161—210	1.30	2.60	5.20	1.95	3.90	7.80
211—290	1.40	2.80	5.60	2.10	4.20	8.40
291—340	1.60	3.20	6.40	2.40	4.80	9.60
341—380	1.70	3.40	6.80	2.55	5.10	10.20
381—420	1.90	3.80	7.60	2.85	5.70	11.40
421—460	2.10	4.20	8.40	3.15	6.30	12.60
461—500	2.20	4.40	8.80	3.30	6.60	13.20
501-1000	2.40	4.80	9.60	3.60	7.20	14.40

Auf den Wiener Verbindungsbahnen beträgt der Personalfahrpreis 3. Kl Personenzug einheitlich 10 Rpf

Wien, im September 1941

Deutsche Reichsbahn
Reichsbahndirektion Wien

854 9 41 180000 — D 0931

Merkblatt
zu den Fahrbegünstigungsausweisen der Reichsbahn-Versorgungsempfänger österreichischen Rechts.

1. Die Ausweise WLV 159 und 160 berechtigen den Inhaber zur Fahrt mit Fahrkarten zum **einfachen**, der Ausweis WLV 161 zum **doppelten** Personalfahrpreis auf sämtlichen **österreichischen** Bahnlinien der Deutschen Reichsbahn bis und ab folgenden Übergangsbahnhöfen (Grenzen):

Engerau	Buchs (St Gallen)
Marchegg Grenze	Brennero
Lundenburg	San Candido
Grusbach-Schöngraf	Tarvisio
Znaim	Rosenbach (Kärnten)
Zlabings	Bleiburg
Gmünd (Waldv) Hbf	Rabenstein (Drau)
Oberhaid (b Kaplitz)	Spielfeld-Straß
Passau Hbf	Radkersburg
Simbach (Inn)	Szentgotthárd
Salzburg Hbf	Strem
Kufstein	Rechnitz
Scharnitz	Kőszeg
Griesen (Oberbayern)	Deutschkreutz
Schönbichl	Loipersbach-Sch Grenze
Lindau Hbf	Wulkaprodersdorf
St Margrethen	Hegyeshalom

1

Figure 3-5. Not all Merkblätter catered solely to the Soldat; this pamphlet, useful to the Soldat and civilian alike, gave instructions for price reductions for the Personnenzug and Schnellzug by class and distance.

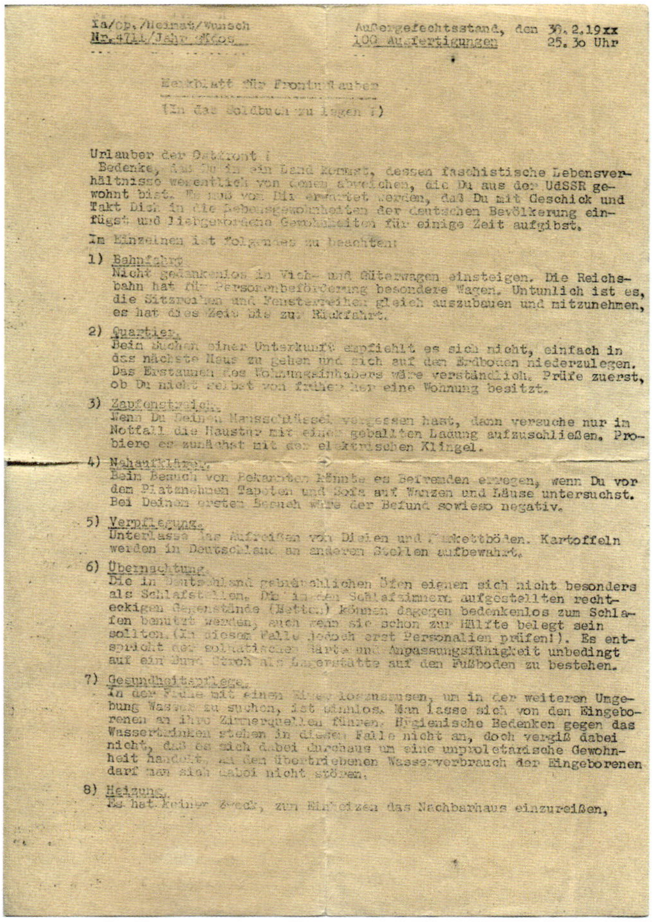

Ia/Op./Heimat/Wunsch
Nr.4711/Jahr gKdos

Außergefechtsstand, den 30.2.19xx
100 Ausfertigungen
25.30 Uhr

Merkblatt für Fronturlauber

(In das Soldbuch zu legen !)

Urlauber der Ostfront !

Bedenke, daß Du in ein Land kommst, dessen faschistische Lebensverhältnisse wesentlich von denen abweichen, die Du aus der UdSSR gewohnt bist. Es muß von Dir erwartet werden, daß Du mit Geschick und Takt Dich in die Lebensgewohnheiten der deutschen Bevölkerung einfügst und liebgewordene Gewohnheiten für einige Zeit aufgibst.

Im Einzelnen ist folgendes zu beachten:

1) Bahnfahrt
Nicht gedankenlos in Vieh- und Güterwagen einsteigen. Die Reichsbahn hat für Personenbeförderung besondere Wagen. Untunlich ist es, die Sitzreihen und Fensterreihen gleich auszubauen und mitzunehmen, es hat dies Zeit bis zur Rückfahrt.

2) Quartier.
Beim Suchen einer Unterkunft empfiehlt es sich nicht, einfach in das nächste Haus zu gehen und sich auf den Erdboden niederzulegen. Das Erstaunen des Wohnungsinhabers wäre verständlich. Prüfe zuerst, ob Du nicht selbst von früher her eine Wohnung besitzt.

3) Zapfenstreich.
Wenn Du Deinen Hausschlüssel vergessen hast, dann versuche nur im Notfall die Haustür mit einer geballten Ladung aufzuschließen. Probiere es zunächst mit der elektrischen Klingel.

4) Nahaufklärer.
Beim Besuch von Bekannten könnte es Befremden erregen, wenn Du vor dem Platznehmen Tapeten und Sofa auf Wanzen und Läuse untersuchst. Bei Deinem ersten Besuch wäre der Befund sowieso negativ.

5) Verpflegung.
Unterlasse das Aufreißen von Dielen und Parkettböden. Kartoffeln werden in Deutschland an anderen Stellen aufbewahrt.

6) Übernachtung.
Die in Deutschland gebräuchlichen Öfen eignen sich nicht besonders als Schlafstellen. Die in den Schlafzimmern aufgestellten rechteckigen Gegenstände (Betten) können dagegen bedenkenlos zum Schlafen benutzt werden, auch wenn sie schon zur Hälfte belegt sein sollten. (In diesem Falle jedoch erst Personalien prüfen!). Es entspricht der soldatischen Härte und Anpassungsfähigkeit unbedingt auf ein Bund Stroh als Lagerstätte auf den Fußboden zu bestehen.

7) Gesundheitspflege.
In der Frühe mit einen Eimer loszusausen, um in der weiteren Umgebung Wasser zu suchen, ist sinnlos. Man lasse sich von den Eingeborenen an ihre Zimmerquellen führen. Hygienische Bedenken gegen das Wassertrinken stehen in diesem Falle nicht an, doch vergiß dabei nicht, daß es sich dabei durchaus um eine unproletarische Gewohnheit handelt, an den übertriebenen Wasserverbrauch der Eingeborenen darf man sich dabei nicht stören.

8) Heizung.
Es hat keinen Zweck, zum Einheizen das Nachbarhaus einzureißen,

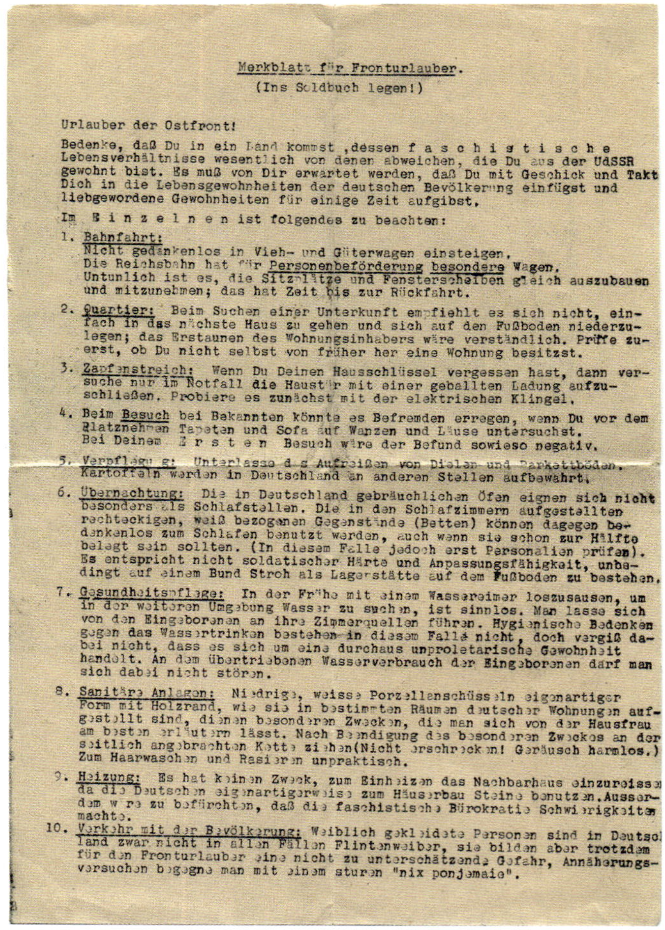

Merkblatt für Fronturlauber.

(Ins Soldbuch legen!)

Urlauber der Ostfront!

Bedenke, daß Du in ein Land kommst, dessen f a s c h i s t i s c h e Lebensverhältnisse wesentlich von denen abweichen, die Du aus der UdSSR gewohnt bist. Es muß von Dir erwartet werden, daß Du mit Geschick und Takt Dich in die Lebensgewohnheiten der deutschen Bevölkerung einfügst und liebgewordene Gewohnheiten für einige Zeit aufgibst.

Im E i n z e l n e n ist folgendes zu beachten:

1. Bahnfahrt:
Nicht gedankenlos in Vieh- und Güterwagen einsteigen.
Die Reichsbahn hat für Personenbeförderung besondere Wagen.
Untunlich ist es, die Sitzplätze und Fensterscheiben gleich auszubauen und mitzunehmen; das hat Zeit bis zur Rückfahrt.

2. Quartier: Beim Suchen einer Unterkunft empfiehlt es sich nicht, einfach in das nächste Haus zu gehen und sich auf den Fußboden niederzulegen; das Erstaunen des Wohnungsinhabers wäre verständlich. Prüffe zuerst, ob Du nicht selbst von früher her eine Wohnung besitzst.

3. Zapfenstreich: Wenn Du Deinen Hausschlüssel vergessen hast, dann versuche nur im Notfall die Haustür mit einer geballten Ladung aufzuschließen. Probiere es zunächst mit der elektrischen Klingel.

4. Beim Besuch bei Bekannten könnte es Befremden erregen, wenn Du vor dem Platznehmen Tapeten und Sofa auf Wanzen und Läuse untersuchst.
Bei Deinem E r s t e n Besuch wäre der Befund sowieso negativ.

5. Verpflegung: Unterlasse das Aufreißen von Dielen und Parkettböden. Kartoffeln werden in Deutschland an anderen Stellen aufbewahrt.

6. Übernachtung: Die in Deutschland gebräuchlichen Öfen eignen sich nicht besonders als Schlafstellen. Die in den Schlafzimmern aufgestellten rechteckigen, weiß bezogenen Gegenstände (Betten) können dagegen bedenkenlos zum Schlafen benutzt werden, auch wenn sie schon zur Hälfte belegt sein sollten. (In diesem Falle jedoch erst Personalien prüfen). Es entspricht nicht soldatischer Härte und Anpassungsfähigkeit, unbedingt auf einem Bund Stroh als Lagerstätte auf dem Fußboden zu bestehen.

7. Gesundheitspflege: In der Frühe mit einem Wassereimer loszusausen, um in der weiteren Umgebung Wasser zu suchen, ist sinnlos. Man lasse sich von den Eingeborenen an ihre Zimmerquellen führen. Hygienische Bedenken gegen das Wassertrinken bestehen in diesem Falle nicht, doch vergiß dabei nicht, dass es sich um eine durchaus unproletarische Gewohnheit handelt. An dem übertriebenen Wasserverbrauch der Eingeborenen darf man sich dabei nicht stören.

8. Sanitäre Anlagen: Niedrige, weisse Porzellanschüsseln eigenartiger Form mit Holzrand, wie sie in bestimmten Räumen deutscher Wohnungen aufgestellt sind, dienen besonderen Zwecken, die man sich von der Hausfrau am besten erläutern lässt. Nach Beendigung des besonderen Zweckes an der seitlich angebrachten Kette ziehen(Nicht erschrecken! Geräusch harmlos.) Zum Haarwaschen und Rasieren unpraktisch.

9. Heizung: Es hat keinen Zweck, zum Einheizen das Nachbarhaus einzureissen da die Deutschen eigenartigerweise zum Häuserbau Steine benutzen. Ausserdem wäre zu befürchten, daß die faschistische Bürokratie Schwierigkeiten machte.

10. Verkehr mit der Bevölkerung: Weiblich gekleidete Personen sind in Deutschland zwar nicht in allen Fällen Flintenweiber, sie bilden aber trotzdem für den Fronturlauber eine nicht zu unterschätzende Gefahr, Annäherungsversuchen begegne man mit einem sturen "nix ponjemaio".

Figures 3-6 & 3-7. Not all informative pamphlets were at all serious, either. These two Merkblatt für Fronturlauber (Pamphlet for Those on Leave from the Front), written and distributed by light-hearted clerks who've signed as the Urlaubsverhinderungskommissar (Leave Prevention Commissar), include such instructions as "... in Germany they have these things called beds,..." and not to speak about the "paradisiacal conditions in Russia or else everyone will want to come and ruin the idyllic convenience we enjoy." (A4)

it had been done. The majority of *Entlausungsstelle* were located on the Eastern Front due to the conditions across such expanses, though as the situation in France and Italy deteriorated in 1944, stations were established along the *Reich's* western and southern borders to accommodate its battle weary troops.

Once a soldier had been declared healthy, his next hurdle was to acquire a ticket, provided he was traveling at his own expense. More often than not, this meant a drive to the train station and a stroll to the window; soldiers leaving the front rarely had to purchase train fare and travel was often at *Wehrmacht* expense.

As mentioned before, the *Soldat* was restricted to certain trains on which he could travel, except when riding on his own. As a courtesy, the *Reichsbahn* had reduced-fare tickets available on a *Wehrmacht-fahrkarte*, or *Wehrmacht* Ticket. Reduced fares were also available on the *Strassenbahn* (Street Train) and *Omnibus* (Semi-bus) once a soldier arrived at his destination, and tickets often reflected this by specially marked stamps.

If a soldier or family member of a soldier wanted to visit a wounded or sick comrade, or to attend his funeral, one could fill out an *Antrag auf Fahrpreisermässigung* (Proposal for Fare Reduction) in an attempt to reduce the cost when the *Wehrmacht* did not provide for travel. This is one instance where conditions presented by the *Wehrmacht* could affect civilian travel; this form could be filed by a *Soldat* or a member of the *Soldat's* family. The *Antrag* was usually reserved for civilians, but if a soldier had attained leave for the expressed purpose of bereavement, a condition that was not normally paid for by the *Wehrmacht*, this form was intended to ease the sorrowful burden of the trip.

There were two conditions in which one's fare could be reduced. The first would be to visit a wounded relation who was home from the front and under a doctor's care in a military hospital. Particulars of the hospitalization were not

Figure 3-8. A World War I postcard (1915), expounding on the humorous conditions and relief experienced by deloused soldiers. During World War II, however, delousing would become second only to examination for infectious diseases in importance to travelling Soldaten. (B7)

Figure 3-9. The Entlaussungsschein or E-Schein (Delousing Certificate) was a very important document that one kept a very close guard over; without it, a Soldat might be forbidden to board his train home. These two E-Scheinen are from the Eastern Front (Brest-Litovsk and Przemysl), but Entlaussungsstellen were established in Naples, Rome, and eventually within the Reich itself, in Mainz and Aachen, for Soldaten returning from the African, Italian, and Western Fronts. (D6 and A6, respectively)

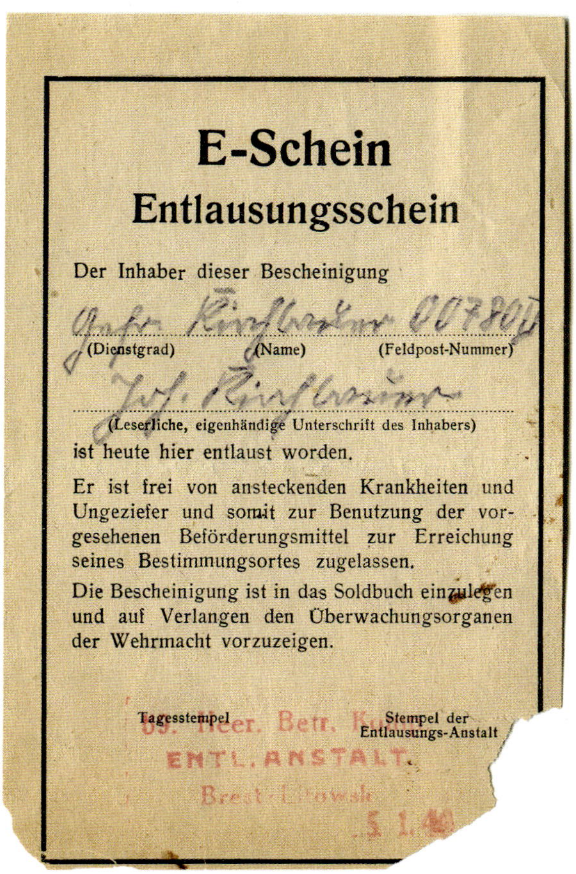

E-Schein

Entlausungsschein

Der Inhaber dieser Bescheinigung

(Dienstgrad) (Name) (Feldpost-Nummer)

(Leserliche, eigenhändige Unterschrift des Inhabers)

ist heute hier entlaust worden.

Er ist frei von ansteckenden Krankheiten und Ungeziefer und somit zur Benutzung der vorgesehenen Beförderungsmittel zur Erreichung seines Bestimmungsortes zugelassen.

Die Bescheinigung ist in das Soldbuch einzulegen und auf Verlangen den Überwachungsorganen der Wehrmacht vorzuzeigen.

Tagesstempel — Stempel der Entlausungs-Anstalt

ENTL. ANSTALT.

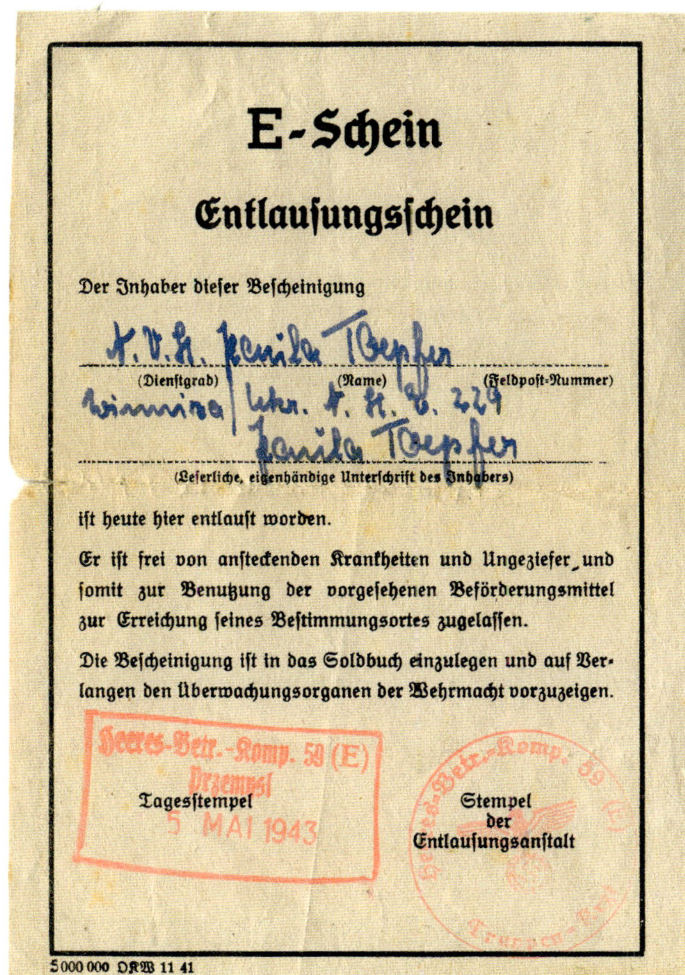

E-Schein

Entlausungsschein

Der Inhaber dieser Bescheinigung

(Dienstgrad) (Name) (Feldpost-Nummer)

(Leserliche, eigenhändige Unterschrift des Inhabers)

ist heute hier entlaust worden.

Er ist frei von ansteckenden Krankheiten und Ungeziefer und somit zur Benutzung der vorgesehenen Beförderungsmittel zur Erreichung seines Bestimmungsortes zugelassen.

Die Bescheinigung ist in das Soldbuch einzulegen und auf Verlangen den Überwachungsorganen der Wehrmacht vorzuzeigen.

Heeres-Betr.-Komp. 59 (E) Przemysl

Tagesstempel 5 MAI 1943

Stempel der Entlausungsanstalt

5000000 DKW 11 41

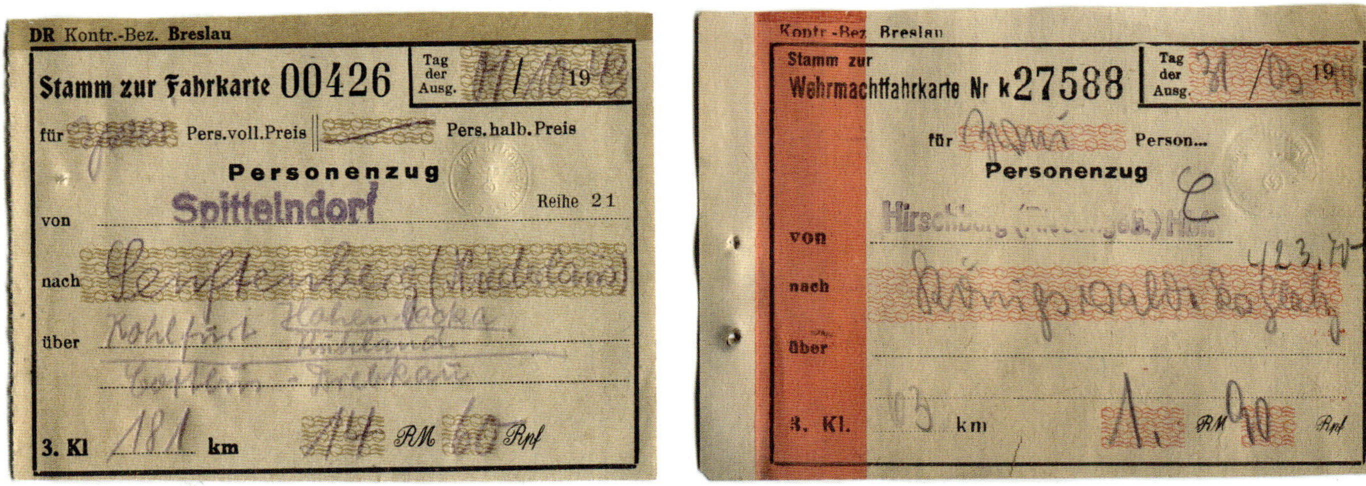

Figure 3-10. The visual difference between civilian train tickets and those reserved for use by Wehrmacht personnel. This made it very easy for Reichsbahn conductors to identify whether someone was using the correct tickets, and whether to ask for additional information. (A7)

Figure 3-11. A military ticket for three from Osterholz-Scharmbeck to Aachen from 1937.

Figure 3-12. Note that even after the war, the Reichsbahn continued to make the distinction between civilian passengers and the many discharged soldiers returning home; this ticket is dated January 9, 1946.

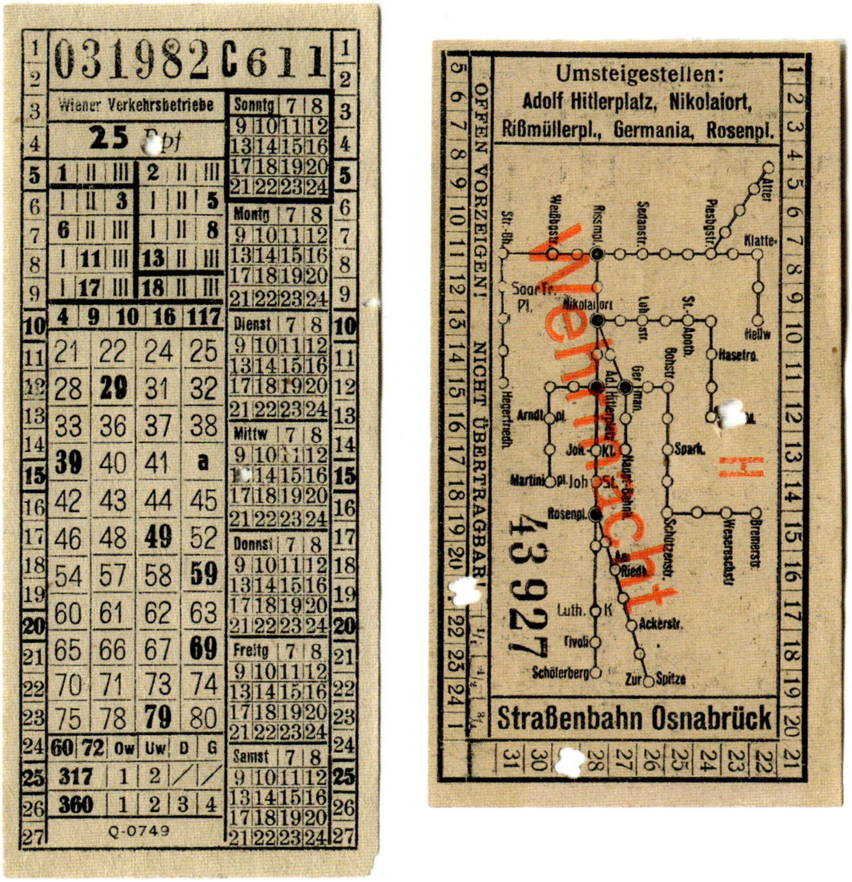

Figure 3-13. Not all Wehrmacht tickets were printed differently, but were still identified by the use of Stempeln. These examples, one from Vienna, Austria, and Osnabrück, Germany, note the similarities and distinct differences between civilian and military Strassenbahn (street train or trolley) tickets.

Figure 3-14. This is a series of Doppelkarten (double tickets), two-way tickets of the shorter route Personnenzüge, reissued following the war using old stocks of invalidated wartime military tickets due to postwar shortages. Note the dates impressed into the top of the tickets; 547 and 647 for May and June of 1947.

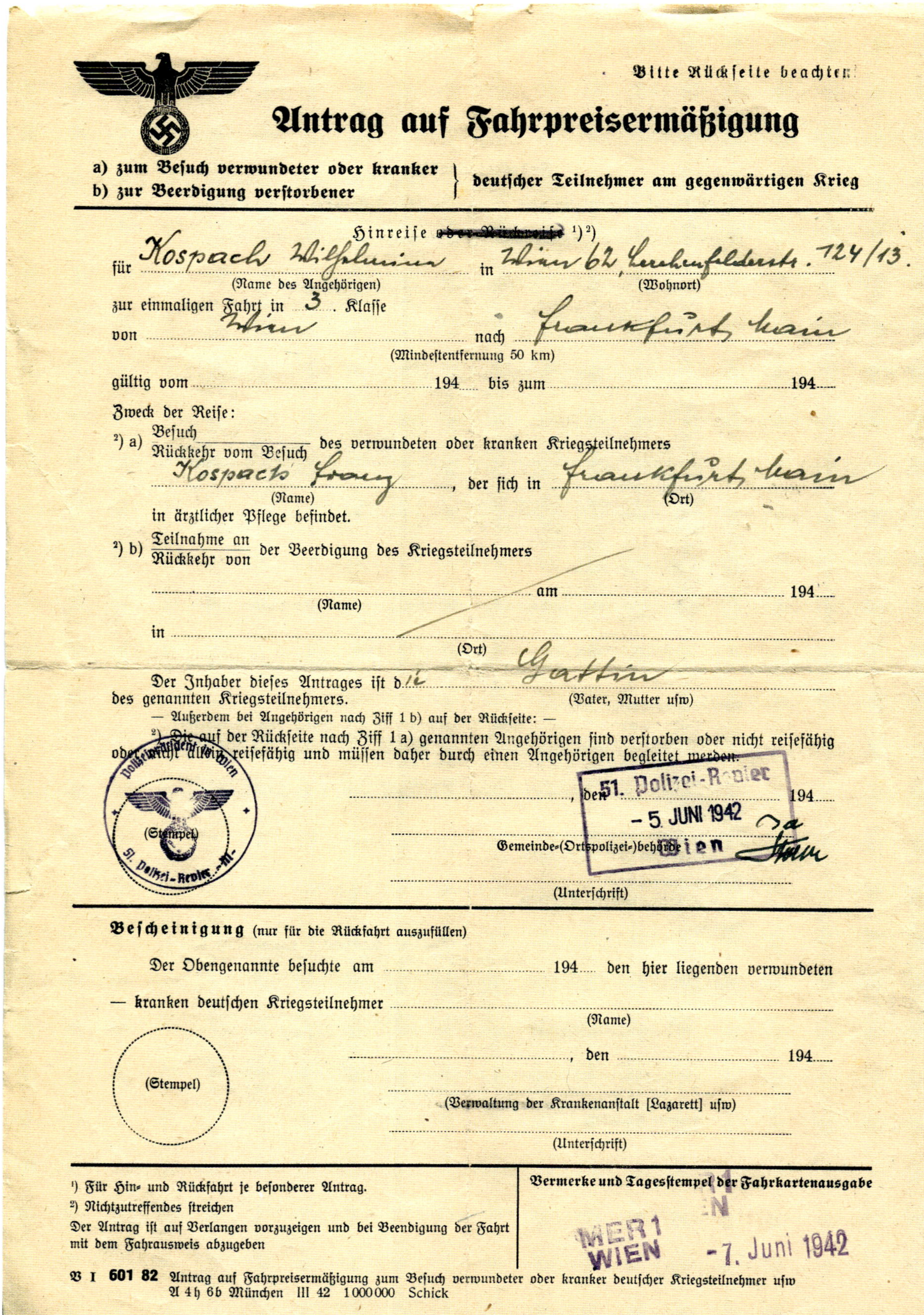

Bitte Rückseite beachten!

Antrag auf Fahrpreisermäßigung

a) zum Besuch verwundeter oder kranker
b) zur Beerdigung verstorbener
} deutscher Teilnehmer am gegenwärtigen Krieg

Hinreise ~~oder Rückreise~~ [1] [2])

für Kospach Wilhelmine in Wien 62, Leuchenfelderstr. 124/13.
(Name des Angehörigen) (Wohnort)

zur einmaligen Fahrt in 3. Klasse

von Wien nach Frankfurt Main
(Mindestentfernung 50 km)

gültig vom .... 194.... bis zum .... 194....

Zweck der Reise:

[2]) a) Besuch / Rückkehr vom Besuch des verwundeten oder kranken Kriegsteilnehmers

Kospach Franz, der sich in Frankfurt Main
(Name) (Ort)

in ärztlicher Pflege befindet.

[2]) b) Teilnahme an / Rückkehr von der Beerdigung des Kriegsteilnehmers

.... am .... 194....
(Name)

in ....
(Ort)

Der Inhaber dieses Antrages ist die Gattin
des genannten Kriegsteilnehmers. (Vater, Mutter usw)

— Außerdem bei Angehörigen nach Ziff 1 b) auf der Rückseite: —

[2]) Die auf der Rückseite nach Ziff 1 a) genannten Angehörigen sind verstorben oder nicht reisefähig oder nicht allein reisefähig und müssen daher durch einen Angehörigen begleitet werden.

(Stempel) Polizeipräsident in Wien — 51. Polizei-Revier

........, den 51. Polizei-Revier – 5. JUNI 1942 Wien 194....

Gemeinde-(Ortspolizei-)behörde

(Unterschrift)

Bescheinigung (nur für die Rückfahrt auszufüllen)

Der Obengenannte besuchte am .... 194.... den hier liegenden verwundeten — kranken deutschen Kriegsteilnehmer ....
(Name)

(Stempel)

........, den .... 194....

(Verwaltung der Krankenanstalt [Lazarett] usw)

(Unterschrift)

[1]) Für Hin- und Rückfahrt je besonderer Antrag.
[2]) Nichtzutreffendes streichen
Der Antrag ist auf Verlangen vorzuzeigen und bei Beendigung der Fahrt mit dem Fahrausweis abzugeben

Vermerke und Tagesstempel der Fahrkartenausgabe

WIEN -7. Juni 1942

V I 601 82 Antrag auf Fahrpreisermäßigung zum Besuch verwundeter oder kranker deutscher Kriegsteilnehmer usw
A 4h 6b München III 42 1000000 Schick

Figure 3-14. A Fahrpreisermässigung (Fare Reduction) form filed by Wilhelmine Kospach of Vienna, Austria to visit her wounded husband Franz in Frankfurt am Main (Germany has two Frankfurts, one on the Main River and the other on the banks of the Oder). Her request was approved by the Chief of Police in Vienna on June 5, 1942. (A4)

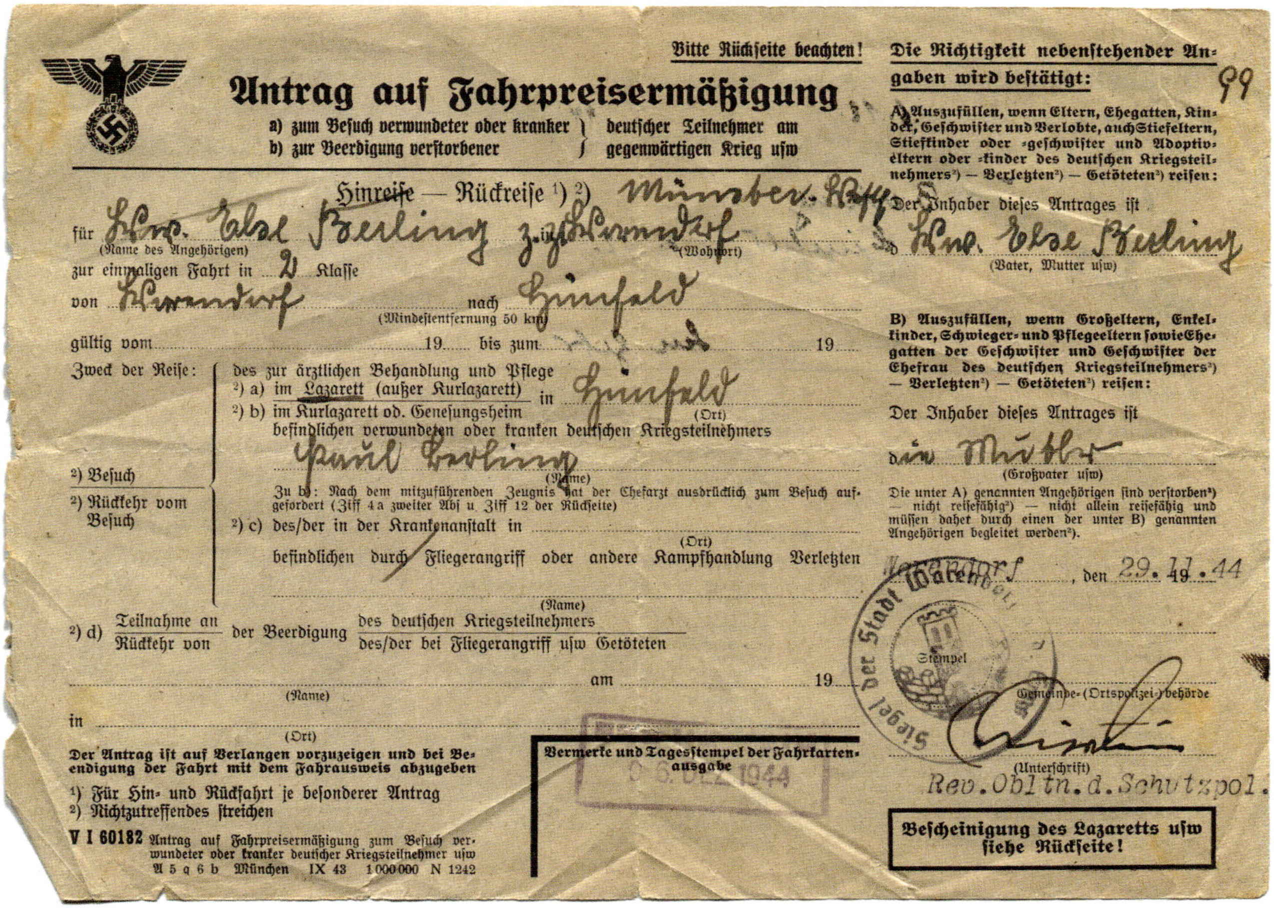

Bitte Rückseite beachten!

Antrag auf Fahrpreisermäßigung

a) zum Besuch verwundeter oder kranker } deutscher Teilnehmer am
b) zur Beerdigung verstorbener } gegenwärtigen Krieg usw

Hinreise — Rückreise ¹) ²) Münster

für Frau Else Berling z.Zt. Warendorf
(Name des Angehörigen) (Wohnort)
zur einmaligen Fahrt in 2. Klasse
von Warendorf nach Hünfeld
(Mindestentfernung 50 km)
gültig vom ......19...... bis zum ......19......

Zweck der Reise: des zur ärztlichen Behandlung und Pflege
²) a) im Lazarett (außer Kurlazarett) in Hünfeld
²) b) im Kurlazarett od. Genesungsheim (Ort)
befindlichen verwundeten oder kranken deutschen Kriegsteilnehmers
Paul Berling
(Name)
²) Besuch
²) Rückkehr vom Besuch
Zu b): Nach dem mitzuführenden Zeugnis hat der Chefarzt ausdrücklich zum Besuch aufgefordert (Ziff 4a zweiter Abs u. Ziff 12 der Rückseite)
²) c) des/der in der Krankenanstalt in ...... (Ort)
befindlichen durch Fliegerangriff oder andere Kampfhandlung Verletzten
(Name)
²) d) Teilnahme an / Rückkehr von der Beerdigung des deutschen Kriegsteilnehmers / des/der bei Fliegerangriff usw Getöteten
...... (Name) am ......19......
in ...... (Ort)

Der Antrag ist auf Verlangen vorzuzeigen und bei Beendigung der Fahrt mit dem Fahrausweis abzugeben
¹) Für Hin- und Rückfahrt je besonderer Antrag
²) Nichtzutreffendes streichen
V I 60182 Antrag auf Fahrpreisermäßigung zum Besuch verwundeter oder kranker deutscher Kriegsteilnehmer usw
A 5 q 6 b München IX 43 1000000 N 1242

Vermerke und Tagesstempel der Fahrkartenausgabe
6. DEZ 1944

Die Richtigkeit nebenstehender Angaben wird bestätigt: 99

A) Auszufüllen, wenn Eltern, Ehegatten, Kinder, Geschwister und Verlobte, auch Stiefeltern, Stiefkinder oder -geschwister und Adoptiveltern oder -kinder des deutschen Kriegsteilnehmers²) — Verletzten²) — Getöteten²) reisen:
Der Inhaber dieses Antrages ist Frau Else Berling
(Vater, Mutter usw)

B) Auszufüllen, wenn Großeltern, Enkelkinder, Schwieger- und Pflegeeltern sowie Ehegatten der Geschwister und Geschwister der Ehefrau des deutschen Kriegsteilnehmers²) — Verletzten²) — Getöteten²) reisen:
Der Inhaber dieses Antrages ist die Mutter
(Großvater usw)
Die unter A) genannten Angehörigen sind verstorben²) — nicht reisefähig²) — nicht allein reisefähig und müssen daher durch einen der unter B) genannten Angehörigen begleitet werden²).

Warendorf, den 29.11.44
Siegel der Stadt Warendorf
Stempel
Gemeinde-(Ortspolizei-)behörde
(Unterschrift)
Rev.Oblt.n.d.Schutzpol.

Bescheinigung des Lazaretts usw siehe Rückseite!

Figure 3-15. An example of a smaller version of the same form as the previous figure, this Antrag (Request) was filed by Else Berling of Warendorf to visit her wounded husband Obergefreiter Paul Berling in Reserve-Lazarett Hünfeld late in the war, in November of 1944. It was not approved until December 6, 1944. (5³/₄" x 8¹/₄")

required on the form, but some proof other than a wife's word was no doubt required.

The second permissible condition for fare reduction was to attend the funeral of an unfortunate *Soldat*. Again, the form did not require proof, though a letter or other notification from the authorities was almost certainly required.

Later versions of the form maintained the two primary conditions for fare reduction, but the first, visiting a wounded relation, was divided into more specific conditions of the visit, primarily distinguishing whether the *Soldat* was in extended care, short-term care, or had been wounded in an air raid.

An A4 form (later, an A5 form was issued), the soldier or relative would fill out their name and particulars of their trip, such as which class they were traveling in, first, second, or third, and the route for which one sought fare reduction. It was approved or denied, not by the *Reichsbahn*, but by the *Polizeipräsident*, or Police President (Chief of Police), of the departure district. Once approved, the form would be turned in at the ticket counter, where one would pay for a reduced-fare ticket.

For those who were wounded and recovering in a local hospital, but well enough to travel, there was the *Verwundeten-Fahrkarte* (Wounded Soldier's Ticket). Frequently accompanied by a *Stadt-Urlaubsschein* and *Ausweiskarte* (Identity Card), since hospitals kept personal items secured, including a soldier's *Soldbuch*, the *Verwundeten-Fahrkarte* was provided by the local city for convalescing soldiers. The reverse of the card stated the conditions of travel, primarily that the card was nontransferable (*nicht übertragbar*) and that soldiers were required to travel in uniform. Both cards were small, A7 size (74mm x 105mm), and often printed on a medium weight card stock.

Soldaten traveling with the *Kleiner Wehrmachtfahrschein* did so if space was available to them. Unless someone was willing to give up their seat, this often resulted in delays for a weary man eager to visit his family, unless he had a *Platzkarte* (Place Card) to guarantee his seat.

The *Platzkarte*, roughly A7 size since many available today appear to have been trimmed, was only valid as a guarantee for the date indicated. If one tried to travel on a different date, he would return to space available status.

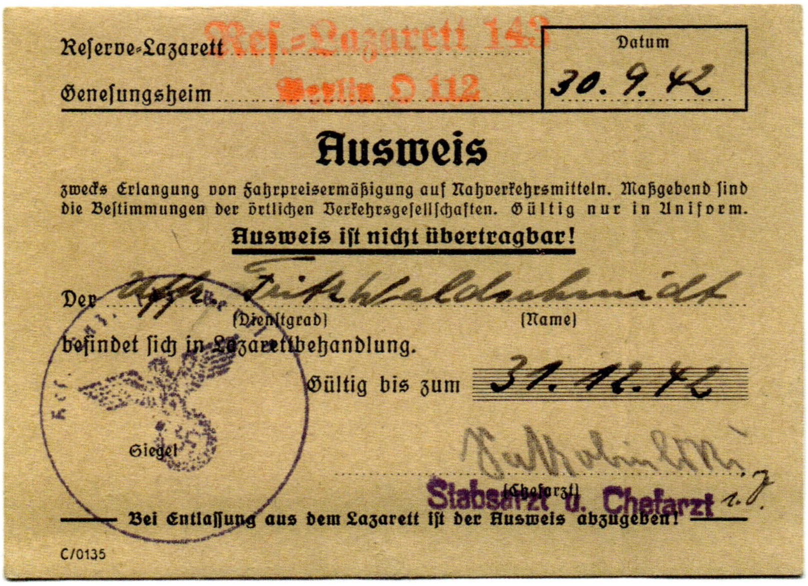

Reserve-Lazarett Res.-Lazarett 143
Genesungsheim Berlin O 112
Datum 30. 9. 42

Ausweis

zwecks Erlangung von Fahrpreisermäßigung auf Nahverkehrsmitteln. Maßgebend sind die Bestimmungen der örtlichen Verkehrsgesellschaften. Gültig nur in Uniform.

Ausweis ist nicht übertragbar!

Der Uffz. Fritz Waldschmidt
(Dienstgrad) (Name)
befindet sich in Lazarettbehandlung.
Gültig bis zum 31. 12. 42

Siegel

(Chefarzt)
Stabsarzt u. Chefarzt i.V.

Bei Entlassung aus dem Lazarett ist der Ausweis abzugeben!

C/0135

Figure 3-16. Issued by Reserve-Lazarett 143 in Berlin, this extension of Fare reduction was issued to Unteroffizier Fritz Waldenschmidt and was valid for short trips from the last day of September, 1942 until the end of the year (December 31, 1942). The bold line at the bottom states that should one be discharged from the hospital that the Ausweis is to be returned.

As you can imagine, these miniature documents would have been quite prized, so clerks in the *Verwaltungsstelle* would often write the number of the *Platzkarte* on the *Kriegsurlaubsschein*, *Marschbefehl*, or the *Sonderausweis*. The base of the *Platzkarte* specifically states that it is only valid if the number is recorded on either of these documents: *Nur gültig in Verbindung mit dem mit der Nummer der Platzkarte versehenen Urlaubsschein oder Dienstreiseausweis* (for example, note the *platzkarten* notations on the *Kriegsurlaubsschein* pictured in figures 2-067, 2-068, and 2-069). The back is often blank, but may at times have additional information written or stamped there.

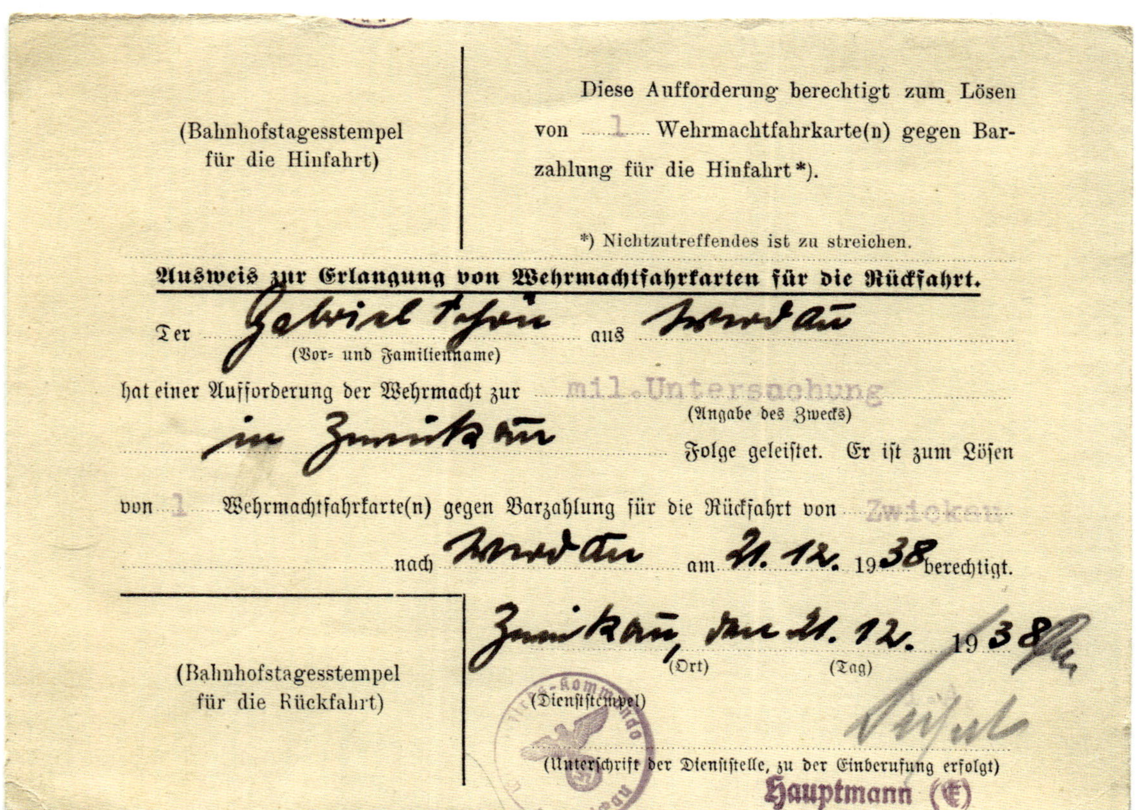

(Bahnhofstagesstempel für die Hinfahrt)

Diese Aufforderung berechtigt zum Lösen von 1 Wehrmachtfahrkarte(n) gegen Barzahlung für die Hinfahrt*).

*) Nichtzutreffendes ist zu streichen.

Ausweis zur Erlangung von Wehrmachtfahrkarten für die Rückfahrt.

Der Gabriel Schein aus Werdau
(Vor- und Familienname)
hat einer Aufforderung der Wehrmacht zur mil. Untersuchung
(Angabe des Zwecks)
in Zwickau Folge geleistet. Er ist zum Lösen
von 1 Wehrmachtfahrkarte(n) gegen Barzahlung für die Rückfahrt von Zwickau
nach Werdau am 21. 12. 1938 berechtigt.

(Bahnhofstagesstempel für die Rückfahrt)

Zwickau, den 21. 12. 1938
(Ort) (Tag)
(Dienststempel)
(Unterschrift der Dienststelle, zu der Einberufung erfolgt)
Hauptmann (E)

Figure 3-17. The lower half of a larger form, the section retained by the bearer, this form was similar to the Antrag, in that it permitted a Soldat to acquire a Wehrmacht ticket for military purposes, rather than having to purchase one on his own.

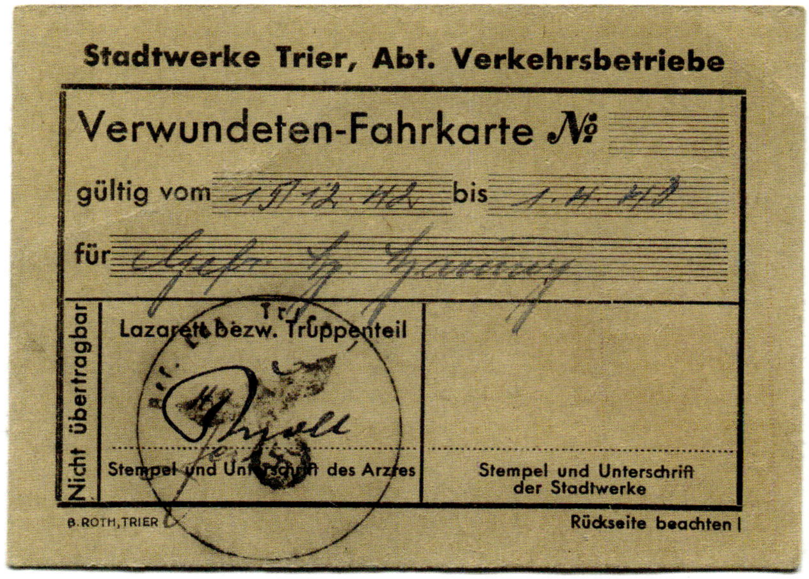

Stadtwerke Trier, Abt. Verkehrsbetriebe

Verwundeten-Fahrkarte №

gültig vom 15/12.42 bis 1.4.43

für

Nicht übertragbar

Lazarett bezw. Truppenteil

Stempel und Unterschrift des Arztes

Stempel und Unterschrift der Stadtwerke

B. ROTH, TRIER

Rückseite beachten!

Figure 3-18. A Verwundeten-Fahrkarte issued by the Reserve-Lazarett Trier, valid (in this case) from December 15, 1942 until April 1, 1943.

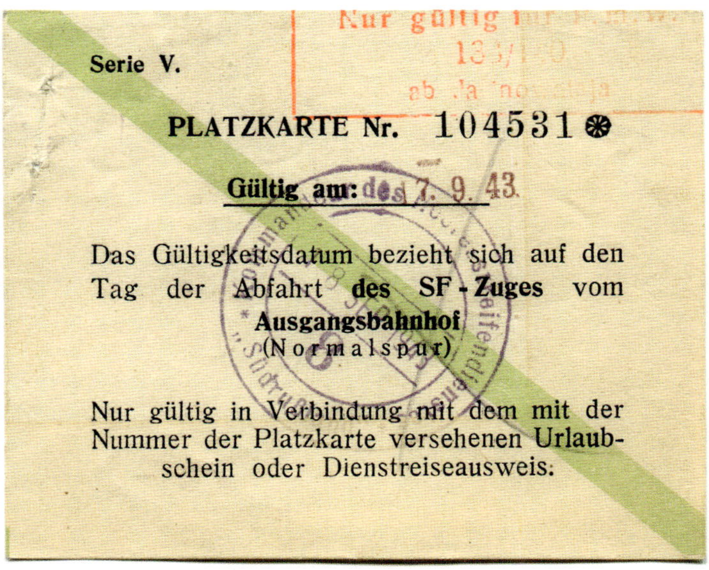

Serie V.

PLATZKARTE Nr. 104531 ✲

Gültig am: des 7. 9. 43

Das Gültigkeitsdatum bezieht sich auf den Tag der Abfahrt des SF-Zuges vom Ausgangsbahnhof (Normalspur)

Nur gültig in Verbindung mit dem mit der Nummer der Platzkarte versehenen Urlaubschein oder Dienstreiseausweis.

II Serie

PLATZKARTE Nr. 0072182 ✲

Gültig am: 9.12.42

Das Gültigkeitsdatum bezieht sich auf den Tag der Abfahrt des SF-Zuges vom Ausgangsbahnhof (Normalspur)

Nur gültig in Verbindung mit dem mit der Nummer der Platzkarte versehenen Urlaubschein oder Dienstreiseausweis.

Figure 3-19 & 3-20. Two examples of Platzkarten, or place cards. These documents guaranteed a seat on a train for a Soldat aboard SF trains, provided he left on time. Each card was numbered and dated, the number of which was often typed, stamped, or written on the Kriegsurlaubsschein or Wehrmachtfahrschein.

Required at One's Destination

The German soldier enjoyed his time away, especially if his unit was stationed at the front. Since many *Soldaten* had never been outside Germany before, due primarily to economic conditions throughout the 1920s and 1930s, they were the consummate sightseers and took advantage of every opportunity presented to them to expand their horizons.

The primary destination of choice for leave, from *Erholungsurlaub* (Recreational Leave) to *Kultururlaub* (Cultural Leave) was Paris. Given the number of soldiers that visited the city, one might almost be led to believe that this was the principal reason Germany invaded France in 1940. Even soldiers just passing through the city were often given a chance to see the city while they awaited their next train.

The *Passierschein für Durchreisende* (Passage Permit for Through-Travelers(was issued at numerous Paris train stations. Single sided and printed on an off-white paper in France for the *Wehrmacht*, it was 108mm x 175mm, and was good for a maximum of two hours, noted at the base of the form. It was issued to *Soldaten* transferring from one Paris train station to another, and although it afforded them an opportunity to see some of the city before departing, it guaranteed that they would not take

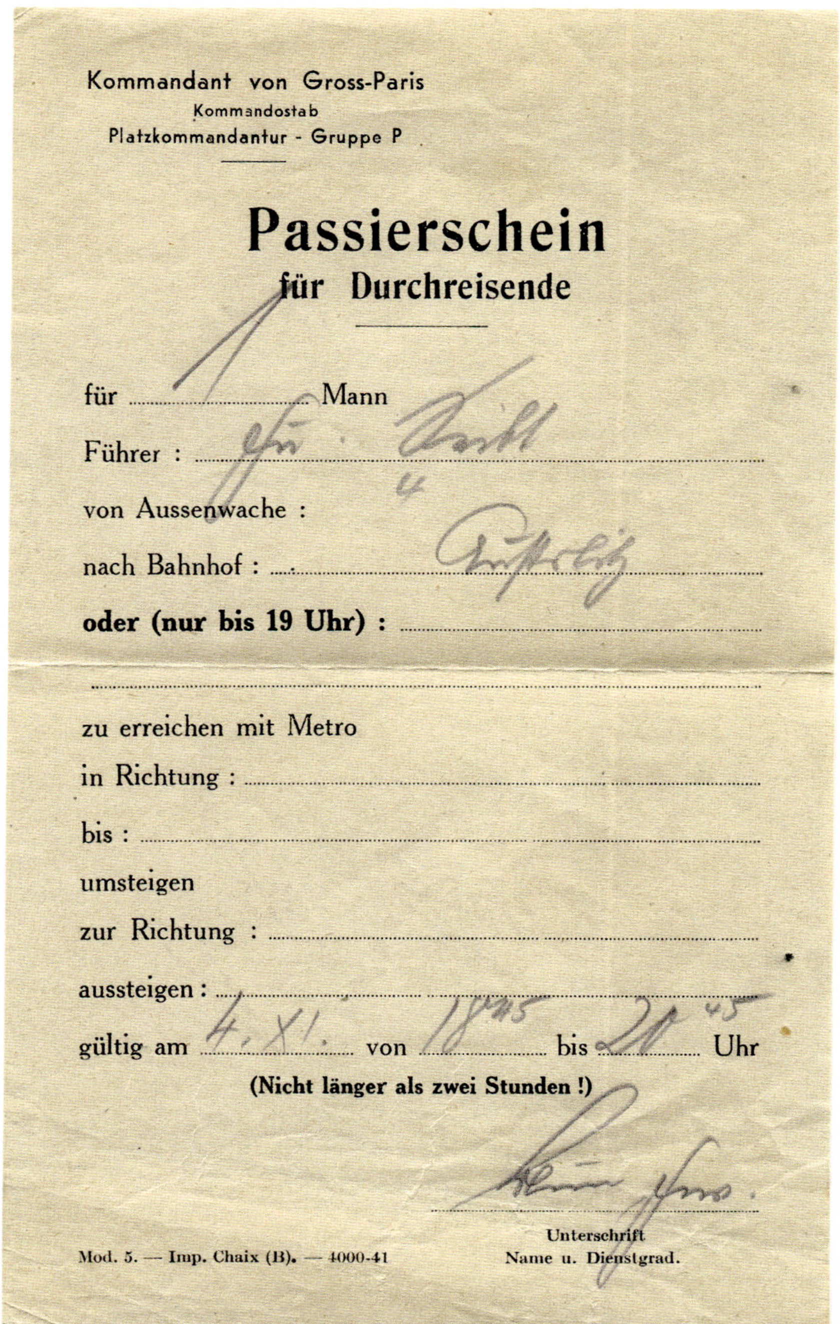

Kommandant von Gross-Paris
Kommandostab
Platzkommandantur - Gruppe P

Passierschein
für Durchreisende

für 1 Mann
Führer :
von Aussenwache :
nach Bahnhof :
oder (nur bis 19 Uhr) :

zu erreichen mit Metro
in Richtung :
bis :
umsteigen
zur Richtung :
aussteigen :
gültig am 4.XI. von 18 45 bis 20 45 Uhr
(Nicht länger als zwei Stunden !)

Unterschrift
Name u. Dienstgrad.

Mod. 5. — Imp. Chaix (B). — 4000-41

Figure 3-21. The Passierschein, or "Passing" certificate, was issued to a Soldat transferring from one train to another in Paris, just to ensure he didn't get "lost."

all day in doing so. This form was important for a Soldat who was not actually on leave in Paris, and did not have a *Befristeter Ausweis*.

For those that had traveled to Paris as their destination, a temporary identity card was used as a pass to identify the soldier on leave and was known as the *Befristeter Ausweis*. This was printed on a heavier white cover stock, a little larger than B7 size, 95mm x 135mm, and was only valid for a maximum of fourteen days (*Längerste Gültigkeitsdauer 14 Tage!*).

The *Befristeter Ausweis* was colorful; in order to determine whether a soldier had overstayed his leave, cards were printed with patterns of crosses, circles, checks, squiggles, and diamonds in different colors. Each Muster (Pattern) was identified by number and printed on the lower left hand corner of the card, Muster 1, Muster 2, etc., and they changed from year to year. Muster 4 in 1941 was different from Muster 4 in 1943, for instance.

Different patterns would be issued at different periods, so the only soldiers who were permitted in the city during a particular span of time would have that particular pattern on their *Ausweis*. Anyone carrying a card printed with a different pattern or color would no doubt be questioned. Thoroughly.

The card was issued by the *Kommandant von Gross-Paris*, the Commander of Greater Paris, and bore the *Dienststempel* of his office: *Kommandant Der Stadt Paris*

Der Kommandant von Gross-Paris

Längste Gültigkeitsdauer 14 Tage!

Befristeter Ausweis № J54501

Der ....
(Dienstgrad, Vor- und Zuname.)

Feldpost Nr. .... MAI 19

ist berechtigt sich am 15. 5. 41 .... bis zum ....
(Datum)

in der Innenstadt aufzuhalten.

Ausgestellt am 15. 5. 41   *Ausgegeben durch :*

Ausgebende Einheit :   Feldpoststempel.

KOMMANDANT DER STADT PARIS

Unterschrift u. Dienstgrad.

Muster 4.

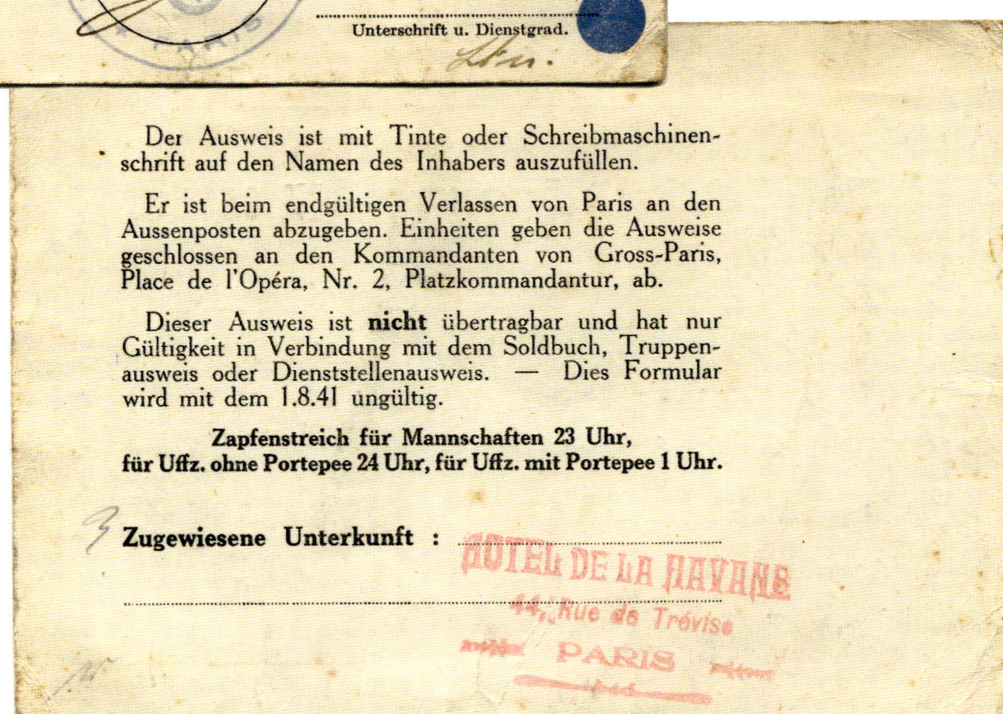

Der Ausweis ist mit Tinte oder Schreibmaschinenschrift auf den Namen des Inhabers auszufüllen.

Er ist beim endgültigen Verlassen von Paris an den Aussenposten abzugeben. Einheiten geben die Ausweise geschlossen an den Kommandanten von Gross-Paris, Place de l'Opéra, Nr. 2, Platzkommandantur, ab.

Dieser Ausweis ist **nicht** übertragbar und hat nur Gültigkeit in Verbindung mit dem Soldbuch, Truppenausweis oder Dienststellenausweis. — Dies Formular wird mit dem 1.8.41 ungültig.

Zapfenstreich für Mannschaften 23 Uhr,
für Uffz. ohne Portepee 24 Uhr, für Uffz. mit Portepee 1 Uhr.

Zugewiesene Unterkunft : ....

HOTEL DE LA HAVANE
44, Rue de Trévise
PARIS

Figure 3-22 (previous page) through 3-25. Temporary identity cards were issued to Soldaten visiting Paris on leave. Cards had different patterns of varying colors on them to distinguish when they were valid, as one can see by this small collection of three different cards issued between May 1941 and January 1943 (miswritten as January, 1942 on the third example). One has to wonder whether overzealous Gendarmes gave Gefreiter Blascun any difficulty when checking his pass.

Der Kommandant von Gross-Paris

Befristeter Ausweis № 139476

Der .... (Dienstgrad, Vor- und Zuname.)

Feldpost Nr. 28 447

ist berechtigt sich am 13 JUIL 1942 bis zum 14 JUIL 1942 (Datum) in der Innenstadt aufzuhalten.

Ausgestellt am 13 JUIL 1942 *Ausgegeben durch :*

Ausgebende Einheit : Feldpoststempel!

Unterschrift u. Dienstgrad.

Muster 4.

Längste Gültigkeitsdauer 14 Tage!

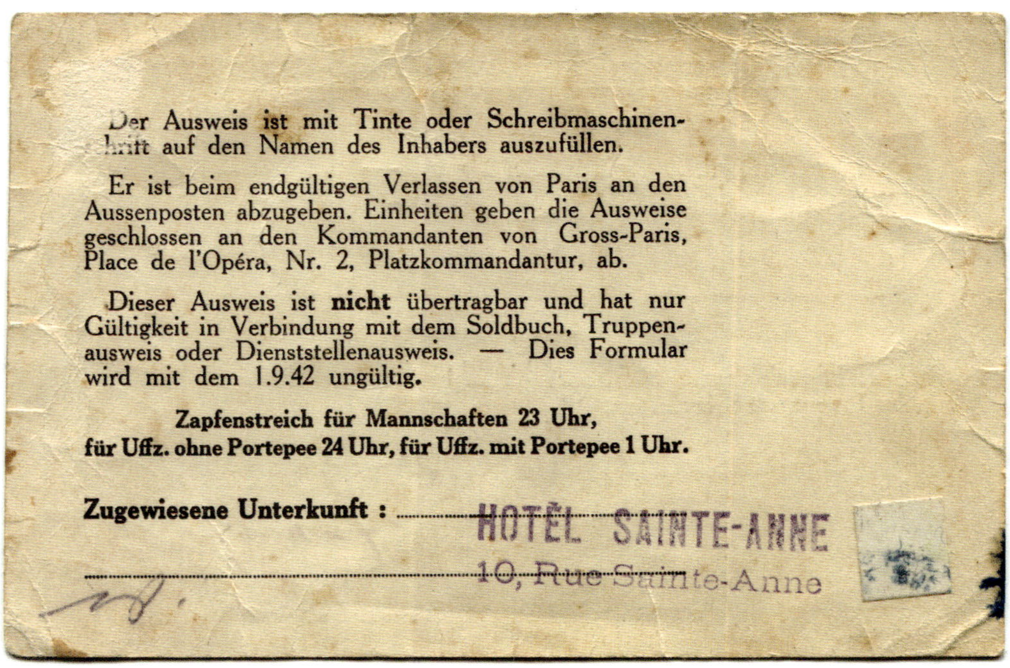

Der Ausweis ist mit Tinte oder Schreibmaschinenschrift auf den Namen des Inhabers auszufüllen.

Er ist beim endgültigen Verlassen von Paris an den Aussenposten abzugeben. Einheiten geben die Ausweise geschlossen an den Kommandanten von Gross-Paris, Place de l'Opéra, Nr. 2, Platzkommandantur, ab.

Dieser Ausweis ist **nicht** übertragbar und hat nur Gültigkeit in Verbindung mit dem Soldbuch, Truppenausweis oder Dienststellenausweis. — Dies Formular wird mit dem 1.9.42 ungültig.

Zapfenstreich für Mannschaften 23 Uhr, für Uffz. ohne Portepee 24 Uhr, für Uffz. mit Portepee 1 Uhr.

Zugewiesene Unterkunft : HOTEL SAINTE-ANNE 10, Rue Sainte-Anne

(Commander of the City of Paris). It was filled out with the soldier's rank and name, as well as the dates for which the pass was valid.

The back of the card was reserved for instructions for the card: that the name of the bearer must be written in ink or typed out, that the card must be mailed or turned in to the *Kommandantur's* office upon leaving Paris, and that the card is not valid unless it is accompanied by the *Soldbuch*, *Truppenausweis* (Troop Identity Card, often issued in areas where carrying the *Soldbuch* might present a security risk), or the *Dienststellenausweis* (Duty Station Identity Card). It also notes when the particular pattern and color expired, again to prevent soldiers from overstaying their welcome.

The last line, often in bold type, gave the curfew for soldiers to be off the streets, *23 Uhr,* or 11:00 p.m. for

Der Kommandant von Gross-Paris

Befristeter Ausweis № 503082

Der Gefreiter Heinrich [illegible]
(Dienstgrad, Vor- und Zuname.)
Feldpost Nr. L 34941 a
ist berechtigt sich am 29. 12. 42 bis zum 11. 1. 42
(Datum)
in der Innenstadt aufzuhalten.

Ausgestellt am 29. 12. 42 *Ausgegeben durch:*

Ausgebende Einheit: Feldpoststempel!

Unterschrift u. Dienstgrad.
Oberleutnant u. Einheitsführer

Muster 4.

Längste Gültigkeitsdauer 14 Tage!

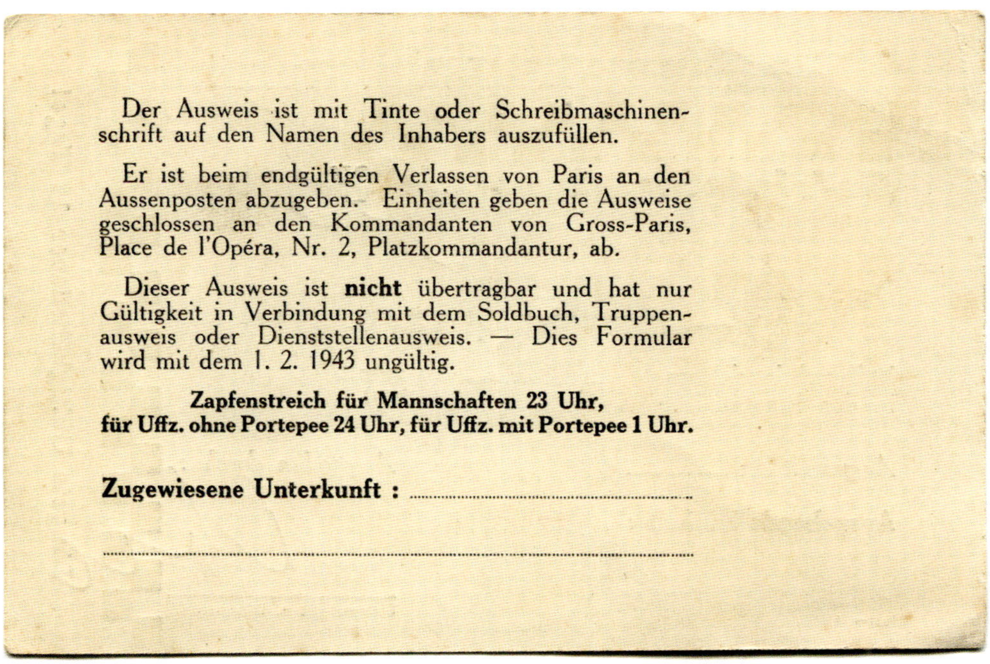

Der Ausweis ist mit Tinte oder Schreibmaschinenschrift auf den Namen des Inhabers auszufüllen.

Er ist beim endgültigen Verlassen von Paris an den Aussenposten abzugeben. Einheiten geben die Ausweise geschlossen an den Kommandanten von Gross-Paris, Place de l'Opéra, Nr. 2, Platzkommandantur, ab.

Dieser Ausweis ist **nicht** übertragbar und hat nur Gültigkeit in Verbindung mit dem Soldbuch, Truppenausweis oder Dienststellenausweis. — Dies Formular wird mit dem 1. 2. 1943 ungültig.

Zapfenstreich für Mannschaften 23 Uhr, für Uffz. ohne Portepee 24 Uhr, für Uffz. mit Portepee 1 Uhr.

Zugewiesene Unterkunft : ....

soldiers, midnight for NCOs without the *Portepee*, and 1:00 a.m. for NCOs with the *Portepee*. The *Portepee* was a decorative tassel that hung from a soldier's sword or bayonet. In the *Wehrmacht*, this signified that an NCO bore additional responsibility as a Senior NCO, such as a *Feldwebel* (Sergeant) or *Oberfeldwebel* (Over-Sergeant).

At times, the back of the *Befristeter Ausweis* would be stamped at the bottom with the name and address of a hotel where a soldier would be billeted. These hotels had made arrangements with the *Kommandantur's* office, which benefitted both; the hotels received constant business, and the *Feldgendarmerie* (Field Police, or MPs) knew where to look should the need arise to locate an errant *Soldat*.

A special identity card, the *Sonderausweis* Paris, was prepared for soldiers stationed at the military garrison (*Dienststellen des Standortes*) for Paris. The card was the same size as the *Befristeter Ausweis*, but printed on different colors of paper to make it easier for the authorities to tell them apart. It had the same conditions printed on them, but listed no expiration date or curfews.

As the war continued and Germany and its territories began to suffer the ravages of the Allied bombing campaign, increasingly more help was needed to man anti-aircraft stations and conduct other essential emergency services. Soldiers visiting from the front were expected to assist, as noted earlier; instructions and directions to

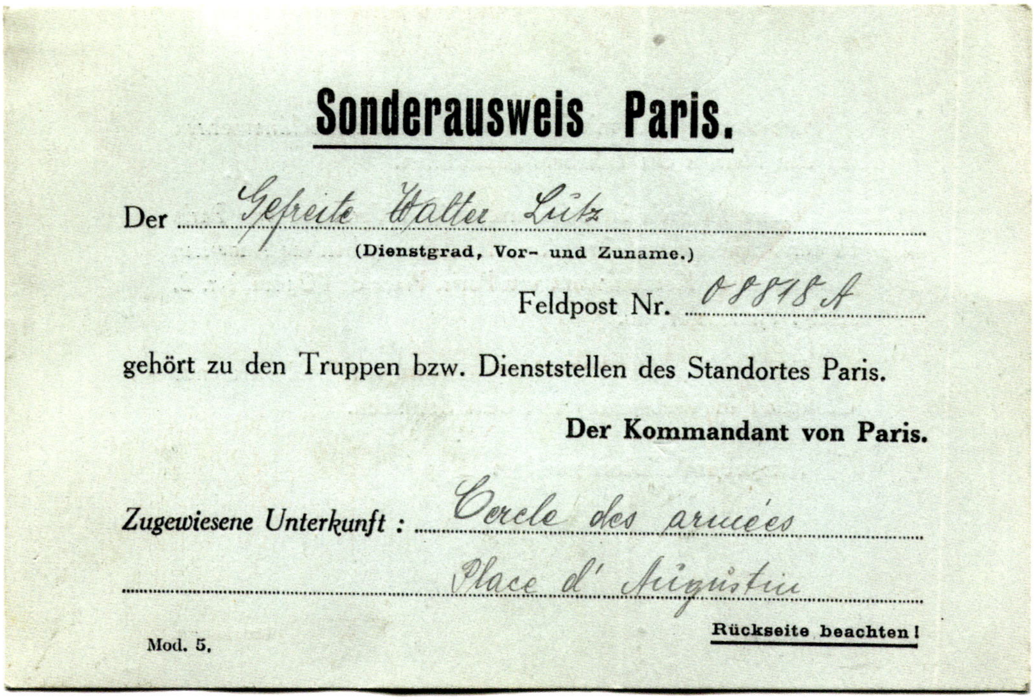

Sonderausweis Paris.

Der Gefreite Walter Lütz
(Dienstgrad, Vor- und Zuname.)

Feldpost Nr. 08818 A

gehört zu den Truppen bzw. Dienststellen des Standortes Paris.

Der Kommandant von Paris.

Zugewiesene Unterkunft : Cercle des armées
Place d'Augustin

Mod. 5.

Rückseite beachten!

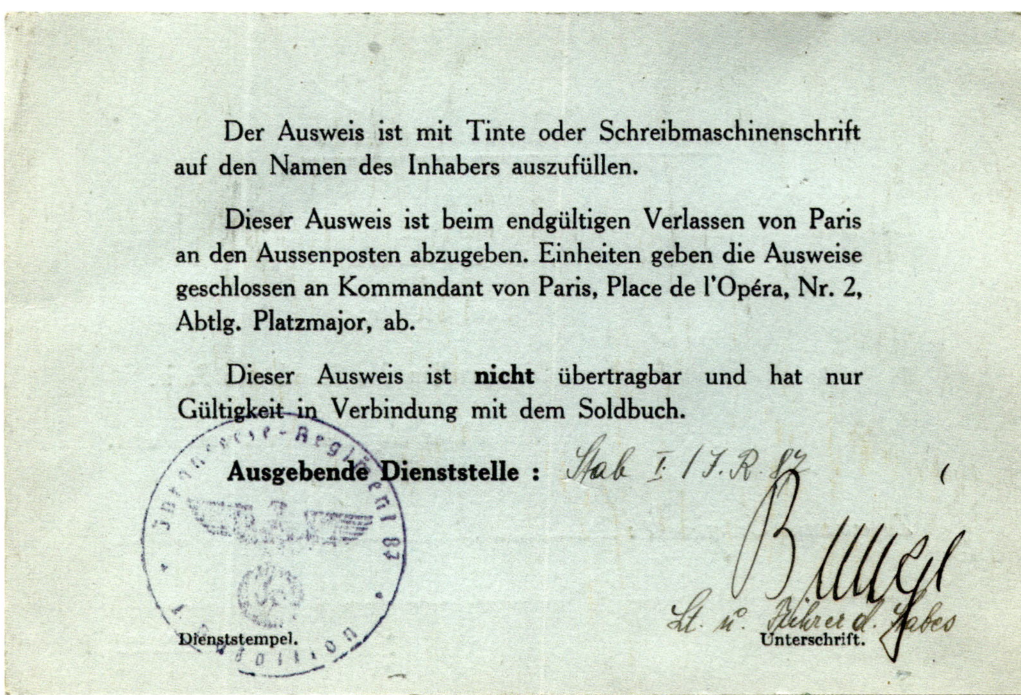

Der Ausweis ist mit Tinte oder Schreibmaschinenschrift auf den Namen des Inhabers auszufüllen.

Dieser Ausweis ist beim endgültigen Verlassen von Paris an den Aussenposten abzugeben. Einheiten geben die Ausweise geschlossen an Kommandant von Paris, Place de l'Opéra, Nr. 2, Abtlg. Platzmajor, ab.

Dieser Ausweis ist **nicht** übertragbar und hat nur Gültigkeit in Verbindung mit dem Soldbuch.

Ausgebende Dienststelle : Stab I/I.R. 82

Dienststempel.

Lt. u. Führer d. Stabes

Unterschrift.

Figure 3-26. Gefreite (sic) Walter Lutz, a member of the Paris Garrison serving with the Company Staff of Infanterie Regiment 82, was issued this card during his tour of duty so he would not be confused with the many Soldaten visiting Paris on leave.

assist during air raids were printed or stamped on many travel forms.

Merkblätter were prepared for *Soldat* and civilian alike, from small informative pamphlets to full-page flyers and even broadsheets, primarily to prepare visiting troops. Many did not know what to do or how to handle themselves in an air raid. Combat is expected by a soldier, but they had not experienced air raids, especially on such a scale and in such concentration; many were simply overwhelmed. Coming home to such devastation, *Soldaten* gained a respect for civilians bearing up to the onslaught, but were saddened that their families were forced to do so.

A common *Merkblatt* was given to the average German household titled "*Was der Luftschutz von Euch fordert!*" (What the air protection service demands of

Figure 3-27. Merkblatt issued by the Wehrmachtkommandantur of Vienna informing visiting Soldaten of the procedures and their duties during an air raid. The pamphlet was published to help them understand how to conduct themselves during an air raid, primarily because it was not something front-line soldiers were used to experiencing.

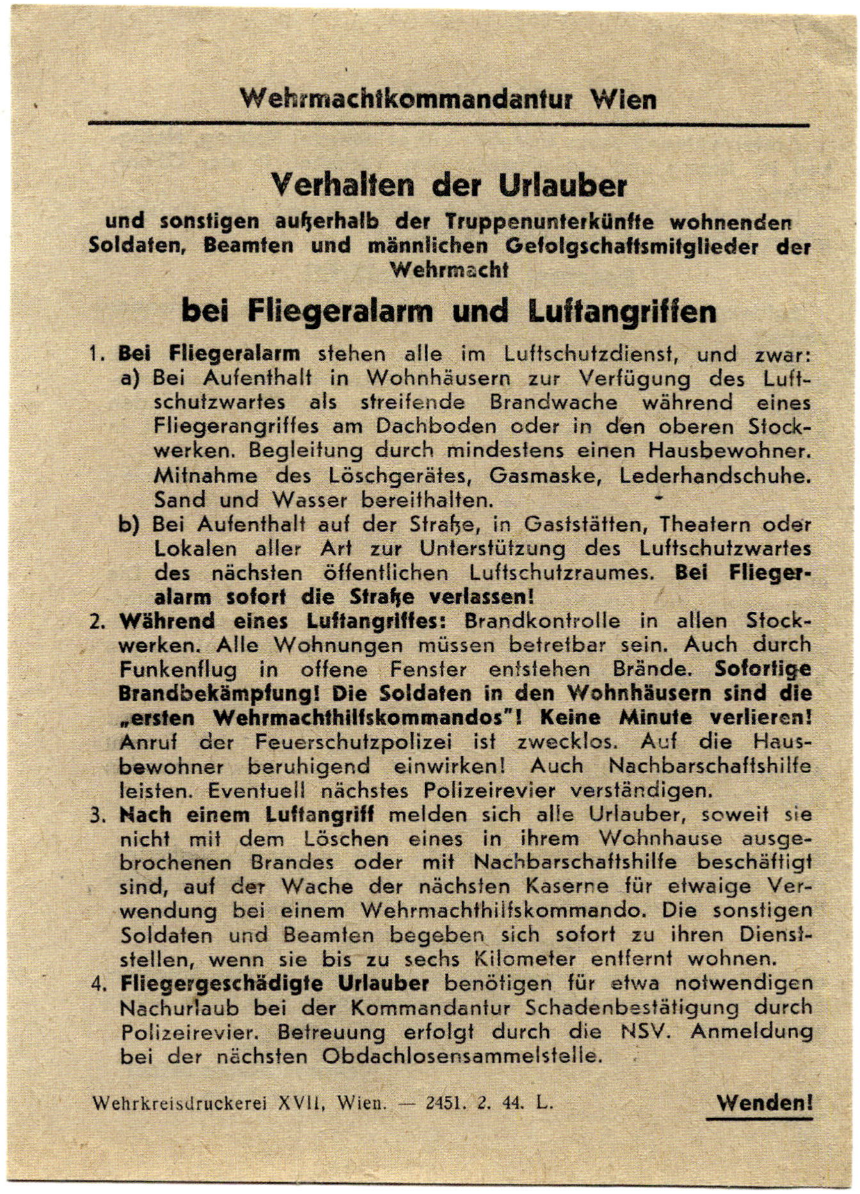

Wehrmachtkommandantur Wien

Verhalten der Urlauber

und sonstigen außerhalb der Truppenunterkünfte wohnenden Soldaten, Beamten und männlichen Gefolgschaftsmitglieder der Wehrmacht

bei Fliegeralarm und Luftangriffen

1. **Bei Fliegeralarm** stehen alle im Luftschutzdienst, und zwar:
   a) Bei Aufenthalt in Wohnhäusern zur Verfügung des Luftschutzwartes als streifende Brandwache während eines Fliegerangriffes am Dachboden oder in den oberen Stockwerken. Begleitung durch mindestens einen Hausbewohner. Mitnahme des Löschgerätes, Gasmaske, Lederhandschuhe. Sand und Wasser bereithalten.
   b) Bei Aufenthalt auf der Straße, in Gaststätten, Theatern oder Lokalen aller Art zur Unterstützung des Luftschutzwartes des nächsten öffentlichen Luftschutzraumes. **Bei Fliegeralarm sofort die Straße verlassen!**
2. **Während eines Luftangriffes:** Brandkontrolle in allen Stockwerken. Alle Wohnungen müssen betretbar sein. Auch durch Funkenflug in offene Fenster entstehen Brände. **Sofortige Brandbekämpfung! Die Soldaten in den Wohnhäusern sind die „ersten Wehrmachthilfskommandos"! Keine Minute verlieren!** Anruf der Feuerschutzpolizei ist zwecklos. Auf die Hausbewohner beruhigend einwirken! Auch Nachbarschaftshilfe leisten. Eventuell nächstes Polizeirevier verständigen.
3. **Nach einem Luftangriff** melden sich alle Urlauber, soweit sie nicht mit dem Löschen eines in ihrem Wohnhause ausgebrochenen Brandes oder mit Nachbarschaftshilfe beschäftigt sind, auf der Wache der nächsten Kaserne für etwaige Verwendung bei einem Wehrmachthilfskommando. Die sonstigen Soldaten und Beamten begeben sich sofort zu ihren Dienststellen, wenn sie bis zu sechs Kilometer entfernt wohnen.
4. **Fliegergeschädigte Urlauber** benötigen für etwa notwendigen Nachurlaub bei der Kommandantur Schadenbestätigung durch Polizeirevier. Betreuung erfolgt durch die NSV. Anmeldung bei der nächsten Obdachlosensammelstelle.

Wehrkreisdruckerei XVII, Wien. — 2451. 2. 44. L. **Wenden!**

you!). It detailed how to make your home ready in the event of an air raid, how to darken the home to prevent light from escaping and giving away the position of neighborhoods to bombers overhead at night, how to proceed to air raid shelters, and so on. There was a great deal of information contained within this leaflet, and the larger A4 size was nearly not large enough to convey it all. By the time soldiers on leave were instructed to assist in air defense, the people of Germany had become well versed in how to cope with air raids.

Other *Merkblätter* were prepared for those traveling, both military and civilian. These were often small leaflets, usually A7 or A8 size, and meant to keep people informed of price changes, limitations of different trains, upgrading which class one would ride in, and so on.

One of the more interesting *Merkblatt* was intended for German civilians traveling prior to the war, but was also given to troops. The *Merkblatt für Reisen in das Ausland* (Leaflet For Travels In Foreign Countries) gave information reminding travelers to respect other countries' customs and traditions, and that those foreigners judged Germany based on one's behavior. The bottom of the *Merkblatt* reminds one in bold *Fraktur,* "*Gedenke, dass du ein Deutscher bist!*" (Remember, that you are a German!).

An interesting note to point out is that the *Merkblatt* reminds the bearer in a familiar German, not as a formal request.

Most Germans address a stranger using the word *Sie*, the formal word for "you." It is considered a polite,

Was der Luftschutz von Euch fordert!

Macht Euer Haus luftschutzbereit!

Der Hausboden

Sorgt für restlose Entrümpelung des Hausbodens!

Stellt reichlich Sand- und Wasservorräte für die Brandbekämpfung bereit!

Entfernt alles, was im Notfall hindernd sein könnte (Verschläge usw.)! Jeder Winkel des Hausbodens muß zugänglich sein.

Vermeidet es, abends auf den Hausböden Wäsche zum Trocknen hängen zu lassen! Sie bildet eine große Brandgefahr und hindert bei der Brandbekämpfung. Nehmt auch die Wäscheleinen ab!

Die Wohnung

Stellt noch mehr Wasser und Sand zur Brandbekämpfung bereit! Wasser auch in den Badewannen!

Überprüft immer wieder die Verdunkelungseinrichtungen! Licht ist nach wie vor das beste Bombenziel.

Zieht abends die Gardinen und Fenstervorhänge möglichst weit vom Fenster zurück, damit sie nicht vom Funkenflug entzündet werden können! Noch besser ist völliges Entfernen der Gardinen und Fenstervorhänge. Nehmt bei Doppelfenstern die inneren Fenster heraus und verwahrt sie bruchsicher, damit Ihr bei Zerstörung der Außenfenster noch Ersatzfenster habt!

Haltet bei Alarm die Türen unverschlossen oder übergebt Eure Schlüssel dem Luftschutzwart zur Mitnahme bei den Kontrollgängen, damit im Falle des Einschlagens von Brandbomben die Bekämpfung ungehindert aufgenommen werden kann!

Der Luftschutzraum

Sorgt für die Anfertigung von Lageplänen der Luftschutzräume und für deren Hinterlegung bei der Nachbarluftschutzgemeinschaft und dem Luftschutzrevier!

Zusätzlich könnt Ihr die Lage Eures Luftschutzraumes zur schnellen Auffindung dadurch kennzeichnen, daß Ihr Pfeile an der Außenwand Eures Hauses anbringt. Verwendet hierfür möglichst Leuchtfarbe!

Schafft Brandmauerdurchbrüche, kennzeichnet sie und haltet die Zugänge zu ihnen immer frei! Der Brandmauerdurchbruch muß leicht und schnell zu öffnen sein. Stellt daneben Gerät zum Durchstoßen bereit und unterrichtet Euch darüber, wie es im Nebenhaus aussieht, durch das Ihr Euch im Notfalle in Sicherheit bringen sollt! Verschließt den Brandmauerdurchbruch nach Verlassen Eures Luftschutzraumes sofort wieder, damit Feuer und Rauch nicht in das Nebenhaus eindringen können.

Entfernt Fenstervergitterungen, die Euch im Notfall das Verlassen des Luftschutzraumes verwehren könnten!

Sorgt für Notbeleuchtung, damit Ihr jederzeit den Weg zum Brandmauerdurchbruch und zu den Ausgängen Eures Luftschutzraumes finden könnt. Haltet Kerzen und Streichhölzer bereit und kennzeichnet die Wege durch Leuchtfarbenanstrich.

Haltet auch in den Luftschutzräumen außer den vorgeschriebenen Selbstschutzgeräten viel Wasser und Sand zur Brandbekämpfung bereit! Versorgt Euch mit Decken und Tüchern, die Ihr im Notfall mit Wasser tränken müßt, um Euch gegen Funkenflug und strahlende Hitze zu schützen, wenn Ihr den Luftschutzraum verlassen müßt!

Legt Euer Luftschutzgepäck rechtzeitig bereit! Hierbei Mundvorrat (z. B. Essen, Trinken, unzerbrechliches Eßgeschirr und Eßbestecke) nicht vergessen!

Der Hof und der Garten

Sorgt für Durchbrüche durch Gartenmauern und Zäune, damit Ihr Euch, falls die Straße versperrt ist, durch Hof und Garten ungehindert in Sicherheit bringen könnt und damit auch Hilfskräfte von dort aus Euer Haus erreichen können!

Liegt Euer Luftschutzraum über Erdgleiche, so schüttet Erde an die Außenmauer und schrägt sie ab! Über die Art der Ausführung geben Euch die Luftschutzreviere und Dienststellen des Reichsluftschutzbundes Auskunft.

Figure 3-28. Heeded by Soldaten when on leave at home, but primarily issued to civilians, the Merkblatt titled Was der Luftschutz von Euch fordert! (What the Air Raid Service requires of You!) was a set of instructions on what to expect during an air raid and how best to protect one's self and others. (A4)

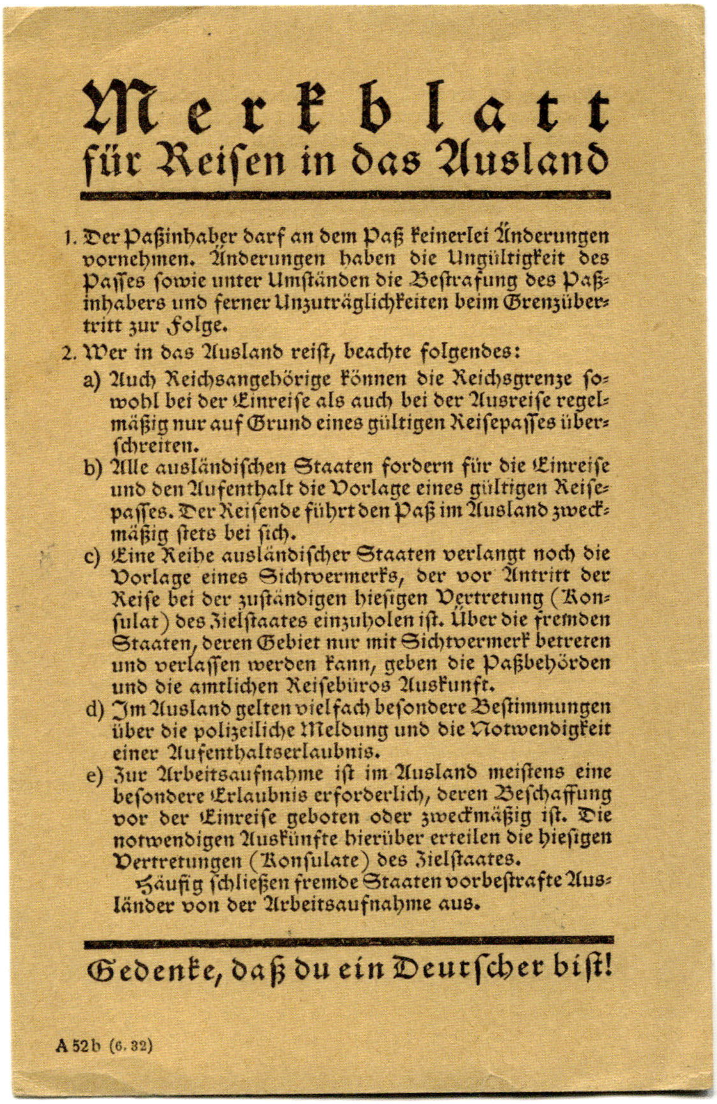

Merkblatt
für Reisen in das Ausland

1. Der Paßinhaber darf an dem Paß keinerlei Änderungen vornehmen. Änderungen haben die Ungültigkeit des Passes sowie unter Umständen die Bestrafung des Paßinhabers und ferner Unzuträglichkeiten beim Grenzübertritt zur Folge.
2. Wer in das Ausland reist, beachte folgendes:
   a) Auch Reichsangehörige können die Reichsgrenze sowohl bei der Einreise als auch bei der Ausreise regelmäßig nur auf Grund eines gültigen Reisepasses überschreiten.
   b) Alle ausländischen Staaten fordern für die Einreise und den Aufenthalt die Vorlage eines gültigen Reisepasses. Der Reisende führt den Paß im Ausland zweckmäßig stets bei sich.
   c) Eine Reihe ausländischer Staaten verlangt noch die Vorlage eines Sichtvermerks, der vor Antritt der Reise bei der zuständigen hiesigen Vertretung (Konsulat) des Zielstaates einzuholen ist. Über die fremden Staaten, deren Gebiet nur mit Sichtvermerk betreten und verlassen werden kann, geben die Paßbehörden und die amtlichen Reisebüros Auskunft.
   d) Im Ausland gelten vielfach besondere Bestimmungen über die polizeiliche Meldung und die Notwendigkeit einer Aufenthaltserlaubnis.
   e) Zur Arbeitsaufnahme ist im Ausland meistens eine besondere Erlaubnis erforderlich, deren Beschaffung vor der Einreise geboten oder zweckmäßig ist. Die notwendigen Auskünfte hierüber erteilen die hiesigen Vertretungen (Konsulate) des Zielstaates.
   Häufig schließen fremde Staaten vorbestrafte Ausländer von der Arbeitsaufnahme aus.

Gedenke, daß du ein Deutscher bist!

A 52b (6. 32)

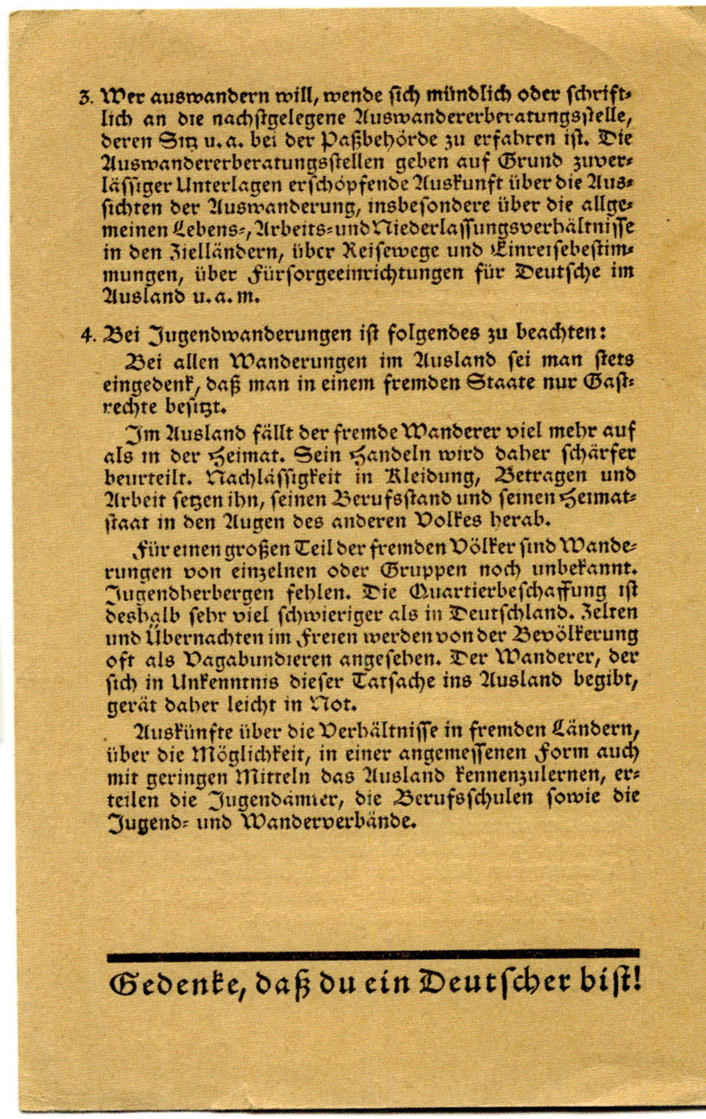

3. Wer auswandern will, wende sich mündlich oder schriftlich an die nächstgelegene Auswandererberatungsstelle, deren Sitz u. a. bei der Paßbehörde zu erfahren ist. Die Auswandererberatungsstellen geben auf Grund zuverlässiger Unterlagen erschöpfende Auskunft über die Aussichten der Auswanderung, insbesondere über die allgemeinen Lebens-, Arbeits- und Niederlassungsverhältnisse in den Zielländern, über Reisewege und Einreisebestimmungen, über Fürsorgeeinrichtungen für Deutsche im Ausland u. a. m.
4. Bei Jugendwanderungen ist folgendes zu beachten:
   Bei allen Wanderungen im Ausland sei man stets eingedenk, daß man in einem fremden Staate nur Gastrechte besitzt.
   Im Ausland fällt der fremde Wanderer viel mehr auf als in der Heimat. Sein Handeln wird daher schärfer beurteilt. Nachlässigkeit in Kleidung, Betragen und Arbeit setzen ihn, seinen Berufsstand und seinen Heimatstaat in den Augen des anderen Volkes herab.
   Für einen großen Teil der fremden Völker sind Wanderungen von einzelnen oder Gruppen noch unbekannt. Jugendherbergen fehlen. Die Quartierbeschaffung ist deshalb sehr viel schwieriger als in Deutschland. Zelten und Übernachten im Freien werden von der Bevölkerung oft als Vagabundieren angesehen. Der Wanderer, der sich in Unkenntnis dieser Tatsache ins Ausland begibt, gerät daher leicht in Not.
   Auskünfte über die Verhältnisse in fremden Ländern, über die Möglichkeit, in einer angemessenen Form auch mit geringen Mitteln das Ausland kennenzulernen, erteilen die Jugendämter, die Berufsschulen sowie die Jugend- und Wanderverbände.

Gedenke, daß du ein Deutscher bist!

Figure 3-29. A pre-war leaflet prepared for civilian overseas travellers, this Merkblatt for Reisen in das Ausland (Trips in Foreign Countries) was widely circulated to German troops as well.

respectful manner of speaking to someone you don't know. As a result, most documents are written using *Sie*. When one is speaking to a family member or good friend, the less formal and more common form of "you" is used: *du*. By using *du* in the phrase at the bottom of the *Merkblatt* instead of *Sie*, it conveys a personal appeal to the reader as a close friend, not a formal request or command. It's one of the more fascinating subtleties of the German language.

Figure 4-1. This Soldat wasted no time in spending his leave in Warsaw. This souvenir sketch by a local street artist of an unknown Wehrmacht Feldwebel was done on October 17, 1939, a scant eleven days after the fall of the city.

4

Souvenirs of Travel

Everyone likes to collect souvenirs of their travels as mementos of their trip, and the *Soldat* was no different. The German soldier was often compulsive about what he collected in his travels; nothing was off-limits, so far as he was concerned. *Soldaten* collected any number of things from leave, from receipts to post cards to photographs and everything in between, each became a commemorative reminder of places they had visited and things they had seen.

Although all manner of items were collected, this work concentrates on ephemera collected by *Soldaten*, paper items that took up very little room in their travels that were associated with good times and fond memories in the midst of the chaos that was the war.

Trade cards are to 1940s Europe what the business card is to us today. Considerably larger than its modern counterpart, trade cards acted as small-scale flyers and advertising leaflets to entice tourists to visit an establishment, or once there, to coax them to return. It was especially useful when printed in the language of the vacationer and not necessarily that of the host nation, so a good many Parisian trade cards were printed bilingually in French and German (until 1944, after which many cards began to appear in French and English).

Figure 4-2.

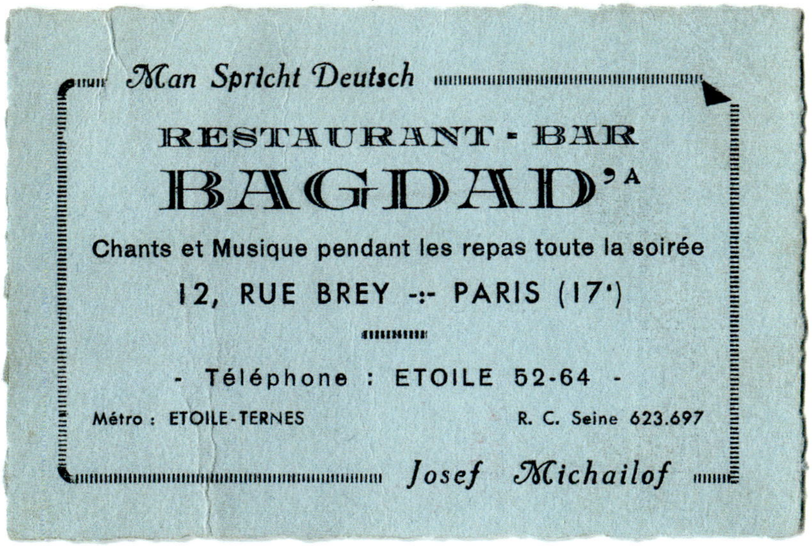

Figure 4-2 (previous page) through 4-7. A collection of Paris trade cards from a Soldat's collection. Notice that the majority are in both French and German; like any tourist industry, Paris during the war knew how to cater to its occupiers and visitors!

Figure 4-3.

Figure 4-4.

Figure 4-5.

Figure 4-6.

Figure 4-7.

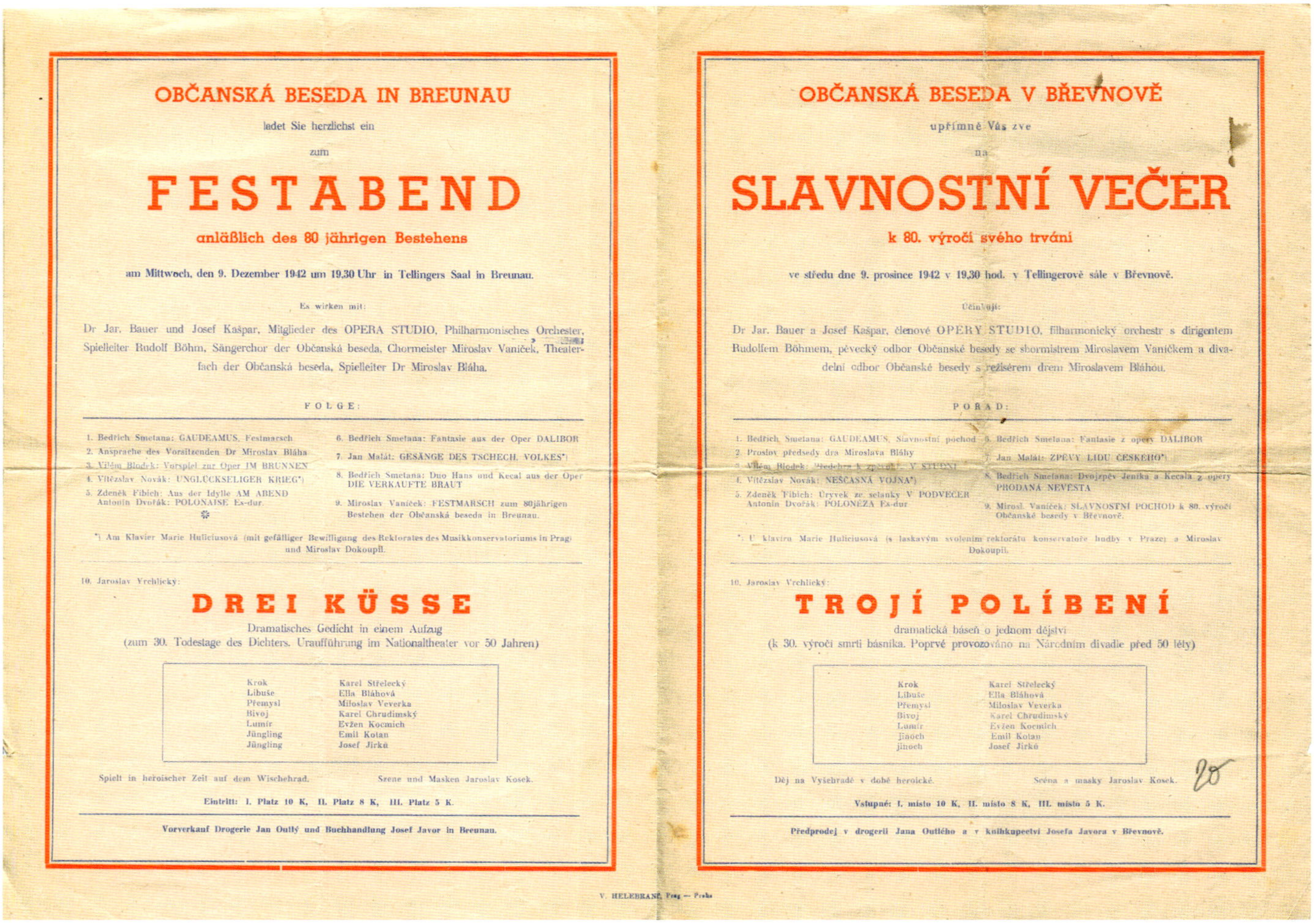

OBČANSKÁ BESEDA IN BREUNAU

ladet Sie herzlichst ein

zum

FESTABEND

anläßlich des 80 jährigen Bestehens

am Mittwoch, den 9. Dezember 1942 um 19,30 Uhr in Tellingers Saal in Breunau.

Es wirken mit:

Dr Jar. Bauer und Josef Kašpar, Mitglieder des OPERA STUDIO, Philharmonisches Orchester, Spielleiter Rudolf Böhm, Sängerchor der Občanská beseda, Chormeister Miroslav Vaníček, Theaterfach der Občanská beseda, Spielleiter Dr Miroslav Bláha.

FOLGE:

1. Bedřich Smetana: GAUDEAMUS, Festmarsch
2. Ansprache des Vorsitzenden Dr Miroslav Bláha
3. Vilém Blodek: Vorspiel zur Oper IM BRUNNEN
4. Vítězslav Novák: UNGLÜCKSELIGER KRIEG*)
5. Zdeněk Fibich: Aus der Idylle AM ABEND
   Antonín Dvořák: POLONAISE Es-dur.
6. Bedřich Smetana: Fantasie aus der Oper DALIBOR
7. Jan Malát: GESÄNGE DES TSCHECH. VOLKES*)
8. Bedřich Smetana: Duo Hans und Kecal aus der Oper DIE VERKAUFTE BRAUT
9. Miroslav Vaníček: FESTMARSCH zum 80jährigen Bestehen der Občanská beseda in Breunau.

*) Am Klavier Marie Huliciusová (mit gefälliger Bewilligung des Rektorates des Musikkonservatoriums in Prag) und Miroslav Dokoupil.

10. Jaroslav Vrchlický:

DREI KÜSSE

Dramatisches Gedicht in einem Aufzug
(zum 30. Todestage des Dichters. Uraufführung im Nationaltheater vor 50 Jahren)

Krok	Karel Střelecký
Libuše	Ella Bláhová
Přemysl	Miloslav Veverka
Bivoj	Karel Chrudimský
Lumír	Evžen Kocmich
Jüngling	Emil Kotan
Jüngling	Josef Jirků

Spielt in heroischer Zeit auf dem Wischehrad. Szene und Masken Jaroslav Kosek.

Eintritt: I. Platz 10 K, II. Platz 8 K, III. Platz 5 K.

Vorverkauf Drogerie Jan Outlý und Buchhandlung Josef Javor in Breunau.

OBČANSKÁ BESEDA V BŘEVNOVĚ

upřímně Vás zve

na

SLAVNOSTNÍ VEČER

k 80. výročí svého trvání

ve středu dne 9. prosince 1942 v 19,30 hod. v Tellingerově sále v Břevnově.

Účinkují:

Dr Jar. Bauer a Josef Kašpar, členové OPERY STUDIO, filharmonický orchestr s dirigentem Rudolfem Böhmem, pěvecký odbor Občanské besedy se sbormistrem Miroslavem Vaníčkem a divadelní odbor Občanské besedy s režisérem drem Miroslavem Bláhou.

POŘAD:

1. Bedřich Smetana: GAUDEAMUS, Slavnostní pochod
2. Proslov předsedy dra Miroslava Bláhy
3. Vilém Blodek: Předehra k zpěvohře V STUDNI
4. Vítězslav Novák: NEŠČASNÁ VOJNA*)
5. Zdeněk Fibich: Úryvek ze selanky V PODVEČER
   Antonín Dvořák: POLONÉZA Es-dur
6. Bedřich Smetana: Fantasie z opery DALIBOR
7. Jan Malát: ZPĚVY LIDU ČESKÉHO*)
8. Bedřich Smetana: Dvojzpěv Jeníka a Kecala z opery PRODANÁ NEVĚSTA
9. Mirosl. Vaníček: SLAVNOSTNÍ POCHOD k 80. výročí Občanské besedy v Břevnově.

*) U klavíru Marie Huliciusová (s laskavým svolením rektorátu konservatoře hudby v Praze) a Miroslav Dokoupil.

10. Jaroslav Vrchlický:

TROJÍ POLÍBENÍ

dramatická báseň o jednom dějství
(k 30. výročí smrti básníka. Poprvé provozováno na Národním divadle před 50 léty)

Krok	Karel Střelecký
Libuše	Ella Bláhová
Přemysl	Miloslav Veverka
Bivoj	Karel Chrudimský
Lumír	Evžen Kocmich
jinoch	Emil Kotan
jinoch	Josef Jirků

Děj na Vyšehradě v době heroické. Scéna a masky Jaroslav Kosek.

Vstupné: I. místo 10 K, II. místo 8 K, III. místo 5 K.

Předprodej v drogerii Jana Outlého a v knihkupectví Josefa Javora v Břevnově.

Figure 4-8. A placard from a December, 1942 Festabend (Festival evening) performance of classical music in Breunau (Brevnov) in Prague. The placard is bilingual, leading one to believe that local civilians, German civilians, and military personnel were all welcome to attend, though this may have just been for show. The performance came soon after brutal reprisals following the June death of Reinhard Heydrich. (A3)

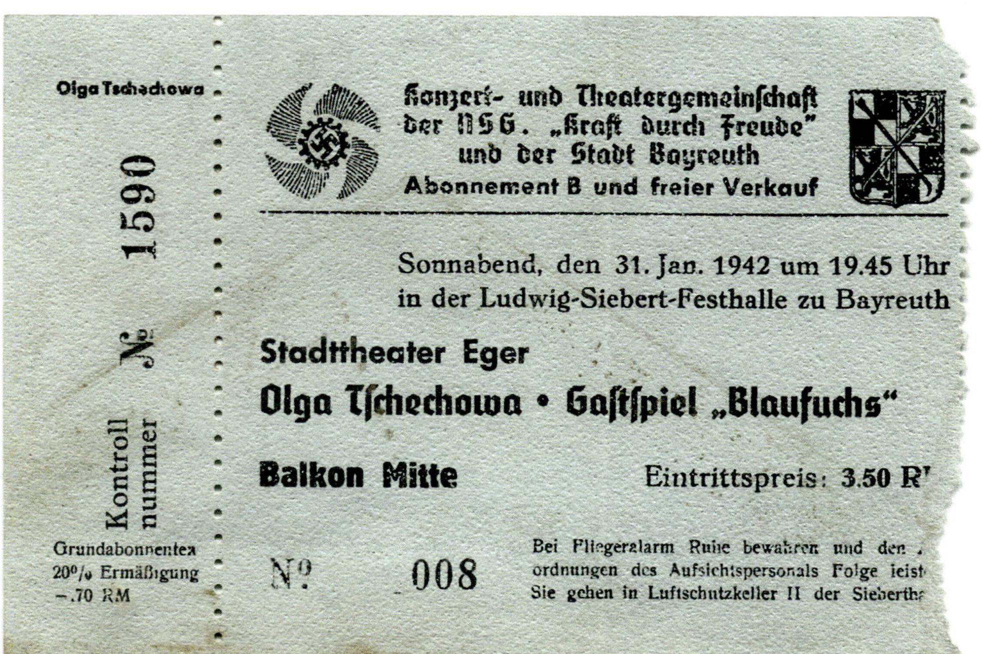

Olga Tschechowa

Kontroll nummer № 1590

Grundabonnentex 20% Ermäßigung –.70 RM

Konzert- und Theatergemeinschaft der NSG. „Kraft durch Freude" und der Stadt Bayreuth

Abonnement B und freier Verkauf

Sonnabend, den 31. Jan. 1942 um 19.45 Uhr in der Ludwig-Siebert-Festhalle zu Bayreuth

Stadttheater Eger

Olga Tschechowa • Gastspiel „Blaufuchs"

Balkon Mitte

Eintrittspreis: 3.50 R

№ 008

Bei Fliegeralarm Ruhe bewahren und den Anordnungen des Aufsichtspersonals Folge leist Sie gehen in Luftschutzkeller II der Siebertha

Figure 4-9. An entrance ticket from an NSG-KDF program of music in the Ludwig-Siebert Festhalle in Bayreuth for a 1942 performance of "The Blue Fox," featuring Olga Czekhova. Ms. Chekhova was a Russian-German actress who, it was rumored, had been pressured by Stalin and Beria before the war to act as a spy in an assassination attempt on Hitler.

NSG. „Kraft durch Freude"
Wehrmachtstournee der
Niedersächsischen Landesbühne • Hannover
Intendant Walter Hitzemann

„Spielzeug"

Lustspiel in 3 Akten von Kurt Sellnick.

Spielleitung: Intendant Walter Hitzemann.

Konsul Erwin Tragberg, Besitzer der „Etrag"-Spielzeugwerke . . . . Carol Härtig

Dagmar Tragberg, seine zweite Frau . . . L. Kinkhorst/E. Scheele

Hannes Tragberg, sein Sohn aus erster Ehe Kurt Frost

Gustav Tragberg, sein Bruder, Abteilungsleiter der „Etrag" . . . . Walter Hitzemann

Alma Silowski } Abteilungsleiter der „Etrag" { E. Attkins/L. Kinkhorst

Willy Amsteg } { Richard Kley

Trude Bast, Sekretärin . . . . Marianne Pick

Erika Berring . . . . Johanna Bauer

Ort der Handlung für alle 3 Akte: Empfangsraum der „Etrag".

Pause nach dem zweiten Akt.

Bühnenbild: Heinz Holzapfel.

Druckerei Karl Otto

Figure 4-10. Playbills were frequently collected by travelling soldiers. A playbill for the comedy Spielzeug (Toy) shows that the performance was sponsored by the National Socialistische Gemeinschaft "Kraft Durch Freude" (National Socialist Fellowship "Strength Through Joy") program, an organization for public morale that had its roots during the Great Depression in the early years of the Third Reich. The KDF is best known as the founders of a savings program which guaranteed a car for every German family, the Volkswagen (People's Car).

Nutzen Sie das vorteilhafte Anrecht!

Bedeutende Verbilligung der Kassenpreise
Umtauschrecht im Verhinderungsfall
Feste Plätze und feste Theatertage
Bequeme und kleine Teilzahlungen

Kein zeitraubendes Anstellen an der Theaterkasse

Das **Anrecht** wird in der Spielzeit 1941/42 erstmalig nur **vierzehntägig** durchgeführt.

Anrechtstage sind Dienstag, Mittwoch und Donnerstag

Jedes Anrecht der Spielzeit 1941/42 **umfaßt 21 Vorstellungen.** Das Anrecht ist in Raten für 3 Vorstellungen zu bezahlen

Bei Fliegeralarm

wird die Vorstellung abgebrochen.
Die Garderobe wird ausgehändigt.
Sämtliche Besucher
haben in größter Ruhe und Ordnung den Anweisungen der Betriebsordner und Platzanweiser Folge zu leisten.
Um eine gleichmäßige Verteilung der Besucher auf die Luftschutzräume entsprechend deren Größe zu gewährleisten, haben die Besucher die Luftschutzräume wie folgt aufzusuchen:

Saalplatz und Saalstehplatz:

Oeffentlichen Luftschutzraum im Ernährungsamt
Eingang Gewandhausstraße 4

I. Sperrsitz **links:**
I. Sperrsitz **rechts:**
II. und III. Sperrsitz
rechts und links: durch das Haupttreppenhaus und den Haupteingang auf den Hauptmarkt.

Rang und Galerie:

Oeffentlichen Luftschutzraum im Rathaus
Eingang Gewandhausstraße 2

I. und II. Rang und Galerie **links:** durch das **linke** Treppenhaus und den Seitenausgang auf die Braugasse,
I. und II. Rang und Galerie **rechts:** durch das **rechte** Treppenhaus und den Seitenausgang auf die Gewandhausstraße.

Wahrt Ruhe und Besonnenheit!

M/1220

Stadttheater Zwickau

INTENDANT PAUL KROHMANN

Spielzeit 1941-42

Sonntag den 10 Mai 1942

Figure 4-11. A copy of a seasonal playbill, this one is for the State Theater of Zwickau's 1941-42 season. Note on the back cover that instructions to various air raid shelters, depending on where one sat, are included under the heading "Bei Fliegeralarm" (In the Event of Air Raid Alarms). (8 1/8" x 11 5/8")

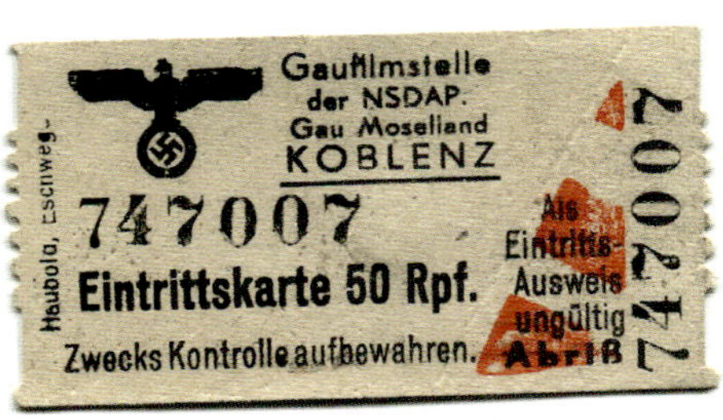

Figure 4-12. This entrance ticket to the Gaufilmstelle der NSDAP (District movie house of the Nazi Party) comes from Koblenz, in the Mosel region.

Figure 4-13. UFA, the Universum Film AG, was the German motion picture studio responsible for such great films as Metropolis and The Blue Angel. Nationalized by the Nazis in 1933, the studio produced many part entertainment/part propaganda feature films under Dr. Joseph Goebbels' direction. The studio, and by default the Nazis, also owned a majority of the theaters in Germany.

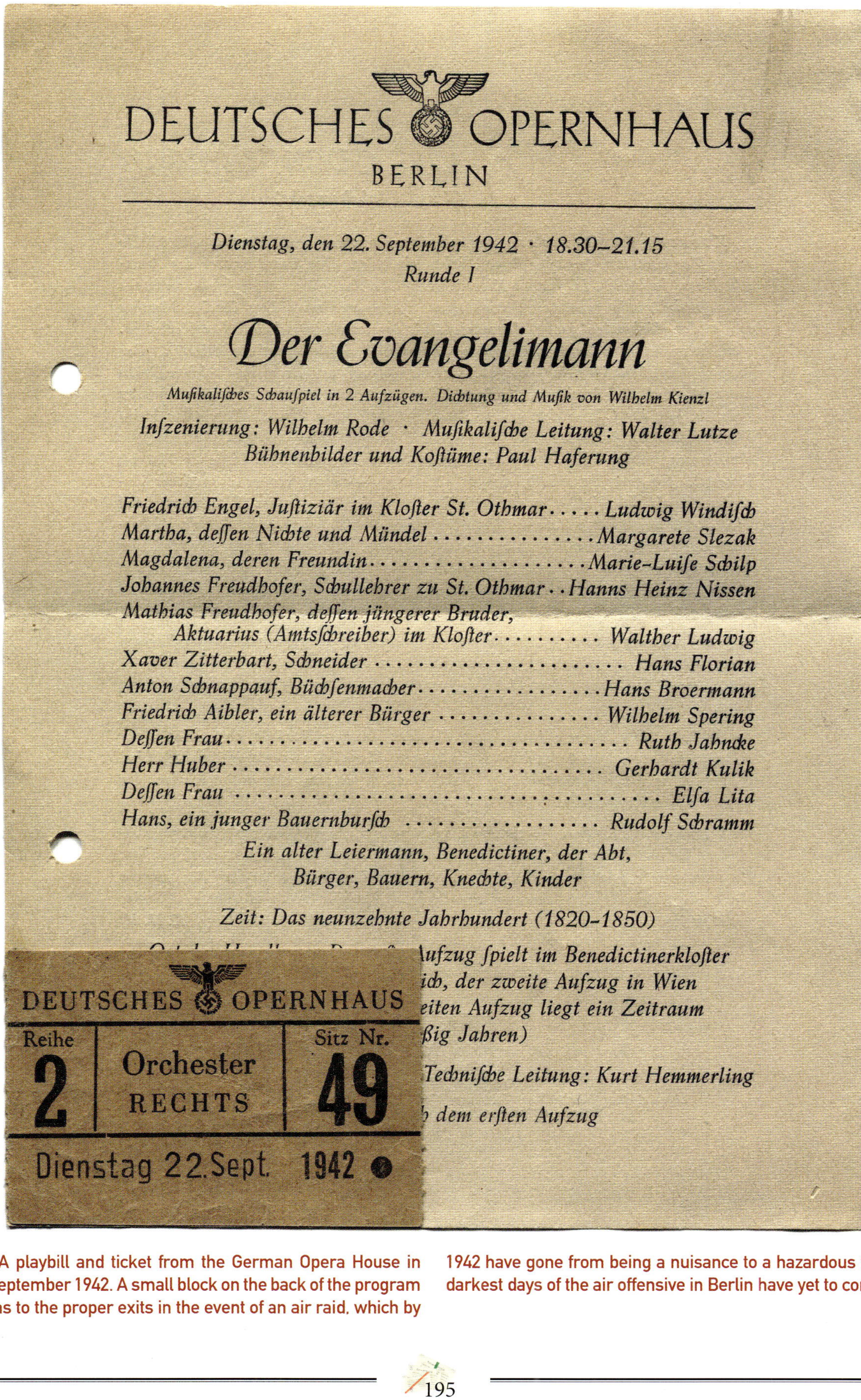

DEUTSCHES OPERNHAUS
BERLIN

Dienstag, den 22. September 1942 · 18.30–21.15
Runde I

Der Evangelimann

Mufikalifches Schaufpiel in 2 Aufzügen. Dichtung und Mufik von Wilhelm Kienzl

Infzenierung: Wilhelm Rode · Mufikalifche Leitung: Walter Lutze
Bühnenbilder und Koftüme: Paul Haferung

Friedrich Engel, Juftiziär im Klofter St. Othmar ..... Ludwig Windifch
Martha, deffen Nichte und Mündel .... Margarete Slezak
Magdalena, deren Freundin .... Marie-Luife Schilp
Johannes Freudhofer, Schullehrer zu St. Othmar .. Hanns Heinz Nissen
Mathias Freudhofer, deffen jüngerer Bruder,
Aktuarius (Amtsfchreiber) im Klofter .... Walther Ludwig
Xaver Zitterbart, Schneider .... Hans Florian
Anton Schnappauf, Büchfenmacher .... Hans Broermann
Friedrich Aibler, ein älterer Bürger .... Wilhelm Spering
Deffen Frau .... Ruth Jahncke
Herr Huber .... Gerhardt Kulik
Deffen Frau .... Elfa Lita
Hans, ein junger Bauernburfch .... Rudolf Schramm

Ein alter Leiermann, Benedictiner, der Abt,
Bürger, Bauern, Knechte, Kinder

Zeit: Das neunzehnte Jahrhundert (1820–1850)

…ufzug fpielt im Benedictinerklofter
…ich, der zweite Aufzug in Wien
…eiten Aufzug liegt ein Zeitraum
…ßig Jahren)

…Technifche Leitung: Kurt Hemmerling

…dem erften Aufzug

DEUTSCHES OPERNHAUS

Reihe		Sitz Nr.
2	Orchester RECHTS	49

Dienstag 22. Sept. 1942

Figure 4-14. A playbill and ticket from the German Opera House in Berlin from September 1942. A small block on the back of the program directs patrons to the proper exits in the event of an air raid, which by 1942 have gone from being a nuisance to a hazardous frequency; the darkest days of the air offensive in Berlin have yet to come.

WB

POSENER WEHRMACHTBÜHNE
Schloßfreiheit 19
Wehrkreiskommando XXI

Liebe auf den ersten Blick!

Kalenderblätter in 5 Abrissen von Peters Arnolds
mit der Musik von Peter Igelhoff

Zwischenaktskompositionen
für das Kalenderblattmädchen von Toni Melzer
mit Texten von Dr. Armas Sten-Fühler

vom 31. Mai — 20. Juni 1944
täglich 19,30 Uhr

Figure 4-15. This playbill comes from the Posen (now Poznan, Poland) Wehrmacht Stage performance of "Love From The First Sight!" which was performed nightly at 7:30 pm from May 31 until June 20, 1944. Announcements inside the playbill, other than the cast, include an announcement that this too was sponsored by the KDF, and that in the event of an air raid this playbill can be used to obtain a refund.

Figure 4-16. An entrance ticket to the first great lighting of the park along the river Enz from 1939.

Figure 4-17. An entrance ticket for a concert by the State Music School in Pressnitz with instructions to see the rules and regulations of the theater on the reverse side.

Figure 4-18. Two adult Eintrittskarten (entrance tickets) for the Stuttgart Reichsgartenschau from 1939. The ad on the back reads "Go to Breuninger's on the marketplace, the place for the family to buy clothing, equipment, sports."

Other bilingual notices happened to find their way into soldiers' souvenir stashes such as theater programs and broadsides. Usually A3 sized or larger, *Plakatten,* or placards, would be posted announcing the dates and times of festivals, plays, operas, and other forms of entertainment to the local population, which often included vacationing *Soldaten*. I can account for at least one such bulletin that made it into the hands of a wayward soldier seeking a unique keepsake.

For the less larcenous, a theater ticket or playbill was usually enough proof of attendance. Many tickets, like tickets to events today, were torn in two pieces, one for the theater to verify its receipts, and the other for the visitor. It bore the title of the program for the evening, possibly the name of the theater, and a seat designation or simply a number in the cases of open seating.

Receipts were also collected and saved, sometimes so a soldier could report or verify how much money he'd spent, and at other times as a souvenir. Because hotels tended to be more expensive, not to mention less secure in occupied countries, the German soldier often availed himself of the *Soldatenheim* (Soldier's Home) or *Heereserholungsheim* (Army Recovery Home).

The *Soldatenheim* was a hotel, lounge, and entertainment center much like an American USO or British NAAFI, owned and managed by the *Wehrmacht*, and open to officer and enlisted man alike. Depending on conditions, soldier's wives were permitted to stay at the *Heereserholungsheim* to visit their recovering husbands.

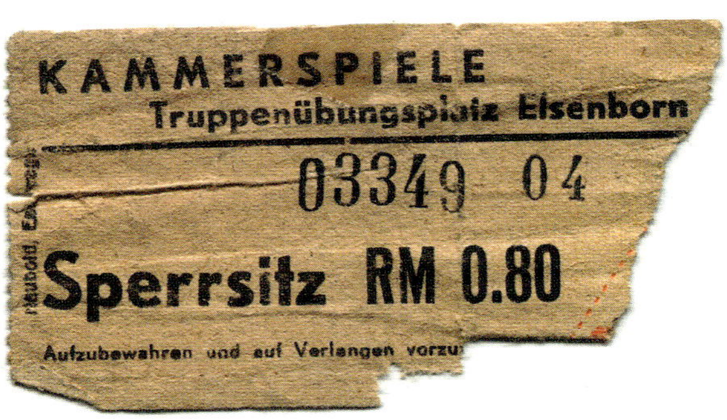

Figure 4-19. This ticket for a chamber performance comes from Truppenübungsplatz (Parade Ground; literally "Troop Practice Place") Elsenborn. Eighty Reichpfennig bought a seat in the Sperrsitz or "stall" seating, which were actually rather good seats in the center of the theater.

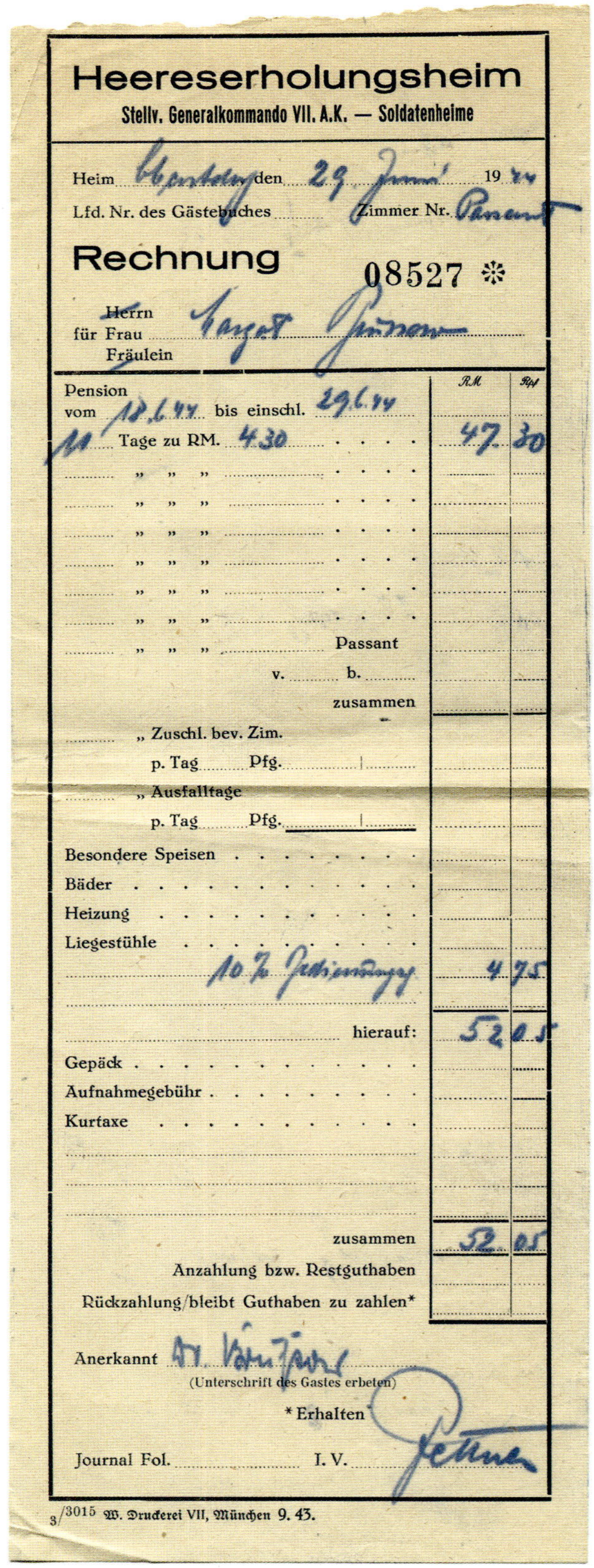

Figure 4-20. A Rechnung (receipt) for an extended stay at the Heereserholungsheim (Army Convalescent Home), which were usually associated with a Soldatenheim. It is uncertain as to where this particular receipt is from, mainly due to the clerk's handwriting, but it records an 11-day stay by a Soldat's wife, Frau Gunssow. (4 1/8" x 11")

Some *Soldatenheim* were located close to military posts, but the most frequented by far were those established in cities and resorts throughout the occupied territories. According to a map published in the *Deutschen Wegleiter* Paris Travel Guide for German Soldiers in June 1941, there were twelve *Soldatenheim*, three *Soldatentheater* (Soldier's Theater), and three *Soldatenkino* (Soldier's Movie House) in Paris alone.

For the homesick *Soldat*, the *Soldatenheim* was a piece of home plucked from his native soil and brought to a foreign land. It offered German meals where none other was likely to be found, as well as German beer and *Spirituosen* (Spirits, such as *Schnapps* and other liquors). The *Soldatenheim* also offered a place where one could sleep with clean sheets, a fresh bath, and fragrant soaps, quite the luxury for soldiers freshly arrived from the field.

To say the least, it was a welcomed respite at low cost, with good food, good security, and a good place to forget that there was a war on.

Figure 4-21. One of the many buildings (almost certainly a hotel) across Europe to be commandeered and pressed into service as a Soldatenheim.

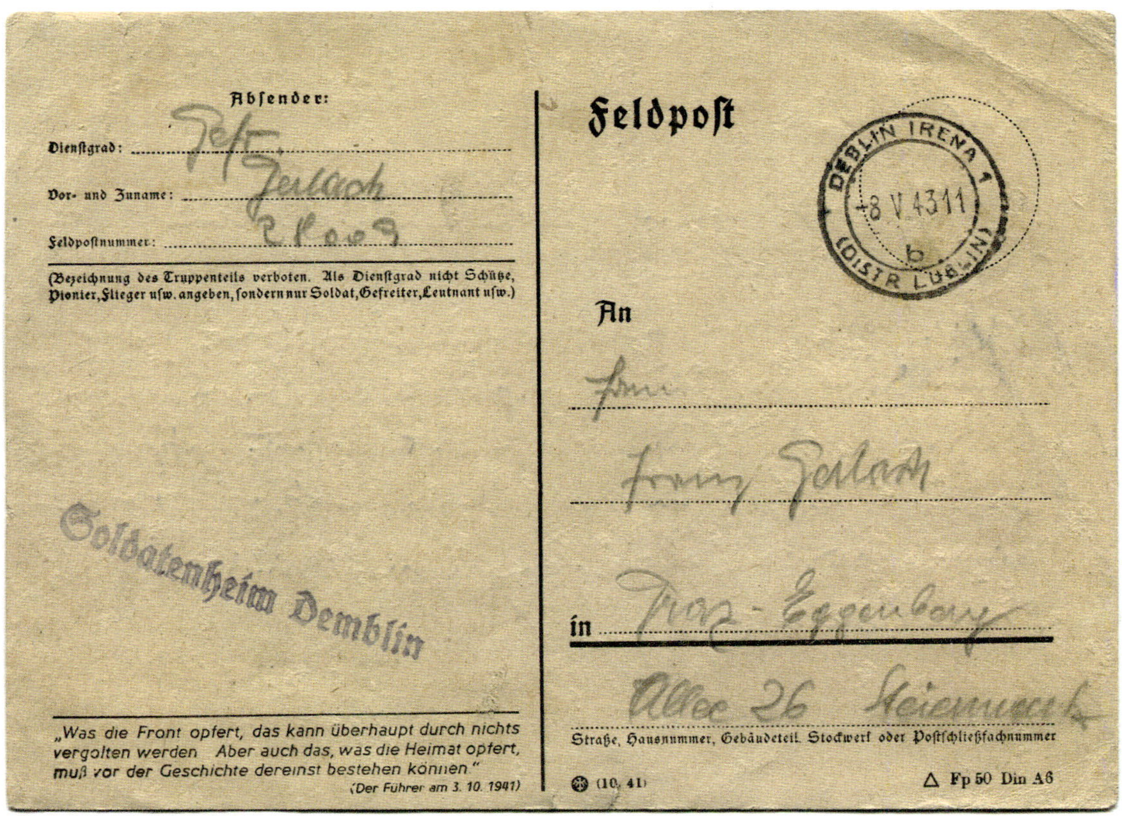
Absender:

Dienstgrad: Gefr.

Vor- und Zuname: Gerlach

Feldpostnummer: 21009

(Bezeichnung des Truppenteils verboten. Als Dienstgrad nicht Schütze, Pionier, Flieger usw. angeben, sondern nur Soldat, Gefreiter, Leutnant usw.)

Soldatenheim Demblin

„Was die Front opfert, das kann überhaupt durch nichts vergolten werden. Aber auch das, was die Heimat opfert, muß vor der Geschichte dereinst bestehen können."
(Der Führer am 3. 10. 1941)

Feldpost

DEBLIN IRENA 1 (DISTR. LUBLIN) 8.V.43.11 b

An

Frau

Franz Gerlach

in Graz-Eggenberg

Allee 26 Steiermark

Straße, Hausnummer, Gebäudeteil, Stockwerk oder Postschließfachnummer

(10. 41) △ Fp 50 Din A6

Figure 4-22. This postcard from Gefreiter Gerlach to his wife in Graz-Eggenberg was posted on May 8, 1943 from the Soldatenheim in Demblin, a village now in Southern Poland.

Figure 4-23. Although many private photos of Soldatenheim exist, postcards were also made as souvenirs for visiting soldiers to send home, and often displayed relaxing, sometimes opulent examples of the comforts there. This postcard hails from a Soldatenheim on the French Riviera.

Figure 4-24 & 4-25. Soldatenkino (Soldier's Movie House) and Soldatentheater (Soldier's Theatre/Playhouse) also graced the landscapes of occupied Europe. These two photos are of the Soldatenkino in Orel, the city around which the pivotal Battle of Kursk would be fought in 1943.

Figure 4-26. This photo of the Soldatenheim and Heereserholungsheim in Kotschka, Germany was taken in January of 1944.

Figure 4-27. These three Soldaten stand in front of a Soldatenheim. The plaque beside the door says Hier spricht die NSDAP! (Here, the Nazi Party speaks!) and is probably a local KDF office for Volksgenossen ("Fellow Germans") requiring Not und Hilfe (emergency assistance and help).

Figure 4-28. Some Soldantenheim served as Fronturlauber-Heim, which catered exclusively to soldiers returning on leave from the front.

Figure 4-29. Three SS Men and their lady friends pose outside a Soldatenheim in occupied Poland.

Figure 4-30. A rather desolate-looking Soldatenheim in Russia.

Figure 4-31. Some Soldatenheimen were very modern. This particular building served as a Soldatenheim in Athens, complete with a recreational sunbathing area on the top floor.

Figure 4-32. This rather chilled Soldat waits outside a playhouse in Toulouse, France in November 1943 for either the Wednesday or Thursday comedic performance of Lache Bajazzo! (Laugh, Bajazzo!) at 7:30 pm.

Figure 4-33. A small map of the Paris Metro, indispensable to Soldaten on leave in the City of Lights, was printed on light paper and affixed to a heavier stock. (6¼" x 7¾")

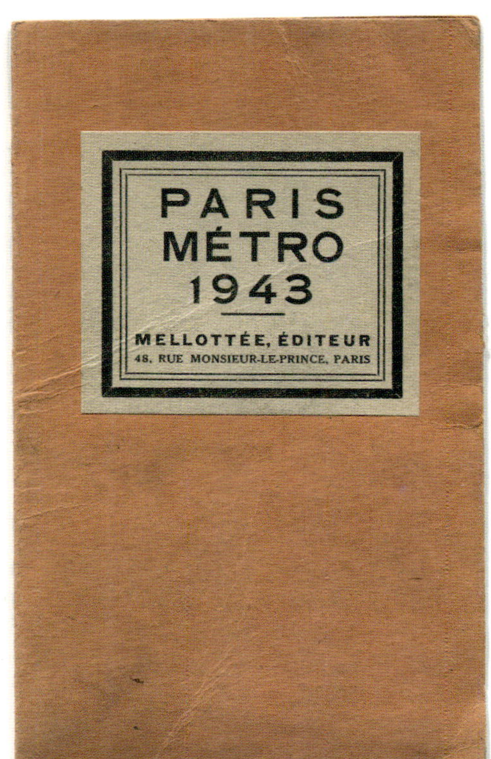

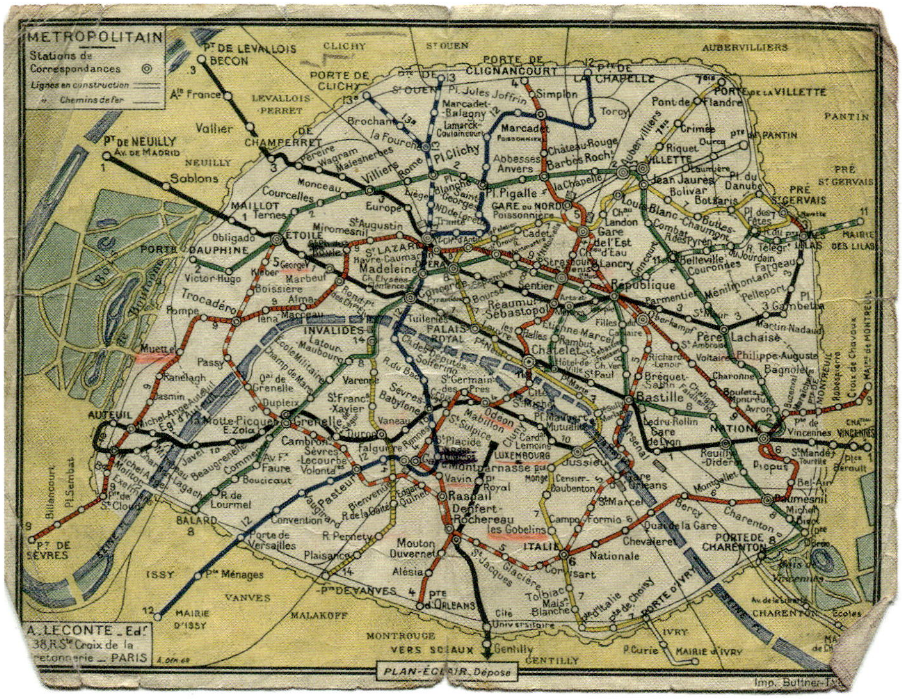

Figure 4-34. Another map of Paris, probably a pre-war print, pressed into service by visiting Soldaten. (5½" x 7")

Figure 4-35. Numerous Wegleiter (Guide Books) were printed in Paris to keep Soldaten both informed and entertained. Each included maps which highlighted Soldatenheim and Soldatenkino, tourist information, and ads for the many approved nightclubs and cabarets.

Figure 4-36. Much more likely to be used than saved as a souvenir, these German prophylactics were a popular item on the streets of Paris.

Figure 4-37. A humorous souvenir postcard, mimeographed onto a blank Feldpostkarte of the Eiffel tower boasting a swastika flag while a visiting Soldat strolls by with his Parisian enchantress. Note that the soldier's gaze is drawn to the young lady's enchanting "eyes," suggesting that the Soldat was no different at heart than his British or American counterpart. ($4^{1}/_{8}$" x $5^{3}/_{4}$")

Figure 4-38. Throughout Europe, miniature booklets of tear-and-mail picture postcards were popular throughout the 19th and 20th century. Bilingual booklets such as these from Laon and Douai in occupied France (even though the postcards from Laon were printed in Belgium) no doubt caught many a visiting Soldat's eye.

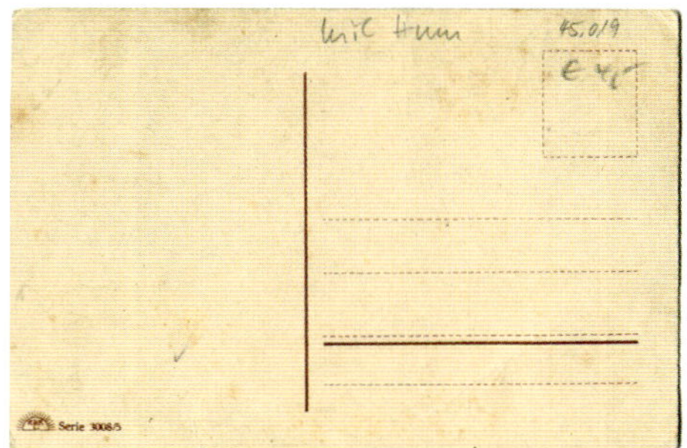

Figure 4-39 & 4-40. Postcards that cast a humorous light on military leave had been popular with Soldaten well before even the previous war. In these World War I postcards, the weeping Soldat on the left laments that he has not been granted leave, while Karle, laden with presents and souvenirs for his family, sets off on his. (3 1/2" x 5 3/8")

Figure 4-41. Front humor, a dark and almost pitiably morose sense of humor, was another popular subject for postcards sent home. This Feldpostkarte bemoans duty at the Austrian outpost of Äpfelgschwendt, "Out where the devil says 'Good night!'"

Soldatenhumor, Soldier's Humor, was often a bleak, dark sense of humor on the front, but once a fighting man was removed from the hazards of combat life, his disposition changed to making light of the very service in which he lived. Postcards of soldierly life and the unique conditions under which he lived were often sent home to family and friends with little clarification. Admittedly, descriptions and explanation was rarely needed, as the nature of the postcards were easily enough understood.

Most postcards were sent from internal *Standortstelle* (Military Posts), *Fliegerhorsten* (Air Bases), and *Dienststellen* (Service Locations) within the *Reich*, i.e., where easy access to printed post cards and a ready mail service was attainable with little to no difficulty. As a result, most of the more humorous *Ansichtkarten* (Postcards) were mailed by soldiers via *Feldpost*, which was free to soldiers.

One of the most frequently seen series of humorous soldier's postcards were those illustrated by humorist and

Figure 4-42. One has to be familiar with the European practice of tipping restroom attendants to understand this card, titled: "The Player – Double or gratis!" ($4^1/_4$" x $5^7/_8$")

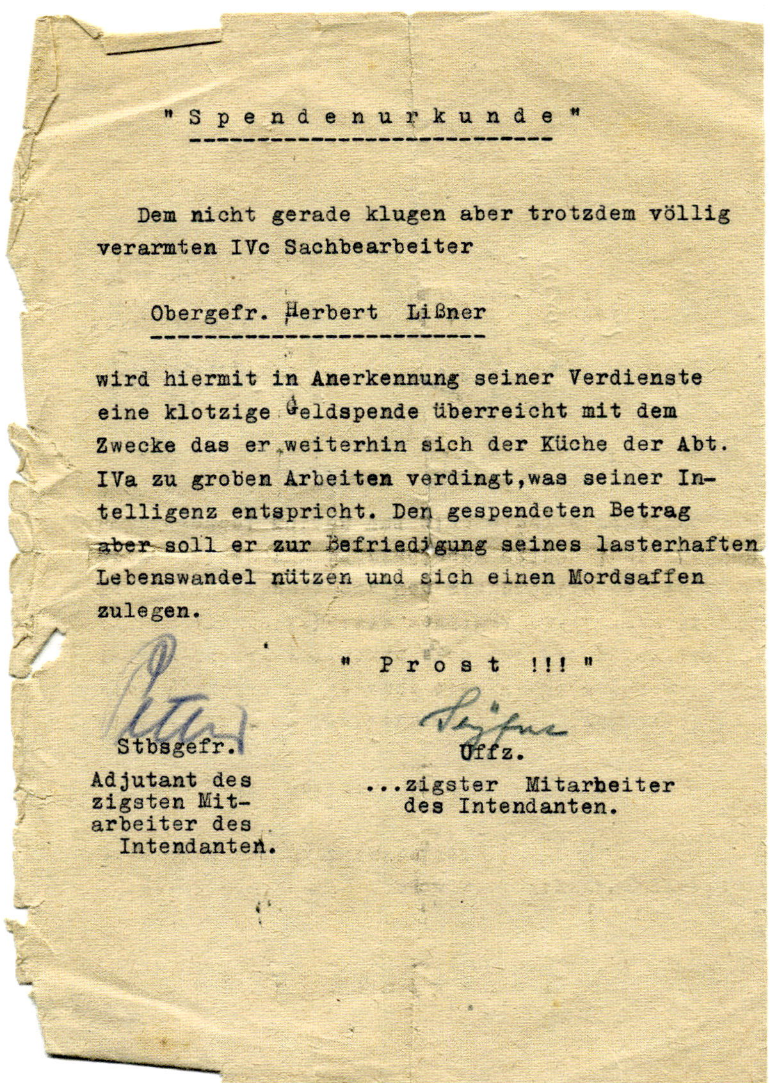

" S p e n d e n u r k u n d e "

Dem nicht gerade klugen aber trotzdem völlig verarmten IVc Sachbearbeiter

Obergefr. Herbert Lißner

wird hiermit in Anerkennung seiner Verdienste eine klotzige Geldspende überreicht mit dem Zwecke das er weiterhin sich der Küche der Abt. IVa zu groben Arbeiten verdingt, was seiner Intelligenz entspricht. Den gespendeten Betrag aber soll er zur Befriedigung seines lasterhaften Lebenswandel nützen und sich einen Mordsaffen zulegen.

" P r o s t !!! "

Stbsgefr.
Adjutant des zigsten Mitarbeiter des Intendanten.

Uffz.
...zigster Mitarbeiter des Intendanten.

Figure 4-43. Front humor was all the more amusing when pointed at one's Kameraden. This Spendenurkunde or donation certificate (a coupon, if you will) was granted to Obergefreiter Herbert Lissner, the "not very clever and impoverished clerk" in recognition of his services in the kitchen at hard labor (fitting his intellect). The certificate is valid for more hard work to fit his depraved lifestyle. (A5)

Figure 4-44. The Völkischer Beobachter (Peoples' Observer) was a popular newspaper of the Nazi Party; they never squandered an opportunity to increase circulation or bolster the party line. They published four volumes of these small booklets, VB-Feldpost, the fourth of which (Landser Lachen, or "Soldiers Laugh") provided humorous anecdotes and cartoons.

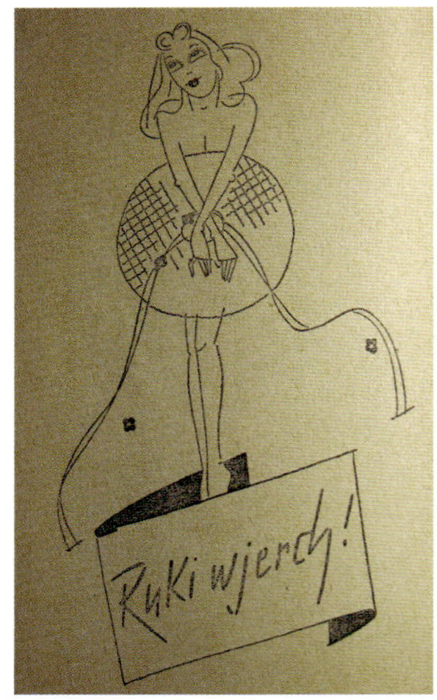

Figure 4-45. The term "rooki vyerkh" is Russian, but used often by German Soldaten advancing through Russia. Even Soldaten who had not yet served on the Eastern Front knew the translation: "Hands up!"

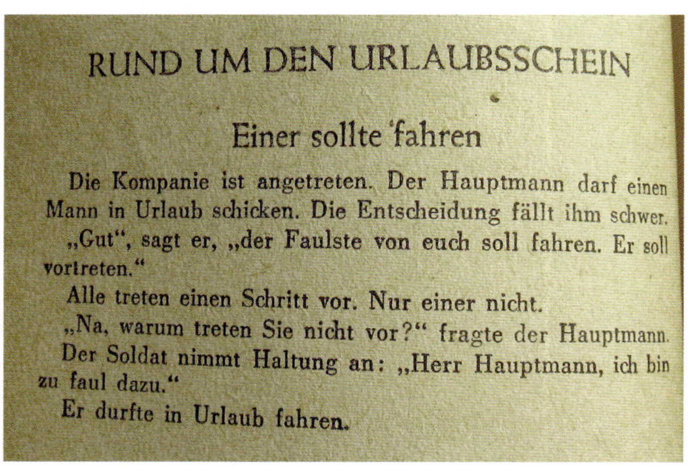

RUND UM DEN URLAUBSSCHEIN

Einer sollte fahren

Die Kompanie ist angetreten. Der Hauptmann darf einen Mann in Urlaub schicken. Die Entscheidung fällt ihm schwer.

„Gut", sagt er, „der Faulste von euch soll fahren. Er soll vortreten."

Alle treten einen Schritt vor. Nur einer nicht.

„Na, warum treten Sie nicht vor?" fragte der Hauptmann.

Der Soldat nimmt Haltung an: „Herr Hauptmann, ich bin zu faul dazu."

Er durfte in Urlaub fahren.

Figure 46. One of the shorter humorous stories from VB-Feldpost Nr. 4: A Captain has been permitted to send one soldier from his company on leave. He tells his men that the foulest (most lice-ridden) may take one step forward and go on leave; they all step forward but one. He asks the one still standing at attention whether he wanted to go on leave. The Soldat replied, "I'm too louse-ridden to go on leave." He was permitted to go on leave.

Figure 4-47. An illustration from VB-Feldpost, Nr. 4; a Soldat returns home to his girlfriend's embrace in this illustration titled "Dream stroll to Germany."

Figure 4-48. A Feldpostkarte titled "Hopes for better times." (4$^{1}/_{8}$" x 6")

Figure 4-49. Another humorous postcard titled "A paratrooper's dream." (4$^{1}/_{8}$" x 5$^{7}/_{8}$")

Figure 4-50. "What the soldiers can only dream of," the embrace of a charming woman and a leave pass. A subtitle could be added, "... and all too rarely receive."

Figure 4-52. Another humorous Feldpostkarte, this one titled "We soldiers dream funny," again feature a pretty woman and a leave permit as well as new vignettes of an island vacation and athletic heroism. ($3^1/_2$" x $5^3/_8$")

Figure 4-51. This long-legged Soldat strides across the front of this Feldpostkarte to the train station for leave. The caption (the Soldat's thoughts) read "The heart beats for me thus 'bomm, bomm, bomm' and I sing along 'I come, I come!" ($4^1/_8$" x $5^3/_4$")

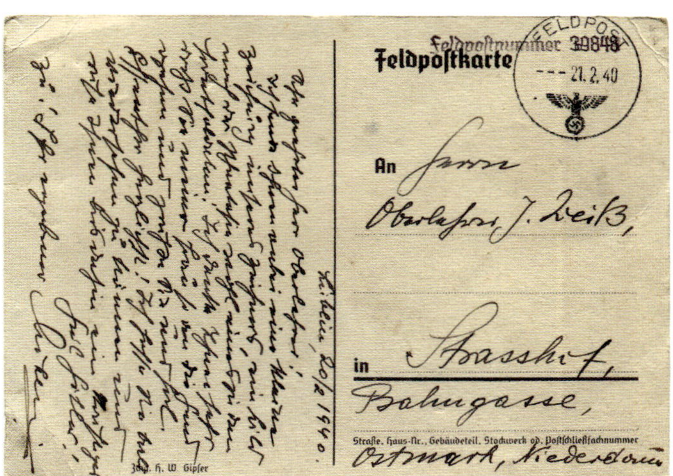

Figure 4-53. Feldpostkarte sent from the 379th Infanterie-Division to Mrs. "Senior Instructor" Zeiss in February 1940 titled simply "the first leave." ($4^1/_4$" x $5^7/_8$")

Wenn ich Urlaub hab'. . . !

Worte von Ralph Maria Siegel   Musik von Gerhard Winkler

Heute gehts hinaus, weit fort von dir, für das liebe Vaterland.
Darum reich nochmal zum Abschied mir deinen Mund und deine Hand!
Nun ade, es muß sein, nun ade, bleibe mein
und vergiß nicht, wenn ich draußen bin, präg dir meine Worte ein:

Wenn ich Urlaub hab', wenn ich Urlaub hab',
lieber Schatz, dann geht's heim zu dir!
Wenn ich Urlaub hab', wenn ich Urlaub hab',
lieber Schatz, dann gehörst du mir!

Halt ich da draußen in der Ferne Wacht, dann gedenk ich immer dein!
Steh ich ganz allein in dunkler Nacht, wird mein Herz stets bei dir sein!
Denn ich weiß, was auch sei, denn ich weiß, du bist mir treu
und ich denk dann nach getaner Pflicht, bin ich ein paar Tage frei:

Wenn aufs neu die Abschiedsstunde schlägt, liebes Mädel, weine nicht!
Ich weiß selber, was dein Herz bewegt, zeig ein lachendes Gesicht!
Sag ade, es muß sein, sag ade, bleibe mein!
Eines Tages kehre ich zurück und ich laß dich nie mehr allein.

Figure 4-54, 4-55, and 4-56. Popular songs were also a common topic for postcards. Two such songs, "When I have leave" and "Brave Little Soldier's Wife," tell of a Soldat's joy at coming home and the sorrow of departure. Note that "The Brave Little Soldier's Wife" was available in both serif and Fraktur versions using the same photo.

Tapfere kleine Soldatenfrau

Lied von Carl Sträßer

1. Als wir im August hinausgezogen sind, / Da hast du mich zum Sammelplatz gebracht. / Du trugst auf deinem Arm unser kleinstes Kind, / Und du hast mich so fröhlich angelacht. / Du sagtest unserem Jungen: „Schau, dort steht der Vater ja!" / Und du warst eine kleine tapfere Frau, / Die ihren Liebsten scheiden sah.

1.—4. Tapfere kleine Soldatenfrau, / Warte nur bald, / Kehren wir zurück. / Tapfere kleine Soldatenfrau, / Du bist ja mein ganzes Glück / Tapfere kleine Soldatenfrau / Ich weiß wie so treu du denkst an mich. / Und so soll es immer sein, / Und so denk ich ja auch dein / Und

Tapfere kleine Soldatenfrau

Lied von Carl Strässer

Als wir im August hinausgezogen sind,
da hast du mich zum Sammelplatz gebracht.
Du trugst auf deinem Arm unser kleinstes Kind,
Und du hast mich so fröhlich angelacht.
Du sagtest unserem Jungen: „Schau,
dort steht der Vater ja!"
und du warst eine kleine tapfere Frau,
die ihren Liebsten scheiden sah.

Tapfere kleine Soldatenfrau,
Warte nur bald
Kehren wir zurück.
Tapfere kleine Soldatenfrau
Du bist ja mein ganzes Glück
Tapfere kleine Soldatenfrau,
Ich weiß wie so treu du denkst an mich.
Und so soll es immer sein,
Und so denk ich ja auch dein
Und ans dem Felde von Herzen grüße ich dich.

Als Abschied ich nahm, da war der Garten bunt,
Viel Rosen waren ringsumher erblüht.
Du gabst mir einen Kuß und dein roter Mund,
Der hat auch wie ein Röselein geglüht.
Du drücktest mir die Hand so fest,
Da hab ich's tief gespürt,
Daß mit Stolz in den Kampf du mich ziehen läßt,
Den Freiheitskampf, den Deutschland führt.

Wenn siegreich der Krieg beendet ist dereinst,
Dann ziehen wir ins Städtchen mit Musik.
Die Fahnen flattern froh und du lachst und weinst
Denn es ist unser schönster Augenblick.
Du trägst denn zwar kein Ordenband,
Du strahlst denn allerwärts,
Als der herrlichste Stern in dem ganzen Land
Dein tapferes goldenes Frauenherz.

Figure 4-57 and Figure 4-58. The roar of the engine and the clatter of tracks sing the song "I am coming on leave," which is precisely what the homesick Soldat below is writing, or so the caption tells us. (3 15/16" x 5 15/16" and 3 1/2" x 5 5/8" respectively)

Ich komme auf Urlaub

Marsch, marsch, zur Straßenbahn um den Urlaub anzutreten

Figure 4-59. Another humorous postcard about leave, this time the caption reads "March, march to the streetcar to kick off leave!" (3 1/2" x 5 5/8")

Figure 4-60. Once again, a joyous Soldat returns home on leave to his eagerly awaiting girlfriend as envious Kameraden peer on. The legend at the bottom reads "When the soldiers return they all meet the same fate; it is necessary to prepare to ward off the final assault." ($3^{1}/_{2}$" x $5^{1}/_{2}$")

Figure 4-61. The illustration on this postcard about going on leave is rather confusing unless one knows of an old Viennese proverb that "the sky is full of violins," meaning to see the world through rose-colored glasses. ($3^{5}/_{8}$" x $5^{1}/_{2}$")

Figure 4-62. Not all postcards about leave involved the Wehrmacht; this postcard titled "Hurray! I have leave!" shows a member of the Reichsarbeitsdienst (RAD), the German equivalent to the American Civil Conservation Corps. Six months' service in the RAD was compulsory for all men between the ages of 18 and 25; in 1939, it became compulsory for women as well. ($3^{1}/_{2}$" x $5^{1}/_{2}$")

Figure 4-63. This postcard depicts Flickstunde, similar to a "make and mend" hour, during which time Soldaten would see to the sewing and repairing of uniforms. As one can see by the Soldat on the right, not everyone was a skilled tailor. ($3^{5}/_{8}$" x $5^{5}/_{8}$")

Figure 4-64. Cartoonist Ferdinand Barlog's own service during the Great War gave him an insight to military life that Soldaten found hilarious, such as this depiction of soldierly bliss, recruits being served pastries and beer by their Sergeants whilst uproariously singing "No Fear, No Fear Rosemarie." ($3^{1}/_{2}$" x $5^{5}/_{8}$")

Figure 4-65. A confused date peers on as her Soldat dashes off to the trumpet's call. The legend below says "Whether soldier or flier, formation remains the victor." ($3^{7}/_{16}$" x $5^{1}/_{2}$")

illustrator Ferdinand Barlog (1895-1955). Drawing from his own military experiences (Herr Barlog was a World War I veteran and former POW of Czarist Russia) and his expertise as a cartoonist for the *Berliner Illustrierte Zeitung* (Berlin Illustrated Newspaper), his rather unique style of simple line art and soft ink washes is immediately recognizable. His postcards struck a humorous tone among civilian and soldier alike, and made light of the situations a soldier encountered during his service, particularly with Officers and Sergeants, not to mention the ladies.

Figure 4-66. The Brandbrief, a letter of "burning" importance, in which this Soldat informs the recipient "Remember, I am out of money." (3¹/₂" x 5¹/₂")

Figure 4-67. As this postcard shows, not all conveyances of the Wehrmacht were mechanized. A Hauptfeldwebel ("Top" Sergeant) drives his drunken charges home as they sing, "From the cradle to the bier is the prettiest life's year." (3¹/₂" x 5¹/₂")

Figure 4-68. This Barlog postcard titled "Geländebesichtigung" (inspection of the terrain), is one of many of his illustrations parodying common courses required of every Soldat. (3¹/₂" x 5¹/₂")

Figure 4-69. Again, Barlog lampoons the reality of Soldatenleben (Soldierly life) by showing precisely what it is not, such as this cartoon of NCOs serving recruits their breakfast in bed. (3½" x 5½")

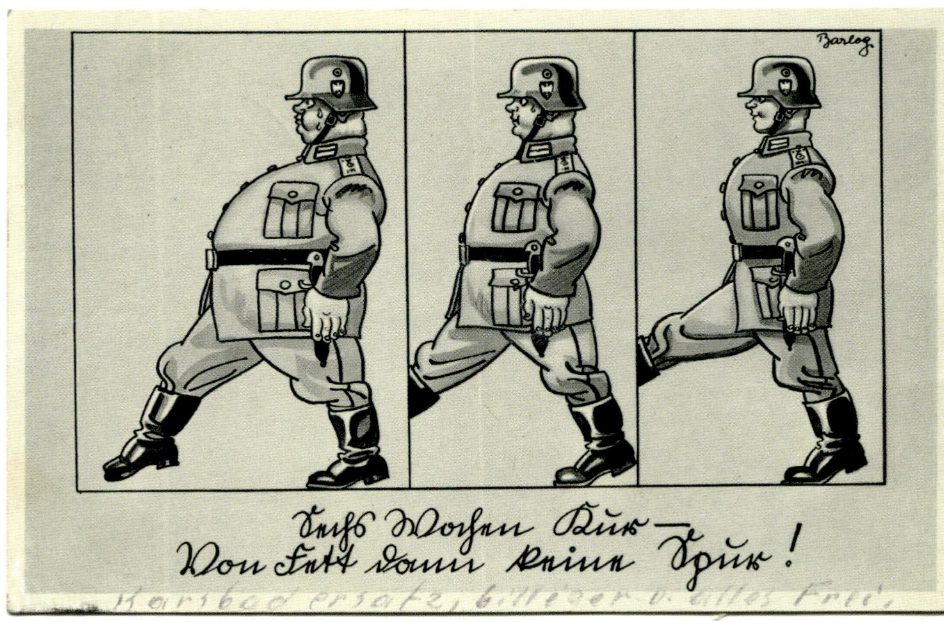

Figure 4-70. Although Barlog satirized a German soldier's life, not everything was unique to Germany; everyone who has gone through military training can appreciate this illustration. "Six weeks, treatment, and then not a trace of fat." (3½" x 5½")

Figure 4-71. This Soldat at a Konditorei (pastry shop) bemoans that his money has not reproduced ("Still only five Pfennig"); the caption states that he has "fired off all his ammunition." (3½" x 5½")

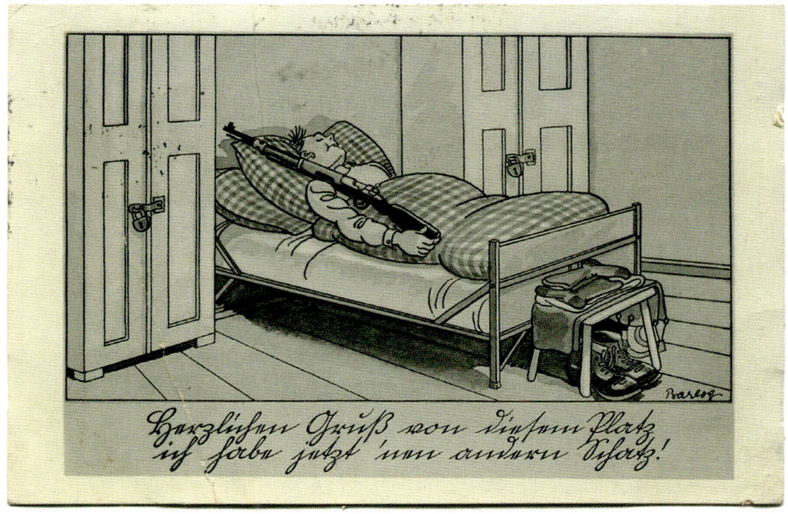

Figure 4-72. Again lampooning soldierly life, Barlog writes "Heartfelt greetings from this place, where I now have a new treasure." Most of the Barlog cards shown here were mailed from a single soldier to his wife, Julia, over the course of two years, from 1939 to 1941. (3 1/2" x 5 1/2")

Figure 4-73. This Barlog postcard has been amended by the sender, adding "to Marie" behind the word "leave," and modifying the caption to read, "I swiftly write you this card; I can't wait until Sunday afternoon!" (3 1/2" x 5 1/2")

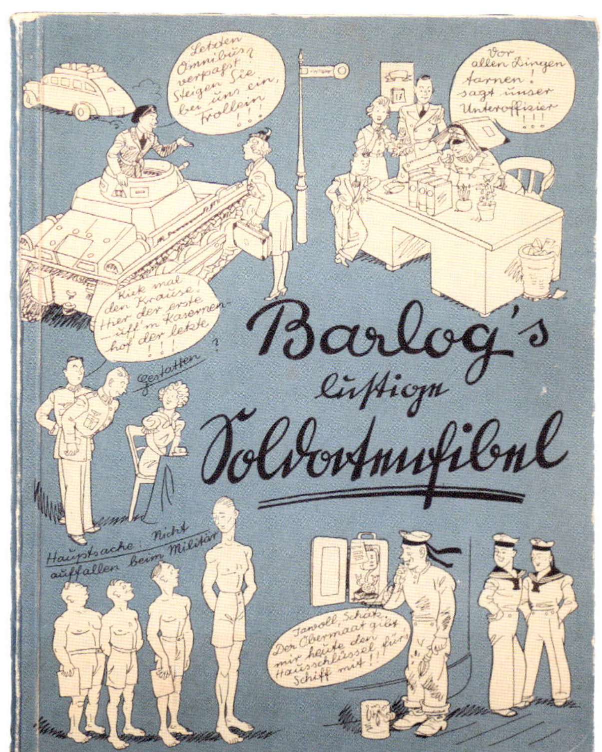

Figure 4-74. A popular book for civilians as well as those in the military, "Barlog's Funny Soldier's Primer" from 1938 is filled with cartoons of not only soldierly life, but also where ever the military (or those in it) influenced the civilian world. (8 1/2" x 10 3/4")

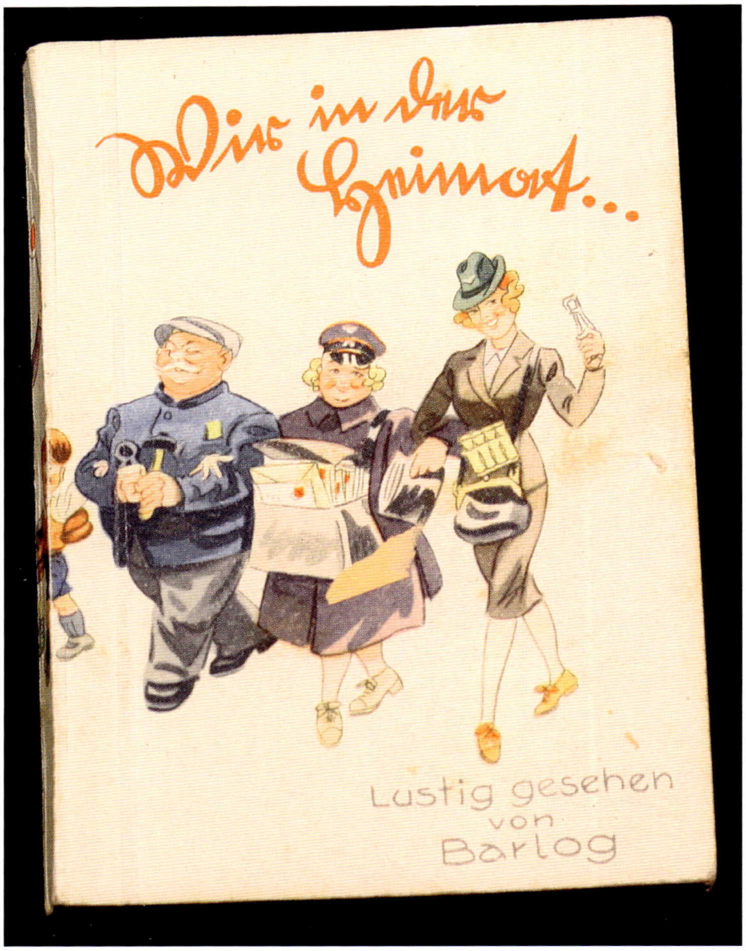

Figure 4-75. In Wir in die Heimat, "We at the Home Front," printed in 1942, Barlog turns his humor toward those suffering through the war on the home front, the lines of which had begun to blur. Although cartoons criticizing the Reich's policies were verboten, cartoons about how people dealt with the conditions those policies created were not, especially for Soldiers returning from the front on leave. (4" x 5³/₈")

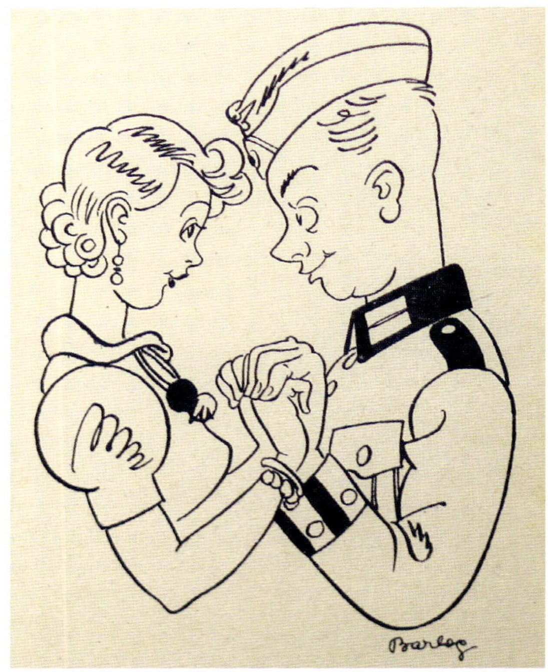

Figure 4-76. In this cartoon titled Urlaubsende, or "leave's end," a woman is informing her Soldat that come Christmastime, they just might be expecting the arrival of a little recruit.

Figure 4-77. This postcard sent to a girlfriend by an amateur illustrator and fan of Barlog's (note that this too has been titled "Urlaubsende") declares that he will "remain true to you my whole life long."

16

Heiratserlaubnisschein

Dem (Dienstgrad, Vor- und Zuname) Stabsgefreiten Otto Weihl

des (Truppenteil) Dienststelle L 26.548 Luftgaupostamt Hamburg I

ist die Heirat mit (Vor- und Zuname) Fräulein Wilma Scheel

Stief-Tochter des zu Hamburg-Harburg wohnhaften Kaufmanns (Ort und Kreis)

wohnhaften oder verstorbenen (Beruf, Vor- und Zuname) Wilhelm Matz

erlaubt worden.

(Ort) Gefechtsstand, den 18. 12. 1944

(Dienststempel) Dienststelle Feldpostnummer L 37881 2

(Unterschrift)

Hauptmann u.stellv.Gruppenkdr.
L 37881 Luftgaupostamt Hamburg
(Dienstgrad, Dienststellung und Truppenteil)

Nr. 564 B. Schabert, Augsburg, Peutingerstr. 9

Figure 4-78. For all intents and purposes, soldiers belonged to the military; if one wanted to get married they had to first acquire permission from their commanding officers. This wasn't unique to Germany; even the U.S. Army required a soldier to get permission to marry well past World War II. A formal request was filed and when the union was approved, a Marriage Permission Certificate was issued, in this case for Stabsgefreiten (Staff Corporal) Otto Weihl, and his fiance, Fräulein Wilma Scheel. (A5)

Soldaten Married while on Leave

For many soldiers, there were two pieces of paper that provided a welcomed peace of mind. The first was the *Heiratsurkunde*, which some saw as an anchor, and others viewed as a harbor. Either way, the Marriage License was a single-sided document that, in many ways, was prized among soldiers.

There were certain conditions for civilians for whom a marriage license would earn a deferment or exemption from military service (though admittedly not very many), but for the soldier it was too late to avail himself of such. Instead, his interests in marriage was much more practical.

Primarily, it meant that there was someone waiting for them at home. Under conditions of extreme stress during combat, that one fact can keep a soldier's emotional well-being high enough to continue; one grasps at what straws one has to maintain some semblance of normalcy. Deplorable conditions become tolerable, so long as one knew that a loving wife (or, for that matter, even an indifferent one) awaited him at the end of such tribulations.

Second, marriage led to progeny, which in a symbolic way, confirmed that a soldier would make it home from the war, if only in legacy. Naturally, it was the act that led to progeny that was on most soldiers' minds.

Third, there was money involved, not in what one would have to pay for a wedding, a home, additional food and clothing, etc., but in what the *Wehrmacht* added to one's earnings.

According to the *Reiseverordnung für die Wehrmacht*, chapter VII, section 69 (1) and (2), soldiers in *Reisekostenstufe V* (the 5th and lowest Travel Cost Ranking), which is where the majority of *Wehrmacht* personnel were classified, i.e., Privates to Sergeants:

> *"Für die Aufenthaltstage am Kommandoort erhalten Kommandierte, auf die die Nr 82 oder Beilage 4 nicht zutreffen, für die ersten 7 Tage ein Kommandoreisegeld in Höhe der Dienstreisetage- und Übernachtungsgelder (45). Vom 8. Tage an wird Kommandogeld gewährt."*

> For days in which one remains at a command location, and conditions of section 82 or supplement 4 are not met, for the first seven (7) days a command travel pay above the service travel per diem allowance and overnight stay allowance permitted under section 45 shall be awarded. This shall be granted on the 8th day.

This *Kommandoreisegeld*, an additional travel allowance at the discretion of one's local level of command, was distributed according to Paragraph (2) as such: married soldiers with their own home received 5 *Reichsmarks* additional pay, per day, for the first seven days of his trip. Married soldiers without their own home and unmarried soldiers with their own home received 3 *Reichsmarks* per day. Single soldiers who were not property owners received 2. (According to Paragraph 3, under certain conditions and hardships, this pay could be extended to fourteen days, but extensions to twenty-one days required prior approval from the *Reichsminister* of Finance.)

This was above and beyond the 5,50 *Reichsmarks* for service travel and 4,50 *Reichsmarks* overnight allowance awarded for each full day of travel according to section 45, which in turn, was added to a soldier's base pay.

Mind you, the *Reiseverordnung* only covered additional married soldiers' pay and allowances allotted for travel. There were additional allowances for housing, subsistence, separation, and so on, all of which was apart from and in addition to the base pay, which single soldier's did not receive. So being married in the *Wehrmacht* could be somewhat lucrative, as is the case in many armies around the world today.

The *Heiratsurkunde* was broken down into two different categories, the F1 form with *Elternangabe* (Parental Indications) and the F2 form without. Both had spaces requiring the name, religious affiliation, address, and birth date of the bride and groom (indicated

Figure 4-79. This engagement announcement from May, 1944 announced the pending union of Pilot and Corporal Rudolf Kirschner to Jutta Kloster. It's quite likely that Unteroffizier Kirschner served at one of the many airfields surrounding Berlin, where this card was printed.

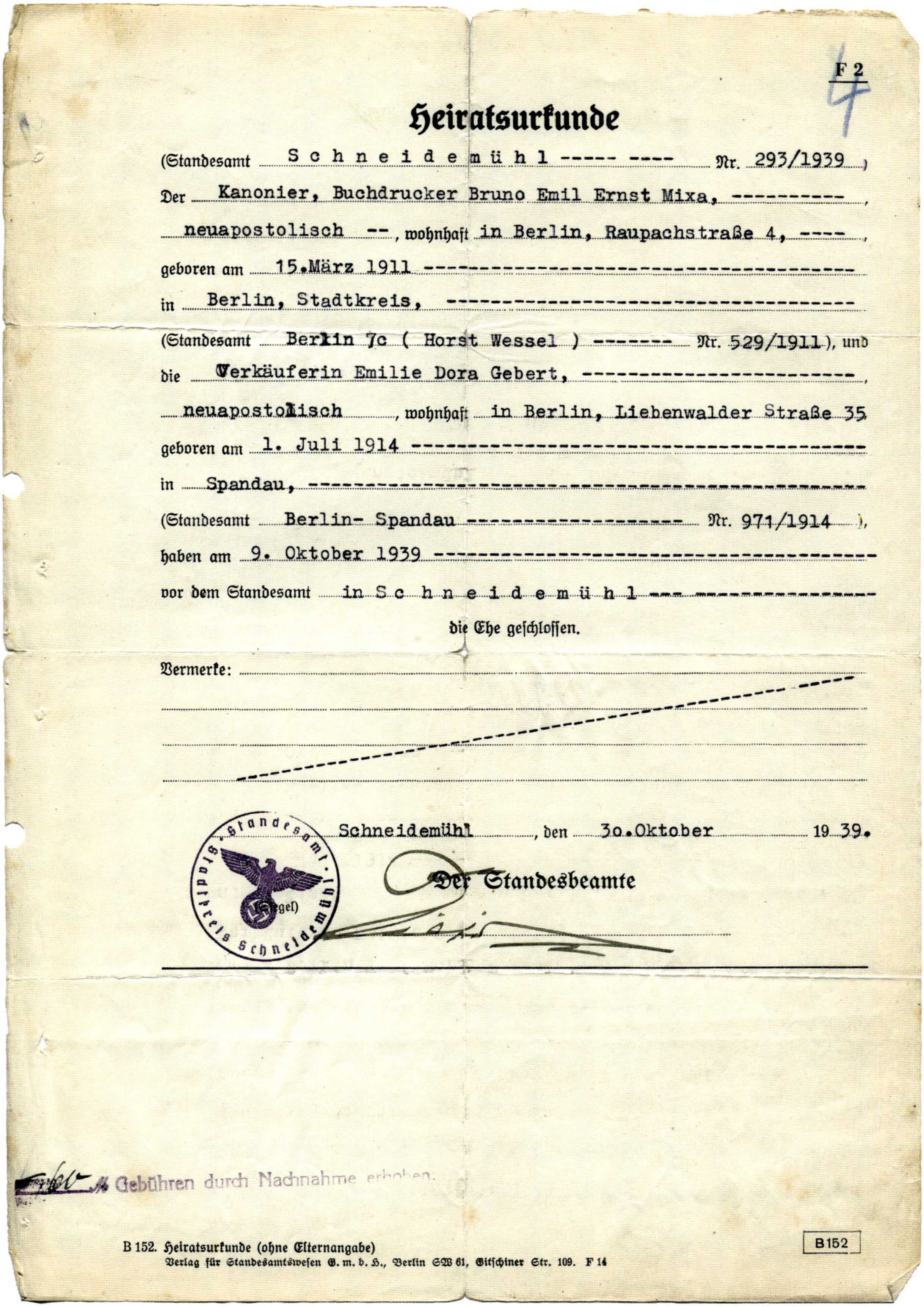

F 2

4

Heiratsurkunde

(Standesamt Schneidemühl ----- ---- Nr. 293/1939)

Der Kanonier, Buchdrucker Bruno Emil Ernst Mixa, ----------,

neuapostolisch --, wohnhaft in Berlin, Raupachstraße 4, ----,

geboren am 15.März 1911 --------------------------------------

in Berlin, Stadtkreis, ------------------------------------

(Standesamt Berlin 7c (Horst Wessel) -------- Nr. 529/1911), und

die Verkäuferin Emilie Dora Gebert, -----------------------,

neuapostolisch, wohnhaft in Berlin, Liebenwalder Straße 35

geboren am 1. Juli 1914 ---------------------------------------

in Spandau, ---

(Standesamt Berlin- Spandau ------------------- Nr. 971/1914),

haben am 9. Oktober 1939 --------------------------------------

vor dem Standesamt in Schneidemühl --- ----------------

die Ehe geschlossen.

Vermerke: ------------------------------

Schneidemühl, den 30.Oktober 19 39.

Der Standesbeamte

(Siegel) Standesamt Stadtkreis Schneidemühl

... M Gebühren durch Nachnahme erhoben.

B 152. Heiratsurkunde (ohne Elternangabe)
Verlag für Standesamtswesen G. m. b. H., Berlin SW 61, Gitschiner Str. 109. F 14

B152

Figure 4-80. This Berlin Heiratsurkunde, or Marriage Certificate, for Cannonier and book printer Bruno Mixa to saleswoman Emilie Gerbert was filed in Spandau in October 1939. This is the shorter F2 version of the Heiratsurkunde, which did not require the parents' names. (A4)

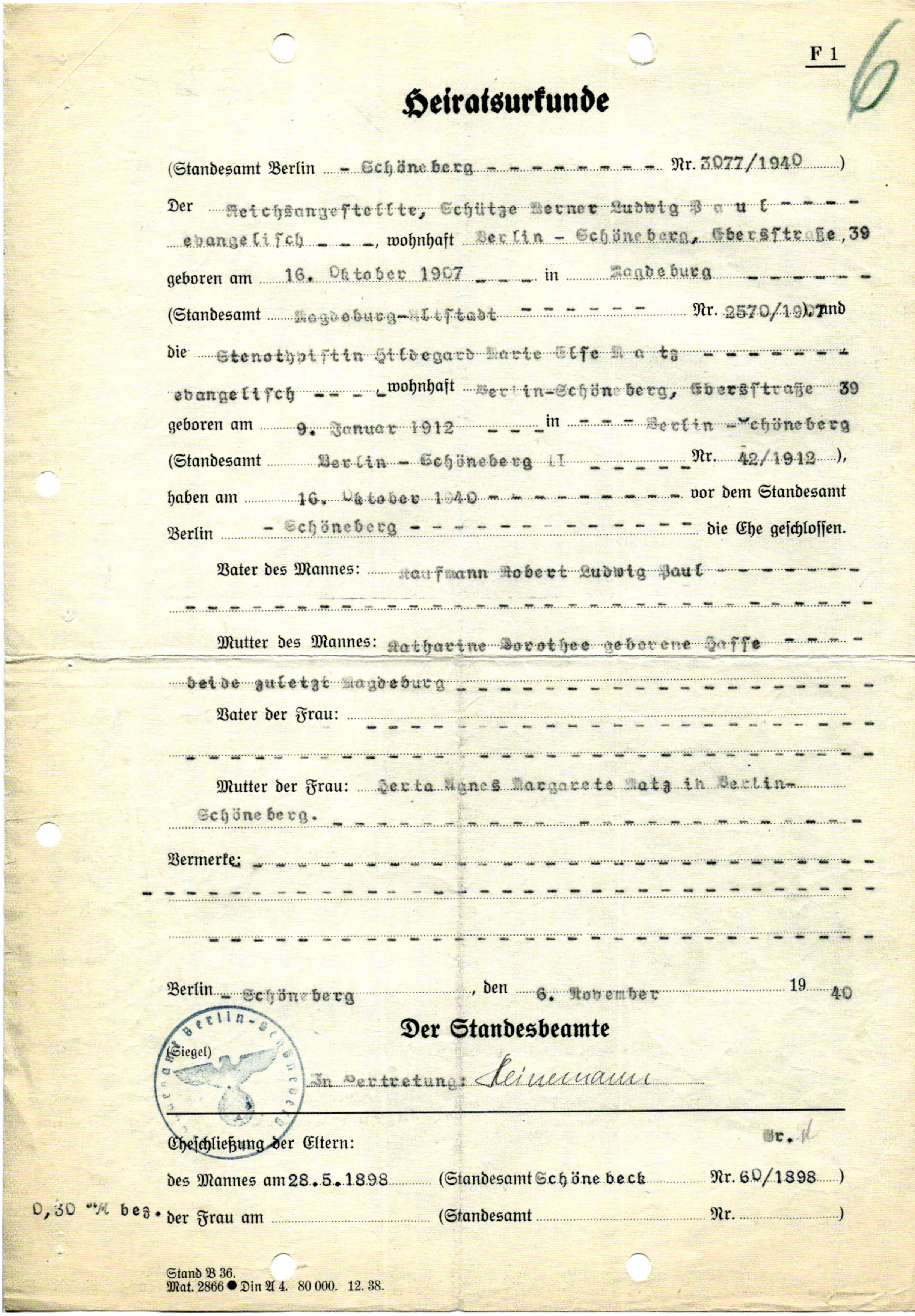

F 1

6

Heiratsurkunde

(Standesamt Berlin - Schöneberg Nr. 3077/1940)

Der Reichsangestellte, Schütze Werner Ludwig Paul
evangelisch, wohnhaft Berlin - Schöneberg, Ebersstraße 39
geboren am 16. Oktober 1907 in Magdeburg
(Standesamt Magdeburg-Altstadt Nr. 2570/1907) und
die Stenotypistin Hildegard Marie Else Katz
evangelisch, wohnhaft Berlin-Schöneberg, Ebersstraße 39
geboren am 9. Januar 1912 in Berlin - Schöneberg
(Standesamt Berlin - Schöneberg II Nr. 42/1912),
haben am 16. Oktober 1940 vor dem Standesamt
Berlin - Schöneberg die Ehe geschlossen.

Vater des Mannes: Kaufmann Robert Ludwig Paul

Mutter des Mannes: Katharine Dorothee geborene Haffe
beide zuletzt Magdeburg

Vater der Frau:

Mutter der Frau: Herta Agnes Margarete Katz in Berlin-Schöneberg.

Vermerke:

Berlin - Schöneberg, den 6. November 1940

Der Standesbeamte

(Siegel) In Vertretung: Heinemann

Eheschließung der Eltern:
des Mannes am 28.5.1898 (Standesamt Schönebeck Nr. 60/1898)
der Frau am (Standesamt Nr.)

0,30 RM bez.

Stand B 36.
Mat. 2866 ● Din A 4. 80 000. 12. 38.

Figure 4-81 and 4-82. The longer F1 Heiratsurkunde required the parents' names as well as those being married. These two certificates, both of soldiers home on leave, were filed in Berlin-Schöneberg in 1940 and 1942 respectively. (A4)

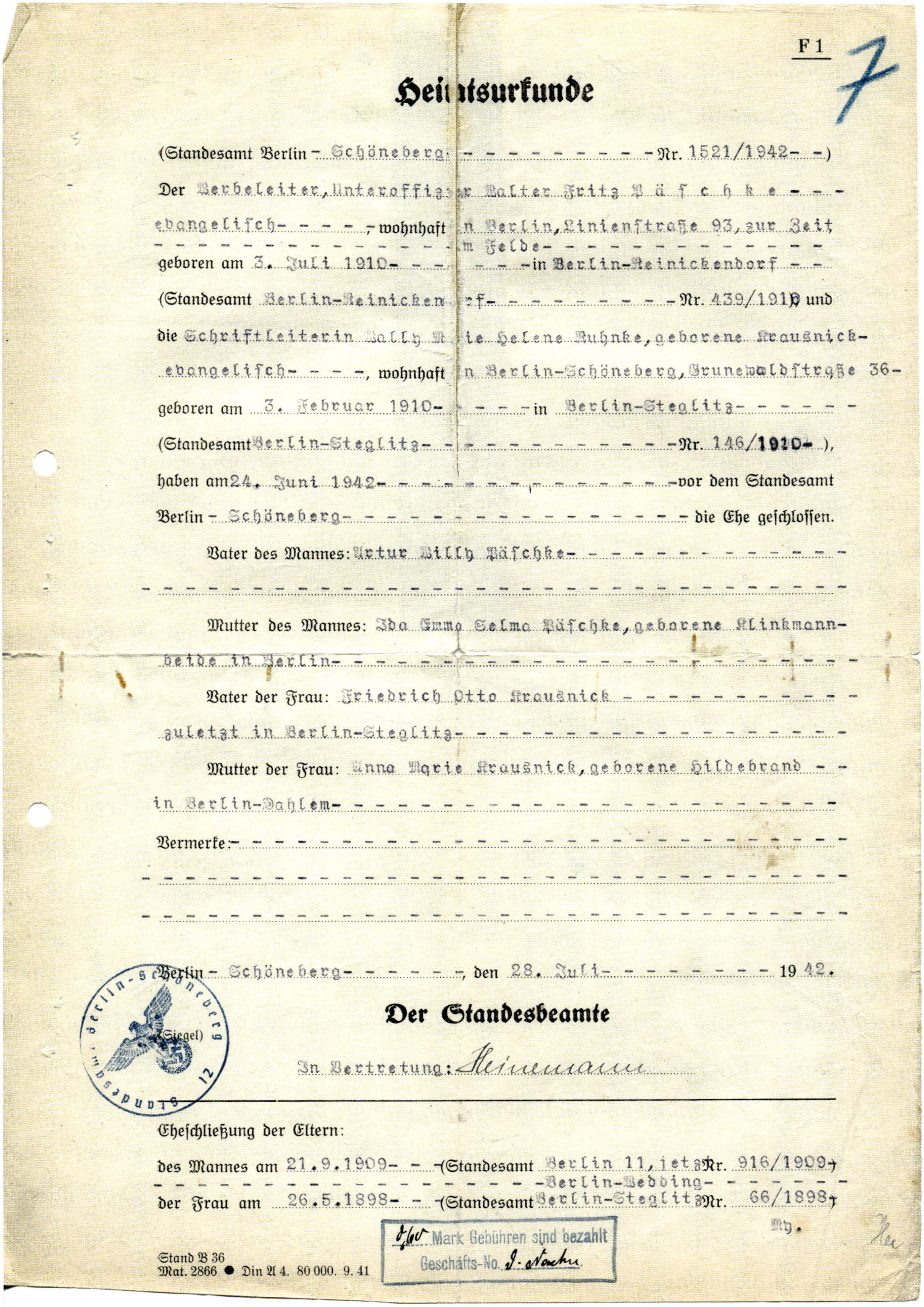

F 1

Heiratsurkunde

(Standesamt Berlin-Schöneberg - - - Nr. 1521/1942 - -)

Der Werbeleiter, Unteroffizier Walter Fritz Päschke - - -
evangelisch - - -, wohnhaft in Berlin, Linienstraße 93, zur Zeit im Felde - - -
geboren am 3. Juli 1910 - - - in Berlin-Reinickendorf - -
(Standesamt Berlin-Reinickendorf - - - Nr. 439/1910 und
die Schriftleiterin Wally Marie Helene Buhnke, geborene Kraußnick -
evangelisch - - -, wohnhaft in Berlin-Schöneberg, Grunewaldstraße 36 -
geboren am 3. Februar 1910 - - - in Berlin-Steglitz - - -
(Standesamt Berlin-Steglitz - - - Nr. 146/1910 -),
haben am 24. Juni 1942 - - - vor dem Standesamt
Berlin-Schöneberg - - - die Ehe geschlossen.

Vater des Mannes: Artur Willy Päschke - - -

Mutter des Mannes: Ida Emma Selma Päschke, geborene Klinkmann -
beide in Berlin - - -

Vater der Frau: Friedrich Otto Kraußnick - - -
zuletzt in Berlin-Steglitz - - -

Mutter der Frau: Anna Marie Kraußnick, geborene Hildebrand - -
in Berlin-Dahlem - - -

Vermerke: - - -

Berlin-Schöneberg - - -, den 28. Juli - - - 1942.

Der Standesbeamte

(Siegel)

In Vertretung: Heinemann

Eheschließung der Eltern:

des Mannes am 21.9.1909 - - (Standesamt Berlin 11, jetzt Berlin-Wedding - - Nr. 916/1909)

der Frau am 26.5.1898 - - (Standesamt Berlin-Steglitz Nr. 66/1898)

Wy.

0,60 Mark Gebühren sind bezahlt
Geschäfts-No. I-Nachw

Stand B 36
Mat. 2866 ● Din A 4. 80 000. 9.41

also by the registry number of their birth certificates by number/year recorded), as well as the date and location in which the ceremony was performed. The F1 form had spaces for the parents of the happy couple to enter their names and in which city they lived as well.

Lastly was a small section for remarks, and a space for the *Standesbeamte* (Registry Official) to record the date and *Standesamt* (Registration Office) in which the nuptials had occurred. The *Standesbeamtestempel* was placed either in the margin or the base of the document, as well as a tax stamp or *Stempel* to note the *Gebühr* or *Gebührnis* (Fee) paid to record the occasion, usually 30 to 60 *Reichspfennig*.

Figure 4-83. A newlywed couple emerging from the church, followed by a member of their entourage (Brother? Best Man?), who happens to be a Luftwaffe officer.

Figure 4-84 & 4-85. A Luftwaffe pilot and his bride, probably later in the war when clothing restrictions often made the acquisition of a complete wedding dress unobtainable.

Figure 4-87. A Gebirgsjäger (mountain soldier) and his bride on their wedding day; note the cap badge and military mountain-climbing boots.

Figure 4-89 & 4-90. These two photos show a well-decorated officer and his new wife as they depart from the church following their ceremony. Note his Adjutant's parade aiguillette, Iron Cross, Eastern Front Medal, and Wound Badge. ($3^{7}/_{16}$" x $5^{1}/_{2}$" each)

Figure 4-91. This is an interesting double exposure photo of a Fahnenjunker-Unteroffizier (Officer candidate corporal) wearing an infantry assault badge and his newlywed wife on their wedding day. One can see where a second exposure was overlaid onto the first, causing a ghostly image of the man's hand.

Figure 4-93. War brides were not unique to the Allies; this Luftwaffe senior NCO and his French bride celebrate their wedding day with this French photo postcard. ($3^{9}/_{16}$" x $5^{7}/_{16}$")

Figure 4-94. The exhaustion of war covers this Eastern Front veteran's face on his wedding day. (4" x 5¾")

Figure 4-95. Another Gebirgsjäger on his wedding day: this Feldwebel also bears a black cuff band of mourning.

Figure 4-96. Although normally a happy occasion, this couple seems less than enthused about their marital status. (3½" x 5½")

The other piece of paper that offered peace of mind to the soldier was the *Entlassungsshein*, a Release from Service Pass or military discharge (not to be confused with the *Entlausungsschein* or Delousing Certificate) which indicated that he had passed from the ranks of active service into that of the "veteran" category.

The form was 217mm x 222mm, a very odd size compared to all other German paperwork, and was not removed or otherwise separated from a larger A4 or B6 form. It was printed on both sides, and the information was presented in five parts.

Part I was filled out naming the soldier being released, his birth date and birthplace, the dates he served, and the date and destination of his release. It also listed the *Wehrbezirkskommando* (W.B.K. or Military District Command) or *Wehrmeldeamt* (W.M.A. or Military Reporting Station) where the soldier was expected to deliver all of his military papers (*Soldbuch*, *Wehrpass*, etc.).

Part II listed pay and equipment the soldier had been given or discharged with. This included *Wehrsold*, rations, and a certain amount of basic military gear he was expected to keep with him if required to return to active duty.

The back was reserved for sections III, IV, and V. Part III allowed for verification of registration at his new residence (*Wohnort*) with the local *Polizeibehörde* (Police Authority) and *Arbeitsamt* (Work District) in order to be issued civilian ration cards. Part IV was set aside for registration with the local Military Registration District, or *Wehrmeldeamt*. Only after parts I-IV had been completed could he complete part V and collect his *Entlassungsgeld* (Separation Pay) of 50 *Reichsmarks*, primarily for the upkeep and maintenance of the equipment listed in part II.

Discharges are often found today in very rough shape; a discharged soldier carried his discharge with him until local civilians, or more particularly local authorities, got used to seeing him. For larger metropolitan areas such as Berlin, Nürnberg, München, and the like, this could take quite a while.

The *Entlassungsschein* was not an exclusively military document, however. The translation means literally a release from service, not just military service. The *Reichsbahn*, RAD, and other paramilitary organizations that used military forms for travel also used military forms for discharge, noted however for civilian service instead. (Civilian *Entlassungsschein*, such as release from a factory or company, are also common, but not within the scope of this work.) In some cases, Ersatz certifications were created using plain paper, letterhead, or even transport forms.

Figure 4-97. The discharge certificate of Obergefreiter Johann Hassler in August 1941. Almost certainly a veteran of the First World War, being 44 years old at his discharge. Hassler was sent home from Sanitäts Ersatz Battailon 17's Convalescent Company, probably after being wounded. ($8^{3}/_{8}$" x $8^{15}/_{16}$")

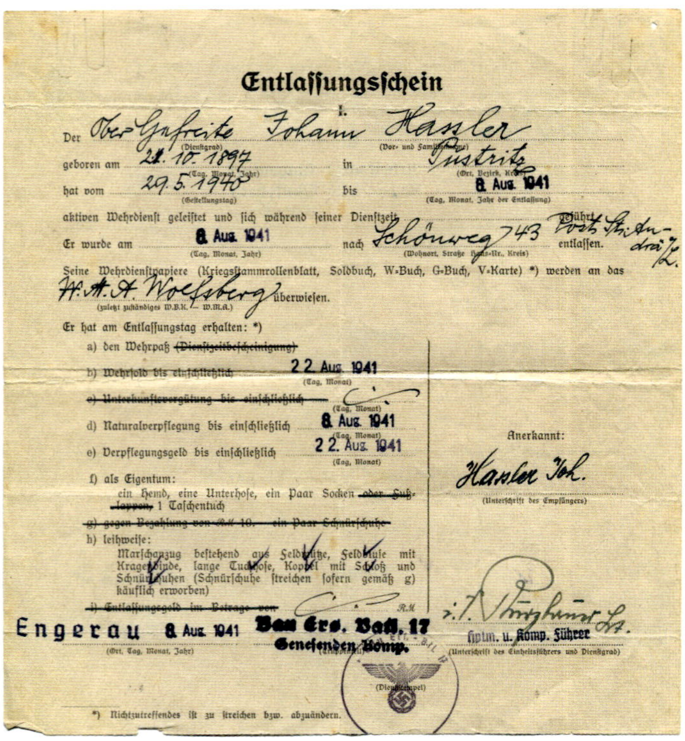

Entlassungsschein

I.

Der Ober-Gefreite Johann Hassler
(Dienstgrad) (Vor- und Familienname)

geboren am 21. 10. 1897 in Pustritz
(Tag, Monat, Jahr) (Ort, Bezirk, Kreis)

hat vom 29. 5. 1940 bis 8. Aug. 1941
(Gestellungstag) (Tag, Monat, Jahr der Entlassung)

aktiven Wehrdienst geleistet und sich während seiner Dienstzeit ... geführt.

Er wurde am 8. Aug. 1941 nach Schönweg 743 Post St. Andrä i/L. entlassen.
(Tag, Monat, Jahr) (Wohnort, Straße Haus-Nr., Kreis)

Seine Wehrdienstpapiere (Kriegsstammrollenblatt, Soldbuch, W-Buch, G-Buch, V-Karte) *) werden an das W.M.A. Wolfsberg überwiesen.
(zuletzt zuständiges W.B.K. — W.M.A.)

Er hat am Entlassungstag erhalten: *)

a) den Wehrpaß ~~(Dienstzeitbescheinigung)~~

b) ~~Wehrsold bis einschließlich~~ 22. Aug. 1941 (Tag, Monat)

c) ~~Unterkunftsvergütung bis einschließlich~~ (Tag, Monat)

d) Naturalverpflegung bis einschließlich 8. Aug. 1941 (Tag, Monat)

e) Verpflegungsgeld bis einschließlich 22. Aug. 1941 (Tag, Monat)

f) als Eigentum:
ein Hemd, eine Unterhose, ein Paar Socken ~~oder Fußlappen~~, 1 Taschentuch

g) ~~gegen Bezahlung von RM 10.— ein Paar Schnürschuhe~~

h) leihweise:
Marschanzug bestehend aus Feldmütze, Feldbluse mit Kragenbinde, lange Tuchhose, Koppel mit Schloß und Schnürschuhen (Schnürschuhe streichen sofern gemäß g) käuflich erworben)

i) ~~Entlassungsgeld im Betrage von~~ RM

Anerkannt:

Hassler Joh.
(Unterschrift des Empfängers)

Engerau 8. Aug. 1941
(Ort, Tag, Monat, Jahr)

San. Ers. Batl. 17
Genesenden Komp.

(Dienststempel)

i. V. ... Lt.
Hptm. u. Komp. Führer
(Unterschrift des Einheitsführers und Dienstgrad)

*) Nichtzutreffendes ist zu streichen bzw. abzuändern.

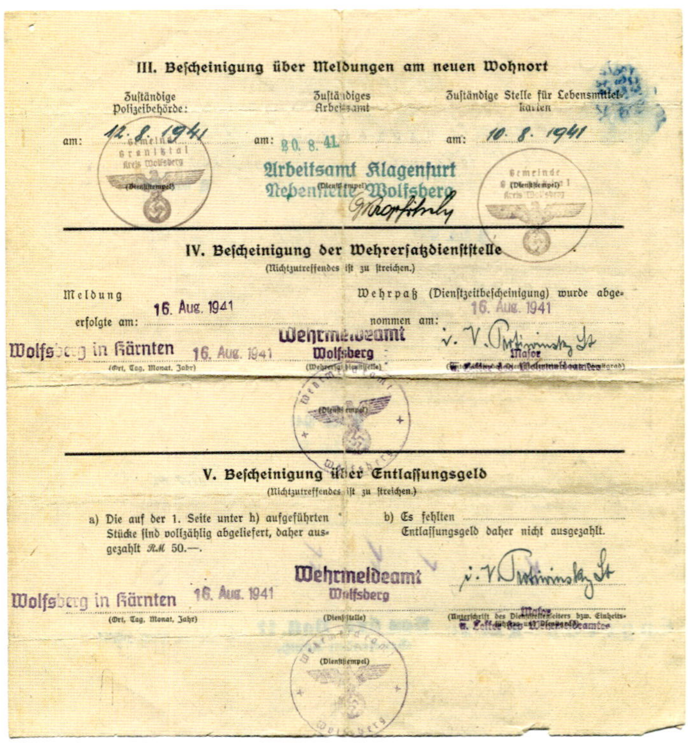

III. Bescheinigung über Meldungen am neuen Wohnort

Zuständige Polizeibehörde:	Zuständiges Arbeitsamt	Zuständige Stelle für Lebensmittelkarten
am: 12. 8. 1941	am: 20. 8. 41.	am: 10. 8. 1941
(Dienststempel)	Arbeitsamt Klagenfurt Nebenstelle Wolfsberg (Dienststempel)	(Dienststempel)

IV. Bescheinigung der Wehrersatzdienststelle

(Nichtzutreffendes ist zu streichen.)

Meldung erfolgte am: 16. Aug. 1941

Wehrpaß (Dienstzeitbescheinigung) wurde abgenommen am: 16. Aug. 1941

Wolfsberg in Kärnten 16. Aug. 1941
(Ort, Tag, Monat, Jahr)

Wehrmeldeamt Wolfsberg
(Wehrersatzdienststelle)

i. V. ... Lt.
Major

(Dienststempel)

V. Bescheinigung über Entlassungsgeld

(Nichtzutreffendes ist zu streichen.)

a) Die auf der 1. Seite unter h) aufgeführten Stücke sind vollzählig abgeliefert, daher ausgezahlt RM 50.—.

b) Es fehlten ... Entlassungsgeld daher nicht ausgezahlt.

Wolfsberg in Kärnten 16. Aug. 1941
(Ort, Tag, Monat, Jahr)

Wehrmeldeamt Wolfsberg
(Dienststelle)

i. V. ... Lt.
Major
(Unterschrift des Dienststellenleiters bzw. Einheitsführers und Dienstgrad)

(Dienststempel)

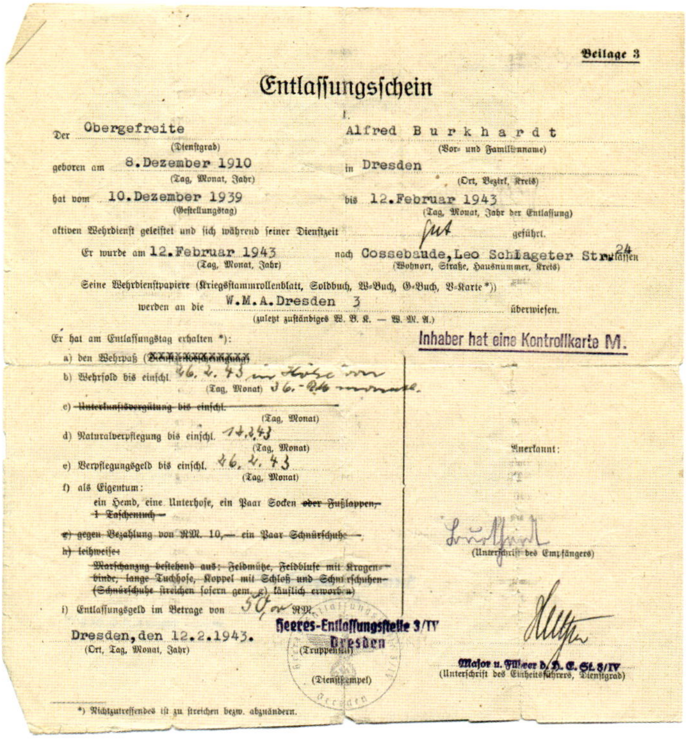

Beilage 3

Entlassungsschein

Der Obergefreite (Dienstgrad) Alfred Burkhardt (Vor- und Familienname)
geboren am 8. Dezember 1910 (Tag, Monat, Jahr) in Dresden (Ort, Bezirk, Kreis)
hat vom 10. Dezember 1939 (Gestellungstag) bis 12. Februar 1943 (Tag, Monat, Jahr der Entlassung)
aktiven Wehrdienst geleistet und sich während seiner Dienstzeit gut geführt.
Er wurde am 12. Februar 1943 (Tag, Monat, Jahr) nach Cossebaude, Leo Schlageter Str. 24 (Wohnort, Straße, Hausnummer, Kreis) entlassen.
Seine Wehrdienstpapiere (Kriegsstammrollenblatt, Soldbuch, W-Buch, G-Buch, V-Karte*))
werden an die W.M.A. Dresden 3 (zuletzt zuständiges W. B. K. — W. M. A.) überwiesen.

Inhaber hat eine Kontrollkarte M.

Er hat am Entlassungstag erhalten *):
a) den Wehrpaß
b) Wehrsold bis einschl. 26. 2. 43 (Tag, Monat)
c) ~~Unterkunftsvergütung bis einschl.~~ (Tag, Monat)
d) Naturalverpflegung bis einschl. 14.2.43 (Tag, Monat)
e) Verpflegungsgeld bis einschl. 26. 2. 43 (Tag, Monat)
f) als Eigentum:
ein Hemd, eine Unterhose, ein Paar Socken ~~oder Fußlappen, 1 Taschentuch~~
~~g) gegen Bezahlung von RM. 10,— ein Paar Schnürschuhe~~
~~h) leihweise: Marschanzug bestehend aus: Feldmütze, Feldbluse mit Kragenbinde, lange Tuchhose, Koppel mit Schloß und Schnürschuhen (Schnürschuhe streichen sofern gem. g) käuflich erworben)~~
i) Entlassungsgeld im Betrage von 50,— RM.

Anerkannt:
Burkhardt
(Unterschrift des Empfängers)

Dresden, den 12.2.1943.
(Ort, Tag, Monat, Jahr)
Heeres-Entlassungsstelle 3/IV Dresden
(Truppenteil)
(Dienststempel)
Major u. Führer d. H. E. St. 3/IV
(Unterschrift des Einheitsführers, Dienstgrad)

*) Nichtzutreffendes ist zu streichen bezw. abzuändern.

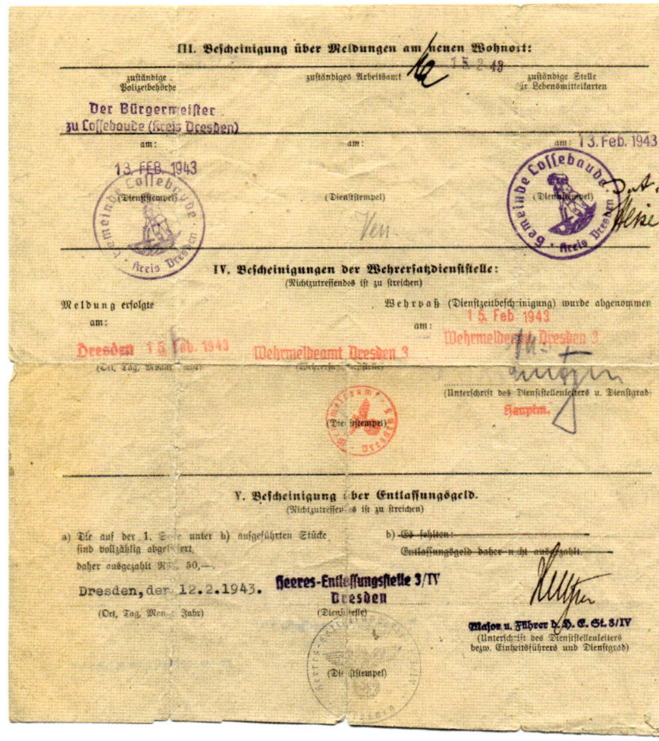

III. Bescheinigung über Meldungen am neuen Wohnort:

zuständige Polizeibehörde	zuständiges Arbeitsamt	zuständige Stelle für Lebensmittelkarten
Der Bürgermeister zu Cossebaude (Kreis Dresden)		
am: 13. FEB. 1943	am:	am: 13. Feb. 1943
(Dienststempel) Gemeinde Cossebaude Kreis Dresden	(Dienststempel)	(Dienststempel) Gemeinde Cossebaude Kreis Dresden

IV. Bescheinigungen der Wehrersatzdienststelle:
(Nichtzutreffendes ist zu streichen)

Meldung erfolgte am: Dresden 15. Feb. 1943 (Ort, Tag, Monat, Jahr) Wehrmeldeamt Dresden 3 (Wehrersatzdienststelle)
Wehrpaß (Dienstzeitbescheinigung) wurde abgenommen am: 15. Feb. 1943 Wehrmeldeamt Dresden 3
(Dienststempel)
(Unterschrift des Dienststellenleiters u. Dienstgrad)
Hauptm.

V. Bescheinigung über Entlassungsgeld.
(Nichtzutreffendes ist zu streichen)

a) Die auf der 1. Seite unter h) aufgeführten Stücke sind vollzählig abgeliefert, daher ausgezahlt RM. 50,—.
b) ~~Es fehlten: Entlassungsgeld daher nicht ausgezahlt.~~

Dresden, den 12.2.1943. (Ort, Tag, Monat, Jahr)
Heeres-Entlassungsstelle 3/IV Dresden (Dienststelle)
(Dienststempel)
Major u. Führer d. H. E. St. 3/IV
(Unterschrift des Dienststellenleiters bezw. Einheitsführers und Dienstgrad)

Figure 4-98. An honorable discharge presented to Obergefreite (sic) Alfred Burkhardt after fours years of good service. Discharged on February 12, 1943 at Heeres-Entlassungsstelle 3 in Dresden (Army Discharge Station 3), one has to wonder how Herr Burkhardt fared in the devastating air raids almost exactly two years later. (8³/₈" x 8³/₄")

Figure 4-99. Typical of many Entlassungsscheinen, the discharge certificate of Obergefreite (sic) Helmuth Platschek doesn't state the conditions of his discharge, only that he has been. (8³/₈" x 8³/₄")

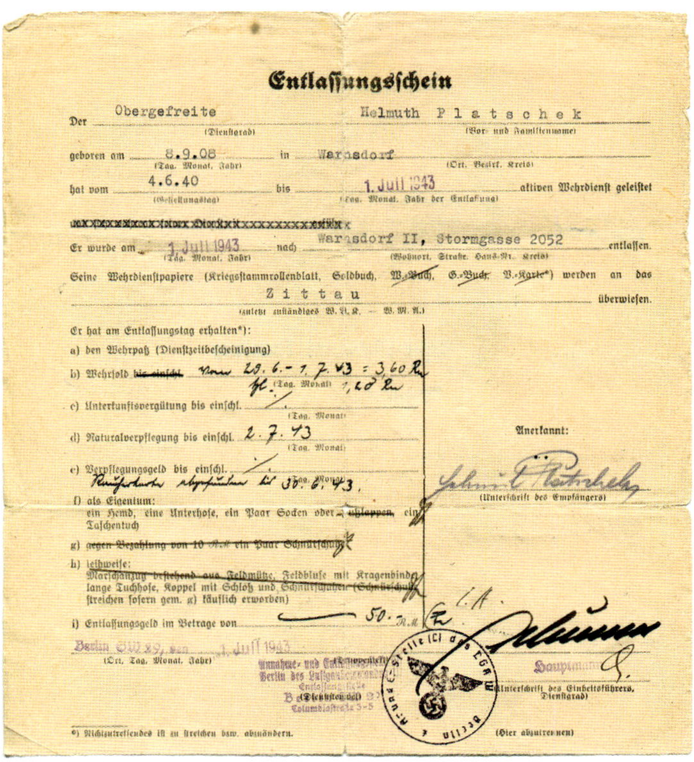

Entlassungsschein

Der Obergefreite (Dienstgrad) Helmuth Platschek (Vor- und Familienname)
geboren am 8.9.08 (Tag, Monat, Jahr) in Warnsdorf (Ort, Bezirk, Kreis)
hat vom 4.6.40 (Gestellungstag) bis 1. Juli 1943 (Tag, Monat, Jahr der Entlassung) aktiven Wehrdienst geleistet
Er wurde am 1. Juli 1943 (Tag, Monat, Jahr) nach Warnsdorf II, Stormgasse 2052 (Wohnort, Straße, Haus-Nr., Kreis) entlassen.
Seine Wehrdienstpapiere (Kriegsstammrollenblatt, Soldbuch, ~~W.-Buch, G.-Buch, V.-Karte~~*)) werden an das Zittau (zuletzt zuständiges W. B. K. — W. M. A.) überwiesen.

Er hat am Entlassungstag erhalten*):
a) den Wehrpaß (Dienstzeitbescheinigung)
b) Wehrsold ~~bis einschl.~~ vom 29. 6. – 1. 7. 43 = 3,60 RM (Tag, Monat) 1,80 RM
c) Unterkunftsvergütung bis einschl. — (Tag, Monat)
d) Naturalverpflegung bis einschl. 2. 7. 43 (Tag, Monat)
e) Verpflegungsgeld bis einschl. — bis 30. 6. 43 (Tag, Monat)
f) als Eigentum:
ein Hemd, eine Unterhose, ein Paar Socken oder ~~Fußlappen~~, ein Taschentuch
g) ~~gegen Bezahlung von 10 RM ein Paar Schnürschuhe~~
h) leihweise:
~~Marschanzug bestehend aus Feldmütze,~~ Feldbluse mit Kragenbinde, lange Tuchhose, Koppel mit Schloß und ~~Schnürschuhen (Schnürschuhe~~ streichen sofern gem. g) käuflich erworben)
i) Entlassungsgeld im Betrage von 50.— RM

Anerkannt:
Helmut Platschek
(Unterschrift des Empfängers)

Berlin SW 29, den 1. Juli 1943
(Ort, Tag, Monat, Jahr)
Annahme- und Entlassungsstelle Berlin des Luftgaukommandos III
(Dienststempel)
Columbiastraße 3-5
i.A.
Hauptmann
(Unterschrift des Einheitsführers, Dienstgrad)

*) Nichtzutreffendes ist zu streichen bzw. abzuändern.
(Hier abzutrennen)

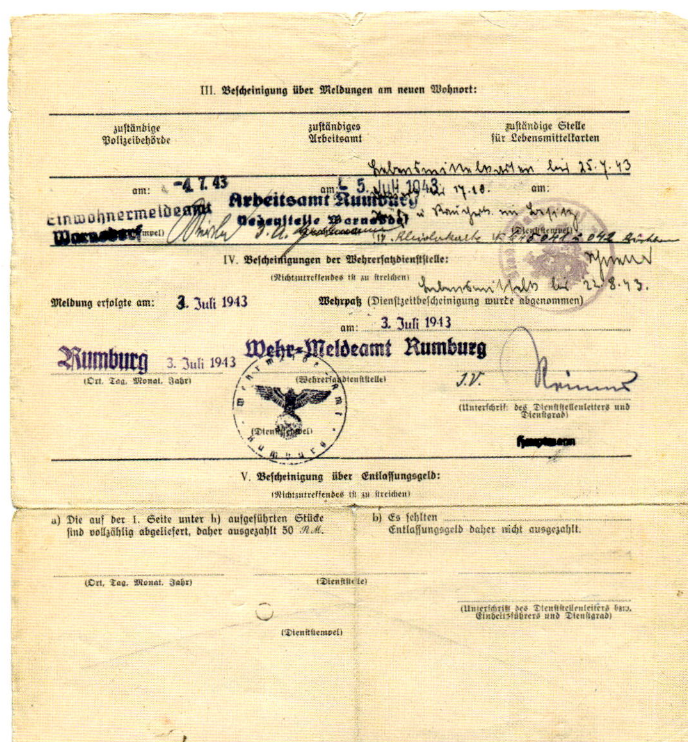

III. Bescheinigung über Meldungen am neuen Wohnort:

zuständige Polizeibehörde	zuständiges Arbeitsamt	zuständige Stelle für Lebensmittelkarten
am: 4. 7. 43	am: 5. Juli 1943	am:
Einwohnermeldeamt Warnsdorf (Dienststempel)	Arbeitsamt Rumburg Nebenstelle Warnsdorf	(Dienststempel)

IV. Bescheinigungen der Wehrersatzdienststelle:
(Nichtzutreffendes ist zu streichen)

Meldung erfolgte am: 3. Juli 1943
Wehrpaß (Dienstzeitbescheinigung wurde abgenommen) am: 3. Juli 1943

Rumburg 3. Juli 1943
(Ort, Tag, Monat, Jahr)
Wehr-Meldeamt Rumburg
(Wehrersatzdienststelle)
(Dienststempel)
I.V.
(Unterschrift des Dienststellenleiters und Dienstgrad)
Hauptmann

V. Bescheinigung über Entlassungsgeld:
(Nichtzutreffendes ist zu streichen)

a) Die auf der 1. Seite unter h) aufgeführten Stücke sind vollzählig abgeliefert, daher ausgezahlt 50 RM.
b) Es fehlten
Entlassungsgeld daher nicht ausgezahlt.

(Ort, Tag, Monat, Jahr)
(Dienststelle)
(Dienststempel)
(Unterschrift des Dienststellenleiters bzw. Einheitsführers und Dienstgrad)

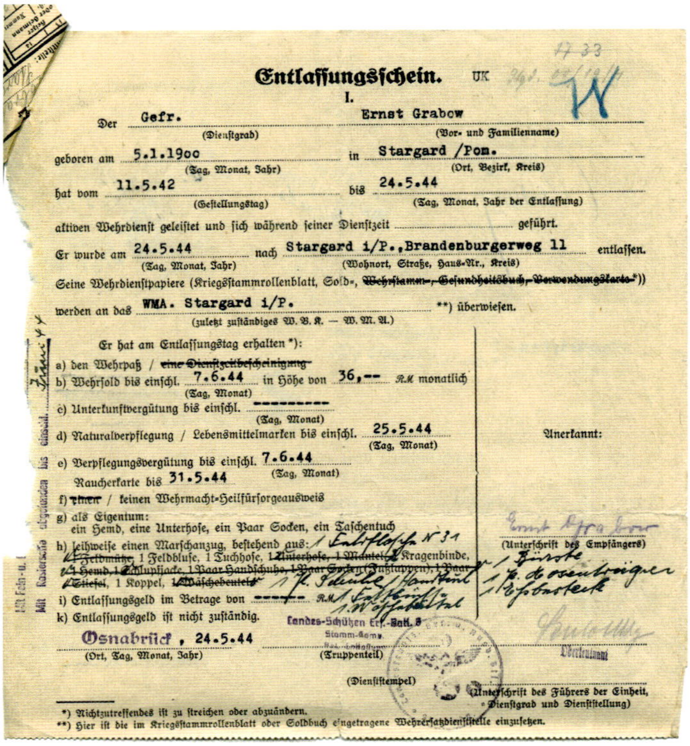

Entlassungsschein. UK

I.

Der Gefr. (Dienstgrad) Ernst Grabow (Vor- und Familienname)

geboren am 5.1.1900 (Tag, Monat, Jahr) in Stargard /Pom. (Ort, Bezirk, Kreis)

hat vom 11.5.42 (Gestellungstag) bis 24.5.44 (Tag, Monat, Jahr der Entlassung)

aktiven Wehrdienst geleistet und sich während seiner Dienstzeit .... geführt.

Er wurde am 24.5.44 (Tag, Monat, Jahr) nach Stargard i/P., Brandenburgerweg 11 (Wohnort, Straße, Haus-Nr., Kreis) entlassen.

Seine Wehrdienstpapiere (Kriegsstammrollenblatt, Sold-, ~~Wehrstamm-, Gesundheitsbuch, Verwendungskarte~~ **))

werden an das WMA. Stargard i/P. (zuletzt zuständiges W.B.K. — W.M.A.) **) überwiesen.

Er hat am Entlassungstag erhalten *):

a) den Wehrpaß / ~~eine Dienstzeitbescheinigung~~

b) Wehrsold bis einschl. 7.6.44 (Tag, Monat) in Höhe von 36,-- RM monatlich

c) Unterkunftvergütung bis einschl. ---------- (Tag, Monat)

d) Naturalverpflegung / Lebensmittelmarken bis einschl. 25.5.44 (Tag, Monat)

e) Verpflegungsvergütung bis einschl. 7.6.44

Raucherkarte bis 31.5.44 (Tag, Monat)

f) ~~einen~~ / keinen Wehrmacht-Heilfürsorgeausweis

g) als Eigentum: ein Hemd, eine Unterhose, ein Paar Socken, ein Taschentuch

h) leihweise einen Marschanzug, bestehend aus: ~~Feldmütze~~, 1 Feldbluse, 1 Tuchhose, ~~1 Unterhose, 1 Mantel~~, 1 Kragenbinde, ~~1 Hemd~~, ~~1 Kalupjacke, 1 Paar Handschuhe, 1 Paar Socken (Fußlappen), 1 Paar Stiefel~~, 1 Koppel, ~~1 Wäschebeutel~~

i) Entlassungsgeld im Betrage von ------ RM

k) Entlassungsgeld ist nicht zuständig.

Anerkannt: Ernst Grabow (Unterschrift des Empfängers)

Osnabrück, 24.5.44 (Ort, Tag, Monat, Jahr)

Landes-Schützen Ers.-Batl. 8 (Truppenteil)

(Dienststempel)

Oberleutnant (Unterschrift des Führers der Einheit, Dienstgrad und Dienststellung)

*) Nichtzutreffendes ist zu streichen oder abzuändern.

**) Hier ist die im Kriegsstammrollenblatt oder Soldbuch eingetragene Wehrersatzdienststelle einzusetzen.

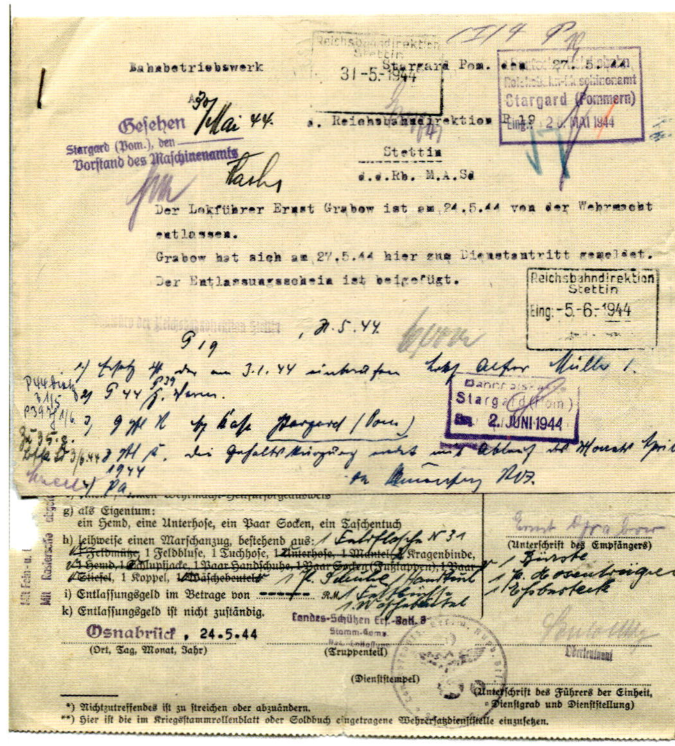

Bahnbetriebswerk Stargard Pom.

Gesehen Mai 44. Stargard (Pom.), den Vorstand des Maschinenamts

a. Reichsbahndirektion

Stettin

d.d.Rb. M.A.Sd

Der Lokführer Ernst Grabow ist am 24.5.44 von der Wehrmacht entlassen.

Grabow hat sich am 27.5.44 hier zum Dienstantritt gemeldet.

Der Entlassungsschein ist beigefügt.

Reichsbahndirektion Stettin Eing.: 5.6.1944

Reichsbahndirektion Stettin 31-5-1944

Stargard (Pommern) Eing. 2 JUNI 1944

g) als Eigentum: ein Hemd, eine Unterhose, ein Paar Socken, ein Taschentuch

h) leihweise einen Marschanzug, bestehend aus: ~~Feldmütze~~, 1 Feldbluse, 1 Tuchhose, ~~1 Unterhose, 1 Mantel~~, 1 Kragenbinde

i) Entlassungsgeld im Betrage von ------ RM

k) Entlassungsgeld ist nicht zuständig.

Osnabrück, 24.5.44 (Ort, Tag, Monat, Jahr)

Landes-Schützen Ers.-Batl. 8 (Truppenteil)

(Dienststempel)

*) Nichtzutreffendes ist zu streichen oder abzuändern.

**) Hier ist die im Kriegsstammrollenblatt oder Soldbuch eingetragene Wehrersatzdienststelle einzusetzen.

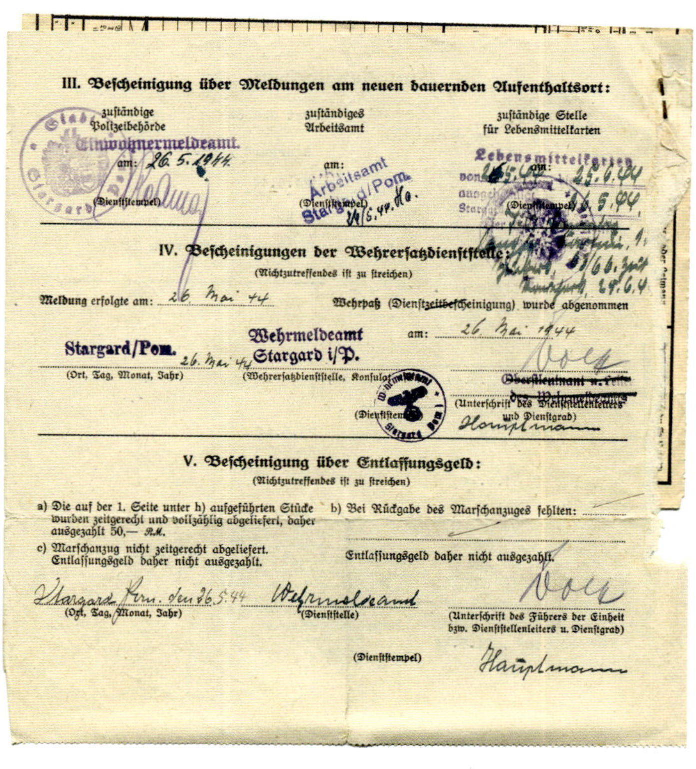

III. Bescheinigung über Meldungen am neuen dauernden Aufenthaltsort:

zuständige Polizeibehörde	zuständiges Arbeitsamt	zuständige Stelle für Lebensmittelkarten
Einwohnermeldeamt. am: 26.5.1944. (Dienststempel)	am: Arbeitsamt Stargard/Pom. 26.5.44 (Dienststempel)	Lebensmittelkarten vom ... (Dienststempel)

IV. Bescheinigungen der Wehrersatzdienststelle:

(Nichtzutreffendes ist zu streichen)

Meldung erfolgte am: 26. Mai 44

Wehrpaß (Dienstzeitbescheinigung) wurde abgenommen

Wehrmeldeamt Stargard i/P. am: 26. Mai 1944

Stargard/Pom. 26. Mai 44 (Ort, Tag, Monat, Jahr)

(Wehrersatzdienststelle, Konsulat)

(Dienststempel)

~~Oberstleutnant~~ (Unterschrift des Dienststellenleiters und Dienstgrad) Hauptmann

V. Bescheinigung über Entlassungsgeld:

(Nichtzutreffendes ist zu streichen)

a) Die auf der 1. Seite unter h) aufgeführten Stücke wurden zeitgerecht und vollzählig abgeliefert, daher ausgezahlt 50,— RM.

b) Bei Rückgabe des Marschanzuges fehlten:

c) Marschanzug nicht zeitgerecht abgeliefert. Entlassungsgeld daher nicht ausgezahlt.

Entlassungsgeld daher nicht ausgezahlt.

Stargard Pom. den 26.5.44 (Ort, Tag, Monat, Jahr)

Wehrmeldeamt (Dienststelle)

(Unterschrift des Führers der Einheit bzw. Dienststellenleiters u. Dienstgrad) Hauptmann

(Dienststempel)

Figure 4-99. This is an interesting discharge certificate, signifying that Lokamotivführer (Engineer) Ernst Grabow has been discharged from the Wehrmacht, but implies that he is still bound by the Reichsbahn. (8¼" x 8¾")

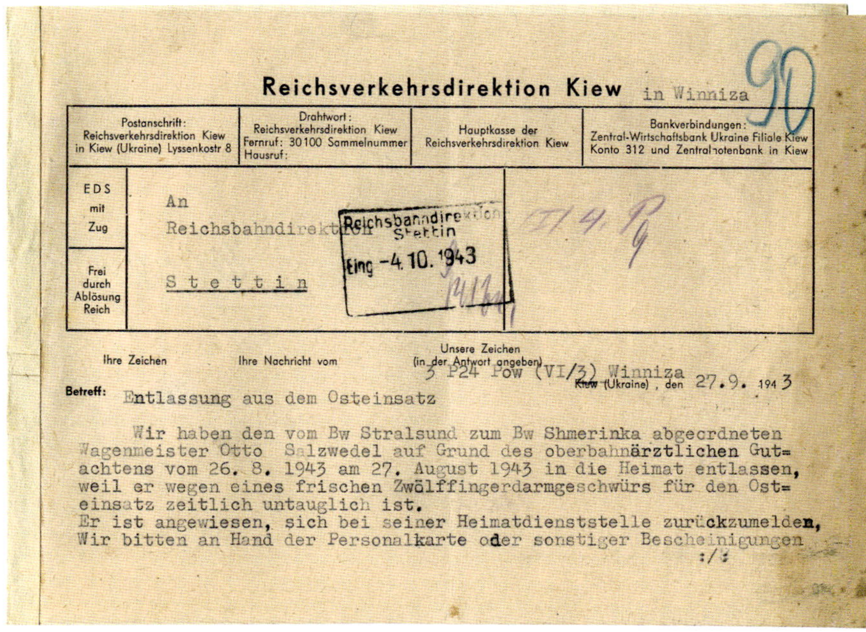

Reichsverkehrsdirektion Kiew in Winniza

Postanschrift: Reichsverkehrsdirektion Kiew in Kiew (Ukraine) Lyssenkostr 8	Drahtwort: Reichsverkehrsdirektion Kiew Fernruf: 30100 Sammelnummer Hausruf:	Hauptkasse der Reichsverkehrsdirektion Kiew	Bankverbindungen: Zentral-Wirtschaftsbank Ukraine Filiale Kiew Konto 312 und Zentralnotenbank in Kiew

EDS mit Zug

Frei durch Ablösung Reich

An
Reichsbahndirektion
Stettin

Reichsbahndirektion Stettin Eing -4. 10. 1943

Ihre Zeichen — Ihre Nachricht vom — Unsere Zeichen (in der Antwort angeben) 3 P24 Pow (VI/3) Winniza Kiew (Ukraine), den 27.9. 1943

Betreff: Entlassung aus dem Osteinsatz

Wir haben den vom Bw Stralsund zum Bw Shmerinka abgeordneten Wagenmeister Otto Salzwedel auf Grund des oberbahnärztlichen Gutachtens vom 26. 8. 1943 am 27. August 1943 in die Heimat entlassen, weil er wegen eines frischen Zwölffingerdarmgeschwürs für den Osteinsatz zeitlich untauglich ist.
Er ist angewiesen, sich bei seiner Heimatdienststelle zurückzumelden.
Wir bitten an Hand der Personalkarte oder sonstiger Bescheinigungen

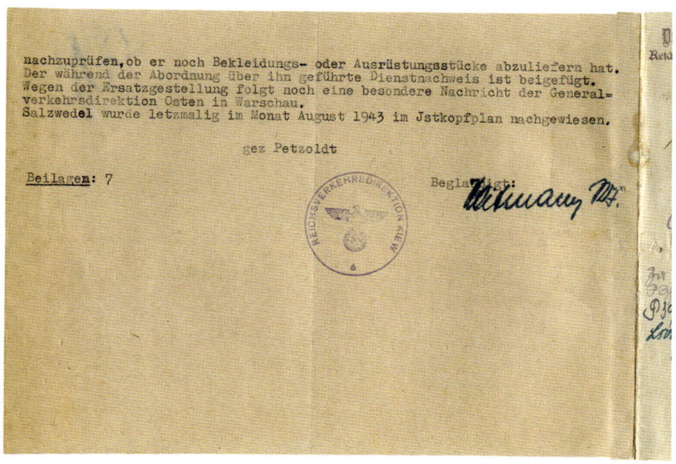

nachzuprüfen, ob er noch Bekleidungs- oder Ausrüstungsstücke abzuliefern hat.
Der während der Abordnung über ihn geführte Dienstnachweis ist beigefügt.
Wegen der Ersatzgestellung folgt noch eine besondere Nachricht der Generalverkehrsdirektion Osten in Warschau.
Salzwedel wurde letzmalig im Monat August 1943 im Jstkopfplan nachgewiesen.

gez Petzoldt

Beilagen: 7

Beglaubigt:

Reichsverkehrsdirektion Kiew

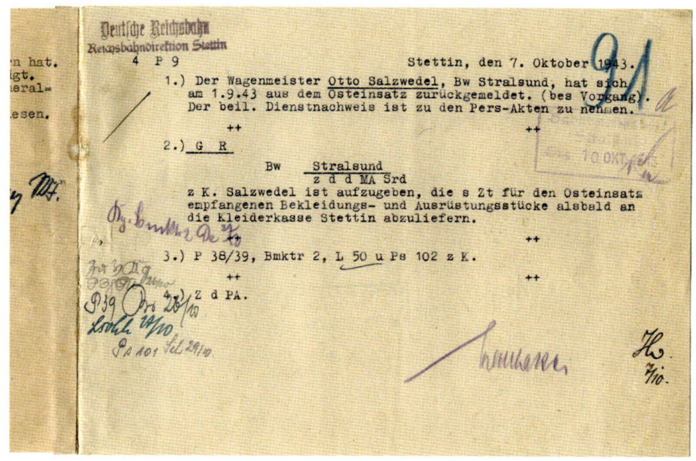

Deutsche Reichsbahn
Reichsbahndirektion Stettin
4 P 9

Stettin, den 7. Oktober 1943.

1.) Der Wagenmeister Otto Salzwedel, Bw Stralsund, hat sich am 1.9.43 aus dem Osteinsatz zurückgemeldet. (bes Vorgang). Der beil. Dienstnachweis ist zu den Pers-Akten zu nehmen.

2.) G R

Bw Stralsund
z d d MA Srd

z K. Salzwedel ist aufzugeben, die s Zt für den Osteinsatz empfangenen Bekleidungs- und Ausrüstungsstücke alsbald an die Kleiderkasse Stettin abzuliefern.

3.) P 38/39, Bmktr 2, L 50 u Ps 102 z K.

z d PA.

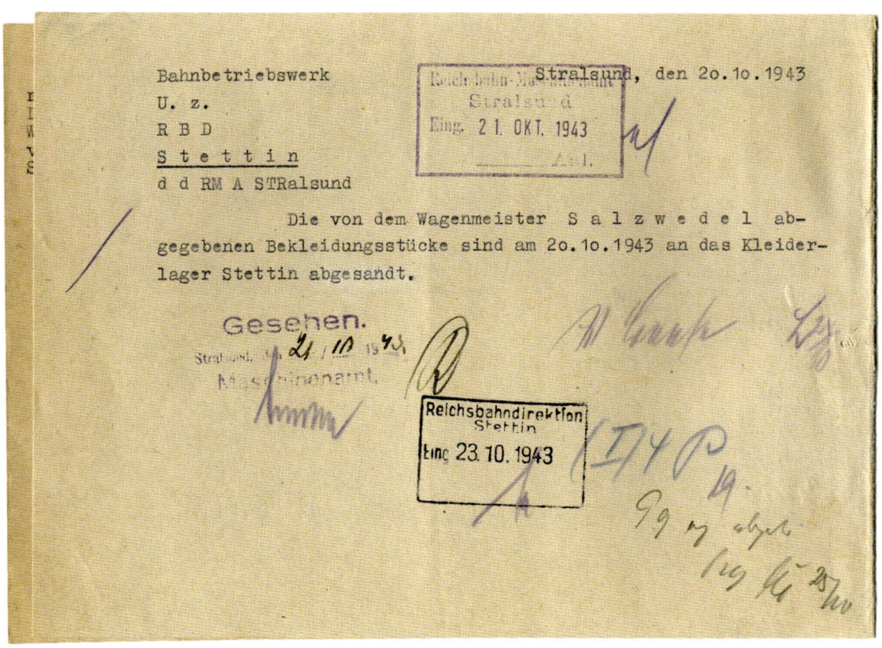

Bahnbetriebswerk
U. z.
R B D
Stettin
d d RM A STRalsund

Stralsund, den 20.10.1943

Reichsbahn-Maschinenamt Stralsund Eing. 21. OKT. 1943

Die von dem Wagenmeister Salzwedel abgegebenen Bekleidungsstücke sind am 20.10.1943 an das Kleiderlager Stettin abgesandt.

Gesehen.
Stralsund, 21.10.1943
Maschinenamt

Reichsbahndirektion Stettin Eing 23. 10. 1943

Figure 4-100. Not all discharges indicated a discharge from all service; this Reichsbahn form simply states that Wagenmeister (Car Leader) Otto Salzwedel has been discharged from service on the Eastern Front, but not from Reichsbahn service. (5⅞" x 8¼")

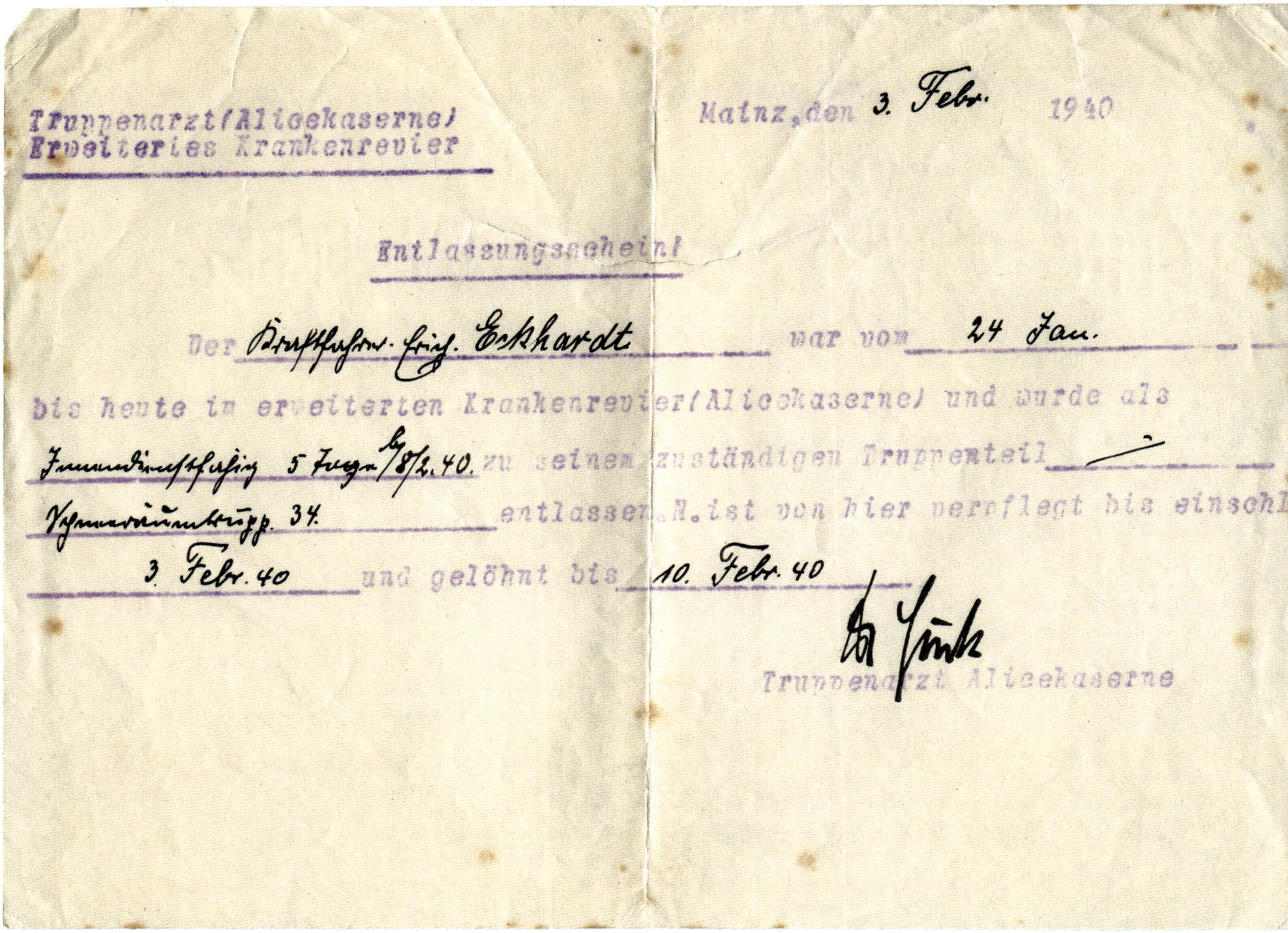

Truppenarzt (Alicekaserne)
Erweitertes Krankenrevier

Mainz, den 3. Febr. 1940

Entlassungsschein!

Der Kraftfahrer Erich Eckhardt war vom 24 Jan.

bis heute im erweiterten Krankenrevier (Alicekaserne) und wurde als

Innendienstfähig 5 Tage [illegible] zu seinem zuständigen Truppenteil

[illegible] 34 entlassen. N. ist von hier verpflegt bis einschl

3. Febr. 40 und gelöhnt bis 10. Febr. 40

Truppenarzt Alicekaserne

Figure 4-101. This mimeographed discharge certificate for Kraftfahrer (Transport Driver) Erich Eckhardt was merely a hospital discharge, issued by the Advanced Infirmary (Erweiterten Krankenrevier) at the Alicekaserne in Mainz, and directs him to return to his unit. (A5)

Souvenir Photography

During the 1920s, 1930s, and 1940s, Germans took to photography like ducks to water. They seem to be natural photographers, and have a love for the hobby much more so it seems than those of other nationalities. It should come as no surprise that the German soldier was an avid shutterbug when on leave, especially in the *Besetzten Gebiet* (Occupied Territories).

The camera differed, but was almost always formatted to the same few sizes of photo paper and film, thanks to DIN standardization. The most common brands of camera carried by German soldiers were Leica, Zeiss, Kodak, and Agfa, though many others were used as well.

There were strict limitations to photography in the field (most of which were ignored), but practically none existed for leave. The *Soldat* was like any other dumbfounded tourist, snapping the typical shots of

Figure 4-102. There are a great number of photo albums from the era available to collectors, both civilian and military.

Figure 4-103. German soldiers wasted no time in taking leave in their newly occupied countries. This snapshot from a French beach in July of 1940 shows both German soldiers and French civilians who would not upset their vacations with such trivialities as a war.

Figure 4-104. This wounded Soldat is home on convalescent leave, though precisely where is a mystery. The rigidity of his left hand and the Silver Wound Badge and Iron Cross suggest that he may have lost at least a portion of his arm in combat.

expected foreign sights, as well as any other scene that struck his fancy.

Photos were kept in albums of all sizes, from miniature albums for individual A8 photos to oversized tomes holding hundreds of pictures, and every size in between. Images range from military ceremonies to weddings to tourist destinations to local women to ... well, the list goes on and on.

Of all the photographs from German soldiers of the Second World War, however; there is one particular genre that I find personally intriguing, and that is photographs of German wives and sweethearts wearing their husbands'

Figure 4-105. Entire families were engulfed during the war in Germany. This snapshot appears to be of a father and son, both home on leave.

Figure 4-106. A group of Luftwaffe officers gather at the Gaststätte Sankt Peter (Restaurant St. Peter).

Figure 4-107. This group of Soldaten couldn't resist having their image struck before the equestrian statue of Louis XIV at Versailles. (3 7/16" x 5 7/16")

Figure 4-109. Not only Soldaten enjoyed leave; this group of four Matrosen (Sailors) enjoy their leave in Wendeburg in 1940.

Figure 4-108. A Feldwebel, home from Africa or Italy; note his tropical cap and how tanned his hands and face appear compared to the ladies to either side of him.

Figure 4-110. It wasn't only the men who enjoyed leave; these two Helferinen (Female Auxiliaries) stroll under the Arc de Triomphe during their leave in Paris.

Figure 4-111 through 4-114. These two family snapshots from before the war were kept by a sailor in the Kriegsmarine, the backs of which he kept as a calendar until either his next leave or his discharge, from January until May, 1935.

Figure 4-115 & 4-116. By Christmas of 1941, the sailor's brother (above, left) has himself joined the Wehrmacht (Heer) and come home on leave.

Figure 4-118. A prewar snapshot of Luftwaffe airmen enjoying a Stadturlaub in what appears to be Hohensalzburg in Salzburg, Austria.

Figure 4-117. This group of Soldaten were bored and wishing they were elsewhere, as one can deduce from this snapshot and their sign which states "Sunday without leave, March 30, 1941."

Figure 4-119. At a train station in the Ukraine, a sign in the background says "Package station for those on leave from the front – Führer's Gift – District of the Nazi Party, Ukraine." Two volunteer soldiers ("Hiwi") pick their way across the tracks, both of which appear to long for a warmer climate.

Figure 4-120. These five Soldaten experience what may be considered by most as the worst part of going on leave; returning to duty. This snapshot from February 20, 1941 shows them in good spirits, however.

Figure 4-121. Three Luftwaffe Signalmen probably returning from leave; only the teletype operator on the right seems to be enjoying himself.

or boyfriends' uniforms. It seems to be a phenomenon perpetrated exclusively by Germans, and dates back to studio shots posed by photographers before the First World War.

Photographs of this type are often simple snapshots, not the formal variety of the previous war. Some photos date to soldiers on leave during the 1930s, but most were taken by soldiers who have come home from the war, evidenced by combat awards and medals on the uniforms being worn. They span all the services, *Heer*, *Kriegsmarine*, *Waffen-SS*, and *Luftwaffe*, and vary from the more formal *Waffenrock* (Dress Tunic) to the standard field uniforms, *Fliegerbluse* (Flight Tunic), and typical *Matrosenhemd* (Sailor's Shirt).

Personally, I find it rather interesting that, for the most part, the uniforms seem to fit. Of course, there's no way to know for sure what cosmetic clamps, belts, and braces had been employed and tucked out of sight for the duration of the photo session. Not all photos exhibit such preparation; I recall seeing one particular photo of a woman who had to be about five feet tall wearing her boyfriend's uniform, the sleeves of which all but swallowed her hands, even as she saluted.

Many of these photos naturally became soldiers' prized possessions, evidenced by the vast number of them still available to collectors today. Albums filled with photos of individual companies and regiments continue to draw respectable prices at auctions and military collectibles shows.

Figure 4-122. This woman wears her husband's Luftwaffe Hauptgefreiter (Head Corporal) uniform. Probably a prewar snapshot, the airman had earned the Luftwaffe sharpshooter's aiguillette.

Figure 4-123. These two ladies wear their husbands' Feldblusen over their own dresses, the left of which has the Eastern Front ribbon on the second buttonhole.

Figure 4-124. Let's hope this woman's sense of balance is better riding a bike than leaning against one. Her husband, a Heer Feldwebel, has both the Iron Cross Second Class ribbon and Black Wound Badge on his uniform, as well as a whistle lanyard leading to his pocket.

Figure 4-125. This jovial Fräulein wears her boyfriend's Kriegsmarine uniform; oddly enough, it is his summer uniform she's wearing, not one befitting the snow-covered yard behind her.

Figure 4-126. A woman wears her boyfriend's Heer uniform over her own clothes; note her dress instead of his trousers.

Figure 4-127. This woman wears her husband's Fahnenjunker-Unteroffizier's uniform.

Figure 4-128. This woman wears her husband's Unteroffizier uniform, though it is doubtful that the shoes are regulation.

Wehrmacht-
Besoldungstabellen
(Gültig ab 1. Januar 1945)

mit

Einsatz-Wehrmacht-Gebührnis-Gesetz
und Durchführungsbestimmungen
In der Neufassung vom 1. November 1944

sowie der

Wehrmacht-Kriegsreiseverordnung
vom 1. Oktober 1944

Textausgaben

19 B&G 44

VERLAG BERNARD & GRAEFE / BERLIN SW 68

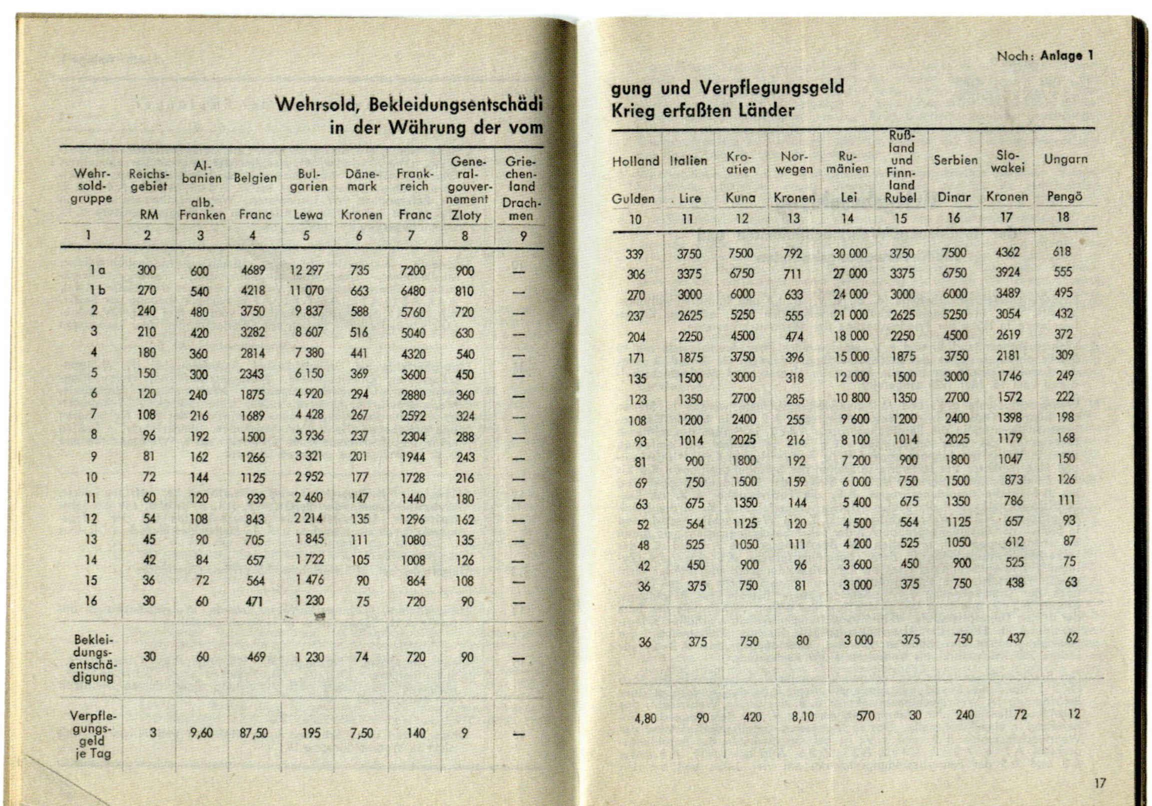

Noch: **Anlage 1**

Wehrsold, Bekleidungsentschädi gung und Verpflegungsgeld in der Währung der vom Krieg erfaßten Länder

Wehrsoldgruppe	Reichsgebiet RM	Albanien alb. Franken	Belgien Franc	Bulgarien Lewa	Dänemark Kronen	Frankreich Franc	Generalgouvernement Zloty	Griechenland Drachmen
1	2	3	4	5	6	7	8	9
1 a	300	600	4689	12 297	735	7200	900	—
1 b	270	540	4218	11 070	663	6480	810	—
2	240	480	3750	9 837	588	5760	720	—
3	210	420	3282	8 607	516	5040	630	—
4	180	360	2814	7 380	441	4320	540	—
5	150	300	2343	6 150	369	3600	450	—
6	120	240	1875	4 920	294	2880	360	—
7	108	216	1689	4 428	267	2592	324	—
8	96	192	1500	3 936	237	2304	288	—
9	81	162	1266	3 321	201	1944	243	—
10	72	144	1125	2 952	177	1728	216	—
11	60	120	939	2 460	147	1440	180	—
12	54	108	843	2 214	135	1296	162	—
13	45	90	705	1 845	111	1080	135	—
14	42	84	657	1 722	105	1008	126	—
15	36	72	564	1 476	90	864	108	—
16	30	60	471	1 230	75	720	90	—
Bekleidungsentschädigung	30	60	469	1 230	74	720	90	—
Verpflegungsgeld je Tag	3	9,60	87,50	195	7,50	140	9	—

Wehrsoldgruppe	Holland Gulden	Italien Lire	Kroatien Kuna	Norwegen Kronen	Rumänien Lei	Rußland und Finnland Rubel	Serbien Dinar	Slowakei Kronen	Ungarn Pengö
1	10	11	12	13	14	15	16	17	18
1 a	339	3750	7500	792	30 000	3750	7500	4362	618
1 b	306	3375	6750	711	27 000	3375	6750	3924	555
2	270	3000	6000	633	24 000	3000	6000	3489	495
3	237	2625	5250	555	21 000	2625	5250	3054	432
4	204	2250	4500	474	18 000	2250	4500	2619	372
5	171	1875	3750	396	15 000	1875	3750	2181	309
6	135	1500	3000	318	12 000	1500	3000	1746	249
7	123	1350	2700	285	10 800	1350	2700	1572	222
8	108	1200	2400	255	9 600	1200	2400	1398	198
9	93	1014	2025	216	8 100	1014	2025	1179	168
10	81	900	1800	192	7 200	900	1800	1047	150
11	69	750	1500	159	6 000	750	1500	873	126
12	63	675	1350	144	5 400	675	1350	786	111
13	52	564	1125	120	4 500	564	1125	657	93
14	48	525	1050	111	4 200	525	1050	612	87
15	42	450	900	96	3 600	450	900	525	75
16	36	375	750	81	3 000	375	750	438	63
Bekleidungsentschädigung	36	375	750	80	3 000	375	750	437	62
Verpflegungsgeld je Tag	4,80	90	420	8,10	570	30	240	72	12

17

Figure 5-1 & 5-2. This booklet, Military Pay Tables (valid from November, 1944 until January 1, 1945), served to update pay regulations allotted to Soldaten in all aspects of their lives, from base pay and marriage allowances to replacement clothing and travel pay. (4 1/8" x 5 7/8")

5

Pay and Rations

Like the soldier of any other country, the *Soldat* was particularly fond of his pay, as were a good many vendors and restauranteurs. This was not a problem within Germany itself, but once soldiers started spending their hard-earned cash beyond the *Reich's* borders, measures had to be taken to keep German currency out of the hands of black marketeers and foreign agents.

Initially, *Soldaten* and any other German citizen in the occupied territories were issued *Reichskreditkassenscheinen* (German Treasury Notes; literally *Reich's* Loan Funds Certificates). Originally printed in Germany as an emergency measure to withdraw silver, copper, or nickel coins from circulation, if needed, they were eventually issued to all German citizens travelling abroad. Apart from differences in design, they were distinguished by the following legends:

> Front:
> "*Ausgegeben auf Grund der Verordnung der Reichskreditkasse*
> *Hauptverwaltung der Reichskreditkassen*"
> Reverse:
> "*Geldfälschung wird mit Zuchthaus bestraft*"
>
> Issued on the grounds of Reichskreditkasse regulations
> Headquarters of Reichskreditkasse
> Reverse:
> Counterfeiting punishable by imprisonment

It wasn't until these notes were used in occupied Poland as an occupation currency that their insidious nature became apparent.

This cash was used in occupied countries to pay for goods requisitioned by German troops, German citizens conducting business, or by German troops on leave. What made these notes unique was that they were not valid inside Germany itself; they were not backed by gold or silver like *Reichsmarks* and were valued at a set exchange rate (favorable to the *Reich*, of course) with the currency in the country in question. Furthermore, establishments in those countries were required by decree to accept them.

For example, if a German officer requisitioned a farmer's livestock to feed his men and paid him in *Reichskreditkassenschein*, that farmer could go to his local national bank to exchange them for their equivalent of his own currency. The foreign bank would then exchange them with the *Reichsbank* in Germany, where they were worth exactly nothing; that bank received absolutely nothing from the *Reichsbank* in return. Instead, the notes were collected and reissued to occupation forces, and the whole cycle started all over.

This shifted all risk of inflation along with the expense of occupation to the occupied country, not the *Reich*. By forbidding their use in Germany, this kept the money supplies separate and protected the *Reichsmark* against inflation.

Needless to say, it didn't take long for these countries to figure out what was going on. The notes became unpopu-

Figure 5-3 through 5-14 (following pages). These elaborate notes were originally intended to be used in the event that silver and nickel coinage needed to be withdrawn from circulation in Germany. Instead, these Reichkreditkassenscheinen were used as currency in occupied countries.

Figure 5-3.

Figure 5-4.

Figure 5-5.

Figure 5-6.

Figure 5-7.

Figure 5-8.

Figure 5-9.

Figure 5-10.

Figure 5-11.

Figure 5-12.

lar, and excuses from the local population to not take the *Reichskreditkassenschein* grew in frequency, as well as creativity and complexity. What truly spelled the death knell of these notes was that different countries suffered from different inflation rates. Enterprising businesses and even a few entrepreneurial *Soldaten* could acquire notes in Poland, for example, and then use them in France where they were worth so much more, not because the exchange rate was better, but because Polish inflation had caused the Zloty to lose its value against the Franc.

As a result, *Reichskreditkassenscheinen* were withdrawn from circulation in the occupied countries, starting with Belgium in 1942 and ending in France by the end of 1943.

In 1940, the *Wehrmacht* attempted to solve this problem by issuing *Behelfszahlungsmittel,* or Temporary Currency, initially with 1 *Reichspfennig* notes in 1940. In 1942, a second series of notes was issued in denominations of 1, 5, 10, and 50 *Reichspfennig* and 1 and 2 *Reichsmarks*. These were printed on one side only, in single shades of blue, green, and red for the *Reischpfennig* and two different colors for the 1 and 2 *Reichsmark* notes.

Soldiers were paid using this form of military scrip and encouraged to spend it at sanctioned *Wehrmacht* venues such as *Soldatenheim*, *Soldatenkino*, etc., where its purchasing power was ten times its face value. It was never intended for use beyond the *Wehrmacht*, and each note was imprinted as such:

> "*Dieser Schein ist kein öffentliches Zahlungsmittel, sondern nur für den Geldverkehr innerhalb der deutschen Wehrmacht bestimmt*"

Figure 5-13.

Figure 5-14.

Figure 5-15 through 5-17. Behelfszahlungsmittel (Temporary Currency) were issued to Soldaten on leave and came in six denominations, five of which are illustrated here: 1, 5, 10, and 50 Reichspfennig, and 1 and 2 Reichsmarks.

Figure 5-15.

Figure 5-16.

Figure 5-17.

> This certificate is not public currency, but only intended for the monetary traffic within the German armed forces

Like the *Reichskreditkassenschein*, this kept German money out of the hands of black marketeers, allowed the *Wehrmacht* to keep more of its own money under its own roof, allowed the *Wehrmacht* to better track soldiers' spending habits, and to a lesser degree controlled the local economy by limiting German soldiers' spending power within it.

Still, German soldiers didn't always want what the *Wehrmacht* venues offered, and often resorted to trading their *Behelfszahlungsmittel* for *Reichskreditkassenscheinen*, which were beyond control of the *Wehrmacht*.

As a result, the *Wehrmacht* issued a new series, the *Verrechnungsschein* (literally – Settlement Certificate), in September of 1944, which was backed by the *Reichskreditkasse* itself (the German Treasury). Notes were valued at their face denominations of 1, 5, 10, and 50 *Reichsmarks*.

This new currency was printed on both sides, and could be used by German military or paramilitary personnel, but only for German military travel traffic and where payment in local currency was restricted. It was not permitted for payments to local vendors, and had to be exchanged for local currency at approved exchange locations, which by September 1944, were swiftly becoming fewer and fewer.

The front of the note was inscribed:

> "*Dieser Schein dient zur Verrechnung im Wehrmachtreiseverkehr sowie zur Zahlung von Gebührnissen in Ländern, in denen Ihre Auszahlung in Landeswährung beschränkt ist. Seine Verwendung im allgemeinen Zahlungsverkehr ist verboten.*"

> This certificate serves for the settlement (of debts) in the armed forces leave traffic as well as to the payment of fees in countries, in which payment in local currency is restricted. Its use in general payment traffic is forbidden.

On the back of the note, an ornate border surrounded an inscription which read:

"*Wird im Rahmen der Zahlungsregelung für die deutschen Wehrmacht in ausserdeutschen Ländern nur an W e h - rmachtnagehörige und Gleichgestellte abgegeben und nur aus der Hand dieses Personenkreises umgetauscht von alle Kassen und Zahlstellen der Wehrmacht, Reichskreditkassen und Wechselstellen, ferner im Reich von der deutschen Reichsbank und den übrigen deutschen Geldinstituten.*"

Issued by the payment regulations for the German *Wehrmacht* in non-German countries only for members of the *Wehrmacht*, and those of equal status, and exchanged only from the hands of this group of individuals at all treasuries and payment locations of the *Wehrmacht*, *Reich* credit treasuries, and exchange locations, as well as within the *Reich* at the German *Reichsbank* and remaining German monetary institutions.

Figure 5-18 through 5-21. Verrechnungsscheinen (Settlement Certificates), three denominations of which are shown here, were only valid in German-occupied countries. By the time these notes were issued, however, Germany occupied very few countries.

Figure 5-18.

Figure 5-19.

Figure 5-20.

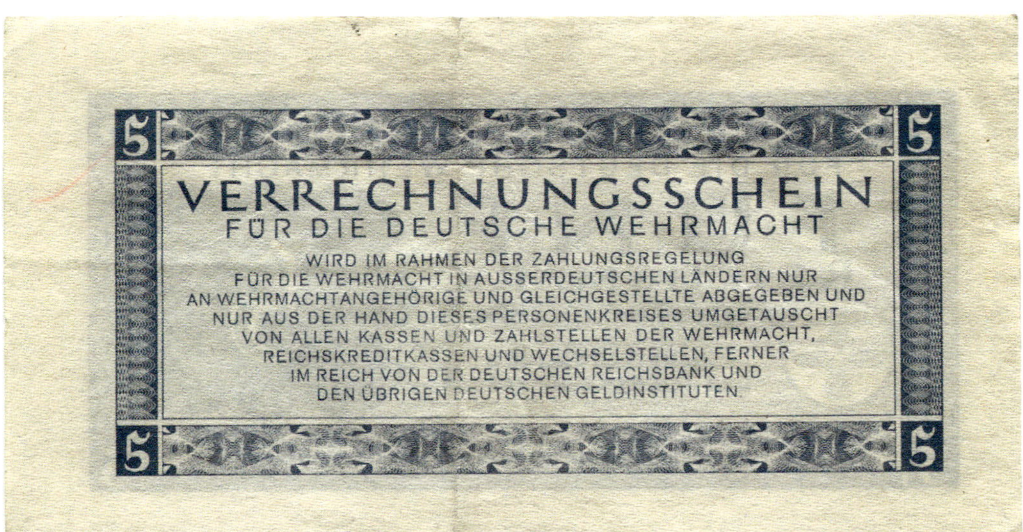

Figure 5-21.

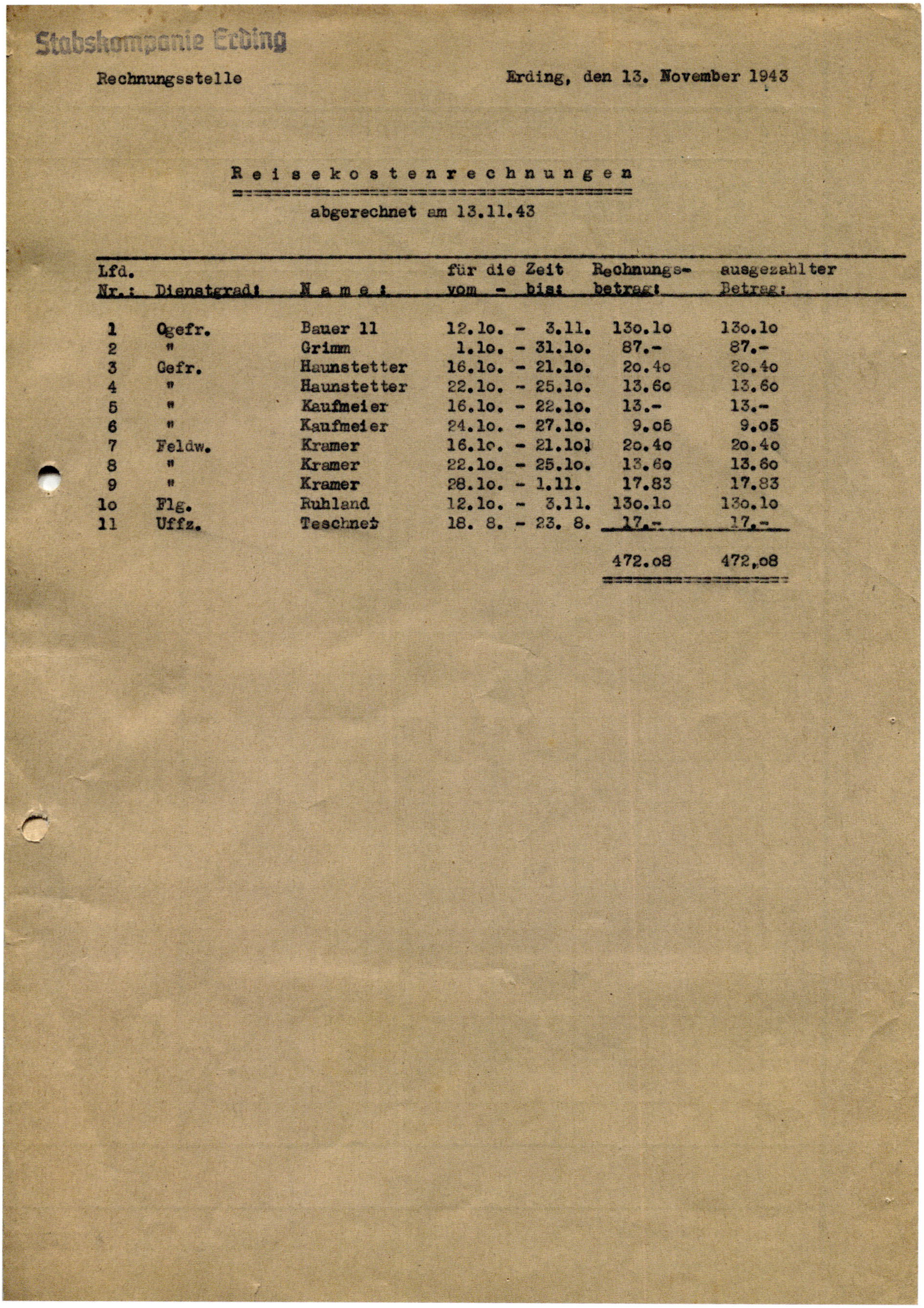

Stabskompanie Erding

Rechnungsstelle

Erding, den 13. November 1943

R e i s e k o s t e n r e c h n u n g e n

abgerechnet am 13.11.43

Lfd. Nr.:	Dienstgrad:	N a m e :	für die Zeit vom - bis:	Rechnungs-betrag:	ausgezahlter Betrag:
1	Ogefr.	Bauer 11	12.1o. - 3.11.	13o.1o	13o.1o
2	"	Grimm	1.1o. - 31.1o.	87.-	87.-
3	Gefr.	Haunstetter	16.1o. - 21.1o.	2o.4o	2o.4o
4	"	Haunstetter	22.1o. - 25.1o.	13.6o	13.6o
5	"	Kaufmeier	16.1o. - 22.1o.	13.-	13.-
6	"	Kaufmeier	24.1o. - 27.1o.	9.o5	9.o5
7	Feldw.	Kramer	16.1o. - 21.1o.	2o.4o	2o.4o
8	"	Kramer	22.1o. - 25.1o.	13.6o	13.6o
9	"	Kramer	28.1o. - 1.11.	17.83	17.83
1o	Flg.	Ruhland	12.1o. - 3.11.	13o.1o	13o.1o
11	Uffz.	Teschner	18. 8. - 23. 8.	17.-	17.-
				472.o8	472,o8

Figure 5-22. A travel cost reimbursement receipt, settled on November 13, 1943, which showed the amount invoiced and the amount paid for seven Soldaten, some travelling for multiple trips. (A4)

Rations and Ration Cards

German soldiers had to eat while traveling, and ration cards were printed specifically for those on leave. Like civilian ration cards, each was subdivided into miniature coupons to either be cut out and collected by the restaurant or grocer, or stamped to render the coupon invalid elsewhere. Each was marked *Reichskarte für Urlauber* (Reich Card for Those on Leave), or some such variation, such as the *Heimatverpflegungszulage für Fronturlauber* (Home Provisions Issue for those on Leave from the Front) or *Lebensmittelsonderkarte* (Special Food Card), indicating that this was not an ordinary ration card, as civilian ration cards were only valid within the district they had been issued.

Variations of ration cards issued throughout the war to those on leave offered the basic food items to the German diet, Brot (Bread), *Fleisch* or *Fleischwaren* (Meat or Meat Products), and *Fett* (literally Fats, but this was often issued in the form of lard, butter, and/or margarine). They were valid for anywhere from one to fourteen days, and each was printed with that number, so it was unmistakable for how long they could be used to keep one fed.

As the number of valid days increased, the ration card expanded its diversity of items, often adding *Zucker* (Sugar), *Marmelade*, *Käse* (Cheese), Nährmittel (literally Foodstuffs, but vegetables, processed foods, etc.), *Eier* (Eggs), and *Speck* (Bacon) in addition to the bread, meat, and fats.

This allowed for reduced amounts of basic foods without sacrificing amounts to the soldier. H.Dv.86/1, the *Vorschrift für die Verpflegung der Wehrmacht bei besonderen Einsatz* (Manual on the Provisions of the *Wehrmacht* by Special Use) requires certain amounts of bread and meat to be issued to a solder per day. By expanding the list of

Figure 5-23.

Figure 5-24.

Figures 5-23 & 5-24. The very center of an original Führergeschenk (Führer's Gift) Ration card and a reproduction from the author's website (reduced), which shows what each separate coupon would have been valid for.

foodstuffs, not only is a variety introduced to the diet, but the draw on available stocks is decreased.

As a result, the average amount of bread (350g/day) and meat (100g/day) allotted can be decreased to as little, at one point, as 285g and 43g, respectively, without forcing the soldier to suffer deprivation.

There were several different styles of ration cards issued, some with a printed expiration date (*Gültig bis 14. November 1943*) or by an imprinted edition number (*2. Ausgabe* or 2nd Edition). Many have a pattern of one form or another printed on the card to prevent counterfeiting. Some were as simple as a different colored *Reichsadler* (Reich's Eagle) printed behind each coupon. Others employed a fine dot pattern overlaid onto another dot pattern of a different frequency or angle to create a moiré effect, making counterfeits much easier to spot. Still others had elaborate sigils over hash marks or moiré patterns.

Each coupon listed the item and weight it was valid for. The person or store collecting the coupons would simply cut away the number of coupons until it totaled the amount given. For example, if someone bought 100g of meat, the grocer would clip away two 50g coupons for *Fleisch*. These coupons only permitted access to food; it still had to be paid for in addition to the presentation of a ration card.

Furthermore, each coupon was marked in one way or another to indicate it had been presented by someone on leave. The word "*Urlauber*," or Vacationer, or the letter "U" was printed or designed into the pattern to make it immediately recognizable.

Ration cards were printed on watermarked paper. This pattern varied from a wide fishnet weave, to a tight fishnet weave, to a small (¼" or so) rosette pattern, again to thwart counterfeiters. This was rather effective against German black marketeers, but proved no more than a minor stumbling block for Ellic Howe and the British Special Operations Executive (SOE).

Howe was a printer before the war who studied German printing processes and had become quite the expert, from typical stocks of paper used to specific typefaces. (Movable lead type was common throughout the world and *Fraktur* was rarely even stocked, much less used, outside of Germany.)

Soon after the war started, Howe was moved to the PWE (Psychological Warfare Executive), a division of the SOE, where he put his expertise to work immediately. Under the pseudonym of Armin Hull, and since he already knew which printing companies in England had purchased German printing presses in the 1930s, he contracted them to produce thousands of forged ration cards that were indistinguishable from the originals, often within days of the release of the originals.

It is quite possible that many of the ration cards available to collectors today are not original German cards, but examples of Howe's work; it is that difficult to tell them apart. Not that this would decrease their value, mind you; they're just as authentic, though for wholly different reasons.

Figure 5-25. An unissued Bezugsausweis für Urlauber, or supplemental ration card, normally given to those on leave by the local Ernährungsamt or food office when their own rations fell short.

Entrahmte Frischmilch für 1 Tag EA: K'he-Ldkrs.
(×6)

Tages-abschnitt für Speisekartoff. EA: K'he-Ldkrs.
(×6)

Bei Warenabgabe haben die Verteiler die Einzelabschnitte abzutrennen und in üblicher Weise abzurechnen. – Die Sonderbezugsabschnitte sind vom Verteiler abzutrennen und bis auf weiteres aufzubewahren.

Der Landrat Karlsruhe Ernährungsamt

Z. U. 4.

Nur gültig im Landkreis Karlsruhe!

Bezugsausweis für Urlauber

(Zusatz zur Reichskarte f. Urlauber, 4. Ausgabe)

(Name)

(Wohnort)

Ohne Namenseintragung ungültig! Nicht übertragbar!

(Kartenausgabestelle) (Datum)

Gemeinde-siegel

Der Landrat Karlsruhe

Ernährungsamt Abt. B

Sonderbezugsabschnitt A
zur Urlauberkarte, 4. Ausgabe
Gültig vom ....
Ernährungsamt Karlsruhe-Land

Sonderbezugsabschnitt B
zur Urlauberkarte, 4. Ausgabe
Gültig vom ....
Ernährungsamt Karlsruhe-Land

O/0470

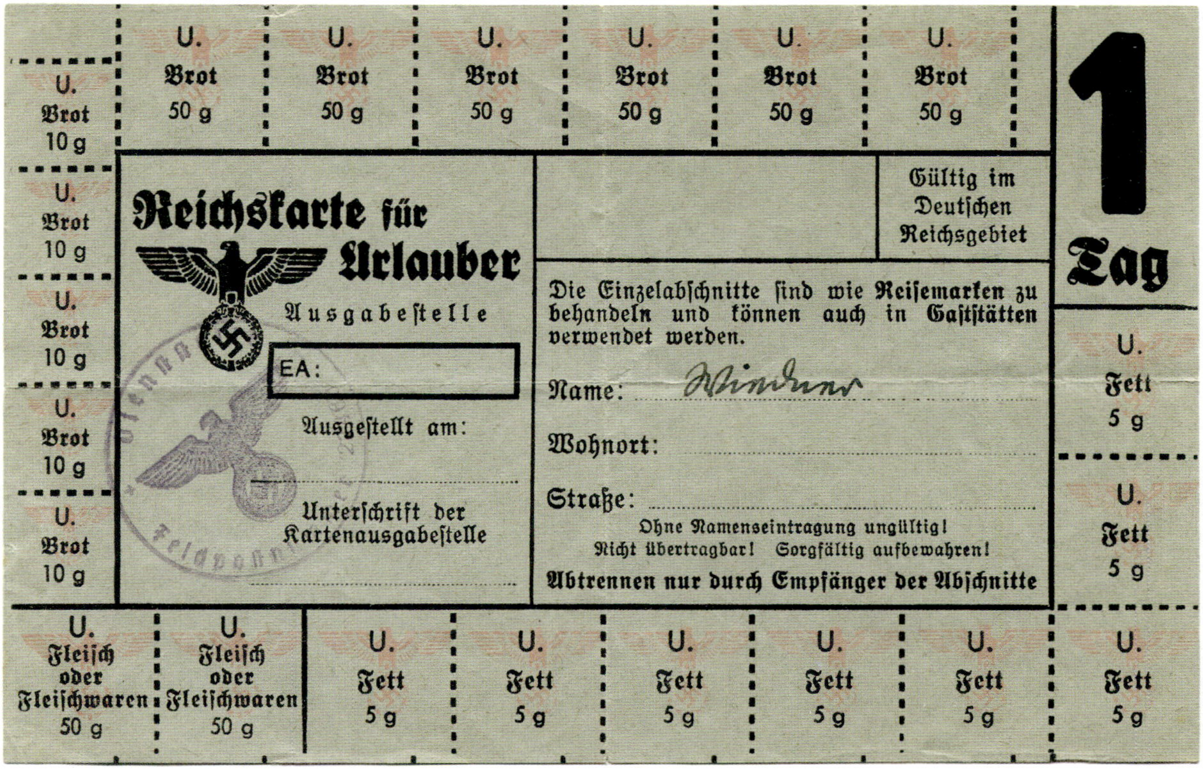

Figure 5-26 & 5-27. Reichskarten für Urlauber were available for rations lasting from 1 day to 2 weeks. These two cards were an early-war pattern. Every coupon for those on leave is marked with a "U" for Urlauber. (below: 8⅝" x 12⅝")

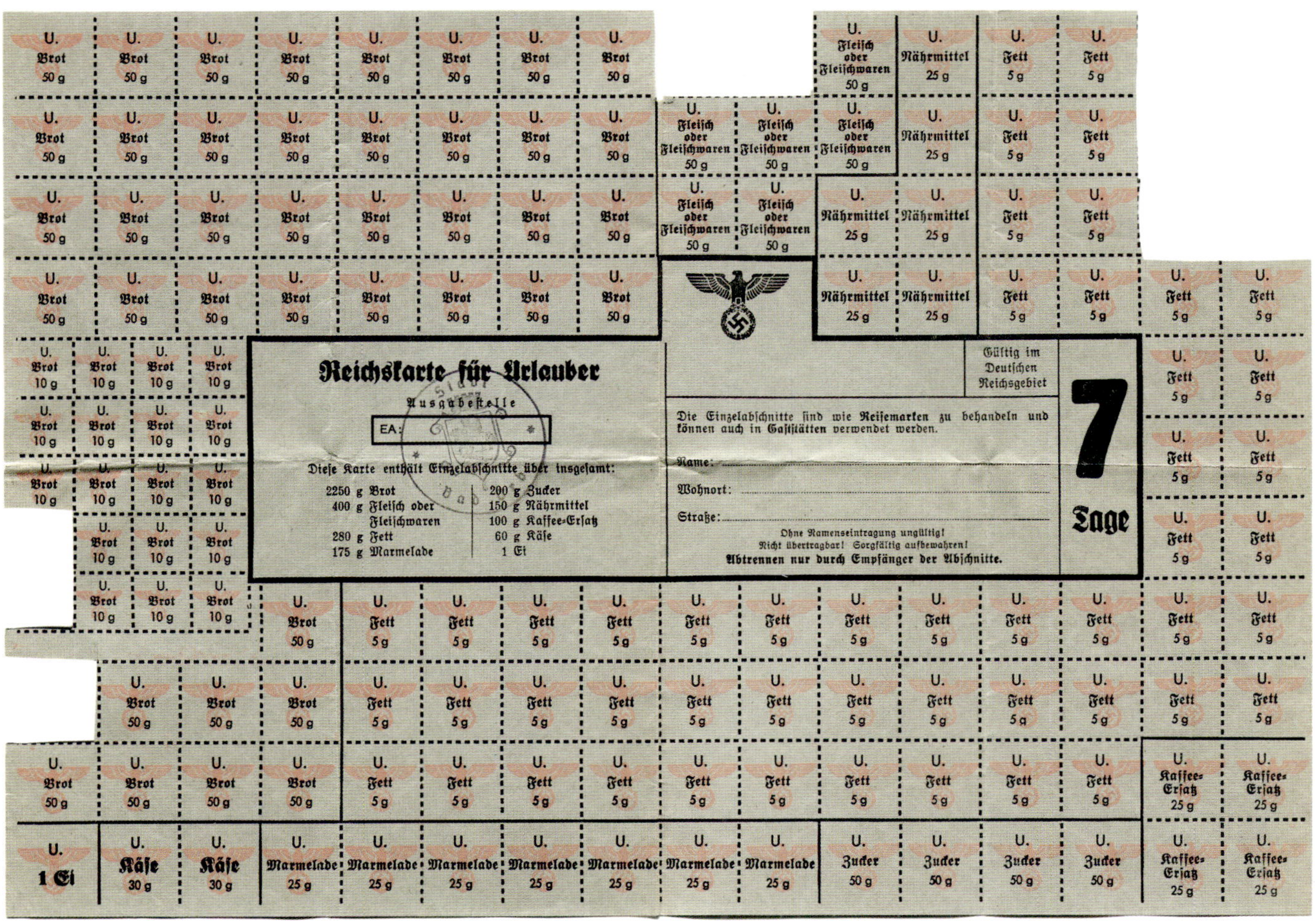

Figure 5-28 through 5-30. These Reichskarte für Urlauber for 1, 2, and 7 days of travel were a pattern similar to the previous examples, but differed in the colors printed to establish a second pattern, valid during different dates. The cards themselves are original, but some enterprising modern seller stamped them with a Geheime Staatspolizei (Gestapo) Stempel in an attempt to pass them off as more valuable than they were. (Original size, 3 15/16" x 7 13/16", and 8 5/8" x 10 1/4" respectively)

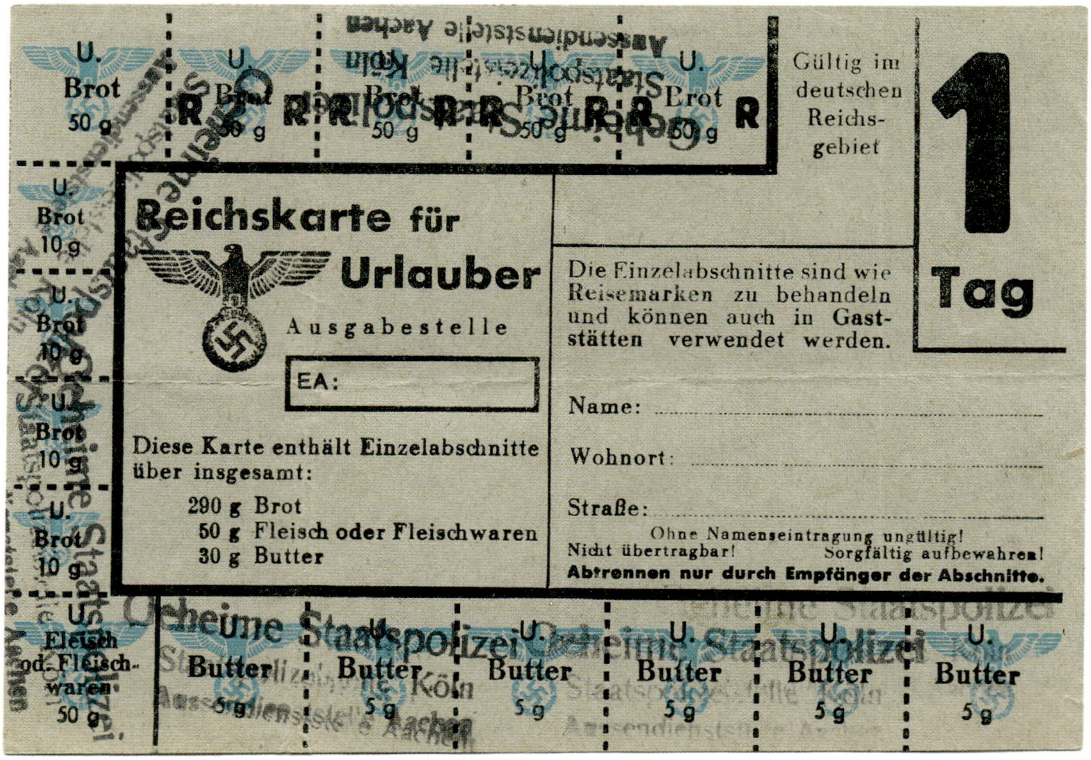

U. Brot 50 g R | U. Brot 50 g R | U. Brot 50 g R | U. Brot 50 g R | U. Brot 50 g R

Gültig im deutschen Reichsgebiet

1 Tag

U. Brot 10 g | U. Brot 10 g | U. Brot 10 g | U. Brot 10 g

Reichskarte für Urlauber

Ausgabestelle

EA:

Diese Karte enthält Einzelabschnitte über insgesamt:

290 g Brot
50 g Fleisch oder Fleischwaren
30 g Butter

Die Einzelabschnitte sind wie Reisemarken zu behandeln und können auch in Gaststätten verwendet werden.

Name:

Wohnort:

Straße:

Ohne Namenseintragung ungültig!
Nicht übertragbar! Sorgfältig aufbewahren!
Abtrennen nur durch Empfänger der Abschnitte.

U. Fleisch od. Fleischwaren 50 g | U. Butter 5 g | U. Butter 5 g | U. Butter 5 g | U. Butter 5 g | U. Butter 5 g | U. Butter 5 g

Geheime Staatspolizei
Staatspolizeistelle Köln
Aussendienststelle Aachen

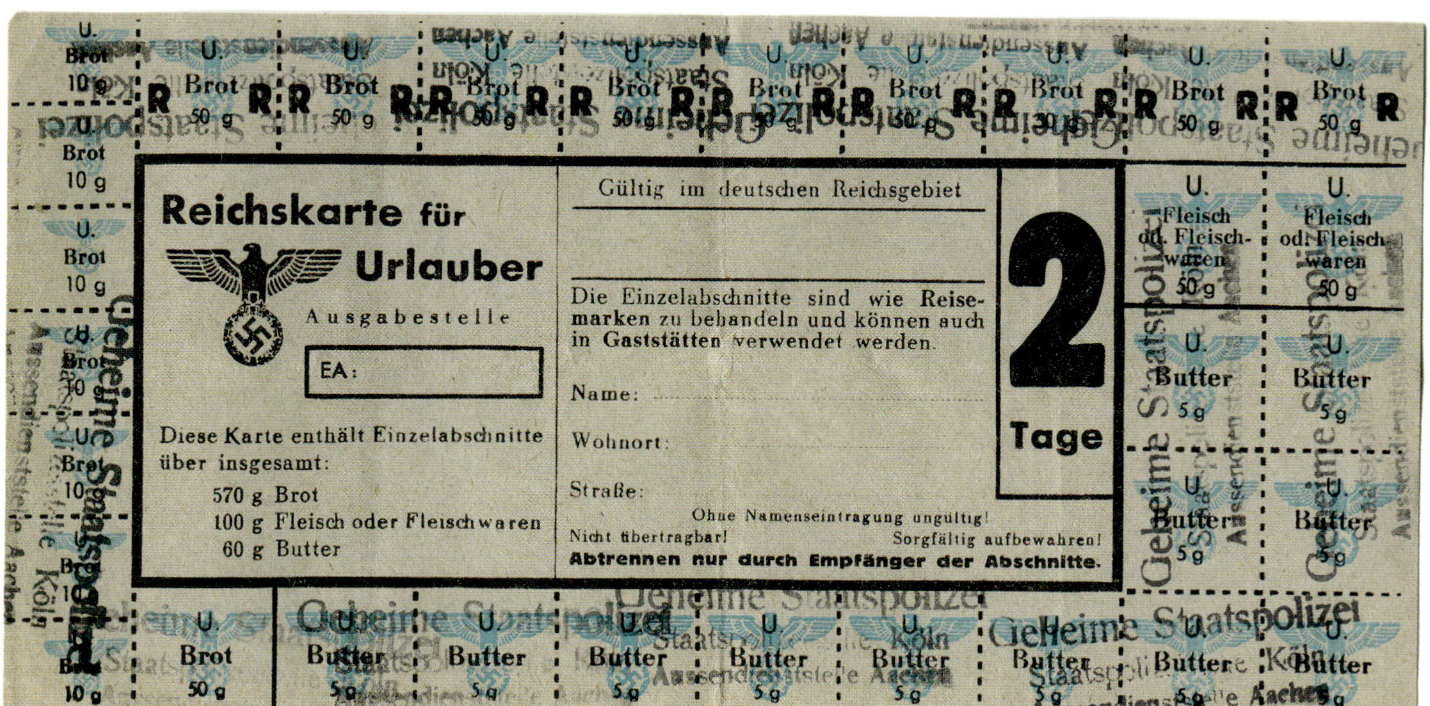

U. Brot 10 g | U. Brot 50 g R | U. Brot 50 g R | U. Brot 50 g R | U. Brot 50 g R | U. Brot 50 g R | U. Brot 50 g R | U. Brot 50 g R | U. Brot 50 g R | U. Brot 50 g R

U. Brot 10 g | U. Brot 10 g | U. Brot 10 g | U. Brot 10 g

Reichskarte für Urlauber

Ausgabestelle

EA:

Diese Karte enthält Einzelabschnitte über insgesamt:

570 g Brot
100 g Fleisch oder Fleischwaren
60 g Butter

Gültig im deutschen Reichsgebiet

Die Einzelabschnitte sind wie Reisemarken zu behandeln und können auch in Gaststätten verwendet werden.

Name:

Wohnort:

Straße:

Ohne Namenseintragung ungültig!
Nicht übertragbar! Sorgfältig aufbewahren!
Abtrennen nur durch Empfänger der Abschnitte.

2 Tage

U. Fleisch od. Fleischwaren 50 g | U. Fleisch od. Fleischwaren 50 g

U. Butter 5 g | U. Butter 5 g | U. Butter 5 g | U. Butter 5 g

U. Brot 10 g | U. Brot 50 g | U. Butter 5 g | U. Butter 5 g | U. Butter 5 g | U. Butter 5 g | U. Butter 5 g | U. Butter 5 g | U. Butter 5 g | U. Butter 5 g

Geheime Staatspolizei
Staatspolizeistelle Köln
Aussendienststelle Aachen

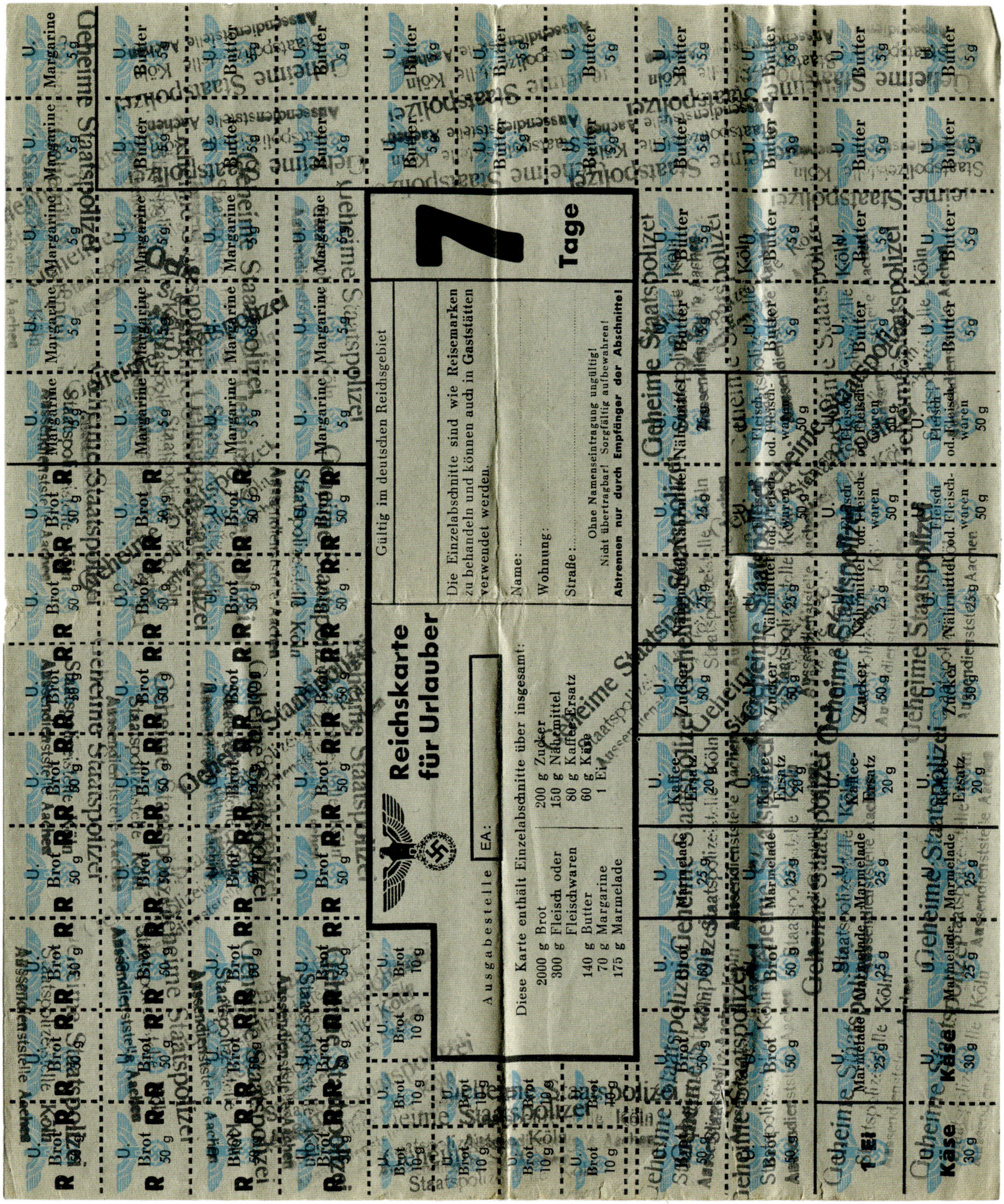

Reichskarte für Urlauber

7 Tage

Ausgabestelle EA:

Gültig im deutschen Reichsgebiet

Die Einzelabschnitte sind wie Reisemarken zu behandeln und können auch in Gaststätten verwendet werden.

Name: ...

Wohnung: ...

Straße: ...

Ohne Namenseintragung ungültig!
Nicht übertragbar! Sorgfältig aufbewahren!
Abtrennen nur durch Empfänger der Abschnitte!

Diese Karte enthält Einzelabschnitte über insgesamt:

2000 g	Brot	200 g	Zucker
300 g	Fleisch oder Fleischwaren	150 g	Nährmittel
140 g	Butter	80 g	Kaffee-Ersatz
70 g	Margarine	60 g	Käse
175 g	Marmelade	1	Ei

Reichskarte für Urlauber

Gültig im deutschen Reichsgebiet bis 14. November 1943

Ausgabestelle

EA:

Diese Karte enthält Einzelabschnitte über insgesamt:
650 g Brot
50 g Fleisch
60 g Butter
25 g Nährmittel

Der Fleischabschnitt berechtigt auch zum Bezuge von Fleischwaren

Name:

Wohnort:

Straße:

Ohne Namenseintragung ungültig! Nicht übertragbar! Sorgfältig aufbewahren!

Abtrennen der Einzelabschnitte nur durch Kleinverteiler, Gaststätten usw.

2 Tage

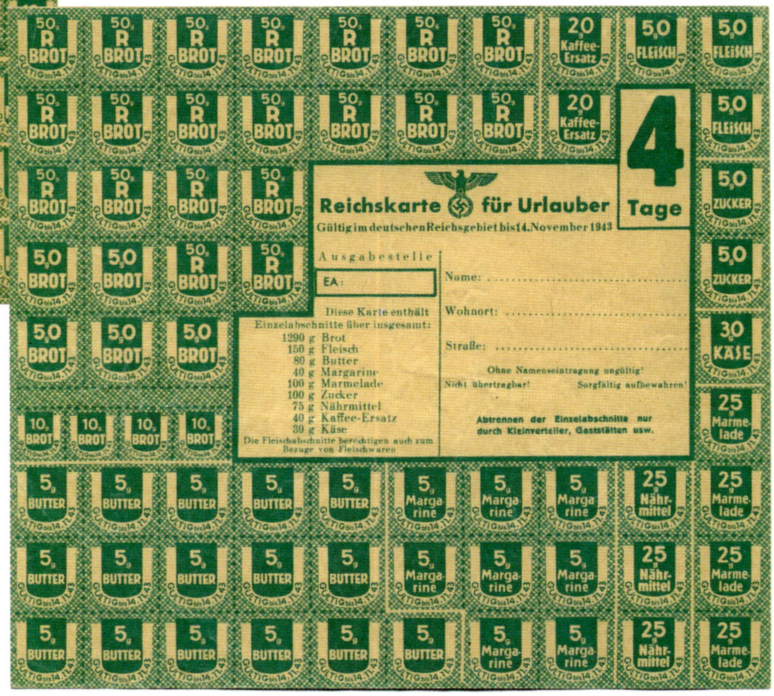

Reichskarte für Urlauber

4 Tage

Gültig im deutschen Reichsgebiet bis 14. November 1943

Ausgabestelle

EA:

Diese Karte enthält Einzelabschnitte über insgesamt:
1290 g Brot
150 g Fleisch
80 g Butter
40 g Margarine
100 g Marmelade
100 g Zucker
75 g Nährmittel
40 g Kaffee-Ersatz
30 g Käse

Die Fleischabschnitte berechtigen auch zum Bezuge von Fleischwaren

Name:

Wohnort:

Straße:

Ohne Namenseintragung ungültig! Nicht übertragbar! Sorgfältig aufbewahren!

Abtrennen der Einzelabschnitte nur durch Kleinverteiler, Gaststätten usw.

Figure 5-31 & 5-32. A different pattern for the Reichskarte für Urlauber, this style was valid until November 14, 1943. Notice that the letter "U" has been incorporated into the design of each coupon. (4" x 7 1/2" and 7" x 8" respectively)

3 Tage

Diese Karte enthält Einzelabschnitte über insgesamt:
1050 g Brot, davon 650 g R-Brot
100 g Fleisch
95 g Butter
75 g Marmelade
100 g Zucker
50 g Nährmittel
20 g Kaffee-Ersatz
30 g Käse

Reichskarte für Urlauber

Gültig im deutschen Reichsgebiet

Ausgabestelle EA:

Name:

Wohnort:

Straße:

Ohne Namenseintragung ungültig! Nicht übertragbar! Sorgfältig aufbewahren!

Abtrennen der Einzelabschnitte nur durch Kleinverteiler, Gaststätten usw.

Diese Karte enthält Einzelabschnitte über insgesamt:
1390 g Brot, davon 850 g R-Brot
150 g Fleisch
85 g Butter
40 g Margarine
100 g Marmelade
100 g Zucker
75 g Nährmittel
40 g Kaffee-Ersatz
30 g Käse

4 Tage

Reichskarte für Urlauber

Gültig im deutschen Reichsgebiet

Ausgabestelle EA:

Name:

Wohnort:

Straße:

Ohne Namenseintragung ungültig! Nicht übertragbar! Sorgfältig aufbewahren!

Abtrennen der Einzelabschnitte nur durch Kleinverteiler, Gaststätten usw.

Figure 5-33 & 5-34. These Reichskarten for 3 and 4 days used both a stylistic Jugendstil motif more befitting the First World War than the Second and a moire pattern, a constructive interference between two frequencies of printed dots, to prevent counterfeiting. (5" x 6" and 5 3/8" x 9 3/8" respectively)

Figure 5-35 through Figure 5-38. These versions of the Reichskarten dispensed with the stylish motif and used only a tighter moire pattern and voided patterns to prevent forgeries. As the war went on, the amounts of food given to visiting soldiers decreased, partly due to availability, but partly because of the deprivations suffered by the civilians they were visiting. (All images are shown at roughly half of original size to indicate scale, relative to one another)

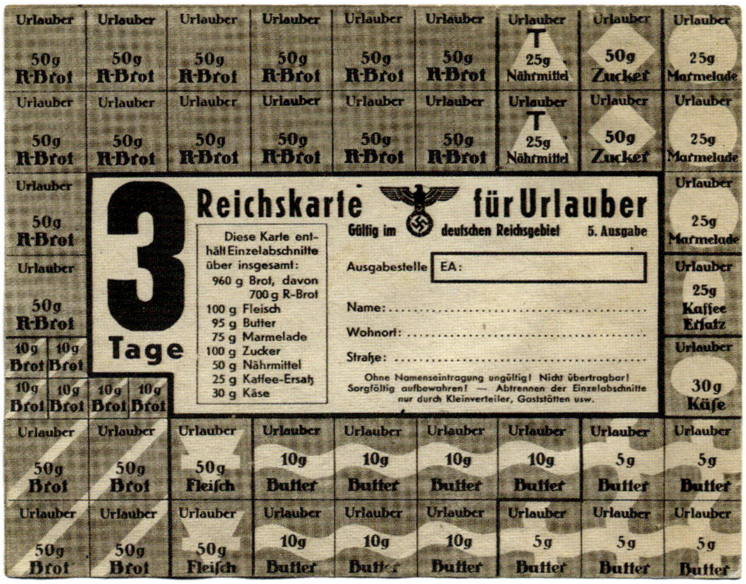

3 Tage
Reichskarte für Urlauber
Gültig im deutschen Reichsgebiet 5. Ausgabe
Diese Karte enthält Einzelabschnitte über insgesamt:
960 g Brot, davon 700 g R-Brot
100 g Fleisch
95 g Butter
75 g Marmelade
100 g Zucker
50 g Nährmittel
25 g Kaffee-Ersatz
30 g Käse
Ausgabestelle EA:
Name:
Wohnort:
Straße:
Ohne Namenseintragung ungültig! Nicht übertragbar! Sorgfältig aufbewahren! — Abtrennen der Einzelabschnitte nur durch Kleinverteiler, Gaststätten usw.

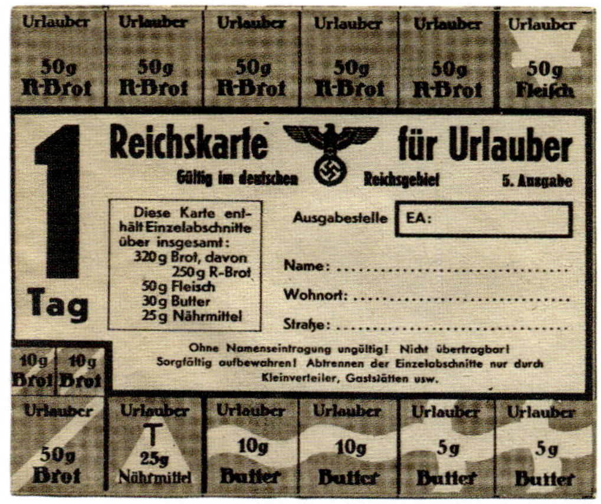

1 Tag
Reichskarte für Urlauber
Gültig im deutschen Reichsgebiet 5. Ausgabe
Diese Karte enthält Einzelabschnitte über insgesamt:
320 g Brot, davon 250 g R-Brot
50 g Fleisch
30 g Butter
25 g Nährmittel
Ausgabestelle EA:
Name:
Wohnort:
Straße:
Ohne Namenseintragung ungültig! Nicht übertragbar! Sorgfältig aufbewahren! Abtrennen der Einzelabschnitte nur durch Kleinverteiler, Gaststätten usw.

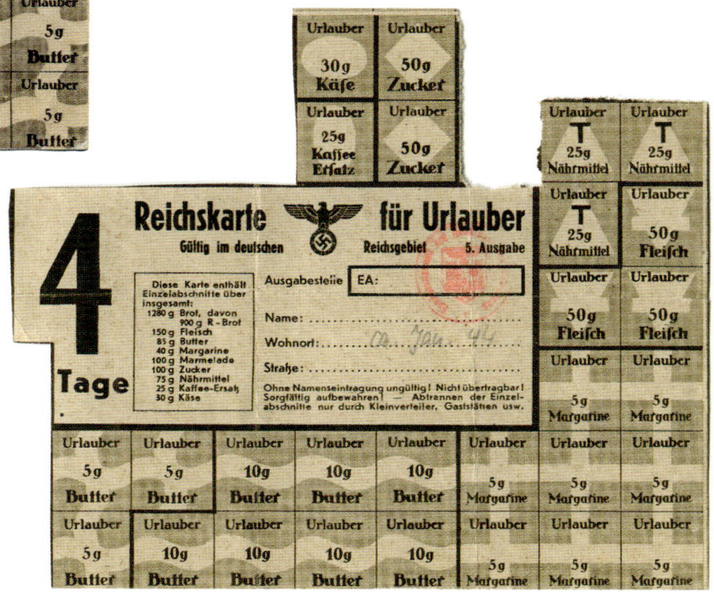

4 Tage
Reichskarte für Urlauber
Gültig im deutschen Reichsgebiet 5. Ausgabe
Diese Karte enthält Einzelabschnitte über insgesamt:
1280 g Brot, davon 900 g R-Brot
150 g Fleisch
85 g Butter
40 g Margarine
100 g Marmelade
100 g Zucker
75 g Nährmittel
25 g Kaffee-Ersatz
30 g Käse
Ausgabestelle EA:
Name:
Wohnort:
Straße:
Ohne Namenseintragung ungültig! Nicht übertragbar! Sorgfältig aufbewahren! — Abtrennen der Einzelabschnitte nur durch Kleinverteiler, Gaststätten usw.

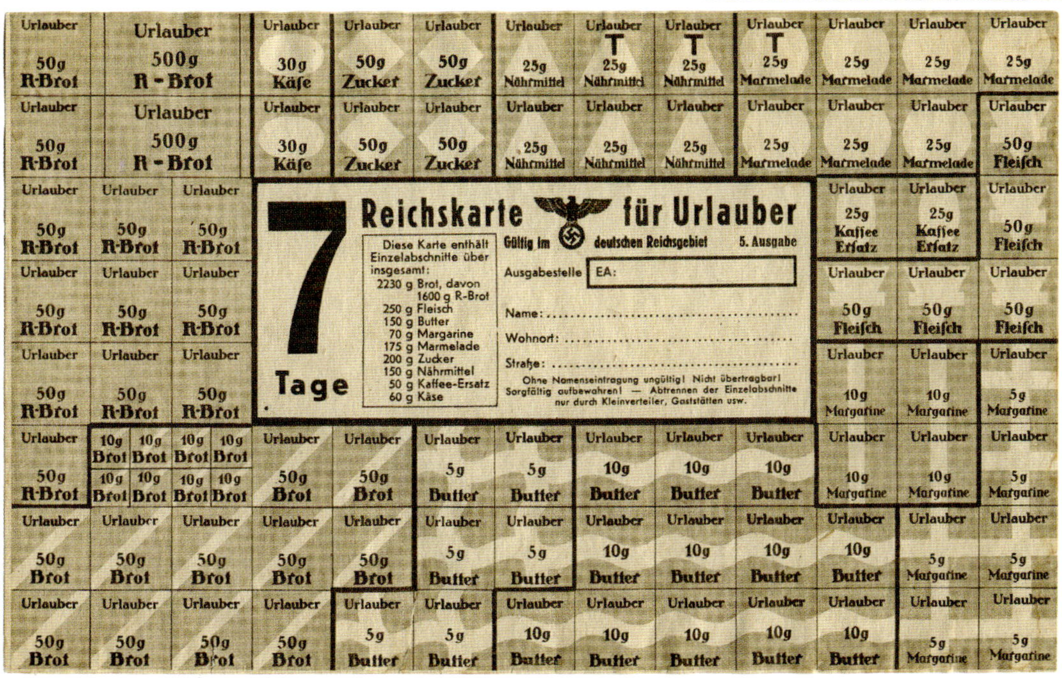

7 Tage
Reichskarte für Urlauber
Gültig im deutschen Reichsgebiet 5. Ausgabe
Diese Karte enthält Einzelabschnitte über insgesamt:
2230 g Brot, davon 1600 g R-Brot
250 g Fleisch
150 g Butter
70 g Margarine
175 g Marmelade
200 g Zucker
150 g Nährmittel
50 g Kaffee-Ersatz
60 g Käse
Ausgabestelle EA:
Name:
Wohnort:
Straße:
Ohne Namenseintragung ungültig! Nicht übertragbar! Sorgfältig aufbewahren! — Abtrennen der Einzelabschnitte nur durch Kleinverteiler, Gaststätten usw.

Additionally specialized ration cards for those on leave included the *Bezugsausweis für Urlauber* (Reference Identifications Card for Those on Leave). This card was used to supplement the fourth edition of the *Reichskarte* for those on leave (*Zusatz zur Reichskarte f. Urlauber, 4. Ausgabe*). Those providing the items listed, specifically *Milch* (Milk) and *Kartoffeln* (Potatoes) were directed to clip the coupons in the usual manner:

Bei Warenabgabe haben die Verteiler die Einzelabschnitte abzutrennen und in üblicher Weise abzurechnen. - Die Sonderbezugsabschnitte sind vom Verteiler abzutrennen und bis auf weiteres aufzubewahren.

Distributors are required to detach the single sections and to deduct in the usual manner. - Distributers are to detach the special reference sections and store until further notice.

A second form of specialized ration card was the *Verpflegungskarte* (Provisions Card). This card functioned in much the same way as a standard ration card, i.e., cut away or

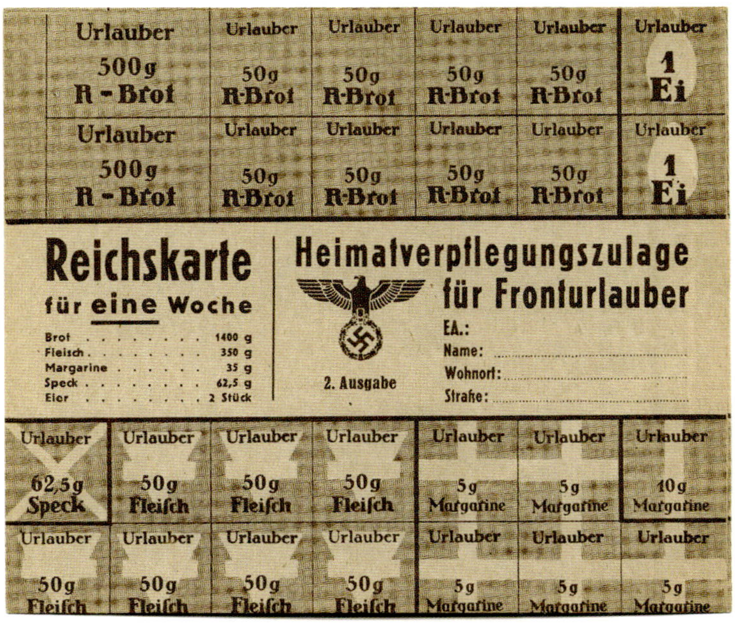

Figure 5-39. This ration card, the Heimatverp-flegungszulage or Home Front Supplemental Ration, similar to the previous pattern and often issued with it, was intended to extend rations of those on leave. (4 5/8" x 5 5/8")

Figure 5-40. The Lebensmittelsonderkarte was, quite literally, a special ration card. It was used as a supplement to ordinary rations. (4 7/8" x 7 1/8")

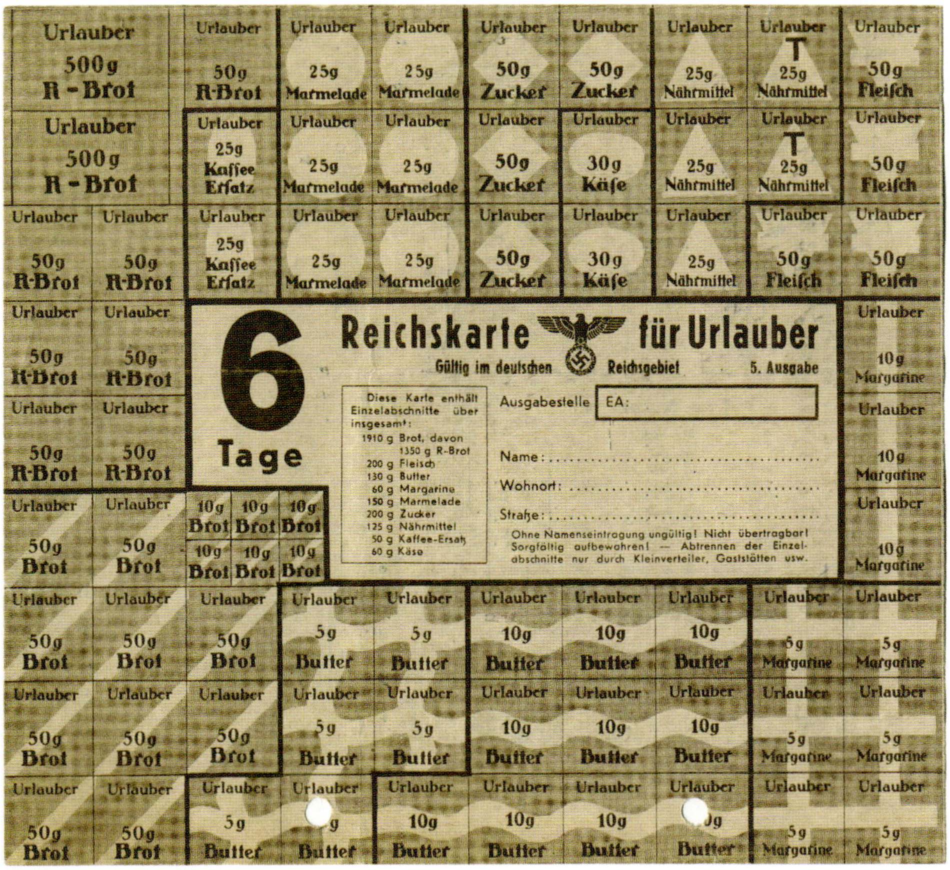

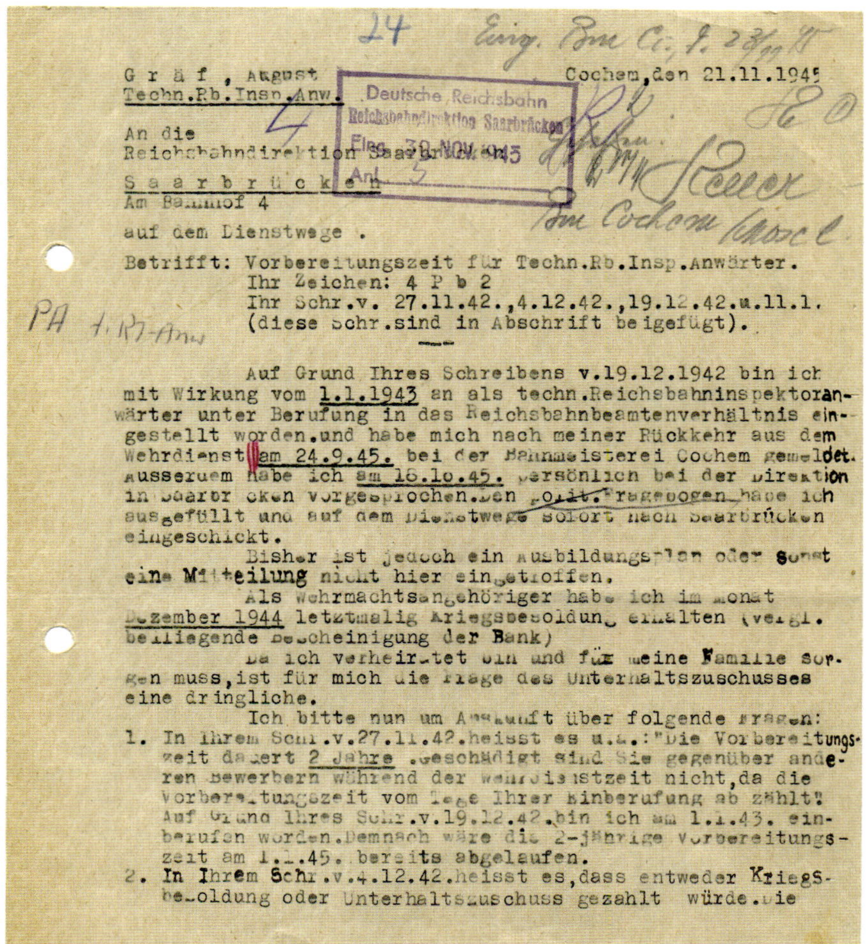

Gräf, August
Techn.Rb.Insp.Anw.

Cochem, den 21.11.1945

An die
Reichsbahndirektion Saarbrücken
Saarbrücken
Am Bahnhof 4

auf dem Dienstwege.

Betrifft: Vorbereitungszeit für Techn.Rb.Insp.Anwärter.
Ihr Zeichen: 4 P b 2
Ihr Schr.v. 27.11.42.,4.12.42.,19.12.42.u.11.1.
(diese Schr.sind in Abschrift beigefügt).

Auf Grund Ihres Schreibens v.19.12.1942 bin ich mit Wirkung vom 1.1.1943 an als techn.Reichsbahninspektoranwärter unter Berufung in das Reichsbahnbeamtenverhältnis eingestellt worden.und habe mich nach meiner Rückkehr aus dem Wehrdienst am 24.9.45. bei der Bahnmeisterei Cochem gemeldet. Ausserdem habe ich am 16.10.45. persönlich bei der Direktion in Saarbrücken vorgesprochen. Den polit. Fragebogen habe ich ausgefüllt und auf dem Dienstwege sofort nach Saarbrücken eingeschickt.

Bisher ist jedoch ein Ausbildungsplan oder sonst eine Mitteilung nicht hier eingetroffen.

Als Wehrmachtsangehöriger habe ich im Monat Dezember 1944 letztmalig Kriegsbesoldung erhalten (vergl. beiliegende Bescheinigung der Bank)

Da ich verheiratet bin und für meine Familie sorgen muss, ist für mich die Frage des Unterhaltszuschusses eine dringliche.

Ich bitte nun um Auskunft über folgende Fragen:

1. In Ihrem Schr.v.27.11.42.heisst es u.a.:"Die Vorbereitungszeit dauert 2 Jahre. Geschädigt sind Sie gegenüber anderen Bewerbern während der Wehrdienstzeit nicht, da die Vorbereitungszeit vom Tage Ihrer Einberufung ab zählt". Auf Grund Ihres Schr.v.19.12.42. bin ich am 1.1.43. einberufen worden. Demnach wäre die 2-jährige Vorbereitungszeit am 1.1.45. bereits abgelaufen.
2. In Ihrem Schr.v.4.12.42.heisst es, dass entweder Kriegsbesoldung oder Unterhaltszuschuss gezahlt würde. Die

Figure 5-41. A 6-day Reichskarte für Urlauber, worth a good deal of food prior to May 8, 1945, was all but worthless immediately following that date. As early as June of 1945, paper was in such short supply that Reichskarten were often used like scratch paper. This particular ration card has been drafted as a Dienstwege, a certificate of service for August Gräf, a Reichsbahn Technical Inspector Candidate. ($7^{1}/_{16}$" x $7^{15}/_{16}$")

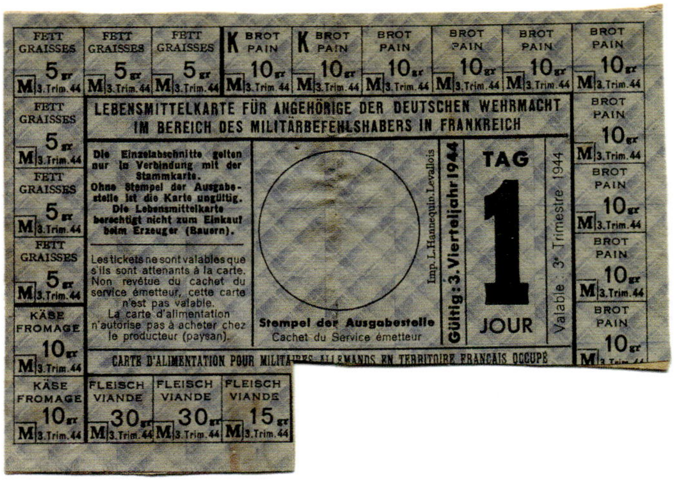

LEBENSMITTELKARTE FÜR ANGEHÖRIGE DER DEUTSCHEN WEHRMACHT IM BEREICH DES MILITÄRBEFEHLSHABERS IN FRANKREICH

Die Einzelabschnitte gelten nur in Verbindung mit der Stammkarte. Ohne Stempel der Ausgabestelle ist die Karte ungültig. Die Lebensmittelkarte berechtigt nicht zum Einkauf beim Erzeuger (Bauern).

Les tickets ne sont valables que s'ils sont attenants à la carte. Non revêtue du cachet du service émetteur, cette carte n'est pas valable. La carte d'alimentation n'autorise pas à acheter chez le producteur (paysan).

Stempel der Ausgabestelle
Cachet du Service émetteur

Imp. L. Hannequin. Levallois

Gültig: 3. Vierteljahr 1944

TAG 1 JOUR

Valable: 3e Trimestre 1944

CARTE D'ALIMENTATION POUR MILITAIRES ALLEMANDS EN TERRITOIRE FRANÇAIS OCCUPÉ

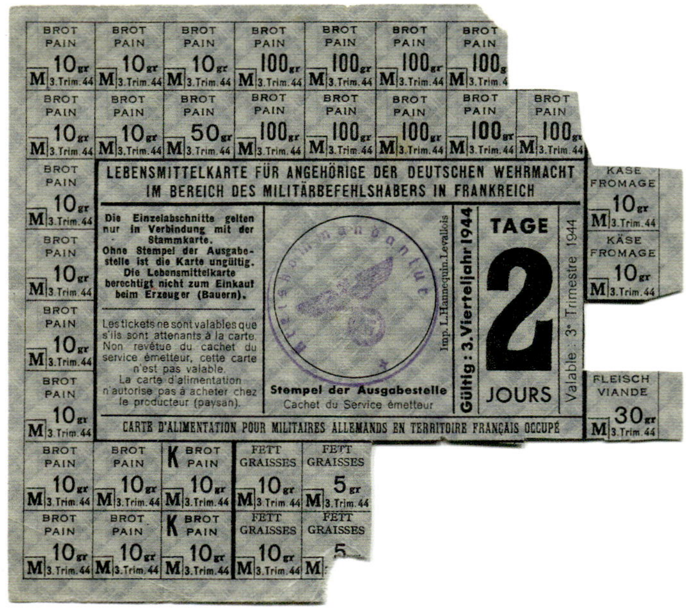

LEBENSMITTELKARTE FÜR ANGEHÖRIGE DER DEUTSCHEN WEHRMACHT IM BEREICH DES MILITÄRBEFEHLSHABERS IN FRANKREICH

Gültig: 3. Vierteljahr 1944

TAGE 2 JOURS

Valable: 3e Trimestre 1944

CARTE D'ALIMENTATION POUR MILITAIRES ALLEMANDS EN TERRITOIRE FRANÇAIS OCCUPÉ

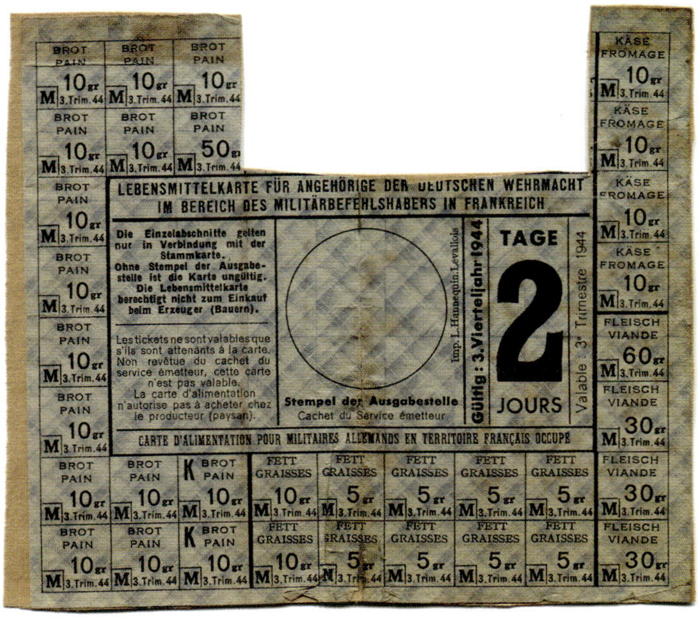

LEBENSMITTELKARTE FÜR ANGEHÖRIGE DER DEUTSCHEN WEHRMACHT IM BEREICH DES MILITÄRBEFEHLSHABERS IN FRANKREICH

Gültig: 3. Vierteljahr 1944

TAGE 2 JOURS

Valable: 3e Trimestre 1944

CARTE D'ALIMENTATION POUR MILITAIRES ALLEMANDS EN TERRITOIRE FRANÇAIS OCCUPÉ

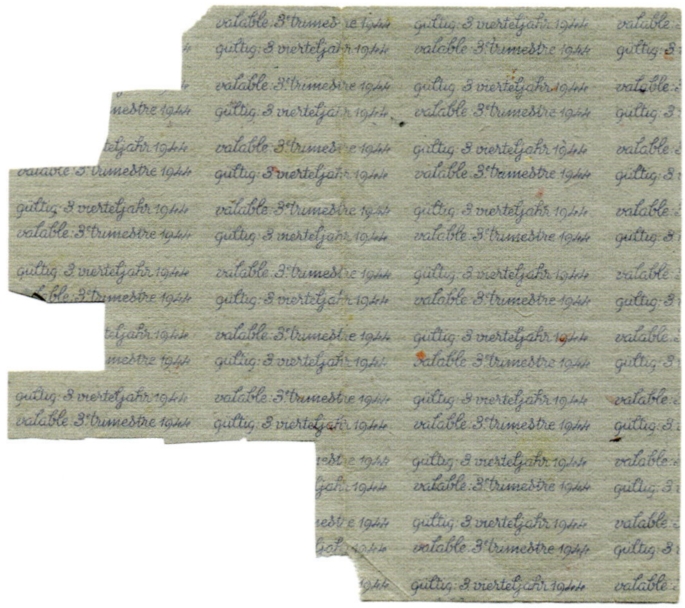

valable 3e trimestre 1944 gültig 3 vierteljahr 1944

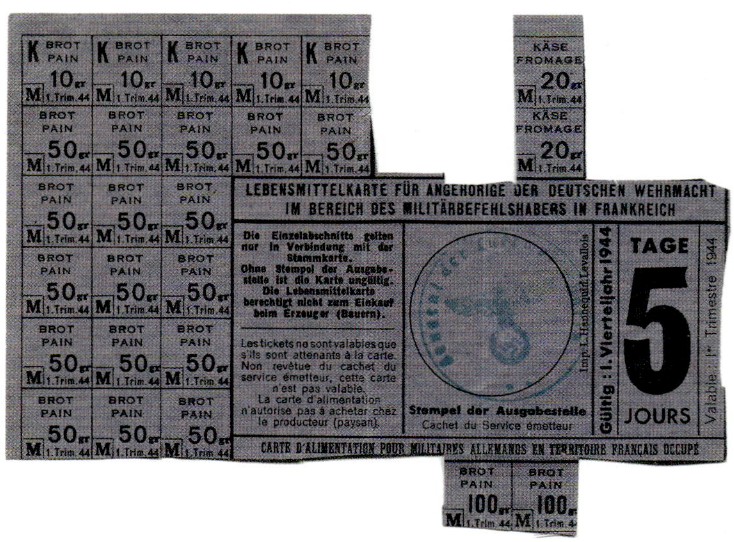

LEBENSMITTELKARTE FÜR ANGEHÖRIGE DER DEUTSCHEN WEHRMACHT IM BEREICH DES MILITÄRBEFEHLSHABERS IN FRANKREICH

Gültig: I. Vierteljahr 1944

TAGE 5 JOURS

Valable: 1er Trimestre 1944

CARTE D'ALIMENTATION POUR MILITAIRES ALLEMANDS EN TERRITOIRE FRANÇAIS OCCUPÉ

Figure 5-42 through 5-46. Members of the German Armed Forces serving in France were often issued special bilingual ration cards that were issued quarterly. Elaborate multicolored moire patterns or even plaids were printed in the background, as the Resistance members were becoming experts at forgeries. Intended for service members separated for service travel or on leave, these cards could be easily understood by Kellner and garcon alike. The backs of the cards were printed with a repeating pattern in both German and French indicating for which quarter the card in question was valid. (All items shown at 64% of original size.)

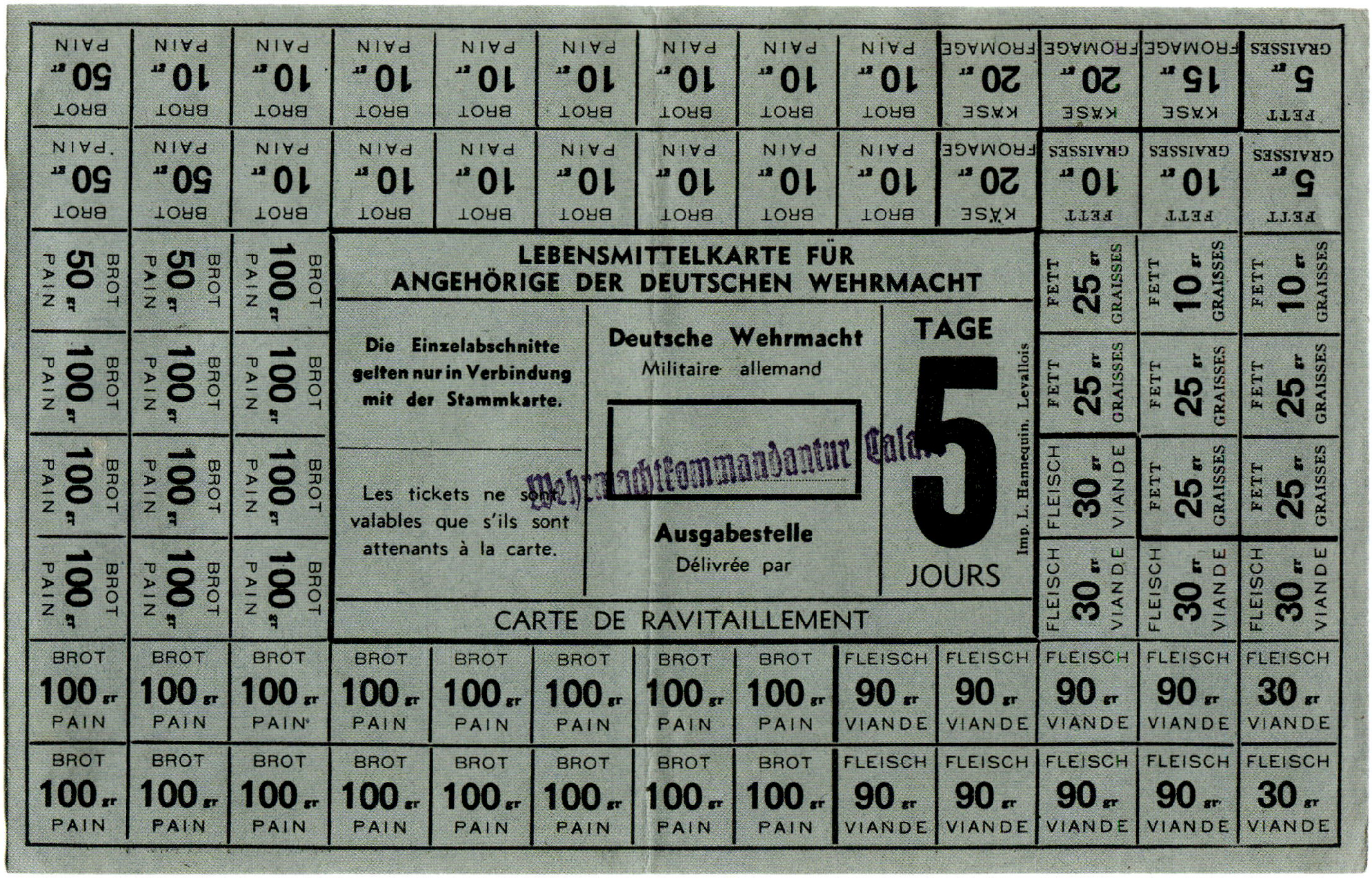

Figure 5-47. An earlier variation of the same ration card, the fonts and pattern more resembles ration cards issued to the French civilian population. By 1942, both had been replaced by more complex designs.

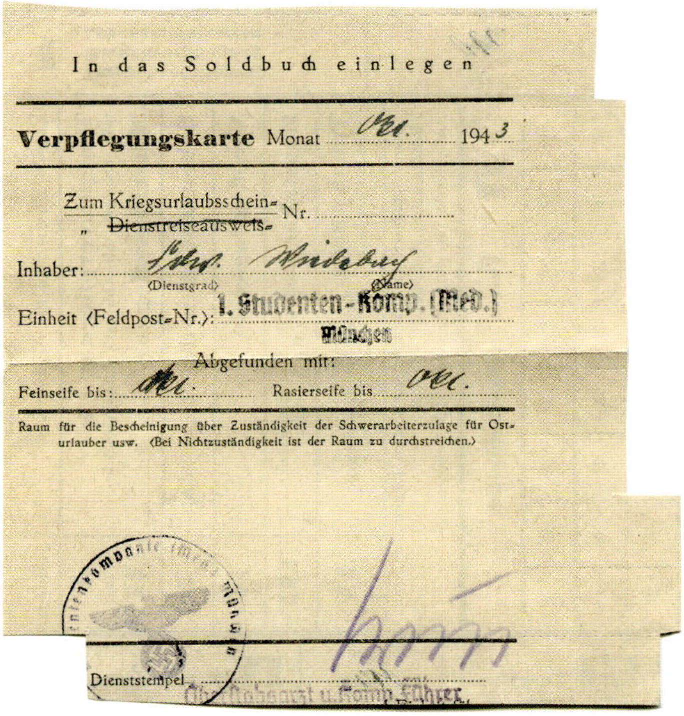

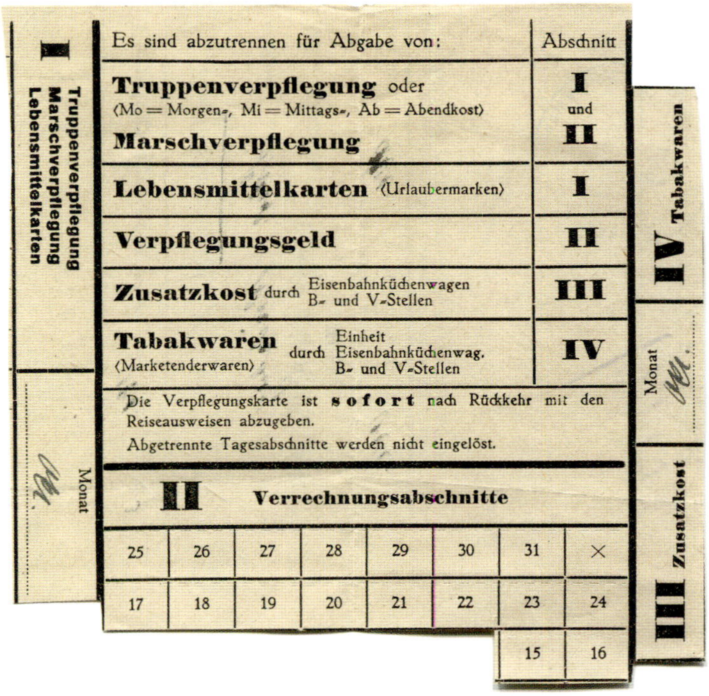

Figure 5-48. A well-used Verpflegungskarte issued for the month of October 1943 to Feldwebel Wiedeburg in conjunction with his Kriegsurlaubsschein. As you can see, Herr Wiedeburg took advantage of nearly every coupon available to him. (5" x 5¼")

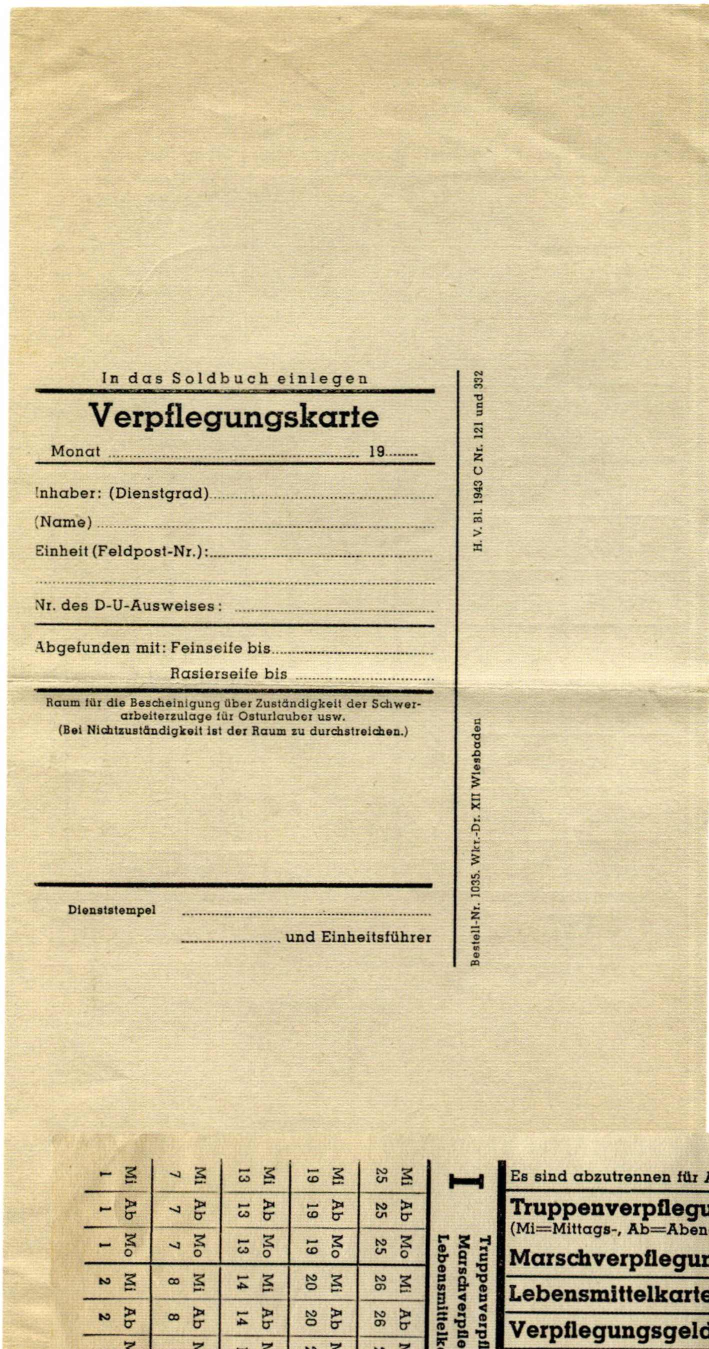

In das Soldbuch einlegen

Verpflegungskarte

Monat .... 19........

Inhaber: (Dienstgrad)..

(Name)..

Einheit (Feldpost-Nr.):..

....

Nr. des D-U-Ausweises: ....

Abgefunden mit: Feinseife bis..

Rasierseife bis ....

Raum für die Bescheinigung über Zuständigkeit der Schwerarbeiterzulage für Osturlauber usw.
(Bei Nichtzuständigkeit ist der Raum zu durchstreichen.)

Dienststempel ....

.... und Einheitsführer

H. V. Bl. 1943 C Nr. 121 und 332

Bestell-Nr. 1035. Wkr.-Dr. XII Wiesbaden

Figure 5-49. An unissued Verpflegungskarte (front and back), or ration card, that was probably issued to troops in a Kaserne or Fliegerhorst (Barracks or Air Field), and not issued to troops on leave. (5" x 9½")

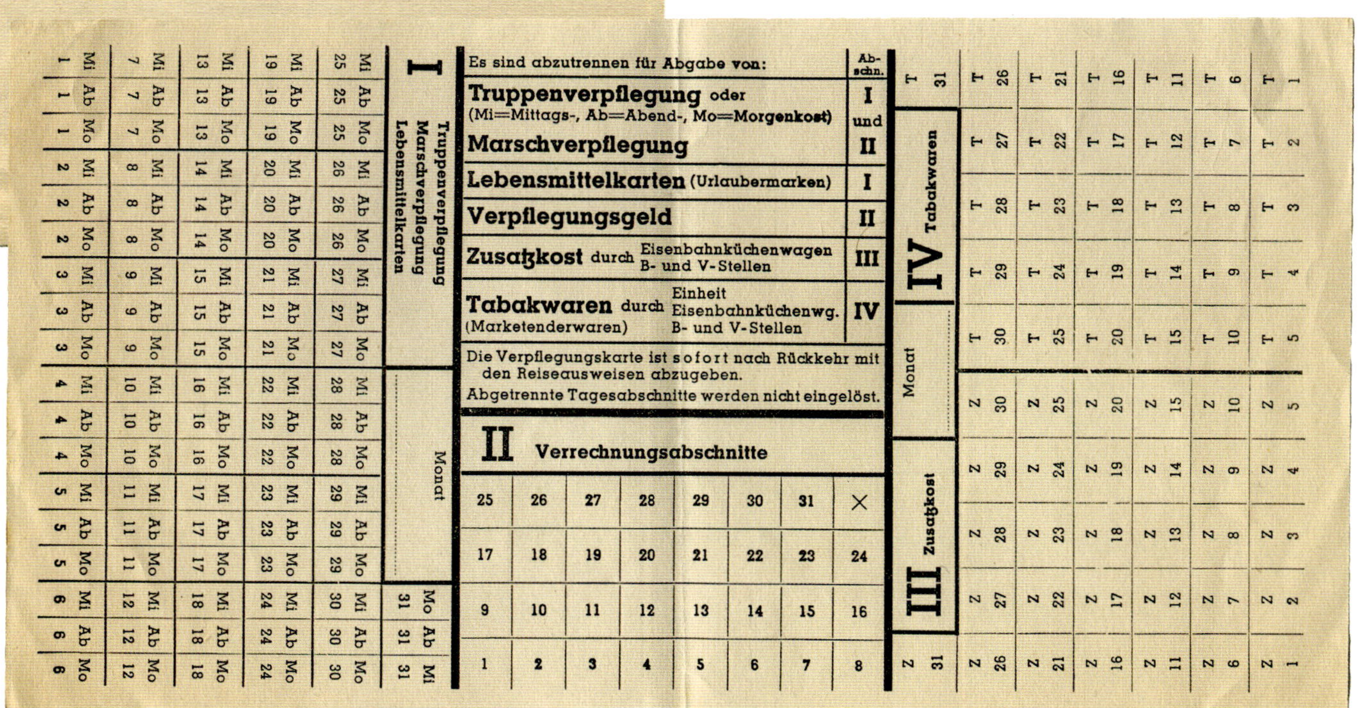

I Truppenverpflegung / Marschverpflegung / Lebensmittelkarten

Monat

Tag			
1	Mi	Ab	Mo
2	Mi	Ab	Mo
3	Mi	Ab	Mo
4	Mi	Ab	Mo
5	Mi	Ab	Mo
6	Mi	Ab	Mo
7	Mi	Ab	Mo
8	Mi	Ab	Mo
9	Mi	Ab	Mo
10	Mi	Ab	Mo
11	Mi	Ab	Mo
12	Mi	Ab	Mo
13	Mi	Ab	Mo
14	Mi	Ab	Mo
15	Mi	Ab	Mo
16	Mi	Ab	Mo
17	Mi	Ab	Mo
18	Mi	Ab	Mo
19	Mi	Ab	Mo
20	Mi	Ab	Mo
21	Mi	Ab	Mo
22	Mi	Ab	Mo
23	Mi	Ab	Mo
24	Mi	Ab	Mo
25	Mi	Ab	Mo
26	Mi	Ab	Mo
27	Mi	Ab	Mo
28	Mi	Ab	Mo
29	Mi	Ab	Mo
30	Mi	Ab	Mo
31	Mi	Ab	Mo

Es sind abzutrennen für Abgabe von:	Abschn.
Truppenverpflegung oder (Mi=Mittags-, Ab=Abend-, Mo=Morgenkost)	I und
Marschverpflegung	II
Lebensmittelkarten (Urlaubermarken)	I
Verpflegungsgeld	II
Zusatzkost durch Eisenbahnküchenwagen B- und V-Stellen	III
Tabakwaren durch Einheit Eisenbahnküchenwg. B- und V-Stellen (Marketenderwaren)	IV

Die Verpflegungskarte ist sofort nach Rückkehr mit den Reiseausweisen abzugeben.
Abgetrennte Tagesabschnitte werden nicht eingelöst.

II Verrechnungsabschnitte

25	26	27	28	29	30	31	×
17	18	19	20	21	22	23	24
9	10	11	12	13	14	15	16
1	2	3	4	5	6	7	8

IV Tabakwaren — Monat

T 1	T 2	T 3	T 4	T 5	
T 6	T 7	T 8	T 9	T 10	
T 11	T 12	T 13	T 14	T 15	
T 16	T 17	T 18	T 19	T 20	
T 21	T 22	T 23	T 24	T 25	
T 26	T 27	T 28	T 29	T 30	T 31

III Zusatzkost

Z 1	Z 2	Z 3	Z 4	Z 5	
Z 6	Z 7	Z 8	Z 9	Z 10	
Z 11	Z 12	Z 13	Z 14	Z 15	
Z 16	Z 17	Z 18	Z 19	Z 20	
Z 21	Z 22	Z 23	Z 24	Z 25	
Z 26	Z 27	Z 28	Z 29	Z 30	Z 31

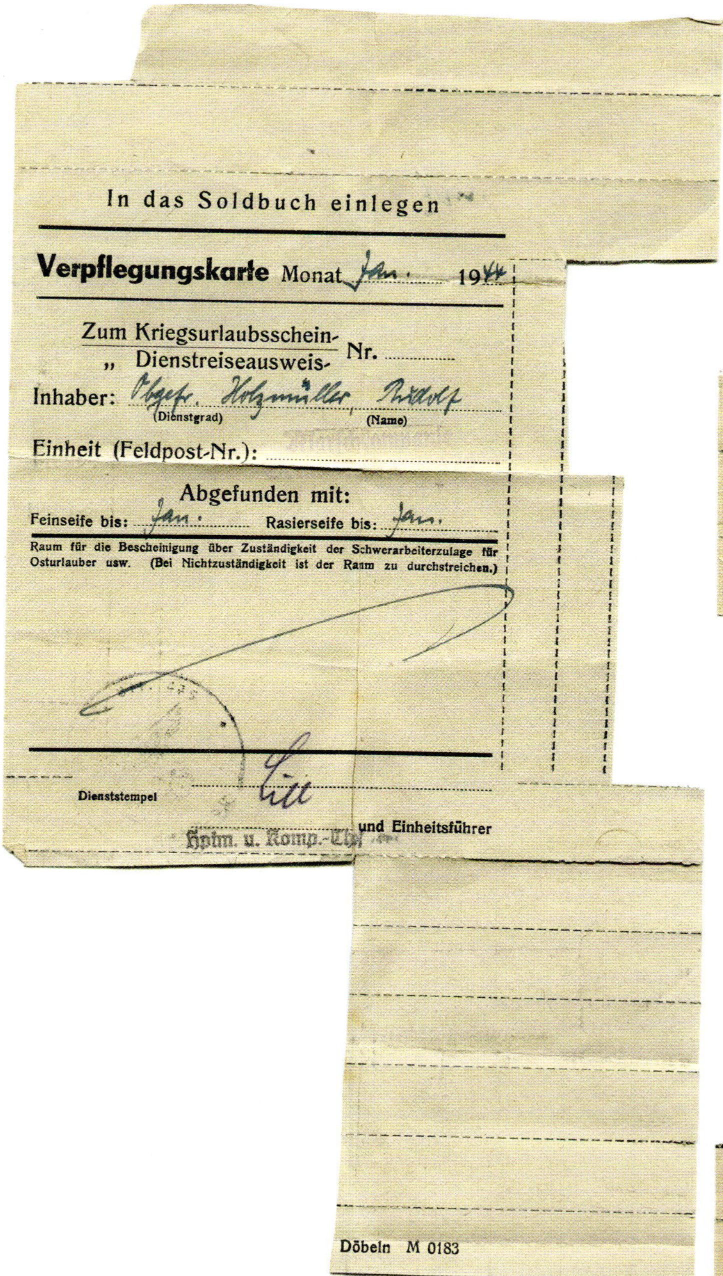
In das Soldbuch einlegen

Verpflegungskarte Monat Jan. 1944

Zum Kriegsurlaubsschein-
„ Dienstreiseausweis- Nr. ....

Inhaber: Obgefr. Holzmüller, Rudolf
(Dienstgrad) (Name)

Einheit (Feldpost-Nr.): ....

Abgefunden mit:
Feinseife bis: Jan. Rasierseife bis: Jan.

Raum für die Bescheinigung über Zuständigkeit der Schwerarbeiterzulage für Osturlauber usw. (Bei Nichtzuständigkeit ist der Raum zu durchstreichen.)

Dienststempel

Hptm. u. Komp.-Chef und Einheitsführer

Döbeln M 0183

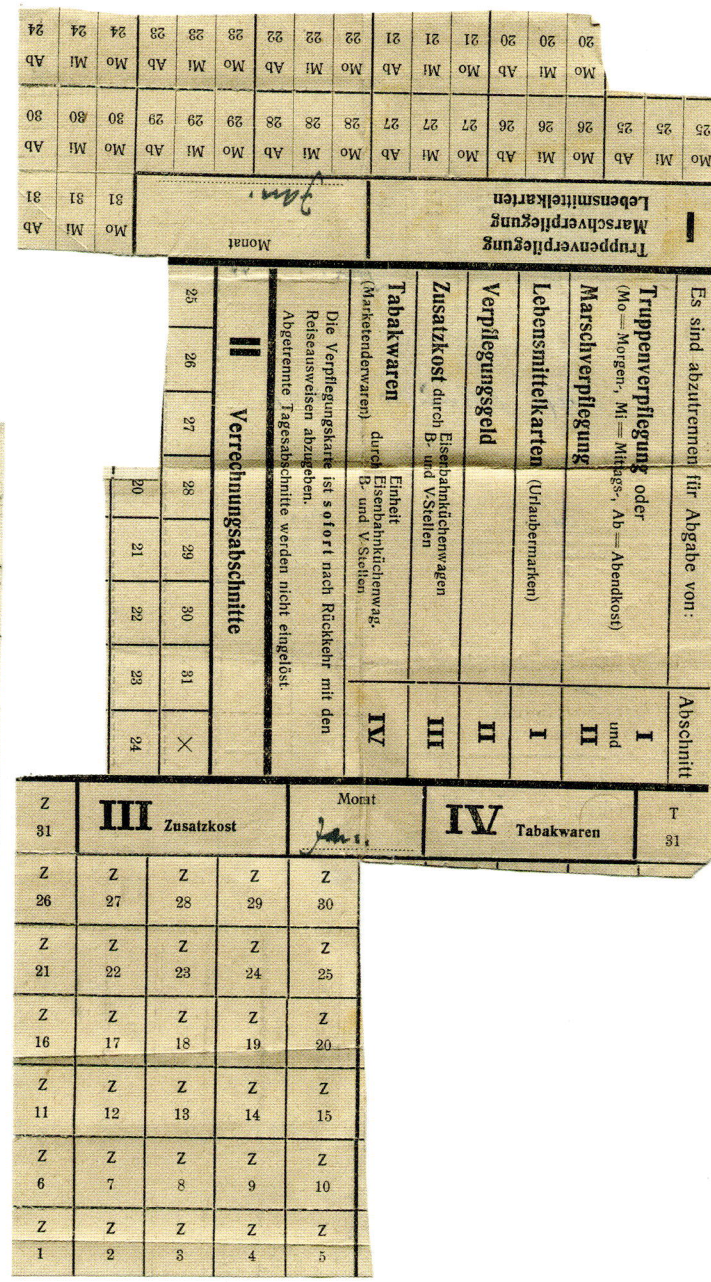
I Truppenverpflegung Marschverpflegung Lebensmittelkarten

Monat Jan.

Es sind abzutrennen für Abgabe von: | Abschnitt
Truppenverpflegung oder (Mo = Morgen-, Mi = Mittags-, Ab = Abendkost) Marschverpflegung | I und II
Lebensmittelkarten (Urlaubermarken) | I
Verpflegungsgeld | II
Zusatzkost durch Eisenbahnküchenwagen und V-Stellen | III
Tabakwaren (Marketenderwaren) durch Einheit Eisenbahnküchenwag. B- und V-Stellen | IV

II Verrechnungsabschnitte

Die Verpflegungskarte ist sofort nach Rückkehr mit den Reiseausweisen abzugeben. Abgetrennte Tagesabschnitte werden nicht eingelöst.

III Zusatzkost Monat Jan.

IV Tabakwaren

Figure 5-50. This Verpflegungskarte was issued for January 1944 to Obergefreiter Rudolf Holzmüller. Although extensively used, many of the coupons remain to give collectors an idea of what the individual coupons looked like. (5³/₈" x 9³/₄")

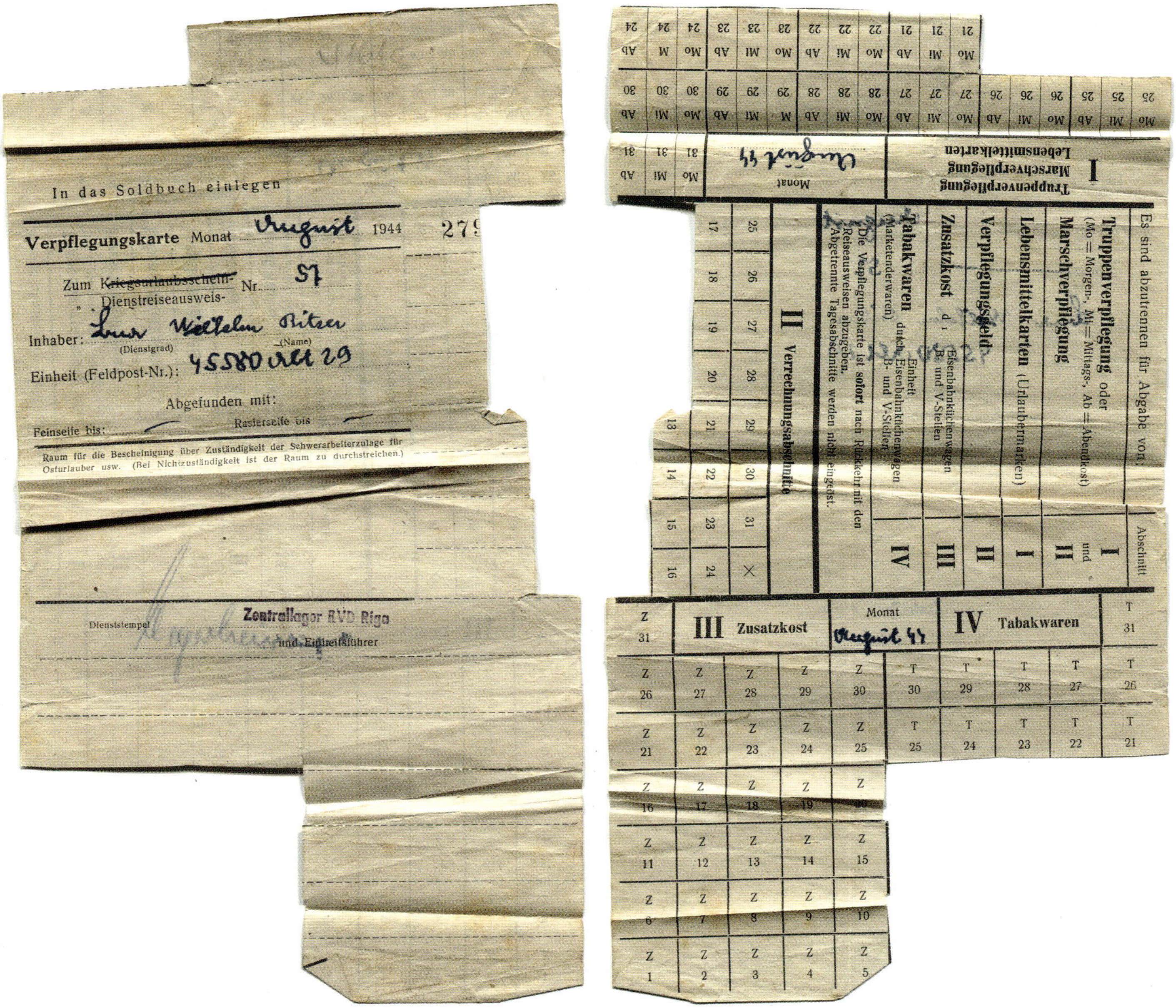

Figure 5-51. A Wehrmacht Verpflegungskarte issued to Reichsbahn employee Wilhelm Ritser in August 1944 in Riga, Latvia, for service-related travel. (5¾" x 1")

stamp the appropriate coupon when used, and was specifically meant for the soldier to keep in his *Soldbuch* (*In das Soldbuch einlegen*).

Apart from food, tobacco was another rationed item dear to a soldier's heart. Despite the harmful nature of the product, recognized by many doctors as early as the 1930s, soldiers continued to request it from home. One letter home from a soldier at the front closes with a short poem:

> *"Willst Du deinem Sohn erröten,*
> *schickt ihm Geld und Zigaretten!"*
>
> If you want to make your son blush,
> send him money and cigarettes!

Nicotine, though highly addictive, has several beneficial effects for people under extreme stress. It enhances the thought process by mimicking the neurotransmitter acetylcholine, a naturally occurring hormone. Nicotine increases circulation, decreases depression, and suppresses appetite. Although Nazi Germany was one of the first countries to engage in an official antismoking campaign, they continued to make cigarettes, cigars, and chewing tobacco available to its troops.

H.Dv.86/1, the *Vorschrift für die Verpflegung der Wehrmacht*, the Manual for the Provisioning of the *Wehrmacht*, lists the exact amount of tobacco products to be provided to the soldier for a single day (I.17(a) and (b)):

> *"...a.) für Raucher als Tabakportion*
> *2 Zigarren und 2 Zigaretten,*
> *oder 1 Zigarre und 4 Zigaretten,*
> *oder 6 Zigaretten,*
> *oder 25g Rauchtabak,*
> *oder 12-1/2g Rauchtabak und 2 Zigaretten,*
> *oder 12-1/2g Rauchtabak und 1 Zigarre,*
> *oder 1 Stück Kautabak (etwa 20g)*
> *--1 Zigarre darf auch durch 2 Zigarillos ersetzt werden--;*
> *b.) für Nichtraucher an den Tagen, and denen die Tabakportion nach a) vorabfolgt wird, als Ersatz 30g Drops oder andere Zuckerwaren."*

...a.) for smokers, the tobacco portion is
2 cigars and 2 cigarettes,
or 1 cigar and 4 cigarettes,
or 6 cigarettes,
or 25g of Smoking tobacco
(tobacco for pipes or rolling papers)
or 12-1/2g of Smoking tobacco and 2 cigarettes,
or 12-1/2g of Smoking tobacco and 2 cigarettes,
or 1 Piece of Chewing tobacco (about 20g)
--1 cigar may be substituted for 2 cigarillos--
b.) for nonsmokers, on those days, the preceding tobacco portion a) maybe be substituted by candy drops of 30g or other sweets.

As was noted in the section on the *Sonderausweis* and *Kriegsurlaubsschein*, soldiers leaving the front were entitled to a tobacco ration in the form of a *Raucherkarte* (Smoking Card), which was initiated with tobacco rationing in November of 1941. The card was a large beige card, roughly A5 in size, and valid for roughly six months with a coupon usable every other day.

Beginning with the tobacco ration of July 1943, *Wehrmacht Raucherkarten* followed the civilian pattern of one coupon per four days over five months, but was printed on red paper. Starting with Ration Period 58 (*Zuteilungsperiode* 58), the *Raucherkarte* was shortened to a two-month validity, with each coupon representing one week.

Another form of *Raucherkarte* was the *Raucherkontrollausweis* (Smoking Control Identity), issued upon leaving the front. It was much more like a small ration card, with coupons valid for daily use, which would have been cut or stamped as the soldier collected his cigars or cigarettes.

If a soldier had left the front without a *Raucherkarte*, he could petition the local authorities to receive one upon arrival. He did so by filling out an *Erklärung*, or Declaration, that he had not been issued one. A *Verzeichnis* (Index, usually understood to be an attestation) would be filled out, verified, and signed by the *Bürgermeister* (Mayor), and the soldier would be issued a civilian *Raucherkarte*.

At the beginning of the war, civilian Raucherkarten were large, much like the military pattern with coupons valid every other day for six months, but gradually shrank in size. By the end of the war, they were often quite small, usually not more than 55mm x 82mm (approximately C8 size). Coupons were valid for a week's worth of tobacco, and the card itself was only valid for a month or less.

Figure 5-52. Even during the stress of rationing and the war, many found a way to lighten the tension with humor. A Reichs-Kusskarte (Kiss Ration Card) "issued" to Gefreiter Unsig while on leave, no doubt by his wife or girlfriend, made light of the ration situation by rationing Dauerkuss (lasting kiss) and Gelegenheitskuss (special occasion kiss) through the provided coupons. Commercially printed Kusskarten were available, but this hand-drawn version was probably just as appreciated. (4 1/4" x 5 7/8")

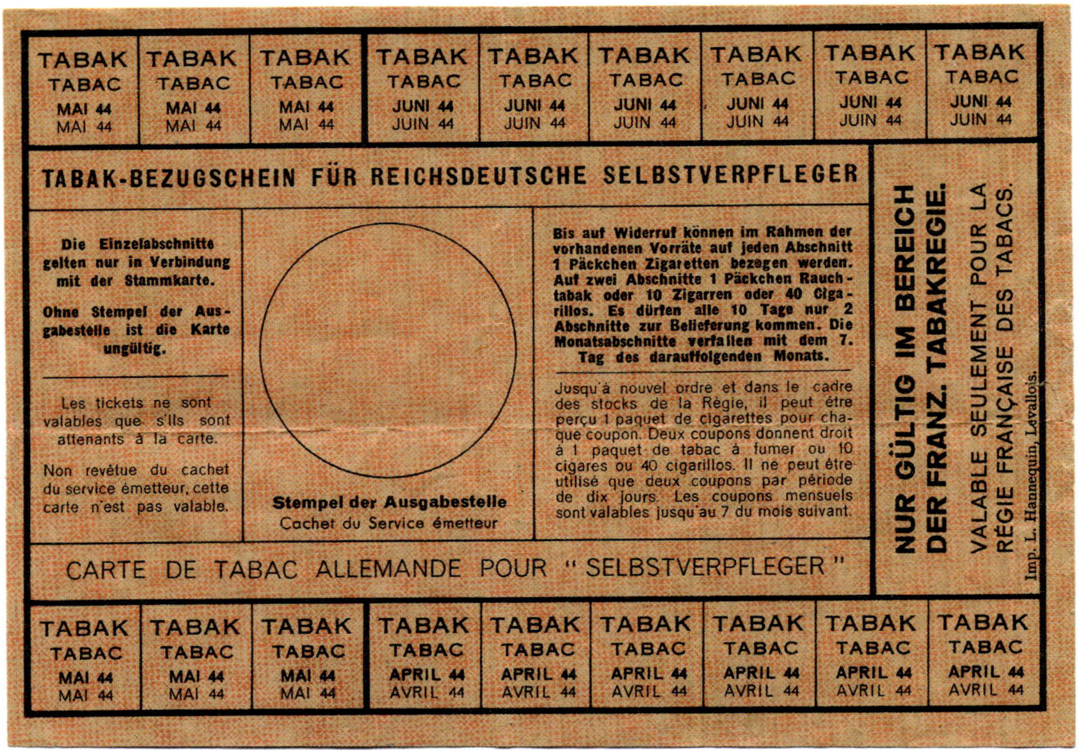

TABAK TABAC MAI 44 MAI 44 | TABAK TABAC MAI 44 MAI 44 | TABAK TABAC MAI 44 MAI 44 | TABAK TABAC JUNI 44 JUIN 44 | TABAK TABAC JUNI 44 JUIN 44 | TABAK TABAC JUNI 44 JUIN 44 | TABAK TABAC JUNI 44 JUIN 44 | TABAK TABAC JUNI 44 JUIN 44 | TABAK TABAC JUNI 44 JUIN 44

TABAK-BEZUGSCHEIN FÜR REICHSDEUTSCHE SELBSTVERPFLEGER

Die Einzelabschnitte gelten nur in Verbindung mit der Stammkarte.

Ohne Stempel der Ausgabestelle ist die Karte ungültig.

Les tickets ne sont valables que s'ils sont attenants à la carte.

Non revêtue du cachet du service émetteur, cette carte n'est pas valable.

Stempel der Ausgabestelle
Cachet du Service émetteur

Bis auf Widerruf können im Rahmen der vorhandenen Vorräte auf jeden Abschnitt 1 Päckchen Zigaretten bezogen werden. Auf zwei Abschnitte 1 Päckchen Rauchtabak oder 10 Zigarren oder 40 Cigarillos. Es dürfen alle 10 Tage nur 2 Abschnitte zur Belieferung kommen. Die Monatsabschnitte verfallen mit dem 7. Tag des darauffolgenden Monats.

Jusqu'à nouvel ordre et dans le cadre des stocks de la Régie, il peut être perçu 1 paquet de cigarettes pour chaque coupon. Deux coupons donnent droit à 1 paquet de tabac à fumer ou 10 cigares ou 40 cigarillos. Il ne peut être utilisé que deux coupons par période de dix jours. Les coupons mensuels sont valables jusqu'au 7 du mois suivant.

NUR GÜLTIG IM BEREICH DER FRANZ. TABAKREGIE.

VALABLE SEULEMENT POUR LA RÉGIE FRANÇAISE DES TABACS.

Imp. L. Hannequin, Levallois.

CARTE DE TABAC ALLEMANDE POUR "SELBSTVERPFLEGER"

TABAK TABAC MAI 44 MAI 44 | TABAK TABAC MAI 44 MAI 44 | TABAK TABAC MAI 44 MAI 44 | TABAK TABAC APRIL 44 AVRIL 44 | TABAK TABAC APRIL 44 AVRIL 44 | TABAK TABAC APRIL 44 AVRIL 44 | TABAK TABAC APRIL 44 AVRIL 44 | TABAK TABAC APRIL 44 AVRIL 44 | TABAK TABAC APRIL 44 AVRIL 44

Figure 5-53. This bilingual tobacco ration card valid in France during the second quarter of 1944 allowed a German citizen (this particular card was not exclusive to the Wehrmacht) a package of pipe tobacco, ten cigars, or forty cigarillos for each coupon redeemed, up to five coupons per month. (4¼" x 6⅛")

Figure 5-54. This Verzeichnis, a directory of items issued, is a receipt of Raucherkarten, tobacco ration cards, collected by the mayor of Hochstadt to be issued to Urlauber who had not been issued their tobacco ration when leaving the front. (5 15/16" x 8¼")

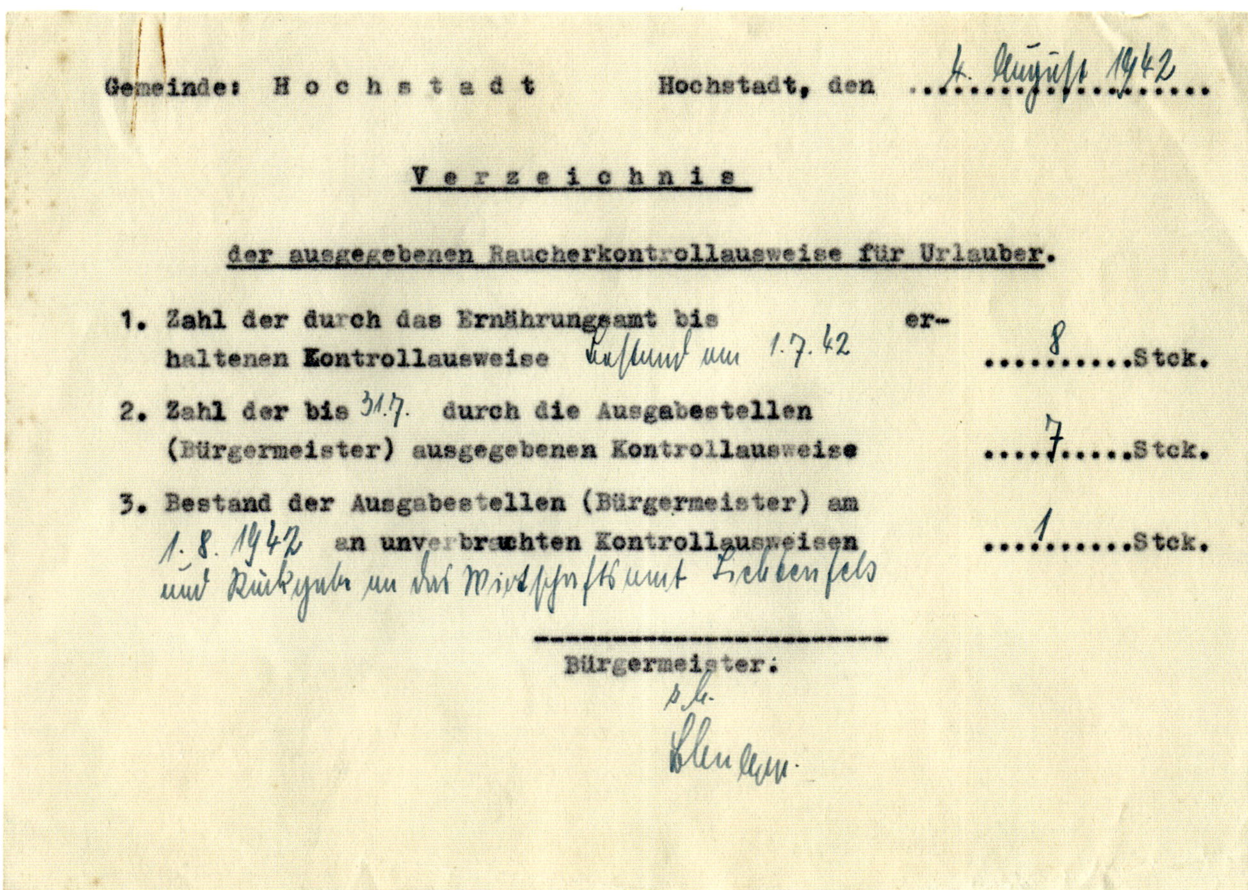

Gemeinde: Hochstadt Hochstadt, den 4. August 1942

Verzeichnis

der ausgegebenen Raucherkontrollausweise für Urlauber.

1. Zahl der durch das Ernährungsamt bis erhaltenen Kontrollausweise Lieferung am 1.7.42 ....8.... Stck.
2. Zahl der bis 31.7. durch die Ausgabestellen (Bürgermeister) ausgegebenen Kontrollausweise ....7.... Stck.
3. Bestand der Ausgabestellen (Bürgermeister) am 1.8.1942 an unverbrauchten Kontrollausweisen und Rückgabe an das Wirtschaftsamt Lichtenfels ....1.... Stck.

Bürgermeister:
i.A.
[signature]

Figure 5-55. If a Soldat hadn't been issued a Raucherkarte, he could acquire one from the mayor's office of the city he was visiting, but only after first filing an Erklärung or declaration that he had not been issued one. (4¾" x 5 15/16")

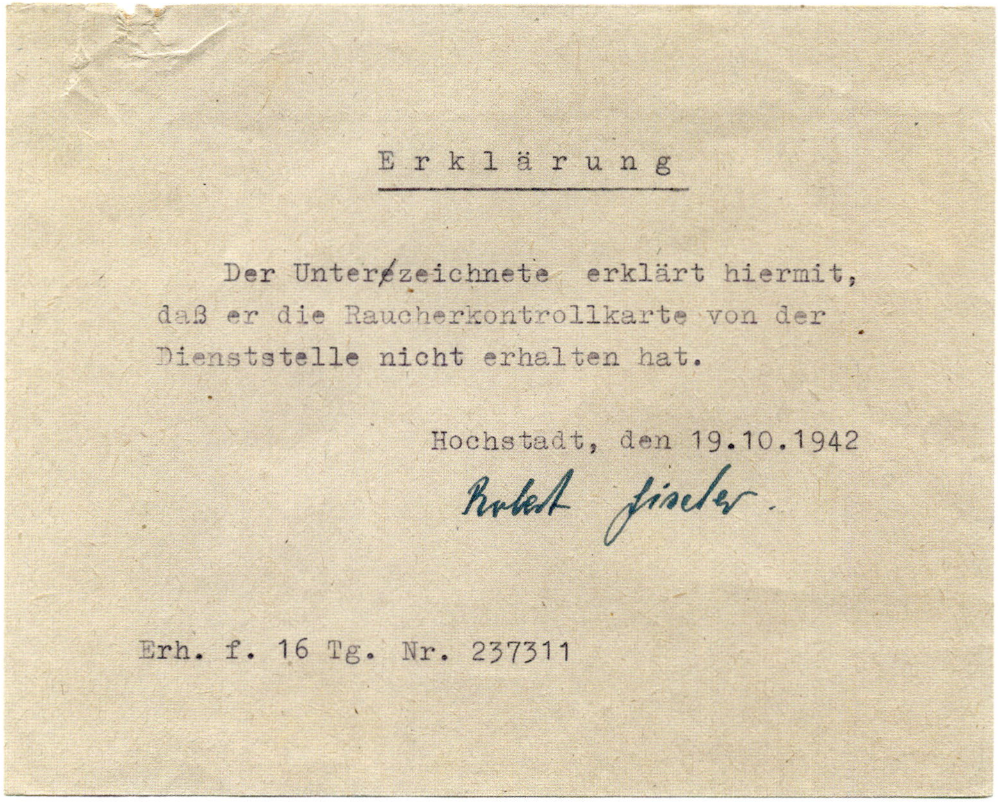

Erklärung

Der Unterzeichnete erklärt hiermit, daß er die Raucherkontrollkarte von der Dienststelle nicht erhalten hat.

Hochstadt, den 19.10.1942

Erh. f. 16 Tg. Nr. 237311

LWA Wien 1 F 64 | LWA Wien 2 F 64 | LWA Wien 3 F 64 | LWA Wien 4 F 64

F

Gültig vom 26. 6. bis 23. 7. 1944

Raucherkarte

Landeswirtschaftsamt Wien

64

Q/0697

Hauptwirtschaftsamt Wien

Inhaberin:
Vor- u. Zuname

Wohnort:
Straße

A F 64 LWA Wien | B F 64 LWA Wien | Ohne Namenseintragung ungültig! Nicht übertragbar!

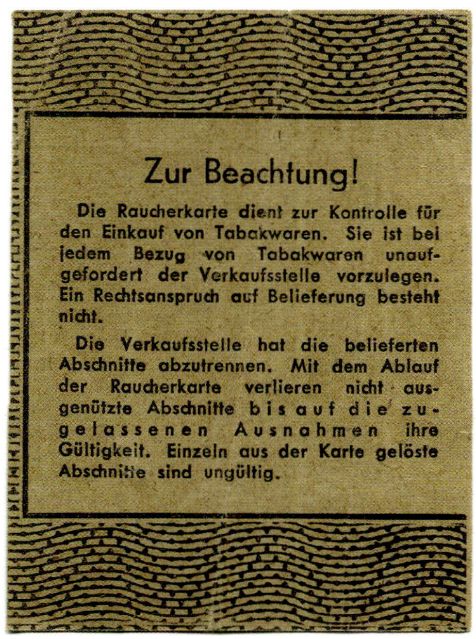

Zur Beachtung!

Die Raucherkarte dient zur Kontrolle für den Einkauf von Tabakwaren. Sie ist bei jedem Bezug von Tabakwaren unaufgefordert der Verkaufsstelle vorzulegen. Ein Rechtsanspruch auf Belieferung besteht nicht.

Die Verkaufsstelle hat die belieferten Abschnitte abzutrennen. Mit dem Ablauf der Raucherkarte verlieren nicht ausgenützte Abschnitte bis auf die zugelassenen Ausnahmen ihre Gültigkeit. Einzeln aus der Karte gelöste Abschnitte sind ungültig.

Figure 5-56. A civilian tobacco ration from Vienna, Austria, similar to what would have been issued to a Soldat who had lost his (although this particular card was a woman's; the "F" denotes use by a Frau or Fräulein). This example was valid from June 26 until July 23, 1944.

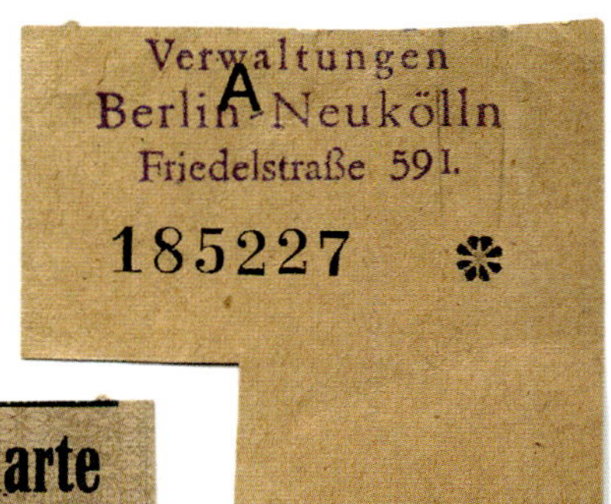

Verwaltungen
Berlin-Neukölln
Friedelstraße 59 I.

A

185227

F

Raucherkarte

Gültig vom 5. 3. bis 1. 4. 45

73

LWA Berlin

A 73 F Stadt Berlin | B 73 F Stadt Berlin

Figure 5-57. This example of a woman's tobacco ration card, this time from Berlin with a very elaborate anti-forgery pattern printed in the background, was the second to last issue period of the Third Reich, valid from March 5 until April 1, 1945. Issue period 75 would be the first of Allied occupation in Germany; rationing would continue until October 1950. Tobacco ration cards, like many other ration cards, continued to be issued up to and after the war, often when the goods themselves were no longer available.

Appendices

Appendix A

DIN 476 Paper Sizes (in millimeters)

Size	A Series	B Series	C Series	D Series
0	841 x 1189	1000 x 1414	917 x 1297	771 x 1091
1	594 x 841	707 x 1000	648 x 917	545 x 771
2	420 x 594	500 x 707	458 x 648	385 x 545
3	297 x 420	353 x 500	324 x 458	272 x 385
4	210 x 297	250 x 353	229 x 458	192 x 272
5	148 x 210	176 x 250	162 x 229	136 x 192
6	105 x 148	125 x 176	114 x 162	96 x 136
7	74 x 105	88 x 125	81 x 114	68 x 96
8	52 x 74	62 x 88	57 x 81	-
9	37 x 52	44 x 62	40 x 57	-
10	26 x 37	31 x 44	28 x 40	-

DIN 476 Paper Sizes (approximate equivalent in inches)

Size	A Series	B Series	C Series	D Series
0	33⅛ x 46 13/16	39⅜ x 55⅔	36 1/16 x 51	30⅓ x 42 15/16
1	23⅞ x 33⅛	27⅞ x 39⅜	25½ x 36 1/16	21½ x 30⅓
2	16½ x 23⅞	19⅔ x 27⅞	18 x 25½	15⅛ x 21½
3	11⅔ x 16½	13⅞ x 19⅔	12¾ x 18	10¾ x 15⅛
4	8¼ x 11⅔	9⅞ x 13⅞	9 x 12¾	7½ x 10¾
5	5⅞ x 8¼	6 15/16 x 9⅞	6⅜ x 9	5⅓ x 7½
6	4⅛ x 5⅞	4 15/16 x 6 15/16	4½ x 6⅜	3¾ x 5⅓
7	2⅞ x 4⅛	3½ x 4 15/16	3⅛ x 4½	2⅔ x 3¾
8	2 x 2⅞	2 7/16 x 3½	2¼ x 3⅛	–
9	1½ x 2	1¾ x 2 7/16	1½ x 2¼	–
10	1 x 1½	1¼ x 1¾	1 1/16 x 1½	–

Appendix B

German Military Ranks (Heer) and Their Equivalents

from the *Reiseverordnung für die Wehrmacht, III, 34 (a)*

Rank	*Reisekostenstufe*	Approximate US Equivalent
Feld Marschall	Ia	General of the Army
General	Ia	General
Generaloberst	Ia	(Colonel General)
Generalleutnant	Ib	Lieutenant General
Generalmajor	Ib	Major General
Oberst	Ib	Colonel
Oberstleutnant	II	Lieutenant-Colonel
Major	II	Major
Hauptmann	II	Captain
Oberleutnant	III	First Lieutenant
Leutnant	III	Second Lieutenant
Stabsfeldwebel★	IV	First Sergeant
Oberfeldwebel	IV	Master Sergeant
Feldwebel	V	Staff Sergeant
Unterfeldwebel	V	Sergeant
Unteroffizier	V	(Lance Sergeant)
Stabsgefreiter	V	(Staff Corporal)
Obergefreiter	V	Corporal
Gefreiter	V	Lance Corporal
Oberschützer	V	Private First Class
Schützer	V	Private

★ The rank of *Hauptfeldwebel*, nicknamed "*Der Spiess*" (the Spear), is an honorific rank, not an official one, and represents the most senior Sergeant in the unit. The US equivalent approximates a Sergeant Major.

Appendix C
Classifications of Leave

Nachturlaub: Overnight leave

Usually only valid for a few hours, from 7:00 p.m. until midnight or 4:00 or 5:00 a.m. the following morning. Some *Nachturlaub* were valid for longer, particularly if on the weekend form as early as 11:00 a.m. until 9:00 a.m. the following morning.

Stadturlaub: City leave

Leave in which the *Soldat* was restricted to the confines of the city. This often lasted anywhere from a few hours to a few days.

Wochenendeurlaub: Weekend leave

- As the name suggests, leave lasting over the weekend. Leave usually began Saturday morning (between 9:00 am and 11:00 am) and lasted until Sunday night to Monday morning.
- This leave was rarely issued to *Soldaten* who weren't in training.
- *Soldaten* were required to remain within 100 km (62.1 miles) from one's duty station.
- No more than 10% of a unit could be granted *Wochenendeurlaub*.
- Married soldiers could be granted up to two *Wochenendeurlauben* during a period of instruction, while single *Soldaten* were restricted to one.

Festtagsurlaub: Holiday or Festival days leave

Leave for special festivals or holidays.

Conditions were often the same as the *Wochenedneurlaub* above.

The following classifications of leave were restricted to once per year, except on rare occasion or extenuating circumstances.

Erholungsurlaub: Recreational leave (Literally: Recovery leave)

This is the regularly earned leave that often lasted up to 14 days, with two *Reisetage* or travel days (later in the war this was frequently extended to as much as five days, due to railroad interdiction from Allied bombing).

No more than 15% of a unit could be granted leave at a time.

Sonderurlaub: Special leave

Leave that was granted for special occasions and could be issued above and beyond annual restrictions for leave; a *Soldat* could be eligible for *Sonderurlaub* and *Erholungsurlaub* within the same year.

Normally granted for 10-14 days, plus two to four days *Reisetage*, but durations often varied by condition:

3 days	To visit family following discharge from a hospital in the same region.
Up to 14 days	Following discharge from a hospital not in the region.
Up to 20 days	Following news of bomb damage to one's family's home (*Bombengeschädigt* or *Fliegergeschädigt*; this was not automatically granted, and even then usually only granted in extreme cases, such as the fire storms in Hamburg or Dresden).
28 days+	Convalescent leave due to combat wounds or severe illness. Also reserved for those about to be discharged for medical reasons or "convenience of the government."
Varied	National athletes competing in a major event.

Arbeitsurlaub: Work leave

Not extended to members of combat units, this periodic leave was reserved for *Soldaten* with vital skills for wartime production, from highly technical factory work to farming, or for those who were only fit for limited service.

Confirmation of one's service had to be verified by the local *Polizeipräsident* (Chief of Police) or the factory principal or farmer where the work was completed.

Lasted up to four weeks.

Other reasons given on documents for leave:

Ambulentenurlaub	Ambulatory leave
Einsatzurlaub	Leave following prolonged duty in combat
Ernteurlaub	Harvest leave (similar to *Arbeitsurlaub*)
Fronturlaub	Leave as a respite from the front
Genesungsurlaub	Convalescent leave
Gesundheitsurlaub	Health leave
Heimaturlaub	Leave to go home
Kulturlaub	Cultural leave (usually in Paris or Rome)
Landwirtschaftsurlaub	Farmers' leave
Tapferkeitsurlaub	Bravery leave
Weihnachtsurlaub	Christmas leave

Appendix D
Glossary

Abzugeben - To return or hand in.
Achsen - Axels.
Afrika Korp - Africa Corps, German forces stationed in North Africa from 1941-1943.
Afrikazulage - Africa Payment, given to soldiers returning from North African or Mediterranean service.
Anhange - Supplement.
Ansichtkarten - Postcards.
Antrag auf Fahrpreisermässigung - Proposal for Fare Reduction, usually reserved for bereavement or funerary travel.
Arbeitsamt - Work District.
Ärztlicher Befundschein - Doctor's Condition Certificate.
Aufenthalt - A Stay.
Ausgabe - Edition.
Ausweis - Identity Affidavit.
Ausweiskarten - Identity Cards.

Bahnhof - Train Station or rail yard.
Bahnhoftagestempel - Train Station Date Stamp.
Bataillon - Battalion, usually consisting of 8-10 companies.
Bescheinigung - Certification.
Befehl - Order.
Befristeter Ausweis - Temporary Identity Card or Pass.
Behelfszahlungsmittel - Temporary Currency.
Beilage - Enclosure.
Berliner Illustrierte Zeitung - Berlin Illustrated Newspaper.
Besetzten Gebiet - Occupied Territories.
Bezugsausweis für Urlauber - Reference Identifications Card for Those on Leave.
Brot - Bread.
Bügermeister - Mayor. Literally, the town master.

Chef der Parteikanzlei - Chief of the Party Chancellory.

Deckblätter - Literally, Cover Sheets, but more appropriately translated to Addenda.
Deutschen Wegleiter - German Travel Guide.
Diensthunde - Service Dogs.
Dienstreise - Service Trip or Service Related Travel.
Dienstreiseschein - Service-Related Travel Pass.
Dienststelle - Service Locations, often implied to mean Military Locations.
Dienstelle der Feldpostnummer - Service Office of the Field Mail Number, the official "longhand" title of the *Feldpostnummer.*
Dienststellenausweis - Duty Station Identity Card.
Dienststellen des Standortes - Service Office of the Base or Garrison.
Dienststempel - Service Stamp, usually indicating an official stamp, or a stamp for official purposes.
Dienstunterrichet in der Luftwaffe - Service Instruction in the *Luftwaffe.*
DIN - *Deutsches Institut für Normung* - German Institute for Standardization.
DIN 476 - *Deutsches Institut für Normung Nr. 476 (Papierformate)* German Institute for Standardization, Number 476 - Paper Formats.
Deutsche Arbeits Front - German Work Front; a para-military construction organization.
Durchgangszug - Throughway Train.

Ei, Eier (plural) - Eggs.
Eilgüterzug - Freight Train with few, swift stops.
Eilzug - Fast Train with a limited number of swift stops.
Eintrittskarte - Admission Ticket.
Einzeltransports - Individualized Loads.
Elternangabe - Parental Indications.
Entlassungsgeld - Separation Pay.
Entlassungsschein - Discharge papers. More appropriately, a release from service.
Entlausungsstelle - Delousing Station.
Entlausungsschein or E-schein - Delousing Certificate.
Entrata - (Italian) Entrance.
Erholungsurlaub - Recreational Leave.
Erkennungsmarke - The *Wehrmacht's* two-piece style of dog tag.
Erklärung - Declaration.
Ersatz - Substitute.
Ersatzteilen - Substitute Pages.

Fahrbefehl - Travel Order, used to identify a vehicle, driver, and itinerary of a service-related trip.
Fahrkarte - Literally, Travel Card; Ticket.
Fascisti - (Italian) Fascist; usually understood to mean the Italian Fascist Party or one of its members.
Feind hört mit! - "The enemy is listening!" A common wartime warning in Germany during World War II.
Feldgendarmerie - Military Police.
Feldlazarett - Field Hospital.
Feldpostnummer - Field Mail Number.
Feldwebel - An NCO (Non-commissioned Officer) or Sergeant.
Festabend - Evening Festival.
Fett - Literally, Fats, but this was often issued in the form of butter and/or margarine.
Fliegerhorst - Air Base.
Fleisch or Fleischwaren - Meat or Meat Products.
Fliegerbluse - Flight Tunic; standard service tunic for *Luftwaffe* personnel.
Fraktur - The heavy, characteristically German typeface used since the sixteenth century.
Fronturlauberpaket - Vacationing Soldier from the Front's Package.
Frontzulage - Front Pay, given to soldiers coming directly from the front.
Führer - Leader. When used as *Der Führer*, it meant *the* leader of the Nazi Party, Adolf Hitler.
Führergeschenk - Führer's Present, given to soldiers returning from front-line duty between October of 1943 and September 1944.
Führer-Paket - Führer's Package, given to soldiers returning from front line duty between October of 1942 and March of 1943.

Gebirgsjäger - Mountain Infantry; literally translated as Mountain Hunters.
Gebühr or Gebührnis - Fee.
Gesundheitsblatt - Health Leaflet.
Gilt als Fahrausweis - This pass is "valid as a ticket."
Grenzübertritt - Border Crossing.
Grenzübertrittsausweis - Border Passage Identity Permit.
Grosser Wehrmachtfahrschein - Large Wehrmacht Travel Pass.
Grund - Ground, as in "ground for travel."
Gültig - Valid.
Güterzug - Literally, Goods Train; a freight train.

Hauptfeldwebel - Literally, Main Sergeant. Equivalent to a Sergeant Major.
Hauptmann und Kompanie-Führer - Captain and Company Leader.
das Heer - The German Army.
Heeres Dienstvorschrift (H.Dv.) - Army Service Manual.
Heereserholungsheim - Military Recovery or Vacation Home.
Heimatverpflegungszulage für Fronturlauber - Home Provisions Issue for those on Leave from the Front.
Heiratsurkunde - Marriage Document or Certificate.
Heiratsurlaub - Marriage Leave.
Hoheitszeichen - High Official Emblem. This is the displayed Nazi eagle and swastika.

Kartenausgabestelle - Distribution station for ration cards or other items pertinent to travel.
Kartoffeln - Potatoes.
Käse - Cheese.
Kleiner Wehrmachtfahrschein - Small Military Ticket.
kombinierte Fahrschein - Combined Travel Pass - not an official designation.
Kommandant Der Stadt Paris - Commander of the City of Paris.
Kommandant von Gross-Paris - The Commander of Greater Paris.
Kommandantur - Commanding Officer.
Kommandoreisegeld - An additional travel allowance granted at the discretion of one's local level of command.
Kompanie - Company, usually consisting of 80-100 men.
Kontrollkart - Control Card.
Krankenblatt - Sickness Report.
die Kriegsmarine - The German Navy during World War II. Referred to as the *Reichsmarine* between the World Wars, it is now referred to as the *Deutsche Marine.*
Kriegsurlaubsschein - Wartime Leave Permit.
Kultururlaub - Cultural Leave.
Kupferstichschrift - Copper Plate Script. Form of German handwriting practiced throughout the nineteenth and early twentieth centuries, that mimicked

a style of copperplate engraving. Common form of handwriting for soldiers during World War I.
Kurrent - Form of German handwriting practiced throughout the nineteenth and early twentieth centuries (see also *Kupferstichschrift*). Common form of handwriting for soldiers during World War I.

Lasciapassare Speciale - (Italian) Special Pass for Through-Travel.
Lazarettzuges - Hospital Train.
Lebensmittelsonderkarte - Special Food Card.
Luftschutz - Air Defense.
die Luftwaffe - The German Air Force, still referred to by this title today.
Luftwaffe Dienstvorschrift (L.Dv.) - Air Force Service Manual.

Marine Dienstvorschrift (M.Dv.) - Navy Service Manual.
Marmelade - Marmalade, Jam, or Preserves.
Marschausweis - Marching Identity Pass or Permit.
Marschbefehl - Literally, "Marching Order."
Marschverpflegung - Marching Provisions or Rations.
Matrosenhemd - Sailor's Shirt; the stereotypical "Donald Duck" style of shirt, with a flap for a collar.
Merkblatt - An informational leaflet.
Merkblatt für Reisen in das Ausland - Leaflet For Trips In Foreign Countries.
Milch - Milk.
Muster - Pattern.

Nacht-Urlaub or Nachturlaub - Night-time Leave.
Nacht-Urlaubsschein or Nachturlaubsschein - Night-time Leave Permit.
Nährmittel - Literally, Foodstuffs, but understood to mean most vegetables, processed foods, etc.
Nicht übertragbar - Non-transferable.
Normalschrift or Romanischeschrift - Normal script or Roman script, taught in German schools after the dismissal of *Sütterlinschrift* in 1941.

Oberfeldwebel - Literally, Over-Sergeant. A Staff Sergeant.
Oberst - Colonel, not to be confused with *Ober*, meaning "waiter."
Ohne - Without.
OKW - *Oberkommando der Wehrmacht* - Central Command of the *Wehrmacht*.
Omnibus – A passenger truck with windows like a bus, but smaller than a traditional city bus.
Organization Todt - A civilian organization of civil and military engineers named after its founder Dr. Fritz Todt.

Panzerjäger - Literally, Armor Hunters; an anti-tank unit.
Passierschein - Permit to pass.
Passierschein für Durchreisende - Passage Permit for Through-Travelers.
Personenzug - Civilian Passenger Train.
Plakatten - Placards.
Platzkarte - Place Card.
Polizeibehörde - Police Authority.
Polizeipräsident - Police President or Head of Police.
Portepee - A decorative tassel that hung from the sword or dagger of a Senior NCO.

Rasierseife - Shaving Soap.
Raucherkarte - Smoking Card, or Tobacco ration card.
Raucherkontrollausweis - Smoking Control Card.
Reichsadler - Reich's Eagle, also referred to as the *Hoheitszeichen*.
Reichsarbeitsdienst - RAD, Reich Work Service or Force, similar to the American Civil Conservation Corps.
Reichsbahn - German State Railroad System.
Reichsbahn Durchgangsstelle - Railway Transfer or Throughway Stations.
Reichsbank - German State Bank.
Reichsheer - Predecessor of the *Wehrmacht*; the German Armed Forces of Imperial Germany.
Reichskarte - Reich's Card, often a ration card, but it could also technically mean any form of officially issued card or paper.
Reichskreditkasse - The German Treasury.
Reichsmarks - The primary form of currency in Germany until 1948, when it was replaced by the *Deutsch Mark* (DM).
Reichspfennig - German Reich's Penny. 100 *Reichspfennig* = 1 *Reichsmark*.
Reise - Trip.
Reisetage - Travel days.

Reiseverordnung für die Wehrmacht - Travel Regulations for the Military. This is the primary manual for travel within the *Wehrmacht*.
Rückreise - Return Trip.
Rucksack - An unframed style of backpack.

Schnellzug - Fast or Express Train with limited stops.
Seilbahn - Closest translation is a cable car.
SF-Zug (Schnellzug für Fronturlauber) - Fast trains reserved for those on leave from the front.
Soldatenheim - Soldier's Home, usually a building much like a hotel, with rooms, restaurant, and bar.
Soldatenhumor - Soldier's Humor.
Soldatenkino - Soldier's Theater or Movie House.
Soldatentheater - Soldier's Theater or Playhouse.
Soldat - Soldier. Used as a title as well as a description.
Soldbuch - Pay Book, the primary form of identification of the German Soldier.
Sonder - Special or specialized.
Sonderausweis - Special Identity Paper, used primarily to identify a soldier and the purpose that he was away from his unit.
Sonderstempel - Specialized stamps.
Speck - Bacon.
Spirituosen - Spirits, such as Schnapps and other liquors.
Stadt - City.
Stadt-Urlaubsschein or Stadturlaubsschein - City Leave Permit.
Stalag Luft - Shortened form for *Stammslager der Luftwaffe* or *Luftwaffe*-run POW camp.
Standesamt - Registration Office.
Standesbeamte - Registry Official.
Standortstelle - Duty Station, Military Post, or Garrison.
Sationsstempel - A stamp indicating a train station, time, and date of departure or arrival.
Stempel - Stamp; can be used to indicate the stamp itself or the impression left by one.
Strassenbahn - Street Train or trolley.
Süd-Ost - Southeast.
Sütterlinschrift - *Sütterlin* Script. Form of German handwriting taught in German schools between 1915 (more completely instituted in 1923) and 1941, when it was banned by a decree of Adolf Hitler.
Teil - Part or page.
Transportführer - Literally, Transport Leader, a *Reichsbahn* loading officer.
Truppenarzt - Military Doctor.
Truppenausweis - Troop Identity Card, often issued in areas where carrying the *Soldbuch* might present a security risk.
Truppenteil - A military troop or unit designation.
Truppenteilstempel - Unit Designation Stamp.
Truppentransports - Troop Trains.

Umwege - Detour.
Unteroffizier - A Senior NCO (Non-commissioned Officer) or higher ranking Sergeant.
Urlaub - Leave or vacation.
Urlauber - Vacationer or one on leave..
Urlaubsgesuch - Leave Request; literally, the "Leave Search."
Urlaubsort - Leave location.
Urlaubsreise - Leave or Vacation Trip.
Urlaubs- und Freifahrnachweis - Leave and Free Travel Report.
Uscita - (Italian) Departure.

Vermerke und Bescheinigung - Notices and Certifications.
Verpflegungskarte - Provisions Card; a form of ration card for German soldiers.
Verpflegungsnachweis - Travel Ration Card.
Verrechnungsschein - Literally, Settlement Certificate; Military Scrip.
Verwaltungsstelle or Verwaltungsquartier - Administrative Office.
Verwundeten- Wounded.
Verzeichnis - Index, usually understood to be an attestation.
Vorschrift für die Verpflegung der Wermacht, H.Dv.86/1 - Manual for the Provisioning of the Wehrmacht.

Waffenrock - Dress Tunic.
Wehrbezirkskommando - W.B.K. or Military District Command
Wehrmacht - The German armed forces of the Third Reich
Wehrmachtangehörige - Military personnel. Literally, Member of the Armed Forces.
Wehrmacht-Fahrkarte or Wehrmachtfahrkarte - Military Ticket, often purchased at one's own expense.
Wehrmacht-Fahrschein or Wehrmachtfahrschein - Military Ticket provided by the military.

Wehrmacht-Marschausweis - Military Marching Identity Pass or Permit.
Wehrmachtzug - Military Transport Train.
Wehrmeldeamt - W.M.A. or Military Reporting/ Registration District or Station.
Wehrnummer - Number identifying a soldier by his home town, year of birth, and military registration roll.
Wehrpass - The soldier's service record, usually kept at the rear areas, and only handled by the soldier when transferring from one duty station to another, where it would be turned over to the new unit.
Wehrstammrolle - Military Draft Register maintained by each town and village in Germany.
Wehrsold - Military Pay above regular, base pay, similar to American hazardous duty pay.
WH - License plate notation for vehicles belonging to the *Wehrmacht-Heer.*
WL - License plate notation for vehicles belonging to the *Wehrmacht-Luftwaffe.*
WM - License plate notation for vehicles belonging to the *Wehrmacht-Kriegsmarine.*
Wohnort - Residence.

Zucker - Sugar.
Zuteilungsperiode - Ration Period. A numerically designated period of time for which certain rations were valid.

Bibliography

Allison, Nigel. *Collecting World War II German Military Pay & Service Books*. Shropshire, England: Ulric of England, 2007.

Barger, Charles J. and J. A. Bowman. *Personnel Documents of the SS*. Lancaster, England: Imperial Publications, 1992.

Barlog, Friedrich. *Wir in der Heimat*. Berlin: Zeitgeschichte-Verlag, Berlin, 1940.

Brandl, Dr. Ralph. *Blitz German*. Harrisburg, PA. Military Service Publishing Company, 1943.

Braun, Hans-Joachim. *The German Economy in the Twentieth Century*. New York: Routledge, Chapman, and Hall 1990.

Burroughs, Michael and Ian Burroughs. *German Identity Disks of World War II*. Shropshire, England: Ulric of England, (Date unknown).

Cowdery, Ray & Josephine. *Papers Please!*. Lakeville, MN: USM, Inc., Lakeville, MN, 1996.

Forman, Adrian. *Forman's Guide to Third Reich German Documents And Their Values, Vol. I & II*. Somerset, England: Adrian Forman, 1995, 1996.

Klose, Dietrich. *Front und Heimat, Teil 2: Geschreibenes und Gedrucktes 1939–1945*. Karlsdorf, Germany: Historicmedia-Verlag, 2005.

Lemkin, Raphael. *Axis Rule in Occupied Europe*. Clark, NJ: The Lawbook Exchange, Ltd, 2005.

Mason, Chris. *Personal Effects of the German Soldier*. Atglen, PA: Schiffer, 2006.

Miller, David. *Fighting Men of World War II Axis Forces*. New York: Chartwell Books, 2010.

Pool, Lt. Col. Jim and Thomas Bock. *Rations of the German Wehrmacht in World War II*. Atglen, PA: Schiffer, 2010.

Pool, Lt. Col. Jim. *Rations of the German Wehrmacht in World War II, Vol. II*. Atglen, PA: Schiffer Military History Books, 2012.

Popp, Diane M. and Gottfried Dulias. *Another Bowl of Kapusta*. Bloomington, IN: Authorhouse, 2004.

Pusey, W. W. and A. G. Steer, ed. *Readings in Military German*. Boston, MA: D.C. Heath and Company, 1943.

Sáiz, Augusín. *Deutsche Soldaten - Uniforms, Equipment & Personal Items of the German Soldier 1939–45*. Drexel Hill, PA, Newberry, Berkshire, England: Casemate, 2008.

Scapini, Antonio and Alberto Gorzanelli. *The Wehrpaß and Soldbuch of the Wehrmacht*. Richmond, MI: B&D Publishing, LLC, 2013.

Stewart, Emilie Caldwell. *German Military Award Documents*. Brigantine Island, NJ: Emilie Caldwell Stewart, 1991.

——. *Military Identity Documents of the Third Reich*. Columbus, OH: Emilie Caldwell, 1986.

——. *Wehrpasses and Soldbuchs*. Columbus, OH: Emilie Caldwell Stewart, 1985.

Tschöltsch, Generalmajor E. Der Dienstunterricht in der Luftwaffe. Berlin: E. S. Mittler & Sohn, 1942.

Young, Jeffrey F. and Daniel W. Meinz. *German Third Reich Era Documents, Volume One-Three*. St. Joseph, MN: Jeffrey F. Young & Daniel W. Meinz, 1996.

——. *Duden Oxford Großwörterbuch Englisch*, Mannheim, Wien, Zürich: Dudenverlag, 1990

——. *Reiseverordnung für die Wehrmacht, H.Dv. 159*, Berlin 1937.

——. *VB-Feldpost, 3. Folge, Darüber lache ich heute noch. Berlin: Zentralverlag der NSDAP*, Franz Eher Nachf. GmbH., 1943.

——. *VB-Feldpost, 4. Folge, Landser lachen - Fronthumor dieses Krieg. Berlin: Zentralverlag der NSDAP*, Franz Eher Nachf. GmbH., 1944.

——. *Vorschrift für die Verpflegung der Wehrmacht bei besonderem*

——. *Einsatz, H.Dv.86/1*, Berlin, 1940.

Electronic Sources

12 O'Clock High (http://forum.12oclockhigh.net/)
About.Com (http://www.about.com/)
Acetylcholine.org (http://acetylcholine.org/)
Das Archiv für technische Dokumente 1900-1945 (http://www.superborg.de/)
Art Fakes (http://www.artfake.net/)
The Avalon Project at Yale Law School (http://avalon.law.yale.edu/)
Axis History Factbook (http://www.axishistory.com/)
Axis History Forum (http://forum.axishistory.com/)
Bundes Archiv (http://www.bundesarchiv.de/index.html.de)
Charles McCain's Blog (http://blog.charlesmccain.com/)
Chronicles of the Vilna Ghetto (http://www.vilnaghetto.com/)
Coin Talk (http://www.cointalk.com/)
Dokumentenarchiv (http://www.wehrmachtlexikon.de/)
Der Bunker (http://wwii-militaria.net/axis.htm)
Der Erste Zug (http://www.dererstezug.com/navigation.htm)
Deutsches Akfrika Korp Forum (http://www.deutsches-afrika-korps.de/)
Ebay
  (http://www.ebay.at/)
  (http://www.ebay.com/)
  (http://www.ebay.co.uk/)
  (http://www.ebay.de/)
  (http://www.ebay.fr/)
  (http://www.ebay.it)
Educational Coin (http://www.educationalcoin.com/)
Feldgrau (http://www.feldgrau.com/)
Fontspace (http://www.fontspace.com/category/fraktur)
Forum der Wehrmacht (http://www.forum-der-wehrmacht.de/)
Fraktur (http://www.frakturweb.org/)
Francisco Miranda Blog (http://chicomiranda.wordpress.com/)
German Postal History (http://www.germanpostalhistory.com/)
Gun Boards Collectors' Forum (http://forums.gunboards.com/)
Helium.com (http://www.helium.com/)
Helmut Weitze, Militarische Antiquitäten (https://www.weitze.net/index_e.html)
The Latvian Legion (http://www.lacplesis.com/)
Lemo Kollektiven Gedächnis (http://www.dhm.de/lemo/forum/kollektives_gedaechtnis/398/index.html)
Lexikon der Wehrmacht (http://www.lexikon-der-wehrmacht.de/)
Militaria 321 (http://www.militaria321.com/)
Militaria Archiv (http://militaria-archiv.com/)
Militaria Sammlergemeinschaft (http://www.militaria-sammlergemeinschaft.com/)
The Norwegian SS Volunteers (http://www.frontkjemper.com/)
Priaulx Library of Guernsey (http://www.priaulxlibrary.co.uk/)
PsyWar (http://www.psywar.org/)
Rare Book Room (http://www.rarebookroom.org/Control/duruwm/index.html)
International Journal of Rationing (http://www.rationcurrency.net/)
Reality Check (http://www.reality-check.ca/)
Soldbuch Web (http://www.soldbuchweb.com/)

Tactical and Technical Trends, No. 37, US Military Intelligence Service, 1943 (http://www.lonesentry.com/intelbulletin/tt_trends.html); see also (http://www.gata.org/node/10457/print)
Typophile (http://www.typophile.com/)
War Relics Forum (http://www.warrelics.eu/)
Wehrmacht Awards Forum (http://www.wehrmacht-awards.com/)
World War 2 Archive (http://www.ww2archive.net/)
World War 2 Shots Photo Archive (http://www.ww2shots.com/gallery/main.php)
World War Militaria Forum (http://www.worldwarmilitaria.com/)
Zweiter Weltkrieg Lexikon Forum (http://zweiter-weltkrieg-lexikon.de/)

Recommended Internet Articles

http://davidmcfall.co.uk/Documents/1944_2%20Ellic%20Howe.pdf
http://www.dererstezug.com/FuhrerandOtherGifts.htm
http://forum.axishistory.com/viewtopic.php?f=46&t=130580
http://german.about.com/od/readinggerman/a/fraktur.htm
http://german.about.com/library/gallery/blfoto_fraktur06.htm